Praise for Carlin Romano's

AMERICA THE PHILOSOPHICAL

"Romano is enlightening when he analyzes American intellectual life and illustrates its liveliness."   —Anthony Gottlieb,
The New York Times Book Review

"Admirable. . . . Romano writes with the snap of a journalist."
—Thomas Meaney, *The Wall Street Journal*

"A comprehensive intellectual history from Emerson to Rawls."
—*The New Yorker*

"Magisterial."   —Patrick Hazard, Broad Street Review

"Romano's remarkable book stands out in terms of ambition, breadth, provocativeness, and, when needed, a delicate touch."
—Howard Gardner, Hobbs Professor of
Cognition and Education, Harvard University,
and author of *Truth, Beauty, and Goodness Reframed*

"Stimulating. . . . Graceful. . . . Exuberant. . . . Succeeds in filling one's mind with the excitement of ideas duking it out."
—Drew DeSilver, *The Seattle Times*

"Both scholarly and entertaining—learned and stimulating—to an equal and extraordinary degree. *America the Philosophical* is one of the best books of the year. . . . A hugely enlightening compendium of intellectual heresy." —Jeff Simon, *The Buffalo News*

"Romano's grip on his subject is fierce. . . . A tour de force—encyclopedic, entertaining and enlightening."
—*Kirkus Reviews* (starred review)

CARLIN ROMANO

AMERICA THE PHILOSOPHICAL

Carlin Romano, Critic-at-Large of *The Chronicle of Higher Education* and literary critic of *The Philadelphia Inquirer* for twenty-five years (1984–2009), is Professor of Philosophy and Humanities at Ursinus College. His criticism has appeared in *The Nation*, *The New Yorker*, *The Village Voice*, *Harper's*, *The American Scholar*, *Salon*, *The Times Literary Supplement*, and many other publications. A former president of the National Book Critics Circle, he was a finalist for the 2006 Pulitzer Prize in Criticism, cited for "bringing new vitality to the classic essay across a formidable array of topics."

AMERICA THE PHILOSOPHICAL

AMERICA
THE PHILOSOPHICAL

CARLIN ROMANO

VINTAGE BOOKS

A DIVISION OF RANDOM HOUSE, INC.

NEW YORK

FIRST VINTAGE BOOKS EDITION, APRIL 2013

The Library of Congress has cataloged the Knopf edition as follows:
Romano, Carlin.
America the philosophical / Carlin Romano.—1st ed.
p. cm.
Includes bibliographical references and index.
1. Philosophy—United States.
2. United States—Intellectual life. I. Title.
B851.R66 2012
191—dc23 2011034753

Vintage ISBN: 978-0-345-80470-9

Printed in the United States of America
10 9 8 7 6 5 4 3 2

To all who seek to persuade without violence and dogmatism

Between us and the universe, there are no "rules of the game." The important thing is that our judgments should be right, not that they should observe a logical etiquette.

—WILLIAM JAMES

What is originality? To *see* something that has no name as yet and hence cannot be mentioned although it stares us all in the face. The way men usually are, it takes a name to make something visible to them.

—FRIEDRICH NIETZSCHE

Philosophy really is "purely descriptive."

—LUDWIG WITTGENSTEIN

The philosophers' own scholastic little definitions of "philosophy" are merely polemical devices—intended to exclude from the field of honor those whose pedigrees are unfamiliar.

—RICHARD RORTY

If the immense reality that is America is addressed to serving man's mind and freedom as well as his body it may well become a civilization comparable to Athens and to Rome.

—SIMONE DE BEAUVOIR

CONTENTS

CONTENTS

AMERICA THE PHILOSOPHICAL

INTRODUCTION

America the *Philosophical*? It sounds like *Canada the Exhibitionist* or *France the Unassuming*: a mental miscue, a delusional academic tic, a dead-on-arrival concept emitting gases of pure intellectual wish fulfillment. Everyone knows that Americans don't take philosophy seriously, don't know much about it, don't pay any attention to it and couldn't name a contemporary academic philosopher if their passports depended on it. As historian Richard Hofstadter drily observed in his Pulitzer Prize–winning *Anti-Intellectualism in American Life* (1963), "In the United States the play of the mind is perhaps the only form of play that is not looked upon with the most tender indulgence."

But if the title phenomenon of Hofstadter's classic indeed boasts, in his view, "a long, historical background," the peculiar attitude directed at philosophy in America is more quizzical than hostile, closer to good-humored wariness than contempt. Philosophy doesn't threaten or bother the practical on-the-go American. The American middle manager confronted with a devoted philosophy type is most likely to yank out the old cliché "What are you going to do, open a philosophy store?" and leave it at that. If, of course, the information has been accurately downloaded. Tell your seatmate on a flight that you're "in philosophy" and the reply is likely to be, "Oh, that's great. My niece is in psychology too."

The infrequent philosophy blips on America's media screens suggest that philosophy doesn't register on the American psyche with the gravitas professors in the field deem warranted. When a blip does occur, it drives that impression only deeper.

"Page Six" of the *New York Post*—the ongoing Ground Zero of American gossip even in the age of TMZ—once featured Lauren Hutton, the nation's fashion model *sub specie aeternitatis*, anointing Camille Paglia as "the greatest living American philosopher" (high praise for someone another newspaper likes to introduce with the phrase "pro-porn femi-nist"). In tiny New York Mills, Minnesota, the town's Regional Cultural Center draws national press every year with its annual "Great American Think-Off." It's a philosophy contest so egalitarian that a finalist one year, Phillip Torsrud, couldn't make the final debate on "Which does society value more, money or morality?"—something about a prior com-mitment in the Wisconsin Correctional System, an inconvenient con-viction for murder. When a wrestler named Nick Baines declared, after entering the University of Northern Iowa, that he planned to become a professor of philosophy, the *Des Moines Register* judged him an oddity to be closely watched. (Local philosophers, historically wiser, noted that Plato, *né* Aristocles, actually pulled a similar career move—he adopted his better-known name, which meant "broad shoulders," while compet-ing in the Isthmian Games.) And when the University of Chicago, in October 2011, simultaneously hosted (in the same building!) a confer-ence on philosophical giant Bernard Williams, and another on the hit reality show *Jersey Shore*, guess which one got the front-page *New York Times* coverage?

Signaling the American media mind-set, it seems, was a publicity release from a New York publishing house, hyping a two-book deal with Dennis Rodman, America's faded, body-pierced, outré, cross-dressing ex–basketball badboy. It offered a sweeping historical perspective on its previously unheralded new thinker in ascending typeface:

Socrates
Confucius
Chopra
RODMAN!!!

Does America take philosophy seriously? One might as well ask whether America takes monarchy seriously. Joking about philosophy in the United States or just ignoring it comes with the territory, like learn-ing the Pledge of Allegiance. Hard-boiled, concrete-minded descen-dants of everyone from the Pilgrims to the slaves to the boat people, we pick it up along the way, like mistrusting politicians, refinancing mortgages or choosing whizbang smartphones. It's the way we're sup-posed to think about a discipline described by Ambrose Bierce (who promptly disappeared into the desert) as "a route of many roads, leading from nowhere to nothing," and by historian Henry Adams as a field that offers "unintelligible answers to insoluble problems."

Alexis de Tocqueville (1805–1859), author of *Democracy in America*, thought no country paid "less attention" to philosophy than the United States.

Tocqueville, that touchstone for all synoptic thinking about America, thought the peculiar attitude of its residents toward philosophy so obvious that he began the second volume of *Democracy in America* by noting it: "I think that in no country in the civilized world is less attention paid to philosophy than in the United States. The Americans have no philosophical school of their own, and they care but little for all the schools into which Europe is divided, the very names of which are scarcely known to them."

Even Tocqueville, however, nodded. For all his general insight into the fledgling United States, he, like many French intellectuals, saw American thought through the prism of European customs and assumptions. The conclusion he drew from that putative intellectual state of affairs—that "in most of the operations of the mind each American appeals only to the individual effort of his own understanding"—was false then, and is even more false now. His misstep came in using the word "only." He should have written that each American "also" appeals "to the individual effort of his own understanding."

For the surprising little secret of our ardently capitalist, famously materialist, heavily iPodded, iPadded and iPhoned society is that

America in the early twenty-first century towers as the most philosophical culture in the history of the world, an unprecedented marketplace of truth and argument that far surpasses ancient Greece, Cartesian France, nineteenth-century Germany or any other place one can name over the past three millennia. The openness of its dialogue, the quantity of its arguments, the diversity of its viewpoints, the cockiness with which its citizens express their opinions, the vastness of its First Amendment freedoms, the intensity of its hunt for evidence and information, the widespread rejection of truths imposed by authority or tradition alone, the resistance to false claims of justification and legitimacy, the embrace of Net communication with an alacrity that intimidates the world: all corroborate that fact.

Mistaking American ribbing of philosophy for what the British call rubbishing, for evidence of a nonphilosophical culture, is only one of the errors traditionally committed by intellectuals in understanding the United States. Even the best philosophical societies, after all, stick it to philosophy once in a while, as Aristophanes caricatured Socrates and his Athenian logic-choppers in *The Clouds* (423 B.C.). American irreverence, far from posing a threat to philosophical activity, fuels and incarnates it.

Has the talk show declined from Socrates to Bill O'Reilly and Jon Stewart? Maybe, but mixing entertainment and argument isn't why. Are those inside-the-Beltway cable-babble shows really talk-*over* shows? Sure, but read some of Plato's dialogues and you'll see Socrates also stepping on the lines of other speakers. In fact, the proliferation and popularity of American radio and television "talk" stars—from Howard Stern or Don Imus recidivus to Charlie Rose, Oprah Winfrey, Stephen Colbert and Stewart—bears a resemblance, albeit imperfect, to the rise of influential celebrity rhetoricians in ancient Greece, even if today's talkers seek more to persuade *and* entertain, and provide forums, than to teach others the arts of persuasion. Was the *Christian Science Monitor* kidding when it marked the end of Oprah's twenty-five years of TV talk in May 2011 with an article headlined "Oprah Winfrey: The Greatest Existential Philosopher Ever"? Was that a smirk as it praised her teaching that the "human project" is "always up for editing, elevation and enlightenment"? It seemed not. The story of philosophy in America is not a short subject about a narrow tributary of high Judeo-Christian culture, once commonly restricted to the university and priesthood, that failed to empty into the great river of American thought. When seen properly and whole, philosophy in the USA is more like a big-budget, *Transformers*-type special-effects movie—*The Big Muddy That Flooded*

America! But it's important to refine and make plain the scope of this metaphorical claim.

To exalt America as the world's philosophical culture par excellence is not just to argue that American philosophers have occasionally swayed everyday society, sometimes in a trickle-down manner, sometimes directly. We've always known that, though the examples bear repeating. Just as we acknowledge that, outside America, the work in logic of philosophers such as England's Bertrand Russell and Germany's Gottlob Frege aided the development of the computer and artificial intelligence, and that Albert Einstein declared his rejection of absolute time was "decisively furthered" by "the reading of David Hume's and Ernest Mach's philosophical writings," we know that Ralph Waldo Emerson spurred American intellectual independence, and John Dewey cofounded the American Civil Liberties Union, with huge consequences for our tradition of freedom of speech. We recognize that William James catalyzed psychology into a full-fledged discipline, and that Alain Locke helped spark the Harlem Renaissance that began the explosion of black artistic self-expression in the twentieth century.

Closer to the present, we're familiar with how even such important scientific accomplishments as the Dendral program that helps chemists identify the structure of molecules, developed by University of Pittsburgh computer scientist Bruce Buchanan from his philosophical work at Michigan State, can be credited to the tribe. Outside natural science, the theory of justice of John Rawls, the economics-accented jurisprudence of Richard Posner, the "end-of-art-history" musings of aesthetician and critic Arthur Danto, affect politics, judicial reasoning and curatorial practice, respectively.

America the Philosophical, however, means more than that.

It is similarly more than the spread of so-called applied ethics, which over the past thirty years has seen American philosophers become business ethicists, medical ethicists, military ethicists and animal ethicists, sometimes taking jobs in corporations, hospitals, service academies, prisons and other institutions to bring their thinking to the problems of those fields. It is more than the effort of individual academic philosophers, such as gay social critic Richard Mohr, or complicated feminist figures such as Martha Nussbaum, to draw attention to terrain traditionally bypassed by the discipline's establishment, and to extend their philosophical work to activism on issues, as Nussbaum has done in regard to poor women in India.

Finally, America the Philosophical is more than a phenomenon it encompasses, but to which it cannot be reduced: the transformation by which America, once urged by Emerson to stand on its own intellectual feet, has become a net exporter rather than importer of professional academic philosophy, an intellectual bank whose bottom line is so much in the black that major thinkers overseas, such as Australian ethicist Peter Singer, head here to shine in a bigger arena. The development is not new. As far back as the mid-1980s, the *Economist* observed that "British philosophy now consists of sophisticated commentary on the bright ideas of Americans." In Germany, leading philosophers such as Jürgen Habermas direct their theorizing toward ideas developed by the American pragmatists, and the twenty-first century has seen the founding of a John Dewey Institute at a German university. In France, Jacques Bouveresse, best known for his maverick promotion of Anglo-American analytic philosophy in the land of sometimes murky "masters of thought," was elected to the prestigious philosophy chair at the Collège de France. In Scandinavia, in Southeast Asia, in South America, professors evoke the names of modern American luminaries, using the field's usual last-name shorthand—Rorty, Danto, Quine, Rawls, Nussbaum—as they once did those of the French, English and Germans.

No, more than all that, acquiescing to America the Philosophical requires seeing America in the new millennium as directly, ebulliently and ordinarily philosophical in a way that remains utterly unappreciated by philosophers, media and the general public alike. It is to see Americans as almost uniquely able, given their rude independence of mind, to pierce the chief metaphorical scam of desiccated, moribund, yet still breathing Socratic philosophy: the "justification language-game" that I examine in Part 6 of this book. It is to see the United States as the exemplar of a paradigm of philosophy long overdue for recognition—one with roots in the pragmatically accented view of the ancient Greek thinker Isocrates—that suits the twenty-first century and jibes with accelerating trends of globalization in economics, politics, culture, ethics and communication.

This is not an easy picture to accept, either within our borders or without. To promote America at home as the world's preeminent philosophical culture is to clash with almost every cliché of American intellectual history, including Tocqueville's and Hofstadter's. To vaunt it overseas is not only revisionary, but offensive, certain to be received as one more example of American cultural jingoism and imperialism, the cerebral equivalent of trying to dominate the film market in France and Japan, bully countries into a "coalition of the willing," or impose our notions of governance on China. Moreover, both here and abroad, it appears to ignore significant evidence for the traditional image of America the Unphilosophical, whose shadings and subtexts, embedded in most domestic handlings of philosophy, appear to seal our local sense of philosophy's unimportance. Consider some evidence, then, for the conventional view of America the Unphilosophical.

In the world of American politics, philosophers appear to play almost no part. A few who did in the past, such as drive-time radio jock and former secretary of education William J. Bennett, or former Boston University chancellor and onetime Massachusetts gubernatorial candidate John Silber, shed their togas fairly early for bare-knuckled politics. A few, like neoconservative icon Leo Strauss, get counted as players only on an extended trickle-down theory, because critics insist that they're beyond-the-grave influences on contemporary figures such as Bush-era neocons. Still others—one thinks of Cornel West, who advised presidential candidate Bill Bradley, or William Galston, who served briefly as a deputy assistant to President Clinton, or the younger PhDs who worked in the past for Representatives Lee Hamilton and Tom Lantos under a Mellon Foundation grant—have come near the actual machinery of policy. But they remain aberrations.

Elsewhere in the world, by contrast, philosophers more directly influence and enter politics, sometimes dominating it. In the Czech Republic, originally founded by philosopher Tomáš Masaryk, people revered their "philosopher-president," Václav Havel, even when they opposed his idealistic vision. In Italy, philosopher Massimo Cacciari, twice the mayor of Venice, looms large on the political scene, and philosopher, novelist and journalist Umberto Eco serves as cultural touchstone of the nation. In England, philosopher Roger Scruton, who played consultant and courtier to Margaret Thatcher, still loudly voices Tory concerns. In France, the likes of Bernard-Henri Lévy, Alain Finkielkraut and Alain Badiou follow in the activist and media-provocateur footsteps of Sartre and Foucault, while Luc Ferry, once a voice of 1968 protest, ran a national ministry.

In Peru, the Shining Path terrorists, founded by philosophy lecturer Abimael Guzmán (sure enough, while on leave from his department), almost brought the country to its knees. In Cuba, a fading Fidel Castro quotes Plato in his autobiography, and Venezuela's Hugo Chávez, visiting Havana for chemo sessions, announces that he's borrowed Fidel's copy of *Thus Spake Zarathustra* to read. In the Soviet Union, philosopher Ivan Frolov advised Mikhail Gorbachev in developing perestroika.

In Israel, the award of the Israel Prize, the nation's highest honor, to the nonagenarian leftist philosopher Yeshayahu Leibowitz—a scathing critic of successive governments—so infuriated top leaders that the cabinet itself debated the prize, with the prime minister at the time threatening to boycott the ceremony until Leibowitz (who once warned that Jews in the West Bank were becoming "Judeo-Nazis") withdrew. Later, Israel awarded the same prize to philosophy professor Asa Kasher, whom the Israeli Defense Forces tapped to create a controversial "ethics of war" for it.

Is America more philosophical than these lands?

In the world of American print media, a similar lack of standing remains the norm. An American philosopher's best shot at coverage is an obituary if he or she lives past seventy, though few get what newspaper people call the "skyline"—a headline *over* the masthead, which French star Jacques Derrida nabbed in the *Süddeutsche Zeitung*. The *New York Times* occasionally grants philosophers print acreage—particularly if they live in or near New York—but nothing like the generous territory now allotted in the *Times's* philosophy blog, the Stone. Some stars of the trade show up once in a while on the op-ed page of the *Times* or other broadsheet papers, but more to announce than to argue. Few if any philosophers write regularly for newspapers or major magazines. Despite a seemingly bottomless appetite for guests, neither the nation's better TV talk shows nor its tabloid trash fests have ever hosted America's great philosophers, even in a compromise format ("Philosophers Who Sleep with Their Ideological Opponents!!!"). If future archivists examine post-1950s American television, they'll find such immortal moments as Drew Barrymore flashing herself on David Letterman's desk, but not a minute of Rawls, widely touted as the greatest American political philosopher of the twentieth century, pondering justice. When 9/11 terrorized Americans into deep and often polemical thought on the meaning of good and evil, a potentially looming clash of civilizations, and the limits of freedom here and abroad, academic philosophers proved noticeably absent from the airwaves, as they have throughout the ongoing turmoil in Iraq, Afghanistan and the Mideast. The first American "reality show" with philosophers awaits its green light.

Again, the situation across the Atlantic differs sharply. In England, philosophers such as A. C. Grayling, Julian Baggini and Scruton write regularly for the newspapers, author Alain de Botton hosts a multipart television series about great thinkers, and two general-interest magazines, *Philosophy Now*, a bimonthly, and *The Philosophers' Magazine*, a quarterly, compete for readers. In France, yet another glossy philosophy magazine, *Philosophie,* can be found at kiosks at Orly and Charles de Gaulle airports, and the French tradition of inviting philosophers on talk shows looms so large that one scholar, Tamara Chaplin, devoted an entire study—*Turning on the Mind: French Philosophers on Television*—to the subject.

America the Philosophical? *Mais non.* And the case for America the Unphilosophical continues.

In the world of broader American publishing, literature, art and culture, serious references to philosophy, in either highbrow or mass-market material, barely register compared to their frequency elsewhere. While a philosopher occasionally breaks into the publishing limelight with a book, such as Harry G. Frankfurt in 2005 with his bite-size *On Bullshit,* it's almost always a fluke, explained by peculiar circumstances. Frankfurt's brief casual essay, smartly repackaged by Princeton University Press with a brash title, appealed to those eager to knock off a serious book without too much time investment. The combination of title and micro size accounted for the book's allure more than Frankfurt's reasoning, which, the retired Spinoza scholar charmingly told one interviewer, he no longer considered cogent. When another philosophy professor, Colin McGinn—well known in the profession as an aspiring public intellectual—tried to capitalize on Frankfurt's strategy by issuing a pocket-size seventy-six-page effort titled *Mindfucking* (McGinn acknowledged in his first sentence that Frankfurt's book "prompted me to undertake a similar enquiry"), it fell stillborn from the press.

Here in the U.S., Socrates is perhaps best known as Sew-crates, the guide in *Bill & Ted's Excellent Adventure,* a successful lowbrow movie about two teenage time travelers who transport the old gadfly to present-day San Dimas, California, which he finds "cool." A *New York Times* article about novelist Rebecca Newberger Goldstein, who temporarily quit teaching philosophy to concentrate on fiction, noted that, while her five books had "received literary raves, their philosophical bent has hardly assured widespread readership."

In England, on the other hand, one can identify a whole genre of art devoted to the celebrated Cambridge philosopher Ludwig Wittgenstein alone. Monty Python immortalized him for a new audience by extolling his beer-drinking prowess. Derek Jarman highlighted his homosexuality in a film. Dame Iris Murdoch plunked Wittgenstein spin-offs into her novels for years after Elias Canetti convinced her to publish her first philosophical fiction, *Under the Net* (1954). Elsewhere in English culture,

Tom Stoppard weaves brilliant theater around philosophical repartee, and the pop group Scritti Politti reprises "I'm in Love with Jacques Derrida." In France, Eric Rohmer made philosophical conversations such as the one in *My Night at Maud's* a signature of elite "French cinema," an art form in which the male protagonist is as likely to be a Sorbonne philosophy professor as a cop. The more philosophical the novelist in France, from Voltaire and Sartre to Michel Tournier and Michel Houellebecq, the quicker the rise to stardom.

Indeed, in fiction throughout Europe and much of the world, attention to philosophy signals literary seriousness without the implication that it estranges readers. Milan Kundera assumed the crown of philosophical novelist from Camus in the 1970s and '80s, and new champions such as Eco and Roberto Bolaño pop up regularly, even outside the largest philosophical cultures. The Turkish philosopher and novelist Bilge Karasu won the International Pegasus Prize for Literature, and Dutch writer Connie Palmen took a European Novel of the Year Award for *The Laws,* which begins with a fourteen-year-old Dutch girl reading Sartre and follows her through to philosophical maturity. Across the continent, *Sophie's World,* by Jostein Gaarder, a novel about philosophy by a Norwegian high school teacher, became an unshakable bestseller on the order of John Grisham or Tom Clancy, but did less well in America. More recently, Ismail Kadare, the Albanian Kafka, won the Man Booker International Prize.

Once again, the comparisons to America seem embarrassing rather than supportive of the U.S. as a dynamic philosophical culture. Attention to yet a fourth area—education—further challenges the notion of America the Philosophical.

In the United States, philosophy remains, despite its image as a bedrock of the Western humanistic tradition, a subject required of almost no one before college and of few during college (except at Catholic institutions), a major whose popularity is eclipsed by business and computer-studies options. In the 1980s, prestigious Rockefeller University simply disbanded its first-rate philosophy department when a cost crunch hit. In the early 1990s, City College of New York came close to eliminating its philosophy department as insufficiently "vocational." Reports of institutions seeking to close down philosophy programs on those grounds remain a regular feature of philosophy blogs. In 2008, the University of Florida announced the shuttering of its PhD program in philosophy, the best in the southeastern U.S., drawing fire from philosophers around the country.

While pro-philosophy counterexamples exist in the world of education—the healthy support given the subject around the country and world by committed American philanthropists such as George Soros, Laurance Rockefeller and Sir John Templeton, and the decades-long efforts to promote philosophy for children by Matthew Lipman at his Montclair, New Jersey, institute—philosophy largely lives hand to mouth. By contrast, in France, all high school students study philosophy and take a nationwide exam in it, familiarizing them with the basics. As for Germany, the country in which philosophy has traditionally enjoyed its greatest prestige, it names intercity trains for philosophers: on a clear or unclear day, you can see the "Hannah Arendt" or "Theodor Adorno" pull out of Frankfurt.

Finally, the views of some of our own intellectuals and authors threaten to put the last nail in the coffin of America the Philosophical. Richard Feynman (1918–1988), the feisty Nobel Laureate in Physics, regularly attacked philosophy as "low-level baloney" and derided philosophers for always "making stupid remarks" about science. Books trumpeting the low intellectual quality of American culture now constitute a genre of their own.

In *Idiot America: How Stupidity Became a Virtue in the Land of the Free,* magazine writer Charles Pierce argued that we live in the land of his title, "the America of the medicine wagon and the tent revival, the America of the juke joint and the gambling den," that we remain "the best country ever in which to peddle complete public lunacy." In *Unscientific America: How Scientific Illiteracy Threatens Our Future,* authors Chris Mooney and Sheril Kirshenbaum warned that America is "home to a populace that, to an alarming extent, ignores scientific advances or outright rejects scientific principles," as well as a culture that "all too often questions the value of intellect and even glorifies dumbness." The most vehement such book came from Susan Jacoby, a thoughtful journalist with a track record of serious works on the Soviet Union, retaliatory justice, secularism and other weighty matters.

"During the past four decades," Jacoby asserted in *The Age of American Unreason,* "America's endemic anti-intellectual tendencies have been grievously exacerbated by a new species of semiconscious anti-rationalism, feeding on and fed by an ignorant popular culture of video images and unremitting noise that leaves no room for contemplation or logic." In Jacoby's view, "This new form of anti-rationalism, at odds not only with the nation's heritage of eighteenth-century Enlightenment reason but with modern scientific knowledge, has propelled a surge of anti-intellectualism capable of inflicting vastly greater damage than its historical predecessors inflicted on American culture and politics."

Jacoby's examples of "junk thought" and "junk culture" encompassed an enormous range: religious fundamentalism (her chief *bête noire*), intelligent-design theory, video and digital culture, iPod cocooning, celebrity infotainment, local control of education, book packaging, innumeracy, youth culture, expert bashing, Baby Einstein videos, Social Darwinism, the anti-vaccination movement.

Jacoby's examples hardly made her case, any more than Pierce's prime evidence—conservative talk-show hosts and intelligent-design advocates—made his. Mooney and Kirshenbaum, as well, despite their spirited call to arms, had to acknowledge that America also happens to be "the world's scientific leader," that Americans "built the bomb, reached the moon, decoded the genome, and created the Internet." Indeed, sound judgments about American culture always depend on how one sifts through large heaps of evidence, not a pocketful of examples.

So while Jacoby's hostility toward religious fundamentalism led her to see its presence in American life as the embodiment of irrationality, other secularists countered that religious thought persists not because believers are dimwitted or can't reason, but because concepts like God, faith, and design possess logical peculiarities that stymie disproof of religious belief in the absence of prior agreement on how one defines terms. A general observation by the MIT philosopher Alex Byrne applied doubly in that realm: "Conclusive refutations of philosophical positions are about as rare as sightings of the ivory-billed woodpecker."

Instead of viewing the rich debate between American secularists and believers as proof of our intellectual vibrancy, Jacoby saw a dumbed-down culture in which rationalists failed to silence believers with muzzles authorized by the Enlightenment. In a similar way, some in American media during the first years of Barack Obama's presidency decried the raucous quality of town hall forums and debates on health care reform and other issues because rude polemicists—the "You lie!" crowd—shared airtime with sensible participants.

Jacoby's overall argument underwhelmed because she stacked the deck. She took forums of cultural life she disdained—dopey TV shows, formulaic drive-time radio, fragmented Internet discourse, newspapers that pander to lowest-common-denominator tastes—as the definitive markers of American intellectual life. But for many thoughtful Americans, life was elsewhere, however occasionally shared with others in such venues. In a nation with more educated people, college graduates, authors, thinkers, books, and general literacy than ever before, philosophically oriented Americans paid attention to quality publications, Web sites, films, and TV and radio shows and dumped those that aimed at bottom-feeding taste. Jacoby piled on *The Da Vinci Code* and *The O'Reilly Factor* while ignoring NPR and BOOK TV. Yet the latter played the same role in the "edifice of middlebrow culture" as the vanished media (e.g., *Saturday Review*) for which Jacoby confessed nostalgia. Because she insisted that edifice had "collapsed," they didn't exist in her inventory.

Still, Jacoby's portrait of America the Nearly Imbecilic added to all the other misgivings, and provided a sorry counterimage to any picture of a New Athens flourishing between the Atlantic and Pacific. Might the only philosophical books right for Americans be Tom Morris's *Philosophy for Dummies* or Jay Stevenson's *The Complete Idiot's Guide to Philosophy*? How can America the Philosophical make sense?

It does, I submit, if one emulates what philosophers ideally do—subject preconceptions to ongoing analysis, and use one's imagination. The traditional clichés get it wrong. Examples that run counter to the vision of this book, such as some of the ones above, prop up the clichés because they imply a musty view of philosophy. They depend too much on activities christened "philosophy" according to antiquated or academic criteria, and pay too little mind to what honest intellectuals increasingly recognize as philosophy today.

For whether one prefers the view of Habermas, Germany's foremost philosopher, that truth issues only from deliberation conducted under maximum conditions of openness and freedom, or the view of Rorty, America's most important recent philosopher, that better conceptual vocabularies rather than firmer truths should be our aim, or South African expatriate John McDowell's belief that a proper relationship between the world and language can yet be articulated if painstaking analysis continues to be done, it's plain that America's philosophical landscape—pluralistic, quantitatively huge, all potential criticisms available—provides a more conducive arena, or *agora*, than any other. If we take the best contemporary thinkers at their word and think of philosophy as an ever-expanding practice of persuasion, rather than a cut-and-dried discipline that hunts down eternal verities and comes pushpinned for media (or internal) consumption, America the Philosophical—a far larger entity than the roughly eleven thousand members of the American Philosophical Association—not only looks more likely, but plainly outstrips any rival as the paramount philosophical culture. In the early years of the twenty-first century, America is to philosophy what Italy is to art, or Norway to skiing: a perfectly designed environment for the practice.

Some evidence of that comes in the very cultural areas that writers such as Jacoby deride. Just as the United Kingdom boasts its independent philosophical writers, such as Baggini and de Botton, who have shown that philosophy transported from ivory tower to street or café can sell books, so America still produces followers in the footsteps of Will Durant, whose *The Story of Philosophy* (1926) sold millions of copies, launched Simon & Schuster as a New York publishing power, filled the coffers of the Book-of-the-Month Club for decades, and introduced more Americans to philosophy than any other work.

Christopher Phillips, an ethnically Greek graduate of the College of William & Mary (class of '81), transformed his student love of conversations about Socrates into a career by conducting "Symposium" gatherings around the country that he called "Socrates Cafés." The venues were inspired—a gambling den in Las Vegas; Billy Graham's last revival meeting; the Wounded Knee memorial on South Dakota's Pine Ridge Indian Reservation; the steps of Capitol Hill with elementary school children. Three books that came out of them—*Socrates Café, Six Questions of Socrates* and *Socrates in Love*—drew both sales and the praise of no less than Robert Coles, who found in them "ancient wisdom in all its complexity brought vividly to life."

At the same time, no fewer than three U.S. publishers—Open Court, Wiley-Blackwell and the University of Kentucky Press—regularly tap into a bustling market with series aimed at connecting philosophy to popular culture, producing, at an amazing pace, titles such as *The Simpsons and Philosophy, The Matrix and Philosophy, Facebook and Philosophy* and *Twilight and Philosophy*. All contain freshly written essays, mainly by professional philosophers who double as rabid enthusiasts of the pop culture subject they write about. Although the books rarely get mainstream-media reviews, they've proved extremely popular. According to David Ramsay Steele, Open Court's editorial director, his all-time bestseller in the series, *The Simpsons and Philosophy*, has sold more than 500,000 copies.

In fact, philosophy books and objects that don't abandon their down-to-earth American sense of humor—or even flaunt it—often turn into hits. In 2007, two middle-aged Harvard alumni who became pals as philosophy undergraduates, Thomas Cathcart and Daniel Klein—neither of whom continued in academe—cowrote a book on their shared enthusiasm for "philogags," jokes that make a philosophical point. In their introduction to *Plato and a Platypus Walk into a Bar,* they explained that "philosophy and jokes proceed from the same impulse: to confound our sense of the way things are, to flip our world upside down, and to ferret out hidden, often uncomfortable truths about life. What the philosopher calls an insight, the gagster calls a zinger."

Aristotle and an Aardvark Go to Washington followed the next year. As both coauthors reached their biblical three-score-and-ten, along came *Heidegger and a Hippo Walk Through Those Pearly Gates* in 2009. More than a few people were laughing, and learning—the same people, possibly, who bought Foucault and Kierkegaard dolls from the Unemployed Philosophers Guild, available in better gift shops everywhere (www .philosophersguild.com), or who asked questions at www.askphilosophers .org, a Web site on which philosophers answer queries "about love, nothingness, and everything else." When the *New York Times* added its philosophy blog called the Stone in 2010, the site, edited by New School philosopher Simon Critchley, drew thousands of comments and 6 million page views.

Similarly, evidence of philosophy's growing appeal to younger Americans continues to mount. According to an overview article in the *Philadelphia Inquirer,* undergraduate philosophy programs (as opposed to those shuttered graduate departments) rose from 765 to 817 in the decade from 1998 to 2008, and schools across the country reported sharp rises in philosophy majors, from City University of New York (a 51 percent increase from 2002 to 2008) to Texas A&M (a 100 percent rise since the 1990s). Some philosophy departments developed links to more empirical disciplines like psychology and cognitive science through such trends as the "experimental philosophy" or "x-phi" movement (symbol: a burning armchair)—x-phi'ers conduct experiments and surveys a la scientists and social scientists to test common intuitions and beliefs. A broader slice of the student body appears to value the field.

The major also increasingly appeals to American undergraduates because evidence shows employers associate its graduates with high intelligence and a flexible, critical, independent frame of mind that helps them master change and new information better than many other entry-level candidates. The *Inquirer* story noted that philosophy majors scored highest of all majors from 2001 to 2004 on the verbal reasoning and analytical writing parts of the Graduate Record Examination, a key test for applicants to graduate school. Citing federal figures, the paper reported that degrees in philosophy and religious studies rose from 8,506 in 1998–99 to 12,444 in 2008–09, a 46 percent rise.

The status of America as a philosophical culture is thus not an open-and-shut case. But to bring the notion of America the Unphilosophical, a deeply embedded commonplace about our country, crashing down like the Berlin Wall, requires more. To defeat the idea on a serious analytic and cultural plane, a full-scale assault on the misconception is necessary, delivered through seven separate efforts at cliché crushing:

1) An overview of the official American philosophical tradition as a tale not of argument machines, but of human beings who got things both right and wrong.

2) A broadly reportorial account of how nonprofessional philosophers have co-opted many of America's philosophical challenges and issues, and how astute cultural criticism recognizes their work as philosophical.

3) An equally concrete picture of how former outsiders—African Americans, women, gays, and Native American thinkers—have expanded America's philosophical tent.

4) A telling chronicle of a wholly fresh and distinctive genre of philosophy in America—cyberphilosophy.

5) A radical explanation of how American philosophy operates under the sign of Isocrates, not Socrates, whose acolyte Plato pulled off one of intellectual history's great public relations triumphs by identifying "philosophy" with Socrates's approach and denying the term to Isocrates's method.

6) A fresh conceptual vision of why Americans reject supposedly airtight "justifications" for confidently asserted positions in philosophy and other areas of life—a tale best told through the mighty achievement, but ultimate failure, of America's most honored modern philosopher, John Rawls.

7) A summing-up that argues how all of these forces help explain why, in the person of Barack Obama, we've ended up with our most cosmopolitan, philosopher-in-chief president since Woodrow Wilson.

America the Philosophical accordingly divides into six parts and an epilogue. It reflects my own multipronged approach to the subject as a longtime literary critic and cultural correspondent for a newspaper, combatant in the philosophy wars, and professor of philosophy at various colleges and universities. As a career critic of books—most regularly as literary critic of the *Philadelphia Inquirer* for twenty-five years (1984–2009)—I think through books, and frequently do so here. As a longtime cultural reporter, I believe close-ups of individual thinkers, gathered over many years, open eyes and change minds, and so, unlike some writers on philosophy—but rather like Mencken when he produced *The American Language*—I provide reportage on the assumption that facts often persuade faster than arguments. Finally, as a teacher of philosophy for thirty years, I've developed my own views—steeped in decades of studying the subject and exploring elusive concepts like metaphor and rhetoric—of how things actually operate in the intellectual world. Be warned, then, or attracted—readers will find philosophy itself laced through this book.

In Part 1, "American Philosophy and the Tradition," I enter the map of mainstream American philosophy. My aim is to walk the reader into the subject through three snapshots of players at both its fringe and center, to ground the reader in some of their lived reality. Accounts of our ongoing national debate on what it means to be an American come next, preceding an overview of the formidable Harvard-and-Ivy-League-dominated tradition of uniformly white-male great philosophers—Emerson, Peirce, James, Santayana, Dewey, Quine and more—that forms what many professionals see as the historic spine of their discipline. Lest that attention to gender seem a quaint, out-of-date exercise, be advised that at the December 2007 annual meeting of the American Philosophical Association in Baltimore, octogenarian Hilary Putnam, the senior living carrier of Harvard's baton, presented a Dewey Lecture on "Twelve Philosophers Who Influenced Me"—all of them American or British white males. Three years later, when intellectual historian James Miller of the New School published his much-reviewed *Examined Lives,* an account of twelve leading philosophers from Socrates to Nietzsche, he chose twelve men, all but one of them (Augustine) white. The idea that philosophy remains a white-male activity dies hard.

That discussion brings the reader up to the revolution spurred by the chief transitional figure in academic philosophy's recent life, Richard Rorty. His broad-minded, internal perspective on the obsessions of his colleagues ended a two-millennium limitation of philosophy to the narrow, bad-faith search for eternal, objective truths. It also liberated others to conceive of philosophy in new ways.

After detailing Rorty's vision of philosophy as a persuasive practice that ought to accomplish its goals through new imaginative enterprises, I then outline in Part 2, "Abandoning Toothless Truth," a comparative, critical assault on America the Unphilosophical by confronting a key elitist prop on which its plausibility rests. After explaining how sophisticated American critics came to reject rigorous divisions of "highbrow," "lowbrow" and "middlebrow" in the arts, I urge the chattering classes to similarly reject those divisions in philosophy (a liberation already accomplished on the American "street"). Among my targets I include blinkered college deans and presidents who, often out of ignorance of the field, continue to permit a supposedly highbrow, rigorous form of epistemological philosophy (the etiolated and decadent one that Rorty brilliantly eviscerated) to dominate academic departments under the protected title of philosophy. Whatever sociological divisions exist between intellectuals and others in American society, our voices effectively crisscross in the great persuasive mix of American public discourse, and the grip upon us of the amorphous content we call "common sense" remains strong.

Part 2 then continues the assault on America the Unphilosophical by piling on reportorial content. I try to counterbalance the old-fashioned, white-male-dominated view of philosophy outlined in Part 1 with a selection of similar white-male thinkers not usually categorized or taken seriously as philosophers: psychologists such as B. F. Skinner; literary thinkers from Kenneth Burke to Edward Said; political scientists, including Francis Fukuyama and Dennis Thompson; scientific storytellers like Oliver Sacks; pop sages ranging from Robert Fulghum to Hugh Hefner; and media philosophers of the caliber of Max Lerner and Bill Moyers.

My strategy is simple, and in line with a broader view of argument than that of syllogistic demonstration, one that emulates the ancient procedure of heaping on relevant information, then seeing if it makes a difference. In essence, I challenge the reader with a question: even if you privately cling to the notion that philosophy and white-male authority figures must be inextricably linked, do you still believe the stereotype of your own culture?

Happily, we're no longer a culture totally dominated by white males, and that bolsters America the Philosophical as well. In Part 3, "The

Rising Outsiders," I offer a similar overview, inevitably imperfect and incomplete, of the contributions made by African Americans, women, Native Americans and gays to expanding American philosophy's big tent: examining figures as know-it-all as Ayn Rand, as say-it-well as Susan Sontag, as find-it-out as Martha Nussbaum, as committed to catalytic prophecy as Camille Paglia and Cornel West. Just modestly setting out their achievements, I believe, communicates the enormous pressure for revision exerted on the traditional misconception of America as a nonphilosophical culture. In a longer book, I might easily have added sections on the growth of Latino philosophy, Asian American philosophy, and other areas worthy of attention.

Part 4 then follows with yet another flank attack on America the Unphilosophical from an up-to-the-minute direction, albeit one rooted in traditional intellectual life: the extraordinary appearance of published work I call "Gutenberg's Revenge: The Explosion of Cyberphilosophy." My hope here is to convince the reader that the body of work I selectively describe, and the thinkers who've produced it, confirm America's place at the forefront of any philosophical thinking we dare to call modern.

Yet, as indicated at the outset, America the Philosophical means more than sheer volume of persuasive activity. It requires a proper understanding of philosophy as a practice in which America snugly fits. In Part 5, "Isocrates: A Man, Not a Typo," I confront America the Unphilosophical with a second remapping of culture that seeks to fulfill the task Rorty urges on the modern philosopher: an imaginative revision of the way we think about both the history of philosophy and American culture, one that might rock some of our clichés in the history of ideas. This reconfiguration of America's place in Western philosophy and of the origins of Western philosophy itself, rooted in ancient history, is long overdue. American philosophers in the twenty-first century, I submit, are the children of Isocrates (436–338 B.C.), the nearly forgotten Greek thinker who insisted that what he did should be called "philosophy," not Socrates (469–399 B.C.), the know-it-all who claimed to know nothing. In their bones and instincts, Americans as well hark back to Isocrates, and not the hero of Plato, who, in the hands of the latter puppeteer, successfully stigmatized Isocrates and his ilk for all posterity as "Sophists" hostile to truth, sharpies doing something other than philosophy.

Our lineage of broad-minded resistance in America to eternal right answers and conventional justifications extends back to Isocrates, whose reflections on how to deal with the ideas of other cultures, and what it meant to be "a Greek" in the ancient world, resemble our own contemporary musings about what it means to be an "American" in the twenty-first century. Just as Rorty's questioning of narrow conceptions of truth and knowledge spurred a more public, democratic conception of how to argue and define concepts within philosophy, so the thought of Isocrates and those who followed him shook up formalistic notions of how persuasion works in society, and articulated a philosophical tradition to which America belongs. It is Isocrates, not Socrates, whom Americans should salute as the hero of classic Greek philosophy.

Finally, America the Philosophical reflects the independent attitude exhibited by Americans in the face of putative justifications posed to them, from the simplest arguments to the most impressive intellectual treatises. In Part 6, "Just Saying No to Justification," I tell the intertwined story of John Rawls—author of *A Theory of Justice* (1971), the most praised book of political philosophy in modern times—and the ultimate failure of his attempt to justify a particular conception of justice in American life. In doing so, I sketch a broad remapping of cultural language—what I call the "justification language-game"—that I plan to flesh out and document more rigorously elsewhere.

I close by reflecting in my Epilogue on how the true nature of American society and culture today, its core philosophical openness and diversity, is ably represented by Barack Obama. Critics mock him as "professorial," but they've got the wrong *p* word. In his commitment to multiple points of view, his pragmatist insistence on data and flexible thinking, his outreach to opponents, his stern refusal to be lured into the gutter of ad hominem denunciations, his acknowledgment of errors, he brings to fruition forces of American philosophical maturity that remain uncredited by almost all scholars and observers of this country.

The image of America the Unphilosophical persists because conventional academics and pundits continue to identify all philosophy with a Socratic approach despite its undermining over the past century and a half by critics from Nietzsche and Wittgenstein to the pragmatists. That identification now stands recognized as wrongheaded in a globalized world in which multiple notions of truth, knowledge, beauty and other core concepts continually open up to new audiences. As scholar and former *Economist* executive editor Anthony Gottlieb concluded when he tried to wrap his arms around the history of philosophy from the ancient Greeks to the Renaissance, "the history of philosophy is more the history of a sharply inquisitive cast of mind than the history of a sharply defined discipline. The traditional image of it as a sort of meditative science of pure thought strangely cut off from other subjects is largely a trick of the historical light."

Americans have thus not so much "evaded" philosophy, in the provocative phrase of Cornel West, as they've sidestepped antiquated conceptions of it. In the post-positivist, post–Cold War, pan-Google era in which we live, America the Philosophical—the country, not the book—can be seen as a coruscating achievement in the pragmatist project that's been unfolding for centuries. It's a rough-hewn implementation of what truth, ethics, beauty and a host of core philosophical notions must be in an interdependent nation and world village no longer able to ignore variant traditions and conceptual categories of others, but equally unwilling to give up the notion that some beliefs are better than others. Our country is not "Idiot America," but "Isocratic America"—a place where the battle between dogma and doggedness in seeking answers never ends, from sea to shining sea.

PART 1

AMERICAN PHILOSOPHY AND THE TRADITION

THERAPISTS, BOOTSTRAPPERS, INFANTRY

The moment wiseguy journalists heard about Lou Marinoff's professional bent—lobbying for philosophers to practice as therapists, to go head-to-head with psychologists and psychiatrists—the jokes and headlines flew fast and funny: "I Shrink, Therefore I Am"; "An Aphorism a Day Keeps the Doctor Away"; "The Uncompensated Life Is Not Worth Living"; "How Many Philosophers Can You Fit on the Head of a Couch?"

Marinoff knew how reporters mock everything, and had the clips to prove it, but the middle-aged CCNY philosophy professor also understood the importance of the counter-jab. Yes, compared with the suicide forced on Seneca by Nero, or getting shot by a student like the German philosopher Moritz Schlick, a little gentle tweaking hardly mattered. Still, it annoyed him.

"This is an example of mass culture's incessant drive for the lowest common denominator," complained the bearded, intense-looking Canadian native, clad in a Plato T-shirt, as he relaxed in his Jersey City apartment and railed against media jollity about his work. "How can we further simplify what we've already oversimplified?" Marinoff asked, his rhetorical questions dripping sarcasm. "How can we further dumb down what we've already made unintelligible by dumbing down? Can we do this with philosophy? That's the challenge!"

Fast-talking, forceful and good-humored, Marinoff resented the simplistic reception his "philosophical counseling" movement received, the droll arrows that greeted his first book, *Plato, Not Prozac! Applying Philosophy to Everyday Problems.* He'd wanted it to become the bible—or *Interpretation of Dreams*—of the movement.

"When people come to see Dr. Marinoff," the book's jacket copy announced, "they do not get endless discussions about their childhoods, quick prescriptions for anti-depressants, or tedious analyses of their behavior patterns. Instead, they learn how the ideas of the world's great thinkers can shed light on the way they live, from Kierkegaard's thoughts on coping with death and Kant's theory of obligation to the I Ching's guidelines on adapting to change and Aristotle's advice to pursue reason and moderation."

Indeed, Marinoff ventured into every messy corner of everyday life—relationship trauma, career frustration, family strife, doubt about life's meaning and coping with loss, while offering a five-step plan for identifying, expressing, analyzing, contextualizing and solving a problem. Case studies about "Vincent," "Doug," "Janet" and "Larry" wove their situations together with insights from wisdom traditions and enough jazzy one-liners to keep even a neurotic reading for more than fifty minutes. Philosophical counseling, in Marinoff's version, targeted the future, not the past. It did not "disease-ify" every human problem but accepted that having problems is normal. Despite the book's absolutist title, Marinoff admitted early on that "[s]ome people may not benefit from Plato, just as others may not benefit from Prozac. Some may need Prozac first, then Plato later, or Prozac and Plato together."

"I work with a person as a human being," explained Marinoff, leaning over his dining-room table, "not as an encyclopedia of aphorisms, or as a database that matches your problem with some fortune cookie." He'd been counseling clients (not "patients") for years, sometimes at $100 an hour, sometimes pro bono.

Marinoff liked to cite the example of a successful Wall Street businessman who came to him because his wife was having an affair, which shook his fundamental beliefs about life. Marinoff said that by careful questioning, he established that the man didn't want to end his marriage, as he initially claimed, but to preserve it. Marinoff then led the man through Kant's principles of forgiveness, compassion and duty, enabling the man to see forgiveness as a strength, not a weakness.

"What the media want," Marinoff said, "is for me to be waving another magic wand, to be someone who says, Plato! You feel better now? That's nonsense." Marinoff was press-savvy enough to know that his book's catchy title bore some of the blame. *Good Reasoning, Not Prozac* wouldn't have been as snappy. But if "philosophical counseling" ever takes off in America, it may be because an idea whose time has come, and a Woody-Allenish philosopher with a jaunty, colloquial style, somehow found each other.

Philosophical counseling, Marinoff acknowledged, was pioneered by philosopher Gerd Achenbach in Germany in the early 1980s. Achenbach urged personal counseling that drew on insights developed in philosophical dialogue. Opposed to dogmatic psychological theories, Achenbach envisioned a freewheeling "dialogic dance" between participants that would produce self-understanding. Achenbach's ideas caught on in the Netherlands, Israel, Canada and other countries, where hundreds of philosophical practitioners now operate. Organizations formed, literature grew, Web sites appeared.

Marinoff entered the scene in the early '90s. Raised in Montreal, where he did a first degree in mathematical physics at Concordia University, he spent much of his twenties questing—as a poet, classical guitarist, and "Dharma bum"—before settling down at age twenty-nine to study philosophy of science at University College, London. In 1991, with a doctorate in academically respectable "decision theory," he moved to Vancouver to take a part-time position at the University of British Columbia's Centre for Applied Ethics.

"Every week," Marinoff recalled, "one of us was on radio or TV or quoted in the newspaper. All of a sudden, people started coming to us, or even walking in off the street and demanding to see a philosopher. . . . I developed protocols. I started seeing people." Marinoff found that many former patients of psychiatrists or psychologists considered them dogmatic, controlling, condescending and/or simply unhelpful, and wanted to try something new. Then an e-mail from Israeli philosopher Ran Lahav led to Marinoff's contributing an article to the leading academic book on the subject—*Essays on Philosophical Counseling* (1995), which Lahav coedited. Marinoff and Lahav followed in the footsteps of earlier intellectual movements and next organized an international conference of their peers, at the University of British Columbia in 1994. The Third International Conference on Philosophical Practice, in midtown Manhattan in 1997, proved a watershed event. A splashy article in the *New York Observer* triggered a sheaf of pieces on Marinoff and company, as well as the book contract that became *Plato, Not Prozac!*

In the United States, two main organizations defined the field. The American Society for Philosophy, Counseling and Psychotherapy conducted academic meetings. The more recent American Philosophical Practitioners Association (APPA), cofounded by Marinoff in March 1998, was an activist trade group pushing for the national licensing of philosophical practitioners. In New York State, it drew support from

Rubén Díaz Jr., a South Bronx Democratic official who believed lower-income constituents should have as much access to philosophical therapy as wealthier clients. He introduced a bill that would enable philosophical therapists to be paid by third-party insurers such as HMOs.

Responses from the psychotherapeutic establishment were generally severe. The New York Health Plan Association, the industry's trade group in that state, mocked the Díaz proposal as an "I think, therefore I bill" plan. Dorothy Cantor, former president of the American Psychological Association, charged that philosophers couldn't handle "something as delicate as a person's mental health," and "totally ignore the role of the unconscious." Herbert Sacks, former president of the American Psychiatric Association, accused Marinoff of "practicing medicine without a license." Practicing psychiatrists gave it an equally frosty reception. "I think it's a big joke," said Michael Miller, a Philadelphia psychiatrist who practiced with his city's Psychiatric Physicians Association. "People who want to talk to philosophers are misguided."

While Miller conceded that individual philosophers might make good therapists in limited situations, the idea of their supplanting trained medical personnel in evaluating people who might have serious mental illness outraged him. "The intellectual tradition of philosophy has nothing to do with real-world problem-solving," said Miller. "They're the least qualified people to do that. They have no clinical experience. Even psychologists, in my opinion, are not qualified to handle most patients that I see." Miller thought the Pennsylvania Psychiatric Society would oppose licensing or accreditation of philosophical practitioners if it became an issue in his territory. "If they get paid, good for them," Miller said. "Anyone who goes to them is a fool. . . . In my estimation, any doctor who sends a patient to a philosopher deserves to lose his license."

Marinoff said he was used to hostility from established psychotherapists. "They try to scare people," he rejoined. "They always say, 'Oh, but they're not trained. What if a person is suicidal?'

"Do you think people are so damn stupid," Marinoff asked, "or inappropriately equipped by evolution, that when a crazy person gets on a subway, a bunch of untrained people—not clinical psychologists—don't know it? How trained do you have to be to recognize someone who's dangerous? It's nonsense."

Psychiatrists and psychologists, Marinoff added, had little to brag about concerning ability to predict behavior. "If only they could predict who the serial killers are, we wouldn't have them," Marinoff gibed. "Don't even get me started." Marinoff said his voicemail and e-mail overflowed when the psychotherapists attacked him. "They drive clients to us because people can see its hubris."

In any case, Marinoff reiterated, while philosophical counselors disagreed among themselves on a number of subjects—the appropriateness of fees, for instance, or government licensing—they aren't generally as dismissive of established therapists as vice versa, and he thought many of the latter misunderstood his movement. One of the philosophical practitioner's first tasks, Marinoff emphasized, was to establish whether a client might have a biologically based problem and be better served by a psychiatrist. Philosophical counseling, Marinoff liked to say, was "therapy for the sane," for "rational autonomous beings" who didn't "need to be patronized."

For Marinoff, the condescension from medical intellectuals didn't matter much; he joked that they were angry because he, unlike psychiatrists, had a pretty open schedule. He savored the large crowds that showed up for his bookstore appearances and resonated to his one-liners. ("The idea that every personal problem is a mental illness is itself a mental illness!") His humor, unusual for a philosopher, prodded some in one Barnes & Noble to give it a shot themselves. ("Have you heard about the sequel?" a retiree in the audience asked. "Voltaire, Not Viagra!")

Marinoff followed *Plato, Not Prozac!* with *The Big Questions,* in which he took the concept of philosophy's usefulness in everyday life "to the next level, by applying centuries of philosophy and literature to the central questions of modern existence." Then came *The Middle Way: Finding Happiness in a World of Extremes,* in which he delved "deeper into the quagmires that define our era" and juxtaposed "the teachings of the three great sages of all time—Aristotle, Buddha, and Confucius (the ABCs)—against all the extremes of religion, politics, and wealth that are increasingly polarizing our world." Each of his books referred to him on their covers as "Lou Marinoff, Ph.D." What Marinoff offered may have been everyday wisdom, but the parallel message seemed to be that it came with authority and expertise.

By 2009, the American Philosophical Practitioners Association, offering multiple certification programs, had celebrated its tenth anniversary with more than 750 members in several dozen countries. Even a few psychiatrists were members.

After the First Annual African American Philosophers Conference wrapped up at nearby Johnson C. Smith University, Johnny Washington, professor of philosophy at Southwest Missouri State, huddled in the lobby of the Doubletree Hotel in Charlotte, North Carolina, and recalled a college encounter.

"When I was an undergraduate at St. Xavier," he said, referring to his Chicago alma mater, "I was interested in social issues and I knew about Marcus Garvey [the Jamaican-born orator who organized an enormous mass movement of blacks in the 1920s]. I mentioned to another student, a white student, something about a black philosopher. And she sort of put me down, and said, 'Well, there aren't any black philosophers. There's no such thing.' So I went and got *The Philosophical Opinions of Marcus Garvey* and showed it to her and she just laughed. Almost insulted me. And said, this is nothing—or this is low stuff. That sort of did something to me. I just kept sort of thinking about it."

Now, decades later, Washington was the author of two books on Alain Locke (1886–1954), the Philadelphia-born impresario of the Harlem Renaissance who became the first black Rhodes Scholar, the first black to receive a PhD in philosophy from Harvard, and the chief black exponent of pragmatism, the distinctly American philosophy developed by Charles Peirce, William James and John Dewey. Decompressing in the same lobby, Archibald Laud-Hammond, a Ghanaian by birth who taught philosophy at Johnson C. Smith, reminisced about his days as a graduate student at the University of Virginia. "It was quite an experience," said the conference host. "Most of it bad."

"They didn't want to hear anything about African philosophy," he explained. " 'No,' they said, 'you have to do traditional philosophy.' Because I wanted to do something in African philosophy for my dissertation. But they discouraged me." So Smith wrote his dissertation on the law of attempted criminal actions, a more conventional topic. Even at Nashville's historically black Fisk University, where Vanderbilt University philosopher Lucius Outlaw did his undergraduate work, the subject of African American philosophy didn't quite exist. There was no discussion of it "at all," recalled Outlaw, who later made it his business to track the black presence in the profession.

In fact, all three men shared a common experience. They never attended a course in African or African American philosophy until they taught one. "This whole business of African American philosophy," explained Outlaw, "is something that got taken up and developed by this generation—by us." If black philosophers kept talking and their white colleagues didn't hear them, did they make a noise? It was a twist on a tired philosophical chestnut, but a pressing one. At a time when

Lucius Outlaw (1947–), professor of philosophy at Vanderbilt University and author
of *On Race and Philosophy*, began his intellectual journey at Fisk University.

black literary studies flourished, with leading scholars drawing lucrative
offers to jump from one school to another, and publishing houses falling
all over one another to issue texts by black writers, African American
philosophers remained where their literary colleagues had been a decade
before: outsiders vis-à-vis their mainstream discipline, yet eager to make
people pay attention. A few universities, such as Temple in Philadelphia,
and later Penn State at University Park, gave prominent focus to African
American philosophy, but they were exceptions.

The conference in Charlotte, hosted by a black institution founded
in 1867, aimed at attracting that kind of notice, but the result showed
both the promise and frustration of the project. Focusing on Anton
Wilhelm Amo, Locke and W. E. B. Du Bois—three controversial black
thinkers—the event drew only one white philosopher not affiliated with
the school, and barely forty attendees, despite national advertising. Why
so few whites?

"'Cause it's black," responded Leonard Harris, professor of philosophy at Purdue University and coauthor of the first definitive biography
of Locke. "Philosophy is among the most raciated professional societies
on earth. You're not going to find one that's any more racist. Nowhere."

Why so few blacks? That was a tougher question. Of the several thousand university teachers of philosophy in the United States, only a hundred plus were African American. Not so long before, only one black woman—Adrian Piper, then of Wellesley College—was a tenured full professor. You could count the number of first-year black philosophy graduate students on one hand.

But as the conference suggested, the numbers reflected a problem in intellectual public relations. The African and African American traditions in philosophy remained little known, even to potential enthusiasts. Laud-Hammond admitted that he had learned of Locke only a few years before, and few philosophers of any stripe knew about Amo, an African who taught philosophy in eighteenth-century Germany. Meanwhile, white philosophers practiced business as usual.

As he opened the conference, former Johnson C. Smith president Robert Albright echoed a theme of Cornel West, along with K. Anthony Appiah one of the few black philosophers to achieve mass-media fame (West was unable to attend). Albright urged that "the study of philosophy must be adopted by black Americans if social change is to come." The speakers then revealed just how vibrant black philosophy had been.

Laud-Hammond led off with a talk on the virtually forgotten Amo (ca.1703–ca.1759), an Ashanti born in the Gold Coast (now Ghana) and brought to Holland at age four. Baptized in 1708 and sent to Germany, Amo studied philosophy, law and medicine at the universities of Halle, Wittenberg and Hemstedt. Laud-Hammond, who was working on a book about Amo, informed the rapt audience that Amo's contemporaries praised him as a "genius" known for "outstanding uprightness." Amo eventually wrote three philosophical works, including *Treatise on the Art of Philosophizing Soberly and Accurately* and a critique of Descartes's theory of the mind, before returning home to the Gold Coast, where he reportedly became a soothsayer.

Yet Amo's most intriguing work, Laud-Hammond explained, was his *Inaugural Dissertation on the Rights of Blacks in Europe.* Unfortunately, only a summary survived. Scholars of black philosophy continued to comb the libraries of Europe for the original. "He was a genuine philosopher of the first class," Laud-Hammond concluded. Of course, it being a philosophy conference, a dispute quickly broke out over whether Amo—given his "Eurocentrism"—should really be considered an "African" philosopher. After spirited debate—enlivened by African philosopher Kwasi Wiredu's suggestion that Ashanti concepts influenced Amo's view of Descartes—the combatants agreed to disagree. The audience's appreciation continued as attention shifted to Locke and Du Bois. Washington provided an overview of the former, who remained best known for editing *The New Negro* (1925)—the anthology that defined the Harlem Renaissance as an artistic movement—despite decades as chairman of Howard University's philosophy department. Locke should be taken seriously as a major thinker, Washington insisted, citing Locke's first-rate articles and the connection between his radical relativism, Einsteinian science and modernism. Further discussion highlighted Locke's resistance to easy pigeonholing: he was a Bahai, a gay aesthete and an elitist whom some critics accused of sharing Booker T. Washington's overly accommodating attitude toward whites. Harris, editor of *The Philosophy of Alain Locke,* stressed how Locke viewed race—a crucial concept in African American thought—as a social rather than biological notion. Outlaw developed the theme later, arguing that Du Bois also thought of race pragmatically, seeing it as a "term of mobilization" rather than a clinical description. And so the conversation continued until closing time, touching on slavery, Afrocentrism, populism, self-deception and Du Bois's concept of "The Talented Tenth" (the educated black elite).

If black philosophers favored social theory more than their peers, it was understandable. They often came from backgrounds that made it hard to ignore real-life struggle. Outlaw's father, a janitor at the leading white Baptist church in his Mississippi hometown, sparred with him about race issues. His mother, a maid who lost six children in childbirth, wanted him to go into the church. Neither of Washington's parents graduated from college. The middle child of six brothers and two sisters, Washington grew up on a farm in Gainesville, Alabama, and first grew interested in philosophy while serving in Vietnam. Harris was the second son of a milkman in Cleveland.

"My family didn't know what philosophy was," Harris recalled. "They'd say it's psychology. I'd go home and my parents would tell people, 'My son's going to graduate school in psychology.' I'd say, 'I'm going to graduate school in philosophy.' They'd say, 'My son's going to graduate school in philosophy of psychology.'"

Outlaw best expressed the sensibility forged in many black philosophers by such memories. He described his waning enthusiasm in graduate school for the ahistorical and often artificial "analytic" philosophy that dominated the profession from 1950 to 1980, and still does. "Increasingly, I thought, wait a minute," he said. "Philosophy of science? Analytic philosophy? Analyzing sentences? I mean, folk are trying to figure out how to stop a war, people are trying to figure out how to get racial justice, I'm going to spend my time analyzing sentences? . . . I didn't come out of Mississippi to analyze sentences." Yet several black philosophers acknowledged that their social concerns played into white media clichés of black thinkers as automatic activists and symbols. Harris bristled at the "expectation that each Negro intellectual is supposed to be a leader of the Negro people. . . . You don't have any of those expectations when it comes to other philosophers. You don't walk up to Hilary Putnam and say, 'Hey Hilary, what do you think of [the president's] situation?'"

The media, he said, "want a preacher." And all recognized that West, an oratorical spellbinder whose Harvard and Princeton pedigrees had helped win him support from white media and academic elites, fit that description. "Cornel is in a league of his own," said Outlaw. But he agreed with Howard McGary, professor of philosophy at Rutgers New Brunswick and author of *Between Slavery and Freedom*, that West had "paid his dues." Musing about the future, Outlaw noted that the lack of a graduate school boasting several black philosophers, instead of one or two, one where "the next generation could be trained," slowed black progress in the field. Like his peers, he hoped the dearth of women would end.

But Outlaw's generation could already count many achievements. A society for the study of black philosophy met regularly in New York and participated in "Philosophy Born of Struggle" conferences. Books on the subject kept increasing. The American Philosophical Association published a "Newsletter on Philosophy and the Black Experience." And just as important, tenured black philosophers now got a say on that touchy matter of what counted as a subject worth discussing in their field. Disciplinary symposia on subjects like "Racism and Philosophy" were increasing. And leading white philosophers, said Harris and Outlaw—even those who thought they had no special link to the subject—were invited.

"To be a real philosopher," observed William James, all you needed was "to hate someone else's thinking." By that standard, both Marinoff and his mockers made the grade, as did black philosophers and racists who derided their work. Marinoff's philosophical counseling took him out of the safe academic setting to which professional American philosophers mainly stuck. His boldness in venturing forth was fueled by such sidelines as playing classical guitar, which added to his obvious comfort in performing to a room. Black philosophers like Laud-Hammond, Washington, Outlaw and Harris, who investigated their own tradition and risked marginalization by white peers as they battled against the grain, exuded the energy of self-made men. But one could see that all also took strength from their status as *official* philosophers—from being professional teachers of philosophy, members of the world's oldest profession without climax or conclusion—more accustomed to giving talks in carpeted and partitioned hotel rooms than in bookstores or bars.

In fact, philosophy professors counted as the only white-collar workers in America who could claim that when they announced, "I'm a philosopher," they were simply filling in a form, like a person who scribbled "lawyer" under "occupation" on an application. Many of them would have responded to James's definition of a real philosopher with an archly phrased, "I'm not sure I agree with that." To be a real American philosopher, they would have countered, meant that you belonged to the American Philosophical Association (APA), headquartered at the University of Delaware in Newark, and also attended the "APA," everyone's shorthand for the association's annual Eastern Division meeting.

It took place at the end of every December, between Christmas and New Year's Day, in a major eastern city—Boston, New York, Philadelphia, Baltimore, Washington or Atlanta. And while professional American philosophy, unlike other academic disciplines, divided into three regional groups, all of which held annual conventions—the APA's "Central" and "Pacific" divisions met separately each spring—it was the huge Eastern Division conclave, where most of the year's job hiring went on, that mattered most. It also counted as the temporary world center of behavior that could only be tagged as quintessentially philosophical, street-level division.

Philadelphia got the APA nod in 2008. And at precisely ten p.m. on Saturday night, December 27, in the "Candidates' Room" at the Philadelphia Marriott where graduate students and others applied for teaching jobs, one could see why philosophy types often didn't play well with others.

Evondra Acevedo, the academic group's employment coordinator, had just announced that the room was closed for the night. She'd been going, after all, since three p.m. A sign on the outside of the door announced that the room would close at ten, but candidates continued to zoom in to check files, exchange horror stories, or simply take stock. She asked the eleven candidates still seeking service to come back in the morning.

One young woman complained that she and her friend had been waiting for thirty minutes. A young man declared that he faced a nine a.m. interview and needed service *now*.

Acevedo politely listened, but stood her ground. She informed them, "Sorry, but I can't help you." That unguarded remark provoked a graduate student standing in front of her to near apoplexy.

"That is *just not true!*" he exclaimed, eyes bulging before his peers as if sharing a logical discovery that had escaped previous generations. "That is *simply not true!*" he repeated, as if expecting her to take up the argument for the proposition that it *was* true. If cooler heads had not prevailed, he might still be there, explaining to her the finer points of modal verbs (e.g., must, can).

It was an emblematic sign over the long weekend of APA—along with the scraggly beards reminiscent of nineteenth-century lithographs and famous philosophers such as Charles Peirce, the pre-Raphaelite women lugging pre-Socratic texts, the tweed, elbow-patched 1950s sports jackets—that days before the annual Mummers Parade, another colorful species had hit town. A species known to hotel staff around the country for sometimes putting lit pipes in their jacket pockets, for questioning why credit cards had to be swiped a second time, for disputing whether the hotel should fairly describe one end of its pool as the "deep end"—a group inclined to argue the fine points of life rather than accept them.

On Sunday night—mayhem having been avoided the evening before—Jeremy Morris, thirty-one, in a one-year visiting position at Ohio University, scrutinized the Candidates' Room bulletin board for last-minute notices. With a doctorate from the University of Miami and a specialization in philosophy of language, Morris said he was encountering the same problem facing job seekers in other academic fields that recession year: freezing of advertised job searches and positions by universities and colleges cutting costs. The APA itself, which usually drew 2,500 registrants, was down closer to 2,000.

"I've had one interview this year," he said, "whereas I had a number last year. I've had letters saying searches have been canceled." The scuttlebutt among APA's roughly 550 job seekers was that more than 10 percent of the 300-plus advertised positions might have been canceled. To be sure, it was the APA job market that often leveled the cruelest blow at one's sense of being a philosopher. For young professional enthusiasts, the notion that they might not make it into philosophy *at all* sometimes bred a peculiarly sharp form of contemplation.

If Morris had been magically whooshed back (perhaps by Bill and Ted) to the APA a decade before, to the Candidates' Room in that same hotel, he might have met Sara Beardsworth, a British postdoctoral student, who appeared pleased with her two possibilities, at Memphis State and Duquesne University in Pittsburgh, but who rued the pressured hiring atmosphere of the APA, remarking, "Philosophers are not the kind of beasts that enjoy that kind of thing."

Or Michael Ialacci, then a newly wed 1995 Brown University PhD accustomed to the gypsy scholar life, who felt his life was "on hold." One semester, he said, "I had the distinction of teaching three different courses at three different institutions in three different states. This will be my last year unless I can get a really good one-year position." He had nabbed just one interview from thirty applications. In fact, most philosophy doctoral programs, for more than three decades, had warned applicants that there was no guaranteed philosophy job down the road.

But Morris, in his second year in the APA market and handsomely outfitted in suit and ponytail, remained upbeat, even playful. "I'm single, good-looking, athletic, six-four, my phone number is . . . ," he joked into a reporter's tape recorder. Asked if he'd be willing to go anywhere to teach philosophy, he replied, "Anywhere on the planet. Anywhere at all. Whether or not I get paid.

"To tell you the truth," he quickly added, "the only thing that could push me out of philosophy is the student loans I've accrued." Passion for the subject marked people in professional philosophy more than it did those in disciplines with better employment options. That remained the same over the years, just as much as APA looked and *was* the same, decade to decade.

There was the old-fashioned bulletin board on which participants thumbtacked real and jokey notes ("To Benedict Spinoza: You're excommunicated from the SAAP party in Suite 2119 tonight"). The hundreds of manila folders in cardboard boxes, holding CVs of applicants seeking jobs. The giant evening receptions (formerly called "smokers," until smoking was banned), at which everyone milled about an enormous ballroom and engaged in informal job seeking.

"This convention," explained APA Executive Director Eric Hoffman at an earlier APA in Philadelphia, "is usually the largest gathering of philosophers in the world." It was, continued Hoffman, a lawyer and philosopher then teaching at the University of Delaware, "for people to share their intellectual work, to engage in philosophical conversation, to test their theories and to keep up their relationships." More informally, he acknowledged, it was part ceremony, part madhouse. Established professors tried to pull off publishing deals at the book exhibition, avoid old spouses or scout new ones. Graduate students mainly hunted employment—preferably tenure-track assistant professorships, though often one-year visiting professorships or adjunct slots.

Of course, one could tell the conventions apart by some of the speakers. At that earlier APA, before an audience of hundreds, the late Harvard luminary Robert Nozick, then APA president, had expounded on "objectivity" at lightning speed while then colleague Cornel West, in the audience, grinned broadly at the rapid-fire performance. On a Sunday panel, "Is the Language of Rights Good for Women?," famed feminist legal theorist Catharine MacKinnon had flashed disgruntled looks as Israeli philosopher Yael Tamir explained the accommodationist tactics Israeli women needed to use to win greater power. MacKinnon, by contrast, demanded an explicit battle for women's rights: "The question really is, Will women get everything we need from rights? This may not be the right thing to say to a group of philosophers, but we're not going to know until we try. This is something we can't really *think* our way through."

Certainly there seemed to be fewer giants walking the Marriott corridors in 2008, for many of the leading American philosophers of the previous thirty years—Nozick, John Rawls, W. V. Quine, Richard Rorty—had passed away. But the topics at the scores of sessions still ranged from the irredeemably musty to the impeccably relevant. At the earlier APA, "Scholastic Influences on Leibniz's Doctrine of Divine Physical Concurrence" seemed to win the first category, with the second accolade going to "The U.S. Supreme Court Opinion on Physician-Assisted Suicide: Critical Philosophical Perspectives." Year to year, professional philosophers also continued to exercise one of their only powers in American society—the right to pun—as in Tulane scholar David Boonin-Vail's edgy "Robbing PETA to Spay Paul: Do Animal Rights Include Reproductive Rights?"

Yet in recent years, APA had displayed far greater openness to diverse philosophical traditions. The 2008 program offered sessions sponsored by the Association of Chinese Philosophers in North America, Concerned Philosophers for Peace, the Ayn Rand Society and more. Joshua Weinstein, forty-one, a native Philadelphian who served as director of studies at Jerusalem's Shalem Center—an Israeli think tank seeking to launch a liberal arts college—decided to make his first visit to APA for precisely that reason. A Princeton alumnus with a doctorate in classical political philosophy from Hebrew University, Weinstein thought philosophy was "becoming much more exciting as long-established presumptions are falling away. . . . There are just a lot of things going on that I did not expect would be going on, and, I suspect, were not going on ten years ago."

To be sure, the panel on "Philosophical Perspectives on Female Sexuality" was not Grandpa's APA. Indiana University's Elisabeth Lloyd, in her paper "Analyzing Bias in Evolutionary Explanations of Female Orgasm," crisply outlined how male assumptions ludicrously distorted "Darwinian" explanations of that explosive adaptation. And Rebecca Kukla, then a professor of obstetrics and gynecology as well as philosophy at the University of South Florida, offered a brilliant analytic comparison, in her "Depression, Infertility and Erectile Dysfunction: The Invisibility of Female Sexuality in Medicine," of male-directed ads for Viagra and ads aimed at female sexual dysfunction, demonstrating the ongoing belief that female sexuality, unlike male, cannot be located in a specific body part.

In 2008, as in the last millennium, it was possible to depart APA satisfied even if one didn't find a job, though some always did. A Google search showed that Sara Beardsworth was still in professional philosophy, albeit far from home—as an assistant professor at Southern Illinois University at Carbondale. A similar search for Michael Ialacci turned up no similar position, suggesting he had left the field.

Only by the 107th annual meeting of the APA in December 2010 did it seem that intimations of modernity and change might be coming to the APA, including in how young professional philosophers find jobs in America and communicate with one another. Held in Boston that year, the meeting suffered scores of cancellations and changes due to a massive northeastern snowstorm on its eve. The APA, still largely functioning in the lead-pencil era with its cardboard boxes, manila envelopes and single bulletin board for messages, found itself ill-equipped to do more than announce the names of five hiring institutions that had cancelled, and to post a printed-out note distinctive for its uncertainty in the midst of hundreds of epistemologists who scrutinized knowledge:

WEATHER-RELATED DISRUPTION

Because of flight cancellations and other difficulties, many session participants have been unable to get to the meeting or are unsure whether they will be able to do so. As a result, numerous sessions will be either disrupted or canceled. In a quickly changing situation, it is impossible to keep track of all these changes to the program. Sessions will occur, if they do occur, at the times and places specified in the program. More than that we cannot guarantee. We ask for your understanding and, if you are a speaker or other session participant, your ingenuity (philosophical and otherwise) in making the best of this very difficult state of affairs.

The note's stoic send-off to attendees only exacerbated an already growing feeling among the APA's highly wired twentysomethings (a similar rebellion was brewing among young literature scholars in the Modern Language Association) that Skype had made the whole APA meat market both passé and a further indignity on top of the recession-repressed market itself (especially when the meat involved was their own tender brains and poorly financed bodies). An increasing number of hiring institutions, weather apart, appeared to be bypassing the APA.

"That's the trend now," remarked Andy Lamey, thirty-nine, a former journalist at Canada's *National Post* who, with his PhD on the ethical status of animals almost in hand from the University of Western Australia in Perth, was sitting outside what he dubbed "Anxiety Central"—the main ballroom where hiring committees interviewed candidates. "It seems like this is a fading institution. The arrival of Skype has particularly had an impact. A lot of people are doing long-distance interviews."

Asked to muse a bit on the convention from the standpoint of a former journalist who once covered such things—he confessed to sometimes being tempted to use a phrase like "sources close to Aristotle" in his academic work—he found that the meeting gave him pause.

"Does anyone really look forward to the APA? I'm not sure—we're here out of necessity, I guess."

Indeed, with the APA itself offering no easy mechanism by which candidates and hiring faculty could rearrange interviews and discuss traditional APA hiring practices, many candidates took their discussion to popular philosophy blogs. On one, a young philosopher declared that APA interviews of financially pressed doctoral students must come to an end, and be replaced by Skype interviews. The candidate's appeal and survey drew hundreds of comments, many as Jesuitically or Talmudically argued as their commenters' dissertations.

The volume of posts reflected a growing generational split among professional American philosophers. While older ones still functioned mostly in a world of paper, books and journals, grad students, as in almost every area and discipline of human interest, devoted major-league time to Web forums and other Internet outlets. For pure information and the orchestration of controversies in the field, many turned to Leiter Reports (www.leiterreports.typepad.com), a blog by the University of Chicago professor of law Brian Leiter. Leiter provided breaking information on the discipline, but also remained controversial among philosophers for his abusive blogging style. Some members of the Chicago philosophy department, who had been criticized on Leiter's blog and elsewhere, objected even to the law school hiring him, though to no avail as he was not only hired but awarded the prestigious Karl Llewellyn Chair of Jurisprudence. Proudly biased toward mainstream analytic departments in his separate and often-criticized rankings of philosophy departments (known as the Philosophical Gourmet Report), Leiter typically took a contemptuous tone toward anyone who disagreed with him or challenged his ex cathedra sense of running the profession from his laptop—Mark Oppenheimer of the *New York Times* described Leiter's style as "verbal soccer hooliganism." Even those who disliked him, however, used his blog as a clearinghouse for information, and it was to Leiter's blog that many 2009 grad students turned to vent their frustrations about APA interviews.

Other blogs, though, provided further options for famously intense philosophy grad students, frantic to be on top of the latest in a field thought by outsiders to operate under the aspect of eternity. Popular sites included New APPS ("A group blog devoted to art, politics, philosophy and science," www.newappsblog.com), which might, on a given day, address the unity of consciousness or the philosophical upshot of cognitive neuroscience. Another, the Philosophy Smoker ("Professional philosophical issues for ABDs, recent Ph.D's and the non-tenured," philosophysmoker.blogpost.com), offered opinions on such trench-level matters as whether giving multiple-choice tests in large lecture classes might damage one's future job prospects. Philosophy Et Cetera, run by a Princeton graduate student with a wry *Jeopardy*-type heading ("Providing the questions for all of life's answers," www.philosophyetc.net), featured a regular round-up of philosophy blogposts from around the Web called Philosophers' Carnival.

Perhaps all that time supposedly on the hands of philosophers—the Web site CareerCast ranked "philosopher" as the seventh least stressful job in America—accounted for the wide choice of philosophical cyberdestinations. Those fascinated by epistemology could visit Certain Doubts ("Devoted to matters epistemic," www.el-prod.baylor.edu/certain-doubts) or Think Tonk (www.claytonlittlejohn.blogspot.com). If interest veered more specifically to a new approach called "Experimental Philosophy," they could visit a site by that name (experimental philosophy.typepad.com), while philosophers of science turned to It's Only a Theory ("A Group Blog devoted to the general philosophy of science," www.itsonlyatheory.blogspot.com). Many women philosophers shared thoughts on Feminist Philosophers (www.feminist philosophers.wordpress.com), where one poster might ask for comment on the way women are depicted in philosophy examples while another observed that "philosophers love the occasional blogosphere shitstorm." Specialists in ethics gathered at Ethics Etc. (www.ethics-etc.com) or PEA Soup ("A blog dedicated to philosophy, ethics and academia," www.peasoup.typepad.com), while those focused on action, agency and free will had a meetingplace at Flickers of Freedom (www.agencyand responsibility.typepad.com).

Public Reason ("A blog for political philosophers," www.public reason.net) and Gender, Race and Philosophy (sgrp.typepad.com) in turn accommodated their audiences. And on top of all that, at least one Twitter feed, @philosophfeeds, conveniently rounded up the best philosophy posts. Professional philosophers might feel cut off from the larger American intellectual marketplace, and graduate students might feel cut off from the profession itself, but the Web enabled them to form and maintain their discrete communities with unprecedented ease. While little sustained philosophy took place on the blogs, they, like the loved and hated APA itself, seemed crucial to the continuation and flourishing of those communities.

None of that online camaraderie, however, could ease the transcendental meatspace reality that the annual market for philosophy professor positions in the U.S. remained a buyer's paradise and a seller's nightmare, and even more so after two years of severe recession in academe. Although available philosophy jobs ticked slightly upward in 2010, the backlog of applicants made the ratio of applicants to jobs among the worst ever.

Andy Lamey, who had sent out forty applications the year before and obtained one interview ("It was my first kick at the can"), sounded delighted at having done better his second time around, with four interviews out of twenty applications. But he cautioned that approaching the job search rationally was an error: "The market's so crazy that you've got to be a little bit deluded even to be in it in the first place. Mere practical or pragmatic concerns have no place here." Asked if he felt committed to becoming a philosophy professor, he replied, "Yes, absolutely." For that very reason, he said, hopeful that his forthcoming book on Hannah Arendt and general reportorial moxie would give him an edge, he explained, "No one is going to stop me."

Others milling about outside the main ballroom, like their peers in past years, mixed notes of gloom with similar ardor. For Sam Butler, a thirty-one-year-old visiting assistant professor in a one-year position at Elon College in North Carolina, making the one interview he'd been granted—by C. W. Post on Long Island—after his flight had been cancelled, required the logistical savvy of George Clooney in *Up in the Air.* Butler sat in the front of the plane on his rescheduled flight, was the first person off it, then grabbed a cab the moment he exited Logan and walked into his interview just in time.

"The market is already brutal enough on self-esteem," Butler confided, explaining that he wasn't spending any time on gossip or scuttlebutt about how bad it was *this year.* "What matters is the numbers in your subdiscipline," he said, and the number of jobs in his—social and political philosophy—was sharply down. But nearby, Anna Gotlib, an assistant professor of philosophy at SUNY Binghamton with a PhD from Michigan State and a JD from Cornell—she was looking for a position at "a more teaching-intensive" school—illustrated why the bad numbers never changed anything at APA.

Yes, Gotlib acknowledged, the number of jobs in her area had dropped about a third since she first went on the market in 2007. Yes, some schools had told her that they had "over 400 applications for one position," leading her to deduce that "your chances of getting a job are about as much as getting a seat playing in the New York Philharmonic." Yes, it was "a bit more desperate" in 2010, with "a lot of people not getting interviews who should be getting interviews because they're good."

But she'd worked as a lawyer for a year and a half and concluded, "Didn't like it, wouldn't want to go back to it." Did that mean she was committed to teaching philosophy no matter how hard it got? "This isn't something I would abandon," Gotlib replied, "unless there were absolutely no jobs, or I just hated my position so much I couldn't stand it. In fact," she added, teaching philosophy "is one of those things I would do even if nobody paid me, because I really love it."

Attitudes like that left David Schrader, beginning his fifth year as executive director of the APA in 2011 after being a loyal attendee since 1975, sanguine about the APA's future.

Chatting outside the second night's "nonsmoker," he granted that the storm's "fairly substantial impact" on attendance, the two "extremely bad years" of the job market, and "the backlog of really fine people out there who are looking for jobs" made APA less than a funfest. (A Carleton College pal had told him that candidates who once would have sniffed at anyplace but Princeton or Harvard now gladly interviewed at the highly regarded Minnesota school.)

A few yards away, in the huge ballroom filled with more than a thousand attendees sipping on beer, munching on pretzels and wandering among scores of tables rented by hiring schools, the usual business of informal lobbying for candidates continued. Schrader, nodding in that direction, remarked, "Nothing in there is ever purely social." The lobbying could be subtle or heavy-handed, he noted: "I have old friends who you'd swear had a career as a used-car salesman somewhere." Still, Schrader pointed out, it remained true that "for younger scholars, to have papers on the Eastern Division program" was "a clear professional plus."

And at one of those tables inside, a young scholar from outside the U.S. took a view of the proceedings that might have lifted the executive director's spirits. Sitting with his Louisville-born American wife, Alison, whom he'd met at Indiana University while doing a PhD on philosophical aspects of cognitive science, Georg Theiner, an Austrian lecturer in philosophy at the University of Vienna who'd garnered three interviews from his thirty or so applications, saw APA as, well, very much in the spirit of the country it called home.

"As much as it's an emotionally draining process," he explained of APA, "it's something you know how to prepare for, you know that it's a market, there are people searching, it's a transparent process, and people find each other. If you don't have that, you have the same people staying at the same schools, there's not the same circulation of ideas.

"In Austria," he continued, "the job market is not as transparent. It's still kind of an old-school process. You sort of know your professor, you write a dissertation, and if you're lucky there's an opening somewhere." Looking around, the young man from the land that gave us modern analytic positivism seemed positively fond of America the Philosophical.

"I think it's something the world should copy," Theiner said of APA with a broad grin, aware that he was speaking sacrilege. "It gets as close as I know of in philosophy to a meritocratic practice."

By the fall of 2011, he'd snared that all-important first job—a full-time position as assistant professor of philosophy at Villanova University.

PARSING AMERICA

Lou Marinoff chasing the mass market in therapy. Washington, Outlaw and Harris seeking solidarity among African American thinkers. The APA's beehive of established stars and young wannabes, doing their thing or competing in the job market.

Three snapshots of American philosophy's continuing experiment in ambition and uncertainty. For Marinoff, whole territories of life owned and operated by other educated professionals remained ripe for sharing by philosophers, if not philosophy's rightful demesne. For men like Washington, Outlaw and Harris, chilliness still pervaded their discipline's air. For young PhDs frustrated by dwindling teaching slots, a mere gypsy position that enabled them to toil in the footsteps of Plato and Aristotle, to call themselves "philosophers"—even if it meant teaching "Intro" at a community college in North Dakota—might make those years of dissertating worthwhile. Across the country, the inchoate adventure of "professional" American philosophy stumbled forward in a variety of forms. APA-stamped professors, devoted custodians of the official and traditional American canon of philosophy from Emerson, Peirce and Dewey to Quine and Rorty, shepherded their wares to students. Eminent giants of the bureaucratically dominant analytic establishment watched their influence trickle down through disciples to new generations. Outside the official field, non-philosophy professors, lacking an official pedigree, found the honorific of "philosopher" imposed on them by a culture eager for textured thoughts that, in James's stinging phrase, made a difference.

As America became almost incomprehensibly diverse and hyper–ethnically aware, altered from the apple-pie clichés once taught in grade school, American philosophy was swelling rather than contracting. The reflex tendency among many professional philosophers and scholars was still to identify American philosophy with the works of great white men, towering figures of the Harvard philosophy department and a handful of other prestigious universities. Historian Bruce Kuklick had subtitled his prizewinning book, *The Rise of American Philosophy* (1977), simply, *Cambridge, Massachusetts, 1860–1930*. But a later book by Kuklick, *A History of Philosophy in America, 1720–2000* (2002), drew criticism for focusing exclusively on white males, his entire mention of African American and women philosophers coming in a single sentence. (Kuklick perhaps took the criticism to heart, later publishing a book on William Fontaine, the first African American philosopher to hold a regular job in the Ivy League.)

Understanding the salient, crucial aspects of the "great white male" tradition remained essential to comprehending America as a philosophical culture, since even our rebels frequently reacted to strains in the mainstream. Accordingly, we will shortly enter that tradition for a while. But we think differently and more inclusively about America today, and so we need to think differently and more inclusively about American philosophy, too. That requires mulling over what we mean by "America," how we expect thinkers to function within it, and what the shaping documents of our political culture imply about our thought.

Empires break up. Associations crumble. The former Soviet Union split into pieces, as did the former Yugoslavia. Sudan became smaller with the advent of Southern Sudan. Might we face the prospect, as America changes, of the former United States of America—the *Untied* States of America?

Imagine Spanish-speaking South Florida, following intense e-mail and Twitter sessions, forming a breakaway state with parts of New Mexico, Texas and California. Our Chinatowns, Koreatowns, and Japantowns, knowing from UN-drawn maps that national borders needn't make geographical sense, seceding and uniting into separate countries. New York City would naturally go its own way (minus Chinatown) after raising bridge and tunnel tolls to $50 a pop. Maybe Redmond, Washington, would join up with Menlo Park and Mountain View in California to declare independence on the principle that the net stock value of Microsoft, Facebook and Google locals exceeded the GNP of scores of UN member states.

Two social scientists, sociologist John Hall of McGill University and anthropologist Charles Lindholm of Boston University, addressed the possibility. Responsible scholars, they helpfully provided context, pointing out that imagining the disintegration of the United States has been a cottage industry for intellectuals since the mid-1980s. *Habits of the Heart* by Robert Bellah et al. suggested that rampant American individualism threatened the nation's sense of community. Books such as Paul Kennedy's *The Rise and Fall of the Great Powers,* Arthur Schlesinger's *The Disuniting of America* and Robert Hughes's *Culture of Complaint: The Fraying of America* soon followed, turning the approach into a booming subgenre.

Dissecting America nonetheless remained an equal-opportunity enterprise, with an open slot for believers in the country's cohesion, stability and even inertia. Hall and Lindholm filled that niche by titling their contribution to the debate *Is America Breaking Apart?* and answering it with an emphatic "No."

The crux of their argument—a sedulous explanation ordinary American boomers and bohos might sloganize as "Breaking Up Is Hard to Do"—came in its drawing of links between accepted truisms of American character and culture and their contribution to American stability. Hall and Lindholm began by marching under Max Weber's flag rather than Tocqueville's. While declaring that the French nobleman still ranked as "the greatest analyst of America," they took issue with his famous worry that, in their words, "apolitical American individuals would be so concerned with their self-interest as to withdraw from their political duties." Weber, on the contrary, stressed the "sect" spirit of America. He argued that Americans "are motivated by an internalized ethic of individual responsibility, personal honor, and principled resistance to immoral authority; they seek membership and participation in the community as a central measure of their own unique worth."

"We," as *USA Today* once headlined it, "Are Natural Joiners," despite the occasional slippages pressed by scholars such as Robert Putnam in *Bowling Alone.* Building on that virtue, Hall and Lindholm suggested a slew of social practices and four crucial turning points in American history as galvanizers of America's social glue. The four crises, Hall and Lindholm argued, were: 1) the organization of the colonies into a strong federal union; 2) the Civil War; 3) the "challenge posed by white workers who rebelled against the confines of the industrial wage contract"; and 4) America's decision to become a world power.

All familiar tales, they produced ultimate ties that bind. Perhaps the most important tie, historically, was linguistic: the sharing of "English in both language and custom." Second, the authors maintained, was America's "shared religion," whose importance could "scarcely be exaggerated." The colonists, Hall and Lindholm reminded us, "were overwhelmingly Protestant," and the influential Virginians and Quakers (unlike the Northeast Puritans) favored tolerance. Third, they suggested, was the much-remarked oddity expressed by the scholar Edward Pessen: "One of the most striking features of class in America is the widespread disbelief in its existence."

Hall and Lindholm smoothly drew the consequences of these truths for America's durability. "By refusing to establish a state religion and giving each individual the right of religious freedom," they noted, "the Founders ensured that religious disputes would not, as so often happened in Europe, layer themselves on top of other sources of conflict." Similarly, the "casualness and absence of deference that are so characteristic of American public culture" intertwine with our resistance to rigid class markers, issuing partly in "the perceived potential for upward social mobility through hard work that stands at the core of the American dream." In the same vein, the harsh finality of the Union's victory in the Civil War spurred greater homogeneity in the country, later abetted by "the spread of radio and television, the impact of Madison Avenue's advertising, Hollywood's endless production of dreams, and the introduction of mass spectator sports, all of which have served to further consolidate the nation as a whole and to bring the South more solidly into the mainstream."

Hall and Lindholm ranged through many intricate sub-issues, including ethnic bonding and political activism, in heading toward their provocative vision of the American mind as a model of flexible, tolerant "contagious vagueness" that allows people of different views to muddle through instead of, as in some locales, disemboweling one another. They perceived that "an ability to ignore contradiction permits Americans to overlook disputes that might tear a more ideologically consistent society apart." Lacking a religion, "America has made a religion of the nation," and so we impute the country's sacred values to our peers. Thus, "citizens tend to assume that to be an American is to act instinctively in righteous and ethical American ways." We trust "that all innately good American citizens will make morally proper decisions," which "helps to maintain social peace." As a result, the authors argued, "it is almost impossible for most Americans even to imagine what serious debate over fundamental principles would entail. Vaguely counting on the general decency of others, and feeling themselves to partake equally in the same sacred national community, Americans also tend to be suspicious of strong opinions and of any sort of zealotry."

In the end, that leads to an "11th commandment" in the air throughout the country—"Thou shalt not judge"—and also to a controversial American attribute. "The characteristic American smiley-faced 'niceness,'" Hall and Lindholm wrote, "so often commented on with varying degrees of amusement or condescension . . . is another expression of the pressure among egalitarian free agents to find the middle ground so as to 'get along' with unknown others. . . . [A]n easygoing, friendly demeanor allows strangers to negotiate a social minefield where there are no clear status markers and where authority is decentralized and relatively weak; this unstable and potentially threatening universe is made livable by the expectation that one's own friendliness and helpfulness will be returned."

It sounds like a wonderful country—a nice place to move if we weren't already here. And Hall and Lindholm's vision helps to frame the notion of a country where, as suggested in Part 2 of this book, effective argument never gets too sharp and unyielding, too stuffy and dogmatic. Yet their theme song can also sound too optimistic. One hears a northeastern, geographically driven voice and ideology sustaining it, as when the authors speak of the South being brought into "the mainstream." Can anyone drive through the ethnic neighborhoods of Los Angeles, where an entire shopping center's signs may be unreadable to a non-Korean or non-Japanese speaker, and believe that "America has become remarkably homogeneous"? What of the view, frequently heard in Texas and New Mexico, that traditional histories of the United States, even in the age of political correctness, reflect a geographical bias (East to West) that should be changed to chronological bias (giving early Spanish settlements their due)?

To be sure, some serious thinkers have been less sanguine about American unity than Hall and Lindholm. No less than the great diplomat and historian George Kennan suggested, in his book *Around the Cragged Hill: A Personal and Political Philosophy,* that the U.S. might operate better if it were "decentralized into something like a dozen constituent republics, absorbing not only the power of the existing states but a considerable part of those of the present federal government." Would anyone take that seriously? When the Daily Kos Web site asked Texas Republicans in 2009 whether Texas would be better off as an independent nation, respondents split 48 percent to 48 percent for each prospect, with 4 percent not sure.

But if Hall and Lindholm are right to probe us for Balkanizing impulses and then pronounce us healthy, to urge that creeping homogeneity is one of the things that will save us, it's because that homogeneity is of a subtle logical sort in America. It would have to be in a country where, as they note, the worst insult you can toss at an American is still "Who do you think you are?," even as more and more Americans answer such questions bluntly, with answers far afield from Protestant, European American stereotypes.

That delicate sort of homogeneity, compatible with the country's diversity while yet parallel to it, increasingly surfaces in the works of social scientists trying to understand America whole. The core question they face almost assaults one. Is character fate for America? Can we celebrate the red, white and blue, those swirling flags that frame presidential candidates, while acknowledging the red, white and black between the lines? Can the balance between sameness and difference remain steady enough that parts of America the Philosophical, the Tea Party and Occupy Wall Street, can argue with one another without pulling guns or resorting to roadside bombs? Is the United States an exception that proves the rule about the us-versus-them nature of political society, or are we a freak political mutation that ends up exhilarating to watch, but ultimately beyond coherent historical and sociological explanation?

Today's Americanists know that from the eighteenth-century musings of the naturalized French American writer J. Hector St. John de Crevecoeur, through the deeper insights in the next century from his countryman Tocqueville and up to today, their predecessors both native and foreign have voted "Yes" to the core question of whether America can be understood. They've employed their quills, typewriters and laptops to bring a nation produced by countless eccentric phenomena and quirks of causation into convincing focus. Almost always, whether the theoretical effort achieves such lasting influence as Frederick Jackson Turner's "frontier" thesis, or fleeting media attention like Michael Lind's "The Next American Nation," the effort requires a suspension of belief on the reader's part—belief that the empirical complexity of America's historical development not only defies the borrowed model of scientific explanation, but belies it.

Still, many of these works persuade. In *Americans: A Collision of Histories,* historian Edward Countryman complicated our view of early America, seeking, like an ambitious director, to recast scenes long ossified by clichés. Countryman insisted that "American" can be both a telling category and a kind of historical fender bender, true to Wittgenstein's notion that a blurred concept is still a concept. Detailing the seventeenth- and eighteenth-century experiences of Anglo-European whites, Native Americans and blacks, Countryman emphasized how the

"Natives and the Africans changed the Europeans even as the Europeans were changing them," producing a unique society separate—no matter how much today's separatists may regret it—from British, European, African or Native American cultures.

Like many historians of his generation, Countryman offered the European colonists only one featured part in the crowded drama of America, making clear that it's a walk-on, even if the Europeans stayed and took over the plot. Unlike some of his peers, Countryman vetted his prose and narrative of hindsight-heavy recrimination, measuring his judgment of villains operating by the mores of their time, recognizing the difference between judging such people wrong and whipping them now with morally superior sentences. Instead, with a marvelous and graceful command of detail, Countryman took us forward through the shared experiences of all Americans, through the Civil War, the women's movement and the building of the nation's infrastructure toward the end of the nineteenth century, showing how "working out common answers" became an inevitability of American history. If the United States turned into an ongoing "disaster for almost all Indians," if the receding "Mexican" Southwest remained a gaping lacuna in many Americans' sense of their own history (unless they live in the Southwest), these marginalized actors nonetheless stayed part of the story.

While the story Countryman told no longer surprises after decades of revisionist multiculturalism in the writing of American history, one remarkable aspect of his compact synthesis of the nation's ethnic history was that it dovetailed with more conceptual accounts by esteemed social scientists of an older generation. For decades, Seymour Martin Lipset, the dean of American political sociologists, had suggested that Tocqueville's America—the land of "liberty, egalitarianism, individualism, populism, and laissez-faire"—could be seen, like a reliable actor, to have kept to the script. And he too, in *American Exceptionalism*, aimed to show how America's "exceptional" state of affairs in world history, captured by Countryman's account, could be rendered analytically manageable by attending to Tocqueville's basket of our enduring ideological bents.

True to the "exceptionalist" tradition, Lipset took on the challenge of explicating why the United States, as democracy, departs in so many ways from other liberal industrial democracies. And true to his own methodology, Lipset drew on a vast array of statistical comparisons between the United States and other countries, intended to show how Tocquevillean imperatives still play out. Lipset, bracingly concrete, therefore committed himself to explaining how the United States can remain "the most religious, optimistic, patriotic, rights-oriented, and individualistic" of nations. How is it, he asked, that we have the highest crime rates, the most people in jail, the most recalcitrant voters and yet the most volunteers? Why is it that our equality of opportunity remains unrivaled, while our income distribution looks shameful among developed nations?

Lipset's smorgasbord of fact daunted, as always, though one could certainly quibble over interpretation of data, wondering whether the United States really stood as more antitax than Britain because we collect 31 rather than 36 percent of our gross domestic product in tax revenue, or whether Americans are vastly more selfish than Italians because far fewer Americans want government to reduce the gap between rich and poor. Far more important was how Lipset's numbers, roughly accepted, jibed with Countryman's story, and with Hall and Lindholm's insights.

White or black, Native American or Chicano, Swedish American or Chinese American, or white *and* black like our current president, we all absorb an ethos by living in the United States that accounts for patterns in Lipset's numbers no one ethnic group could create. If, as Lipset stressed, American "exceptionalism" is "double-edged"—causing both welcome and antipathetic social consequences—it appears to be psychologically better distributed than our wealth. And it bolstered the old truism that Americans rarely perceive their unique identity as sharply as when they think they're visiting their homelands—African Americans seeking chords of memory in Africa, Asian Americans trying to make sense of radically unfamiliar customs in their parents' lands, Arab Americans no longer comfortable with Islamic expectations from another time and place. The best articulation of that subtle sense of identity tracked by Lipset was offered by another shrewd, though more philosophical, social scientist: the political theorist Michael Walzer.

Walzer cared about the "similarity amidst difference" so many detect in Americans. It is, to be sure, an idea familiar enough for commentators and comedians to poke fun at. When Bill Clinton, before his first inauguration, announced his intention to pick a Cabinet that "looks like America," one glib editorial cartoonist portrayed model Cabinet members with signs around their necks: "Lawyer with Corporate Firm"; "Lawyer with Activist Experience"; "Lawyer Who Went to School with Hillary." When President-elect George W. Bush began to appoint, like a latter-day Noah, one of every kind to his Cabinet—a Latino, a black, a Japanese American—pundits dripped sarcasm. Yet years of "diversity

Michael Walzer (1935–), the author of twenty-seven books and professor emeritus at the Institute for Advanced Study in Princeton, coedited *Dissent* magazine for many years.

consciousness" have helped commentators to notice a kind of mathematical formula about America: that the number of American types is equal to the imagination of the numberer. Given that truism, articulating the nature of "Americanness" required the kind of precise, commonsense approach found in all of Walzer's work.

One traditional view of "Americanization," Walzer asserted in *What It Means to Be an American,* holds that "the process requires for its success the mental erasure of all previous identities." On the contrary, he said, we are a "nation of nationalities" that tries to decipher what that means. "It is peculiarly easy to become an American," Walzer wrote, thinking conceptually rather than legally, because the "adjective provides no reliable information about the origins, histories, connections or cultures of those whom it designates." Some theorists of America, such as philosopher Horace Kallen in *Culture and Democracy in the United States* (1924), translated the motto of the Great Seal of the United States—*E pluribus unum*—as "From many, one." But Walzer argued that the "From" amounts to a "false preposition. There is no movement from many to one, but rather a simultaneity, a coexistence: once again, many-in-one."

He supported that by pointing to the history and nature of the United States, with its careful, formalist politics, aimed at preventing the government from identifying itself with any particular culture, religion or creed: "It never happened that a group of people called Americans came together to form a political society called America. The people are Americans only by virtue of having come together. And whatever identity they had before becoming Americans, they retain (or, better, they are free to retain) afterward." Put in flintier terms, "American" is "not one of the ethnic groups recognized in the United States census. Someone who is only an American is, so far as our bureaucrats are concerned, ethnically anonymous. He has a right, however, to his anonymity; that is part of what it means to be American."

Efficiently rebuking the thinking that fuels right-wing tirades about real Americans and "cultural war," Walzer expanded on his principles to sketch why "British-Americans" aren't justified in feeling more American than others. Walzer pointed out that "the symbols and ceremonies of American citizenship could not be drawn from the political culture or history of British-Americans. Our Congress is not a Commons; Guy Fawkes Day is not an American holiday; the Magna Carta has never been one of our sacred texts. American symbols and ceremonies are culturally anonymous, invented rather than inherited, voluntaristic in style, narrowly political in content: the flag, the Pledge, the Fourth, the Constitution."

The analysis helps us focus on exactly what we park on each side of the hyphen that governs our ethnic identity as American—and what we signal when some of us choose to toss our hyphens out. As Walzer saw it, we "have come to regard American nationality as an addition to rather than a replacement for ethnic consciousness. The hyphen works, when it is working, more like a plus sign. . . . [A]n ethnic-American is someone who can, in principle, live his spiritual life as he chooses, on either side of the hyphen." So, for Walzer, many of our self-images and habits of talk hide profound truths. "Most often," he wrote, "when individual men and women insist on 'being themselves,' they are in fact defending a self they share with others." Our public life might even improve, in a more diverse United States, rather than disintegrate into a "new tribalism," if we noticed that the "politics of difference" usually goes through three stages. In the first, groups "articulate" their value as a group and demand gestures of public recognition. In the second, they find they must "negotiate" with other groups, and acknowledge that the limits of their own rights are "set by the legitimacy of others." In the third, a kind of nonrepressive "incorporation" takes place, in which past wrongs and "unjust incorporations" are redressed.

In all this, Walzer emphasized, "fragmentation" and "cacophony" come with the territory, and shouldn't be feared. If the United States is to remain a "political community of engaged and active men and women" who enjoy both their particularity and Americanness, Walzer advised, we must observe several rules of the road. We should, he counseled, not "shut the gates" to new immigrants. We should focus public education on the history and contemporary form of "democratic politics" and "the immigrant experience." We should "maintain the neutrality of the state," include all groups in the mix of public life, and not "give way to the silliness and intermittent nastiness that inevitably accompanies democratic politics in multicultural societies."

One could not ask for a better description—or social recipe—for America the Philosophical, with its thinkers (a Marinoff, a Johnny Washington) so putatively different on the surface, so remarkably linked in their depths. Elsewhere, Walzer provided a rounded portrait of what the American philosopher could be in such a state with his meditation on the authentic "social critic"—that being a more comfortable phrase for many Americans than "philosopher." By "critic," of course, Walzer didn't mean the species *Ebertiana,* composed of otherwise sensible grown-ups sticking their thumbs up or down while scooting between screenings and TV gigs. He meant more dangerous figures: Socrates and Jesus, George Orwell and Albert Camus, Simone de Beauvoir and South African poet Breyten Breytenbach—men and women who dared to challenge their societies without resigning from them. What made such catalysts tick differed from case to case, but all kept time with the societies they sought to instruct.

"Ideally," Walzer wrote, "the critic is a masterless man, a masterless woman, who refuses to pay homage to the powers-that-be." The social critic "speaks out loud, in defiance of the established powers. He is a hero. . . . The critic challenges friends and enemies alike; he is self-sentenced to intellectual and political solitude." Walzer's bionic critic also commits himself or herself "to question relentlessly the platitudes and myths of his society," and he may do it through "political censure, moral indictment, skeptical question, satiric comment, angry prophecy, utopian speculation." At the same time, an effective critic must "express the aspirations of his people." The "arrogance of power" should not "find its secret ally in the arrogance of opposition." If "courage is one of the chief virtues of a social critic . . . so, sometimes, is loyalty and connection." The effective critic remains within his community, speaks its language, incarnates its hopes.

Like Richard Rorty in *Achieving Our Country* years later, Walzer in *The Company of Critics* implicitly attacked the sometimes obscure, rarefied social criticism of the left, which could veer in such dubious directions as the precious nihilism of Michel Foucault, or the revolutionary fervor of Herbert Marcuse (whose *One-Dimensional Man* found modern life flat, but brought no pump beyond retooled Marxism to inflate it). The philosopher-critic should work from within a community's core beliefs, rather than snipe from the rooftops. Walzer's early work on moral obligation, published when he taught political philosophy at Harvard, both reacted to and influenced the modern liberal theory of civil disobedience, so these issues cut close to home. As a man of the left, a Jew, a distinguished academic privileged to write about social conflict from such comfortable academic settings as Princeton and Harvard, Walzer experienced the complexity of the social critic's role as if it were so much small-arms fire on his chosen mission. "It is one of the discoveries of modern democracy . . . ," he trenchantly remarked, "that by not killing the critic, we acquire the right not to admire him." Although some American critics today face violence or imprisonment, most don't: "The angry and alienated social critic bangs his head against a rubber wall. He encounters infinite tolerance when what he would like is the respect of resistance. Detachment under these conditions doesn't mean much more than withdrawal; its likely effect is apathy and resignation or bohemian idiosyncrasy."

Must one sacrifice one's life to be a critical or philosophical hero? Should one stay detached from actual political activities and leaders, lest they poison one's intellectual purity, as French writer Julien Benda argued in his controversial *Treason of the Intellectuals*? Can the endlessly captious operate within society without losing their credentials as members of the community? These are the questions that gnawed at Walzer, and he rejected some academic truisms about social critics out of hand. Contrary to the modernist conceit of many contemporary thinkers, Walzer argued that all criticism arises from common complaint—the gap between the cave dweller angry about his poor heating and Marx's *Das Kapital* is not so immense. Social criticism is not a modern, self-conscious child of the Enlightenment, and it's no more obscure today than ever, because criticism always pushes its practitioners toward specialized language. Today's social naysayers "are not peculiarly hostile to the societies in which they live; they are not peculiarly alienated from those societies."

Walzer corroborated this by examining the career choices and writings of eleven modern philosophical intellectuals committed to social criticism: Benda, Randolph Bourne, Martin Buber, Antonio Gramsci, Ignazio Silone, Orwell, Camus, Beauvoir, Marcuse, Foucault and Breytenbach. Walzer gathered enough body parts to construct the social critic he wanted to herald. The factory model might be some mix of Bourne's patriotism, Camus's adherence to principle, Orwell's prose style and so on, minus corresponding diseased organs like Marcuse's jargon or Buber's superior tone. Walzer's super-critic managed to stay close to his society in both language and commitment, without surrendering to hypocrisy. He "agitates, teaches, counsels, challenges, protests from within." Intellectuals who adopt such a model "can't just criticize, they must also offer advice, write programs, take stands, make political choices, frequently in the harshest circumstances."

The role model Walzer opposed was the one famously advanced by Benda, whose imperious tract expressed the view that, in Walzer's words, "the intellectual's kingdom is not of this world." Benda's "true intellectual must be indifferent to the passions and attachments" of ordinary people. Nationalists who justify and lend cachet to political agendas exemplify false intellectuals, who "locate themselves" in the real world. As a result, false intellectuals "lend to politics the aura of morality and teach politicians not so much to do evil . . . as to think it good."

As far back as 1932, French writer Paul Nizan deftly skewered Benda's views in *The Watchdogs*, pointing out, as Walzer put it, that "when one leaves the world to Caesar, one doesn't serve the ideal; one serves Caesar." Walzer also plainly rejected Benda's model. His other intellectual specimens illustrated approaches to end-running Benda without abandoning the persuasive core of Benda's position—the fact that all intellectual independence requires some detachment. Bourne, for instance, while opposing America's World War I policy, nevertheless retained a certain nationalistic bent for "city on the hill" Americanism. Gramsci, the brilliant cofounder of the Italian Communist Party, found the choice of activist or detached commentator decided for him when Mussolini jailed him for eleven years. Breytenbach operated during apartheid by reinventing his identity, going from Afrikaner to South African. Marcuse insisted on abandoning the language of the people. Foucault tore into systems of state control without offering any improvements—in Walzer's view, an irresponsible act for a social critic. Buber remained a committed Zionist while criticizing Israeli policy on "a thousand small decisions." "We cannot refrain from doing injustice altogether," Buber wrote in 1945, opposing a Jewish state, "but we are given the grace of not having to do more injustice than absolutely necessary."

What Walzer observed in his chapter on Buber holds true generally as his standard for social critics/philosophers: "Success as the world measures it is not the measure of social criticism. The critic is measured by the scars his listeners and readers bear, by the conflicts he forces them to live through, not only in the present but also in the future, and by the memories those conflicts leave behind. He doesn't succeed by winning people over—for sometimes it just isn't possible to do that—but by sustaining the critical argument."

Fanatics and cynics might quarrel with that model, the first arguing that winning is the only thing, the second that moderation in the pursuit of virtue is the final vice. For others, the more natural criticism of Walzer is appropriately internal—that he hasn't thought out the full dimensions of being a "connected" social critic. The cavil arises because all of Walzer's models remained literary intellectuals, writers of books read only by small percentages of their communities. Outside the academy, it's natural to ask whether modern literary social critics can prove effective when, in media lingo, their audience share is so low. Is Oprah Winfrey, with her urge to examine social problems, a better "connected critic" of our time? Or issue-oriented filmmakers like Errol Morris and Michael Moore? What happens to Walzer's connected social critic, an outsider may wonder, when the language of the people is no longer "book" language or philosophy language?

The fact remains that for most of our history, and still today, the landscape of American philosophy occurs chiefly on the page. If the wisdom of today's Americanists tells us anything, it is that this landscape, comprising both venerable monuments in the canon of American thought—Emerson, James, Dewey—and those added to the tour by a broader vision, may communicate compelling lessons about consistency in American philosophy, especially when thickened by biographical detail. For just as specialists in America continue to correct our once-too-white-bread view of our country, so their peers in cultural criticism and biography continue to expose the human reality that has accompanied canonized American philosophy from its beginning, dating from our founding documents.

If the Constitution and *The Federalist*—the series of articles Alexander Hamilton, James Madison and John Jay wrote to urge the former document's ratification—offer the first indisputably American (as opposed to colonial) philosophy about government and the nature of man, then we should take heart from the gritty realities in which they were grounded. Charles Beard, the trenchant political scientist whose interpretation of the Constitution once stirred great controversy by emphasizing its economic origins, showed little respect for the way later intellectuals picked apart the reasoning of *The Federalist.*

Hamilton, Madison and Jay, Beard acidly wrote, "were not closet philosophers. They were not dust sifters engaged in dissecting the ideas of other dust sifters." Maintaining a sarcastic tone, Beard observed that "the authors of *The Federalist,* poor fellows," lacked "the benefit of modern sociology, psychology, economics and political science," and "did not discuss the problems of epistemology, or 'appearance and reality,' which have long occupied the attention of armchair philosophers."

Beard was hardly a lone carping voice in constitutional scholarship. Robert Schuyler, in *The Constitution of the United States: An Historical Survey of Its Formation* (1923), contended that "only a decent sense for the proprieties of political discussions required" the framers to make "at least occasional references to [John] Locke and Montesquieu." In the 1950s, Arthur Lovejoy, the eminent historian of ideas, expressed related views. Against this chorus of voices, others have pushed for strong philosophical appreciation of both the Constitution and *The Federalist.* A few years back, historian Forrest McDonald's fine study, *Novis Ordo Seclorum: The Intellectual Origins of the Constitution,* won the acclaim of a Pulitzer Prize jury, and the lure of the Constitution's bicentennial in 1989 tempted a slew of intellectuals to reexamine the ideology behind the Constitution, from historian Richard B. Morris to *Encyclopaedia Britannica* maven Mortimer J. Adler.

But the most important point to emerge from all this attention is one that reappears throughout our history: how enduring aspects of American intellectual reality—the urgency of its challenges, the lack of luxury for idea spinning in perpetuity—governed the framers and the *Federalist* writers. Morton White, one of the magisterial scholars of social thought in America, recognized that Madison, Jay and Hamilton largely asserted, rather than argued, their fundamental philosophical beliefs about natural rights, the aims of government and many other matters, mostly drawing on Locke and David Hume to form them. White demonstrated how *The Federalist* proposes two aims of the Constitution, the protection of natural rights and the seeking of the public good, which inevitably had to clash. He also made plain that the authors, particularly Madison, argued inconsistently at times, and compromised their philosophical principles in the face of intractable opposition on issues like slavery.

White's careful examination of the logic of *The Federalist* led him to reject the view, held by such scholars as Gordon Wood, that the "philosophy" of the Constitution changed radically from the thinking that fueled the Declaration of Independence, however much he agreed with Wood's view that "the Constitution was in some sense an aristocratic doctrine designed to curb the democratic excesses of the Revolution." Charles McIlwain observed in *Constitutionalism Ancient and Modern* that "the most lasting of the essentials of true constitutionalism still remains what it has been almost from the beginning, the limitation of government by law." Because the framers tried to limit the power of their government at a definite point, they stayed forever open—as have courts that shaped the Constitution since—to the criticism that they placed the limits too far short, or beyond, the spot where our political goals might wish them to be. In short, both the framers and the *Federalist* authors—two of them also framers—were practical men, accomplishing a practical deed.

It should not surprise us, then, that the Constitution became less a frequently discussed text of philosophy in American life than a kind of totemic object for patriotic celebration—and even that a muted one—except when political differences roared. Looking back in 1887 on the confused centennial gala, A. Loudon Snowden, the chief marshal, complained of "the entire absence of any interest or general sentiment in favor of the proposed celebration on the part of the public at large." Given the bungling that led up to it, one sympathizes with the public. A popular historian named Benson Lossing kept fighting for June 21, 1888, as the proper celebration date—the 100th anniversary of New Hampshire's clinching vote. The *New York Times* steadfastly pushed April 30, 1889—the anniversary of Washington's inauguration. Others argued for March 4, 1889—one hundred years after the convening of the first Congress.

More shenanigans followed. Alexander Hamilton, the statesman's grandson, refused to attend the Philadelphia celebration because his state, New York, had fought hard to defeat ratification. The federal government stiffed the city on money. The commemorative poem fell through after every poet solicited—including James Russell Lowell—refused to participate. (Walt Whitman, officials deemed, "would not be safe.") As if that weren't enough, someone botched the invitations to the states. Colorado's governor later testily explained that he hadn't replied because the Centennial Commission had persisted in addressing its letters to "a gentleman who is not and never has been Governor of Colorado."

We know much of the reality of the Constitution's life in our history—its near removal at times from the realm of philosophy to the arena of social symbol—thanks to historian Michael Kammen's fine work in *A Machine That Would Go of Itself: The Constitution in American Culture.* The Cornell historian slogged through court-packing fights, opinion polls on constitutional issues, immigration procedures and endless public speeches praising our "Ark of Covenant" (Chief Justice Taft, 1922) and our "cement of the Union" (James Madison, 1809), in order to describe "the place of the Constitution in the public consciousness and symbolic life of the American people . . . the perceptions and misperceptions, uses and abuses, knowledge and ignorance of ordinary Americans."

By steeping us in that popular history, denying the Constitution's rigid identification with political philosophy proper or Supreme Court jurisprudence (while monitoring all linkages), he was able to drive home his theme that "a glaring discrepancy exists in the history of American constitutionalism between the recurrent declarations of reverence . . . and the ongoing reality that most of us do not adequately understand the Constitution." In a 1943 poll, only 23 percent of Americans could identify or state some part of the Bill of Rights correctly, and subsequent polls show little improvement. Americans, Kammen contended, "have taken too much pride and proportionately too little interest in their frame of government." By tracing that wan interest, Kammen developed important lessons for understanding the role of philosophical scripture in an America writ large.

A key one arises from his conclusion that "Americans have known the Constitution best when they have revered it least." During battles over slavery and Franklin D. Roosevelt's court-packing, Kammen wrote, citizens eagerly took to constitutional issues, just as they later did during President Clinton's impeachment and legal controversy over the 2000 presidential election. That compensated, in some degree, for the terrible job done by both schools and the Supreme Court in explaining the Constitution. As Kammen developed these ideas, he put the Constitution's success in perspective by framing it with scores of political facts. By 1910, 1,736 amendments to the Constitution had been proposed to Congress. From 1789 to 1974, the states made 356 requests for a new constitutional convention. Of 160 national constitutions existing in 1983, 101 had been established since 1824.

Kammen made plain that strict constructionists and activists, and partisans and opponents of judicial review, have been battling since the opening bell. He also drove home, in the special context of the Constitution, the casual, irreverent approach that Americans bring to philosophy whenever it looms too pompously. Where did the Supreme Court declare the Constitution unconstitutional? Why, in George S. Kaufman and Lorenz Hart's musical *I'd Rather Be Right*. Kammen also cited a classic line, elsewhere attributed to the legendary Tammany Hall pol Timothy J. Campbell, that one as easily imagines spoken in twentieth-first-century Washington, DC. When President Grover Cleveland refused to support a bill deemed unconstitutional, Campbell reportedly remarked, "What's the Constitution between friends?"

Kammen, better than any previous scholar—most of them legal or political sorts cool to the materials of popular culture—established that the Constitution was a remarkable feat of political spadework and ideological symbol, more a float to be drawn past American minds than a scripture to be chanted, a script to be read, a philosophical treatise to be parsed outside of all human context. And yet *inside* a human context, its ideas had always resonated in American life.

As far back as 1852, Frederick Douglass, in his historic Rochester speech best known as "What to the Negro Is the Fourth of July?"—with Lincoln's Gettysburg Address, the greatest American speech of the nineteenth century—had burned its importance into the minds of his listeners: "Standing with God and the crushed and bleeding slave on this occasion, I will, in the name of humanity which is outraged, in the name of liberty which is fettered, in the name of the constitution and the Bible, which are disregarded and trampled upon, dare to call into question and to denounce, with all the emphasis I can command, everything that serves to perpetuate slavery—the great sin and shame of America."

Similarly, as recently as 2011—if in a less fiery tone—Rodney Smolla, one of the nation's foremost First Amendment scholars, could argue in his *The Constitution Goes to College* that there is "scarcely any constitutional question that arises in the United States that does not devolve, sooner or later, into a campus question," that "the brilliance of the American Constitution" and its protection of free speech had shaped the "idea of the American university," whose own unparalleled ideal of free speech flowed back into American life from its graduates.

The perspective suggested by Kammen—recognition that even our biggest ideas in American life exercise their influence by messy, flesh-and-blood engagement with our lived reality—should be kept in mind in pondering the great figures of mainstream American philosophy, whether Emerson and the Golden Age icons of Peirce, Dewey and James, or their successors, men like Dworkin, Danto and Rorty. Exact and intricate as their argumentation may be on a given page, their enduring power in an age of nanosecond attention spans, among a people who check their smartphones every minute, rests predominantly in the headlines they communicate to us, not the footnotes. It's the messy amalgam of their ideas, predilections and personalities we respond to, which can coalesce into a persuasive punch. Contemporary scholars and biographers, no longer fearful of compromising a great thinker's dignity by reporting human details, increasingly give us philosophers with flesh on their bones. The gap between the anointed few in that category and the many thinkers we shall meet in Part 3 grows ever smaller.

It is important, then, to take a look at the grand parade of American philosophy as most have understood it. But not to mark a different plane of thinking, somehow beyond the human. On the contrary, it enables us to see the continuity between those traditionally seen as "America's" philosophers, and those who should be as well.

GREAT WHITE MEN AND THE
IVY LEAGUE CAVALCADE

Fourteen months after his cherished wife, Ellen, died of tuberculosis at age twenty, young Ralph Waldo Emerson, on course to become nineteenth-century America's most influential thinker, was still making his daily pilgrimage from Boston to her tomb in then-distant Roxbury. But on one of those painful March days in 1832, the twenty-eight-year-old widower did something few of his worldwide admirers today would imagine of him.

He opened Ellen's coffin and examined his wife's body. According to Robert D. Richardson Jr., the Wesleyan professor who reported the incident in *Emerson: A Mind on Fire,* a biography that reflected years of immersion in his subject, Emerson admitted the act in his journal, but untypically said nothing else about the event. To Richardson, an Emerson enthusiast who returns to the incident several times, the act crystallizes his reinterpretation of the great Transcendentalist as a man who "lived for ideas," but "did so with the reckless headlong ardor of a lover." Far from being the "passionless Sage of Concord" known to tradition, a bold advocate of American individualism and self-reliance whose life nonetheless looked withdrawn and cerebral to outsiders, Emerson was more authentically that "mind on fire," a "complicated, energetic and emotionally intense man who habitually spoke against the status quo and in favor of whatever was wild and free."

It was a revisionist twist of some import for those who care about American intellectual life, its original umbilical link to European culture and its relation to values we now take for granted as quintessentially American: unrepentant individualism, hands-on ingenuity, a cocky unwillingness to be cowed by earlier cultures, a generous common sense

Ralph   Waldo   Emerson
(1803–1882) stood as the first
American thinker to insist
that his countrymen could
have "an original relation to
the universe."

marked by tolerance for difference. Behold, in short, an Emerson who's
nearly as radical as Thoreau.

The portrait rightly corroborated the growing sense in the literature
of American intellectual history that Emerson constituted a necessary
touchstone for elements peculiar to our philosophical ethos, explaining
why he has always been, with the possible exception of Benjamin Franklin and William James, the American prose writer who most influenced
how other world-class writers saw us.

Figures as disparate as Nietzsche, Baudelaire and Jorge Luis Borges
famously cited their fascination with Emerson. From poor Boston boy
to indifferent minister and teacher to undisputed mandarin of Boston
intellectual life, Emerson was the first American thinker to dare, like
Nietzsche or Kierkegaard, to declare his philosophy in biting maxims that
led one critic to call his prose "an army, all officers." Whereas Nietzsche
urged philosophizing "with a hammer," Emerson boasted, "I am a rocket
manufacturer." If no nineteenth-century American thinker survives so
pungently in the thought of contemporary American critics—famous

philosophers, literary theorists, theologians and poets regularly vie to be seen as his heir—it is not for want of an ambition as up-to-date as today's fervor to be a digital billionaire or social-network savant. Emerson was the first American thinker to unabashedly insist that he would dwell with the greats of his world, and world literature, and that Americans could have "an original relation to the universe." For all his railing against book learning and in favor of experience and nature ("Life is our dictionary," he advised), he drew on such an unparalleled range of august sources—among them Confucius, Plato, the Bible, Montaigne, Mme de Staël, Goethe, the Quakers—that his individualism, love of nature and ultimate faith that a person's experience and judgment forms the transcendental center of the universe coalesced into a quiet American melting pot of the mind.

Those characteristics keep Emerson a crucial way station on the American philosophical landscape rather than a once prominent figure now largely forgotten, like Theodore Parker or Chauncey Wright. Who ever declared the American religion of self-regard so ringingly? It was Emerson who taught us that "if the single man plant himself indomitably on his instincts, and there abide, the huge world will come round to him." It was Emerson who assured us that "nothing is at last sacred but the integrity of your own mind." He could strongly champion the individual's right to stay apart. ("[T]he great man is he who, in the midst of the crowd, keeps with perfect sweetness the independence of solitude.") It was an entitlement that his friend and disciple, Thoreau, would transmute into a personal religion. And yet, as much a proto-pragmatist as Douglass or Franklin, he could warn that "inaction is cowardice," that ideas must matter, that one must seize the world by its lapels and make it listen. "I do not wish to expiate," insisted Emerson, "but to live. My life is not an apology, but a life." Americans by the millions have emulated him in that goal.

His own life, for the most part, lacked drama. "I have no history, no fortunes that would make the smallest figure in a narrative," Emerson once wrote to a person who sought biographical details about him. "My course of life has been so routinary, that the keenest eye for point or picture would be at fault before such remediless commonplace." He often wrote a starchy, stately, antique New England prose that tests the reader in large swatches, though such classic essays as "The American Scholar" remain teaching tools (Oliver Wendell Holmes Sr. called it America's "intellectual declaration of independence"). His most enduring aphorisms both endure and pin their author like a name tag. ("A foolish consistency is the hobgoblin of little minds.")

Still, musty or not, Emerson corroborates Richardson's central claim: that by apotheosizing the individual's direct, emotional and street-smart approach to life and nature (and therefore God), he shaped the American temperament so exactly that a century and a half later, we still find him crucial to our self-portraits. That Emerson could, despite the harsh realities of his life—his wife's tragic death, that of several brothers and his firstborn son, and his own physical infirmities—hang on to his celebrated optimism and ebullience made him all the more winning and emblematic. "Emerson dealt with trouble by turning to life," wrote Richardson. That made him a quintessential American thinker—a mind on fire that never consumed itself, but instead cleared dry forest for others.

The next colossus to whom historians of American philosophy traditionally leap, Charles Sanders Peirce (1839–1914), has similarly emerged as more of a recognizable human being in recent years. For a long time, Peirce (pronounced "Purse"), the oddball maverick credited with inventing "pragmatism" as a philosophical bent, semiotics as a radical new discipline and the "community of inquirers" as the key to all truth, appeared to philosophy students as a virtual code name for theses, rather than a man. Then historian Joseph Brent published his resourceful, bristly *Charles Sanders Peirce: A Life*—the first incisive investigation of this quirky thinker since his death nearly eighty years ago—and Peirce turned out to be as colorful a philosopher as Ludwig Wittgenstein (once dubbed the "Elvis of philosophy" by the English magazine *Harper's & Queen*).

Peirce may yet get his show-business day should Terrence Malick or some other philosophical filmmaker find a script worthy of this often debauched metaphysician. The handsome son of Harvard professor Benjamin Peirce, America's leading mathematician and astronomer in the mid-nineteenth century, Peirce began with all the privileges that might have won him his lifelong goal: a tenured Harvard professorship in philosophy. Eminent figures, including Emerson, graced his home, where his father educated him as boldly as James Mill trained John Stuart Mill. Charles entered Harvard at sixteen, graduated at twenty, and brimmed with intellectual ambition throughout his life. In an 1887 article, he wrote of his aim to "outline a theory so comprehensive that, for a long time to come, the entire work of human reason, in philosophy of every school and kind, in mathematics, in psychology, in physical science, in history, in sociology, and in whatever other department there may be, shall appear as the filling up of its details."

The standard view of Peirce for most of the twentieth century was that while he didn't achieve that syncretic overview, his ground-laying work on pragmatism—a concept he was so sure James stole that he redubbed his own version "pragmaticism"—makes him a figure of crucial historical importance. Peirce, all agree, set out several foundational ideas that came to govern American pragmatism.

Always down-to-earth in his epistemological inclinations, he argued that all thought begins from doubt, but not the phony doubt ("Does anything exist?") of the seminar room, or Descartes's programmatic doubt, which the French rationalist believed we should apply to everything. Peirce, like the pragmatists who followed him, insisted on "real and living doubts," urging that we should "not pretend to doubt in philosophy what we do not doubt in our hearts." Real doubt, Peirce contended, "is an uneasy and dissatisfied state from which we struggle to free ourselves. . . . The irritation of doubt causes a struggle to attain a state of belief." As creatures with purposes, we seek to solve our problems and overcome obstacles through action. Although Peirce never "nationalized" his insight, it sounded almost like a description of mainstream American character.

The "whole function of thought," Peirce asserted, "is to produce habits of action." Once we do that, we don't like to go on thinking any longer than necessary. "Thought in action," Peirce pithily observed, "has for its only motive the attainment of thought at rest." We are thus always, in a phrase that became the title of a key Peirce essay, seeking "the fixation of belief." But Peirce also recognized that we can't usually do that alone. "Unless we make ourselves hermits," Peirce observed, "we shall necessarily influence each other's opinions; so that the problem becomes how to fix belief, not in the individual merely, but in the community." Thus truth inevitably ended up a communal project. It was, Peirce submitted, no more than "the opinion which is fated to be ultimately agreed to by all who investigate, and the object represented in this opinion is the real."

Peirce made a key contribution to pragmatism in his 1878 paper "How to Make Our Ideas Clear," by setting forth pragmatism's basic way of understanding the "meaning" of concepts. He argued for the notion, later popularized by James, that "our idea of anything is our idea of its sensible effects. . . . [T]here is no distinction of meaning so fine as to consist in anything but a possible difference in practice." To make sure the idea sank in, Peirce issued another canonical formulation in the same essay: "Consider what effects, which might conceivably have practical bearings, we conceive the object of our conception to have. Then our conception of these effects is the whole of our conception of the object."

Despite these fine philosophical feats, a hand-me-down image of Peirce as brilliant but unstable emerged from the sparsely described, yet familiar version of his life. Although he gave a few lectures on logic and philosophy at Harvard and Johns Hopkins early on, Peirce never secured a full-time teaching post at Harvard or elsewhere, working instead for thirty years as a research scientist in the U.S. Coast and Geodetic Survey. Peirce's difficult personality, tradition advised, led him to burn bridges wherever he turned. "I yield to no one in admiration of his genius," wrote James, who befriended Peirce throughout his life, "but he is paradoxical and unsociable of intellect, and hates to make connexion with anyone he is with." After 1891, Peirce supposedly left his research post to concentrate on philosophy, and soon ran into financial woes. He tried to make ends meet through literary journalism, including scores of anonymous book reviews for the *Nation,* but matters worsened. Eventually marrying Juliette Froissy, who claimed to be a European princess, Peirce repaired to a farm in Milford, Pennsylvania, where he lived the rest of his life. His hair and beard grew longer and more unkempt, he never finished any of his planned books and he became an eccentric recluse long before his death, which followed several years of illness.

Harvard subsequently purchased his papers—Peirce did finish hundreds of articles—and it was their slow publication between 1931 and 1958 that accounts for his present stature. Peirce's intellectual reputation also soared on his polymathic efforts in a variety of other fields: mathematics, astronomy, chemistry, cartography, philology, medicine, lexicography. In 1989, more than four hundred scholars from around the world attended a congress at Harvard—the university that repeatedly denied Peirce a position—to celebrate the 150th anniversary of his birth.

Brent's great accomplishment was to do for the canonized biographical sketch of Peirce what Peirce hoped posterity would do for his philosophy: fill in the details. A vintage Polaroid snapshot slowly sharpening into focus, Peirce the man proved to be the untamable spirit everyone suspected. Acolytes and skeptics read of his drunkenness as a student, his strained relationship with his first wife, Zina (a racist and feminist), and his fateful estrangement from Charles Eliot, future president of Harvard, by cutting up a bench in the then chemistry professor's classroom. (Eliot later frustrated Peirce's teaching goals for years.) According to Brent, Peirce's personality problems grew out of severe pain: he suffered from what is now called trigeminal neuralgia, an excruciating facial affliction that Peirce tried to counter with morphine and opium. The disease and opiate use probably accounted for his often violent mood swings, which offended potential supporters.

Like Richardson, and unlike earlier biographers of philosophers, Brent rarely suppressed his subject's flaws or oddities, permitting yet another giant of the canon to grow three-dimensional. He reported Peirce's peccadilloes with unprecedented exactness, then tried to understand why Peirce acquired them. Noting the secrecy that long surrounded Peirce's life—a result of Harvard's longtime suppression of some of his personal papers—Brent acknowledged that it "led to rumors about homosexuality, sexual promiscuity, chronic drunkenness, violence and drug addiction," then added casually, "In fact, many of the rumors were true." Peirce, it seems, was "impulsive, quick-tempered, and often perverse and arrogant." He dressed with dandified gentility, "loved luxury and taking risks," and was "a lady's man of considerable notoriety." Inevitably, "his contempt for convention, his difficult character, his reckless involvement in get-rich-quick schemes, and recurring questions about his morals caused him to fail at every turn of his career."

Indeed, the man now widely accepted as one of America's most original philosophers was "dismissed from every important professional position he held," and suffered many other ignominies during his lifetime. "So strong was the Harvard Corporation's antipathy to Peirce" that, after 1870, when he was thirty-one, it refused to allow him to lecture on the Harvard campus, despite James's periodic requests, until he was in his sixties. Peirce's abrupt dismissal from a lectureship at Johns Hopkins came because of "unspecified moral grounds after five years." His thirty-year position with the geodetic survey ended because "he was forced into retirement on grounds of dereliction."

Denied grants because of his morals, funded by friends as he teetered on the edge of bankruptcy, occasionally driven from Pennsylvania by impending lawsuits against him, Peirce threatened suicide several times. In Brent's view, Peirce was "profoundly confused about himself," if not about his beliefs in philosophy. Yet the newly discovered Peirce could only be considered a major contribution to a more realistic view of American philosophers and philosophy. If the kind of biography Joyce Carol Oates fiercely denounced as "pathography" permitted a subject's ills to unfairly eclipse a subject's worth, Brent presented an "empathography," where the subject's weaknesses always received sensitive handling in the context of the subject's work. In doing so, he'd helped to show that even philosophers working the abstract terrain of epistemology and metaphysics lived fleshy, erratic lives, and their work could not be wholly divorced from their settings.

Peirce, one imagines, would have been pleased. Although he resented James—who was legendarily generous toward others—for building upon his theory, Peirce venerated him nonetheless: "He is so concrete, so living; I a mere table of contents, so abstract, a very snare of twine." Thanks to Brent, the man who insisted that no concept made sense without a firm impact on reality could now be seen in full color himself, undermining the habit of professor-packed philosophy departments to "rationally reconstruct" American thinkers into skeletons made of their theses and arguments.

James, the usual next character in American philosophy's canonical cavalcade, never faced that problem, thanks to family ties. While Frank and Jesse long ago won the battle to be the James Gang of choice in popular American sagas, ballads and B movies, philosopher William, novelist Henry and diarist Alice—those neurasthenic Kennedys of culture spawned by a wealthy Irish American eccentric—corralled the biographers and critics. The boom for William began with Ralph Barton Perry's two-volume masterpiece, *The Thought and Character of William James* (1935), which spread its subject's reputation as a vigorous, outgoing, altruistic spokesman for the pragmatic American mind. Among other works, F. O. Matthiessen's *The James Family* (1947) tried to capture the whole family in one volume, Leon Edel's *Henry James* (1953–1972) dissected the novelist in five, and Jean Strouse's *Alice James: A Biography* (1980) gave the pair's frustrated sister her long-overdue due. A score more books on William and family followed in the next three decades. The rich appeal of all three to biographers makes sense, since an ambitious Boswell can discern whole strains of American culture in their lives. In Henry James's, it is easy to map the Euro-worship that Emerson warned against, that still gives us restaurants named Chez New Jersey. In Alice's struggle for a writing career, we see all the historical oppression of talented women.

And in William, so the story has gone, we see the triumph within philosophical theory of the tough-minded American emphasis on action, the concrete and the practical over airy European metaphysics, and the tender-minded openness to whatever experience brings. Standard accounts have painted the household of Henry James Sr. in which William grew up as a remarkably edifying salon. Henry Sr., who presided over it, was a quirky, peripatetic, amateur scholar who lived on inherited wealth, sang the praises of Swedenborgian theology (a mystical creed that interpreted divinity as infinite love), tested wits with luminaries such as Emerson and Thomas Carlyle, and encouraged his children to think for themselves. William, born sixteen months before Henry in 1842, got his early schooling in England, France, Switzerland, and Germany.

According to Henry Jr.'s autobiographical writings, William set standards of intelligence, confidence, and common sense that intimidated his siblings. William, resisting his father's strong desire that he become a scientist, pursued painting until adolescent study convinced him of his mediocrity. He next studied chemistry, and then anatomy and physiology under Harvard scientist Louis Agassiz. Still dissatisfied, he shifted to Harvard Medical School in 1864. A collecting expedition to Brazil with Agassiz in 1865–66 lifted his dissatisfied spirits despite a bout with smallpox that temporarily blinded him. While in Brazil, he

William James (1842–1910), before becoming pragmatism's turn-of-the-century champion, declared in his diary that "my first act of free will shall be to believe in free will."

wrote to brother Henry, "When I get home, I'm going to study philosophy all my days."

For the next few years, James wandered between Europe and Cambridge, Massachusetts, studying and suffering his share of the backaches, insomnia and stomach upsets that also plagued Henry and Alice. Receiving his MD degree in 1869, he experienced a deep emotional crisis the next year. Some biographers have pinned most of the blame on despair over the then-widespread philosophical view that man was a mere machine. James wrote that his rejuvenation came upon reading the French philosopher Charles Renouvier. Renouvier defined free will as "the sustaining of a thought because I choose to when I might have other thoughts"—a stark foreshadowing of twentieth-century Sartrean existentialism. James decided to adopt the credo. "My first act of free will," he wrote in his diary, "shall be to believe in free will."

From then on, the neurasthenia seemed to have dropped away. He began teaching psychology at Harvard in 1875, married in 1878, and the great career began. *The Principles of Psychology* (1890) revolutionized its subject and helped establish it as a separate discipline. Later works such as *The Varieties of Religious Experience* and *Pragmatism*—the latter with its oft-stated notion that action and experience are the true test of correct beliefs—offered what seemed a wondrous combination of acute introspective insight and magisterial thumbnailing of American common sense. Willing to take on the role of public philosopher, James opposed big business, championed underdogs, denounced the Spanish-American War and scorned U.S. imperialism in the Philippines. At his death in 1910, a newspaper mourned him as "the greatest American of his time," the leading philosopher and psychologist of his era, and a beloved educator who'd won the widest public any American thinker had until his day.

That status, noted John Dewey, fifty-one years old at the time of James's death, came partly because of a literary "clearness and a picturesqueness that will long be the despair of other philosophers." Coining long-lived phrases like "stream of consciousness," "moral equivalent of war" and "the bitch goddess, success" seemed a special talent with James. More important still was James's articulation of a philosophy that suited the American predilection for practical thinking. Philosophy, he declared, should direct us to "concreteness and adequacy, towards facts, towards actions and towards power." Experience, he argued, had a way of "boiling over" and adjusting our beliefs. His "pragmatism" insisted that abstract ideas were simply conceptual tools employed in everyday life to achieve particular purposes. If examined in that context, James wrote, and tested for what difference they made to everyday life, they would yield their "cash value"—their meaning.

Truth, he controversially contended, might be seen as whatever "proves itself to be good in the way of belief." In his view, "[i]deas become true just so far as they help us to get into satisfactory relations with other parts of our experience." With yet another startling image, James signaled that he endorsed Peirce's idea of truth as an intersubjective group project: "Truth lives, in fact, for the most part on a credit system. Our thoughts and beliefs 'pass,' so long as nothing challenges them, just as bank-notes pass so long as nobody refuses them." The notion outraged some critics, but it won a permanent hold over many American minds.

James also lent authority to a tendency in American thought—an openness to experience, a resistance to cookie-cutter precision about the imprecise—that Morton White would later dub "the revolt against formalism." In one of his most daring formulations, James echoed the Italian thinker Giovanni Papini's claim that pragmatism "unstiffens" our theories, saying of it: "She has in fact no prejudices whatever, no obstructive dogmas, no rigid canons of what shall count as proof. She is completely genial. She will entertain any hypothesis, she will consider any evidence." In that respect, James took pragmatism beyond the scientistic approach of Peirce, advocating its application to every area of human life. For James, writing at the end of his career in *A Pluralistic Universe* (1909), pragmatism suggested "the open air and possibilities of nature, as against dogma, artificiality, and the pretence of finality in truth."

That capacious approach inevitably affected James's conception of philosophy itself. "No philosophy," he wrote in *A Pluralistic Universe,* "can ever be anything but a summary sketch, a picture of the world in abridgement, a foreshortened bird's-eye view of the perspective of events." Our universe, he insisted, contains "no complete generalization, no total point-of-view, no all-pervasive unity, but everywhere some residual resistance to verbalisation, formulation, and discursification, some genius of reality that escapes from the logical finger, that says 'hands off,' and claims its privacy, and means to be left to its own life." Finally, as a psychologist, James maintained that mental phenomena such as consciousness could only be understood as streamlike successions of experiences—not entities. He stressed that the interests and purposes of particular beings attending to particular stimuli in particular circumstances determined those activities. In doing so, he anointed himself one of the most powerful foes in psychology of all attempts to formalize or reduce to simple principles the riches of mental life.

At least one biographer, nonetheless, turned reductivist on James. In *Becoming William James*, Howard Feinstein described a figure startlingly at the mercy of his phobias. No less than Leon Edel, Henry's master biographer, judged Feinstein's book "the best biographical work I have read on the philosopher and psychologist." Since Edel ranked as the éminence grise of psychoanalytic biography, his nod compared to Ernest Hemingway praising Norman Mailer for manly sentences. But the biography was instructive in adding yet another layer of graphic reality to the psychological facets of James's life.

Feinstein's revisionist story began with William of Albany, the Irish-born family founder who came to New York and made a fortune in real estate. The author traced it through the rebellion of William's son, Henry James Sr., against his father's commercialism. William of Albany tried to disinherit Henry Sr. for his idleness, but after fourteen years of litigation, Henry Sr. defeated the will in court and won himself a life of moneyed leisure. Despite his Swedenborgian writing, Henry Sr. assumed no profession. From this slender reed, Feinstein developed an alleged ongoing crisis over Jamesian vocation. He repeatedly referred to the struggle over work choice that "plagued the next two generations" after William of Albany, and presented William as so suspicious of a permanent job that he wondered whether the "Jamesian species" was biologically "fixed and immutable" in its indecisiveness. Dismissing the importance of mechanism and Renouvier to James's depression, Feinstein attributed it to William's need to free himself "from the web of confusion spun around him by his father's vocational struggles with his father."

Feinstein detected support for his views about William's thinking in the latter's drawings and other activities, recounting William and Henry's bowel movements at one stage. Arguably, he provided enough evidence to undermine his theory. He acknowledged, for instance, that Henry Jr. sprang toward a literary life from the starting gate and never hesitated, and admitted that Henry Sr. "urgently required his son to succeed in a worldly profession." He showed William constantly reading in philosophy and science, building up the erudition that would set him apart as a thinker. Feinstein also seemed oblivious to the old saw that "a writer is working when he is looking out the window."

Facing this "prodigal son" theory of his life, William, who once intimidated young Henry Jr. by correcting him on the causal order of thunder and lightning, might have been the first to correct the author's fallacy of *post hoc, ergo propter hoc*—after this, therefore because of this. After all, Feinstein virtually conceded that neither William nor Henry Jr. even knew about their father's problems with his inheritance. He simply took the "Freudian" view that subconscious intuition was at work, and "the James children acted as if they knew of their father's shame, though they did not have the details."

In the end, Feinstein's explanation of how James became James hardly stood up against the shrewder portraits available: Gerald Myers's *William James: His Life and Thought* (1986); Jacques Barzun's brilliant *A Stroll with William James* (1983); Gay Wilson Allen's *William James: A Biography* (1967); or Perry's classic. The psychoanalytic biographer showed little sign of giving James's published writings, or his widely remarked kindness and goodness—Bertrand Russell opined that James "probably committed as few sins as any man who ever lived"—the same attention he gave musty wills. Yet by putting in play the alleged mental fragility of a mandarin American thinker more typically viewed as stable, resourceful and solid, a brother described by novelist Henry as "my protector, my backer, my authority and my pride," Feinstein contributed to the gathering appreciation of classic American thinkers as complicated forces, not easily translated into scholastic salesmen of premises, corollaries and conclusions, containing the seeds of heretical impulse wildly apparent in contemporary thinkers of far less canonical stature. Even the standard bios and studies suggested that James often threw rigorous, syllogistic argument to the wind, asserting himself past intellectual obstacles—and getting others to share the assertions. Perhaps American philosophy packed more tricks of persuasion up its sleeves than mere proof, more peculiarities than nineteenth-century propriety conceded.

The career of George Santayana, a comparable giant in the Ivy cavalcade, suggested no less. Those who forget Santayana (1863–1952) are not doomed to be reminded. When the first posthumous biography of him in several decades arrived, John McCormick's *George Santayana* promised, in the ceremonial tone familiar to dust jackets, to "restore its subject to his rightful place in the intellectual history of our times." It didn't quite happen. Around the same time, the MIT Press launched a nineteen-volume critical edition of Santayana's complete works with *Persons and Places,* a thick volume that included the text of Santayana's memoir by that title, as well as its sequels, *The Middle Span* and *My Host the World*.

Persons and Places sought to settle the issue of Santayana's relevance by casting the reader off into 545 pages of Santayanan reminiscence, a calm sea whose gentle waves are wry and Latinate, full of bobbing memories that often seem mere lures to lush generalization. A book whose antique marginal headings included "I am impervious to moralising" and "My body and my mind disagree about the sea" elicits a provisional acknowledgment of charm from anyone who dips into it. And an authorial voice that disarms would-be opponents by describing reason as "a harmony among irrational impulses" has its crosshairs set on the modern relativist as well. Lovers of languorous, cultured commentary, warmly welcomed at the outset of *Persons and Places*, might have wished to break a lance in Santayana's favor on that count alone.

McCormick's answer to the question of Santayana's relevance took a more hard-nosed line, one implicit in the MIT project as well—that Santayana the philosopher demands contemporary attention. In his preface, McCormick wrote of philosophers who ignored Santayana's work in the analytic heyday after 1950 that Santayana "may well come to be seen for what he was, the master of them all." One of his leitmotifs was the suggestion that Santayana's work foreshadowed that of some fashionable later thinkers, such as Saussure and Chomsky.

The truth is that recovering Santayana for the world of contemporary American philosophy requires making sense of him first, a task as tricky as unpacking certain gnomic sages of the East. For readers in the early twenty-first century, accustomed to Derrideans, Habermasians, Rortyans, semioticians, queer theorists and other philosophers who arrive with name badges and party lines, Santayana intrudes as a puzzling figure, a "Mona Lisa of philosophy" in the phrase of his contemporary, Baker Brownell. A moody thinker, he has been described over the years as a naturalist (everything is just matter in motion), Platonist (scratch the naturalist part), Grecophile aesthete, conservative martinet, pessimist in an optimist's country, Fascist sympathizer, and believer in "essences." Yet while different scholars have placed their emphases here and there, all agree—as did Santayana—on the intensely personal spine of his philosophy. The odd circumstances of Santayana's childhood and career partly explain why, in McCormick's words, his thought has "slipped out of the education and sight of an entire generation."

Santayana came into the world as "Jorge," in Madrid, in 1863. His mother, Josefina, had previously been married to a Boston merchant named George Sturgis, with whom she had three children before he died in 1857. Santayana's father, Agustín, was a former Spanish governor of Batang in the Philippines, where he first met Josefina. Shortly after George's birth, the marriage faltered, and Josefina, fulfilling a promise to her first husband, returned to Boston to raise her other children there. George remained with his father in Ávila until the age of eight, when Agustín decided that his son belonged in Boston. He dropped the pre-pubescent philosopher there, then returned to Spain. George began a new life and language in Boston, growing up with his mother and half siblings.

Thus, by the age of eight, Santayana had been deserted once by each of his parents. In *A History of Philosophy in America,* Elizabeth Flower and Murray G. Murphey commented that "one can hardly repress the conviction that [Santayana's] subsequent pessimism and fatalism about life must have had roots in the tragedies of his early years." McCormick's spadework on Santayana's parents fleshed out this early period, and confirmed that view. Although McCormick argued later that, after graduation from Harvard, Santayana was basically "a happy man," and not the morose figure some assumed him to be, the direction of Santayana's thought into elitism, authoritarianism and anti-Semitism suggested otherwise—as did his definition of life in *Persons and Places*: "something confused, hideous, and useless."

In 1882, Santayana entered Harvard, where he studied under giants of the time such as James, and also took turns as a student editor, cartoonist and actor. After graduation, he briefly studied ancient philosophy in Berlin before returning to Harvard as a philosophy instructor. There, from 1889 to 1912, he taught in the country's foremost philosophy department. McCormick made new sense of Santayana's personal life during his Harvard years. He pulled aside some of the drapes that obscured the scene in *Persons and Places,* exploring matters that had only been alluded to before.

"A small coterie of students idolized him," wrote McCormick. "His fastidious black dress—he wore an exotic European cape—and his aloof, removed demeanor epitomized for them the only sane style of life. For most others he was supercilious, vain and offensive." In a Harvard used to the widely loved and duty-conscious James, Santayana cut an unusual figure, and not only for his manners. According to Sidney Hook's autobiography, *Out of Step,* Bertrand Russell's "stories about Santayana left little doubt that even in his younger days, Santayana had been a suppressed prissy queen and a prig." But McCormick was not eager to flash dirty linen. So while he wrote of Santayana's "frank preference for homosexual over heterosexual attachment," he failed to report a single sexual encounter in Santayana's life, despite eighty-eight years of biographical play-by-play to call on.

That dovetailed nicely with Santayana's own approach to the subject in *Persons and Places*. When relatives thought of fixing him up with his Spanish cousin, his "circumstances" made "any marriage impossible." Referring to a time when he became exceptionally close to Elizabeth Russell, wife of his friend Frank Russell, he wrote, "Not that he [Frank] imagined for a moment that Elizabeth and I were making love; that would have been absurd"—particularly in light of Santayana's own "physical affinity" for Frank.

Although McCormick couldn't say whether Santayana acted on his impulses at Harvard, he was sure that the philosopher's homosexual reputation contributed to his discomfort there. In an 1898 letter to Hugo Münsterberg, which dealt with Santayana's proposed appointment as an assistant professor of philosophy, Harvard president Charles William Eliot, who felt Santayana didn't comport with his New England vision of a proper young scholar, raised questions about promoting "a man so abnormal as Dr. Santayana." McCormick wrote that Eliot "probably meant 'homosexual.'" James, however, stuck up for Santayana, arguing that his difference from the rest of the faculty was the very reason they needed to keep him—so he could challenge them. Eliot relented. Here, as in other works on the period, James came across as immensely generous and open-minded, an attitude that later disappeared from the Harvard philosophy department.

Santayana eventually became a full professor and esteemed member of the department, thanks to the publication of *The Sense of Beauty* (1896), with its famous definition of beauty as "pleasure objectified"; *Interpretations of Poetry and Religion* (1900), in which he introduced his equation of poetry and religion; the five-volume *Life of Reason* (1905–06), which first set out his unusual compromise between pure materialism and idealism; and *Three Philosophical Poets* (1910), in which he argued that Lucretius, Dante and Goethe "sum up all European philosophy." He thus became a key figure in American philosophy's so-called Golden Age.

But Santayana never really felt comfortable at Harvard. In a letter to James, he bridled at the school's atmosphere, which he described as "an unintelligible, sanctimonious and often disingenuous Protestantism." When, in 1912, his mother's death left him with a small inheritance, Santayana—who later claimed he'd never enjoyed being a professor—stunned his colleagues by resigning. Josiah Royce, his dissertation adviser, later observed that Santayana was "passing away to his own region in his own heavens, where he discourses with the seraphs of his own order and choir."

Although he lived forty more years, Santayana never returned to America—even for a brief visit. For a while, he moved about in England and France, and began writing more cultural criticism, including *Winds of Doctrine* (1911) and *Egotism in German Philosophy* (1916). *Character and Opinion in the United States* (1920) brought to center stage Santayana's sharp tone about America, which would become a staple of his writing. In it, Santayana observed how American life "seems to neutralize every intellectual element, however tough and alien it may be, and to fuse it in the native good will, complacency, thoughtlessness, and optimism." He openly flailed America's Protestant, capitalist, democratic ethos, preferring the skeptical, cynical, aristocratic ideals of Greece and the Mediterranean. "If I had been free to choose," he wrote in 1940, "I should not have lived [in America], or been educated there, or taught philosophy there or anywhere else."

The 1920s proved a productive period, and it was during that decade, thanks to attention from the English writer J. B. Priestly and others, that Santayana began to enjoy a wide reputation as a critic. In *Scepticism and Animal Faith* (1923), he started to revise the psychological approach to human existence that dominates *The Life of Reason*. In 1925, he settled permanently in Rome, living luxuriously in the Bristol Hotel on Piazza Barberini and becoming even more productive. From 1927 to 1940, he published *Realms of Being*, the four-volume work that gives fullest expression to his mature philosophy. His only novel, *The Last Puritan* (1935), proved heavily autobiographical and made him famous far beyond his previous celebrity—it became a Book-of-the-Month Club selection.

In 1941, wartime currency restrictions forced him to move into the Clinica della Piccola Compagna di Maria, the hospice of the "Blue Nuns" in Rome. After the war, American soldiers came regularly to visit him, and periodicals vied for interviews. Even in old age, when he usually wore pajamas, he hired a tailor to customize them. ("I have always been attentive to clothes, and careful about my own," he said in *Persons and Places*.) He died at the convent in 1952, a Spanish citizen until his death.

Santayana's isolation from both America and professional philosophy during his last four decades explains, in part, the dimming of his star. Although as a teacher he influenced such important students as

T. S. Eliot and Walter Lippmann (each of whom served as his teaching assistant), Wallace Stevens, Robert Frost and others, he left no disciples. In addition, he often gave confused directions to critics who might have helped shape his reputation. Shifting from poet to critic to novelist to philosopher from book to book, he suggested on some occasions that he wished to be judged primarily as an American philosopher. On others, he emphasized the part of the civilized man of letters. With divided loyalties himself, he left many possible preservers of his shrine similarly divided.

Literary figures tend to think of Santayana as a philosopher who wrote some literature, and many philosophers, while sympathetic to some of his positions, dismiss him as a man of letters and pre-professional philosopher. "[Henri] Bergson and Santayana," wrote Lewis White Beck, the late dean of American Kant scholars, "are warnings to other philosophers not to write *too well*. Their lush style is as evocative as Swinburne, and the richness of their imagery exhibits philosophical ideas when the reader has a right to demand analysis and proof, an argument, not an aphorism."

That "analysis and proof" don't always trump aphorisms and intellectual body language as tools of persuasion is, of course, the anthem of *America the Philosophical,* making Santayana, in that and other respects, a proto-rebel against pinched professional assumptions about philosophy. But Beck was not alone. Santayana's contemporaries commented frequently on the weakness of his philosophical writing as *philosophy.* According to Peirce, *The Life of Reason* offered "a shimmer of rapidly passing thoughts that are hard to make out through a medium more glittering than lucid." Of the same work, James wrote, "It has no rational foundation, being merely one man's way of viewing things. . . . He is a paragon of Emersonianism—declare your intuitions, though no other man share them." Flower and Murphey gave a judgment much closer to the general contemporary view of Santayana than McCormick's: "His writings, despite their unquestionable literary merit, have often seemed almost unintelligible." McCormick's claim that "among philosophers writing in English, only Bertrand Russell comes close" to Santayana's clarity was, to be kind, eccentric.

McCormick recognized, however, that restoring Santayana's luster required demonstrating that at least one of three Santayanas—man, writer, philosopher—was a titan. The weakest candidate was Santayana the man. Always a consummate snob, Santayana went further. His later letters, McCormick conceded, are "unpleasantly eloquent" on fascism and full of epithets like "Jew critics." In one of his rare departures from hero worship, McCormick found both Santayana's anti-Semitism and his vicarious fascism unworthy of him.

He was more accepting of the pompous, Olympian manner that grew irritating in Santayana. Quoting his most famous letter to James—in which he wrote, "it is not I that speak but human reason that speaks in me"—McCormick calls it "the only surviving evidence of Santayana's pomposity." But his own book and *Persons and Places* teemed with examples.

Santayana's stature as a writer is trickier. Most interested parties concede that his early sonnets are dead rather than deathless. William Archer effectively sealed their tomb, quipping that Santayana the poet treated the "visible universe merely as hearsay." McCormick's admiration for the prose, by contrast, was gushy—he described Santayana as "Montaigne, Henry Adams and Proust" rolled into one, raising the hope that Santayana might return to the pantheon on literary merit alone. To be sure, beyond his now terminally recycled maxim about people who refuse to remember the past, he fashioned some useful aphorisms that circulate as memes in the culture: "That life is worth living is the most necessary of assumptions, and, were it not assumed, the most impossible of conclusions"; "Fanaticism consists in redoubling your effort when you have forgotten your aim"; "Culture is never mentioned by those who have it"; "Scepticism is the chastity of the intellect, and it is shameful to surrender it too soon or to the first comer."

His prose, despite occasionally antiquated syntax, is "rich in casual intuitions"—the judgment he himself rendered on Alain's collected writings. The proud Spaniard who described the Harvard faculty as "an anonymous concourse of coral insects, each secreting one cell, and leaving that fossil legacy to enlarge the earth," was more than a maxim machine. He was a thinker who saw novelistic exposition of one's own intuitions as what all philosophy amounted to—not a "science," as he wrote in *Persons and Places*, but a "balance of mind and temper."

That solipsistic approach to his own system, however, is the trapdoor that has swallowed the crucial Santayana—the philosopher. He continues to suffer among professionals because of a widespread feeling, even among some who reject mathematical and scientific models in philosophy, that he disdained argument excessively, favoring well-phrased assertions coated with irony. He claimed, for instance, that the only proof his naturalism needed was "the stars, the seasons, the swarm of animals, the spectacle of birth and death, of cities and wars"—an argument comparable to Dr. Johnson's celebrated kicking of a stone to dispute Berkeley's skepticism, but more in fashion today than twenty years ago.

Critics have also maintained that Santayana's early system (*The Life of Reason*) and late one (*Realms of Being*) clashed with the purity of his materialism, or posed a distinction without a difference. In *The Life of Reason,* and indeed throughout his life, Santayana maintained a thoroughgoing naturalism—the position that the natural world's deterministic unfolding constitutes the whole of reality, and that gods, supernatural causes, abstract entities and the like have no place in the physical business of reality. That permitted him to take what seem clear-eyed, "rational" twentieth-century positions on specific areas of cultural life.

Religion, for instance, was regarded by Santayana as a kind of poetry, and the Catholic religion, which he inherited but rejected, as sublime poetry. A professed atheist, Santayana's espousal of the aesthetic merits of Catholicism made him the spiritual forefather of all yuppies and bohos who attend mass at St. Patrick's Cathedral because the colors are, "like, spectacular." Bertrand Russell, who alternately admired and condescended to Santayana, provided the best one-line precis of Santayana's theology: "God does not exist, and Mary is his mother."

Yet in his later systematic work, *Realms of Being,* Santayana argued that a kind of "animal faith" nonetheless allows us to know a realm of "essences"—a nonmaterial realm containing what most of us call ideas. In Santayana's view, essences included ideas, meanings, perceptions, possibilities and universals—such as colors, tastes and odors—that do not "exist" in a material sense, but somehow "subsist." The language of essences led many to charge that Santayana had become a fuzzy Platonist, and to dismiss him. McCormick acknowledged that Santayana "refused to argue, and argument is the staff of life of academic philosophy." He also mused that Santayana "wrote for himself to clarify his own mind and . . . was not interested in proving others right or wrong." That accounts for the neglect of him by younger philosophers committed to discovering something more enduring than one man's opinion. But it also makes him eerily contemporary in the twenty-first century, in a philosophical America less certain about such commitments.

In fact, the ironies and adumbrations continued to multiply around this quizzical figure who, Royce cattily remarked, would teach metaphysics "unwillingly, as one led to the slaughter." No less than Miguel de Unamuno, sage of Salamanca and author of *The Tragic Sense of Life,* supposedly said of Santayana, "There is nothing Spanish about him. He is a

New Englander to the core with a Spanish name." Be that as it may, in the late twentieth century a request went out to Santayana aficionados such as MIT philosopher Irving Singer, asking them to participate in a documentary about his life and work "directed toward teen-age Hispanics in America."

Who knows? A rising tide lifts all boats. Multiculturalism may put wind in Santayana's sails, just as John Dewey now bobs about on revived tides of pragmatism. Unquestionably, Santayana betokens elements now billowing in America the Philosophical. If he doesn't rise, the judgment may stand that those who refuse to live in the future are doomed to stay in the past. That is not a judgment, however, that could ever be made about John Dewey, who carried the baton of great white-male American philosophy into the 1950s.

As a young high school teacher in Oil City, Pennsylvania, the twenty-two-year-old Dewey gamely sent an article entitled "The Metaphysical Assumptions of Materialism" to William Torrey Harris, editor of the *Journal of Speculative Philosophy*. It was spring 1881 and Dewey, the transplanted son of a Vermont grocer, was still struggling to find his way. Uneasy amid the "derricks, refineries and crowded river wharves" of that Allegheny town, Dewey added a personal plea to the editor of America's leading philosophy journal. He asked the older man if he could evaluate whether the article demonstrated "ability enough of any kind to warrant my putting much of my time on that sort of subject."

Harris's positive answer helped Dewey decide to abandon high school teaching. History provided an even clearer reply to the novice's question. A shy teenager, born in 1859 in Burlington, Vermont, and powerfully influenced by his Catholic activist mother until his University of Vermont education steered him toward a noninstitutional spirituality, Dewey went on to become "the most important philosopher in modern American history," according to his biographer Robert Westbrook, "honored and attacked by men and women all over the world." His professional activity "spanned three generations of American life and thought, and his voice could be heard in the midst of cultural controversies from the 1890s until his death in 1952 at the age of 92." Historian Henry Steele Commager observed at mid-century that Dewey had become "the guide, the mentor, and the conscience of the American people; it is scarcely an exaggeration to say that for a generation no major issue was clarified until Dewey had spoken." Philosopher Morris

John Dewey (1859–1952) wed philosophical pragmatism to social and political activism throughout his life and wound up, in one biographer's view, "universally acknowledged as his country's intellectual voice."

Cohen observed that "if there could be such an office as that of national philosopher, no one else could be properly mentioned for it." A recent grand scrutinizer, Oxford political theorist Alan Ryan, agreed, saying he was "universally acknowledged as his country's intellectual voice."

Dewey's influence, particularly as a leader in progressive education, became international—he was a "fad" in China in the early 1920s, a huge influence in Europe. When the University of Paris awarded Dewey an honorary doctorate in 1930, it described him as "the most profound, most complete expression of American genius." How did a diffident professor of psychology and philosophy achieve such renown? Here, again, recent biographers complicate earlier pictures of pragmatist thought as simply hanging in the American air, successfully inhaled for no obvious reason, unrelated to the qualities of personality that fanned it.

Westbrook stresses Dewey's straight-shooting, indefatigable approach to everyday problems. Unlike James, Dewey enjoyed neither a commanding personality nor a spirited prose style. U.S. Supreme Court Justice Oliver Wendell Holmes remarked in a much-quoted jab that

Dewey wrote as "God would have spoken, had He been inarticulate." Nor did Dewey overwhelm the intellectual world with rigorous argument, or win it over by expressing conventional views. For decades, Bertrand Russell notoriously treated Dewey as a kind of mental defective. H. L. Mencken, bemoaning the harm done American schools by notions he traced to Dewey, asserted, "I believe he is the worst writer ever heard of in America, and probably the worst philosopher known to history. All the while, of course, he remains an extremely amiable and honest man. This is a familiar combination." That backhanded compliment partly explained Dewey's success. His colleague J. H. Randall Jr. described him as "simple, unpretentious, quizzical, shrewd, devoted, fearless, genuine." Of modest social stock, and a veteran of humble jobs, Dewey approached philosophy with the common man's touch.

Because he never lost that, despite decades of increasing intellectual sophistication and celebrity as a professor at Michigan, Chicago, and Columbia, he brought philosophy down from the clouds for Americans. In "The Need for a Recovery of Philosophy" (1917), he argued that its recovery could take place only "when it ceases to be a device for dealing with the problems of philosophers and becomes a method, cultivated by philosophers, for dealing with the problems of men." It could do that, he added, by bringing to wide consciousness America's "own implicit principle of successful action." Soldiers in World War II could soon be found carrying copies of *Reconstruction in Philosophy* (1920) and other accessible books by Dewey.

A "can-do" attitude informed all of Dewey's thought. As an educational theorist, Dewey profoundly reformed American schooling with his forceful opposition to rote learning and his emphasis on developing a child's whole potential. Westbrook showed that Dewey got wrongly blamed for the worst excesses of "progressive" schools, that villainous notion best expressed by "a famous New Yorker cartoon in which a gloomy child in such a school asks her teacher: 'Do we have to do what we want today?' "

As a mature "pragmatist" philosopher, Dewey viewed life as an organic process in which man, always with focused aims, uses his intelligence to solve real problems in concrete situations. Eager to bridge the gap between thought and action, and hostile to philosophy's traditional "quest for certainty," Dewey's so-called instrumentalism had little patience for what he called "paper doubts," the hypothetical problems of that same seminar room rejected by Peirce and James. His appetite for grasping the world in its concrete, touchable reality reflected a characteristic American bent stretching from Franklin to the present. The "non-social individual," Dewey warned, "is an abstraction arrived at by imagining what man would be if all his human qualities were taken away." Democracy, he endlessly urged, could not be reduced to numbers, majorities and voting rules, but could only be a "social" and "ethical" conception that required participation and deliberation of real people, from every class: "To say that democracy is *only* a form of government is like saying that home is a more or less geometrical arrangement of bricks and mortar; that the church is a building with pews, pulpit and spire. It is true; they are certainly so much. But it is false; they are so much infinitely more."

For Dewey, linking thought to action also meant, as it did for James, engaging in real-life causes. Philosophical commitments to fairness and justice fired his long-standing social activism: his involvement with Jane Addams's Hull House settlement project in Chicago, his journalism for the *New Republic,* his campaign to outlaw war after World War I. They fueled his chairing of the 1937 Mexico inquiry into the Soviet Union's charges against Leon Trotsky and his cofounding of the teachers' union of New York, the American Association of University Professors, and other lasting organizations in American life.

In pulling the life and thought together, Westbrook demonstrated that Dewey, far from being the wishy-washy liberal attacked by conservatives, was in fact a radical democrat who rejected the "elite liberalism" in which intellectuals act as surrogates for the masses. Other biographers and critics in recent years, such as Ryan and Mary Dearborn, have also helped us to better understand Dewey's personal life, and the way it both tested and exemplified his principles. The material, particularly on his relations with women, is provocative.

Dewey's first wife, Alice, possessed the feisty personality he lacked. A devoted activist, she once told reporters, "I would rather starve and see my children starve than see John sacrifice his principles." Her strong-willed views added adrenaline to his ideas, but the marriage worsened as "her zeal for reform and perfectionism degenerated into resentment and insistent nagging." By the time of her death in 1927, cultural critic Max Eastman remarked, Alice Dewey had become "impossible except for saints to live with." Long after Alice's death, Dewey, this amazing stalwart who had lived through both the Civil War and World War II, married, at the age of eighty-seven, forty-two-year-old Roberta Lowitz Grant and quickly adopted two children. Yet it is Dewey's relationship with Anzia Yezierska, the immigrant novelist twenty-five years his junior, that has finally gained broader attention in recent years, and helped humanize Dewey the man.

"I have been educated in social rather than physical terms," Dewey wrote in 1915, "a one-sidedness I regret but am too old to rectify." Yezierska (1880–1970), by contrast, was the passionate Russian-born "Sweatshop Cinderella" whose novels of immigrant life (*Bread Givers, Salome of the Tenements*) brought her sudden but fleeting fame in the 1920s. "I am a Russian Jewess, a flame—a longing," one of Yezierska's autobiographical heroines announces to her shy, Deweyan suitor. "I am the ache of unvoiced dreams, the clamor of suppressed desires." In November 1917, when Dewey, fifty-eight and married, was teaching philosophy at Columbia and Yezierska, thirty-seven, was a struggling writer supporting herself as a public school cooking teacher, she burst unannounced into his office, seeking his help in resolving difficulties she was having with the New York Board of Education. Charmed by her boldness, Dewey accompanied her to the Lower East Side, watched her conduct a class, then declared that she ought to concentrate on writing, not teaching. In the months that followed, he supported her in various ways. He gave her the first typewriter she'd ever had, permitted her to attend his seminar in social philosophy, got her first story published in the *New Republic,* and included her among an elite group of students who attempted to apply Dewey's experimental principles to a survey of Philadelphia's Polish community.

It was only, however, with the publication of Dewey's poems in 1977 that a more private side of the relationship emerged. By combining an analysis of those poems ("I am overcome as by thunder / Of my blood that surges") and Yezierska's fiction, filled with cold, rational, Deweyan men who shrink from Yezierska-like heroines, Mary Dearborn arrived at what she believed was an "intense and intimate relationship," an electric social drama played to the theme of "He Done Her Wrong." According to Dearborn, Yezierska looked for a "personal messiah" in every new acquaintance, and Dewey fit the role. At first, Dearborn implied, he held out the hope of passionate involvement, writing that Yezierska stood for "fire and sunshine." But then, just as quickly, he cooled off. Dearborn argued that after an initial fascination, Dewey increasingly viewed Yezierska as an interesting social datum, not a woman. "Though numerous factors contributed to the romance's end," Dearborn wrote, "finally it was Dewey's failure. What his poetry documents is tragical emotional cowardice."

Yet was there any real "romance"? Dearborn conceded that "Yezierska's daughter, Louise Henriksen, did not believe her mother's relationship with Dewey was ever consummated," and her own thesis rested only on Dewey's poems and Yezierska's fiction. Even as Dearborn spoke of "Yezierska's readiness to alter facts as she wished" in her novels and acknowledged that "the skill with which Yezierska took to self-invention is astonishing," she accepted Yezierska's fictional "Dewey"s as versions of the man himself and repeatedly ascribed their actions to Dewey.

Dewey, Dearborn concluded, treated Yezierska "very shabbily" just as he acquiesced silently in the anti-Semitism of his art collector friend, Albert Barnes. She suggested that while Dewey was a feminist on intellectual principle, he personally proved an uncommitted skunk. Finally, the failure of the relationship "tolled a very real failure on the part of native-born America in accepting immigrant America."

Thankfully, for admirers of Dewey who disliked that conclusion, Louise Henriksen wrote her own book. It began with a prominent reader's note: "Although Anzia Yezierska's seemingly autobiographical work was always fictional, it incorporated small chunks of verite." That skepticism toward the reliability of her mother's fiction informed Henriksen's account of the relationship, as well. She believed that Dewey, true to his reputation for great generosity, mainly sought to help Yezierska as an encouraging friend. Unlike Dearborn, Henriksen reported that Dewey tried to cool Yezierska's ardor by reminding her that he was married. Yezierska didn't seem to care.

According to Henriksen, Dewey plainly felt passionate urgings, but successfully quelled them—except once. Based on an incident in Yezierska's novel *All I Could Never Be,* which Dearborn passed over quickly, Henriksen believed that Dewey once attempted to kiss and embrace Yezierska, and was rebuffed. (Henriksen reported that her mother always remained more of a talker than a doer when it came to passion.) At that moment in 1918, Henriksen surmised, Dewey quickly recovered and realized that there's no fool like an old fool. He treated Yezierska more coolly from then on, and the relationship effectively ended.

Dewey obsessed Yezierska for the rest of her life, Henriksen conceded, but unlike Dearborn, she implied that Yezierska had herself to blame—that the ring came around only once in regard to drawing out America's most respected, and diffident, philosopher, and that Yezierska missed it. Also, as befit a thorough biographer and daughter, Henriksen did not use Yezierska as a banner, but set her out with warts and beauty marks. As a result, though Henriksen pulled no punches on her mother's instability or self-promotion, Yezierska came off as a fascinating writer deserving of further study—just as she did in Dearborn's apologia.

In one of his poems to Yezierska, Dewey wrote, "If I have not wholly stood / Neither have I wholly bent." That flexible solidity, that spirit of compromise, explains why Dewey, like Emerson and James before him, remains so fixed in the hearts of American intellectuals. His ability to move between tenements and ivory towers, to swing between urgent articles and lasting books, betokens the fine-tuned balance. At a time when our own supposed top policy intellectuals specialize in slicing opponents in cable TV sound bites, Dewey's depth rebukes them from the grave. "His Collected Works," Ryan noted in his own fine study, "fill thirty-seven volumes and spell out Dewey's views on persons from Plato to Franklin Roosevelt and on subjects from immortality to the place of cooking in primary education."

Yet if Dewey served no better purpose today than to clarify, by example, how intellectual standards have fallen, he'd hardly be exerting the ongoing sway he does.

One spectacular achievement of Ryan's book was to show how relevant Dewey's philosophical vision and liberalism remain to social life today. With great acuity, Ryan, an Englishman whose outsider status yielded fresh insights, argued that the step-up to the millennium was "turning out to be astonishingly like the 1890s." For when Dewey first arrived at the University of Chicago to teach in 1894, Ryan noted, in the whole city of Chicago "only one person in four had an American parent.

"Dewey's America," wrote Ryan, "was one in which the problems of the inner city were appalling. In the early 1890s, homelessness in Chicago sometimes reached 20 percent; unemployment frequently hit one of four of the working population. Disease was rife, and medical services were out of the reach of the poor. Social conflict was everywhere. Strikes were physically fought out with a level of violence we have not seen for sixty years. The upper classes were apparently indifferent to the fate of the poor and even to the fate of the working near poor. In the cities, the response of the better off was to remove themselves to the suburbs."

How did Dewey respond? By evolving a philosophy, Ryan argued, that proved "immensely popular" in a world where many readers shared "his sense that the world was in a critical but not a hopeless state, that neither standpat nor bloody revolution would do." Dewey's mature and optimistic philosophy, Ryan maintained, "spoke to a deeply felt need to believe that science would not undermine faith, that radicalism did not mean chaos, that a faith in individualism did not lead to wild individualism, and that a faith in community did not lead to an oppressive collectivism."

In doing so, that philosophy slipped away from the sort of simpleminded "liberal" and "conservative" labels now slapped on political actors. Which is the John Dewey who, as Ryan recalled, "spent the 1930s criticizing Roosevelt's New Deal as a feeble, unimaginative, and inadequate attempt to prop up a dying economic and social system"? If Dewey were alive today, Ryan suggested, he'd despise politicians who indulge in polarizing rhetoric, as well as policy minions who convert every new event into a political advantage, rather than thinking imaginatively about how problems can be solved. Dewey was not, as often portrayed, "a fire-breathing leftist, and he never became one." You suspect he'd be serving in the Obama administration.

Yet perhaps the most telling aspect of Dewey's all-encompassing vision, as one traces the canonical backdrop of America the Philosophical, is how quickly unfashionable it became. It was, Ryan synopsized,

> a genuine liberalism, unequivocally committed to progress and the expansion of human tastes, needs, and interests; its focus is on the self-development and autonomy of the individual; it is, if not rationalist in outlook, certainly committed to the rule of intelligence. Nonetheless, it comes complete with a contentious world view and a contentious view of what constitutes a good life; it takes sides on questions of religion, and it is not obsessed with the defense of rights. What makes it an optimistic and expansive liberalism is its insistence that the individual whom liberalism wants to encourage is neither the rip-off artist favored by the economic changes of the 1980s nor the narcissist bewailing (or for that matter celebrating) the state of his or her psyche. The individual it celebrates is someone who is thoroughly engaged with his or her work, family, local community, and its politics. . . . In practical politics, such a liberalism has little use for the idea of the state at all but is happy to think about the positive contributions of government.

Decades after Dewey's death, Rorty, the single most powerful influence on turn-of-the-millennium American philosophy and its unfolding dimensions, would comment that at the end of every blind alley in modern intellectual life, Dewey appeared. The old Vermonter's presence faded, however, in the years after 1950, when attachment to the real world seemed more an embarrassment than a goal for American philosophy, which, to some academics, increasingly became identified with the perspective and output of a single university department.

By identifying the rise of American philosophy with events at a modest redbrick university in Cambridge, Massachusetts, Bruce Kuklick didn't have to plow through the papers of departments around the country. Virtually the whole of American philosophy, he explained in the introduction to his 1977 history, amounted to the "lengthening shadow" of the Harvard philosophy department—a metaphor deftly lifted from that profoundly influential Harvard man for whom they named the building housing the Harvard department, Emerson himself, and his essay, "Self-Reliance."

Of all the great American philosophers, only Dewey, settled for most of his career at Chicago and Columbia, practiced in the "hinterlands" and lived to tell his tale. As in other fields, Harvard presumably drew the best and the brightest, with minor glory left over for toilers at Princeton or other prestigious campuses. From 1950 on, Harvard philosophers disproportionately dominated internal views of the discipline. Whether their work will endure like the writings of James and Dewey—or retreat to more modest status as America's expanding conception of philosophy takes hold—is unclear. But the key Harvard professors of the last part of the twentieth century significantly defined the academic landscape of American philosophy, through both their admirers and foes.

Without doubt, the towering figure in the traditionally core areas of epistemology and metaphysics was Willard Van Orman Quine (1908–2000). After he died, on Christmas Day, 2000—as if scripted to bring down the curtain on an era of American philosophy—few readers of the *New York Times* probably recognized the name in the next-day obituary. The world's most authoritative newspaper itself seemed unsure of how to portray the profession he'd so powerfully influenced. His obituary, taking up two-thirds of a page, testified to his nonpareil stature. Yet on the same day, the *Times* ran a story about that year's APA convention in which the reporter portrayed American philosophy as hopelessly irrelevant.

Quine, to be sure, symbolized modern analytic philosophy's distance from the engaged activity associated with James and Dewey. After 1930, Kuklick observed, philosophy became thoroughly professionalized, and Harvard thinkers "mostly abandoned interest in the culture for a preoccupation with technique." In the era from 1950 to 1980, when technical prowess ruled the academic field, Quine was often described as the most distinguished philosopher in the English-speaking world. He believed himself engaged in a scientific examination of problems in logic and language that needn't concern the man in the street. True to that conception, his ideas never became available to general readers in the way that, say, the ideas of Sartre did, in secondary works, *Cliffs Notes,* and *Sartre for Beginners* trots. There is no *Quine for Beginners.*

Quine accepted the end of monarchism in philosophy early in his career. He considered philosophy not the king or queen of the sciences, but a kind of teammate, keeping out of the way when spadework needed to be done in biology, chemistry or physics, but always on the scene to point out when procedures like inductive reasoning or the positing of abstract entities went awry. Philosophy for him served as a finicky methodological overseer, reporting back to the crew on problems at the site—the border between language and the world. The scientists could then tinker with their plans (i.e., theories) so everything would work smoothly (i.e., be true).

Generally, he loathed abstractions. Excluding some abstract objects like numbers or sets that are necessary to fill out our system of the natural world, Quine thought nothing existed but physical objects in space-time, and even those were merely cultural posits of an "epistemologically superior" kind. That partly explained how he managed (for those swayed by such claims) to undermine the commonsense view that there are ever brute facts of the matter from which we build our theories.

At the heart of his work was the problem of how language connects with the world—how we can know and talk about what exists. In examining the link, Quine questioned some of our most basic notions—causal and logical necessity, the concept of laws of nature, the coherence of the idea of "meaning." One tenet of common sense, for instance, is that while we would instantly revise some of our beliefs about the world in the face of contrary evidence, we cling to others as necessary. Quine, however, argued that there is no belief in our conceptual scheme that's not in principle revisable, and, to many, he argued this ingeniously. In his view, we live in a world of "ontological relativity," in which what exists very much depends on how we slice the world.

For Quine, how we gerrymander the world of experience into objects resembles how we slice a country into states—so-called natural boundaries are really fences we erect for practical purposes (to be good neighbors, epistemologically speaking). Thus "facts" about these objects are more like tenured claims about the world, unlikely to be laid off in a conceptual crisis forced by stubborn new evidence, but not immune to dismissal. "My concern," he wrote in *Pursuit of Truth,* his late-in-life summary of his work, "has been with the central logical structure of empirical evidence." Because Quine saw matters outside these broad methodological areas as the province of the rest of science, he rarely wrote about them, and then only cavalierly.

Quine's overarching attitude about philosophy best came across in a collection of essays, *Theories and Things.* Of the twenty-six articles included, most involved with technical concerns like "On the Individuation of Attributes" and "Predicates, Terms, and Classes," the four-page "Has Philosophy Lost Contact with People?" was a kind of throwaway. Atypically written for the Long Island newspaper *Newsday,* it appeared in the volume chiefly, it seemed, because Quine didn't care for the edited version *Newsday* had published. As he had in various forums before, the great logician used it to quickly puncture any romantic notion readers might have about the social role of philosophers or philosophy. Aristotle, Plato, Descartes and Leibniz, he emphasized, were also physicists. Locke, Berkeley, Hume and Kant "were in part psychologists." Philosophy, he implied, progressed only where it was "continuous with science." Our "traditional introspective notions" of such things as meaning, idea and concept, we had learned, "afford a hopelessly flabby and unmanageable foundation for a theory of the world."

Fortunately, he advised, scientific philosophy that is not "spotty" or "incompetent" had learned its lesson. Philosophy may have paid a high price for that insofar as the subjects left to treat are recondite, but Quine didn't see "why the layman should care about much that concerns me in philosophy." Even where competent philosophy in his view treated moral or aesthetic values—subjects of keener interest to the layman—Quine didn't hold out much hope for edification: "The student who majors in philosophy primarily for spiritual comfort is misguided and is probably not a very good student anyway, since intellectual curiosity is not what moves him."

It was not an inference worthy of a "competent" thinker—that leap from motive to ability—but Quine, after all, was slumming it in a newspaper. He concluded, "Inspirational and edifying writing is admirable, but the place for it is the novel, the poem, the sermon, or the literary essay. Philosophers in the professional sense have no peculiar fitness for it. Neither have they any peculiar fitness for helping to get society on an even keel, though we should all do what we can."

Robert Nozick (1938–2002) won
the National Book Award for
Anarchy, State, and Utopia (1974)
and taught philosophy for many
years at Harvard University.

Quine's contempt for philosophy's traditional engagement with the
rest of culture, a charged part of the atmosphere of postwar analytic
philosophy in America, stayed with him until his death. Always a crisp
writer, he seemed content to continue merrily on his abstruse metaphi-
losophical way, developing materialist points he'd emphasized for years
in a chirpy ex cathedra style addressed to his several thousand fellow
analytical philosophers and no one else. But the weakening hold of that
contempt even on younger Harvard thinkers could be seen in the oscil-
lating attitudes of Quine's brilliant junior colleague, Robert Nozick,
whose confidence in the narrow, purely professional approach of his
department's patriarch appeared to ebb and flow.

If every academic field boasts a "cleverest young technocrat,"
Nozick owned the part in American philosophy during the 1970s. A
Brooklyn-born graduate of Columbia University, the dashing young
man first attracted attention as an ingenious doctoral student at Princeton, where he took his PhD at age twenty-four and dazzled older professors with a striking gift for counterexamples that undermined the claims
of other thinkers. He quickly went on to teach at Harvard, where, at
thirty-one, still turning out brain-crunching analyses of "rational deci-

sion" dilemmas, he received a tenured full professorship. His first book, *Anarchy, State, and Utopia* (1974), a spirited manifesto of libertarian political theory that won the National Book Award, outraged many thinkers on the left with its biting attacks on the welfare state. "Individuals have rights," it began imperiously, "and there are things no person or group may do to them." The book's lively style and flashy theses—that taxation without consent is forced labor, that the state should leave "capitalist acts by consenting adults" alone—also made him, briefly, an unusual public intellectual: influential and cheered by the ascending New Right, but disinclined to exploit media invitations.

Critics, at least, were happy for that. One, the political theorist Brian Barry, slammed the book as "indecent" and accused Nozick of "proposing to starve" people. What angered critics most was the book's combination of "analytic" style and arbitrary assumptions. Analytic philosophers, dominant in the academic profession, specialized in supposedly precise, piecemeal arguments about philosophical problems using the tools of logic, the model of science, no history, and—these critics added—very little common sense. Nozick's fame for *Anarchy, State, and Utopia*, in their view, came not because his book shed light on how these three concepts actually developed or operated in political language and society, but because its often clever thought experiments invited further work by academic drones. Nozick simply assumed that people have certain rights—the rights Nozick gave them—and as a result various actions, such as a redistribution of their holdings, could not be justly undertaken by the state (which he argued would have to be a minimal one, limited to narrow duties of protection and keeping the peace).

Nozick's next book, the mammoth *Philosophical Explanations* (1981), fanned similar reactions in the end, but betrayed signs of uncertainty on Nozick's part about his methods. By that time, his reputation loomed large enough for Harvard University Press, the book's publisher, to run "Publisher of Robert Nozick's *Philosophical Explanations*" at the bottom of its general trade ads. At the book's outset, Nozick announced that he sought to "explain" rather than solve traditional philosophical conundrums such as the identity of the self, why there's something rather than nothing, the conditions of knowledge, how free will can be possible, the nature of objective ethics, and even a topic that might have made Quine shudder: the meaning of life. For twenty-four pages, it sounded as though Nozick had courageously rebelled against his surroundings in Harvard's Emerson Hall. He pondered the logic-chopping coerciveness of much contemporary philosophy and asked, "Is that a nice way to behave toward someone?" Better to instruct, to learn together. He advocated philosophical pluralism, keeping track of "different philosophical views." For critics, though, that introduction formed the most satisfactory part of the book. Afterward, Nozick was quickly back to business, upholding the notion that a "philosopher's seriousness is judged by the quality of his arguments," bringing out formal apparatus borrowed from symbolic logic for no useful purpose, and producing an almost complete lack of concrete examples to test his claims.

In one odd passage, the young dynamo of Harvard philosophy recalled the movie *Charly,* in which Cliff Robertson portrayed a retarded man who briefly changes into a brilliant scientist. By Nozick's lights, Robertson failed to convince as a scientist. Ergo, "Seeing this film led me to conjecture that actors and actresses cannot convincingly portray people of significantly greater intelligence than themselves." That is, all those stammering professors we know. But thus spake Nozick at times in his nearly eight-hundred-page Meistertreatise—one example, one theory. Then back to "qua" this and "modulo" that.

Even in the section on the foundations of ethics, a place where readers eager to learn from Nozick might have hoped for familiar signposts—something as visible and connected to everyday behavior as Dewey's public or James's workingman—he disappointed. His sterile world offered nothing about the church, the state or the interest throughout history of different groups—slaves, aristocrats, middle managers. Ethics, apparently, had been founded in a classroom with a piece of chalk. Nozick's listless discussion of "value" as "a degree or organic unity" sounded like an imposter concept, a thief stealing the name of a word well known in the culture. Even the precious clarity identified with Harvard philosophy à la Quine often flagged badly.

"The disunifying character of the anti-V verbs," wrote Nozick in one particularly opaque passage, "can match the disunity of the disvalues. In taking an anti-V stance toward disvalues, our relationship mirrors its object, and so the total situation has its own degree of unity. Some writers have written of the fittingness of behavior to its objects, and of moral judgment to particular situations; however, the mode and nature of the fittingness they had in mind were left unclear. Here we might say that anti-V-ing is a fitting response to disvalue. That response in its character as disunifying matches and mirrors the character of the disvalue as it rends organic unity or produces clashes."

Only eight years later, when Nozick published his first book with a commercial trade house—*The Examined Life,* with Simon & Schuster—

did the murmurings of that introduction burst forth. Suddenly it was good-bye—at least partly—to "Bertrand" Nozick, best logic-chopper on the block, and welcome to "Jean-Paul" Nozick, even-tempered existentialist, able to be superbly exact and touchy-feely too. Nozick now described his political view in *Anarchy, State, and Utopia* as "seriously inadequate" because it minimized the "reality of our social solidarity and humane concern for others." For some readers at the time, it was as if Rush Limbaugh had started pushing the ACLU, or Yasser Arafat were turning to Kabbalah.

Nozick criticized himself in *The Examined Life* as too "opinionful" when younger. He set aside the analytic philosopher's customary insistence on pure rationality and said to the reader, "I would like to speak to your whole being, and to write from mine." He turned his eye and heart to real-life subjects that many of his analytic colleagues tended to dismiss as softheaded mush: "Dying," "Parents and Children," "Sexuality," "Love's Bond," "Emotions," "Happiness," "Selflessness," "The Holocaust." "I want to think about living and what is important in life," Nozick wrote.

"Life or living is not the kind of topic whose investigation philosophers find especially rewarding," he reflected, because it doesn't provide "clear standards of success." A decade before, that alone might have kept Nozick from addressing it. Instead, he wrote that "thinking about life is more like mulling it over, and the more complete understanding this brings does not feel like crossing a finishing line while still managing to hold onto the baton; it feels like growing up more."

Undoubtedly, some copies of the book ended up in New Age sections of bookstores, routed there by a clerk who'd read a paragraph or two. A beguiling modesty, a new tolerance for appropriate imprecision and down-to-earth conceptual criteria, ran through the book. "My thoughts do not aim for your assent," Nozick announced in the introduction, "just place them alongside your own reflections for a while."

Who or what retooled Nozick from emotionless argument machine reminiscent of Mr. Spock to mellow thinker skeptical about machinelike arguments? The etiology intrigued people in the field, especially since Nozick acknowledged that a philosopher's beliefs should be understood in the context of his life. In 1982, Nozick and his first wife had divorced. Word passed in the philosophical world that Nozick was writing a book on "creativity," a notably unorthodox topic for analytic sorts. Gossips reported him to be involved with actress Barbara Feldon and the poet Ai. Indeed, a friend reported that to prepare for his plunge into creativity, he'd browsed the shelves of Widener Library's poetry section, cruising the flap photos of women poets and reading their work. Then, in 1987, he married the award-winning young poet Gjertrud Schnackenberg, to whom he dedicated *The Examined Life*. Nozick's more intimate contact with poetry undoubtedly helped account for his newfound joy in both the sensuous pleasure of the concrete and its importance to conceptual analysis. His chapters on sex and love, his footnoting of his children's arguments as he ignored prominent thinkers, his references to the feelings generated by becoming a parent to his own ailing eighty-two-year-old father, his self-criticism of his teenage posturing vis-à-vis philosophy—all revealed a man deeply touched by new roles, freshly humanized beyond the mainly intellectual ambitions that formerly (one sensed) dominated his life.

Ethical and aesthetic themes now ran through his approach ("Our fundamental connection to the world is not explanatory, but one of relation and trust"), and sounded more heartfelt than the syllogistic noises Nozick also made in passing. Would any reader of *Anarchy, State, and Utopia* have believed that Nozick would one day repeatedly invoke Jesus and Gandhi, offering among his "reality principles" that one should "become a vessel of light"? Or expect him to speak of the "purity and dignity of an apple, the explosive joy and sexuality of a strawberry"? He wrote like an epistemologist in love.

Ultimately, the causes of Nozick's shift mattered less than the effect. Nozick hadn't abandoned precision so much as anchored it in the real world. He still frequently pressed topics into formal modes, suggesting, for instance, that we view "regret" as the ratio of important things left undone to important things done, and "satisfaction" as the opposite ratio. He still used thought experiments to corroborate or undermine our intuitions. He still demonstrated a gift for asking fresh questions ("Is there such a thing as sex that is too slow?"). And the smooth coiner of "capitalist acts between consenting adults" continued to exercise his aphoristic talent to good purpose: "A mood is like a weather prediction that could affect the weather."

The difference was that Nozick now permitted the conventional values that weighted many of our ethical and political notions to exert their proper force in arguments about them. Whereas in *Anarchy, State, and Utopia* he suggested that "correctness in ethics is not found in what we naturally think," in *The Examined Life* he insisted that an answer to the question of why God allows evil in the world must be "something we can actually utter and bring ourselves to say to somebody who is undergoing suffering." In short, no clever intellectual trick, no stipulative definition, would do. He rightly appealed to ordinary usage in finding "creative" a notion logically linked to a creator's experience, rather than to what previously existed in the world (for example, we wouldn't think Picasso's *Guernica* not "creative" simply because we discovered an identical painting in some newly opened pharaoh's tomb). There, as elsewhere in the book, Nozick proved no more historical than before in his approach, but far more respectful of the links between ideas and our palpable lives. The combination of that respect and his continued analytical verve added power to his positions without subtracting from them. Readers may already have felt that "happiness is not the only important thing in life," but probably had never seen the point argued so subtly. The sheer philosophical firepower remained. If any world that God created has to have finite value, Nozick explained at one point—since the sum total with Him is always infinite—isn't it inevitable that any world that God creates must not be the best of all possible worlds? Since He can always create another one with more finite value? Even where Nozick seemed to go awry—as in taking a notion such as "perfection," which by definition doesn't permit gradation, and spinning arguments about higher and lower "perfection"—one still had to pay perfect attention to devise a suitable counterargument.

It was smooth, provocative. Philosophy types wondered whether *The Examined Life* pointed toward a new lasting connection between rigor and reality in Nozick's work, or simply reflected one man's journey in changing philosophical times—a temporary joining of Bertrand Russell and Martin Buber at the hip. The answer remained unclear—Nozick's subsequent publications suggested divided loyalties.

Only two years later, Nozick returned to the spirit of his earlier analytic work—and to a university press publisher—with *The Nature of Rationality,* in which he argued that rational belief is evolutionary. Then came *Socratic Puzzles,* a collection of twenty-two essays, reviews and short pieces from Harvard University Press. According to the publisher, the gathered articles were "as up-to-date as the latest reflections on animal rights" while also showing the "timelessness" of Nozick's thinking. In fact, the book was part time capsule, with nineteen of the selections more than ten years old. Was it, then, a deserved vanity publication, reflecting little about Nozick close to the millennium, or evidence of his ongoing commitment to the formal bent of his early papers?

At the very least, *Socratic Puzzles* continued Nozick's moderate move back to the love of analytic rigor. He emphasized that the "vast majority" of his writing had been on nonpolitical subjects, and he found it "disconcerting" to be known primarily for *Anarchy, State, and Utopia.* Colleagues at Harvard reported that he ritually repelled efforts to engage him on the topics of that book, saying they no longer interested him. The unifying element of his work, he wished to point out, was his belief that "philosophy's understanding is structural." For Nozick, that meant the central task of philosophy is "to formulate and justify rules, norms and principles to help guide us through the welter of possibilities we face."

Many thinkers of all stripes would accept that as one worthy goal. But for Nozick, the goal implied utilizing the strain of philosophy called "decision theory," a structure of thought (game theory is its best-known subcategory) that he liked to "keep in mind, and use, and tinker with." That approach, however, full of stipulated abstract "preferences," "maximizations" and other precision-fantasies of economists, strikes critics as deeply ahistorical and ivory-tower, false to the way real choices are made. It is philosophy's version of "irrational exuberance": rational behavior that gets ahead of itself. Nozick's notion that "philosophy's understanding is structural" reverberated like an unfortunate counter-slogan to Wittgenstein's wiser urging that philosophers shouldn't impose false grids of precision on concepts—such as "games"—that don't historically or sociologically possess them. In that respect, Wittgenstein echoed Aristotle, who urged philosophers to seek only that degree of exactness appropriate to a concept. But rational-decision theorists specialized in such grids.

Nozick, however, argued that his approach mirrored that of Socrates, to whom the book's title "pays homage." The work in his volume, Nozick said, grew "out of what Socrates did and is continuous with it. Sometimes an interesting question motivates analyzing a concept, sometimes a central notion leads to a new and puzzling question, and sometimes these links iterate to form a longer chain of reasoning."

Nozick differed from Socrates in two ways. First, as he admitted in *Socratic Puzzles,* he had "not responded to the literature" on his writing, despite or because of its massive size. In his books, Nozick conversed mainly with himself. He never seriously confronted, as Socrates did in the *Gorgias* and other dialogues, premises and approaches sharply different from his own, such as those of philosophical "rhetoricians" who believed "right" answers depended on decisions made in contingent historical circumstances. Also, Socrates's method tracked with a logic of concepts educated Greeks could understand, while Nozick often operated—with indisputable technical brilliance—in a realm of decision-theory inferences foreign to mainstream thinking. Whereas Socrates drew on tacit beliefs of Greek society to get his opponents to concede points and advance his dialectic, Nozick preferred contextless variables, the better to quickly formalize principles, as in an essay on coercion:

"If the alternatives among which Q must choose are intentionally changed by P, and P made this change in order to get Q to do A, and before the change Q would not have chosen (and would have been unwilling to choose) to have the change made (and after it's made, Q would prefer that it hadn't been made), and before the change was made Q wouldn't have chosen to do A, and after the change is made Q does A, then Q's choice to do A is not fully his own."

When Nozick threw himself into such frenzies—and the notation could get worse—the image of him as updated Socrates seemed far-fetched. Given that style of explication, particularly in Nozick's earlier pieces, *Socratic Puzzles* alternately delighted and deadened.

Only in the last two parts did Nozick control his reflex toward excessive formalization and recall the author of *The Examined Life*. As Nozick approached sixty, one had to credit him with striking sincerity in acknowledging the technical instincts that steered him. He wrote that after stomach cancer in 1994 forced him into "serious surgery followed by months of chemotherapy and radiation treatments," and confronted him with "dire statistics" about his chances, his first thought was whether such statistics were cued to "the most relevant reference class." You could take the whiz kid out of the classroom—even put him in intensive care—but . . .

That fastidious intellectual style gave ironic force to one observation Nozick passed along in the collection's title essay about Socrates's Elenchus: the Athenian's method of forcing others to modify their beliefs by exposing inconsistencies. Nozick quoted the late Gregory Vlastos, his Princeton mentor in classical philosophy, about Socrates:

I have already argued that he does care for the soul of his fellows. But the care is limited and conditional. If men's souls are to be saved, they must be saved his way. And when he sees that they cannot, he watches them go down the road to perdition with regret but without anguish. Jesus wept for Jerusalem. Socrates warns Athens, scolds, exhorts it, condemns it. But he has no tears for it. . . . One feels there is a last zone of frigidity in the soul of the great erotic; had he loved his fellows more, he could hardly have laid on them the burdens of his "despotic logic," impossible to be borne.

Socrates's logic, though, seemed accessible—even democratic—when compared with the perplexing symbols and variables of later rational decisionists. It is that hard-core symbolization and inference mongering of technocrat logicians that hits many outsiders as a kind of "despotic logic," impossible to be borne by the rest of us. Heading toward his grand-old-man years, Nozick appeared to be a brilliant mind whose energy for abstract ratiocination in the service of structure hadn't mellowed as much as some had wished. As always, he impressed and challenged readers able to follow him. There just weren't many of them. And then, before anyone expected it, the stomach cancer killed him at age sixty-three.

While Quine and Nozick defined the epistemological and metaphysical core of Harvard philosophy, the third of the department's three unquestioned superstars in the late twentieth century was John Rawls, author of *A Theory of Justice* (1971). Many intellectuals around the world came to regard it as the most important book of English-language political theory since John Stuart Mill's *On Liberty* (1859). Scholarly citations to Rawls numbered in the tens of thousands. Some academics credited him with singlehandedly reviving political philosophy. Yet knowledge of Rawls, like that of Quine and Nozick, divided along a familiar line in the modern media age. To any who studied law or political theory at an elite Anglophone college or university, Rawls stood as an ineluctable point of reference. The power elite regularly dealt with his vision of the liberal welfare state, particularly through the distributionist policy inclinations of government technocrats.

However, to other Americans who trusted newspapers, magazines or trade books to tell them what they ought to know, Rawls remained missing in action. Rawls rarely granted interviews. As noted in the introduction, a computer search through past decades would churn out hundreds of profiles of logic-challenged rappers and starlets, but nary a piece or television report on modern America's most respected political theorist. That played some role in why Rawls's lifelong aim to successfully justify his theory of justice ultimately failed—a revelatory tale of American resistance to formalistic argument that I examine in Part 6.

In reviving the "social contract" tradition associated with thinkers like Hobbes, Locke and Rousseau, Rawls sought a theory of "justice as fairness" that would satisfy all types, from liberals who believed that justice protects individual rights to socialists who thought justice demands redistribution of property. Although Rawls's precise arguments could be notoriously complex, a few basic ideas stood out. His most striking notion was to combine two standard ideas in justice theory—that justice issues from a social contract among individuals and that "formal" justice ("Treat equals equally") forbids arrangements that improperly favor any one person's interests.

Rawls urged that we think of principles of justice as those that people would choose if they pondered a social contract in what he dubbed the "Original Position": a hypothetical setting in which they reasoned from behind a "veil of ignorance." As Rawls described this veil, participants mulling potential principles or arrangements do not

> know how the various alternatives will affect their own particular case and they're obliged to evaluate principles solely on the basis of general considerations. First of all no one knows his place in society, his class position or social status; nor does he know his fortune in the distribution of natural assets and abilities, his intelligence and strength, and the like. Nor again, does anyone know his conception of the good, the particulars of his rational plan of life, or even the special features of his psychology, such as his aversion to risk or liability to optimism or pessimism.

Rawls even assumed that these contractors did not "know the particular circumstances of their own society." What they did know, he stated, are "general facts about human society," including "the principles of economic theory" and "the laws of human psychology." Rawls wasn't suggesting that the "Original Position" actually took place in ancient or later societies. Rather, he posed it and the "veil" as tools for conducting a thought experiment. What feasible, desirable principles of justice would his impartial contractors choose? Rawls argued that they'd first choose to guarantee core individual liberties such as those of speech and worship. Second, they'd abide by the so-called difference principle, which ensures "that social and economic inequalities are arranged to offer the greatest possible benefit to the worst-off in society, while upholding fair equality of opportunity."

Rawls developed a labyrinthine argument to defend these views and their consequences. But critics immediately went on the attack. Some objected that Rawls's theory pretended to be a universal account of justice, but really amounted to a rationalization of modern welfare capitalism. Other, "communitarian" critics accused Rawls of assuming that "radically disembodied" subjects can create their own values, countering that human values come shaped by preexisting communities. Many observers pointed out that Rawls's "veil of ignorance" so completely stripped people in the "Original Position" of distinguishing human features that they effectively became the same person. As a result, the "contract" became more of a metaphor, the image of someone making a contract with himself.

In his work after the 1970s, Rawls found some of these criticisms just. Once the most sophisticated pursuer of a comprehensive, "objective" and universal standard of justice, he came to see his theory as articulating intuitions of justice that more accurately fit modern American democracy. More important, Rawls came to see his theory of justice as a "political," not philosophic, doctrine. Shrewd criticism over the years tended to show that a "neutral" theory of justice was impossible. Rawls slowly came to describe his work as looking to what kind of justice is "reasonable" in a pluralistic democracy. In such a society, he believed, the chief goal must be to maintain stability and to avoid battles between factions whose absolutist notions of justice threaten social unity by inviting the state to choose sides.

Rawls, in short, arguably evolved from a champion of objectivism to a pragmatist who emphasized not "true" principles of justice, but principles Americans can live with. His mature theory of justice, like jurisprudence itself, taught that no one theory of justice compels rational assent by sheer logic alone. Any theory of justice requires a choice among value-laden premises—particularly the relative weight one gives such factors as needs or wants. A judge must "take sides" on basics if he's to judge. The fuller story of Rawls's evolution outlined in Part 6—a story rooted in his own autobiographical experiences of injustice—arguably made him American philosophy's poster boy for why ambitious philosophical systems don't succeed in a country that amounts to a landscape of persuasion, not a citadel of proof.

But Rawls's book sparked a widely remarked revival of political and legal philosophy in America. Over the final two decades of the twentieth century and into the first decade of the present one, a pair of men in the orbit of prestigious universities outside Harvard—Ronald Dworkin, long a professor at both Oxford and New York University, and the prolific Judge Richard Posner, a University of Chicago lecturer who kept pumping out books even after being appointed by President Reagan to the Seventh Circuit Court of Appeals—proved to be the major legal philosophers of the era. The work of both men devolved from the long history and context of jurisprudence, yet both also opposed the syllogistic instincts of the Rawlsian construct, making American legal philosophy another engine for a potentially more tactile, relevant American philosophy.

Long a subspecialty of philosophy departments, and even more so in the analytic age, philosophy of law enjoyed a healthy share of attention from philosophical judges and scholars in the American tradition such as Oliver Wendell Holmes, Roscoe Pound and Benjamin Cardozo. Beyond that, it could trace its lineage to at least the late fifth century B.C., when sophists as well as Socrates and Plato began tangling with the concepts of justice, authority and obligation. Should we obey the law simply because it's the law? (Should we run stop signs in the dead of night?) How do we decide when punishment fits a crime? Do retroactive laws violate the moral fabric of law? And what about the granddaddy of all such queries—what is the very nature of law itself?

Over the centuries, Christians, Marxists and secular humanists constructed full-blown theories to provide answers. But most views fell under one of two rubrics: natural law and positivism. Natural law theory held that higher laws govern all man-made laws. As the British jurist William Blackstone put it, the law of nature, "dictated by God himself, is of course superior in obligation to any other. It is binding over the whole globe, in all countries and at all time." Natural law thinking surfaced in matters as controversial as the Nuremberg trials, and as honored as the civil disobedience of Gandhi and Martin Luther King Jr. Positivism, most identified in the last years of the twentieth century with the late British philosopher H. L. A. Hart, identified law with man-made rules and denied that law must be moral. Positivists, for example, tended to hold that Nazi jurisprudence counted as law—just bad law.

It was Dworkin, through influential essay collections such as *Taking Rights Seriously* (1977) and *A Matter of Principle* (1985), and regular pieces in the *New York Review of Books* on hot topics like affirmative action, press freedom and pornography, who began to challenge the positivism Hart set out in *The Concept of Law* (1961)—that is, to outline a legal theory that sought common ground between positivism and natural law. A native of Rhode Island who won a Rhodes Scholarship and studied with Hart at Oxford, he had clerked for the legendary Judge Learned Hand

and practiced with Sullivan & Cromwell in New York before turning to law school teaching. In *Law's Empire*, he made a 470-page attempt to unpack his vision of law in a style accessible to educated laymen.

Unlike Hart, Dworkin believed no ultimate test existed for determining what constitutes law in a particular system. Law, he claimed, consisted not just of rules on the books or in past opinions, but also of "principles" that undergird the system and make it morally coherent. Whereas positivists believed that in "hard cases"—cases where statutes and precedents don't provide an easy answer—judges must appeal to policy or personal values and thus exercise legislative discretion, Dworkin insisted that there is almost always a right answer in every legal dispute—that is, a party entitled to win on legal grounds—if jurists simply dig deep and extract their legal system's fundamental principles. One case Dworkin repeatedly invoked was *Riggs v. Palmer,* an 1889 New York State decision concerning a young man, Elmer Palmer, who sought to inherit his grandfather's property despite an awkward detail—he'd poisoned the old man and been convicted of murder for it.

The grandfather's last will bestowed the bulk of his estate on Palmer. While the New York Statute of Wills didn't explicitly bar a person named in a will from inheriting just because he'd murdered the testator, the grandfather's daughters argued that Palmer should be barred from inheritance. The New York Court of Appeals declined to follow the implied directive of technical probate law, instead invoking the principle that a wrongdoer should not profit from his own wrong. Though a dissenting justice interpreted the statute literally and voted for Palmer, the majority appealed to the presumed intentions of the legislators. While Dworkin appreciated the possible rationales of both judicial approaches, he plainly favored the decision as a paradigm of how legal systems depend on implicit moral principles. Judges, according to Dworkin, never run out of law. In hard cases, they must discover (not invent) the moral theory that "best explains and justifies" rights established in settled law—that is, easy cases.

In spotlighting the case, Dworkin wanted to emphasize that the principles drawn on aren't external pointers dragged into court by stymied judges, but rather internal elements of the law that "fit" legal tradition. Judges, he maintained, naturally discover them through creative interpretation. Such principles may lack the specificity of holdings, and should lack the contingent agenda of mere policies or politics—they carry a kind of philosophical weight that judges are honor bound to recognize. In Dworkin's view, the greatest judges and philosophers of law search beyond the conflict of black-letter rules to find principles that persuade everyone. Dworkin consequently rejected the separation of law and morality that forms a fundamental tenet of positivism.

Dworkin's jurisprudence sounded simple when reduced to themes, but *Law's Empire* teemed with intricately spun considerations, examples and counterexamples. They were frequently presented as dilemmas for "Hercules," the ideal judge Dworkin posited as a device for exploring the field. Along the way Dworkin exhibited a new interest in such European theorists as German philosopher Hans-Georg Gadamer, who emphasized the interpretation of cultural matters in their historical contexts, and expressed his heightened dislike for semantic bickering over the proper use of words like "legal" and "moral." Law, Dworkin contended, is a social institution, not a set of linguistic definitions; competing theories about law ought to battle things out in the marketplace of persuasion. His new focus on "law as integrity" repackaged his ongoing belief that the best interpretation of law is one that, "all things considered, makes the community's legal record the best it can be from the standpoint of political morality."

But Dworkin also drove his influence home to a wider audience, and sought to exemplify his theory despite a lack of judicial robes, by ex cathedra tackling of America's concrete social issues, as he did with abortion in *Life's Dominion*. A would-be Solon above the battle, Dworkin placed the blame for abortion's roiling of America on "intellectual confusion" that he could "identify and dispel." Once that was accomplished, "a responsible legal settlement of the controversy, one that will not insult or demean any group, one that everyone could accept with full self-respect," was indeed "available."

According to Dworkin, most people mistakenly believed the abortion debate centered on a "polarizing" question: "Is a fetus a helpless unborn child with rights and interests of its own from the moment of conception?" If so, abortion is murder. If not, pro-lifers are "bigots." Dworkin rejected that "conventional, pessimistic understanding." He insisted on an "absolutely crucial distinction" between two different objections to abortion. Some people, he observed, "claim that fetuses are creatures with interests of their own right from the start, including, preeminently, an interest in staying alive, and that therefore they have the rights that all human beings have to protect these basic interests, including a right not to be killed." Dworkin called that the "derivative" objection: it assumed fetuses are persons.

The second approach was the belief that "human life has an intrinsic, innate value; that human life is sacred just in itself; and that the sacred nature of a human life begins when its biological life begins." Dworkin labeled that the "detached" view, because it doesn't presuppose fetus rights or interests. Confusion between these two anti-abortion reasons, Dworkin believed, had "poisoned" the debate. He wrote, "Almost everyone who opposes abortion really objects to it, as they might realize after reflection, on the detached rather than the derivative ground." But because so many believe they think otherwise, we ignore the "markedly less polar disagreement about how best to respect a fundamental idea we almost all share in some form: that individual life is sacred."

Dworkin bolstered that unorthodox take with a smart mix of material: X-ray exposures of ideological contradictions, detailed analysis of key constitutional cases and concrete reportage on European policies toward abortion. Combining his lean if occasionally haughty, *New York Review of Books* style with tenacious proferring of reasons, he took abortion debate far from the lie-down-in-front-of-the-clinic (or shoot-the-doctor) crowd, and stationed it in the arena of civilized analysis. What he did not achieve was the consensus his Hercules might ideally gather around a principle. At the heart of Dworkin's analysis, after all, was a disputable drawing of conceptual lines. In his opening chapter, he'd asserted that "it is hard to make any sense of the idea that an early fetus has interests of its own, in particular an interest in not being destroyed, from the moment of its conception."

Fanciful examples then flowed as expected from one trained in analytic reasoning, with its outré hypotheticals. It was not "against the interests of a baby carrot that it be picked early and brought to the table as a delicacy." It was not against the interests of the assemblage of body parts on Dr. Frankenstein's table—just before Doc pulled the lever that brought "it" to life—that someone smashed the apparatus. The reason, according to Dworkin, was that "it makes no sense to suppose that something has interests of its own . . . unless it has, or has had, some form of consciousness: some mental as well as physical life."

On top of that arguably arbitrary "consciousness" criterion for having rights and interests—a standard pro-life advocates might oppose by positing some version of fetal consciousness or discarding the criterion altogether—Dworkin added another: awareness that one's interests are being violated at the very moment the violation takes place. Thus, for Dworkin, it is in the interests of every human being now alive, we might assume, that the earth did not explode in a collision with a gigantic meteor millions of years ago. But it does not follow that it would have been against any human being's interests if the earth had exploded then, because there would then never have been any human beings against whose interests that could have been. It is in my interests that my father didn't go on a long business trip the day before I was conceived. But it would not have been against anyone's interests in that way, if he had done so because, once again, there would never have been anyone whose interests it could have harmed.

Dworkin's "crucial distinction" view did capture some common intuitions. It proved most effective in showing how certain opponents of abortion plainly held the "detached" view. At the time, he noted that both former president George Bush and vice president Dan Quayle had expressed "pro-life" views, then added that they would support a daughter's choice for abortion. Dworkin remarked, "They would hardly do that if they really thought that abortion meant the murder of their grandchildren or great-grandchildren."

But Dworkin's "crucial distinction," and much of the book, rested on an assumption that didn't square with ordinary moral thinking: his claim that only an existing consciousness can have violable rights and interests. Just as Dworkin claimed we couldn't range back before his birth to condemn his father for harming his interests by traveling rather than "conceiving," Dworkin contended in one chapter that if we unleashed radioactivity certain to extinguish humans by the twenty-second century, it would be "absurd to argue that we would then have done terrible injury or injustice to people who would otherwise have lived."

In fact, our moral judgments permitted greater futuristic sweep than that. Had Dworkin been more historically inclined, he'd have acknowledged that influential political philosophers such as Edmund Burke and Thomas Paine famously lunged at each other's throats over the obligations of the presently living to the unborn. When we judge that a pregnant mother is harming her not-yet-conscious fetus by "unsafe life"—drugs, drink, unprotected sex—we ascribe interests and rights to the identifiable victim in just the way Dworkin suggested we can't, even if the unlucky one's pain/pleasure receptors haven't kicked in. It's just a normal case of moral thinking involving speculative hypothetical consequences. Few people outside a seminar room would accept the idea that we never recognize the rights and interests of those we expect to exist.

Dworkin's criterion, in the tradition of dogmatic premises everywhere, simply ignored the familiar notion that we bear moral obligations toward people still unborn—those "children's children" politicians love to talk about. Taking seriously the idea that the unborn can't have rights or interests would have impugned the entire environmental movement and its commitment to justice between generations: Exactly whom, Dworkin might have been asked, did we have in mind? In ordinary moral thinking, as in future-oriented federal policy decisions about the Social Security system, it's not necessary for us to have the Social Security numbers of future victims to know there will be some.

Dworkin's abortion arguments didn't solve America's battle over abortion, any more than his subsequent writings on euthanasia or presidential impeachment won unanimous consent. Their chief flaw—a stinginess about candidates for rights and interests that also prompted him to bar "animal species"—was easily identifiable. In *Life's Dominion* and later books such as *Freedom's Law, Sovereign Virtue* and *Justice for Hedgehogs,* in which Dworkin also ventured into political philosophy proper, he exhibited some worthy instincts that even analytic American philosophers felt compelled to follow in recent years: the layering on of detail; the putting forth of multipronged considerations; the unabashed concern for reaching one's fellow citizens, and not just professional peers. The motivation for his drive and productivity perhaps came out clearest in his remark, at the end of a lecture, "that volumes of philosophy speak in the fall of every judge's gavel." But the strain of smugness and oracular certainty that marred his analysis in *Life's Dominion* grew stronger as Dworkin headed toward *Justice for Hedgehogs,* published as he approached the age of eighty. Where a textured, overarching perspective once compensated in his work for less than argumentative rigor, Dworkin increasingly leaned toward the announcement of fundamental principles, accompanied by a personal certification of them as "mutually supportive."

"I believe," he wrote in the "Baedeker" or introduction to *Justice for Hedgehogs,* "that there are objective truths about value. I believe that some institutions really are unjust and some acts really are wrong no matter how many people believe that they are not." As in much of his work, Dworkin simply assumed that values held by many well-educated, elite, liberal Westerners—such as, for example, aiming to make one's life a kind of work of art, or respecting human dignity in one and all—are beyond question.

A fundamental shaping principle for Dworkin had become that every life should be a "successful performance rather than a wasted opportunity"—that is, we should place extraordinary value on our own lives. Yet that view is shared around the world more by aggressively careerist professionals than by humbler, selfless sorts. In similar fashion, Dworkin's notion of democracy stressed an ideal of citizens as partners rather than competitors—a welcome goal, perhaps, but hardly necessary as a part of the traditional conception. Law, as always in Dworkin, amounted to a "branch of morality."

It seemed as if Dworkin had followed an opposite trajectory from Rawls (as we shall see in Part 6), moving even more forcefully in his later years toward universalist claims. In *Justice for Hedgehogs,* Dworkin went so far as to say that even if no one existed to believe some of his fundamental judgments, they would still be true. He similarly contended that "one cannot defend a theory of justice without also defending, as part of the same enterprise, a theory of moral objectivity," even though it seemed plain logic that one could. Rawls, particularly in his later work, did not take such a leap. In contrast to the imperiousness of Dworkin's later work, Rawls in his final, internationally oriented writings sought principles that would keep a society both just and stable in the absence of agreement on shared, demonstrable, objective moral truths.

Dworkin, for all that, kept publishing analyses in the *New York Review of Books* of newly appointed Supreme Court justices and key Court opinions, sometimes revisiting his theory of judicial decision making. And he won respect from high quarters: in a contribution to a volume of essays on Dworkin's jurisprudence, Associate Justice of the Supreme Court Stephen Breyer observed that "Dworkin's theses are highly practical. . . . They, like the bulk of his constitutional thought, have had considerable impact upon American constitutional law." Nailing absolutely right answers—Dworkin surely believed in them—may have remained important to him, but one could value Dworkin's work without sharing his aim.

Richard Posner, like Dworkin, frequently found himself embroiled in the subject of judicial reasoning, and brought his evolving judicial pragmatism to it. The issue dominated philosophy of law as developed by the great American judges, turned up on front pages whenever judges or justices seemed too "activist" (note the clashes over Sonia Sotomayor), and had been irking philosophers forever. "When your dog does anything you want to break him of," wrote Englishman Jeremy Bentham, the founder of utilitarianism, in 1823, "you wait till he does it, and then beat him for it. This is the way you make laws for your dog. And this is the way judges make law for you and me." Bentham believed legislators should eliminate judicial discretion by passing laws to cover every possibility.

One of Posner's first "outings" on the issue came when Supreme Court Justice David Souter, whose seat President Obama nominated Sotomayor to fill, underwent his confirmation hearings. At the time, senators wondered whether Souter (who much later declined to vote for the overthrow of *Roe v. Wade*) would kill abortion rights if he got on the Court—the same concern that occupied pro-choice forces during the more recent confirmation hearings of Chief Justice John Roberts and Justice Samuel Alito. Souter expressed the view that he shouldn't comment, because the issue would be coming before the Court.

That attitude, among others, spurred then senator Paul Simon (Democrat of Illinois) to brandish and selectively cite before Souter *The Problems of Jurisprudence,* Posner's then recently published study in philosophy of law. At one point, Simon asked, "Where does the judge turn for the knowledge that is needed to weigh the social interests that shape the law?" He then read Posner's "answer," a quote from legendary Supreme Court Justice Benjamin Cardozo: "I can only answer that he must get his knowledge . . . from experience and study and reflection; in brief, from life itself." Simon didn't continue with Posner's next three sentences, a comment on Cardozo's dictum: "This is vague, but points in the right direction. The judge is not merely an interpreter of legal materials. He is not only a finder but a maker of law."

What senator or savvy jurisprude, whether Posner that year or Sotomayor in 2009, would publicly concede that judicial activism is an inescapable part of judging? When Sotomayor admitted as much in a videotaped talk, supporters feared the tape would scuttle her nomination. Posner's observation, though, typified his bent: pragmatic, down-to-earth, candid. It led him to be an asker of more and broader questions than usually occupied Dworkin, whose jurisprudence Posner pooh-poohed in *How Judges Think* (2008): "[R]eally what he has done is relabel his preferred policies 'principles' and urged judges to decide cases in accordance with those 'principles.'"

Consider this "brief" list of queries Posner raised in his introduction to *The Problems of Jurisprudence,* to all of which he eventually returned:

What is law? A system of rules? Of rules plus judicial discretion? Of principles? Or is it just organized public opinion? Is it a thing, entity, or concept at all—and, if not, does this make the original question ("What is law?") meaningless? Where does law come from? Can there be law without lawyers and judges? Is there progress in law? How do we know when a legal question has been answered correctly? . . . What conditions are necessary or sufficient to make law objective? Should law even try to be objective? Can legal findings of fact ever be verified? Is there really a distinct form of legal reasoning or is it identical to some other form, such as moral and economic reasoning? Is law an autonomous discipline? . . . Does the criminal law presuppose the existence of minds? Of free will? Does the case for free speech depend on the existence of truth? Is objective interpretation of statutes and constitutions a chimera? What is the purpose of law? . . . Is law a science, a humanity, or neither? If a law is sufficiently vicious, does it cease to be law? Does "law" mean the same thing in all these questions and, if not, what is the range of meanings of the word?

That passage alone might have led many readers to slam the book shut. If a first date asked you more than twenty questions in a row, would you stay for tiramisu? Jurisprudence, like philosophy, could make both laymen and ordinary lawyers feel that way. Hyper-attentiveness frustrates the normal mind. As Supreme Court Justice Hugo Black observed in 1971, "The layman's Constitutional view is that what he likes is Constitutional and what he doesn't like is unconstitutional."

Yet over the years, Posner's clear, incisive and reportorial development of analytic legal issues, from the 2000 Bush-Gore election to the 2008 Wall Street debacle that he jumped on in *A Failure of Capitalism: The Crisis of '08 and the Descent into Depression*—sprinkled at times with commentary on other legal philosophers such as Dworkin and Roberto Unger—pulled in readers beyond intellectual sophisticates. That proved even truer when he began the Becker-Posner Blog with his Nobel Prize–winning colleague, economist Gary Becker.

When Posner first appeared on the intellectual scene as a professor at Chicago, he won his initial reputation as the chief spokesman for the so-called economic school of law, which held that judges decide hard cases to maximize social wealth. Years of actual judging and further reflection, however, plainly put distance between Posner and the theory. He gradually argued for "pragmatic jurisprudence" and "reasonable" answers in law against absolute "right answers." He described his position as a "functional, policy-saturated, non-legalistic, naturalistic and skeptical, but decidedly not cynical, conception of the legal process."

Posner's astonishing productivity, which led one observer to dub him the "Joyce Carol Oates of jurisprudence," implied almost superhuman feats of reading for a full-time scholar, let alone a full-time judge. Yet precisely that heavily empirical side of his work, so different from the pocketful of examples favored by analytic philosophers, explained the media's attention to *Sex and Reason,* his characteristically ambitious attempt to explain, dispassionately, an entire area of human existence that most Americans were conditioned to see (and would probably defend to the death) as a matter of passionate unanalytical happenstance. Wasn't it true that even Masters and Johnson couldn't work out their problems as a couple, and that no volume of public health information about AIDS could stop thousands of teenagers and others from behavior that defied common sense? But Posner forged ahead, while admitting that "judges know next to nothing about the subject beyond their own personal experience" and that he himself was "very dispassionate" about the subject. If Posner wrote with the flair of a court stenographer, his vision nonetheless remained synoptic, his arguments advanced him to unexpected positions, and he anticipated nearly every criticism one might bring against his project.

Two events prompted Posner's attention to sex, he reported. One was his reading of Plato's *Symposium.* The other was his court's hearing of a case that became *Barnes v. Glen Theatre Inc.* (1991), about the constitutionality of a state statute that had been interpreted as prohibiting total nudity by strippers. The conjunction of the two convinced him that judges ignored at their peril the vast cultural material available about sex. So he conceived his book in part as summarizing that material's "principal findings, as far as they bear on law, in a form accessible to the legal profession."

His larger ambition, he conceded, was to present an "economic theory of sexuality," a two-part effort that would explain both existing regularities in sexual behavior and legislation, and also suggest reforms. Posner described the theory in one place as "libertarian," in another as "functional, secular, instrumental, utilitarian." It operated on the premise that sexual behavior is a case of "volitional human behavior," in which rational choice is paramount, without denying that sexual desire or preference "is rooted in our biological nature" and so without ignoring "the intense emotionality of the sexual act."

The theory thus permitted Posner to apply many of the concepts of economic analysis—e.g., search costs, substitution, inferior goods, demand curves—to sexuality, though without the rigidity or intellectual hubris that marked his early work. One aim, he asserted, was to "strip away" the "moral and emotional overtones" of sex, our "customary attitudes" about it, so we could analyze sex in a "morally indifferent" way, as we supposedly analyze our behavior in regard to food.

The result was an incisive tour through theories of sexuality and legal regulation of such matters as marriage, pregnancy, homosexuality, sexual revolution in the courts, erotic art, pornography and nudity, sexual abuse and the separation of reproduction from sex. By combining his economic concepts and empirical data from diverse cultures with attention to key social variables—the two most important of which to Posner were the economic dependence of women in a given society and the presence of "companionate marriage" (modern marriage "between at least approximate equals")—he came to judgments that inclined to the libertarian, and therefore didn't sort out conventionally along liberal/conservative lines:

> The case for forbidding abortion in the early months of pregnancy, for criminalizing homosexual acts between consenting adults, for banning homosexuals from teaching jobs, for flatly forbidding them to have custody of children, for discouraging contraception and premarital sex, for seeking to alter the birth rate in the United States (in either direction), for refusing to enforce contracts of surrogate motherhood, for regulating adoption as strictly as we do, for trying to stamp out prostitution, and for banning pornography by recognized artists is unpersuasive on the basis of present knowledge. . . . But an economic case can be made for publicly subsidizing the dissemination of contraceptive advice and devices to teenagers and for stepping up efforts to prevent the sexual abuse of children, so the implications of the analysis are not entirely laissez-faire.

Sex and Reason invited philosophical challenge to many of its axioms, and spurred a large scholarly response. Its most controversial premise was the notion that "emotionality" attaches to the sexual act itself, but not significantly to all the thinking that precedes and follows it. Life and literature (if not scholarly literature) and the movies, of course, suggested otherwise. In fact, there was no area in which we so regularly acted contrary to our rational interests. Posner's ideological commitment to rational choice analysis made him oblivious to certain commonsense objections to his economic schema. He didn't fathom, for instance, that "search" was not automatically a "cost" when dealing with romance and sex. The notion that "getting there is half the fun" did not quite compute in Posner's world, opening him to the charge that he might, at heart, be legal philosophy's ultimate "juris-prude." Still, his oddities forced readers to experience the useful intellectual pain that came from reassessing cultural ideas they were loath to reexamine. In the years after, whether dissecting President Clinton's impeachment, public intellectuals, the "9/11 Constitution" or dastardly Wall Street credit swaps, Posner remained a model of intelligent self-criticism, tweaking the persistent offshoots of his "wealth-maximization principle" in judicial decision making to accommodate that "pragmatic jurisprudence." It was perhaps no surprise that when Posner defended Clinton's impeachment as legally justifiable, if misguided, Dworkin wrote of Posner that "many of his most confident and important judgments are highly doubtful or plain wrong."

Posner plainly sought the sensible, no-nonsense image of a philosopher-judge on the order of Cardozo and Holmes, two figures he'd associated himself with through an exaltation of book projects. In doing so, he provided, with Dworkin, an unusual opportunity for laymen to examine the spectral assumptions that ruled their current jurisprudential thinking. For what John Maynard Keynes wrote of practical businessmen—that they are "usually the slaves of some defunct economist"—held equally true of citizens in regard to deceased legal philosophers.

One might just as smoothly detect yet a third subtle relationship in American intellectual life—between aestheticians and appreciators of art. Painter Barnett Newman's withering observation that aesthetics interests artists the way ornithology interests birds never packed the same force within philosophy as outside it. Even at the height of analytic philosophy's obsession with language and meaning in the 1950s and '60s, the philosophy of art in America held its own, often contorting itself toward such obsessions. Here, too, if one fairly assessed whose thinking mattered most to other philosophers, and to outsiders looking to the field for direction, the answer was two charismatic white men from the Ivy League: Columbia's Arthur Danto, and Harvard's black sheep, Stanley Cavell.

In 1964, Danto published a philosophy journal article entitled "The

Artworld." Its focus? A puzzling exhibition—Andy Warhol's effigies of Brillo cartons. Why, Danto asked, were these objects "art" when ordinary Brillo cartons weren't? If physical differences between the boxes couldn't account for the difference "between art and reality," what could? The answer, he suggested, was "something the eye cannot descry—an atmosphere of artistic theory, a knowledge of the history of art; an artworld."

Within the academic world of aesthetics—where philosophers, musicians and art historians tended to make the American Society of Aesthetics one of philosophy's livelier subgroups—Danto sometimes got credit or blame for making the idea of "the artworld" a serious component of aesthetic analysis. Less happily, he was occasionally cited as father of the "institutional theory of art," a Pirandellian thesis assiduously worked out by another American aesthetician, George Dickie. According to it, art is, more or less, what art world institutions say it is. Danto called the theory "quite alien to anything I believe."

The fullest statement of Danto's own views came in his book *The Transfiguration of the Commonplace*. There he maintained that works of art are best understood as objects requiring interpretation. Drawing for inspiration on Wittgenstein's distinctive approach to the philosophy of mind, Danto recalled Wittgenstein's question about the link between mental intentions and bodily movements: "What is left over if I subtract the fact that my arm goes up from the fact that I raise my arm?" Applying the query to art, Danto imagined a square red painting entitled *Red Square* and asked, "What is left over when we subtract the red square of canvas from 'Red Square'?" That kind of question, he believed, had to be answered in order to address another: "Why is something a work of art when something exactly like it is not?"

His own answer stemmed from the insight that artworks make points about the presentation of their content not offered by identical objects that simply present that content—points that require interpretation. Danto explored the implications by analyzing related notions like style, rhetoric and metaphor. In a subsequent book, *The Philosophical Disenfranchisement of Art*, the onetime painter continued to unpack "interpretation" as the "lever with which an object is lifted out of the real world and into the art-world." Pondering his usual wealth of examples—ox-herding pictures, Matisse's *The Green Stripe*, performance art—Danto moved toward an even grander theme in his concluding chapter. Art, he emphasized, had "exhausted its conceptual mission," passed outside history and turned into philosophy. The shift began when painting and sculpture, challenged by the cinema, became self-conscious as a means of survival. Art, he argued, now seemed "but a name for an infinite play with its own concept."

For Danto, it was Marcel Duchamp's "readymades" that forced such self-consciousness on the art world more than anything else. Once Duchamp commenced such gestures as picking out a urinal and dubbing it *Fountain,* an adequate theory of art afterward had to be a "philosophy of the history of art." So his tale of disenfranchisement began with two movements "made against art by philosophy"—both initiated by Plato. The first was the "effort to ephemeralize art by treating it as fit only for pleasure." The second was "the view that art is just philosophy in an alienated form." Opposing both movements, Danto argued that despite the art market, which "thrives on the illusion of unending novelty," we had entered "a period . . . where the need for constant self-revolutionization of art is now past."

Danto's work drew various objections. Some critics argued that he took "art" too seriously as a class term by assuming that all things called "art" had to possess a shared relationship to the outside activity of interpretation. That led him, they complained, to ask inappropriate questions—such as what a Duchampian snow shovel has in common with *Tristan und Isolde.* Others deemed him obsessed with modernism, speechless in the face of counterexamples from landscape painting or from sociobiological directions. A few aestheticians submitted that Danto begged a key question by assuming, rather than proving, that objects like Warhol's Brillo boxes were works of art. For instance, Mary Mothersill, a longtime doyen of aesthetics across the street from Danto at Barnard College, suggested that Danto erred in taking Duchamp's gestures as breakthrough phenomena rather than cultural marginalia. Caligula, she once wrote, apropos of the Duchampian challenge, also sought to make a statement by declaring his horse a senator, "but suppose he had replaced the entire senate. Wouldn't the joke have begun to wear thin?"

The history of modern art, however, did not appear to be wearing thin, and seemed to be irrevocably on Danto's side as the twenty-first century got moving; Duchamp wasn't going anywhere, except up in value. The same might be said for Danto's corpus. Like Posner in jurisprudence, he radiated questions. Does art make anything happen? Is philosophy of art "a massive political effort" to emasculate or supersede art? Can something be an artwork in one period but not another? Can art be separated from philosophy, given that its meaning depends on "what it is philosophically believed to be"?

Beyond the Brillo Box and other collections of essays continued Danto's scrutiny of his core subjects: the non-perceptual criteria by which we distinguish art from non-art; the necessary link between reasoned interpretation and art; the importance of understanding art, criticism, art history and philosophy as connected elements of an organic culture. But as he updated and adjusted, Danto progressed to new examples and consequences, making his collections showcases of how a resourceful philosopher never quite left his subject, yet never quite returned to it in the same way.

Danto's introduction in *Beyond the Brillo Box* summarized his evolving views. It noted the "dismantling" of the traditional concept of art in the West since the 1880s, the "aestheticization" of the commonplace and the supposed upshot that we can no longer "teach the meaning of art by examples." But it also made clear that his newer writings sought to engage the resulting "Post-Historical Period of Art." In such an era, Danto believed, "art can be externally dictated to, in terms either of fashion or of politics, but internal dictation by the pulse of its own history is now a thing of the past." Post-historical, to Danto, meant post-narrative, because in an age of extreme aesthetic pluralism, "the master narrative of Western art is losing its grip and nothing has taken its place. My thought is that nothing can."

But something could—smart essays of the sort Danto turned into his signature genre. In that volume's "Animals as Art Historians," he contrasted the picture-making capacity of humans with the pictorial competence of animals, playfully analyzing Mark Tansey's provocative painting *The Innocent Eye Test,* in which a cow (under the observation of scientists) stares at Paulus Potter's 1647 painting *The Young Bull.* Danto's conclusions offered a new way of approaching his belief that "reasons for presenting" are crucial to an object's status as a work of art. Similarly, in "The Art World Revisited," Danto showed how reasoned discourse in art survives in postmodern times. He reexamined the way institutionalized behavior—sometimes in the form of rote responses from working critics—shaped our sense of art, provoking us with his unerring eye for intriguing examples (a typical one, ripe for deconstruction, was the 1959 effort of Wendell Castle, dean of the Studio Furniture movement, to bring his work under the aegis of sculpture by titling a piece *Stool Sculpture*). Toward the end of the essay, Danto cited Wittgenstein's claim that his own ambition rested "in showing that things which look the same are really different."

"That's my whole philosophy of art in a nutshell," Danto commented, "finding the deep differences between art and craft, artworks and mere things, when members from either class look exactly similar." Modest as always, Danto occasionally resembled other art critics, but grew to form a class of his own. Four decades after his initial forays into aesthetics, readers of the *Nation* knew Danto as the weightiest critic in the Manhattan art world, honored with the George Polk and National Book Critics Circle awards in criticism. He'd become the one contemporary thinker about art that every intellectual interested in the subject had to read, the one critic simultaneously reviewing current shows and offering a broad aesthetic theory that explained both past and recent developments.

In contrast to Danto, Stanley Cavell had grown best known, after straying from the epistemological rigidities of the Harvard philosophy department, for cheering, "Hooray for Hollywood!" in a discipline largely immune to popcorn and weekend grosses. Which didn't mean that his stage luck was any better than the standard philosopher's.

On a visit to the University of Pennsylvania, an event titled "Cavell and Hollywood" meant to honor him for decades of urging philosophers of art to pay attention to movies, he glanced up uncertainly at the ceiling as his hosts anguished over their sudden problem—a finicky light.

"Did you try the maximum button there?" asked Drexel University's Craig Bach, the symposium's moderator in recently restored Logan Hall, trying to figure out why the auditorium's state-of-the-art lighting system was on the blink.

"We only spent about $10 million to rehabilitate this building," sighed Paul Guyer, Penn's distinguished Kant scholar, from the front row. The one bulb over the speaker's podium kept flickering, perfect for Marilyn Manson or an elder rock star turned visiting lecturer but inconvenient for a discipline whose production values—symbolized by the large movie screen that went unused at the front of the auditorium—still called for the reading of papers without visual frills.

Fortunately, their guest was the one American philosopher who knew that in the beginning, there was lighting—and it mattered. Cavell, past his biblical allotment of years at the time and a traveling star on the intellectual circuit, sat patiently until his hosts made the tough decision: to hit another button, operate by sideways illumination, and get past the trailer and on to the feature attractions.

Those were to begin with three papers ruminating on Cavell, widely regarded as the thinker who made it possible for American intellectuals to think philosophically about movies by bringing together *Stella Dallas* and Descartes, Buster Keaton and Heidegger, *It Happened One Night* and Kantian epistemology. Middlebury College's Stanley Bates took on the introductory task of explaining Cavell's two most famous studies of film genre: *Pursuits of Happiness: The Hollywood Comedy of Remarriage*, about screwball comedies from the 1930s and '40s, and *Contesting Tears: The Hollywood Melodrama of the Unknown Woman*. In the latter book, Cavell argued that his newly discovered genre of movies about women unsuited to marriage—he cited as definitive examples *Gaslight, Letter from an Unknown Woman, Now, Voyager,* and *Stella Dallas*—shared with "remarriage comedy" the imperative of moral perfectionism he earlier traced back in American thought to the very non-Hollywood figure of Emerson. For Cavell, Bates noted, a film genre did not have easily mapped necessary or sufficient criteria, was "not a solution to a critical problem," but was a beginning of analysis that links traditional philosophical problems to real life.

William Rothman, a noted Hitchcock expert then at the University of South Florida, in turn praised Cavell (while delivering more technical insights) for a love of film "that's as alive in him as it ever was," and for acknowledging, philosophically, "the massive way we involve movies in our lives." Karen Hanson of Indiana University concluded the homage by taking off from Cavell's readings of Hollywood genre to ponder why philosophy pays so little attention to parenthood, a subject historically better explored by film directors.

If all three speakers came off as attempting footnotes to a main text, the difficulty was the usual one of trying to synopsize an overarching career, a task comparable to conveying the yearlong activities at Lincoln Center in a sound bite. Born in Atlanta to a mother who played piano for silent movies and vaudeville, Cavell graduated from the University of California at Berkeley in 1947 as a music major, and his student days included playing lead alto in an otherwise black swing band in Sacramento. That passion for music also led him to Juilliard for studies in composition before he wound up a graduate student in philosophy at Harvard.

It was there that the so-called ordinary language philosophy of visiting English luminary J. L. Austin captured his imagination, steering him toward his eventual position as Harvard's longtime Walter M. Cabot Professor of Aesthetics and the General Theory of Value. His writings on film, literature, opera and theater, as well as his attempts to draw links between those arts and such thinkers as Emerson, Thoreau and Wittgenstein, influenced generations of Harvard graduate students, if not necessarily the ones in philosophy. Cavell's desire to include movies among the standard subjects pondered by philosophy first became clear in 1971 with the publication of *The World Viewed: Reflections on the Ontology of Film*. (The book began, "Memories of movies are strand over strand with memories of my life.") His declaration of continuing independence on the matter, cited by several symposiasts, was his epigraph to *Contesting Tears*: "To my way of thinking, the creation of film was as if meant for philosophy—meant to reorient everything philosophy has said about reality and its representation, about art and imitation, about greatness and conventionality, about judgment and pleasure, about skepticism and transcendence, about language and expression."

When the time came for him to deliver an overview and response, Cavell hardly backed off those large claims or his original assertions in *The World Viewed* that philosophy can no longer avoid film, that classic American movie comedies such as *Adam's Rib* are every bit as profound as European film masterpieces, and that certain classic Hollywood films are in fact the chief twentieth-century expression of the American transcendentalism of Emerson and Thoreau. Rather, while noting that his "recurrent praise of these Hollywood films has caused some consternation"—especially among academic critics concerned that such praise might "preempt" their ability to criticize the America such films often communicate—Cavell, like a John Ford hero, stuck to his guns.

"I'm reaffirming the extravagant claims I make for them," he said, driving the point home with an incisive analysis of a Fred Astaire dance in *The Band Wagon*. Yet Cavell expressed regret that philosophy and film's "promises for each other" had hardly been "fulfilled," that serious thinking about film remained a marginalized academic endeavor. "One hundred years after its invention," he observed, "eighty years after its first masterpieces, film is still rather condescended to by intellectuals," instead of being "on a par with study of the other great arts." The closing Q-and-A session, however, suggested that film's ultimate status in our intellectual adventures remained for Cavell, like many philosophical matters, uncertain. Responding to a question about whether popular music had superseded film as the most important art among young people, Cavell remarked, enigmatically, "We don't know where we are with the status of film any more than we know where we are."

By the turn of the century, nonetheless, many professionals in American philosophy thought they knew where they were, for better or worse. There was before Richard Rorty, and after Richard Rorty.

RORTY'S REVOLUTION

On a warm spring day in the late 1980s, a middle-aged man with white, flouncy hair entered a University of Virginia classroom for his graduate seminar on Freud. Suddenly, faster than you could say *petitio principii*, the cliché of the philosophy professor hung heavy. There, in the empty room, on the pushed-together tables that form the flat arena of the modern seminar, lay scattered notes. His notes. From last week's class. Utterly undisturbed by man or Zeitgeist. With no students yet in sight, Richard Rorty scooped them up with an expression of unruffled resignation, but no wisecrack, though one was practically de rigueur to clear

Richard Rorty (1931–2007), the most important American philosopher of his era, revived pragmatism within American philosophy and urged academic colleagues to abandon epistemology.

the sudden instant of near caricature in the room. Too many complicated thoughts were coming together. A casual observer, quick to judgment, might have concluded that, yes, the great philosophers had always been this way—it began when Thales, the first Greek metaphysician, stumbled into a ditch while looking at the sky. But the casual observer, as often in matters of philosophy, would have been wrong. This man was no conventional philosopher.

The air of cliché faded rapidly as Rorty sliced through *Beyond the Pleasure Principle*, his Freudian text, before seventeen rapt students, his speech bristling with the everyday phrases of a major-league sportscaster, or the knockabout journalist his father once was. He described how one psychological mechanism in Freud's schema tells another to "knock it off," and a few students laughed, taken aback by the slang. Remarking on Freud's sudden leap to a definition of the "instinctual" in that work, he said, "This is the big jump that everyone has always bitched about." His speech bristled with phrases like "the whacked-out Freud," "whooping it up" and "hiring these outside guns."

Attention was paid, as it has been to Richard Rorty, both inside and outside philosophy, for more than three decades, ever since his publication of *Philosophy and the Mirror of Nature* in 1979 set the American philosophical world on its ear. The recognition of his impact built over the 1980s. Yale literary critic Harold Bloom, a graduate school pal, bluntly called him at the time "the most interesting philosopher in the world today" and "the legitimate heir in contemporary American philosophy" to the grand tradition of pragmatism, of daring to ask, in James's words, "What difference would it practically make to anyone if this notion rather than that notion were true?" Bernard Williams, the distinguished British theorist of ethics—no particular fan of Rorty's—acknowledged that Rorty exercised "quite a galvanizing effect in some of the larger places" in England. Vincent Descombes, author of *Modern French Philosophy*, described him at the time as "one of the best-known names in France. He is becoming a *somebody* in our culture."

Why did Rorty's star shoot so high and so fast? Professional philosophers skirmished over the issue as frequently as they did over his ideas. Many pointed to Rorty's unusual midlife break with his then recent professional past as a scientific, "analytic" philosopher who believed that "philosophy makes progress"—a break so extreme that it shocked many of his colleagues on a deeply personal level. Some also noted his flashy journalistic writing style. All, however, mentioned the sweep of his stark, historical view of philosophy, and its crucial implications for the field. In some ways, Rorty was the red-white-and-blue Nietzsche, a comparison he invited himself.

In one essay, he wrote that it was key to his view of modern philosophy "to construe Nietzsche and the American pragmatists as saying the same things in different tones of voice." Like that German maverick, who ridiculed Christianity for producing two millennia of distorted values, Rorty, in *Philosophy and the Mirror of Nature* and *Consequences of Pragmatism,* an essay collection, dismissed philosophy's 2,500 years of analyzing capitalized blimps like "Truth," "Knowledge" and the "Good" as a sham. Just as Nietzsche broke with Wagner and romanticism, so Rorty ranked as chief traitor to the European positivism, adapted to American tastes by émigrés such as Rudolf Carnap, that dreamed of turning philosophy into the handmaiden of science. Nietzsche called for an "artistic Socrates" to replace the tradition, and Rorty declared that the philosopher could be nothing more than that. To Nietzsche's declaration of the death of God and Christianity, Rorty added the death of Plato, Aristotle, Kant and the last pillar of philosophy as a separate discipline—the theory of knowledge.

Unlike Nietzsche, however, who fumed about the "steady decline of German earnestness, German profundity, and German passion in things intellectual," Rorty was an intellectual patriot. A later op-ed piece for the *New York Times,* "The Unpatriotic Academy," and the book that grew out of it, *Achieving Our Country: Leftist Thought in Twentieth-Century America,* would bring down the wrath of some fellow liberals upon him. In his books and papers, Rorty celebrated the modest, democratic, public-minded pragmatism of James and Dewey as "the chief glory of our country's intellectual tradition."

He was not, to be sure, the first contemporary American philosopher to sing pragmatism's praises. Specialists in American philosophy had been doing it for years. In *Purpose and Thought,* a 1978 study, Yale's John E. Smith, a leading expert on the field, had praised the insistence of the great pragmatists on the provisional nature of knowledge and on understanding all concepts in the active, purposeful context of real life. The tenet could be found in Peirce's maxim that "there is no distinction of meaning so fine as to consist in anything but a possible difference in practice," and James's repeated scrutiny of the consequences of beliefs, his declaration that "the whole function of philosophy ought to be to find out what definite difference it will make to you and me, at definite instances in our life, if this world-formula or that world-formula be the true one."

But Rorty, as Smith recognized, had many cannons firing in addition to his reverence for the pragmatists, his belief that the test of philosophical ideas ought to come in an experimental, liberal marketplace of persuasion. Like Nietzsche, Rorty wanted to philosophize with a hammer and smash the mold of "professional" philosophers who pursue the "meaning of meaning" while other intellectuals tune out. Like many academics in other disciplines, Rorty mourned the way intellectual conversation had become distilled into so many varieties of shoptalk, and questioned the supposedly yawning gap between scientific and literary disciplines. Then, finally, there were those helpful credentials as a former analyst at Princeton, ranked at the time as America's leading philosophy department. "Since the people who belong to what he's criticizing have never learned from anybody but themselves," Smith himself quipped, referring to Rorty's impact on the analytic establishment, "they have to learn from someone who has a union card."

The gibe was fair. When *Philosophy and the Mirror of Nature*, Rorty's first book, was published by Princeton University Press, American philosophy largely remained under the sway of Quine and other analysts such as Princeton's Saul Kripke, both of whom looked to science and logic for their methodological models and took certain aims of proper philosophy for granted—particularly the justification of narrow knowledge claims by piecemeal and supposedly scientific argument. That year's edition of *The Philosopher's Index*, which recorded virtually all professional articles on philosophy, reflected the profession's interests—it listed sixty-eight articles on Quine, and only three on Rorty, who had been publishing journal articles for more than a decade.

Then came *Mirror of Nature* with its radical view that the theory of knowledge was dead, that scientific method in philosophy was a myth, that philosophy and science are both forms of literature, that philosophy should be no more than a kind of sophisticated, cosmopolitan conversation among intellectuals. Parting company with analytic philosophy's longtime condescension toward "continental," historically minded thinkers like Martin Heidegger, Rorty celebrated Heidegger (along with his other intellectual heroes, Dewey and Wittgenstein) as a wise man who could save philosophers from their mistaken paths.

The response of reviewers was powerful and immediate. The *Australasian Journal of Philosophy* declared the book to be perhaps "the most fundamental and challenging contribution to metaphilosophy since Kant created philosophy roughly as we know it today." The *New Republic* acknowledged it as "the closest thing to a cult book" in philosophy.

Other philosophers started finding it necessary to address Rorty's challenge. Slowly, a groundswell developed. By the turn of the millennium, philosophers in centers as diverse as Helsinki, Paris, Oxford, Seoul, São Paulo and Los Angeles jumped to state their position on his work, friendly or belligerent, the moment his name was mentioned.

Both personal and professional achievements marked Rorty's rise in the 1980s and '90s. The MacArthur Foundation bestowed one of its first "no strings attached" fellowships on him—one of only a handful awarded to an academic philosopher. Prestigious lecture invitations built up: the Friedrich Lecture at Harvard; the Northcliffe Lectures at University College, London; the Clark Lectures at Trinity College, Cambridge. Translations of *Philosophy and the Mirror of Nature* appeared in multiple languages, and Cambridge University Press quickly issued two more volumes of his essays. He became a standard name in the indexes of cutting-edge books in the humanities, and at conferences his work regularly began to be discussed with that of such already famous thinkers as Germany's Habermas and France's Derrida. By 2001, when Posner published his notorious lists of the most mentioned world intellectuals, Rorty ranked first among American philosophers in scholarly citations from 1995 to 2000, and sixteenth overall behind such figures as Dewey, Max Weber and Foucault.

In American philosophy itself, Rortyism blew in like a gust through a dusty attic. While the profession's mood ten years before could still be described as logicist and scientific, the key words became "historical" and "pragmatic." Neo-positivists turned further inward among themselves, seeking to preserve the fiefdoms they'd carved out at leading universities by convincing deans—who rarely knew much about philosophy—that the scientism of analytic philosophy remained the most prestigious form of philosophy, regardless of the way it bored undergraduates and drove numbers down in philosophy classes. Some thirty years later, that desiccated view of philosophy still issued from the Philosophical Gourmet Report, run by University of Chicago law professor Brian Leiter, who sought to influence deans and schools into hiring fellow analysts.

Beyond the literature, signs of the profession's rumbling were also apparent. At Harvard, so synonymous with the field for a century, allegiances were shifting. Cavell, as noted, had pledged his fealty less to Quine than to Wittgenstein, Heidegger, Emerson and Thoreau. Nozick seemed shaky on his loyalties. Hilary Putnam, who had specialized in the philosophy of mathematics and language a decade before, suddenly praised Rorty's erudition and started referring to many of the same continental thinkers. In one paper, Putnam remarked that "the great differences in style between French philosophy and 'Anglo-Saxon' philosophy conceal deep affinities"—a claim Rorty had been making for years. The profession, observed Putnam, had become "less smug and better educated. There are fewer things that people think you don't have to read." And Quine, he asserted in a Cain-like blow, was not "one bit clearer than Derrida." Describing himself as a pragmatist and "post-analytic philosopher," Putnam uncharacteristically published an article in the journal *New Literary History*, a publication run by Rorty's then University of Virginia colleague Ralph Cohen. Even Berkeley's Donald Davidson, a top analytic philosopher and student of Quine, found himself close enough to Rorty on some issues that he'd been enlisted by the latter into the pragmatist ranks.

Rorty's impact, however, had not been restricted to philosophy alone. The influence of *Philosophy and the Mirror of Nature* on scholars in literary criticism, economics and other fields had been pronounced. Jonathan Arac, coeditor of *The Yale Critics: Deconstruction in America*, and later chairman of the Columbia University English department, credited Rorty with the "renewal of American pragmatism" and wrote that one reason for his importance was his "ability to speak for literature to philosophy"—to hold up the model of literature to philosophers as more than a debased form of intellectual discourse. Economist Donald McCloskey of the Institute for Advanced Study and the University of Iowa, a leading critic of pseudo-science and excessive quantification in economics, cheerfully conceded in *The Rhetoric of Economics* that he'd "cribbed" from Rorty in arguing that economists should recognize their true "method" as being shot through with devices of rhetoric and metaphor, and that the aspiration of economics to scientific method was "obsolete in philosophy." (Whether McCloskey further "cribbed" from Rorty in his bent for wholesale life changes was unclear—he subsequently underwent a sex-change operation and became the even more distinguished Deirdre McCloskey.) One result of all the prominence was that, just as the philosophical dilettante of the 1950s had to know a pocketful of facts about Sartre and existentialism, the cocktail-party philosopher of the 1980s and '90s quickly gave himself away without an opinion or two on "Rortyism," the death of epistemology, philosophy as "conversation" and the importance of classical American pragmatism.

The sudden academic stardom startled Rorty, an outwardly glum native of New Jersey, born in 1931, who'd gone off to the University of Chicago at the age of fifteen to enter the experimental "Hutchins" program that admitted students after two years of high school. As a graduate student at Yale, he had continued to favor the systematic philosophical bent of thinkers such as Aristotle, Hegel and Alfred North Whitehead. After his expertise in Aristotle won him a junior position at Princeton from no less a classicist than top Plato scholar Gregory Vlastos, Rorty found himself surrounded by his generation's top analytic thinkers. He began, he later wrote, "striving to make myself over into some sort of analytic philosopher," spending much of his early academic career at Princeton teaching survey courses in philosophy and publishing narrow articles on the philosophy of mind, which examines phenomena such as consciousness and mind-body interaction. Despite his best efforts, however, he found many of the problems explored by analytic philosophers artificial. Even worse, he wrote, he "came to see the analytic philosophy 'establishment' as defensively reactionary" when its goals and methods were challenged. That led to his apostasy with *Philosophy and the Mirror of Nature*.

Increasingly a jet-set star of the international humanities circuit, he became a traveling gadfly, invited to a global congress in Mexico one month, a gathering in Paris the next, or to stellar think tanks such as Berlin's Wissenschaftskolleg for a year. The irony was not lost on him. Writing about the ills of globalization much later in *Achieving Our Country*, he observed that "platoons of vital young entrepreneurs fill the front cabins of transoceanic jets, while the back cabins are weighted down with paunchy professors like myself, zipping off to interdisciplinary conferences held in pleasant places."

Still, Rorty's ordinary lifestyle reflected the all-American equanimity associated with his pragmatist masters, not the flamboyant presence associated with such guru-like humanists as the Frenchman Jacques Lacan. Arriving in Charlottesville in 1982 as a University Professor of the Humanities at the University of Virginia, Rorty largely concentrated on his own work, remaining the same diffident workhorse he'd been at Princeton. When teaching there, before moving to Stanford in 1998 as a professor of comparative literature to be closer to family members, he commuted to campus from a five-bedroom Adirondack-style farmhouse some ten miles from town. There he lived on three acres with his second wife, Mary Rorty, also a philosopher, and their two children, Patricia and Kevin. His homelife seemed more Cosbyan than Nietzschean. As his family prepared for dinner one evening, it was not Wagner one heard in the living room, but Patricia, crooning, "Hey, Mr. Sandman, sing me a song." His son, Kevin, wore a scout's uniform, and his puckish father was not above answering his son's query about what he was doing by replying, "Just positing theoretical entities." Having grown up close to mountains in northwestern New Jersey, Rorty, a birder, enjoyed the closeness of the Blue Ridge range. Unlike Dewey, he seemed more on the outlook for sightings than political battles.

In fact, while Rorty had long admired the way Dewey wrote a weekly column on current issues, produced serious books of philosophy, and still chaired committees on every liberal cause "worth joining for fifty years," he himself tended, in the early years of his fame, to be more withdrawn, not given to city hopping for chitchat with political intellectuals, or using his academic stardom as a route into middlebrow cultural and political journalism. Addressing the Eleventh Inter-American Congress of Philosophy in Guadalajara, Mexico, in 1985, Rorty declared to hundreds of philosophers from around the hemisphere that "we should not assume it is our task, as professors of philosophy, to be the avant-garde of political movements."

That initial unwillingness to politicize his intellectual position beyond a reverent bow to democracy—to get into day-to-day policy questions—also contributed to Rorty's audience. His vehement rejection of analytic philosophy's fetish for eternal verities, unmarred by the Marxist overtones about power that attached to the related views of France's "archeologist" of ideas, the late Michel Foucault, won Rorty special respect from democratic thinkers like Germany's Habermas. Habermas applauded Rorty for the fact that he did "not climb aboard the 'antihumanist' bandwagon, whose trail leads back in Germany to figures as politically unambiguous as Heidegger and Gehlen." In Habermas's view, Rorty retained from the pragmatist tradition "the conviction that a humane collective life" depends on "unforced egalitarian everyday communication."

More important, Rorty's refusal to politicize his position in the 1980s had, perhaps strategically, made clear that the battle over Rortyism would be fought on the epistemological ground Rorty chose. For the most controversial arrow he had taken from pragmatism's quiver, the one that attacked the discipline at its core, was total hostility to the theory of knowledge. *Philosophy and the Mirror of Nature* attempted nothing less than a death blow against epistemology's role as the main business of philosophy. The book urged professional philosophers to drop both that specialty and the general search for eternal truths. Rorty's aim, he wrote, was "to undermine the reader's confidence" that he ought to have a philosophical view about the mind, a foundational theory about knowledge, and a grasp of something called "philosophy" since Kant.

As Rorty interpreted the tradition, the seventeenth century bequeathed us "the notion of a 'theory of knowledge' based on an understanding of mental processes." Influenced by Descartes's adoption of the Greek metaphor of "the mind's eye," it introduced "the notion of 'the mind' as a separate entity in which 'processes' occur." A metaphor of the mind emerged as a "mirror" of nature that contained representations of the outer world—representations that Descartes thought philosophers could scrutinize and classify in order to determine their accuracy. "Without the notion of the mind as mirror," Rorty wrote, "the notion of knowledge as accuracy of representation would not have suggested itself."

Descartes, though, won the day. By the eighteenth century, Kant, presupposing general assent to these ideas, was taking the theory of knowledge a step further, giving us "the notion of philosophy as the tribunal of pure reason, upholding or denying the claims of the rest of the culture." Yet these concepts, according to Rorty, were historical accidents, scholastic "inventions" and metaphors masquerading as "intuitions." We should neither resolve them nor ponder them, Rorty argued, but set them aside along with a certain view of philosophy.

To help us do so, Rorty suggested we emulate an unlikely twentieth-century trio: Wittgenstein, Heidegger and Dewey. Each of them, wrote Rorty, in a description that might just as well have fit himself, "tried, in his early years, to find a new way of making philosophy 'foundational.'" Eventually, each came to view that effort as "self-deceptive" and switched to the "therapeutic" task of warning others against it. The foundational approach that led to epistemology's virtual identification with philosophy, Rorty argued, was self-deceptive because it grew partly out of a longtime confusion between what "causes" knowledge (sense impressions) and what "justifies" it (complex sociological and rhetorical strategies in particular societies). Furthermore, it had depended on traditional distinctions between what nature gives to the senses and what the mind provides, and between the necessary and contingent in knowledge.

Yet three of analytic philosophy's greatest technicians—Harvard's Quine, Pittsburgh's Wilfred Sellars and Berkeley's Davidson—undercut these distinctions. Quine, according to Rorty, showed in his work that hard, permanent distinctions between the conceptual and the empirical, language and fact, statements true by virtue of their meaning and those true by virtue of the way the world is, did not hold up under analysis. Sellars, similarly, demolished the difference between "the given" and the postulated in his articles on how we perceive the world. Davidson, lastly, had noticed that while neither of those two thinkers was willing to give up the distinction overturned by the other, we both *could* and *should.* We could also jettison a third unhelpful distinction Davidson called the "dualism of scheme and content, of organizing system and something waiting to be organized." With that accomplished, according to Rorty, epistemology collapsed.

We could then go on to believe, with Quine and Sellars, that truth and knowledge depended on "the standards of the inquirers of our own day." That truth, as Davidson had convinced him, was a property of linguistic entities and not the world, and was ultimately "indefinable." We could recognize, according to Rorty, that we always justify things by reference to what we already accept. We can't, in other words, step outside our language and beliefs. Those who resist that view, Rorty suggested, needlessly hold on to the heirloom belief that philosophy must appeal to "a permanent neutral matrix for all inquiry and all history." They would be wiser, Rorty believed, to enter a post-epistemological world where the philosopher, no longer pretending to be a "cultural overseer," could, so to speak, enter the "salon" and engage in "conversation" with other thinkers rather than pointless assessment.

In *Consequences of Pragmatism,* the collection of his essays that followed *Mirror of Nature,* Rorty fleshed out those ideas, stating his notion of pragmatism more fully and considering its implications for contemporary thinkers such as Foucault and Derrida. Putting his appreciation for Dewey and James in the strongest possible terms, he wrote that they "were not only waiting at the end of the dialectical road which analytic philosophy traveled," but also at the end of the road on which continental philosophers like Foucault were traveling. *Consequences* was also the book in which Rorty sharpened his attack on so-called capital *P* "Philosophy," the notion of the field as some kind of natural object with preestablished rules and methods. In an essay entitled "Pragmatism, Relativism and Irrationalism," he linked his harsh attitude toward his calling to a concrete appreciation of the low regard in which professional philosophers were held by fellow intellectuals.

This century's philosophers, he declared, had become "isolated from the rest of culture." Even worse, fellow intellectuals took as "merely comic" their attempt "to guarantee this and clarify that." In Rorty's view, laymen since the time of Kant had caught on to the philosopher's ability to "supply a philosophical foundation for just about everything." Yet that spirit continued to rule much of the field. As long as it did, Rorty intimated, fellow intellectuals would continue to see philosophy professors "as caught in a time warp, trying to live the Enlightenment over again." To counter that image, Rorty urged his peers to take a "pragmatic" turn. He characterized pragmatism as "anti-essentialism applied to notions like 'truth,' 'knowledge' . . . and similar objects of philosophical theorizing." The pragmatists, he argued, urged us to throw off "the Kantian strategy" of finding principles that defined such big ideas—a central premise of the analytic enterprise. Rather, we ought to understand philosophical inquiry as a practical matter. We ought to follow Dewey in his experimentalism, testing claims about such big ideas by asking not "Do they get it right?" but "What would it be like to believe that? What would happen if I did?"

Such a shift, Rorty acknowledged, was not easy for philosophers. The "common urge to escape the vocabulary and practices of one's time" for "something ahistorical and necessary" had informed virtually the whole "Western philosophical tradition." Dewey and James, like Nietzsche and Heidegger, he believed, asked us to abandon that tradition. Their work, Rorty asserted, offered professional philosophers "a hint of how our lives might be changed."

If colleagues and other appreciators of engaged philosophy took Rorty's ideas to heart in the 1980s and '90s, changing their lives a bit by moving out into hospitals, businesses and think tanks, and reaching out to address real-world issues like abortion and the future of art, it may have been because they, like Rorty, regretted that philosophy in America wasn't what it used to be in pragmatism's heyday. Back in the so-called golden age of American philosophy, between the 1880s and the First World War, James and Dewey had straddled the academy and the wider culture, taking public stands on public issues, bringing their presumed intellectual depth to bear on what Dewey liked to call "the problems of men."

"In the period following World War I," wrote H. Standish Thayer in *Meaning and Action,* one of the fullest conceptual histories of pragmatism, the doctrine "had become broadly entrenched in the universities and established effectively, even stridently, in American intellectual life." Morton White, in his book *Social Thought in America,* remarked on the links between pragmatism and such successful applications as

Oliver Wendell Holmes's legal realism and Thorstein Veblen's economic insights, noting how the triumphant doctrines of twentieth-century America had all maintained a suspicious distance from "excessively formal" approaches and a wish to "come to grips with reality."

By the late 1930s and '40s, however, analytic philosophy had begun to take hold in America, fueled by the immigration to the United States of such European thinkers as Carnap and Hans Reichenbach. Their special variant of analytic philosophy, known as logical positivism, denied that such traditional philosophical enterprises as ethics, aesthetics and the philosophy of religion had any meaning or cognitive value at all. Suddenly, several of the traditional bridges between philosophy's more abstract concerns and the man in the street's real-life dilemmas were not just considered unfashionable, but worthless. The bottom fell out of pragmatism, except in the rarefied epistemological vein that Quine could be said to pursue it.

Scholars of American intellectual history continue to argue about the relative strength of the causes. Some cite the prestige of Bertrand Russell and Alfred North Whitehead's logical achievement in *Principia Mathematica* and philosophy's embarrassment in the face of modern science's success. Others stress the professionalization of philosophy in universities, and the notions of philosophy as linguistic analysis urged by J. L. Austin at Oxford and Wittgenstein at Cambridge. All agree that the vulgarization of the word "pragmatic" by ordinary Americans, who used it as a synonym for crass everyday practicality, did not help.

But the result was clear. Philosophical pragmatism, wrote Thayer, ended up "so quickly eclipsed by the movements of logical positivism and analytical philosophy" in the 1940s that "a decade later pragmatism was not even a respectable subject of interest in most departments of philosophy." By the mid-1970s, the decline was so great that at a bicentennial convention on the topic "Philosophy in the Life of a Nation," Bruce Kuklick felt compelled to remark on the irony of the symposium's title, asserting that "philosophers have nothing to do with that life." America's leading analysts—such as Quine—remained happily unknown to both the general public and many intellectuals. So Rorty's invitation to philosophers to abandon arid epistemology and converse with their intellectual peers had been like offering a jug of cool water to parched survivors in a lifeboat. It had raised the hope of some American philosophers that their discipline might recapture a more respectable cultural role than Kuklick's bicentennial image of an "undead vampire, robust even corpulent, though parasitic on really living organisms."

Yet Rorty's growing reputation also attracted fierce opponents. They not only questioned his arguments but sought to explain away his influence by emphasizing two unusual factors in it—his dramatic defection from analytic philosophy, and his journalistic style. Rorty, above all else, had become the most notorious renegade in the history of professional philosophy. As editor of one of analytic philosophy's most widely used anthologies, *The Linguistic Turn* (1967), Rorty was a member of the establishment in good standing. But in the mid-1970s, he dramatically abandoned ship by beginning to write sympathetically about two philosophical traditions banned from the American mainstream for decades: the historical, continental approach to philosophy associated with figures like Hegel, Nietzsche and Heidegger; and pragmatism. The move was tantamount to treason.

That was not too strong a word. Analytic philosophers had traditionally dismissed continental philosophy as murky and poorly argued, and classic American pragmatism as a technically inept attempt to formulate crucial philosophical issues. Philosophers in both those traditions, in turn, tended to dismiss analytic philosophy's belief in "scientific" approaches to problems as empty and misguided. Instead, they looked to, in the case of the continental tradition, literary and historical models of understanding, and, in the pragmatic tradition, how the real problems of everyday life are solved. As a result, bad blood grew up between analytic philosophers and their opponents in the 1950s, with each side competing for jobs in American philosophy departments. Different camps claimed particular campuses and departments, and showed hostility toward candidates for appointments coming from the enemy's territory. Within professional philosophy, Rorty's switchover could be compared to William F. Buckley suddenly declaring he'd seen the light and proposing a program of New Deal liberalism. The move infuriated some of Rorty's former colleagues.

"I don't think he honestly intended it to be taken personally," said his second wife, Mary Rorty, of the furor. "I don't think he can quite understand why so many of them do take it personally." A few former colleagues, however, not only took Rorty's turn in personal terms, but saw it as motivated by personal concerns. Stuart Hampshire, the distinguished British philosopher and former warden of Wadham College, Oxford, was chairman of the Princeton philosophy department in the 1960s. According to Hampshire, Rorty enjoyed a large undergraduate following at Princeton, but felt "he wasn't taken seriously by the top people at Princeton." "The predominant tradition in the department,"

said Hampshire, "was very strict, very good, and, by my standards, aus-
tere, and he certainly was very embittered, because people wrote and
told me so. He was just not taken seriously by his peers, and I think that
finished it for Dick. I mean, if you want a subjective explanation, he just
felt, 'Here are Tim Scanlon, Tom Nagel, Gil Harman [three Princeton
professors at the time], all these people who just regard me as an old
survey man, rather useful for teaching.' And he got very angry about
that." Hampshire believed Rorty "just got fed up, and made a bolt for
freedom, very successfully."

Rorty, predictably, saw it differently. He claimed he simply changed
his mind about a lot of things after years of reading and thinking. Yet
whatever the cause of his conversion, analytic philosophers, comfortable
with Rorty's clear prose and still confident in his training, continued to
look to him as a window onto traditions they knew little about.

The late Elizabeth Flower of the University of Pennsylvania, coauthor of *A History of Philosophy in America*, observed that Rorty was "the
product of a very bad division. It seems to me that he was the product
of a crisis, and contributed to the solution. He came at the right time.
He had credentials. No one could say he wasn't competent." Part of that
contribution was to tempt younger philosophers from both camps to
explore what had been a kind of demilitarized zone between analytic
and continental philosophy.

The contribution of Rorty's literary talent to his rise was also
a matter of consensus. "He writes like a newspaperman," carped one
colleague, derisively. Yet others who sought his writing—like the editors of the *New Republic* and the *London Review of Books*—were not so
snippy. Commenting in the latter publication, Paul Seabright praised
Rorty's unusual literary flair and credited his prose with "energy, humor,
great tolerance, an exemplary clarity that can illuminate even the darkest reaches of Heidegger, and above all, a rare ability to communicate
enthusiasm and sheer love of ideas."

Rorty acknowledged that he might have inherited some of that style
from his father, James, a noted poet and journalist who wrote for the
Nation and other magazines, and his grandfather Walter Rauschen-
busch, the famous nineteenth-century social gospel theologian. Some
who know Rorty's background wondered whether he might have inherited a taste for radical conversion from his father as well—James Rorty
moved from being a communist to writing for William F. Buckley's
National Review.

"I was brought up to respect the ability to go to the typewriter and knock out a piece," Rorty once said. "It was his early training really," agreed Mary Rorty, who met her husband at a 1981 Bennington College conference on ancient Greek philosophy. She recalled that his first writing involved helping his parents edit their manuscripts—his mother, Winifred Rorty, was a sociologist who worked in race relations. In Mary's eyes, he was still a kind of instinctive journalist in the sense that "if your parents are chicken pluckers, you pluck a lot a chickens in your childhood, even if you never open your own chicken farm."

Still, a few philosophers also attacked Rorty's syncretic style, calling him a namedropper who attempted to wow less erudite readers by his range of intellectual references. In his 1979 presidential address to the American Philosophical Association, his own declaration of independence from earlier views, he referred, in no special order, to Protagoras, Pythagoras, Socrates, Plato, Aristotle, Aquinas, Galileo, Descartes, Newton, Paracelsus, Machiavelli, Milton, Kant, Hegel, Marx, Mill, Holderlin, Spencer, Nietzsche, Pasteur, Peirce, Husserl, Einstein, Russell, Dewey, James, Lenin, Orwell, C. I. Lewis, Freud, Heidegger, Kuhn and Habermas. The habit especially disturbed analysts, many of whom learned at their masters' positivist feet that they didn't need to read any work older than the latest articles from peers. Even a Rorty critic like Hampshire, however, acknowledged that Rorty was far more "well read" than most philosophers. And Putnam defended the authenticity of Rorty's erudition: "I don't know anyone who reads more than Dick does."

The attempts to dismiss Rorty's growing influence as a matter of style or academic melodrama did not seem to disturb Rorty much, eliciting no more than a shrug in response. He was aware that his full-force attack on capital *P* Philosophy had resulted in both personal resentment and some concrete retribution. In the early 1980s, for instance, when he'd begun looking for a new job in order to leave Princeton, Rorty aimed particularly at Yale, with its influential group of like-minded literary critics. The Yale philosophy department said no. Asked by a colleague in religious studies about opposition to the appointment, department member Ruth Barcan Marcus, a notoriously activist champion of analytic philosophy, reportedly replied, "Look, you don't want a death-of-God theologian in your department. Well, we don't want a death-of-philosophy philosopher in ours." The University of Virginia job offer, unsurprisingly, came from literary theorist E. D. Hirsch Jr., an old acquaintance of Rorty's from graduate student days at Yale.

The more difficult criticisms came from thinkers Rorty respected, who attacked his syntheses themselves. Two of the modern spadesmen of Rorty's tale, for instance—Quine and Sellars—responded coolly to his work. Sellars commented that Rorty's view of philosophy made it "seem more trivial than it is." Quine labeled it "defeatist." Quine, already in his seventies and retired at the time Rorty's star ascended, maintained that Rorty didn't have his views "altogether right." Nor did he care for Rorty's general outlook. "I deplore it," remarked Quine, "because it seems to me to come to pretty much the notion that philosophy is a matter of expressing oneself, one's attitude toward things. That it's like writing a poem or doing an abstract painting, and that true or false in a really interesting sense doesn't apply. My attitude is that philosophy is, and should be, a continuation of science. That one is going after the truth. So all this negativistic debunking approach of Derrida and Rorty—I think of it as anti-rational."

Davidson similarly took issue with many of Rorty's claims. He believed that "true" was a primitive notion, "and anytime you try to analyze it in terms of something else—like coherence, or correspondence, or what works—what you say is wrong." He thought Rorty had come to understand that, so he didn't understand why Rorty wanted to enlist him as a pragmatist. Davidson also rejected the claim that analytic philosophy's research programs had self-destructed. On the contrary, he asserted, analytic philosophers toward the end of the century were just "getting down to the nitty-gritty" on such projects as a "semantical theory for English." To the statement in *Post-Analytic Philosophy* that analytic philosophy "showed in great technical detail that the problem of 'how words hook onto the world' does not admit of a solution," Davidson replied, "I don't see why, for example, a truth definition of the type that [the Polish logician Alfred] Tarski gave isn't *exactly* that." Whereas Rorty believed *Philosophy and the Mirror of Nature* knocked out the enterprise of epistemology itself, Davidson believed Rorty properly attacked a *way* of doing epistemology.

Even philosophers who might be expected to welcome Rortyism raised tough questions. Like Rorty, Danto, for all his prominence in the philosophy of art, ranged over disparate fields, from Nietzsche to action theory. Yet Danto thought Rorty had boxed himself into relativism, a position many philosophers consider logically self-contradictory: "In the end, people really do want answers, they want it all laid out. Dick is not going to give them that." Similarly, Putnam, while welcoming Rorty as an "ally" in opening up the profession, complained that Rorty talked too often like a relativist. Holding to middle ground between Rorty and the tradition, Putnam disagreed that the problems of philosophy were "just optional." And he found he couldn't give up the belief that "there's something right in realism. There's something right to the idea that truth is a characteristic, that it isn't just a word of praise."

Another line of attack came from historical scholars of pragmatism, who questioned the version of intellectual history Rorty offered to bolster his positions. They charged that Rorty's pragmatism was too passive, emphasizing Dewey's negative attack on metaphysics at the expense of his far more important belief that experimental philosophy contributes positive things to the world. Kuklick, who admired Rorty's work despite disagreeing with it, didn't think Rorty was "recapturing the intentions" of the pragmatists. Emphasizing the negative side of pragmatism, Kuklick believed, was "a major mistake." If Dewey came back, Kuklick remarked, he'd accuse Rorty of "a failure of nerve," of losing his "sense of the potential of philosophy."

Confronted with his critics, Rorty accepted a certain amount of what they said. He conceded, for instance, that his history was selective. "It's the kind of oversimplification that Dewey did," he commented, adding that "everybody has a more or less simple picture of the history of philosophy in the back of his head" and it did no harm "to spell it out." Despite that feeling, he conceded surprise that people read *Mirror* as "a debunking of analytic philosophy" rather than of *positivistic* analytic philosophy. "Analytic" as a description of philosophy, he explained, meant no more to him than a certain style of writing philosophy, marked by clear and careful argumentation, which he didn't oppose. He still deeply respected the work of Quine, Sellars and Davidson, but not because he considered them more "precise" than the continentals. Rather, he thought they shared the "sheer imagination" of his continental heroes.

While Rorty still valued a good argument, he'd come to realize that some elliptical writers, such as Derrida, presented points that couldn't "be made very well argumentatively." Thus, since he wasn't "anti-analytic," Rorty didn't think the term "post-analytic philosophy" conveyed much. He attributed it to people "groping around for some phrase to mark a break." Pragmatism, however, did seem to him a useful term for capturing his wish to redirect attention in philosophy from isolated individual claims to persuasive narratives about real experience—the recognition of philosophy's literary character that made him attractive to literary theorists. As a result, Rorty didn't see his view as necessarily causing the death of small *p* philosophy—as opposed to the death of epistemology. Narratives, he urged, could do some of the work "philosophy is traditionally supposed to do. Namely, make you question your presuppositions, realize that things haven't always been this way, that they might be different."

In the early years of his fame, Rorty thought the mutual relations between his pragmatism and his understated politics had sometimes been misunderstood. Those politics were sufficiently opaque at times to put Rorty in the unusual position of drawing fire from both sides of the politicized world of middlebrow intellectual journals. The vaguely leftish *Raritan* scored him for "political complacency," a view echoed by philosopher Alasdair MacIntyre, who called Rorty "an ideologist of the status quo." At the same time, he absorbed attacks from the *New Criterion* and *Commentary*. Rorty accepted the suggestion that his notion of "conversation" could be construed as "an attempt to make American liberalism look good." Though he shared Ronald Reagan's view of the Soviet Union as "an evil empire" and loathed "the implicit anti-Americanism of fashionable French and German thought," he nonetheless rejected the neoconservative label. "I try to be as old-fashioned a liberal as possible," he once quipped. "I think Irving Howe is just right."

The link between his pragmatism and his politics, he asserted, was straightforward. "If you give up the idea of criteria," he pointed out, "then all you have is appeals to persuasion rather than force." The natural route was toward what Habermas called "communicative consensus," what Americans might call democratic deliberation and decision making. Rorty even wrote a paper entitled "The Priority of Democracy to Philosophy." Yet that paper provoked dismay among old philosophical allies such as New School philosopher Richard Bernstein, who accused Rorty of offering "little more than an ideological *apologia* for an old-fashioned version of cold war liberalism, dressed up in fashionable 'post-modern' discourse."

Rorty responded by fleshing out his "political credo" to an unprecedented degree. He stated his belief that the world was "currently divided between a rich, relatively free, reasonably democratic, notably selfish and greedy, and very-short-sighted First World; a Second World ruled by ruthless and cynical oligarchies; a starving desperate Third World." He nodded toward a system of mixed socialism and capitalism. It was a middle-of-the-road position, one from which Rorty could continue to hold that philosophy was literature, not a propaedeutic to political strategy. Sympathetic to Orwell's view that thugs are thugs regardless of ideology, Rorty suggested that intellectuals treat "thugs as thugs and theorists as theorists, rather than worrying about which theorists to pair off with which thugs."

Still, democracy had a way of pressing intellectuals to take specific stands on policy issues, and some critics found Rorty cornered in those situations—forced to defend his alleged Achilles' heel of relativism. His appearance at one American Philosophical Association convention in Boston dramatized the conflict. Appearing on two panels, he began by once again trying to hammer home his literary vision of intellectual life.

"What intellectuals contribute to moral and political change," he advised one panel gathered to discuss *Consequences of Pragmatism,* "is not methodology, but brilliant new redescriptions of what's going on—for example, Marx's description of modern industry, or Richard Wright's description of being black in America." That called for Deweyans—"flexible, creative, unprofessional, and imaginative." Dewey, he asserted, "kept reminding his fellow intellectuals that they were simply the cutting-edge of the public, and the public just a sort of out-of-date version of them." Dewey believed intellectuals "could imagine possibilities which their community did not yet envisage." His model for the intellectual's independence, Rorty asserted, was "the freedom of the creative artist from the tradition, rather than the priest's access to a higher sphere."

Yet judging by the reception Rorty got from at least one disgruntled philosopher in Boston, some thinkers in the trenches still wanted priests and phrases.

"Pick the issue," challenged a young man at the other panel, on "The Social Responsibility of the Intellectual."

"Let it be nuclear weapons, anything that's specific." The young man wanted Rorty to tell him "the moral consensus of the nation," a concept Rorty had used in a published abstract. But Rorty wouldn't bite. He refused to give the man "a neat little phrase" to deal with "a concrete issue." After badgering Rorty some more, calling his answers "empty" and "offensive," the man gave up.

The next day, at the *Consequences* symposium, a questioner complained that Rorty didn't provide a way for people to choose among the creative "languages" for reality that Rorty invited from his new storytelling type of philosopher. He pointed out that Rorty, nonetheless, continued to have no problem making judgments about better or worse "languages" used by other philosophers.

"I think my own work is disappointing in this respect," answered Rorty. "What I can't imagine any systematic treatise ever doing is giving criteria for choice of vocabulary. In what vocabulary would one give criteria for choice among all possible vocabularies?" Yet, his pragmatist impulses returning, he struggled to deny the picture he was being asked to assume. "The tradition has conditioned us to say, 'If we have no criteria, then of course they're all equal,'" he continued. "As if somehow it would be unfair to even the lousiest language, a language that nobody would ever dream of using, to say, 'It's a bad language,' without having criteria."

"I don't know how you get around that," retorted the questioner, "because if it's just a matter of 'I like Smith,' and you don't like Smith, and he likes Smith, and that's the end of it, I don't know where we go with that."

"How about onward and upward?" replied Rorty. "When Galileo replaced Aristotle and Schiller replaced Dryden, it wasn't that we had criteria for good science or good poetry in the back of our heads and said, 'By George, this one is better by these criteria.' It's just that we looked at the two and said, 'Well, we used to think this one was good but look at the competition.' And that doesn't seem to me to leave us in a position of relativism, or intellectual egalitarianism, or irrationalism. It just leaves us doing what we've been doing all the time."

In short, making decisions and trying new things in the real world. Rorty's pragmatic answer to relativism—that it doesn't exist in the real world—had been stated in his abstract. Conceding that relativism is logically self-refuting, he asserted the difference "between saying that every community is as good as every other" and saying that we have to work out "from the communities with which we presently identify." No pragmatist needed to worry about relativism, because the "view that every tradition is as rational or as moral as every other could be held only by a god, someone who had no need to use (but only to mention) the terms 'rational' or 'moral,' because she had no need to inquire or deliberate. Such a being would have escaped from history."

Both conference encounters crystallized the difficulty of reconciling pragmatism with traditional philosophy, if not with American life. In everyday life, we're free to adopt criteria for this or that decision in good pragmatic style—according to our purposes in concrete situations. But traditional philosophy's concrete situation remained the academy, the classroom, the convention hotel, the journal—places where the questions remained academic and the overriding purpose to find criteria.

Given that very practical snag, the growing number of academic philosophers leaving "non-pragmatic" classrooms, and entering "applied" areas like medicine, law and business, offered one hopeful route for philosophy. On the surface, Rorty's pragmatist revival and the spread of applied ethics seemed like locomotives going in opposite directions—as one side decided "philosophy" had no goods to deliver, the other side delivered them. But leading applied ethicists like Syracuse University's Samuel Gorovitz, who worked in a Boston hospital, and the University of Delaware's Norman Bowie, who did time in a Texas corporation, pointed out that applied ethicists tended to follow a Rortyan method in their practice—not handing down theories or edicts, but talking to their new colleagues, questioning hidebound assumptions. Hilary Putnam thought the two tendencies could "be mutually supportive" because he saw part of the fallout from post-analytic philosophy, and its attack on traditional theories of truth, as requiring a giving up of the dichotomy between facts and values—the hard-line positivist assertion that the two are simply apples and oranges, and one can't deduce values from facts. Putnam said at the time that he wanted to "push people like Quine" to take what they believed about science—"that there's no better reason to accept something as justified than that you in fact find it indispensable"—and apply it to ethics too. "If we pragmatists do what we're trying to do right," he remarked, "we can actually strengthen the hand of the people who are doing applied ethics."

By the 1990s, Rorty's enduring importance made him target practice for any intellectual with a beef about "deconstruction," any philosopher still wedded to positivism. Standard clauses like "America's most famous academic philosopher" or "the preeminent cultural philosopher in the United States today" accompanied most mentions of his name. His moment of true media crossover, however, came in 1998, with the publication of his first overtly political work, *Achieving Our Country*, the widely reviewed tip of his secular, reformist, anti-epistemological iceberg. The charges of aloofness, it seemed, had hit their mark. The book opened him up to harsh comment from the political right.

To Roger Kimball in the *American Spectator*, America's philosophical maverick was a "happy nihilist" and "the official philosopher of postmodern academic liberals," even though Rorty had prominently zapped "postmodernism" in a "Most Overrated Idea" symposium sponsored by the *New York Times.* (He branded it "a word that pretends to stand for an idea," and one "it would be nice to get rid of.") According to David Brooks in the *Weekly Standard,* Rorty predicted in *Achieving Our Country* that "we were about to become a dictatorship," even though a glance at the text showed that Rorty was extrapolating from Edward Luttwak's suggestion that "fascism may be the American future." To Arnold Beichman in the *Washington Times,* Rorty sought "to resuscitate a moribund Marxified radicalism," an odd size-up, given Rorty's statement in the book that "Marxism was not only a catastrophe for all the countries in which Marxists took power, but a disaster for the reformist Left in all the countries in which they did not."

The most disingenuous criticism, however, came in George Will's *Newsweek* attack on Rorty's "remarkably bad book." Will charged that Rorty "radiates contempt for the country" and "seems to despise most Americans." Asking, "When was the last time Rorty read a newspaper?," Will declared that Rorty "knows next to nothing" about the "real America." It seemed unfair to a book that variously touched on the Wagner Act, Stonewall and other non-ivory-tower events. Nowhere did Will advise his *Newsweek* readers that he'd been derided by Rorty within *Achieving Our Country* as one of those "columnists" who base their "know-nothing criticisms of the contemporary American academy" on believing "everything they read in scandalmongering books by Dinesh D'Souza, David Lehman and others. They do not read philosophy, but simply search out titles and sentences to which they can react with indignation."

No matter. For those who did read philosophy on the eve of the millennium, *Truth and Progress,* Rorty's fourth volume of essays from Cambridge University Press, came at an apt time. A selection of his philosophical essays from the 1990s (along with two earlier pieces), the volume undermined widespread shibboleths about Rorty: that he never argued; that he rejected analytic philosophy; that he considered philosophy dead; that he celebrated all continental philosophers, including Foucault, Lacan and Derrida; that he didn't believe in truth. The book showed him vulnerable to criticism, but hardly on the sloppy grounds advanced by enemies.

Helpfully organized into three sections—truth, moral progress and the role of philosophy in human progress—it enabled new readers, as *Achieving Our Country* did not, to trace the full arc of Rorty's beliefs. It also permitted media sorts, suddenly finding Rorty on their radar screens, to locate the challenges of his work accurately, to understand the linkage between his philosophical beliefs, his intellectual autobiography and his politics.

"Although frequently accused," Rorty had drily commented in an autobiographical precis for a reference work, "of raving irrationalism and unconscionable frivolity by the political right, and of insufficient radicalism, as well as premature anti-communism, by the political left, I think of myself as sharing John Dewey's political attitudes and hopes, as well as his pragmatism. In my most recent work, I have been trying to distinguish what is living from what is dead in Dewey's thought."

Truth and Progress helped confirm that by exhibiting the dazzle and idiosyncrasy of Rorty's literary style and eristic habits—the sharp insider wit, the hyperactive thumbnailing of other thinkers to hawk fresh images of their thought, the will to eponymy and syncretism, the vote-with-one's-feet reaction to what Imre Lakatos called "degenerate research programs" in philosophy. In it, he kept to his own program, making clear that the pragmatist conception of truth anchored all else. What American pragmatists from Peirce, Dewey, and James to Sellars, Quine, and Davidson established, in Rorty's view (he continued to enroll the last three as pragmatists, without obtaining their signed membership forms), is that we understand truth better when we abandon such notions as "the intrinsic nature of reality" and "correspondence to reality" for something like James's famous phrase that "the true is the good in the way of belief." We needed, however, to understand James to be saying that "we have no criterion of truth other than to form a justification," and that justification will always be relative to audiences.

While Rorty accepted (contrary to his caricaturists) that "true" is semantically "an absolute term," he noted that "its conditions of application will always be relative." For complex reasons whose articulation Rorty continued to credit to Davidson, Rorty believed pragmatists could not sensibly attempt "to specify the nature of truth" because truth's very absoluteness makes it indefinable. In practice, it, like "objectivity," amounted to intersubjective agreement within a particular community. Rorty saw the substitution of "objectivity as intersubjectivity" for "objectivity as accurate representation" as "the key pragmatic move." The link between independent reality and thinking is causal, not rational.

Rorty's first eight essays explored nuances in his views on truth by grappling with those very epistemologists he described as engaged in "sterile quarrels." In those essays, Rorty took on the work of Davidson, Crispin Wright (a realist completely at odds with Rorty's views), Hilary Putnam, John Searle, Charles Taylor, Daniel Dennett, Thomas Nagel,

Robert Brandom, John McDowell and Michael Williams. He acknowledged that his tone was "dismissive," that his aim was "discouraging further attention" to the topic. Yet sentence by sentence, he argued—that is, he presented complex theoretical considerations meant to persuade us to abandon realism. In "Is Truth a Goal of Inquiry?," for instance, Rorty answered no, because pragmatism doesn't permit the notion that we ever get closer to a capital T Truth that trumps all others for all times and communities. But not before he entered the nomenclature of his opponent, Wright, and explored the possibilities.

Similarly, in "Hilary Putnam and the Relativist Menace," Rorty painstakingly sought to identify the differences between their pragmatist positions, and accepted some rebukes. He agreed, for instance, that for pragmatists "the question should always be 'What use is it?' rather than 'Is it real?'" Throughout the essays, Rorty did his homework. That stayed true whether he was pondering everyday phrases like "representing accurately" or manipulating such peculiar notions as prestigious British philosopher P. F. Strawson's that facts are "sentence-shaped objects," or training intense attention on the signature phrases favored by lead actors in the realist/anti-realist follies—McDowell's "answerability to the world," Bernard Williams's "how things are anyway," Taylor's "in virtue of the way things are."

Along the way, he also explained the philosophical hats he was and wasn't willing to wear (for lovers of nomenclature, he owned up to being a naturalist, holist and psychological nominalist, but not a reductivist). And always and ever he elaborated, coloring in his big picture. The pragmatist conception of truth, Rorty admitted, should not claim to be "commonsensical," because most people hold on to "realist" and "representationalist" intuitions. Rather, pragmatists must be, like Dewey, reformers "involved in a long-term attempt to change the rhetoric, the common sense, and the self-image of their community." He also aired the Darwinism that structured most of his other beliefs. By Darwinism, Rorty meant the view that humans are "animals with special organs and abilities," but those organs and abilities "have no more of a representational relation to the intrinsic nature of things than does the anteater's snout or the bowerbird's skill at weaving." Those who continued to charge Rorty with simplistic relativism could consult this and other parts of *Truth and Progress* to confirm that he knew the traditional "self-contradiction" charge against relativism, and easily slipped it. He agreed, in fact, with Putnam: "Like Relativism . . . Realism is an impossible attempt to view the world from Nowhere." Rorty wrote that his "strategy for escaping the self-referential difficulties into which 'the Relativist' keeps getting himself is to move everything over from epistemology and metaphysics to cultural politics, from claims about knowledge and appeals to self-evidence to suggestions about what we should try."

It was in such observations that Rorty indicated that big, non-epistemological choices—linkages—followed from the knowledge situation he describes: "Once one gives up the appearance-reality distinction, and the attempt to relate such things as predictive success and diminished cruelty to the intrinsic nature of reality, one has to give separate accounts of progress in science and in morals." That is, pragmatist accounts, which require that the answers reflect our interests as problem-solving organisms and that the distinctions they utilize make a difference in ordinary practice. Scientific progress becomes "an increased ability to make predictions." Moral progress turns into "becoming like ourselves at our best." Philosophical progress occurs when we "find a way of integrating the worldviews and the moral intuitions we inherited from our ancestors with new scientific theories or new sociopolitical institutions and theories or other novelties."

In his second section of essays, on moral progress, Rorty similarly eschewed representation for creativity. We should, he suggested, stop asking, "What is our nature?" and ask instead, "What can we make of ourselves?" He rejected foundationalism as quickly in human rights as in epistemology. The "question of whether human beings really have the rights enumerated in the Helsinki Declaration," he remarked, "is not worth raising." While strongly supportive of feminism, he wished certain feminist writers would abandon realist "rhetoric" that suggested women have a "nature" or that oppression needed a "theory." Stories, not principles or definitions, led to moral progress, so "the difference between the moral realist and the moral antirealist seems to pragmatists a difference that makes no practical difference." Instead of theories, we needed "sentimental education" of the sort movies, journalism and novels provided, which would expand the set of "people like us." In morality, as elsewhere, we made progress, Rorty insisted, by becoming bold narrators and Romantic inventors of better vocabularies.

In his final section, Rorty drove home a related point about philosophy. For him, philosophy made progress "not by becoming more rigorous but by becoming more imaginative." Geniuses like "Frege and Mill, Russell and Heidegger, Dewey and Habermas, Davidson and Derrida" sparked that kind of progress, not "underlaborers" like himself, who did the useful "dirty work" of clearing philosophical rubbish and "drum-beating" for new narratives and vocabularies. Geniuses induced "Gestalt-switches," which no method can guarantee. Because "the history of philosophy is the history of Gestalt-switches, not of the painstaking carrying-out of research programs," Rorty denied he had "any views about what form philosophy ought to take." Philosophy should have the freedom we offer, at our most liberal, to art. He concluded that to "give up on the idea that philosophy gets nearer to truth, and to interpret it as Dewey did, is to concede primacy to the imagination over the argumentative intellect, and to genius over professionalism."

Which narrative shifts appealed to Rorty? Here, unlike in *Achieving Our Country*, with its moralizing story of political activism and hope, Rorty did not offer a full-scale vision. But in assessing candidates, he favored Sartre's view that we should "attempt to draw the full conclusions from a consistently atheist position," a goal he later described as a "perfect secular utopia." At various points in his essays, Rorty returned to a dark notion that drew his epistemology and ethics together in a surprising way. Throughout history, Rorty believed, man had evinced a "desperate hope for a noncontingent and powerful ally"—God, Reason, Truth, Name Your Poison. In his essay on McDowell, Rorty put it bluntly: "I agree with Heidegger that there is a straight line between the Cartesian quest for certainty and the Nietzschean will to power." In Rorty's view, our traditional seeking of "authoritative guidance"—from God, Reason, "the fierce father," "a nonhuman authority to whom we owe some sort of respect"—debilitated us as free agents. He opposed the "ambition of transcendence" that Thomas Nagel saw as crucial to philosophy. We should drop all that.

Rorty knew that the subtleties of his debates with Nagel and other peers were "as baffling to nonspecialists as are those among theologians who debate transubstantiation or who ask whether it is worse to be reincarnated as a hermaphrodite or as a beast." Yet his larger themes made clear that both the political right's objection to Rorty as a wishy-washy, postmodernist believer in nothing, and the left's gentler charge that he devalued cultural analysis, misconstrued the challenge Rorty posed to all intellectual "stories." His vision of philosophy and art was nakedly Darwinian: Let a thousand narratives bloom, and those that survived would survive (not necessarily the fittest, since there was nothing to fit except differing purposes).

More appropriate criticisms of Rorty, it seemed, were those that held him to his pragmatist standards, then evaluated his narratives by how well they persuaded us. Vulnerabilities suggested themselves on the stylistic, rhetorical and moral fronts.

Rorty was, for instance, unquestionably the best philosophical writer since Bertrand Russell, gifted at lacing details and abstractions together with a punch few could rival. Yet his most famous stylistic signature remained his runaway eponymy—he was the biggest philosophical namedropper, the most inveterate cartographer, in the history of the field. "Brandom is, in this respect, to Davidson," he wrote in his essay on the first thinker, "as McDowell is to Sellars." He began a sentence in his essay on McDowell, "From a Sellarsian, Davidsonian, Brandomian, or Hegelian viewpoint."

Pedantry? Mastery? Regardless, one had only to ponder the adjective "Rortyan" to fathom that adjectives aimed at capturing entire webs of a philosopher's beliefs were like webs themselves—full of holes. Could Rorty's narratives, fastened together at so many knots by these eponymous adjectives, win a long-range battle of persuasion? Would Americans bother to learn *that* vocabulary? In another doozy of a sentence, Rorty wrote about the imagined conversations of great philosophers across time: "The Fregean, the Kripkean, the Popperian, the Whiteheadian, and the Heideggerean will each reeducate Plato in a different way before starting to argue with him." A key question was whether anyone would be able to speak "Rortyese" after its head griot passed on.

Rorty also practiced a kind of therapeutic proselytization, a blend of Wittgenstein and Nancy Reagan. His most common argumentative move was to urge the reader to "Just Say No!" to concepts he disliked. In *Truth and Progress,* Rorty announced we should "rid ourselves" of the notion of intelligibility. We should notice that talking about the "real" has been "more trouble than it was worth." We should "dissolve rather than solve the problem of freedom and determinism." We should dump such mental faculties as "thought" and "sensation." We should "just stop trying to write books called *A History of Philosophy.*" We should know that "the time has come to drop the terms 'capitalism' and 'socialism' from the political vocabulary of the Left." And we already knew from *Philosophy and the Mirror of Nature* what he thought about Descartes, representation and realism. We should do all this, he added, in Humean good spirits, to achieve a Wittgensteinian peace.

Rorty appeared to end up, for better or worse, the Rhett Butler of professional American philosophy: a man willing, in the end, to walk away from what had been most important in his life—and discipline—with a fine crusty confidence. The problem was, one couldn't clearly determine why others would want to join him in hitting the road.

Take realism. For someone hostile to countless old distinctions, Rorty could be awfully binary. In *Achieving Our Country,* he wrote that "objectivity is a matter of intersubjective consensus among human beings, not of accurate representation of something nonhuman." Yet most battles over objectivity concern a third category—accurate representation of something *human.* Recognizing our hand in shaping narrative, we still think some stories more accurate than others. In his zeal to launch a thousand narrative ships, Rorty paid little mind to the journalistic truth that the first step in establishing a new tale may be to discredit the old one already in the clip file. It was a job he regularly performed—his apostate rendition of modern philosophy as the mirror of nature being a classic—but never overtly honored.

On the contrary, he tended to pooh-pooh the enterprise of getting stories right, a possible case of Sartrean self-deception for this fine conceptual reporter who sweated to make his dispatches on other thinkers exact. In *Achieving Our Country,* Rorty asserted that there was "no point in asking whether Lincoln or Whitman or Dewey got America right. Stories about what a nation has been and should try to be are not attempts at accurate representation, but rather attempts to forge a moral identity." But if one took Rorty at his word in *Truth and Progress*—that pragmatism required imaginative stories that solve problems—then there was a point, and not just an epistemological point. The point was that we want to know which is better for us.

Too often, it seemed, Rorty let his fear of epistemological echoes lead him into diction that played into the hands of those who branded him a relativist. It made him sound as if he thought no one story was better than another, which was the opposite of what he believed. Finally, Rorty scanted another problem that arose from his belief in nonfoundational ethics propelled by humanizing stories. He almost never acknowledged that clearheaded pragmatism might mandate the use of absolutist, realist speech in a culture where absolute, realist intuitions persisted. The only place in *Truth and Progress* where Rorty partly conceded this was in "Feminism and Pragmatism," where he wrote, "Although practical politics will doubtless often require feminists to speak with the universalist vulgar, they might profit from thinking with the pragmatists."

But why, if the "universalist vulgar" did the job? Rorty remarked in his final essay that his least favorite thought in Foucault's writings was the idea that "to imagine another system is to extend our participation in the present system." One could just as well have said that to ignore the tenacity of the present system—or the vocabulary of a present culture—is to ensure that one's imagined system will not prevail. For all his vaunting of future imaginative labor, Rorty underestimated how current "objectivist" tales are themselves imaginative, exploitable work.

Rorty's lack of interest in this "prudential" form of realism was best explained by the starkest lacuna in his philosophical ecumenicism: the absence of any appreciation for the reviving insights of classical rhetoric, the sensible human persuasion of others without bowing to eternal verities. One would have expected greater affection from Rorty toward figures from Protagoras and Isocrates down to Gramsci (who knew that cultural battles matter) and Chaim Perelman, the Belgian philosopher (and leader of the Belgian resistance in World War II), who abandoned analytic philosophy once he studied how lawyers actually argued cases in real life. Rorty often gave the impression that any attempt to persuade beyond simply standing up and reciting one's story, or screening one's film, or offering a fresh vocabulary, smacked of surrender to old-fashioned realism. It was yet another irony of Rorty's ironism that this steadfast foe of realism so insisted that philosophers talk a correct meta-language.

Other weaknesses in the Rortyan front lines could be detected, such as his deafness to the jurisprudential overtones of "justification" that render it, in the average American's ear, a more aggressive and realist notion than he noticed. But *Truth and Progress* demonstrated that Rorty remained not only the master philosophical expositor of his era but a thinker who had raised (some would say lowered) philosophical historiography to an art form.

His good-bye wave to the century, as he approached seventy, came a year later, in *Philosophy and Social Hope*. Just as *Achieving Our Country* enabled him to break past longtime inhibitions on making overt political noises, *Philosophy and Social Hope* extended his autobiographical self-positioning. Right-wingers, he admitted, viewed him "as one of the relativistic, irrationalist, deconstructing, sneering, smirking intellectuals whose writings are weakening the moral fiber of the young." Yet leftists such as Sheldon Wolin saw "a lot of similarity between me and Allan Bloom: both of us, he says, are intellectual snobs who care only about the leisured, cultured elite to which we belong." *Achieving Our Country,* to be sure, had clarified his status as a man of the left who thought the left could use some reform. Still, he knew he was hardly out of the woods with naysayers. "Some postmodernists," Rorty noted, "who initially took my enthusiasm for Derrida to mean that I must be on their political side decided, after discovering that my politics were pretty much those of Hubert Humphrey, that I must have sold out."

While much of *Philosophy and Social Hope* recapitulated and reexplained old themes, it predictably added twists of vocabulary, "more useful" descriptions, as in contending we can "substitute hope for the sort of knowledge which philosophers have usually tried to attain." More striking was Rorty's growing willingness to respond to how critics interpreted his work through the prism of his personality, supposedly bent on philosophical sensationalism. He acknowledged that some opponents "from both ends of the political spectrum" suspected that he would "say anything to get a gasp." To be sure, his notions often tested common sense, as when he remarked that "what is called common sense is simply the habit of using language inherited from the Greeks, and especially from Plato and Aristotle." Their "descriptions of our relation to the rest of the universe . . . are no longer good enough for us," he asserted. "We can do better."

Cheap lunge for a gasp or philosophical nerve? A remark Rorty offered in another essay—"Philosophy is not a field in which one achieves greatness by ratifying the community's previous intuitions"—put that instinct in context. For contrary to the long-standing caricature of his position that had once damaged his prospects of moving from Princeton to Yale, Rorty did not think the "philosopher" culturally obsolete. Rather, he found that word "the most appropriate description for somebody who remaps culture—who suggests a new and promising way for us to think about the relation among various large areas of human activity." If many philosophers stayed hostile to his fancy cartography, it was possibly because, as he noted, you can always "increase the amount of consensus among philosophers by making your philosophizing more scholastic and minute, and decrease it by making your philosophizing more ambitious."

What continued to anger enemies most was Rorty's ability, abundant in *Philosophy and Social Hope,* to articulate his fey insights in unaccented American—a droll merging of high and low diction and snappy images. Working out a fine meditation on American education, Rorty confided, "Even ardent radicals, for all their talk of 'education for freedom,' secretly hope that the elementary schools will teach the kids to wait their turn on line, not to shoot up in the johns, to obey the cop on the corner, and to spell, punctuate, multiply and divide. They do not really want the high schools to produce, every year, a graduating class of amateur Zarathustras."

Driving home that acerbic take on how Nietzsche served the hormonal imperatives of philosophical teen males as efficiently as Bart Simpson does those of normal adolescents, he commented elsewhere, apropos of moving on from philosophical puberty: "A further state is reached when, upon rereading *Thus Spake Zarathustra*, one comes down with the giggles. At that point, with a little help from Freud, one begins to hear talk about the Will to Power as just a high-falutin euphemism for the male's hope of bullying the females into submission, or the child's hope of getting back at Mommy and Daddy."

The same wry tone informed his sprinkled tidbits of autobiography. Recalling his schoolyard days in "Trotsky and the Wild Orchids," a brief foray into memoir, he wrote, "At fifteen I escaped from the bullies who regularly beat me up on the playground of my high school (bullies who, I assumed, would somehow wither away once capitalism had been overcome)."

Yet it was a rare anecdote early on in *Truth and Progress*—an ironic one, given the main character's own assessment of Rorty—that captured a core truth about him. "When I was a thrusting young academic philosopher," Rorty recalled, "I heard an admired senior colleague, Stuart Hampshire, describe a starstudded international conference on some vast and pretentious topic." Hampshire, who'd attended, had been asked to sum up the results. " 'No trick at all,' Hampshire explained, 'for an old syncretist hack like me.' At that moment, I realized what I wanted to be when I grew up."

As it turned out, Rorty overachieved. He climbed the ranks over the last decades of the twentieth century to become American philosophy's chief syncretic downsizer and designated Gestalt-switch-hitter. By 2007, dying of pancreatic cancer, he spent his last working days racing to finish his replies to more than a score of essays in the most prestigious book with which a world philosopher could be honored: a volume in "The Library of Living Philosophers," issued for some seventy years since the first volume honored John Dewey.

To no one's surprise, the great champion of exciting new vocabularies still hadn't given up on the shocking sound bite, the quest for new ways to express his "pragmatist propaganda." Kant's main value had been in "exasperating Hegel," thus leading him from epistemology to narrative. What American philosophy needed most was Dewey's experimentalist attitude, a "constant supply of wide-eyed visionaries," acceptance of "the importance of imaginative (as opposed to argumentative) writing in facilitating moral and political progress," and the next "big swooshy narrative of the history of Western thought."

Modest to the end—which came for him at age seventy-five on June 8, 2007—he mused in his "Library of Living Philosophers" comments that his own greatest attempt at that genre, *Philosophy and the Mirror of Nature*, "was now out of date." Only, one had to think, if the conceptual home run it hit—making it possible to think of America the Philosophical as far more than a lineup of epistemology fanatics—counted for nothing.

PART 2

ABANDONING TOOTHLESS TRUTH: OTHER WHITE MALES MUSCLE IN

PERSUASION AND THE BROWS

Can philosophy, one of Western civilization's most highly revered "highbrow" activities, flourish as a practice of Rortyan persuasion and decision? The thought discombobulates some admirers. A discipline not capable of churning out proofs seems diminished, down in the gutter with far more humble, unsavory and dubious forms of swaying people. If recognizing America the Philosophical requires accepting that, in Rorty's words, "rational persuasion is simply one social practice among others"—and perhaps not a very effective one at that—is the name of "philosophy" worth the candle?

An antidote to that reaction lies in paying attention to the many forms of persuasion that surround us. Professional philosophers typically don't. Here, as in many areas, other thinkers have filled the gap. "Persuasion shows up in almost every walk of life," pointed out University of California at Santa Cruz psychology professors Anthony Pratkanis and Elliot Aronson in their *Age of Propaganda: The Everyday Use and Abuse of Persuasion.* But it doesn't always take the form we expect—knockdown argument—or stay in the contexts traditionally called to mind, such as courtrooms and seminars. "Every time we turn on the radio or television," the authors advised, "every time we open a book, magazine, or newspaper, someone is trying to educate us, to convince us to buy a product, to persuade us to vote for a candidate or to subscribe to some version of what is right, true, or beautiful."

That is particularly true in America, which ranks as the world's top persuasion culture because of its emphasis on democratic decision making. Start, in one year that the authors documented, with 1,220 TV stations, 9,871 radio stations, 11,328 magazines, and hundreds of major newspapers (now supplemented or replaced by endless Web sites and smartphone apps). Factor in the average American's annual load of 37,822 TV commercials watched and 216 pieces of direct-mail advertising received. Add a federal government that spent $400 million a year and employed eight thousand employees toward the annual production of ninety films and twelve magazines in twenty-two languages. Stir in hundreds of thousands of lawyers arguing for a living, more than three hundred companies that supplied "image consulting," and more than five hundred marketing and research polling firms. Top it off with journalistic pundits, artsy-fartsy critics, special-interest lobbyists, community activists, academics ranging beyond their specialties and the obnoxious guy at the deli. Some forms of persuasion are quick and subtle, almost (but not quite) beneath notice. Think of the brand names of batteries: Eveready, Duracell, DieHard. The manufacturers are trying to tell us something. Even insistent laugh tracks on sitcoms seek our surrender.

Pratkanis and Aronson found America's persuasion scene both comprehensible and controllable. The purpose of their book, they wrote, was "to look at the nature of persuasion in our everyday life—to understand how it influences our behavior, how we can protect ourselves from unwanted propaganda, and how we can ultimately come to use persuasion wisely." Is persuasion in America on a one-way nosedive toward simplemindedness and away from careful argument and evidence, as *Idiot America* and other books argue is true of almost all American cerebral activity? If so, the blame rests on a crowded culture's increasing pressure on everyone's time, as well as on our weakness of character in letting that free us from fairness and precision. Drawing on psychology experiments as well as historical and journalistic material, Pratkanis and Aronson reported on a world in which consumers, voters, politicians, managers, journalists and everyone else increasingly shoot from the hip when they try to persuade, and go by the seat of their pants when they decide to be persuaded.

Supermarket managers, for instance, assume that shoppers will buy products stocked at eye level more readily than those at floor level, and stock accordingly. Manufacturers know that telling aspirin buyers "no other pain remedy is more effective than Brand A" will impress most consumers, with only cagey sorts concluding that no other pain remedy is less effective either. But it is also possible to expose intellectual habits that encourage simplemindedness. One is our urge to eliminate "cognitive dissonance," the desire to falsely reconcile contradictory positions rather than decide between them (the hopeless smoker who starts attacking the surgeon general's credibility). Another is the tendency to concede accuracy to higher-ups rather than lower-downs in a hierarchy instead of determining truth in the particular case (the CEO who automatically backs a VP over a whistleblower, regardless of the facts). A third is the impulse to let heuristics—simple rules for solving a problem—determine one's judgment. ("Well, he's an expert, so he must be right.")

Indeed, the authors offered some good news about present-day persuasion follies. They assured us that American society still exacts a price from sloppy thinkers—it still renders a kind of justice in many matters of persuasion—because its few remaining forums of careful analysis also remain the most important ones, such as courtrooms and hospitals. Consumers too lazy to see through deceptive "arguments" by cigarette advertisers pay for their laziness in the hospital. Managers who make cursory decisions by relying on factoids rather than careful argument or evidence pay for it in the legal system or stock market. Voters who settle for symbols of a candidate's intentions, rather than on-the-record exposition and commitment, get the candidate they deserve. We can, in short, avoid heading for an "'ignorance spiral'" if we simply stop standards of persuasion from deteriorating by not being persuaded by third-rate goods. America the Philosophical doesn't have to descend to a *Clockwork Orange* world of pulling guns on people to get them to agree to propositions. It can be as rigorous or casual as we choose to make it, like every other philosophical culture since the dawn of time.

For a large part of American history, the chief brand of elite persuasion ordinary Americans faced wasn't philosophical reasoning in treatises, but the sermon. And was the sermon a perfect specimen of calm Socratic procedure? Jonathan Edwards, the fiery eighteenth-century Congregationalist, used such scary tactics in his famous "Sinners in the Hands of an Angry God" (1741) that he provoked "distress and weeping" among the Connecticut parishioners, and had to ask for silence. "God," Edwards warned the unregenerate among his flock, "will crush you under his Feet without Mercy; he'll crush out your Blood, and make it fly, and it shall be sprinkled on his Garments, so as to stain all his Raiment. He will not only hate you, but he will have you in the utmost Contempt; no Place shall be thought fit for you, but under his Feet, to be trodden down as the Mire of the Streets." If you've been wondering why *America the Philosophical*—the book, not the place—doesn't begin with Edwards, the Puritans and the pre-Franklin hyper-religiosity that marked so many early intellectual histories of the United States, roll those hubristic sentences off your tongue one more time. One must choose between visions of the early American past.

Moses Coit Tyler (1835–1900), the first historian of American ideas, thought the Puritans "were thinkers in some fashion." Perry Miller (1905–1963), their great twentieth-century champion, praised the "majesty and coherence of Puritan thinking." In contrast, V. L. Parrington (1871–1929) argued in his Pulitzer Prize–winning *Main Currents in American Thought* that Puritan ideas constituted "an absolutist theology that conceived of human nature as inherently evil, that postulated a divine sovereignty absolute and arbitrary, and projected caste divisions into eternity—a body of dogmas that it needed two hundred years' experience in America to disintegrate."

In short, that "adventurous pioneer" Roger Williams could not in his Puritan dissidence outweigh men like Samuel Sewall and Increase Mather, forever "inhibited from bold speculation," or Timothy Dwight, whose mind "was closed as tight as his study windows in January." As for Edwards, Parrington charitably concluded that he set "the apologetics of the theologian over the speculations of the philosopher." Historian Daniel Boorstin (1914–2004) would later write accurately of the Puritans, "Theirs was not a philosophic enterprise; they were, first and foremost, community-builders."

When one has read America's early thinkers, game, set and match go to Parrington and Boorstin. We leave "Colonial America the Dogmatic" to seventeenth- and eighteenth-century specialists.

Edwards's venom in any event was enough to make one grateful for the relatively benign glee with which revivalist Billy Sunday ended his famous 1925 sermon attacking rationalist visions of God, "Spiritual Food for a Hungry World": "I come out with the cross of the son of God—it is a flaming cross, flaming with suffering, flaming with triumph, flaming with victory, flaming with glory, flaming with salvation for a lost world!"

Both Edwards and Sunday probably knew they needed to jazz up earlier forms of the sermon. According to Rutgers University English professor Michael Warner, who examined some 3,000 specimens for a 939-page anthology of classic American sermons, "We have evidence that people have thought of sermons as boring and painful and moralistic from the very beginning." Warner acknowledged shepherding a genre whose baggage included more than occasionally woolly prose: "You can see that one of the things that preachers are often doing is trying to compensate for that through folksiness, through humor, through appealing metaphor, through plain speech."

As acts of persuasion, sermons benefited from their speakers truly preaching to the congregation, or, as the saying has it, the choir—people already, in some sense, persuaded. Warner's anthology, for instance, spanned fifty-two preachers from three religions (Protestantism, Catholicism, Judaism) over 340 years. It began in the seventeenth century with such classic, still-quoted examples as Puritan John Winthrop's "A Modell of Christian Charity" and its admonition that "wee must Consider that wee shall be as a Citty upon a Hill," an image Ronald Reagan rebroadcast in his farewell address three hundred years later. The eighteenth-century section touched on politics with Jonathan Mayhew's "Discourse Concerning Unlimited Submission." In the nineteenth century, with speakers like Emerson and Absalom Jones, the sermon expanded from Protestant exegesis of scriptural text to wider forms and subjects.

Yet "sermon" still carries a sense of overbearing speech that seeks to impose belief upon the listener. Or does it? What did it mean to be a "sermon"? The English word, derived from the Latin, *sermo/sermonis,* talk or discourse, traditionally denoted a formal discourse, on a religious subject, delivered from a pulpit during group worship. In the Protestant tradition, it typically focused on a specific scriptural text. Expositions of scripture, however, date to early Christian services. Some Old English sermons survive from Aelfric (late tenth century), and the sermon had a distinguished history in early modern England.

In the nineteenth century, American preachers began to shorten sermons, abandon formal conventions and speak extemporaneously. Moreover, according to Warner, religions "that had not historically revolved around preaching" reacted to the Protestant sermon's impact on American culture, making America's "the culture, of all national cultures, that has been most prominently defined by the sermon.

"Rabbis did not really preach sermons," Warner explained, "until Reform rabbis in America began to do so . . . and the same with Catholic priests. . . . There's no set of beliefs or doctrines that will tell you what a sermon is." Yet in thinking about which forms philosophical persuasion might take in a post-Rorty culture, the sermon provides some sensible criteria. "Sermons," observed Warner, "have a kind of narrative arch. They always want to bring things down home to the hearer at the end." That requires "preacherly eloquence."

"If you stand up to preach to a congregation," Warner maintained, "you know you have to take people out of their ordinary frame of reference. . . . You have to get them to stand outside of that and bring them in touch with something that they think is truer, more permanent, wiser."

That, of course, also describes what a fine book, powerful movie, or excellent play can do. Which may explain why the sermon itself hardly flourishes in the early twenty-first century as a role model of persuasive discourse, however readable the best of them. Cultural trends and technological primitiveness (not that you want a sermon on your iPhone) probably militate against its revival as a major persuasive form. As Warner pointed out, book publishers no longer compete to bring out the sermons of leading preachers, and the *New York Times* no longer prints weekly excerpts from its city's most prominent sermons, as it did until the middle of the twentieth century.

Not that preachers aren't trying to keep up. The Lutheran Theological Seminary in Philadelphia sometimes runs an ecumenical conference for preachers eager to improve their skills, and sermons in mainline denominations increasingly average twelve to fifteen minutes—about the time it took Edwards to warm up. Warner, though, thought the literary sermon's golden era was probably past. "Now what tends to happen," he mused, "is that preachers who would have collected their sermons write self-help books instead."

One might see that transition as standard American streamlining and efficiency. The genre that Harvard pastor Peter Gomes once called "America's characteristic form of speech" gets broadened to what sermon scholar Larry Witham, in his *A City upon a Hill: How Sermons Changed the Course of American History,* defined as any "stream of words transporting ideas."

But if America abandons or marginalizes the treatise and sermon and other literary forms traditionally categorized as philosophy, might we hurtle down into what critic James Twitchell denounced as a "Carnival Culture" in which all good taste and proper standards get trashed? Might defining philosophy down, if not completely dumbing it down to whatever persuasive acts people perform, equal "vulgarizing" it despite English critic William Hazlitt's wise caveat—"A thing is not vulgar merely because it is common, but there is no surer mark of vulgarity than thinking it is"?

Twitchell, in *Carnival Culture,* argued that we were losing our ability to tell the difference between high and low, between vulgar and refined. For him, vulgarity as a concept in our culture was "rapidly disappearing because of the relentless economic demands of show business." The clash between democratic taste and elite aesthetics repeatedly resurfaced at the battle lines of his subject. According to Twitchell, "We live in an age distinct from all other ages that have been called 'vulgar' because we are so vulgarized that we have even lost the word in common use. . . . It is not that we think it bad manners to criticize someone else's taste, as much as it is that we have lost the concept of taste as a measure of criticism." For Twitchell, the concept of the "vulgar" no longer figured in cultural judgments "not because it has been transcended, but because it has triumphed. The vulgar has become the norm."

His own eye trained on developments in media, where he reported "the worldwide commodification of culture" in recent decades, and the remarkable extent to which American culture in particular had become almost exclusively "market driven" rather than determined by "editor approval," the taste of creators in words, images or music. From a distance, Twitchell could sound like a fuddy-duddy, vaguely Marxist complainer about capitalist culture, an unremittingly abstract academic crank. But he wasn't. On the contrary, he wrote in the bemused voice of a middle-age parent with extremely skeptical teenagers. Yet his dated 1990s harangue to his kids about vulgarity in the arts, looked at almost two decades later, shows one reason why vulgarization—of the arts as of philosophy—poses less of a danger to America the Aesthetic or America the Philosophical than Twitchell feared: the vulgar, whatever else it may be, also tends to be the ephemeral:

> I tell them that Madonna videos are vulgar, as are Stephen King novels, *Screw* magazine, Van Halen, John McEnroe, Las Vegas, the Trump Tower, dances like the Lambada, Mr. T, professional wrestling, Batman, Opal Gardner, "graphic novels," Velcro, Cher, costume jewelry, almost anything reported on in *People,* Joan Rivers, clothing with someone's name on it, Geraldo Rivera, anything that the adjective "loud" can be used in front of, Rupert Murdoch, Richard Simmons, Houston, Texas, Joan and Jackie Collins, Benny Hill, the late Billy Martin, *USA Today,*

confrontainment television with Mort Downey Jr., paintings on velvet, electrified musical instruments, monstrous bodybuilding, Barry Manilow concerts, Ed Koch's campaigns (when he was running for mayor of New York City), political advertising in general, the second edition of the *Random House Dictionary,* Brian Bosworth, Mick Jagger, Donald Trump, any Aaron Spelling production, men's suits that shine, the Philip Morris Company trucking around the Bill of Rights, Countess Mara ties, Rodeo Drive boutiques, almost all Top 40 music and rap music, diamond jewelry for men, any movie with a sequel, music by Michel Legrand, Forest Lawn, paintings by Leroy Neiman, full-length leather coats, George Steinbrenner, Larry Flynt, Jerry Falwell, Hawaiian shirts, Tammy Bakker, Disneyland and World, Chuck Barris, anything on prime-time television with a market share of more than 10, any large building by John Portman, belt buckles that look like silver dollars, roller derbies, anything that shines.

The Lambada? Tammy Bakker? Mr. T? To be sure, a few of Twitchell's targets are still going strong, but as a time capsule of vulgarity from the 1990s, his cache now contains the evidence of its own impotence. One can imagine a similar jeremiad from that time, rolling down from the heights of academic philosophy: "Deepak Chopra, Marianne Williamson, any remark by Bill O'Reilly, any book with the title '. . . *for Dummies.*'" Of course, it makes sense that we need to classify this way, if we're to retain the ability to distinguish between quality and junk. "When we can no longer classify certain entertainments as vulgar," Twitchell noted, "we will also be unable to classify their opposites as art." He emphasized that "the speed of descent has increased dramatically." At some point, he warned, "there will be no border between Lower Aesthetica and Upper Vulgaria." The gatekeepers, he feared, would not be able to find the gates. In time, greeting cards would become "our epic poetry, MTV our heroic opera, and Walt Disney our Michelangelo." So, one might complain, America the Philosophical threatens to make Howard Stern our Plato, Michael Moore our Kant.

But the analogy of a dumbing down in philosophy to dumbing down in the arts falls short in one respect. Not every thinker outside the academic profession of philosophy, as we will shortly see, represents a steep fall into vulgar standards. America the Philosophical overflows with other academics and intellectuals who have supplanted philosophers as public disputants and are not popularizers and lowerers of standards. In remapping the contours of American philosophy, however, it's helpful first to examine the controlling triangle of metaphors behind fears of vulgarization: highbrow, middlebrow and lowbrow. Those cranial images, like much else in America the Philosophical, invite scrutiny.

We know from Joan Shelley Rubin, the leading historian of "brow" categorization, that "brow metaphors" came from nineteenth-century phrenology's equation of physiognomy and intelligence. They caught on because in "the three decades following the First World War, Americans created an unprecedented range of activities aimed at making literature and other forms of 'high' culture available to a wide reading public." Because that twentieth-century democratization of Matthew Arnold's version of culture—"The best that has been thought and said in the world"—met resistance and exposed America's aesthetic class divisions, those divisions needed labels.

In the 1880s, according to Rubin, highbrow meant "refined" and lowbrow denoted a "lack of cultivation." In a 1933 *Saturday Review* article, Margaret Widdemer argued that middlebrows represented "the general reader," sandwiched between the "tabloid addict class" and the "tiny group of intellectuals." Virginia Woolf, in an essay in *The Death of the Moth* (1942), attacked the middlebrow as a person dedicated to "no single object, neither art itself nor life itself, but both mixed indistinguishably." Woolf warned both highbrows and lowbrows against the "pernicious pest who comes between," and her association of middlebrow with commercial corruption of taste still sticks to the term.

After World War II, other writers weighed in. Art critic Clement Greenberg denounced middlebrow culture for "devaluating the precious, infecting the healthy, corrupting the honest, and stultifying the wise." *Harper's* editor Russell Lynes genially defended the middlebrow in 1949, popularizing the term while dividing it into upper and lower territories. Dwight Macdonald, in a famous 1960 *Partisan Review* article entitled "Masscult and Midcult," savaged middlebrow culture because it "pretends to respect the standards of High Culture while in fact it waters them down and vulgarizes them." He cited such institutions as the Book-of-the-Month Club and *Saturday Review*.

Where did philosophy connect to this regime? Among the middlebrow institutions and products of the 1920s, '30s and '40s that Rubin examined—all specializing in "mediating between elitism and democracy"—Will Durant's *The Story of Civilization* and *The Story of Phi-*

losophy figured prominently, along with the *New York Herald Tribune*'s Books section, the Book-of-the-Month Club, the Great Books series and book-chat radio shows. Rubin argued that middlebrow culture began by repackaging Arnold's Olympian wares, but ended by watering them down for commercial reasons.

Yet did Durant (1885–1981) represent a watering down? If one grew up with the Book-of-the-Month Club, some corner of a book-shelved house remained forever *The Story of Civilization,* his eleven-volume, six-million-word chronicle written over half a century and coauthored in later years with his wife, Ariel. The club offered it for decades as an inducement to join, and sold thirteen million of them. An independent scholar who operated outside academe's protections and won both the Pulitzer Prize (1968) and Presidential Medal of Freedom (1977), Durant jump-started then fledgling Simon & Schuster in 1926 with *The Story of Philosophy,* the all-time best-selling book about its subject if one excepts the Bible.

It's at least arguable that Durant's maverick life and stimulating prose cross-fertilized each other. Born in North Adams, Massachusetts, Durant headed to St. Peter's Academy in New Jersey in his teens. At first a Catholic seminarian, he soon turned agnostic and socialist, got a job as a reporter at the *New York Evening Journal,* and merged his progressive interests with a passionate desire to bring the pageant of Western thought and culture to the masses. Having become a teacher at a libertarian school, he turned so progressive that he scandalized some by marrying his lifelong love and partner Ariel when he was twenty-eight and she was fifteen—and his student. (In hindsight, Durant may have been too well informed about the betrothal ages of early European royalty.) That led to his excommunication by the Bishop of Newark. The May-December beginning perhaps also explained the rococo, guilty-sounding, but apparently heartfelt apologies Durant gushed forth in a preface when he finally admitted Ariel to coauthorship decades later in Volume 7.

Yet love him or jail him, one wandered happily with Durant through his lush, well-constructed sentences, splendid hallways connecting gilded rooms in a Byzantine palace. As old-fashioned as could be imagined in his overarching take on Western history, Durant accepted the traditional divisions—the Renaissance, the Reformation, the Age of Reason—and promoted an upbeat, even noble great-man-and-woman vision of history. Still, he brought a warm, smooth appreciation, and consistently lively style, to peaks of Western thought. His ambitiously conceived volumes suggested you could yet stroll through the best in human history if you just elegantly walked through the ages with him at your side.

Where, then, the watering down? Were the thinkers he emphasized (Plato, Aristotle, Kant) different than those that academe apotheosized? No. Were his judgments about them so off? No. With remarkable prescience, Durant wrote in his introduction to the 1926 edition, "The author believes that epistemology has kidnapped modern philosophy, and well-nigh ruined it." In an even more spot-on insight in his preface to the second edition, Durant caustically observed, "Doubtless now that epistemology is dying in Germany, it will be exported to America, as a fit return for the gift of democracy."

Explaining why he thought Confucius the most important thinker of all time, Durant observed, "By this alone: that he was a moral philosopher rather than a preacher of religious faith; that his call to the noble life was based upon secular motives rather than upon supernatural considerations; that he far more resembles Socrates than Jesus." That seemed to line up three for three with a traditional analytic philosopher's privileging of reasoned, secular, argumentative method. In fact, philosophers have found little fault with Durant's accuracy as a philosopher. It's just that his style proved so, well, entertaining and popular.

Rubin, however, allowed the music of the Three Brows to form the soundtrack of her book. She accepted standard equations: "academic culture equals highbrow," "media culture equals middlebrow," "working-class culture equals lowbrow." That reflexive academic value system showed in her discussion of H. G. Wells's *The Outline of History*. Having cited comments on it by academic historians, Rubin wrote, "The *Outline*'s reception among intellectuals, however, had little bearing on its fortunes with the American public." Professors, then, equaled "intellectuals." To her, it seemed, Simone Weil's belittling put-down in *The Need for Roots* might better be interpreted as straightforward fact: "Culture is an instrument wielded by professors to manufacture professors, who in turn manufacture more professors."

"Intellectuals" and "the American public" formed non-overlapping sets for Rubin. Those commitments mattered, for while Rubin purported to be "dedicated to democratic values," she also declared herself an advocate of "aesthetic standards." She regretted that "middlebrow popularizers accommodated consumer priorities," and bemoaned "a situation in which market considerations rush in to fill the vacuum created by an unchecked relativism." Rubin might have read less Matthew Arnold and more John Stuart Mill. She didn't grasp the aesthetic implications of the democratic culture she supported.

In Mill's marketplace of ideas, truth and other values emerge from clashing worldviews. In Rubin's, the old Arnoldian values still held pride of place—they were to be brought to market, then distributed to the plebs. Oblivious to her own academicism, Rubin missed an important dimension of her subject, which operates as well in America the Philosophical—the condescension that the "highbrow," or learned and savvy nonacademic, often feels for the "middlebrow" academic. She never weighed whether her chosen institutions of middlebrow culture, far from watering down highbrow material for the masses, might have imposed quality control on a university culture with low standards of clarity, originality and style, as when good editors turn a normally turgid academic intellectual into a readable reviewer in the *TLS* or *London Review of Books*.

More important to assessing how the Three Brows might impact the vision of American philosophy as a broader activity than traditionally conceived, Rubin overlooked dimensions of her triangular classificatory scheme noticed by other writers. Berkeley historian Lawrence Levine, for example, in his *Highbrow/Lowbrow*, spotted something in its application to the arts that might have given pause to Twitchell and to protectors of academic canons in philosophy as well: the tendency of formerly low-rent cultural items to rise with time, and formerly high-rent ones to sink.

In 1839, lowbrow William Burton, performing in *As You Like It* at Philadelphia's American Theater, shared the bill with a "magnificent display" of gymnastic position, courtesy of "Il Diavolo Antonio and His Sons." In 1915, middlebrow D. W. Griffith aimed his *Birth of a Nation* at the masses and hit the box-office bull's-eye. In ancient Greece, highbrow wrestlers clinched for glory without peroxide ponytails or even a cable network on hand. So much for yesteryear. Later, the only acrobats at Shakespeare would be reluctant corporate attendees trying to keep their sleepy heads from bouncing off their chests. *Birth of a Nation* became an art film wrapped in a dissertation inside a revival house, while Hulk Hogan, Jesse Ventura and other modern practitioners pulled wrestling's profile down.

Brow labels, in short, like art itself, shift over time. Yet Levine pushed the point beyond mere notice of changing cultural taste. Critical labels such as "highbrow" and "lowbrow," he indicated in *Highbrow/Lowbrow,* played the anchoring role in culture that parents do in family life. At first, growing up in their company, we find life unimaginable without them. In time, we realize that they arose from a definite beginning, and face a definite end as well. In both realms, he implied, it's a mark of maturity to accept the loss of former absolutes without casting them away as useful influences.

Levine's project began when he discovered, to his shock, that Shakespeare counted as popular entertainment in nineteenth-century America. The discovery started him thinking generally about hierarchy in the arts. "Everywhere in the nation," he wrote, "burlesques and parodies of Shakespeare constituted a prominent form of entertainment." Tocqueville observed that "there is hardly a pioneer's hut that does not contain a few odd volumes of Shakespeare." Levine documented the performance of the Bard in mining towns as well as metropolises, often on bills that included folk singing, magicians or comics. He rejected the explanation that Americans liked Shakespeare because producers edited or sensationalized the material. Rather, he said, nineteenth-century Americans easily fit Shakespeare into their culture because "so many of his values and tastes" squared with their own.

To Levine, those were the good old days—living in a pluralistic culture without class divisions. It disintegrated toward the end of the nineteenth century, Levine argued, because a "sacralization of culture took place in regard to the opera, symphonic music, and the fine arts." Music acquired "unique aesthetic and spiritual properties that rendered it inviolate, exclusive and eternal." In the concert hall, mixed genres and rude habits were out. Deprecating popular music and stressing the quality gap between American and European music were in. The very word "culture," Levine noted, became "synonymous with the Eurocentric products of the symphonic hall, the opera house, the museum, and the library, all of which, the American people were taught, must be approached with a disciplined, knowledgeable seriousness of purpose, and—most important of all—with a feeling of reverence."

It sounded like the sacralization of culture that developed in academic philosophy as well when it professionalized in the late nineteenth century, treating the PhD as a Golden Calf, leading to a world where doctoral students would speak reverently of "Davidson" or "Derrida" (first names being déclassé) while sniffing at the notion that anyone outside department precincts might deserve surname status.

In the arts, Levine attributed the decline of our shared public culture to increased immigration, which drove people to create class distinctions. He quoted psychologist Robert Sommer's view that "society compensates for blurred social distinctions by clear spatial ones," and detailed how once egalitarian theater spaces became stratified. He invoked Henry James on how the "huge democratic boom" ushered in an age of "the new, the simple, the cheap, the common, the commercial, the immediate, and, all too often, the ugly."

In explaining those transformations, Levine elaborated on how culture became browified. For the new middle class, "following the lead of the arbiters of culture promised both relief from impending disorder and an avenue to cultural legitimacy." The upper class engineered

> an escape into Culture, which became one of the mechanisms that made it possible to identify, distinguish, and order this new universe as strangers. As long as these strangers had stayed within their own precincts . . . they remained containable. . . . But these worlds of strangers did not remain contained; they spilled over into the public spaces. . . . This is precisely where the threat lay and the response of the elites was a tripartite one: to retreat into their own private spaces whenever possible; to transform public spaces by rules, systems of taste, and canons of behavior of their own choosing; and, finally, to convert the strangers so that their modes of behavior and cultural predilections emulated those of the elites.

If Levine too strongly implied that highbrow/lowbrow ideas sprang fully from the circumstances of late-nineteenth-century America, rather than boasting a long pedigree back to Plato, he nonetheless highlighted a key truth: the process by which arbiters associate cultural activities with one brow or another is a complex sociological one bearing close attention. It's a truism worth keeping in mind when one ponders, as we will in the next part of *America the Philosophical,* whether the pugnacious political-philosophy claims of a journalist-thinker such as Christopher Hitchens, or the ruminative questions of a broadcaster-philosopher like Bill Moyers, are highbrow, lowbrow or middlebrow. Is the test the company they keep, or some external standard of rigor?

Over the past thirty years of arts culture, the voices of highbrowism still cried out. One example was art critic Hilton Kramer, founder of the neoconservative journal the *New Criterion,* whose warnings about the decline of "serious culture" and the "revenge of the philistines" echoed comments made by late-nineteenth-century defenders of the genteel tradition. Against it, one might set the "growing cultural eclecticism and flexibility" that Levine found in modern culture, which possibly signaled an end to passive audiences of "sacralized" culture, trained to "submit to creators and become mere instruments of the will, mere auditors of the productions of the artist."

The thrust in late-twentieth-century and twenty-first-century arts criticism, if not in hidebound academic philosophy, militated against allowing tired old binary symbols and metaphors—highbrow and lowbrow, serious and superficial, elitist and populist, weighty and lightweight—to interfere with Americans who wanted to talk with one another, persuade one another, philosophize with one another. Absolute scales of cultural values, like other absolutisms, appeared to be withering away.

One could trace the development back at least as far as the protean reviewer Gilbert Seldes (1893–1970), a kind of anti-Twitchell who helped spark the collapse of high/low distinctions with his commentary on the arts. Cornell historian Michael Kammen rightly subtitled his mammoth biography of Seldes "The Transformation of Cultural Criticism in the United States." Seldes, the Harvard-trained managing editor of the *Dial* and pro-modernist pal of James Joyce and E. E. Cummings, made no bones about his position. He became a champion of vaudeville, comics, TV, radio, movies and jazz—of Charlie Chaplin, Al Jolson, Krazy Kat and the Ziegfeld Follies.

Born into an anarchist community in Alliance, New Jersey (now Vineland), he grew up in a freethinking family that also produced his brother George, the maverick founder of American press criticism. A member of Harvard's Class of '14, Gilbert Seldes shared the secular, aesthetic and independent bent of the time. But his sympathies for the high and the pretentious waned as the communications revolution raged. Late in life, he wrote with pride that he had "witnessed more changes in the modes of communication than occurred in all recorded history before." As Kammen reported, resistance to serious criticism of the newer arts lingered in the 1920s and '30s: "When Nunnally Johnson proposed to Harold Ross that he contribute film reviews to the *New Yorker,* Ross replied scornfully that 'movies are for old ladies and fairies.'" Seldes responded in the opposite direction. Believing, in Kammen's words, that "popular culture could be both democratic and distinguished" (could he have foreseen the death of Michael Jackson becoming the world's number one news story?), Seldes constantly sought to see the revelatory in new art, the useful in the demotic.

Seldes may well have stretched himself too far over the years, dabbling in every job associated with language: editor, playwright, screenwriter, historian, novelist and more. Still, it was in a worthy cause. Kammen emphasized that the critic's own expansion forced his contemporaries to grow as well. Seldes "challenged intellectuals and the informed public" to reconsider their judgments about arts such as jazz and the musical, to widen "the targets of inquiry and the criteria that cultural critics applied." The Cornell scholar made an even stronger claim for his man, arguing that Seldes could "properly be regarded as a progenitor of the discipline known as cultural studies—a mixture of communications theory, film and television analysis, historical and literary investigation."

Today, if Seldes is remembered at all, it's for believing that popular art provides as many intellectual vitamins as high art. His most influential book, *The Seven Lively Arts* (1924), cast the rise of populist taste in the arts as another robust example of America's Emersonian impulse for change in its own exceptional direction. Happy to write for "middlebrow" publications such as *Esquire* and the *Saturday Evening Post,* Seldes didn't "deride middle-class mediocrity." Not for him was the belittling posture academic philosophers often take toward thinking expressed in popular magazines and newspapers, forgetting—or never knowing—that such heroes of theirs as Peirce wrote for the *New York Post* and published one of his most important philosophical articles in a popular science magazine.

Because Seldes publicized his personal associations with major artists such as Picasso, Stravinsky and Fitzgerald, he transferred cultural cachet to whatever he approved. No less a rival than the endlessly pontificating Edmund Wilson credited him with a key role, along with Mencken, in "the liquidation of genteel culture in America." Kammen contended that just as we look back to figures such as Jefferson, Madison and Paine for our political ethos, we should look back to Seldes for the principles of the democratized, brow-removed culture we've become—at least outside of philosophy. The result would be an ever-expanding tent where no self-anointed "art form"—be it schlock video, mindless graffiti, puerile podcast or inept fringe-festival performance art—is automatically criticized for falling short of depth, meaning or artistic status.

Yet Seldes's own career demonstrated how difficult it could be for even the most enthusiastic opponent of high/low distinctions in culture to resist their lure over a lifetime. As Kammen reported, Seldes's own views took a bittersweet turn in later years. They especially migrated in the 1950s, during his time as founding dean of the University of Pennsylvania's Annenberg School for Communication. Having briefly and unsuccessfully served as the first "program director" for CBS Television, Seldes, making noises similar to Twitchell's much later, charged that America was "being engulfed into a mass-produced mediocrity." Seldes by then thought an intelligible distinction could be drawn between the popular art he'd praised in his youth and the meretricious mass-media values represented (to his eye) by the rise of television and movies. Yet to our perspective today, the latter appear only to have extended the characteristics of new art that Seldes once praised. In fact, in an instance of Levine's lowbrow/highbrow shifts, scholars now regard the 1950s TV that drove Seldes to distraction as television's "Golden Age." One lesson of Seldes's life, Kammen implied, was an old one: Beware of what you wish for when you're young—you may get heaps of it later.

In 1925, Seldes had declared that "the significance of a critic is measured by the problems he puts to us." If that's so, the man's ghost lingers, urging arts critics to keep their antennae tuned, their eyes wide open, their pomposity in check as every week, whether in movies, popular music or literature, they face the assault of the binaries once again. In the arts, Seldes won his critical battle against rigid high/low distinctions. Susan Sontag and others continued the demolition job on them in the next generation. Now, in the early twenty-first century, one rarely hears sophisticated objections when critics pronounce a television series like *The Wire* or *The Sopranos* a masterpiece, or award a Pulitzer to a graphic novel, or publish hermeneutical secondary trots about hip-hop culture. Even the *New York Times* Sunday Arts & Leisure section, long the gatekeeper of high culture for the American elite, declared at one stage that it would devote greater space to what faded conservatives might have considered "lowbrow" arts, hiring a twenty-seven-year-old online journalist to run the show.

Only in philosophy have the high/low binaries continued to rule, with professors typically belittling popular thinking and being ignored by popular culture in turn. Yet just as Seldes, Sontag and others smashed the high/low clichés in the arts, America on its own is slowly smashing them in philosophy.

To be sure, surviving, post-Rortyan epistemologists, like Rosicrucians oblivious in their inbred conventions to time and intellectual culture passing them by, continue to focus on narrow syllogistic arguments in the theory of knowledge, seemingly governed by the ethos that baseball umpire Ed Vargo once said faced people in his trade—"You're expected to be perfect the day you start, and then improve." The hostility of academic philosophy's epistemological alpha males and females toward any vision of philosophy as an activity that takes place outside philosophy departments as well as within them—that also needs to be validated outside them—could be seen at Harvard's well-publicized September 2011 "Symposium on Philosophical Progress," cosponsored by the philosophy departments of both Harvard and Australian National University. It brought a slew of analytic epistemologists together.

To many gathered in the Barker Center's Thompson Room (with Joseph DeCamp's enormous portrait of Teddy Roosevelt towering over all), philosophy after Rorty still meant what a disciplinarily dominant class of English-language epistemologists did, separated from an outside world too untrained and illiterate in the field's issues and nomenclature to matter much. Jason Stanley, a cocky analytic epistemologist at Rutgers University—one monastery favored by the priestlike order of experts in the theory of knowledge—explained to the packed audience that certain advances in philosophy, such as Ruth Barcan Marcus's work in modal logic (i.e., the logical properties of verbs such as "can" and "must") couldn't be communicated to the "unwashed masses," or "even some of the washed masses."

Yet if one recognized "philosophy" as a word and activity that preceded this professional sect into the world, didn't the burden fall on those identifying "philosophy" with rarefied "research programs" that sought universally satisfying definitions for contested everyday words such as "truth," "meaning" and knowledge" (not to mention "can" and "must") to justify their artificial narrowing of the terms?

Stanley's own work indicated that analytic epistemology did not so much teem with brilliant insights beyond the layman's grasp as lumber along with artificialities that exposure to sunlight quickly dissolved. In his 2005 book, *Knowledge and Practical Interests*—a volume, he explained, that demonstrated his daring within the field by connecting the two subjects of his title—Stanley discussed how some current thinkers in epistemology (dubbed "contextualists" in the ritual taxonomizing of fellow theorists that professional philosophers cherished), believed in the phenomenon of "semantic blindness." Stanley quoted John Hawthorne, a philosophy professor (who had coined that phrase without accepting the hypothesis) as saying it stood for the thesis "There is a real sense in which users of the word 'know' are blind to the semantic workings of their language."

That is, we the people needed analytic epistemologists to explain to us how to use the word "know," as well as what it means.

Given that sort of nonsense within professional philosophy, is it any wonder that Americans increasingly turned elsewhere for their wisdom?

As large issues loomed in the new millennium—war, terrorism, globalization, abortion, sustainable energy, stem-cell research, immigration, animal ethics—Americans largely listened to others.

A good instance of genuine if merely "popular" philosophical argument in American society, over a jagged, homegrown concept, was the struggle over political correctness—PC—which began in the 1980s and has remained a subtext of cultural debate ever since. Like everything else in America, PC quickly became a product. Texts on "political correctness" tracked the mainstreaming of the phrase from academe into the media world. The social phenomenon that drove warring faculty members to swear eternal enmity, that tore campuses into verbal Baghdads, mushroomed into guides and anthologies. Their editors hoped they'd be the thinking person's beach books.

PC took off as a media event in late 1990, after a *New York Times* article produced its standard snowball effect, leading to front-page articles in *Newsweek,* the *Atlantic* and other national publications. The first President Bush gave it headline status in his 1991 University of Michigan commencement address, and Dinesh D'Souza's best-selling *Illiberal Education: The Politics of Race and Sex on Campus* kept its media profile high. Once a phrase used, with collegial irony, by leftists to mock their own pieties, political correctness came to operate as an epithet middle-of-the-roaders and right-wingers all brandished to describe the behavior of an alleged new generation of extreme-left college teachers, reared in the 1960s and said to wield disproportionate power in American universities.

Critics charged them with pushing two pedagogical agendas, one philosophic, one curricular. Philosophically, they were accused of teaching "postmodernism," a view that purportedly abandoned the distinction between truth and falsehood, regarded the meanings of words and texts as relative, and deemed literature largely an exercise in power politics. PCers stood accused of translating that ideology into aggressive educational policies. They supposedly sought, in the face of an increasingly multicultural student population, an egalitarian political revolution in which all cultures received equal respect, and no culture enjoyed "hierarchical" privilege over any other. "Multiculturalism" thus deemphasized Western classics, which were considered to represent the oppressive artifacts of an imperialist civilization. PC allegedly sought to eliminate "elitist" standards of quality literature, to give entitlements (George Will called them "reparations") to minority, female and Third World writers, bringing them into the canon by literary affirmative action. Socially, according to PC opponents, the agenda created campus repression through speech and behavior codes, and a culture of euphemism.

It's instructive, now that the phrase "PC" feels passé even as it still surfaces in American culture, to reflect on how philosophical battles over it took place. Search the academic philosophy journals of the 1980s and '90s and you'll find barely a mention. Too new, too amorphous, too media connected for folks still analyzing Truth, Knowledge and Meaning. Instead, it fell to the journalists, the commentators, the comedians, to drive the debate.

At the height of PC's controversial life, Paul Berman's *Debating P.C.*, a collection of essays, provided the best—or most rotationally prior—introduction to the subject, delivering a broad intellectual survey tilted to the right. Berman, a longtime culture critic for the *Village Voice*, the *New Republic* and other journals, and later the author of fine books such as *A Tale of Two Utopias* and *The Flight of the Intellectuals*, admitted that the PC debate could seem, even after close study, "a puzzle without a solution." But he valiantly attempted to explain its roots, concluding that PC in the 1990s was "the fog that arises from American liberalism's encounter with the iceberg of French cynicism." Ironically for a debate in which canonical texts served as chief targets, the PC controversy quickly produced its own.

Berman provided a slew of them, including three that had generated considerable commentary: an address by English professor Catharine Stimpson to the Modern Language Association; an article by Roger Kimball on an MLA convention in Chicago; and a piece by philosopher John Searle for the *New York Review of Books*, "The Storm over the University." Searle was notable for being the only professional philosopher among twenty-one contributors. Elsewhere, the argument took flight through four important literary critics—Irving Howe, Edward Said, Henry Louis Gates Jr., and Katha Pollitt—First Amendment experts Nat Hentoff and Patricia Williams, linguistics researcher Richard Perry, literature scholar Stanley Fish, Afrocentrist Molefe Kete Asante and then assistant secretary of education Diane Ravitch.

The richness of dialogue the book captured made it hard to remain simpleminded about PC, or to view contributors as predictable. D'Souza, far from disparaging non-Western cultures, argued that multiculturalism distorted them. Old socialist Irving Howe, who might have been expected to support younger leftists stigmatized as PC, contended that classical Marxists actually exhibited great respect for Dead White European Male culture. The kind of concrete philosophical debate stirred, angled slightly from the right, shared shelf and media space at the time with balanced but pointed counterattacks on anti-PC forces, tilted to the left, such as journalist and communications professor Patricia Aufderheide's *Beyond PC.* Her volume helpfully reprinted basic documents from two key battle groups formed in the PC wars: the National Association of Scholars, which opposed PC, and Teachers for a Democratic Culture, which favored multiculturalism.

Yet the kind of text that probably exerted the most influence throughout America in making PCers reassess their reflexive positions was *The Official Politically Correct Dictionary and Handbook,* an environmentally sound guide offered to every verbally abled human animal. Taking a more Conan O'Brien approach, it operated on the sound theory, known to the ancient rhetoricians (but lost to almost all contemporary academic philosophers), that parody and sarcasm make powerful tools of persuasion.

In such serious company as the Berman and Aufderheide volumes, *The Official Politically Correct Dictionary and Handbook* might have seemed a dopey lark. With a wise-guy handbook tone, advising the prospective reader that you "desperately need this book to survive" in these "be-sensitive-or-else" times, its authors claimed to be in cahoots with the American Hyphen Society, based in Wilkes-Barre, Pennsylvania. They evinced no high theoretic purpose or ideas. But like Adam Smith's invisible hand, or John Rawls's veil of ignorance, clever tone could steer minds, and even orient them. Suggested new euphemisms communicated contempt for the PCer better than any philosophical essay might manage. The authors suggested "Canine-American" to refer to any dog that lived in the United States, and "mineral-companion" as the preferred term for the once sought-after pet rock. "Non-traditional shopper" sounded better than shoplifter, and "persons with difficult-to-meet needs" rang well as the sensitive phrase for "serial killers."

By the time one hit the acknowledgments, paraphrasing Sir Isaac

Newton—"If we have seen further, it is by standing on the shoulders of heightism survivors"—it was hard to take PC credos seriously. Arguably, such a droll tone—paralleled by similar commentary from talk-show hosts and water-cooler pontificators—cut through force fields of dogmatism and arrogance and contributed to the gradual move toward more reasonable, commonsense positions. In that respect, the authors stood in the tradition of sardonic and effective American popular thinkers like Benjamin Franklin. The multiculturalists admitted not rejecting the idea that some books are better than others. Traditionalists confessed to liking the idea of broadening curricula, so long as standards of excellence endured. Parties on both sides recognized that while all literature and culture might be political, reducing either to politics distorted reality.

The PC debate hinted that Rorty's revolution, and the intuitive rejection by Americans of high/low clichés, might be pushing America the Philosophical toward renewed respect for that most solid expression of everyday truth—common sense. Not a common sense in which everyone thought the same thing, or argued the same way, or held the same literary, aesthetic or political positions. Rather, a common sense in which no one tried to bulldoze anyone else about the parameters of what can be true, or justified, or what it took to get everybody from disagreement to agreement.

The notion of common sense had long intrigued and divided philosophers. Descartes, founder of modern "scientific" philosophy, seethed with sarcasm on the subject when launching his *Discourse on the Method,* quipping that common sense must be "the most equitably shared thing in the world" because "every man is convinced he is well supplied with it." The puzzles that surrounded "common sense" drove onlookers to profound territory. Was common sense a kind of knowledge or a kind of judgment? Was it a repository of accumulated provincial prejudices, as many eighteenth-century *philosophes* thought? (The notion took a nosedive in prestige once Enlightenment thinkers identified it with ignorance.) Was it a collection of the self-evident principles beneath all belief, as the Scottish "common sense" thinker Thomas Reid insisted? Was the whole notion a rhetorical device for silencing sophisticated opponents, or a set of tenets people had voted for so often that it seemed far more than a matter of decision? Could we define it, or only appeal to it?

Such concerns already troubled the concept when Aristotle originally used the expression *koine aisthesis* to label a faculty that, he believed, gathered the data of the five senses into coherent judgments. They persisted when Cicero popularized the Latin translation *sensus communis* to apply to a body of general knowledge shared by everyone. They still provoked uncertainty when experimental psychologists began to test whether four-year-olds possess enough smarts to evade an oncoming object (usually rolled at them by a researcher). Getting a headlock on even the tricky first word of the two wasn't easy. Was "common" a term of praise or put down? "God loves the common man," Lincoln announced, "because he made so many of them." Oscar Wilde, irked by the thought, replied, "God hates the common man because he made him so common."

At least one American writer took on the topic whole. "Common sense," Lawrence Joseph began gamely enough in an accessible book on the idea, "is the good sense that everyone should have. It is the quality of judgment necessary to know the simplest truths, to recognize striking absurdities and to be shocked by palpable contradictions. As sayings go, common sense is the ability to tell your shoes from Shinola . . . your butt from your elbow, chalk from cheese." Joseph's tone in *Common Sense: Why It's No Longer Common* came across as warm, chummy, corny, and aw-shucksy, the style stridently concrete, as though the author took his marching orders from humorist Will Rogers, once world famous as the "Cowboy Philosopher." But that drove home something about unshackled American thinking: its hunger for the particular, its innocent confidence that common sense doesn't have to be defined in an academic thinker's pompous, semantic fashion ("Common sense indicates those propositional beliefs, held by all rational beings"), but could be formulated through a series of concrete objects and situations: "Common sense is small potatoes, a bran muffin for breakfast, double coupons on Wednesday, long underwear in winter even if it makes you look bulky, no-label blue jeans, his-and-hers bicycle helmets, short hair in summer, SPF-15, a Timex watch, Lite Beer, what Sears used to make, an ox instead of a horse, buying another Honda Accord."

Granted, Joseph's common sense deteriorated into a pop-psych commodity as he worked it out, including as it did the proposed founding of a "National Common Sense Society" modeled on the National Honor Society, and, of course, clear rules ("Common sense always rings true"). But even a glib, hype-conscious book could scratch itches. Joseph communicated some of the topic's inevitable appeal in freewheeling America. Our fast-changing world was "stretching our parameters of commonality to distant and alien places," and "a great many 'universal' assumptions" were turning out to be "nothing more than parochial biases." So while Icelanders might have their version of "common sense" too (*allmen skynsemi*, if you're taking notes), we needed to shape ours.

Was it common sense, then, that America might be a place where philosophy flourishes in a far broader form than the APA might admit? So far, we've tried to soften the ground beneath the idea that American philosophy means only what a pantheon of elite white male argument-machines have produced on the page. The first assault was historical, highlighting the human dimensions of the parade of great white male philosophers usually seen to constitute our elite "tradition," while spotlighting how Rorty upended a hijacking of that tradition by fanatics about epistemology. The second, in this section, has sought to extend the dissolution of "Three-Brow" angles on art, and the demise of archaic high/low distinctions in culture, to how we see philosophy. The next and third assault is full-scale and reportorial.

To wit, look at all the white male thinkers who follow, all the philosophers in America who haven't been philosophy professors—that is, who don't or never did belong to that eleven-thousand-member black hole in American media and public life known as the "philosophy profession." Admittedly selective, this panorama of American intellectual energy outside philosophy departments, spanning the past fifty years, offers us a cadre of—what else?—white males. Even in the age of Obama, this is America the Philosophical we're talking about, not a Hypatian fantasy. That beginning, however, will soon be followed, in Part 4, "The Rising Outsiders," with an account of women, African Americans, Native Americans, and gays—the outsiders heading in.

The idea is to add another bulwark to America the Philosophical by asking a straightforward, politically incorrect question: Even if you can't free yourself from the picture that philosophy is a white male practice, does a country with the following white male thinkers merit any lesser title?

PSYCHOLOGISTS AND PSYCHIATRIST

According to the third law of intellectual motion, every bold thinker provokes an equal and opposite name-calling campaign. Burrhus Frederic Skinner (1904–1990), the twentieth-century's foremost behavioral psychologist, received his reinforcement on that point firsthand. At the height of his fame, legions of ordinary people came to consider him a rat. The occasion was his publication in 1971 of *Beyond Freedom and Dignity*, a brash outline of the scientific and social-engineering beliefs that made the Harvard psychology professor and best-selling utopian novelist (*Walden Two*) one of America's most controversial academic theorists. First, *Time* magazine put the lean, redoubtable-looking scientist on the cover of a September issue under the headline "B. F. Skinner says: WE CAN'T AFFORD FREEDOM." Then came the deluge.

Poet Stephen Spender denounced the book as "fascism without tears." *TV Guide* described Skinner's ideas (particularly his notion that humanity would best be served by scientific conditioning of our environmentally determined actions) as "the taming of mankind through a system of dog obedience schools for all." Novelist Ayn Rand, perhaps the world's greatest champion of autonomous heroes, savaged the book as "a corpse patched with nuts, bolts and screws from the junkyard of philosophy, Darwinism, Positivism, Linguistic Analysis, with some nails by Hume, threads by Russell and glue by the *New York Post*." Could such evil be generated by a mild-mannered type born and reared in the friendly little rail town of Susquehanna, Pennsylvania? By a man whose worst boyhood crime had been maniacal ingenuity in rigging up amateur roller-skate scooters, merry-go-rounds, catapults, telegraphs, cigar-box violins and other impromptu concoctions?

Apparently, the answer was yes. America's details about the real Skinner came mainly after his death, from his biographer Daniel W. Bjork, a Texas history professor. Bjork deserved to have a few pellets

B. F. Skinner (1904–1990) wrote influential books such as *Walden Two* and
Beyond Freedom and Dignity and forced
Americans to confront the claims of
behavioral psychology.

of cheese dropped onto his plate to thank him for a job well done. He
braided his biographical and philosophical narratives together so one
could see how the ideologically severe experimenter with the Harvard
hauteur grew naturally out of the small-town Pennsylvania oddball. As
Bjork explained, Skinner remains a fiercely contested figure in intellectual circles:

> Some view him as a reductive, mechanistic behavioral scientist
> who denied the existence of a creative purposeful mind or an
> inner person free to choose and accept responsibility for one's
> actions. He wrongly equated the behavior of rats and pigeons
> with humans, they say, maintaining that despite the obvious
> higher mental capacity of the latter, all organisms could be con-
> trolled or manipulated through a psychology of behavior called
> positive reinforcement. By belittling superior mentality and dis-
> avowing free choice, Skinner degraded what was most human

in humanity. . . . For others, however, Skinner was the brilliant originator of radical behaviorism, a science that yielded the most controllable and hence most predictable experimental results in the history of psychology. . . . Techniques of positive reinforcement and cultural design could, if applied over time and on a grand scale, save the world from the catastrophes of urban decay, ecological ruin and uncontrolled population growth. Far from being an evil, antihumanist scientist, Skinner was the greatest humanistic scientist of our time.

Aided by the archive of Skinner materials at Harvard and the psychologist's own 1,300-page autobiography, Bjork illustrated how Skinner's own consistent personality probably inclined him toward determinism—certainly a "philosophy" if any "ism" is. Even during his first eighteen years in Susquehanna, Skinner, son of a lawyer, displayed fascination with boxlike environments of the sort that later marked his professional approach to behavioral control. As a child, young "Fred" fashioned a private reading place out of a cardboard case. That presaged his "Skinner Box," in which he studied rat behavior, the thermostatically controlled "baby tender," in which he reared his own daughter (an enclosed crib with a safety-glass front, filtered air and a stretched-canvas floor), and his mechanical "teaching machine" that rewarded student learning.

Other startling patterns stood out in Skinner's character. Young Fred, for instance, looked at emotionally charged situations as mere cases of matter in motion (when his sixteen-year-old brother died of a massive cerebral hemorrhage in front of Skinner's eyes, he watched it with "remarkable detachment," treating it as a matter-of-fact physical collapse of a system). Skinner also condescended at an early age to most people he disagreed with, particularly his parents with their social-climbing aspirations (later he would be accused by many academic colleagues of "opinionated arrogance"). By the time he entered Hamilton College, Skinner wanted to be a writer. He received encouragement from Robert Frost, who read some of his work. Skinner began to throw himself into literary and academic pursuits. After graduation, he spent what he called a "dark year" trying to write a novel, then living in Greenwich Village. Only when he gave up on the idea did he apply to graduate school in psychology at Harvard, where his career took off.

Once there, Skinner quickly fastened onto a behavioral approach to his subject and threw himself into inventive research. He earned a reputation as a brilliant young man and a dogmatist whose behaviorism became a "militant conviction." Bjork paints an acid portrait of a conceited young genius who was also "sensitive, unhappy, slightly cynical," and searching "for something not to be cynical about." He found it in the idea that there was nothing more to an organism than its behavior. Skinner "never denied that feelings existed," but he didn't believe a scientist should "appeal to the unseen" for facts. Influences on him ranged from Ernst Mach, the Austrian physicist/philosopher, to writer Sinclair Lewis, whose novel about an idealistic scientific researcher, *Arrowsmith* (1925), strongly affected him. Skinner's technical methods and experiments with lever-pressing rats and pecking pigeons produced achievements in "operant science," which rested on his ability to construct devices that provided predictable, measurable rates of an organism's behavioral responses, permitting the postulation of behavioral "laws." His lifelong attempts to capitalize on his social inventions included the baby tender (once atrociously marketed as the "Heir Conditioner"), which brought Skinner his first fame in 1945 after he publicized it in a *Ladies' Home Journal* article. His long but apparently not blissful marriage continued as he confronted misunderstanding of his use of the baby tender with daughter Deborah (contrary to widespread belief, however, he did not keep her locked in the device for long periods).

Skinner had many failings. A "womanizer," he also "liked the limelight" and sought commercial self-aggrandizement. Like any ambitious novelist, Skinner charted the sales of his first, *Walden Two,* a stark vision of a behaviorally engineered community, after it took off as a countercultural bestseller in the communal 1960s. But his biographer rightly defended Skinner against the many critics who distorted his views by comparing him to dictators such as Hitler and Mussolini. Skinner's eccentricities—the timer he used to keep his work sessions regular; his insistence on sleeping alone for most of his married life; his sedulous records of how many hours he spent on particular tasks—correlate remarkably with his faith that the self is "a repertoire of behavior appropriate to a given set of contingencies." Unlike so many fashionable intellectuals, Skinner never chased bandwagons, hoping to leap aboard. He preferred to build his own and then peer down at the world from it.

Skinner's slightly younger but less academically privileged contemporary, maverick psychologist Abraham Maslow (1908–1970), projected no less self-confidence. While dining in Harvard Square one night in the

1950s, journalist and scholar Max Lerner ran across him. "What have you been up to lately?" Lerner asked. Maslow said he'd just written a book on values and the higher way of life.

"Plato already wrote that book, Abe," Lerner said with a smile.

"Yes, Max," Maslow replied, also smiling, "but I know more than Plato did."

As an indicator of gentle hubris, the remark fell entirely in line with the personality of the Brooklyn street kid who, while decrying narrow empiricism in psychology, also liked to remind friends that he had an IQ of 195. The son of an immigrant in the barrel-repair business, Maslow started out by studying the dominance behavior of monkeys through standard techniques and ended up the patriarch of humanistic psychology in the United States—psychology as a route to higher experience.

"He had a messiah complex," recalled historian Frank Manuel after Maslow's death, "but he never sought to impose it on others."

He didn't need to. Maslow's key books, such as *Motivation and Personality* (1954) and *Toward a Psychology of Being* (1962), flipped modern psychology's negativity on its back and fueled the Zeitgeist of the 1960s with positive notions, such as "self-actualization" and "peak experiences." At Esalen, the California hideaway devoted to hippie hedonism and consciousness raising, Maslow became an intellectual and philosophical mentor. Former students, such as Abbie Hoffman, sang Maslow's praises to the Movement. His upbeat ideas, while still marginal in psychology departments devoted to experimental research—one must remember that many psychology departments don't even teach Freud—continued to exert a lingering influence in such philosophically tinged areas as management theory, education, social counseling, psychotherapy and theology. In psychology itself, his legacy could be traced forward to the "positive psychology" work advanced by Martin Seligman.

Edward Hoffman's *The Right to Be Human* offered the fullest probe into Maslow's life. Largely uncritical of Maslow's work, Hoffman, a New York clinical psychologist, presented a balanced view of Maslow's personality while acknowledging the intuitive nature of his work. He recognized the accuracy of Maslow's own description of himself as an "idea man" rather than a "rigorous" thinker—hardly a disqualifying philosophical characteristic in an era when American existentialist William Barrett claimed "the illusion of technique" was losing steam. For better or worse, Maslow functioned as an Isaiah Berlin "hedgehog" in intellectual history—he pushed one fundamental idea that challenged the mainstream assumptions of his discipline.

Only in America, of course, could someone growing up in the shadow of Ebbets Field become a self-appointed guide to the Elysian Fields. Maslow came of age in mundane lower-middle-class Flatbush, the mythological Brooklyn territory of Duke Snider and Woody Allen. He played punchball, evaded anti-Semitic gangs, and dreamed of becoming a bodybuilder. He married his first cousin Bertha Goodman—"the only woman he ever dated"—and the marriage lasted more than forty years. After attending Boys High, where reading Upton Sinclair made him a lifelong socialist and idealist, Maslow continued on to City College of New York and ultimately the University of Wisconsin, where he began his primate studies. In the 1930s, he conducted research on female sexuality and dominance, which led to a dispute with Alfred Kinsey. But those years also provided him with a prestigious fellowship at Columbia, enabling him to hobnob with major European analysts driven to Manhattan by Nazism. In time, he won a low-level appointment to Brooklyn College's psychology department, where he began the work that made him famous.

The field of psychology in the 1940s largely divided into two camps: behaviorists like Skinner, and Freudians. Behaviorists believed in controlled experiments that tested reaction to stimuli. Freudians believed unconscious sexuality determined most action. But the increasing sophistication of these approaches didn't impress Maslow. He believed that both Freudian pessimism and behaviorist relativism ignored mankind's great accomplishments, narrowly focusing on "crippled people and desperate rats." Maslow rejected "the fundamental premise of modern psychology: that we can devise accurate theories about human nature by studying the mentally ill or the statistically average."

Instead, from the 1950s on, he stood for the view that psychology should study the healthiest people, the "great people" he called "self-actualizers." Turning to historical examples, he found self-actualizers more autonomous, spontaneous, democratic, altruistic and aesthetically sensitive. They also seemed more open to transcendent experiences, accepting of themselves and others, and possessed of genial rather than cruel humor.

At the time Maslow came to these judgments in the 1940s, Hoffman wrote, "the very concept of studying healthy people was too alien to be aired publicly in professional gatherings." But contemporaries, such as Carl Rogers, hailed Maslow's notion as a conceptual breakthrough, and his reputation gradually grew.

In elaborating on his research, Maslow outlined a "hierarchy of needs," ranging from basic ones for food, safety and love to higher ones for beauty, truth and similar goals. Every human being also begins with "fundamental and inborn human tendencies" toward altruism, compassion, love and friendship. But the deprivation of lower needs usually blocks them. According to Maslow, once basic needs are met, higher needs emerge and dominate man—particularly the need for self-fulfillment. "What a man can be," he wrote, "he must be."

In Maslow's later years, the concept of a "peak experience" became one of his major preoccupations. He cited twenty features peculiar to such moments, among them "feelings of wonder and awe." Unlike some 1960s thinkers, however, he consistently rejected any religious basis for these epiphanies. Self-actualizers who have them, Maslow wrote, can give us "a better report of what reality is like . . . just as canaries can be used to detect gas in mines before less sensitive creatures can."

In Hoffman's view, Maslow's name remained "misidentified with the excesses of the 1960s," though it must be said that few thinkers (consider Nietzsche and the Nazis) have been able to control their associations once they become well known. Despite points of congruence between his humanistic psychology and 1960s sensibilities, Maslow remained a political centrist, supporting Hubert Humphrey in 1968. Although he conducted seminars at freewheeling Esalen, he remained monogamous. And detesting the popular countercultural slogan "Nirvana Now!," he warned that one had to "sweat" to reach "peak experiences." In addition, although some mistakenly viewed Maslow as "an enemy of reason," he criticized Esalen for becoming too anti-intellectual in its approach to higher planes of experience. "Where," he once asked, referring to its Big Sur setting of hot tubs perched on a cliff over the Pacific, "is the library at Esalen?"

In the course of *The Right to Be Human*, Hoffman brought to light the clash between Maslow's worldwide reputation for warmth and kindness and his implacable hatred for his mother. Psychologist Gregory Bateson, husband and collaborator of Margaret Mead, once remarked (crossly), "He was always so good." But Maslow found his mother, Rose, cruel, ignorant and unloving—so much so that he refused to see her for decades and declined to go to her funeral. Hoffman also remarked that Maslow combined "a strong sense of his intellectual power and superiority" with "an intense desire, perhaps born of some deeper insecurity, to be accepted by the finest scholars." He treasured the academic respect that came when, after fourteen years on the tenure ladder at Brooklyn College, he became chairman of Brandeis University's newly formed psychology department in 1951.

Now, some forty years after Maslow's death, one is tempted to strip his general philosophy of its jargon and label it "Commencement Addressism"—the commonsense view that everyone should become all he or she can be in life. But, as we've seen, common sense is not necessarily second-rate philosophy in a post-certainty culture. Indeed, it's not bad advice, which explains why it proliferates every spring on campuses. "The only thing anybody had against him," Walter Anderson wrote of Maslow in *The Upstart Spring,* a history of Esalen, "was that sometimes he seemed too nice, too warm and generous." Maslow undoubtedly would have considered that a reasonable cross to bear.

"Psychologist philosophers," whatever else one might attribute to them, could go either way when it came to kindness and empathy, as the contrast between Skinner and Maslow indicated. On the whole, they appeared more on the side of the angels than professional philosophy's logic choppers, always more prone to savor the next counterexample that might ruin a rival's theory than to worry about the happiness of others. Among those in the next generation of psychologically oriented thinkers that rose highest in most observers' moral estimation was the child psychiatrist among them, Robert Coles.

In his Adams House office at Harvard, at least one reason why the celebrated author seemed to carry the weight of the world—and history—on his narrow shoulders could be easily spotted.

"Franklin Delano Roosevelt," read the plaque on the wall, "lived in this room, 1900–1904, a student in Harvard University." Surrounding Coles in the office were the tools and bric-a-brac of his career: old tape cassettes; the V8 juice that got him started; photos of admired friends or mentors, such as novelist Walker Percy, poet/physician William Carlos Williams, Catholic worker Dorothy Day; a poster marking the eight hundredth year of the birth of St. Francis. "If I hadn't come back here and started working with Erik Erikson," said Coles, recalling the influence of the great psychiatrist on his early career plans, "and appreciated the power and strength of his work, and how much it had to teach me . . . I don't know what I might have done."

Figuring out what he has done isn't easy, either. "Who and what is Robert Coles?" the Rev. Andrew Greeley once asked, and Father

Robert Coles (1929–), author and child psychiatrist, received the Pulitzer Prize for his
series of books, *Children of Crisis.*

Greeley's answer wasn't simple: "Social scientist, humanist, political
activist, psychiatrist, minstrel, wandering storyteller, mystic, wiseman,
poet, dissenter, and yes, I'll use the word, secular saint." He might have
added "philosopher." To the cynic, Coles was Harvard's slippery way of
appointing Art Linkletter, St. Francis and Sigmund Freud to the faculty
while granting tenure only once. To the media, he was an intellectual
with a profile that has remained distinct through a cascade of books
about the psychology of children, the importance of stories, the call of
social service. But to Harvard students for several decades, Coles was
that short, lean fellow with the craggy face and thick eyebrows, typically outfitted in a slapdash mix of faded preppy and early Movement (a
familiar outfit offered gray sweater, brown shoes, red windbreaker). He
was the dreamer whose salt-and-pepper hair seemed perennially choppy,
as though he'd just gotten up. The "prof" in charge of "The Literature
of Medicine" at Harvard Medical School, and the "Literature of Social
Reflection" at Harvard University.

Born in Boston in 1929, Coles received his BA from Harvard in 1950.
Perry Miller, the great scholar of Puritanism, had advised Coles to do
his thesis on William Carlos Williams, the folksy family medical prac-

titioner in Rutherford, New Jersey, who occasionally bartered food for checkups and carried Hershey's Kisses in his pockets for young patients. Coles sent Williams his thesis. Williams replied with a note—"Not bad for Harvard"—and an invitation to drop in some time. Abandoning thoughts of becoming a high school teacher, Coles switched gears after getting to know (and revere) Williams personally. Coles turned to medicine, receiving his MD from Columbia University in 1954. Over the next few years, he did his pediatric and psychiatric residencies at Boston hospitals. But his career turning point came afterward, while serving for two years as an Air Force physician in the South. Coles watched local pro-segregationists harass a black first grader named Ruby Bridges as she attended school, and watched her keep her dignity through it all.

Moved and outraged, Coles dropped plans for a conventional practice in child psychiatry and began, in 1960, to study school desegregation in New Orleans. Over the next three decades he became a traveling oral historian of the lives of children and women in "crisis." His wife, Jane, and his three sons, Bob, Danny and Mike, often accompanied him and contributed to his fieldwork around the country and the world (Appalachia, New Mexico, Alaska, Northern Ireland, Brazil, South Africa). Talking warmly and wisely to ordinary people, Coles turned their tapes into a new genre—not oral history, but oral epiphany and philosophy. The result? More than one thousand articles and the writing or coauthoring of more than fifty books, among them the five-volume *Children of Crisis,* in which he listened to the children of migrants, sharecroppers and mountaineers, of Eskimos, Chicanos and Indians; *Erik H. Erikson: The Growth of His Work; The Mind's Fate;* and *The Call of Stories.* The list of awards and accolades included the Pulitzer Prize, a MacArthur Fellowship and more than forty honorary degrees. Some attribute the achievement to Coles's simple wisdom. Unlike many psychiatrists, he had never forgotten that the "history" of a person or patient always takes place in the thick of what ordinary people mean by "history": the everyday story of our lives. He also knew that therapy begins at home.

As his undergraduate class settled into the Paine Hall lecture room one autumn day, Coles, in beige chinos, paced the enormous stage. The sleeves of his blue work shirt remained rolled up, his hands in his pockets. He was lost in thought. The class assignment had been a John Cheever story, "The Housebreaker of Shady Hill," but Coles could hardly begin before a young woman asked him what students should think about Iraq. "It's the same question as always," he said in his low, faint, gravelly voice. "How to live our lives." He started to talk about an incident that morning as he rode his bike to the post office in Concord, the small town where he lives. An impatient driver had cut him off at a traffic circle, startling another driver at the same time. Coles could see the road-rage look in the driver's face. "He wanted to murder me," he said with a shrug. It was a segue into his own anger, into Cheever's character, into the line one can draw to Stalin and Saddam and Osama and the whole world of us-against-them thinking.

"It's a long way from Cheever and Percy to Baghdad," he said, "but not that far." The students listened, oblivious to the large klieg lights on both sides of the room, placed there by local producers shooting a segment on Coles for a PBS series.

A few hours later, Coles arrived across town at Harvard Medical School, red knapsack over his shoulder, red windbreaker ajar, one shirt collar in, the other out. It was time for his seminar, "Literature and Medicine." Eight mikes dotted the table—PBS still taping. As the students discussed a Chekhov tale, the close relationships already established in the class played out. One student, in a caring tone, asked Coles about his sick dog. Coles told her that he'd had to take it to the vet to be put to sleep. Suddenly an older friend rather than a "professor," Coles confided how depressed the experience had left him. He'd been struggling over whether to tell his own patients, especially when they remarked that he was being unusually quiet or not concentrating. The discussion meshed well with analysis of the story, with its core issue of a doctor's responsibility to patients when facing his own personal pain. At times, Coles digressed—or perhaps didn't—recalling the cultural distance he once felt with an Indian child in New Mexico, or expressing his prudery over borderline child pornography. Driving back to Cambridge, he voiced satisfaction with the class and students. He talked casually about trying to be a sensitive human being in Harvard's citadel of privilege.

People often seem surprised, he said, that he drove a red BMW instead of a dilapidated Volkswagen. Grinning, he added, "I never know what to say except that I like it." In his later years of teaching, Coles pretty much became William Carlos Williams—a model for medical students determined not to refer their own humanity to specialists. He said he'd been touched by the decision of all three of his sons to go into medicine. "It's been wonderful," he remarked of his family life. "We're very private. We never go out. We live kind of a quiet, isolated life." Coles acknowledged that many medical students sought him as a mentor: "I'm not very helpful, because I keep on bringing up the truth of my life, that it's a series of accidents, incidents that cannot be programmed, and luck—pure luck."

"If I hadn't been sent by the Air Force down to Biloxi, Mississippi," he noted, expressing the same sense of happenstance before fate that he'd earlier acknowledged in regard to encountering Erik Erikson, "I don't know what I'd be doing."

"I almost didn't get into medical school," he bragged, jogged into memories of breaking a flask in lab, of failing to tie knots properly: "I was a very poor pre-med. Williams got me in. He called up a biochemist and said, 'Take a chance.'" Later, Coles was told by a faculty member, "'We take in two or three like you.' I said, 'What do you mean, like me?' He said, 'People who are a little confused.'" Coles grinned and shook his head. Feeling like a writer at last, he saw himself as a narrator who, "like Cheever or Carver or anyone," works hard to shape his material, "going for important, dramatic moments, going by the artistic impulse."

"How do you convey a laugh?" he asked. "How do you convey a kid suddenly with tears rolling down his face as he describes a death in the family, which has got him becoming metaphysical and introspective in a spiritual way? How do you do that?"

"The wonderful part of this work," he continued, "is that you hear this all the time from kids, as they exercise their humanity. Their capacity for metaphor, for allusion, for attribution, for putting themselves in the shoes of others. And especially for moral imagination."

One of Williams's greatest achievements, Coles believes, was to teach doctors honest self-scrutiny, to show how "we become full of ourselves, self-preoccupied, so caught up in either our importance or our own affairs that we can't listen and pay attention to other people, even our patients at times." Students, he urged, should get used to "seeing a patient's history as a story, and taking it very seriously, and trying to give it that kind of dignity." Williams, he recalled, helped him appreciate that dignity by expressing, toward the end of their friendship, his own attitude toward his dual career: "He said, 'You know, I go to those cocktail parties in Manhattan, with all their talk, and I can't tell you how happy I am to come back across the river, and walk up the stairs, and knock on a door, and have something to do.'" Robert Coles smiled his radiant, "Isn't that something?" smile. The one with a lifetime behind it.

In his books, such as *The Spiritual Life of Children,* Coles made that deference to others an art. Who ever heard of a philosopher that actually listened to others, let alone children? But Coles listened.

"I think He gets rained on a lot," offered Betsy, a fourth grader in Lawrence, Massachusetts, sharing her fledgling form of deism in talking about God. "Just because it's heaven doesn't mean there's no rain."

"God is up there looking down on us every single second," believed Sophia, the twelve-year-old daughter of a New Orleans maid. "He adds things up later. For every line on his forehead, He'll do something later." Mark, the twelve-year-old son of Seventh-Day Adventists near Chattanooga, Tennessee, felt that God occasionally had to do something right away. The boy remembered an awful highway accident, witnessed by his father, in which a careening truck killed a family of five: "Daddy got right down on his knees and he prayed for the family, that God should take them into His house, and be extra nice to them, considering. It's times like that He must be in tears Himself. Probably those folks were crying on the way to meet Him, and He must have been crying awaiting them."

They could only have been the children of Robert Coles. *The Spiritual Life of Children,* like so many of Coles's books, exhibited this homespun explorer's gently self-critical mind, always ready to report, examine and feel at the same time. It radiated a humane yet firm sensibility, the upshot of a courageous professional life. Yet it also exhibited the soul of the true philosopher: a self-critical spirit. In his books on children's humble lives, Coles probed their notions of citizenship, of right and wrong. Yet no less than Anna Freud, who urged Coles to review his earlier research, to look for things he'd missed, Coles came to feel that he, of all people, hadn't been listening closely enough. In the pages of *The Spiritual Life of Children* he repeatedly castigated himself for what he'd "managed to avoid examining all those years," for not following up on the "constant mention of religious matters," key factors in shaping the lives of the "young pilgrims" with whom he spoke. His avoidance, he acknowledged, was inevitable given his psychoanalytic training. Freud, after all, disdained religion as an illusion "derived from human wishes," mocked its "fairy tales" and described it as a "universal obsessional neurosis." In *The Future of an Illusion* (1927), Freud expressed the hope that someday, when children were "sensibly brought up," religion would disappear.

In that culminating book on children, Coles tried to "come to tentative terms" with the question of faith. He relied on later psychologists, such as Ana-Maria Rizzuto, who reject Freud's easy analogies between childhood neurosis and the religious impulse. Coles's conclusion hardly amounted to conversion, but it enabled him to respect religious inclinations—and his children's words—without sacrificing his secular intellectual beliefs. He decided that "the mind's search for meaning and purpose through fantasy and storytelling, through a faith in received legends, handed down in homes and places of worship, in songs and poems and prayers, is not to be construed necessarily or arbitrarily as a lie or a form of self-delusion." Armed with that tenet, plainly consistent with the respect for narrative that he championed in *The Call of Stories* (1989), Coles returned to his métier, dwelling on what comes out of the mouths of babes. Bounced by one child's words to the memory of another, candid in confessing his own moments of boredom, evasion or arrogance, he guided the reader through ruminations on God's face and voice, philosophical and psychological themes expressed in youthful spirituality, visions and pictorial representations of God, discussions of Christian salvation, Islamic surrender, Jewish righteousness and secular soul searching. He closed with thoughts on "The Child as Pilgrim."

There, in his willingness to absorb as well as disgorge, Coles demonstrated that philosophy as a practice of persuasion also leaves itself open to shifting thoughts. Coles's "investigation of the ways in which children sift and sort spiritual matters" was a way of making amends, but also of salvaging insights from the past. Children, like adults, Coles learned, often need to weave the clashing demands of personal spirituality and institutional religion together. Children, like adults, grow more pensive and theological when faced with tragedy. Children, unlike many adults, welcome unconventional questions about God, don't consider them beside the point, and aren't afraid to get personal. One boy in Coles's book wondered "whether God needs to eat or drink." Another insisted, "He isn't a person who wants people fighting over Him!" Still another figured God can't be on call all the time, considering "all the people He has to keep up with." An unnamed girl in a fourth-grade art history course in Cambridge suggested that even God, like a good analyst, sees some people without appointments: "He can't do everything, not until you go to the next world—and He's the boss there. But he'll listen to you if you really want to talk with Him. He will." Coles also learned that cultural differences matter in some respects, but not others. His Islamic children, for instance, shared a sense of God's great power ("He wouldn't be Allah if he didn't know everything!" declared twelve-year-old Asif), but remained distinctive in their desire for complete surrender before it.

Could the intense childhood spirituality that Coles delicately elicited persuade nonbelievers that Freud and the Enlightenment were wrong, and the great religions right, just as effectively as—more effectively than?—a traditional philosophical treatise? It was one of the questions that a thinker like Coles, and an America the Philosophical that produced him, needed to address. Ever the honest researcher, Coles conceded that children often parrot what adults pour into them. He knew that if parents dispatched their children to Sunday analysis rather than Sunday school, or cultures inculcated youngsters with Freud rather than Christianity, Islam and Judaism, kids might be wondering whether it ever rains on the super-ego. No matter. By coming not to proselytize, but to behold, Coles suggested how reportage itself could fulfill Rorty's admonition that we philosophize through narrative, using stories to shape new imaginative visions.

In a later book, *The Call of Service*, Coles extended that philosophical marshaling of story and narrative to autobiography. From the standpoint of Adam Smith, one might say, Coles grew up in a dysfunctional home. His mother rolled bandages for the Red Cross, served meals in a soup kitchen, sewed clothes for poor children, and visited hospital patients. She loved FDR, sent checks to the *Catholic Worker*, read to the blind and occasionally irritated her son with her "pietistic side." His engineer father, a "skeptical scientist," inclined more toward Republicans Wendell Willkie and Robert Taft. Philip Coles worried that New Deal legislation might "weaken the spirit" of the poor and turn them into "a class of dependents." Yet Coles's father, after retiring in his mid-sixties, also worked as an unpaid volunteer with poor elderly men and women in Boston, keeping it up until his mid-eighties. He took on battles for people confined to nursing homes and hospitals, and confronted bureaucrats who made already difficult lives worse. No one in the Coles family, it seems, thought much about golf or tennis. None spent much time arguing about baseball.

What his parents did clash over, Coles recalled, was how—or even whether—one should describe such do-goodism. His mother, Jane, an outgoing sort, used blunt moral notions such as "idealism" and "goodness of heart." Coles's father, a laconic, practical type, didn't like to be psychoanalyzed by his son, or pressed by his wife on his inner motives. "Your mother was trying to figure out why I do what I do," his father once replied when Coles queried him about an attempt by Jane to grasp her husband's motivations. "I told her not to bother! I told her I like talking to the people I meet!" Coles eventually extracted enough information from his father to understand Philip's "unspoken faith" in service to others. And he went on to emulate his parents' moralism.

Beyond his devoted teaching and prolific book writing, Coles tutored indigent schoolchildren, lived and worked in a *Catholic Worker* hospitality house, participated in the civil rights movement and shepherded voices from Nicaragua, New Mexico, Israel, Alaska and many other places to a worldwide audience. Still, typically self-reflective, Coles found himself wondering about the ambiguities of idealism, needing to explore the circuitry that makes altruism possible. So he decided to examine the satisfactions and costs of service to others, the "trials and opportunities."

In *The Call of Service,* this preeminent investigator of subjective moral notions probed for symptoms of the magic that overrides selfishness, turning his theme over many times so he could view it from every angle, mulling each part in the light. He mixed oral history and meditation, and distinguished different kinds of service, such as social and political struggle, community work, personal gestures and encounters, charity, religiously sanctioned action, government-sanctioned action and service to country. He scrutinized the satisfactions—among them, personal affirmation and fulfillment of moral purpose. He detailed the hazards, ranging from weariness, resignation and cynicism to harsher pitfalls such as arrogance, anger, bitterness, despair and "burnout." He pondered the differences between older and younger idealists, the nature of mentoring, the nexus between doing and learning.

And the persuasion came, as always, in a style welcome to ordinary Americans: through story and example. In his earlier *The Call of Stories,* Coles wrote of how well-wrought tales nourish the moral imagination because they "convey two summonses my mother and father heard and repeatedly took very seriously. . . . They knew that stories are a means of glimpsing and comprehending the world; they knew that service is a means of putting to use what has been learned." In *The Call of Service,* his sharp eye and ear for epiphany characteristically pulled together hard-to-forget phrases and incidents.

Brushing off Coles's fear of whether he might risk "burnout," a committed Harvard student cheered Coles with a simple reply: "My whole life before I started the work was a long stretch of burnout." Another electric moment came when Ruth Ann, Coles's fourth-grade student at the Martin Luther King, Jr. School in Cambridge, grilled him on "why you come over here to us." After Coles mentioned that he got his loafers "in the Square," she drilled a verbal bullet into his forehead. "Why do a lot of you folks always talk about 'the Square,' " she asked, "as though there is only one square?"

Several of Coles's people struggled to understand their own motivations for community service. Students accused one another or themselves of doing it for their CV or "brag sheet." Older idealists acted faintly embarrassed, often presenting their kindness as a gift to themselves. A lawyer in her late twenties started to chide herself for sounding missionary about her public interest work, apologized, then reversed field again, realizing that her apology itself symbolized a selfish culture ashamed of altruism. At the same time, Coles showed that humility of spirit, resistance to the sin of pride, is essential for those who do good. Recalling George Eliot's character Dorothea Brooke in *Middlemarch,* whose idealism breaks the bounds of common sense, Coles noted that "Eliot warns us, by implication, that a high-minded devotion to the call of service can turn into a nightmare of sorts."

Weaving together his illustrations, Coles delivered them in a conversational style that never descended to the chatty, maintaining proper dignity for his topic. He knew when to let his guests talk and elaborate, and when to return to the microphone, bridging their tales with his own notion of where their memories and concerns led. Why did they do it? The motivations—and answers—were many. But Coles received his pithiest answer decades ago when a young civil rights volunteer named Dion Diamond told him, "The satisfaction, man."

Finally, he returned to that other form of reporting as philosophy— autobiography—candidly tracing his career, acknowledging his occasional flashes of ego, moments when he didn't like the great humanist in the mirror. Coles recalled wrapping up an interview with his heroine, Dorothy Day, informing her that he was just about finished with his task of reporting on her and the *Catholic Worker* movement, having talked with her coworkers and academic experts. "I'm not sure you're as close to the end of this as you hope," she said. Day then pointed out that Coles still hadn't spoken to the "most important people" in her life: her "guests," by whom she meant the indigents who came to her Lower East Side soup kitchen. Coles felt reprimanded. "I still remember," he wrote,

> the words that crossed my mind: "Many of them are drunk when they arrive and still drunk when they leave—Bowery bums." So much for one researcher's methodology: an eager interest in intellectuals, in writers and theologians, in the "interesting" array of volunteers who came to give their time and energy; in the ideas and actions and hopes and disappointments of a well-known essayist and moralist who had a complex relationship to a host of eminently recognizable people, from Eugene O'Neill and Mike Gold to W. H. Auden and Hannah Arendt.

But, alas, I had no apparent desire to "expand the sample," as they say in the social sciences, by talking to the folks she sat with every noon after preparing and serving them food and asking them to pray with her, pray for her.

His method since shows that he learned his lesson. At various points in *The Call of Service*, such moments remind us of how a handful of writers whose consciences proved as mighty as their talent—Day, Tolstoy, George Eliot—turned up repeatedly in the lives and minds of those who commit themselves to helping others. You couldn't know from reading Robert Coles that he, early in the twenty-first century, played the same role for many young Americans. But he wouldn't have been Robert Coles if you could.

Some of Coles's broad influence and success—like Skinner's—also had to be attributed to the institution behind him. In psychology as in philosophy—the Harvard psychology department parted company only in the early twentieth century from the philosophy department—Harvard's influence loomed large. That continued into a younger generation of psychologist-philosophers as well. And true to their rambunctious independence, they didn't necessarily work in the department, or stick to the expected subjects.

By the late twentieth century, for instance, anyone curious about the time-honored concept of genius might have thought that dialing 1-800-GENIUS would get you Howard Gardner's private line at the Harvard Graduate School of Education. It didn't. But it was the right call to make.

"I'm surprised at how many letters and phone calls I'm getting—including Thursday night at eleven thirty and Sunday morning at eight thirty," confided Gardner, once the hottest kid pianist in Scranton, Pennsylvania, but by then Harvard's and the country's hottest educational theorist for his twelfth book, *Creating Minds*. In his spare Longfellow Hall office, a modest rectangle outfitted with metal file cabinets and a framed *New York Times* review of legendary psychologist Jean Piaget's *The Grasp of Consciousness*, he shifted uncomfortably. "There are people calling me up to either ask if they're geniuses," he said of the unusual phone traffic, "or to say that they finally realized that they're geniuses."

Perhaps they'd been driven into a buying frenzy despite the rather complicated subtitle of his study, *An Anatomy of Creativity Seen Through the Lives of Freud, Einstein, Picasso, Stravinsky, Eliot, Graham, and Gandhi.* The buzz had started with a magazine mention. In a recent issue, *Newsweek* had splashed a story called "The Puzzle of Genius" across its cover. There inside, with a sizable sidebar all to himself, was Gardner, his powerhouse academic career fine-tuned to six columns under the cheeky headline "He's the Next Best Thing: A Student of Genius." The headline writer seemed out of step with *Newsweek*'s own reporter and most of the sidebar's sources. The latter inclined toward giving the small, slight, ironic Gardner—visualize Woody Allen passing up show biz for academe—the benefit of the doubt on the big G.

Newsweek's staff writer began full-gush: "Mention Howard Gardner's name to a growing cadre of educators, and the response verges on the reverence teenagers lavish on a rock star." For the first time, a national newsmagazine readership got to meet the man who, with his earlier book *Frames of Mind,* had driven a stake into the commonplace that "intelligence" is a single intellectual capacity, thus reducing designers of IQ tests to midlife crisis and fueling the vibrant "multiple intelligences" movement in childhood education. The magazine's readers also learned about the middle-age scholar's "gurulike status" with progressive teachers around the country, his MacArthur Fellowship and his eclectic learning from gifted children, brain-damaged adults, Chinese preschoolers and his own four children from two marriages.

Gardner, who said he didn't use the word "genius" much himself, admitted to being delighted because he is, he conceded, a thinker who wants to have impact. "I had no idea that I was going to be featured," he recalled, "and that the whole structure of the article came out the way I've been thinking about things, which is only apparent if you've read the book." Indeed, the article substantially reflected the thesis of *Creating Minds* that genius is what Gardner called a "social judgment," a culturally constructed cachet rather than a measurable mental ability. At the same time, the article recognized that paradigms of genius display enough similarities to make talking about patterns worthwhile. "I reserve the word 'genius,'" explained Gardner, rocking gently back and forth in his office chair, "for an individual who discovers a basic truth. It can be a basic truth about the outside world, such as the kind scientists discover, or it can be a basic truth about experience, which is what artists do."

That truth, however, must also be of "universal significance," and it must change the nature of the domain, or area of life, in which it appears. "Ultimately," he elaborated, "what people do in that particular domain is different because of what the genius did." Think of physics after Einstein, or art after Picasso, or dance after Martha Graham, and even a non-genius can absorb the point.

Creating Minds suggested a number of generalizations about genius drawn from Gardner's seven modern giants, whose lives he investigated in all their carefully chosen diversity: a psychologist, a physicist, a painter, a composer, a poet, a choreographer and a political activist. Gardner found, for instance, that his examples (except for Picasso) all experienced ten years of dues paying before their first significant breakthrough. He argued that geniuses often suffered a sharp sense of hurt in childhood, required early support and enthusiasm from intimates, enjoyed a knack for handling different audiences, and—perhaps most saliently—exhibited a fierce, Faustian determination to toss aside conventional goals such as friendship and marriage to achieve their obsessive goals.

"They are difficult people, these geniuses," Gardner said. "They cause a lot of damage around them. You have to ask whether you'd want you or your child to be that kind of person." Indeed, even as he reported the selfish habits of genius—Picasso's exploitation of women, young Einstein's short fuse with inferiors—Gardner expressed his moralism, insisting that genius is "not a license for 'to hell with everybody else.'" How, though, does one know these geniuses, when they come around, without a name tag? Gardner agreed that initial attention and sustained PR muscle make a difference in the history of genius.

"We shouldn't ignore the fact," he commented, "that the early returns are quite important. If what you do is ignored by everybody, or condemned by everybody, whatever potential you may have could be rubbed out. If you're not on the map, it's almost a miracle if your work is ever discovered. I assume in Widener Library [Harvard's main library] there are hundreds and hundreds of people who said, in effect, the same thing around the same time, or even earlier, as people whose name everybody knows. And for some reason, they never got that little window of exposure."

Nonetheless, you can't really credit careers like Einstein's and Picasso's to a good publicity machine. Or can you? "It differs across domains," Gardner conceded. "In painting now, it might well be the case that PR is 90 percent of it. In science, that's not true. If you solve Fermat's last theorem, whether you're a good PR person doesn't make a lot of difference. There's 350 years of expectation around you. In fact, the guy who did it seems to be very shy." Gardner emphasized one thing across the disciplinary spectrum that's clear to him: genius isn't a sure thing. It's a verdict the culture renders (sometimes only hundreds of years later) upon momentous accomplishment wrought through hard work and discipline. Gardner never quoted Thomas Edison's familiar maxim about genius being "99 percent perspiration," but a hint of it ran through the book.

"One of the obvious lessons of the book," Gardner said, "is that these people were very bourgeois. They came from households where work was the name of the game, where love was contingent on being productive. One of the things I do with my own kids is that I try to counter the notion that their father is easily successful. So I show them when I really get dumped on, and when things I do don't get funded, or they get ignored. One stereotype is that certain people are born successful and everything works out for them. That's not true, as these biographies indicate."

Gardner explained that he chose his final team of seven—not "an affirmative-action list," he notes—partly to get a sample who lived more or less during the same cultural age. His decisions—such as putting aside near misses like Virginia Woolf—depended more on personal likes and dislikes than scientific rigor. He also wanted a group "remote enough from the present that we already had some distance." Distance seems the operative word when he's asked whether the theory of genius being provoked by early emotional hurt might apply to him as well.

In a freak accident, Gardner's older brother, Eric—the first son of Gardner's German-Jewish parents, who immigrated to Scranton in 1938—was killed in a sleigh accident at age eight while his mother looked on. She was pregnant with Howard at the time. Gardner grew up with photographs of Eric around the house. Only as he neared age ten did his parents tell Howard that the boy was not really a neighborhood friend, but his dead older brother. His parents, he wrote in a memoir, *To Open Minds,* told him that if his mother hadn't been pregnant with him at the time of the accident, they might have killed themselves. Did the whole experience affect him greatly?

"I'm sure it did," he said, "but I'm not psychodynamic enough to be able to say how it happened. . . . My parents were doing the best they could, and probably had a terrible difficulty dealing with the thing. My father, now, fifty-five years later, he still can't deal with it."

Gardner, however, more than fulfilled whatever hopes were placed upon him. After excelling as both pianist and student in public school in Scranton, and then at Wyoming Seminary in Kingston, Pennsylvania,

Gardner arrived at Harvard to feel a shudder familiar to freshman hot-shots: "When I walked into the Union here, and heard everyone playing Rachmaninoff's Third Piano Concerto, I realized I might have been special in Scranton, but I was completely unspecial here. On the other hand, it was the first time in my life where I felt I could come out of the closet, so to speak, meaning that I didn't have any ambiguity about talking to everybody about anything I was interested in, pushing myself as hard as possible. For people like me, Harvard was wonderful, because you could be yourself, and nobody cared."

So he stayed on for graduate school in psychology, studying under masters such as Erik Erikson. Right after college, he went to work for Jerome Bruner, the distinguished professor emeritus of psychology at Harvard, who has juggled psychology and education for most of his long career. Gardner later got involved with Project Zero, a renowned Graduate School of Education project to study creativity and intelligence. He was thus ideally positioned for what happened a decade ago: "*Frames of Mind,* which was written as a contribution to psychology, was picked up much more by education people. I suddenly found an audience, and, as my own theory would say, the field had some effect on me." He was persuading folks, all right, but like many thinkers in America the Philosophical, not precisely the ones he expected to reach.

Asked about his theory of seven intelligences—linguistic, musical, logical-mathematical, spatial, bodily-kinesthetic, interpersonal (dealing with other people) and intrapersonal (understanding oneself)— Gardner denied that there's any hard and fast scientism to the concept of an intelligence, or to the number of them he settled on. "An intelligence is a biopsychological potential," he explained, but it doesn't really take form except in a cultural activity like mathematics or dancing that gives it an avenue for expression. So, like genius, it's less a physical attribute than a latent ability.

Moreover, Gardner resisted any effort to sanctify his theory or guru-ize him. He saw his rise as champion of new educational thinking as a serendipitous event. ("The opportunity arises because people come to you, and then you have to decide how much you want to do.") He doesn't want to abuse his influence. "I don't go round and recommend or not recommend anybody who does work in multiple intelligences," he said. "I simply serve as an information center. I have a book called *Multiple Intelligences: The Theory in Practice.* . . . The last part of the book is simply lists of people who do this stuff, making it available to people. But I don't give a *Good Housekeeping* seal."

Gardner later moved on to other subjects and topics, such as leadership and "good work," where he combined his rambunctious boundary breaking with other hard-to-define thinkers like Mihaly Csikszentmihalyi, the California-based theorist of "flow." With nineteen books and eighteen honorary doctorates at last count, he looked likely to have more than a few future tangents to play out—especially in light of the way he articulated his basic credo as a thinker. "When I was in college," he said, "my hero was [literary critic] Edmund Wilson. I loved the way he wrote—in a very clear way about technical issues. But the other thing was that, whatever interested him, he wrote about it. I don't like to feel that because I was trained in psychology, or that I'm in the education school, it means that anything I want to study or write about is foreign to me."

It might have served as a credo for Harvard's psychologist-philosophers as a whole, from William James to Steven Pinker, who kept up the tradition in 2011 with *The Better Angels of Our Nature,* his meditation on the decline of violence in modern life. Gardner's nod to Wilson made perfect sense. Because just as much as the psychologists, literary critics had long since occupied their part of America the Philosophical.

THE LITERARY CRITICS

In a poorly furnished, dilapidated apartment near Emory University in Atlanta, eighty-six-year-old Kenneth Burke—once described as "the finest literary critic in the world, and perhaps the finest since Coleridge"—anxiously scanned the cheap Formica kitchen table where he worked. Somewhere on it lay that "dull" paper about him, the one he planned to savage at an upcoming three-day Burke conference in Philadelphia, the paper that got his dander up. Somewhere. Unfortunately, only his battered blue Royal typewriter—a manual with weathered keys—stuck out. Crowding it were decomposing paperbacks, scattered photocopies, scrawl-ridden reprints. An indoor thermometer, still factory sealed in its plastic and cardboard casing, hung from a nail on the wall. Empty bottles of vermouth and vodka dotted the sink top. A soiled orange rug curled up in the corners. It was not a scene in which one expected to find a National Medal of Literature winner, let alone a visiting research fellow at rich Emory.

Yet this is America, and Kenneth Burke was, as he once quipped, just "a word man." More important, he was Kenneth Burke, once called "the most controversial literary figure of the past 50 years in America" for more than his complex theories. Whatever his guise—former Pittsburgh factory worker challenging the academy without a BA, "agro-bohemian" living on an Andover, New Jersey, farm for decades without plumbing or electricity, gypsy scholar without a regular academic appointment until age forty-six, husband of two sisters, songwriter for his grandson Harry Chapin—Kenneth Burke never lived by the rules.

He gave up looking for the article.

"I understand I don't have to do anything, anyway," laughed Burke, stooped but incredibly spry, referring to his critic-at-large duties at the conference. "If I just want to sit around and jaw, I can do it."

Burke's general philosophical concerns were easier to state than his theories. Starting in *Counter-Statement* (1931), his first book, and the one he still believed contained the essence of his ideas, he sought a theory of literary form. "I started out with a theory of art as self-expression," said Burke. But in studying Shakespeare, he became increasingly intrigued by the psychology of the audiences at which the plays were aimed. His interest shifted from a theory of form to the whole nature of human relations. In confronting that larger subject, which became his enduring one, Burke approached man as the "symbol-using animal." The focus on linguistic symbols and their effects prompted him to reexamine and help revive the ancient field of rhetoric—the study of persuasion.

Some Burke experts, in fact, thought of him mostly as a rhetorician who treated any use of language—scientific, poetic, dramatic—according to its strategies for affecting the audience. Burke, however, recognized other functions of language—he simply appreciated that every kind of language exhibits some rhetorical aspect. His system, dubbed "Dramatism," analyzed concrete "acts" of language by making the actors, their purposes, their audience and the context of the interactions all fair game for study. "The misunderstanding that's most common," said Burke of his critics, "is that I make the world all words. The thing is, you can't talk about the world without using words."

Yet it was not so much Burke's general direction that caused fireworks as his inclinations. Always keeping close to texts, he favored scatological interpretations. His most famous, reducing John Keats's line "Beauty is truth, truth beauty" to a bathroom image, outraged many academic critics. Another jarring Burkean tendency was to jerk unfamiliar things together to achieve "perspective by incongruity." Some critics considered him the champion mixer of apples and oranges. Behind it all, apparently, lay Burke's aim to "purify" us of warlike impulses, to eliminate differences that defeat a sense of oneness. An anti-technological strain ran through his work.

"For a darn good reason, fella," he said, recalling his rough Pittsburgh youth. "One summer I worked in one of these damn factories down there." The smell of the burned oil that cooled the lathes would stay in his hair for months. "He's like Buckminster Fuller," said Trevor Melia, a University of Pittsburgh rhetoric professor who co-organized the symposium on Burke's work. "I suspect if you canvass this conference, you'll find people willing to say that this is the greatest American genius of the twentieth century. You'll also find people with exactly the opposite opinion."

Everyone agreed that Burke was difficult to read because of his puns, digressions, odd punctuation and fondness for abstract language. Everyone agreed that his ambition had taken him far beyond literary criticism, into philosophy, history, psychology, science, theology and politics. It was the evaluations of those moves that clashed. The formalist New Critics of his generation—R. P. Blackmur, Allen Tate, John Crowe Ransom—questioned his going outside the text for interpretations. John Simon, pondering candidates for the great American critic, once said it couldn't be Burke because he didn't write English. Academic philosophers like Max Black and Sidney Hook bemoaned the "turbid prose" and "absence of developed argument in his work."

Yet the kudos also went back a long way. Writing in 1941, W. H. Auden called him "unquestionably the most brilliant and suggestive critic now writing in America." The prestigious University of California Press republished his collected works. And in 1981, Burke won the National Medal of Literature, selected for the honor before such worthies as Saul Bellow and Isaac Bashevis Singer.

Though few scholars made such extravagant claims for him as Trevor Melia ("He is, in my opinion, probably the most significant contributor to rhetorical theory since Cicero") or State University of New York professor William Rueckert ("There is no question that Burke is one of the major critical minds of the twentieth century"), Burke's star clearly shone in many quarters. "I think he's the most important man of letters of our time," said Wayne Booth of the University of Chicago, whose own critical works stress a rhetorical approach to literature. "Burke is to American thought what Charles Ives was to music," observed literary critic Alfred Kazin. "Burke is an original. One can't really compare him with other people."

"He probably will turn out to be the most significant critic of the 1930s," said Geoffrey Hartman of Yale. Hartman, along with his Yale colleagues, largely redirected American literary criticism away from the New Critics to European thinkers who resemble Burke in ranging across academic disciplines.

Yet the acclaim for Burke hardly counted as universal. Hook, for example, pulled no punches late in life in dismissing Burke. "He has a reputation among literary people who find him so obscure that they figure he must be profound," said Hook. "I think he's a man devoid of common sense and political judgment. He has no philosophical standing whatsoever." Advised of that remark, Burke cracked, "I'll piss on Sidney Hook's grave." (He did, so to speak, surviving Hook by four years.)

For the vibrant five-foot-four-inch Burke, however, who liked to boast that he towered over Balzac (five foot three) and shared the same birthday as Kierkegaard and Marx, no such talk could blunt the pleasure he took in his rising philosophical reputation. As one talked to him, his long, hard fight to escape his father's working-class world burned through. Born in Pittsburgh, where he began a lifelong friendship with writer Malcolm Cowley, he knew he "wanted out." His father focused on a clerical job "when he had a job at all."

"The trouble with him," mused Burke, "was that he believed in nothing but money, and he never made any. His stories were just told for nothing. They were marvelous. He just didn't appreciate himself at all."

After brief stints at Ohio State and Columbia, he dropped out and moved to Greenwich Village to write. In 1921 he joined the *Dial* magazine, serving as a music critic, among other roles. In 1929, he won the Dial prize for service to letters, but then the magazine folded. The 1930s were probably the key decade of his life. A man of the left, he caught heat from people like Hook for not abandoning Stalin in those years. "At that time, I didn't believe any of the stories about him," said Burke. "I thought the stuff was totally done by people like Hitler."

From the 1930s on, though, Burke's work became less overtly political. *Counter-Statement* was followed by such major books as the novel *Towards a Better Life*, *Permanence and Change*, *The Philosophy of Literary Form*, *A Grammar of Motives*, *A Rhetoric of Motives*, *The Rhetoric of Religion*, *Language as Symbolic Action* and *Collected Poems 1915–1967*.

"There was a period in my life," he said proudly, talking of years when he believed he was blacklisted, "when I had to tell myself, Look, you think that people are down on you, keeping you out of those jobs, you mustn't do that. I never in my life missed one meal because I didn't have the money."

By his later years, he had become the family patriarch, with three daughters, two sons, and a very close grandson who'd playfully tease him. "Harry would call him," recalled Melia of folksinger Harry Chapin, "and say, 'You're doing very well, old man, but I just sold out the XYZ arena.'" So in his days of doing well, Burke made no apologies for the myriad distinctions in his work. "Every distinction we've got," he says, "someone put it there." And one couldn't knock the benefits for longevity of Burke's intensity. In fact, Burke credited his hard-drinking, hard-driving intellectual life for keeping him in shape.

"Basically, I'm still terribly interested in what I'm doing," he said, "and I want to get it cleared up. Malcolm [Cowley] says if I ever get it cleared up, I'll die the next day." He did not say it like a worried man.

For unlike many professional philosophers, sentenced to a lifetime of teaching the same texts, from the same ossified canon, with the same bureaucratic boundaries constraining their imaginations, Burke concentrated his attentions where they made the most sense to him at any given moment. He made up his philosophical life as he rolled along. The style fit literary critics more naturally than it fit official philosophers. Irving Howe could tell a similar tale.

"When I was a kid, I wanted to be a tribune of the socialist movement," recalled Howe one summer evening in Washington, D.C., relaxing before a speech organized by supporters of peace in Israel. "Something like Norman Thomas. But I didn't have those gifts. I wasn't as good a speaker." So he turned to the typewriter, writing and editing political and literary studies. By his sixties, Howe had become an elder statesman of democratic socialism in the U.S., which often took him away from his work. Fidgeting in a small, sparsely furnished room at the Tabard Inn on N Street, lacking a wished-for desk, but at least away from the "carbolic" odor of the plastic-and-glass hotels he detested, Howe tugged at his socks and sandals, reflecting on the life of a graying eminence.

"One of the curses of my life is the growth of obligations," he lamented, "each of which has its own validity, but the sum of which can drive one crazy." That day, at least, the frustrated intellectual deferred to the activist, seeking to draw more people to the evening's discussion of peace issues at the Jewish Community Center of Greater Washington in Rockville, Maryland. The virtue of the Israeli peace movement, he said, explaining his support, "is that it proposes certain immediate measures—it doesn't propose a long-range solution." Howe listed them as "a cessation of all settlements," an announcement by Israel that it is willing to "cede the West Bank under proper security guarantees," and a readiness "to negotiate with any Palestinian body that recognizes Israel and ceases terrorism." Howe thought the Israeli government could encourage moderate Palestinian leaders by adopting such measures.

On the activist stump, Howe could give as good as he got. That night in Rockville, in Israeli-like heat of more than 90 degrees—and some American heat generated by concerned local Jews—Howe shared panel space with a former chief of education of the Israeli Defense Forces. Several audience members objected to the requirement of written questions, but the panel continued. The IDF man, mopping his brow, emphatically recounted the history of the Israeli peace movement, stressing its "moderate nature" and reminding the audience of the tradi-tion "of the Zionist movement to have a dialogue with the Diaspora."

Howe tried to dampen tension in the room with a brief observation in Yiddish, after which he stated his reasons for backing peace. He spoke, as he had in the afternoon, of what most disturbed him: the threat of violence down the line by Jewish extremists against other Jews—a viola-tion, he said, of the cherished Jewish rejection of force. "It is sometimes said that these people are taking the law into their own hands," intoned Howe. "That is not true. They are taking lawlessness into their hands."

Objections came quickly, centering around the supposed absence of Palestinian leaders with whom Israelis could talk. Both Howe and the IDF man replied that the imperative was to create such leaders. One written question implied that Arab money supported Howe. He denounced the innuendo as an example of the increase of intolerance in Jewish debate. Yet all the political heat didn't wilt his literary instinct, or his inclination to make a philosophical point through a story. He told a tale in Yiddish and English about trying to write a letter large enough for a deaf man to read and understand. His accuser, he said, was such a man.

Earlier, in the afternoon, Howe had bristled slightly at the sugges-tion that his political opinions might be discounted by public policy types wary of literary intellectuals playing political philosopher. "A lot of lawyers," he said, "despite their jargon, are very fuzzy-minded—often there's only the appearance of precision. There may be such attitudes, but we return them 'with interest.' "

Howe never showed any inclination to apologize for his literary background. He latched on to books early, and they took him from a Yiddish-speaking, working-class family in the Bronx to public schools and university in New York. He considered himself a Marxist by the time he attended CCNY, but he opposed Stalinism while there, begin-ning his lifelong opposition to all tyrannies. Finally he made it all the way to a Distinguished Professorship at City University of New York, despite the lack of a PhD. Howe credited his eighteen-month Army tour in Alaska during World War II with making him a scholar. Dur-ing that "frigid sabbatical," as he liked to call it, he read roughly four hundred books. He thought only a heart attack could slow him down enough to repeat the feat.

Asked what kind of reputation preceded him among his enemies, Howe shot back, "Intellectually rigid," and "not scholarly enough, spread out too far, journalistic." He blamed part of that on academic revenge for his years of baiting professors as "pedants and dullards," but admitted the "spread out too far" view hit home. "There's a Yiddish proverb—you don't have to dance at every wedding," he chuckled, conceding he might have danced at too many. Still, apart from *The World of Our Fathers*, his history of Jewish immigrant life, he considered his greatest achievement a philosophical and political one reflected in his twenty-six years editing the journal *Dissent*: his attempt to "keep the idea of democratic socialism in America alive during hard times." The regrets of such a full life struck him as few. "Where you lose out," mused the eternal book lover, "is in that large, indiscriminate, promiscuous reading that Samuel Johnson said is the mark of a literate man. Just the luxury of picking up a book because it captures your attention. You lose that."

His readers didn't notice that he'd fallen down in that respect. Remembering the New York intellectuals, his second-generation street gang of literary and social critics, Howe recalled that they all possessed "a mania for range"—a drive that expressed a "profoundly Jewish impulse; namely, you've got to beat the goyim at their own game. So you have to dazzle them a little." For all his modesty, Howe's writings, particularly the many scattered essays that began to be gathered in the 1980s and '90s, revealed that will to dazzle, and some large, promiscuous reading behind it.

Early on in his career, few ascribed a Nietzschean bent to this voracious culture critic, author or editor of more than thirty books, former professor at Brandeis, Stanford, and CUNY, wobbly onetime planet in the *Partisan Review* solar system, socialist tribune (after all), and sedulous analyst of American, European and especially Jewish literature. The adjectives typically ascribed to Howe made him sound like a date arranged by your liberal aunt: sane, lucid, idealistic. Yet impress he did. Not wildly, like the Dadaist critic Jacques Vaché, who pulled a gun at a Paris theater and promised to shoot the first person who applauded a play he hated. Not with Randall Jarrell's flashy wit, or Norman Podhoretz's malleable cast-iron ideology, or Susan Sontag's powerfully implied erudition, or Harold Bloom's effortful stretching.

Instead, Howe dazzled by always making sense. Whether rescuing Sholom Aleichem and Émile Zola from their deteriorated reputations, or outlining the genus New Leftist, or explaining the assault upon the city by literary Romantics, Howe didn't magically and automatically convince, but he routinely delivered clear, elegant positions to tussle with. In an era when literary academe's herd of unheard independent theorists settled for far less—smugly thinking it had achieved more—Howe's greatest hits rewarded repeated listening.

His selected writings offered a "reasonably fair picture" of his career, he said when they appeared. They did better. A major critic's essays often surpass a fresh study in importance, for they force author and reader to experience a sensibility's development free of the publisher's urge to nudge awkward protuberances into the artifice of a book. Reading a critic's essays, like watching an actor in the same play over several nights, permits one to distinguish reflex and technique from inspiration and pure gift. Throughout Howe's work, one saw the high seriousness, the resistance to duking it out with pop culture that marked and somewhat limited him. In a brilliant 1962 essay entitled "T. E. Lawrence: The Problem of Heroism," he began by announcing that his subject's image was "mercifully" no longer "Lawrence of Arabia"—never mind the unmentioned Oscar-winning film of that year. Similarly, in "The Idea of the Modern" (1967), we heard the voice of the immigrant polymath concerned (half ironically) about covering all the bases, noting how he "should speak about J. G. Frazer . . . should speak about Marx . . . should speak about Freud . . . should speak, above all, about Nietzsche."

A more enduring and edifying element was Howe's gift for sound, by-the-by generalization. In "Dreiser: The Springs of Desire" (1964), he noted "the fate that often besets writers caught up in cultural dispute: their work comes to seem inseparable from what has been said about it." And in "This Age of Conformity" (1954), an essay worth downloading in any age, he included his classic brief against how "the Ph.D. system . . . grinds and batters personality into a mode of cautious routine."

"What one finds among these young people," he wrote, "for all their intelligence and devotion and eagerness, is often appalling: a remarkable desire to be 'critics,' not as an accompaniment to the writing of poetry or the changing of the world or the study of man and God, but just critics—as if criticism were a subject, as if one could be a critic without having at least four non-literary opinions, or as if criticism 'in itself' could adequately engage an adult mind for more than a small part of its waking time."

A true critic offered many possible legacies: singular taste, adjusted reputations, interpretations destined for consensus, spontaneous writing turned required reading, memorable lines such as Virginia Woolf's on *Ulysses* ("The work of a queasy undergraduate scratching his pimples"). Howe left us all of these. Yet as his autobiography, *A Margin of Hope*, confirmed, Howe's contributions moved us most when embedded in concrete memoir.

"Strangers," an essay on the Jewish American intellectual's encounter with American literary tradition, hardly rivaled the autobiography's depth, but it delighted with entertaining asides, such as the memory of older writer Isaac Rosenfeld trying to persuade young Howe that Chekhov wrote in Yiddish. If Howe's literary essays impressed more than his political ones, life took the blame. Despite the heartfelt forensics of pieces such as "Lillian Hellman and the McCarthy Years," they reminded readers that quotidian political battles fade fast. In the former essays, Howe wrote like a charged autodidact, bounding out of the library to change the world. In the latter, he sounded as though he were chairing a panel, with endless hours left on the clock.

In *A Margin of Hope,* Howe acknowledged his youthful ambition, after giving on becoming Norman Thomas, of turning into a social critic like George Orwell, "one of those free-ranging speculative writers who grapple with the troubles of their time yet command some of the accumulated knowledge of the past." His essays explained why during his life and afterward, so many American intellectuals modeled themselves on Irving Howe.

Not all literary critics of philosophical stature shared the political, class-conscious bent of Howe and Burke, or reified Michael Walzer's vision of the social critic as philosopher in the manner Walzer might have liked. Harold Bloom, for instance, evinced an equal passion for changing people's minds without taking on the mission of winning their hearts at the voting booth.

Magisterially stretched out on a brown leather recliner in his Washington Square North apartment, the white hair, etched wrinkles and dark eyebrows confirming that he'd reached patriarchal age, Bloom on a fall afternoon fired away at a bête noire of the moment reflected in Christmas displays and bric-a-brac: the way New Age types distort such venerable aspects of religious experience as prophetic dreams, near-death experiences and the meaning of the millennium. Nearby sat his assault on those "popularizations," *Omens of Millennium: The Gnosis of Angels, Dreams, and Resurrection.*

"It's kitsch," Bloom remarked about wimpy cherubim on lapel pins and prime-time "touchers" who act like personal trainers from some great health club in the sky. "It's namby-pambyism. They're sentimentalized. Angels are horrifying creatures." That is, they are in the great religious and literary traditions absorbed with astonishing energy by a world-famous scholar so coveted that for a number of years he held *both* the Sterling Professorship of Humanities at Yale and the Berg Professorship of English at New York University. In recent years, Bloom explained, he'd come to feel that much "New Age" religiosity amounted to a "contemporary debasement" of the so-called Gnostic tradition (named after the Greek word for "knowledge"). That controversial, anti-institutional strain in religious thought assumed a transcendent God who predated the creator of the universe, but fell to pieces in the tragedy of material creation. It exalted the individual's direct knowledge of a "spark" of that original divinity within oneself. As a result Gnostics, typically uninterested in worldly power and seeing little need for orthodox institutions of religion, had usually clashed with the latter and been persecuted by them. To Bloom, many New Agers resembled religious Americans since the eighteenth century in their "desire to be unchurched, to break with dogmatic, institutional and historically European Christianity." In their inwardly directed religiosity, they were essentially "Gnostics without knowing it." Unfortunately, he felt, they'd begun to practice a particularly "adulterated or travestied" kind.

So after working out his view of American spirituality a few years earlier in *The American Religion,* he decided to write *Omens,* a "spiritual autobiography" that sought to lure fans of the New Age ("an endlessly entertaining saturnalia of ill-defined yearnings"). Instead of leaving them to books marked by a "vacuity not to be believed," he wanted to lead them to the more challenging literature that vacuous books simplify. "In that Gnostic sermon I preach at the end," Bloom observed, commenting again on angels, "I say that maybe it would be better to start thinking of them as our prison wardens." That, of course, would be a lot of wardens. According to a poll Bloom cited, 69 percent of Americans believe in angels.

Phony "angelology" wasn't the only problem in the New Age surge propelled by wind chimes and instant astrology. In religious traditions, Bloom pointed out, prophetic dreams are also "terrifying. They're not pacifying or mollifying phenomena." As for near-death experiences, popularized as a kind of celestial high in which one is "blessed by the light," Bloom saw them as "parodies of authentic shamanism." He sardonically remarked (as he did in the book) that "all of life is a near-death experience."

"I tried to organize the book around those three images," Bloom explained, "and then, in a very tentative way, to do what I know is an outrageous and oxymoronic thing: preach a Gnostic sermon. How can there be such a thing? There is no congregation and should not be.... So all you can do is hope to purify what we have now.... [T]he book is really directed to that great mass of seekers out there who are unchurched.... It's not so much that I want them to read me. I want them to use me as an introduction to their reading Henry Corbin [the great scholar of Iranian Shi'ism] or Moshe Idel [the great scholar of Jewish Kabbalism] or Hans Jonas [the great scholar of Christian Gnosticism]."

"A Tour Guide to Gnosticism" seemed an odd job to attract Bloom. In books such as *The Visionary Company, The Anxiety of Influence* and *A Map of Misreading,* he made his name as a provocative interpreter of romantic poetry and of the influence earlier literary figures exert on later ones. Yet as he related in *Omens,* he had experienced, since childhood, intense, epiphanic aesthetic experiences, particularly in reading the visionary verse of William Blake. They resembled the kind of private "knowing" described by Gnostics. In the mid-1960s, he experienced a serious depression that began to lift only after a kind of "conversion" produced by reading *The Gnostic Religion* by Jonas. Bloom found multiple points of contact between Gnosticism and his earlier inklings. But he also saw many connections with a thinker he was then restoring to a supreme place in the American canon: Emerson, who once wrote, "That is always best which gives me to myself" (a virtual Gnostic prayer, in Bloom's view).

In the years since, Bloom's scholarly and philosophic interest in religion had grown so strong—in addition to *The American Religion,* his *The Book of J* spurred controversy by arguing that a woman wrote one part of the Bible—that he was now widely seen as a thinker about both literature and religion. In the four main sections of *Omens,* Bloom provided an entertaining and provocative overview of "Angels," "Dreams," "Not Dying" and "Gnosis," followed by a brief excursus on millennial behavior and his "Gnostic sermon." He waved the reader through medieval Sufism, Zoroastrian dualism, Jewish Kabbalism, Christian Gnosticism and modern Hollywood. He introduced the lustful angels of the Gnostic Book of Enoch, eager to copulate with human females. He presented the star of that story, the prophet Enoch, who is swooped up into heaven and made over into the greatest of the angels, Metatron. Driving home the fearsomeness of "real" angels, he reminded readers that the mere sight of the angel Gabriel caused the prophet Muhammad to faint. A philosopher of religion on holiday, and perhaps on a lark, Bloom also devoted some time to Shirley MacLaine, Arianna Huffington, Newt Gingrich, Mormon Joseph Smith and punitive caning in Singapore.

Many critics applauded Bloom's enormous ambition, while splitting on *Omens* itself. Religion scholar Mark Taylor complained that "a melancholy world-weariness haunts its pages." Georgetown professor and *Fresh Air* critic Maureen Corrigan judged it "staggeringly erudite." British scholar Marina Warner praised Bloom for a "true teacher's refusal to give up the job of stimulating and informing." With twenty-two books and more than forty years of teaching under his belt, Bloom had been up before the critical tribunal many times before. He expected that a "second wave" of scholarly reviews would upbraid him for one sin or another. But as he escorted his visitor to the door, parting company with the courtliness familiar to generations of students ("You go ahead, my dear, and then we'll hug goodbye"), it was plain that on this project a different sort of authenticity mattered to him.

He recalled a visit to his home years before by Bentley Layton, one of the foremost translators of the Gnostic scriptures. Layton wanted him to be one of four plenary speakers at an international conference on the subject. Bloom protested that he was not really a scholar or philosopher of ancient religion. Layton, in a characteristic gesture, held up his finger to make a point. "Ah," he replied. "But you are something better. You are a native speaker."

Bloom's willingness to range far beyond his seeming scholarly expertise made him perhaps the foremost poster boy for the philosophical boldness often evinced by American intellectuals outside the professional discipline of philosophy—their determination to take on any and all writers or thinkers within their ken. By 2011, if you looked up "Bloom, Harold" under "Author" in the University of Pennsylvania's main library catalog, the computer shot back 846 entries. Most were his Chelsea House collections of critical essays on authors, each one "Edited and with an Introduction" by Harold Bloom. At eighty, Yale's never-say-die polymath had knocked out volumes on, for starters, A. E. Housman, A. R. Ammons, Agatha Christie, Albert Camus, Aldous Huxley, Alexander Pope, Alexander Pushkin, Alexandr Solzhenitsyn, Alfred Lord Tennyson, Alice Munro, Alice Walker, Amy Tan, André Malraux, Andrew Marvell, Anthony Burgess, Anton Chekhov, Arthur Miller, Arthur Rimbaud, August Wilson, Ben Jonson, Bernard Malamud, Blaise Pascal, C. S. Lewis, Cervantes, Charles Baudelaire, Charles Dickens, Christina Rossetti, Christopher Marlowe, Cormac McCarthy and Cynthia Ozick.

And those volumes didn't include the collections by Bloom, also "Edited and with an Introduction," on specific works of literature such as Aeschylus's *Oresteia*, Camus's *The Stranger*, and Aldous Huxley's *Brave New World*. And the volumes by Bloom on categories of writers, such as *African-American Poets; American and Canadian Women Poets, 1930–Present; American Fiction 1914–1945; American Naturalism; American Poetry 1915–1945; American Poetry 1946–1965;* and *American Poetry Through 1914.*

Whether such prolific publishing enhanced Bloom's reputation as a critic and thinker remained open to question. No one doubted his prodigious reading habits and singularly capacious mind—he once responded to the "myth" that he could read a thousand pages an hour by explaining that he could read only four hundred. It might have been that he actually did know enough about all the writers, books and literary groups on which he'd edited essays to make his spectacle of 360-degree opinion magnificent rather than tawdry. But the publication in 2011 of Bloom's *The Anatomy of Influence: Literature as a Way of Life,* intended as a kind of magisterial sum-up, suggested that allowing one's reach to exceed one's grasp was not a quality that automatically enhanced one's status as a philosopher.

At the outset of *The Anatomy of Influence,* Bloom told us he'd be updating his controversial *The Anxiety of Influence* (1973) by commenting on about thirty writers, all of whom he'd written on before. A third of the book would go to Shakespeare, whom Bloom conceded had long been his "obsessive concern," sharing a God-like position with Emerson in Bloom's literary universe. But the first warning sign of the slapdash came early: in just the first thirty pages, the author repetitively called the book a "final reflection upon the influence process," his "final statement on the subject," his "virtual swan song" and his "last reflection upon influence."

The promise of updating also proved shaky. In "The Point of View for My Work as a Critic," Bloom recalled yet again his early infatuation with Hart Crane and Blake, his appreciation of Samuel Johnson, his insistence that literature is life itself, his "possession" of much immortal literature by memory, his antipathy to nonaesthetic approaches to literature. In regard to the last, he made clear his continued hostility to that "rabblement of lemmings" and "resentniks," as he memorably labeled his critics, whose ranks he saw filled by "feminists, Marxists, purple-haired semioticians, new historicists, Lacanians, De Manians."

Also familiar rather than fresh was Bloom's instant, characteristic need to clear his op-ed throat. "Twenty-first century America is in a state of decline," he reported, sounding like Susan Jacoby or the author of *Idiot America*:

> It is scary to reread the final volume of Gibbon these days because the fate of the Roman Empire seems an outline for the imperial presidency of George W. Bush retraced and that continues even now. We have approached bankruptcy, fought wars we cannot pay for, and defrauded our urban and rural poor. Our troops include felons, and mercenaries of many nations are among our contractors, fighting on their rules or none at all. Dark influences from the American past congregate among us still. If we are a democracy, what are we to make of the palpable elements of plutocracy, oligarchy, and mounting theocracy that rule our state? How do we address the self-inflicted catastrophes that devastate our natural environment? So large is our malaise that no single writer can encompass it. We have no Emerson or Whitman among us. An institutionalized counterculture condemns individuality as archaic and depreciates intellectual values, even in the universities.

If professional philosophers shunned the oracular, Bloom gladly handled the task for them. When the *Paris Review*'s interviewer in the early 1990s had asked Bloom who edited him, Bloom replied, "No one edits. I edit. I refuse to be edited." That still seemed the case, with sad results. Officially, *Anatomy* reappraised *Anxiety*, that tract on influence—excoriated by the poet Howard Nemerov as "nonsense"— that declared all poets to be intimidated by earlier poets, and great ones to be committed to "misreadings" of predecessors as the price of originality. Bloom now called it "a brief, gnomic theory of poetry, free of all history except literary biography." He conceded that "it is a hard read, even for me," because it carried "an undercurrent of foreboding," and constituted "an attempt to forge a weapon against the gathering storm of ideology that soon would sweep away many of my students."

In conceiving *Anatomy* as a chance to look back on his work, to wed his thinking about influence from 1967 to 1982 with "more public reflections" of the past decade, he wished "to say in one place most of what I have learned to think about how influence works in imaginative literature." Now, he declared, "I define influence simply as *literary love, tempered by defense.*"

Yet it wasn't clear that much had changed for Bloom. Literary folk in the trenches knew that many poets don't care terribly about specific predecessors. Bloom countered that he'd always been talking about "an anxiety *achieved* in a literary work, whether or not its author ever felt it." So it was not necessarily a psychological state in the later poet. Even if you'd never met a writer who felt "[t]hreatened by the prospect of imaginative death, of being entirely possessed by a precursor," who felt he or she would "suffer a distinctively literary form of crisis," Bloom was not necessarily wrong in his theory. You didn't have to be Sir Karl Popper (the Austrian-born philosopher who believed a thesis must be falsifiable to be potentially true) to see the problem with Bloom's claim. When "students ask me why great writers cannot start out fresh," Bloom confided, "without any past at their back . . . I can only tell them that it just does not work that way." As fellow literary man John Hollander once remarked to the *New York Times,* Bloom was not "a particularly good explainer."

Indeed, perhaps unhelpfully for a literary scholar who'd transmuted himself into a would-be philosopher and man of ideas about everything from angels in heaven to U.S. foreign policy, Bloom was, even in his native habitat of literature, a consummate assumer. Bloom continued to posit art "as a contest for the foremost place," and *agon,* or conflict, as "a central feature of literary relationships," even though he knew that it is for some artists, and isn't for others. He still took pride in being an "incessant canonizer." He still talked of the "poet-in-a-poet," by which he meant "precisely" a poet's "daimon, his potential immortality as a poet, and so in effect his divinity."

For a critic fond of literary crushes, and celebratory of the panache with which so many American writers and thinkers took on philosophical themes—yet also eager for clear concepts, convincing evidence about links among writers, and aesthetic coherence in shaping a canon of greatness—Bloom disappointed. His literary passion came soaked in so much bile toward those who love literature differently that at times it seemed more a personality disorder than healthy judgment. When he practiced a fundamental critical task of his trade in interpreting one writer's link to another, we often got arbitrary foolishness: that Leopardi's "possession" of Dante and Petrarch was "miraculous" rather than wholly natural, or that Milton in any sensible way suffered a "humbling defeat" at the hands of Hamlet!

Such misfires recalled all those hasty introductions to the Chelsea House editions, reminding one of Bloom's high comfort with arbitrary promulgations and convenient ex cathedra salvos. In his introduction to the Zora Neale Hurston volume, Bloom had begun (perhaps dictating from his car phone to the dozen or more graduate students who helped him pump out the Chelsea House volumes), "Extra-literary factors have entered into the process of even secular canonization from Hellenistic Alexandria into the High Modernist Era of Eliot and Pound, so that it need not much dismay us if contemporary work by women and by minority writers becomes esteemed on grounds other than aesthetic."

It was a shabby lead, considering that Bloom actually liked Hurston—or at least *Their Eyes Were Watching God*. But could anyone not trapped behind elite Europhile glasses believe that "Nietzsche's vitalistic injunction, that we must try to live as though it were morning, is the implicit basis of Hurston's true religion"? The off-base philosophical conceit made as much sense as Bloom's fey judgment, in his introduction to the Rudyard Kipling volume, that "Kipling writes in the rhetorical stance of an aesthete, and is very much a Paterian in the metaphysical sense." If Bloom's instant Chelsea House intros had been his comp exams, his first book might have been called *The Flight to Another Career*.

"It may be," Bloom wrote at the outset of *Anatomy*, referring to Robert Burton's *The Anatomy of Melancholy*, which he took as a model, "that all I share with Burton is an obsessiveness somewhat parallel to his own." That seemed right. In regard to Emerson, Bloom appeared bent on the Concord sage's promise that "if the single man plant himself indomitably on his instincts, and there abide, the huge world will come round to him."

But the smart money was that Bloom might have a long wait on that score. With *Anatomy*, Bloom sounded grimly like the lit-crit equivalent of an unsteady Mideast autocrat, used to declaiming on whatever struck his fancy, oblivious as his ritual apostrophes fell on deaf ears.

One couldn't say that Bloom had been alone in acting out the distinctive moves of the distinguished literary theorist gone philosophical—ranging beyond one's disciplinary territory with a visceral pledge to interweave

Edward Said (1935–2003), University Professor of English and Comparative Literature at Columbia University for many years,
was seen as the founder and inspiration of
"postcolonial" theory.

one's personal experience and ethos, to mix scholarly erudition, sharp
judgment and political ideology. Among slightly younger literary scholars, no American intellectual more reflected a similar combination of life
and learning, or stirred greater loyalty or hatred, than Columbia University literary theorist Edward Said.

Even more than Noam Chomsky, the linguistics theorist who (we
shall see) generated comparable heat in both his academic specialty and
his part-time job as anti-imperialist watchdog, the urbane Palestinian
American activist matched every article published with a blast filed by
an enemy, every honor received with a death threat logged (the NYPD,
concerned by the threats, once installed a "panic button" in his apartment). It amounted to a birthright. For the critical brawl that Edward
Said triggered with almost every utterance—and that his magnum
opus, *Culture and Imperialism,* reignited—wasn't just a media reflex. It

exploded because Said, born in Jerusalem, raised in Cairo and later educated in America, grew up sufficiently divided in his soul to make it inevitable that he'd divide others.

If *Culture and Imperialism* sometimes read like a book patched together on flights between lecture stops, or hammered into shape during office hours, it fit with its author's experiences. Smooth organization and tone, the ambience of ivory-tower calm, would have been as false to Said's life and thinking as blazing-pink covers on an Anne Tyler novel. *Culture and Imperialism,* with its water-bug dartings between Matthew Arnold and Kuwait, its dubious leaps from Verdi's *Aida* to Desert Storm, arrived as rough-and-ready scholarship from an ongoing street fight in the humanities—a manuscript wrestled between covers by a thinker fated to play the role of world ideological referee. It proclaimed an "astonishingly direct" link between imperialist ideology and modern Western culture, and if the book reflected the man, it was because the book refracted his émigré life—bending and intellectualizing it at the same time.

The son of a wealthy Christian Arab father who sold office equipment, and a Palestinian-Lebanese mother whose father served as the first Baptist minister in Palestine, Said, born in 1935, spent his early adolescence in Cairo, amid luxury and servants, after his parents moved there in December 1947, following the UN vote to divide Palestine into Arab and Jewish states and place Jerusalem under international control. Research published by an Israeli scholar in a 1999 issue of *Commentary* magazine, a conservative Jewish monthly, showed that Said had not been a forced exile from Palestine, as he'd suggested in a memoir, but that his father, who had already been living in Cairo since 1929, left Jerusalem again with the family when Said was only two.

Having attended elite Middle Eastern schools, he finished his BA at Princeton, then earned a PhD from Harvard in comparative literature. Classically educated and reportedly able to read seven languages, Said first established his scholarly reputation as an expert on Polish-born English novelist Joseph Conrad. He next developed into an early enthusiast of French philosophical approaches to literature in *Beginnings* (1975), which won Columbia's Lionel Trilling prize. But by then the 1967 Arab-Israeli War had spurred his rediscovery of himself as an Arab. Only when his scholarly interests and personal history coalesced did Said send sparks flying.

Orientalism (1978), his breakthrough book, boldly attacked a whole tradition of European scholarship for promoting Arabic stereotypes in the service of Western imperialism. Its main thesis held that colonialism, racism and centuries of political exploitation distorted the West's image of the East. It prompted a sharp public assault from Middle East scholar Bernard Lewis, who savaged the book. Nearly three decades later, the maverick Muslim scholar Ibn Warraq similarly attacked its accuracy point by point in *Defending the West,* charging that Said had "taught an entire generation of Arabs the art of self-pity." But Said's reputation not only survived, it flourished—the book's influence spread until it created a whole field of "postcolonial" study.

Subsequent books by Said about Western views of Arabs and Islam—among them *The Question of Palestine* (1979), *Covering Islam* (1981) and *Blaming the Victims* (1988)—soon became essential texts for those who accused the West of abusing the Third World. Over the decades, Said became prominent and controversial for challenging Western policy toward Palestinians and other Arabs, and for launching postcolonialism as a perspective from which to examine earlier ideology in Western thought and literature. He also became more than an outside onlooker in Palestinian affairs, serving as a member of the Palestinian National Council (its parliament in exile) from 1977 to 1991, one of the key drafters of the Palestinian declaration of independence, and a continuing adviser to Yasser Arafat of the Palestine Liberation Organization.

To his political opponents on the right, Said acted as a smooth front man for the PLO's international agenda, its face of academic civility. A 1989 *New York* magazine profile of Said fanned that image with its title, "Arafat's Man in New York." Tel Aviv professor Edward Alexander, in an article in *Commentary,* denounced Said as "The Professor of Terror," claiming that Said justified the Palestinian National Council's alleged "spilling of blood" by supporting the murder of collaborators by the intifada, the Palestinian rebellion against Israeli occupation. But Said rejected those charges, describing himself as an independent activist who took orders from no one and opposed terrorism by Palestinians or Israelis. To his supporters on the political left, Said deserved praise as a courageous scholar who stood up for his people despite the option of an apolitical Ivy League life.

A clash only slightly less vitriolic also persisted over the "literary" Said. Traditionalist scholars regarded Said as a key influence behind reformist efforts to shake up American academe's Western canon of masterpieces, to open it (in the traditionalists' view) to mediocre writers from the Third World, to subject the "greats" to "postcolonialist" analysis. Many of those reformist scholars, devoted to such projects and angry at insinuations of Third World mediocrity, in turn celebrated Said as an inspiration.

Culture and Imperialism alternately pleased and infuriated many of these people. A rambling meditation on the links between the two title concepts, it sought above all to demonstrate that imperialist ideologies lurk where we least expect them. Said began by reminding readers of Western stereotypes about the East, "the notions about bringing civilization to primitive or barbaric peoples, the disturbingly familiar ideas about flogging or death or extended punishment being required when 'they' misbehaved or became rebellious." As Said paraphrased the thinking, Eastern types "deserved to be ruled" because " 'they' were not like 'us.' " But Said confessed that he left out something crucial in *Orientalism*: the story of Third World resistance to imperialism, which ultimately led to decolonialization: "Never was it the case that the imperial encounter pitted an active Western intruder against a supine or inert non-Western native; there was always some form of active resistance."

Said told that story in *Culture and Imperialism* by first examining individual works of the "Western empire"—restricted there to nineteenth-century Britain and France, and twentieth-century America—focusing on writers such as Rudyard Kipling and Albert Camus, then moving on to "resistance" heroes such as Frantz Fanon. But instead of asking readers to concentrate on obvious material, such as Conrad's direct treatment of imperialism in *Heart of Darkness* and *Nostromo*, Said urged them to recognize far subtler cases in which imperialist assumptions "infiltrated" culture: Jane Austen's scant attention to Sir Thomas Bertram's Antiguan slave plantation in *Mansfield Park*—even though it supported the "poise and beauty" of his home—or the "threatening presence" of Bertha Mason, Rochester's deranged West Indian wife, in *Jane Eyre*.

According to Said, "the empire functions for much of the European nineteenth century as a codified, if only marginally visible, presence in fiction, very much like the servants in grand households." But Said wanted astute readers to confront the blindness of great novelists to their imperialist prejudices, their obliviousness to the perspective of subjugated colonials. Even major critics whom Said otherwise admired, such as Raymond Williams, faced the charge that they "simply ignore imperialism." Yet Said did not believe that the novel or culture "caused" imperialism. Rather, nineteenth-century British fiction helped "keep the empire more or less in place," even if, like much culture, it was "somehow excused for its role." As a result, the nineteenth-century novel and imperialism ended up "unthinkable without each other."

Conservative literary scholars eager to trash Said found that he made matters difficult for them, staking out a middle position between traditional, Eurocentric dismissal of the Third World and the rejectionist stance of so-called nativist scholars who wanted to eliminate anybody who wasn't them. Said's own moderation about nineteenth-century fiction stemmed from his insistence that one shouldn't throw out art with the artist's ideology. Imperialist masterpieces, he believed, retained their intrinsic richness—that's what made them masterpieces—even if we should rightly read them "contrapuntally," or against a broad historical context that balances aesthetic and political values. Indeed, Said remained inordinately fond of Kipling's *Kim,* the classic boy's tale by the preeminent voice of British imperialism, which dovetailed with his view that "European culture was no less complex, rich or interesting for having supported most aspects of the imperial experience."

Thus, in an interview published in one of many secondary collections either of, or about, his work, *Edward Said: A Critical Reader,* Said rejected Nigerian novelist Chinua Achebe's view of Conrad as simply a racist whose attitudes Achebe, a black man, reviled. "There's no reason for me to perform acts of amputation on myself," said Said, "intellectual, spiritual or aesthetic, simply because in the experience of other people from the Third World, a black novelist from Nigeria like Achebe . . . can make my Proust or Conrad into someone who is only despicable." It was a sensible position, part of the complex commitment to worldliness in interpretation that remained Said's signature as a literary theorist. To his credit, he read passionately and bravely, counterposing "resistance" writers like Trinidadian C. L. R. James with imperialist interpreters of the West, yet spurning ugly forms of nationalism and separatism. He deftly applied insights from his mentors—Foucault's axiom that power politics always shapes societal institutions like the prison, the hospital and sex itself; Gramsci's notion of how a society exercises hegemony (subtle and often unvoiced cultural control over its citizens' imaginations)—and applied them to broad West-East issues formerly outside normal Western academic scrutiny. Occasionally criticizing Arab totalitarianism, he challenged everyone to read fiction in the most comprehensive manner possible—as the product of the entire "earthly context" in which a writer operated. In that expansive tone, his philosophical aspiration spoke for itself.

But Said contained multitudes, and not all deserved praise. To his shame, he exaggerated wildly when describing the First World's view of the Third, and constantly attributed the most racist possible view of Arabs to the West. In an era when American universities routinely supported the study of scores of world cultures, and long before the post-9/11 reassessments of civilizational clash, he falsely claimed that a "prevailing Western consensus" regarded "the Third World as an atrocious nuisance, a culturally and politically inferior place." Said might deserve some credit for that pluralism, but his refusal to acknowledge that establishment goodwill helped his cause—just as it fueled his climb to star status at Columbia—diminished him and damaged his credibility.

However, it was when Said discussed the Persian Gulf War, the Arab-Israeli conflict or American interventionism—which he did frequently—that he abandoned evenhanded approaches entirely, ignored evidence opposed to his beliefs and scattered about one-sided bromides. Seething with anger over the diaspora of Palestinian Arabs, and the American foreign policy he often blamed for it, he stated, for instance, that the "entire premise" of American foreign policy in the first Iraq war "was colonial: that a small Third World dictatorship, nurtured and supported by the West, did not have the right to challenge America, which was white and superior." Lost in the logic were Iraqi atrocities, the international coalition behind the United States in *that* war, the wishes of Iraq's nonwhite neighbors, the endless face-saving offers made to Saddam Hussein, and any number of other factors. It was a view that would be heard once again—in the voice of no less than Nelson Mandela—a decade later as the U.S. geared up for its second Iraq war.

Said's attitudes toward Israel remained so hostile that even his core interpretive principles in music criticism, one of his chief side activities, became contradictory. Many pages of *Culture and Imperialism* put forth the argument that Verdi's *Aida*, like any nineteenth-century European work of art, retained the "inflection and traces" of the ideologically contaminated artist who conceived it. He asserted that "the embarrassment of *Aida* is finally that it is not so much about but of imperial domination." Yet in a later *London Review of Books* article titled "Wagner in Israel," Said ridiculed as "ludicrous" the notion that Wagner's music was inseparable from his anti-Semitism.

The irony of *Culture and Imperialism,* but also a defining feature of Said's intense embodiment of the high academic expander of philosophy, was that the bracing intellectual passion that enabled Said to look afresh at a writer like Austen—to understand her attitudes without accepting her imperialist baggage—couldn't reach the bitter part that ruled his political reasoning. "No one today is purely one thing . . . ," he wrote on his last page. "It is more rewarding—and more difficult—to think concretely and sympathetically, contrapuntally, about others than only about 'us.' But this also means not trying to rule others, not trying to classify them or put them in hierarchies."

Said didn't seem willing to extend his conciliatory spirit to Israelis and Americans, however much he offered it to imperialist novelists. But as he came to realize late in his career, his black-and-white vision of West and East—and particularly the West's supposed humiliation of the East—had become unquestioned gospel for young postcolonialist scholars. It was not the happiest of legacies for a thinker who liked to say that he rejected all "totalizing narratives." Conscious of the situation he'd created, he wrote cannily in *The World, the Text, and the Critic,* with just a hint of self-rebuke, that criticism "is most itself and, if the paradox can be tolerated, most unlike itself, at the moment it starts turning into organized dogma."

THE POLITICAL THEORISTS

Francis Fukuyama's first book, *The End of History and the Last Man,* a bold explanation of the triumph of liberal democracy over communism, found itself anointed at birth as part of an idiosyncratic tradition in American philosophical nonfiction: the intellectual book that lands on America's front pages because its content and provocative title permits it to be sloganized, simplified, sensationalized and sold to better bookstores everywhere.

Did Charles Reich's predicted *Greening of America* ever take place? How gauche of you to ask! Just raising the question suggested a degree of cultural naïveté. Had the title phenomenon of Allan Bloom's much bemoaned *The Closing of the American Mind* continued despite his warning, or been halted by covert action during the Reagan administration and those of the two Bushes? Again, the appropriate response seems a smile, not an inquiry. Given his provocative title, Fukuyama joined this crew by birthright.

Back in the summer of 1989, Fukuyama, then deputy director of policy planning at the State Department, had published a sixteen-page article titled "The End of History?" in the *National Interest,* the influential neoconservative journal. Catching the Beltway crowd in the summer of its fading discontent, when Washington's "Cold Warriors" grew slaphappy cheering the liberal West's string of victories over the crumbling East, Fukuyama detected some capital-*H* History in breaking lower-case history: free elections in eastern Europe, expanding glasnost in the Soviet Union, rising reform in China. "What we may be witnessing," Fukuyama wrote, "is not just the end of the cold war, or the passing of a particular era of postwar history, but the end of history as such: that is, the end point of mankind's ideological evolution and the universalization of Western liberal democracy as the final point of human government."

Fukuyama was not making the dubious suggestion that all world events would cease at five p.m. Eastern time on a particular date. Rather, he placed himself in the grand tradition of speculative philosophers of history such as Hegel and Marx, who thought history slouched toward an end or goal, and would eventually reach it: the liberal state for Hegel, a classless, communist society for Marx. Invoking Hegel by name—itself an unusual and intimidating move within the social science precincts of Washington policy journals—Fukuyama contended that political ideology in the late 1980s had reached its final evolutionary point of progress: liberal democracy. Mankind in general had come to the conclusion that all the traditional alternatives to liberal democracy—including hereditary monarchy, fascism and socialism—didn't work, and only liberal democracy enjoyed legitimacy as a system of government. As a Harvard PhD in government and Kremlinologist, Fukuyama plainly recognized that theses beginning "The End of . . ." signaled the decisiveness rewarded by media but frowned upon by cautious academics. Daniel Bell's classic *The End of Ideology* established the device decades ago, to be followed by George Leonard's *The End of Sex,* Bill McKibben's *The End of Nature* and similarly pumped-up teleological tomes.

Equally clear was that Fukuyama boasted a fine pedigree for his line of work. As an undergraduate at Cornell, he'd lived in Telluride House, where no less than Bloom himself ran the philosophical show. After brief intellectual flirtations in New Haven and Paris, where Fukuyama rejected the fashionable thinking of literary theorists Paul de Man, Jacques Derrida and Roland Barthes, he'd ended up doing his PhD on Soviet foreign policy in the Middle East. Fukuyama's article predictably excited Washington policy intellectuals and poli-sci junkies around the country. Translations appeared in Paris, Rome, Copenhagen and Tokyo. Intellectuals struggled to get on the record about it. *Time* and *Newsweek* provided space, and the BBC moved in with cameras. Neoconservatives in particular perked up. They knew the title was really "We Won! And It's a Pretty Profound, Intellectually Deep and Last-Forever Victory at That!"

Yet criticisms abounded. "At last, self-congratulation raised to the status of philosophy!" sneered Christopher Hitchens, while others accused Fukuyama of slighting the Third World, celebrating too early and misreading Hegel. Even a few conservatives questioned Fukuyama's complacency, and regretted his Bloom-like lack of enthusiasm for the consumerist culture that had won. Probably there was only one thing all hands could agree on: history would not end until someone had signed up Fukuyama for a book. Predictably, the question mark came off the title, possibly pried loose by the publisher's marketing director. And Fukuyama, with still more breaking history in his corner in the Year 1 A.G. (After Gorbachev), forcefully attempted to answer critics and flesh out his thesis. He widened his political and philosophical playing field, drawing on everything from the economies of Asia's "Four Tigers" (Hong Kong, Taiwan, South Korea and Singapore) to an elaborate use of Nietzsche's notion of the "last man."

The result called to mind a line from Nietzsche that Fukuyama understandably didn't quote: "The historian looks backward. In the end, he also believes backward." Or, as German philosopher Friedrich Schlegel opined still earlier, the historian is "a prophet in reverse." When Fukuyama elaborated on some of the concrete causes of liberal democracy's run of victories, he illuminated. But when he slid into philosophical overdrive by simply assuming that the human desire for recognition plays a major role in history, or signed on to the necessary, progressive "directionality" of history just because it happened to go in one direction on one occasion, he disappointed. Fukuyama stood by his article's views about liberal democracy, seeing two "visible" hands guiding history to liberal democracy's triumph.

The first was "modern natural science," which Fukuyama saw as "cumulative" and proceeding "according to certain definite rules laid down not by man, but by nature and nature's laws." In a provocative argument, Fukuyama contended that science, through its technological impact on the military preparedness of nations, and its economic impact on their production capabilities, eventually pushed them in the direction of capitalism and structural identity with one another. Yet he conceded that modern science alone couldn't explain the boom in democracy, since technologically advanced capitalism has often coexisted with political authoritarianism, as in Meiji Japan. Plainly wishing to avoid Marxist-style reduction of man to mere economic creature, Fukuyama turned for his second visible hand to Hegel's "non-materialist" concept of man's "struggle for recognition."

That desire "to be recognized as a human being . . . as a being with a certain worth or dignity," wrote Fukuyama, arose out of the part of the soul that Plato called "*thymos*," or "spiritedness," which fuels such ordinary emotions as anger, pride and shame. This "irrational" desire was, according to Fukuyama, the "motor of history." And advanced industrialization, especially through its usual concomitant of universal education, tended to "liberate" that desire "among poorer and less educated people," driving them toward liberal democracy. Fukuyama concluded the book by reflecting on the quality of life in "liberal democracy." He focused on Nietzsche's notion of the typical figure in a modern democracy as a "last man," the nihilistic victim of a slave morality that keeps him from wanting to be recognized as greater than others. He suggested that a vibrant liberal democracy requires citizens with greater ambition than that, even though the desire for unequal recognition, if it gets out of hand, can spark the kind of "prestige battles" that originally led mankind into war.

The End of History deserved better than the reductionism its title invited. A lucid writer, Fukuyama won strong credit for his consistent clarity, and neoconservatives celebrated the book as they had the article: George Gilder called it "awesome . . . profoundly realistic and important . . . supremely timely and cogent." Fukuyama brought light to an area (anywhere within a thousand miles of Hegel) thought by professional philosophers to produce Absolute Obscurity more than Hegel's Absolute itself. Yet Fukuyama failed to convince in several respects. He tended, like many authors of broad-brush treatises, to exaggerate whenever it served his purpose. He stated, for instance, that liberal democracy "remains the only coherent political aspiration that spans different regions and cultures around the globe." In fact, socialism and Islamic fundamentalism also fit that description—they'd simply been less successful in winning power. Similarly, he asserted that "recognition" is the "psychological ground for political virtues like courage, public-spiritedness, and justice," a premise that accounted for its huge importance in his system. But one wondered whether Mother Teresa, or many of the faceless do-gooders of our world—the altruists who toil for Doctors Without Borders, or the Red Cross—would agree.

Fukuyama's inferences also leaned toward the careless. He seemed to feel that it followed automatically from liberal democracy's success after 1989 that a "remarkable consensus concerning the legitimacy of liberal democracy as a system of government had emerged throughout the world." Yet the inference was no more automatic than a similar inference would have been, in the late 1930s, that a consensus had emerged in favor of the legitimacy of dictatorship. International developments early in the twenty-first century hardly counted in favor of his thesis. As Fukuyama acknowledged, the attribution of "legitimacy" to a system of government remained a highly sophisticated one, "legitimacy" being, in his words, "a relative concept that exists in people's subjective perceptions." Many eastern Europeans opposed to communism in the 1990s were more accurately seen as loathing communism's consequences on a visceral level than as understanding or loving democracy on a theoretical level. To presume that recent events had transformed them all into steadfast Thomas Jeffersons was a leap not of faith, but of theoretical jingoism.

Indeed, Fukuyama's whole position appeared flawed by a fatal contradiction. On the one hand, he acknowledged that "consensus" judgments, such as the widespread acceptance of liberal democracy's legitimacy that he claimed existed, were time and culture bound. On the other hand, he recognized throughout *The End of History* that looming environmental dangers, such as global warming, might threaten mankind or individual nations. Yet he never put the two thoughts together. As a result, he ignored in that book how crises in man's circumstances might leave liberal democracy a few steps short of the finish line.

Suppose, for instance, that global warming or nuclear winter threatened mankind, or even a particular country, with disaster? In such a continuing crisis, would citizens prefer the endlessly argumentative, glacially slow process of democracy over a form of benevolent authoritarianism? Did it even take extreme examples to make the point? In argument-weary Russia after the fall of the Soviet Union, exhausted democracy boosters watched Boris Yeltsin govern by decree with less public resistance than Mikhail Gorbachev encountered trying to emphasize parliamentary approval. Vladimir Putin's initially popular authoritarianism demonstrated the same countervailing reality. Indeed, the Chinese/Russian model of successfully mixing economic liberalism with political fascism twenty years after Fukuyama's greatest hit effectively undermined it. Fukuyama admitted as much in a 2011 *Wall Street Journal* essay, "Is China Next?," in which he answered "No" to the question of whether that year's Arab uprisings for democracy would reach China, citing the government's success there in raising incomes.

Fukuyama, in short, failed to acknowledge that his confident closing of the casebook on liberal democracy belied his own acceptance of the way specific cultural contexts govern evaluative judgments. It was exactly there that the dual meaning of "end"—its sense as "goal," and its other sense as the "chronological halting of events"—folded in on itself. Liberal democracy couldn't be the end of history, even in the sense of "goal," because history as a succession of events hadn't ended, and a culture had the right to change its mind. But Fukuyama's stab at reinvesting history with grand purpose naturally appealed to late-twentieth-century Americans short on eternal verities, to intellectuals and philosophy buffs up for decisiveness in the wake of Rorty's revolution, and ordinary folks fond of crisp segmenting of time, the kind who made a best-selling bumper sticker out of "Life's a bitch, and then you die."

That thought may be cheapened by its pop vulgarity, but it fits with a venerable, secular and skeptical Western tradition that assumes history possesses no innate meaning or internally designed pattern—a view more respectably expressed in Lord Chesterfield's remark that history is "only a confused heap of facts," or Gibbon's that it's "little more than the register of the crimes, follies and misfortunes of mankind." In an era with few comforts from official theology or philosophy, Fukuyama's political-philosophy equivalent of "Beauty and the Beast" carried the natural appeal of any fairy tale. Yet Fukuyama, of all people, might have wanted to recall the most famous person to say, with gusto, that "Whether you like it or not, history is on our side." That would have been Nikita "We will bury you" Khrushchev, who ended up just another out-of-work Hegelian leader.

As things turned out, Fukuyama proved his own best counter-example. In subsequent books, such as *The Great Disruption, Our Posthuman Future* and *State-Building*—the second of which argued that liberal democracy would mutate under the pressure of the biotechnology revolution—Fukuyama himself evolved into a more conventional and less grandly philosophical policy analyst. By the time he published *America at the Crossroads: Democracy, Power, and the Neoconservative Legacy* (2006), both right-wingers and left-wingers wanted his head on a plate for—oops!—changing his mind about a few things.

Despite having cosigned a 1999 open letter from the Project for a New American Century advocating strong action against Iraq, and a post-2001 letter stating that "any strategy aimed at the elimination of terrorism and its sponsors must include a determined effort to remove Saddam Hussein," Fukuyama, by then a professor at the School of Advanced International Studies at Johns Hopkins University, judged the war to bring democracy to Iraq a mistake.

He still believed in core principles of neoconservatism—that the "internal character of regimes matters," that force must sometimes be used for moral purposes, that ambitious social-engineering agendas often go wrong, and that the ability of "international law and institutions to achieve either security or justice" is limited—but he thought they'd been misapplied in Iraq. Unilateral preemptive force, aggressive nation building and indiscriminate promotion of democracy didn't work. They needed, he argued, to be balanced by a "realistic Wilsonianism," a use of "soft power," cultural influence, rather than hard weapons. We also needed to stop making allegedly foolish inferences drawn by the Bush administration from what happened in Germany after World War II, or Poland after 1989, in judging what was possible for a country with barely any democratic consciousness and history. Fukuyama could, as he put it, "no longer support" the neoconservative's view of where history should be heading, even if it meant crossing swords with former allies such as columnist Charles Krauthammer, who had welcomed *The End of History* as "bold, lucid, scandalously brilliant." By 2011, with his publication of *The Origins of Political Order: From Prehuman Times to the French Revolution*—the 585-page first volume of a promised two-book account of why societies end up forming states, and why some states succeed and others fail—Fukuyama appeared to be tilting, à la Jared Diamond in *Guns, Germs, and Steel,* toward an empirical rather than philosophical account of political history, drawing on findings in sociology, biology and economics.

Fukuyama's big "end of history" splash in America the Philosophical showed that Harvard credentialism retained its force even in a philosophical culture attracting expanders ("interlopers" being a nasty word) from many directions. Another representative, as influential within the academic world of political theory as Fukuyama proved to be in policy circles, was Dennis F. Thompson, a Harvard political scientist soon to become a leading on-site orchestrator of greater concrete political thought than offered by Rawls. An early instance came in his book *Political Ethics and Public Office,* a study of ethical judgments about political action that showed an atypical grasp, for a political theorist, of the real political world.

For media types, professorial political philosophers of the Rawls/ Nozick variety exerted no impact on their cerebral lives. TV talkers stole their sharpest wisdom about the link between ethics and politics not from great tomes of political thought but from compendia of one-liners. On the idealism side of the ledger, you might patch in Jefferson, writing that "the whole art of government consists in being honest." On the lighter side, one might sample the decidedly less immortal Simon Cameron (1799–1889), perpetrator of the classic maxim "An honest politician is one who, when he is bought, will stay bought."

The explanation fell into no-brainer territory. The vast punditocracy (the columnists and Sunday talk-show hosts, and later the bloggers and

Tweeters) didn't have time for complicated political philosophy. Even when a classic political philosopher got off a provocative line—like Plato's proviso in *The Republic* that "if anyone at all is to have the privilege of lying, the rulers of the state should be such persons"—the danger was that everyone knew it came with a complex political philosophy attached, and someone might call you on the attachment. Far better to pepper one's commentary with irreverent riffs on government like Henry Kissinger's twist on an old Army motto: "The illegal we do immediately. The unconstitutional takes a little longer."

That said, Thompson tested the traditional resistance. He represented the ongoing supplanting of professional philosophers in areas putatively their own—such as classic political philosophy—by intellectuals from other disciplines. Thompson proved willing to get his hands dirty with heaps of empirical fact, but remained committed to broad philosophical explanation. He recognized, of course, that the polis occasionally resembles a circus (already a win for realism over the starchier conceptions of Rawlsian political theory). In one choice anecdote, he related how leaders in the Tennessee senate, following a political scandal, tried to institute an ethics code. Opponents, reluctant to fight reform, found a better way. When the code came to the floor, a resistant senator proposed the Ten Commandments and Golden Rule as a substitute. He figured no local legislator would dare vote against them. Politics being flexible, a compromise was reached that could accommodate both Moses and no-show jobs. Reported Thompson, "From Article IV with its detailed procedural rules, the document jumped immediately to Article V, which read in its entirety: 'Thou shalt have no other gods before me.'"

Thompson's book made clear why serious analyses of the tie between ethics, said to be unyielding, and politics, wedded to the almighty compromise, presented a challenge. Appreciating those realities, he still rejected the view that "moral talk" had no place in government thinking. He worked out his theory by emphasizing "the mutual dependency of ethics and democracy." One early focus was the traditional problem of "dirty hands"—the violation by officials of ordinary moral rules (such as truth telling) in the service of the public good. Ranging over such landmarks as Machiavelli, JFK's deceptions during the Cuban missile crisis and the stealthy moves built into nuclear deterrence, Thompson argued for as much public discussion as possible, concluding that "partly democratic dirty hands are less bad than just plain dirty hands."

He then resourcefully moved on to the related problem of "many hands"—the way government policies often appear to have no specific author, raising the question of whether moral responsibility can be attributed to an organization. Rejecting simpleminded solutions such as the "hierarchical" model ("The buck stops here"), Thompson stood fast for intelligent methods of locating appropriate moral agents within organizations that do wrong (a kind of hunt that doesn't give the government problems when the corruption lurks in multinational corporations). The discussion there touched, for instance, on J. Robert Oppenheimer and his responsibility for nuclear weapons.

Grabbing on to an issue that became only more important as the Clinton-Lewinsky follies produced their progeny in subsequent years (Governors Eliot Spitzer, Mark Sanford and David Paterson among them), he then explored "The Private Lives of Public Officials." Unlike many media commentators, Thompson contended that we can't easily separate the privacy of public officials from the privacy of ordinary citizens. While acknowledging that the privacy of public officials "should receive less respect," he argued that "by respecting the privacy of public officials, we may also encourage greater respect for the privacy of citizens."

Repeatedly, covering such topics as organizational crime, paternalism and the ethics of legislators and social experiments, Thompson articulated subtleties in the logic of political ethics that journalistic commentary papered over. Though not the first scholar to write extensively on those issues, he brought more consistent philosophical focus to many of them. In a chapter on "Legislative Ethics," he noted that the ethical demands on a legislator clash with certain "generic" requirements of morality: "Ethics demands a general perspective," he wrote, "but legislators are also obligated to look after their own particular constituents. Ethics requires autonomous judgment, but legislators are also expected to defer to electoral decisions." A similar incoherency, Thompson pointed out, attached to the idea of "conflict of interest" on the part of an official—that rare slab of conceptual red meat that lures reporters. Expressing a view common among thinkers about ethics, yet virtually unexplored by journalists, Thompson sketched the vagueness of "conflict of interest" as an ethical notion:

> By itself, the idea of conflict of interest in democratic representation is paradoxical. To avoid a conflict of interest, legislators are not supposed to do anything that would appear to further their own interests. Yet, as Madison emphasized, a legislator

must share "a communion of interest" with his constituents. A legislator cannot adequately represent the interest of constituents without also representing some of his or her own. The most common way of resolving this paradox has been to say that a conflict of interest exists only when the representative would personally benefit from some piece of legislation in a way or to a degree that other people would not. In practice, however, virtually the only conduct such a rule would exclude is a member's voting on a controversy about his or her own seat in the legislature.

In the years following *Political Ethics and Public Office,* Thompson's supplanting of political philosophers fond of "clean hands"—freedom from too much empirical detail—took many forms. As founding director of the University Center for Ethics in the Professions, he made that Harvard think tank a gathering point for those committed to political thought that confronts political institutions as they actually operate. As a consultant, he mixed it up with the Joint Ethics Committee of the South African Parliament, the U.S. Office of Personnel Management and the American Medical Association. As an author, he kept his eye on the ball, publishing a timely tome called *Just Elections: Creating a Fair Electoral Process in the United States,* which, in typical Thompson style, applied justice theory to the nitty-gritty of elections: redistricting, term limits, ballot designs and other details often beneath the notice of political philosophers. Ironically, his supplanting of official philosophers won a sort of bureaucratic confirmation. By 2003, his academic title—in Harvard's John F. Kennedy School of Government—read "Alfred North Whitehead Professor of Political Philosophy." Whitehead, the great founder of "process" philosophy, probably would have regretted seeing his name grace a process by which the Harvard philosophy department ceded priority over political philosophy that mattered.

In America the Philosophical, projects about politics and ethics expanded to law faculties as well. To be sure, legal giants such as Holmes, Benjamin Cardozo and Pound had always functioned as philosophers of law in their broader work. More pronounced in recent decades, though, as America the Philosophical expanded, was the sight of law professors stretching to wrap their minds around political and legal concepts once largely in philosophy's demesne. Early in the twentieth century, Josiah

Royce, a giant of the Harvard philosophy department, had published *The Philosophy of Loyalty*. In the changing intellectual milieu of America nearly one hundred years later, the key book on the subject came from a Columbia law professor, George Fletcher.

In *Loyalty*, subtitled *An Essay on the Morality of Relationships*, Fletcher made no pretense of approaching the subject through legal technicalities. He wrote as a philosopher—and a man. The sophisticated second-generation son of a Hungarian immigrant, and a graceful writer awarded an American Bar Association Silver Gavel Award for his very public-oriented law book, *A Crime of Self-Defense* (about Bernhard Goetz, a New Yorker whose shooting of muggers became a cause célèbre), Fletcher explained in his preface that if he'd been asked about loyalty even a decade earlier, he'd have vilified the concept, as many of his liberal friends still did. He might have identified its role in patriotism "with the breast-beating zealots who threatened my generation with those billboards, 'America: Love it or Leave it,' " and seen an ethic of loyalty as smacking of "the rhetoric of anti-Communist fanaticism."

Over his last decade of teaching jurisprudence, however, Fletcher said he'd grown skeptical of what he called "impartial ethics." As he reconsidered the axioms of his moral outlook on life, he evolved into a believer that "the normal commitments of our lives—expressed as 'loyalties'—provide a sounder basis for the moral life than an Enlightenment ideal." Did he mean the kind of grand sentiment expressed by Albert Camus's famous declaration, "I believe in justice, but I will defend my mother before justice"? What about the German people's loyalty to Hitler?

Fletcher attempted a revival of loyalty, not just as a sensible ethical goal but as a foundation for ethical life itself. He began with an intriguing observation: "The exemplar of the marketplace has conquered neighboring arenas. Today we think about relatives, employers, religious groups, and nations the way we think about companies that supply us with other products and services. If we don't like what we are getting, we consider the competition. Conventional free-market theory teaches that leaving is a virtue." More troubling, Fletcher pointed out, is the creeping consensus that "leaving has become the increasingly popular option. In the marketplace, where all that is at stake is the performance of the product or the quality of the service, the best thing to do is leave—that is, to find the competitor who better supplies the needed good."

Shrewd, wide-ranging, edgy, it was philosophy, all right—just not the kind that would let a counterexample here and there obstruct a general truth obvious to many. Implying that yet another revival of greed in American life bore the blame, Fletcher asserted that "shifting loyalties" was "an increasingly common way of coping with a weak friendship, a shaky marriage, a religious community that takes the wrong stand on an important issue, or a nation that has come into the hands of the wrong political party."

To counter that belief, Fletcher set out to describe the kind of "loyalty" he considered vital glue for any community that hoped to survive as more than a tankful of barracuda. Analytic at heart, Fletcher sought to shape the concept before moving to its applications in the public sphere. He observed that the "minimal demand of loyalty is maintenance of the relationship, which requires the rejection of alternatives that undermine the principal bond." He also conceded that loyalty can become overwrought, and quickly noted that "blind adherence to any object of loyalty—whether friend, lover or nation—converts loyalty into idolatry." But while loyalty comes with "a built-in element of contingency," it also brings the promise of altruism and stability, and can be distinguished, in the best of cases, from idolatry. The important question, Fletcher insisted, and one that he rightly permitted to dominate his book, was behavioral and moral: "If we do act loyally, do we do so as a matter of inclination or habit or by virtue of a well-grounded duty of loyalty?"

Ideally, Fletcher concluded, in a Kantian vein characteristic of his thought, our act is a well-grounded duty. Loyalty, for Fletcher, had to grow out of the "historical self" and its experiences—one couldn't just suddenly declare loyalty to a stranger and expect it to count for much. Loyalty sometimes implied "merely the avoidance of betrayal and sometimes a deeper, romantic unity sustained by rituals expressed in patriotism, religious devotion and erotic love." Once he established his conceptual footing, Fletcher moved on to more complicated territory: loyalty in ancient Greek drama; the checkered history of treason; the distinction between patriotism and loyalty; and finally, returning to his field, the implications of loyalty for privacy law and the line of U.S. cases regarding loyalty oaths, the Pledge of Allegiance and flag burning.

It was a bravura performance, despite Fletcher's writing it in tenured safety. While he remained an analyst with a taste for clarity, he also came across as a European soul. Existentialist blood raced through his sentences, and a sure Pascalian credo—that the heart always has its reasons—never lay far from his thought. As he wrote in one chapter, "There comes a point at which logic runs dry and one must plant one's loyalty in the simple fact that that is MY friend, MY club, MY alma mater, MY nation." One could also hear between the lines: My check may come to a law professor, but when I write as a philosopher, I write with my whole soul, my whole body, my whole heart and experience.

That bent continued with Fletcher's *Defending Humanity: When Force Is Justified and Why* (2008), cowritten with his Columbia colleague Jens David Ohlin. The book's chief argument held that the "legitimate defense" concept in the UN Charter frees states to use force against other sovereign states even without the twin justifications of self-defense or Security Council approval. But one could be forgiven for detecting its motivation in the moral belief that decent states must intervene when dictators seriously violate the human rights of their own people, a doctrine President Obama later appealed to in justifying U.S. intervention in Libya. As Thompson seemed determined to wed political theory with the nitty-gritty of politics, Fletcher permitted himself to channel his moral emotions through his philosophical and legal expertise, in this case his mastery of international law. His voice reverberated: I'm philosophizing here, and don't anyone try to stop me.

A fourth and final arrogator of the prerogatives of American political philosophy in the late-twentieth and early-twenty-first century took his paycheck as a theorist of linguistics, but that didn't stop MIT's Noam Chomsky from becoming the most controversial of the lot. He illustrated, with apologies to psychologists, the mind-brain problem in contemporary philosophy. As a brain, he stood as the patriarch of the Chomskyan revolution in linguistics, the man whose revolutionary *Syntactic Structures* (1957) stampeded the behaviorism and historical philology that ruled the field before him with a vision of "transformational grammar," his comprehensive theory of how innate language abilities are not so much learned as biologically "grown." But another Chomsky was known for producing complex tomes of radical political analysis that ambitiously dissect global problems, always in solidarity with the downtrodden.

Chomsky the mind, in his chosen hobby as radical political commentator, author, and pop-off, was viewed by many as a fanatical anti-American who could find American or Israeli culpability behind almost any misdeed in the universe. Chomsky could also be famously captious, self-righteous and splenetic—prone to belittle the integrity and mental ability of those who disagreed with him, to exaggerate points and impute foul motives to others. In one pamphlet, *Media Con-*

trol: The Spectacular Achievements of Propaganda, Chomsky wrote that "the last legal victory for labor was really 1935," that the media's depiction of international politics had "only the remotest relation to reality," that everybody "goosestepped on command" during the first Iraq war. Regarding that war, Chomsky added, "No reason was given for going to war that could not be refuted by a literate teenager in about two minutes. That again is the hallmark of a totalitarian culture." He did not follow up with a quote from any of the Kuwaitis who had been butchered, raped or mutilated by Saddam Hussein's troops.

Long mostly absent from mass-media outlets—because of ideological censorship, according to him; because of his terrible judgment, according to others—Chomsky combined an extraordinary generosity toward humble folk who sought his counsel with a take-no-prisoners venom toward professionals who clashed with him in print. Considering the dimensions of his fame and influence—in one survey, the Arts and Humanities Citation Index listed him as the only living figure among the ten most-quoted humanist thinkers of all time, ahead of Hegel and Cicero and gaining on Freud—it was odd that no one before Robert Barsky bothered to publish a straightforward biography of him. Studies of Chomsky's thought abounded—from John Lyons's early monograph in the Penguin Modern Masters series to the eight-volume Routledge collection of articles in its Critical Assessments series—but not nuts-and-bolts accounts of his life.

Barsky's effort, *Noam Chomsky: A Life of Dissent,* might have been labeled a hagiography in the days when people believed in living saints. The term "apolography" made more sense, because Barsky, then an assistant professor of English at the University of Western Ontario, had invented a new genre. Not only did he take Chomsky's side on every issue (Chomsky's work contained "some of the most accurate analyses of this century"), but his routine way of repelling any intellectual challenge to his hero involved yanking Chomsky in—courtesy of snippets from interview transcripts with the all-knowing one—to answer the charge.

Thus when Barsky introduced Chomsky's controversial debate with B. F. Skinner about behaviorism, he immediately brought in Chomsky to describe Skinner's work as a "fraud." When Barsky contrasted Chomsky's activism with Irving Howe's alleged lack of similar commitment, Chomsky beamed down and nastily attributed Howe's move toward moderate socialism to his "bitter resentment of the student movement and the New Left for failing to pay enough attention to him." Barsky's defenses of Chomsky's long-standing affiliation with MIT, despite its Defense Department contracts, and Chomsky's concern with the free-speech rights of French Holocaust denier Robert Faurisson, proved even more embarrassing.

Anyone inclined to view Chomsky's irascibility in the face of criticism as a factor merely in his political life needed only to turn to Randy Allen Harris's *The Linguistics Wars,* which recorded bloodbaths in that discipline. Barsky echoed Chomsky's belittling of Harris's book, dubbing it "gossipy." In fact, Harris drew on scores of sources and interviews, while Barsky's book strung together Chomsky's phoneme bites with a clip-job approach. To be sure, fellow linguists knew Chomsky best. In a *New York Times* article, Berkeley's George Lakoff remarked, "He's a genius, and he fights dirty when he argues." According to Robin Lakoff, Chomsky thought he was "in possession of the Truth, and that everybody should listen when he speaks." Barsky, certainly, listened like a good apparatchik. Late in the book, he observed, absurdly, "Once one has assimilated Chomsky's objections and grasped his criteria for identifying what constitutes valid academic research, it becomes difficult to credit much of what is proposed as serious scholarship in the social sciences and the humanities."

Barsky's main service came in setting out the intensely "left-libertarian" milieu of Chomsky's upbringing in Philadelphia, particularly the history and positions of such Jewish groups as Avukah and Hashomer Hatzair. As he detailed the various stations of Chomsky's upward trek in prestige academe—from University of Pennsylvania student, to member of Harvard's Society of Fellows in 1951, to full professor at MIT in 1961 at the age of thirty-three—Barsky also detailed the development of Chomsky's activist career. Reading about Chomsky's intense teenage reaction to the fall of Barcelona during the Spanish Civil War, and his enduring love affair with anarchism, one absorbed a crucial truth way before Barsky stated it: "Unlike the many members of the left who captivated him as a young man—such as Dwight Macdonald, George Orwell, and Bertrand Russell—Chomsky himself did not come to left-libertarian or anarchist thinking as a result of his disillusionment with liberal thought. He quite literally began there."

He also seemed to end up there. Sure enough, even before the smoke and ash stopped belching from Ground Zero, before loved ones had even finished with funeral services for "vaporized" victims, Chomsky produced *9-11.* From the imperial safety of his suburban Massachusetts home, from the cushy protectorate of his lifetime perch at one of the Pentagon's top academic partners, Chomsky informed readers that "[w]e should not forget that the U.S. itself is a leading terrorist state." He maintained that Osama bin Laden had been "eloquent" in expressing the concerns of Palestinians under occupation, that "[m]any who know the conditions well are also dubious about bin Laden's capacity to plan that incredibly sophisticated operation from a cave somewhere in Afghanistan," and that "[t]he 'war on terror'" was "neither new nor a 'war on terror.'"

In the world according to Noam, America's 1998 attack on the Al-Shifa pharmaceutical plant in Sudan, which killed one or two people, constituted a far greater terrorist act than the September 11 assaults. Moreover, the loss of pharmaceuticals to the Sudanese population could be considered to have caused, Chomsky estimated, tens of thousands of deaths. ("What would the reaction have been," Chomsky asked, "if the bin Laden network had blown up half the pharmaceutical supplies in the U.S. and the facilities for replenishing them?") Chomsky gave lip service to some sentiments he appeared to view as the price of admission for saying more peculiar things about September 11. The attacks were "a particularly horrifying terrorist crime." But then, boilerplate recorded, it was on to America's almost genocidal wickedness in Indonesia, Turkey, Nicaragua, the Mideast, and elsewhere. He repeatedly mentioned that bin Laden's activities had been counterproductive for the poor Muslims he claimed to champion, yet asserted that we had to take bin Laden "at his word" in assessing his motivations—a courtesy he never extended to U.S. leaders.

"Nothing can justify crimes such as those of September 11," Chomsky wrote, before immediately adding, "but we can think of the United States as an 'innocent victim' only if we adopt the conventional path of ignoring the record of its action and those of its allies, which are, after all, hardly a secret."

Chomsky's analytic methods when it came to politics remained consistent from year to year, a triumph of doublespeak. When a mainstream news article supported some point of his, he cited it as though no further proof were necessary. He summarized reports about the Sudan attack, for instance, with the addendum that those accounts came from "respected journalists writing in leading journals." But when mainstream articles more typically challenged his view, the authority of such journalists vanished. The reports were worse than false—they were corrupt.

In similar style, Chomsky traditionally launched ad hominem attacks on those who disagreed with him, often suggesting that anyone who could surf the Web knew he was right. In *9-11*, Chomsky knifed the immensely more thoughtful philosopher Michael Walzer, who urged confrontation with and rejection of "all the arguments and excuses for terrorism." Rather than accept Walzer's stance—the view that a ban on killing innocents should anchor any coherent morality—Chomsky disingenuously wrote, vis-à-vis Walzer's view, "[I]n effect, this translates as a call to reject efforts to explore the reasons that lie behind terrorist acts that are directed against states he supports." Chomsky both reversed Walzer's call to confront such reasons and slimed him as duplicitous at the same time.

Chomsky's problem as a political thinker did not come from introducing irrelevant examples or information, however much he expanded the range of American political philosophy by his sheer extremism. Who, after all, could argue that Americans didn't need to think about and criticize the Sudan bombing if it was wrongheaded? Who wouldn't have agreed that we should ponder whether the U.S. behaved wisely when it refused to honor the judgment of international courts, or even join them? But Chomsky's hammering on about such matters always came with an overwhelming absence of goodwill toward the intelligence and judgment of others, as if any explanation but his was preposterous.

That arrogance backfired, as usual, when he discussed international law, a subject in which he exhibited either illiteracy or bad faith. He ritually treated international law as if it were, or ought to be, binding upon states in exactly the way domestic law binds citizens. Yet one of the first truths that all law students learn, and international lawyers live with, is that international law remains peculiar because it arises from the voluntary submission of sovereign states, leaving it in many circumstances with nonbinding force. Like Chomsky's reiterated mantra that the perpetrators of September 11 should have been treated as mere violators of domestic terrorism laws (a distinctive case of Chomskyan reverence for federal legislation), his positions on U.S. violations of international law often seemed rooted more in political reflex than reason.

World events, in any event, usually proved Chomsky wrong. In *9-11,* he railed at America's supposed demand that Pakistan cut off food aid to Afghanistan, an effort to harm the Taliban thieves who stole it. According to Chomsky, U.S. policy was essentially, "OK, let's proceed to kill unknown numbers, maybe millions, of starving Afghans who are victims of the Taliban." Meanwhile, ordinary American soldiers and international caregivers risked their lives to bring food and medicine to grateful Afghans. Chomsky also predicted that attacking Afghanistan would drag America into bin Laden's "diabolical plot," provoking the Middle

East street to rise up against the U.S. But it didn't. Instead, the Arab street rose up against its own oppressors.

Amid the vacuum of professional philosophers willing to reflect philosophically on American foreign policy, Chomsky seized and stood his ground over the years, adding uncommon viewpoints to America the Philosophical. He simply lacked supportable truths most of the time. Champions of Chomsky frequently complained that in an era of nonstop cable punditry by intellectual nonentities, American media disgraced themselves by the scant airtime they offered, over the decades, to one of the world's greatest thinkers.

The best explanation probably lay in a point made by one of those top American officials whom Chomsky habitually accused of fascism or worse. "The right to be heard does not automatically include the right to be taken seriously," Hubert Humphrey once told a University of Wisconsin audience. "To be taken seriously depends entirely on what is being said." Major American media, for better or worse, did not take Chomsky seriously as a political philosopher.

That nonetheless left Chomsky's star power in academe untouched. In October 2010, the throngs who showed up for his scheduled appearance at a linguistics conference at his alma mater, the University of Pennsylvania, forced school officials to move his lecture from Claudia Cohen Hall (a building Chomsky might have been annoyed to learn was named after a founder of the *New York Post*'s Page Six). Instead, everyone flocked to the enormous auditorium of Penn's Museum of Archeology and Anthropology. "This is like opening for Bob Dylan," quipped Charles Yang, the Penn linguistics professor and former Chomsky PhD student tapped to introduce his former adviser before the packed hall.

Chomsky, still feisty at eighty-two, even after admitting that he had forgotten his hearing aid at home, didn't disappoint. Casual in a blue sweater, keeping to linguistics as agreed, he tore into "scientists" who simply collect data and worry about predictions, lacerating attempts to undermine the theoretical, explanatory approaches to language that he and his progeny in linguistics specialize in. Certain procedures of scientific thought, he declared, had been "unquestioned for the sciences at least since Galileo," and "to give a general argument against abstraction and idealization is to abandon rational inquiry."

Of course, many of the most influential twentieth-century philosophers of science—thinkers such as Thomas Kuhn, Stephen Toulmin and Paul Feyerabend—didn't think scientific procedure had been at *all* consistent since Galileo. But you couldn't keep Noam down.

The same remained true when it came to politics. After American Special Forces killed Osama bin Laden in May 2011, Chomsky posted his reaction. He deemed it "a planned assassination, multiply violating elementary norms of international law." Obama, he stated, had lied in reiterating to the country that "the 9/11 attacks were carried out by al Qaeda." As for former president George W. Bush, Chomsky wrote, "Uncontroversially, his crimes vastly exceed bin Laden's."

LINGUIST, MATHEMATICIAN, NEUROLOGIST

In the heyday of positivistic analytic philosophy, with resources marshaled to corner "truth," "knowledge" and "meaning," attention to other concepts waned. As the nation's philosophical lens widened, however, other concepts made a comeback as subjects of attention—again with the help of outside thinkers.

"Reason" was one. Humiliated and marginalized by twentieth-century politics and war, belittled by psychoanalysis, stripped of its capital letter by everyone except the Germans, it had hobbled along in the humanist vocabulary, mainly surfacing in musty older-generation conversation ("Won't he listen to reason?"). Even intellectuals who treasured its Enlightenment glory days treated reason like a rickety emeritus worthy of deference during chance encounters, but not mentioned in one's current work. Many philosophers and cognitive scientists excluded it from their books and indexes, ignoring it like some embarrassing cousin of phlogiston.

Linguist George Lakoff, working with philosopher Mark Johnson, bucked that trend. The two attempted to restore reason's conceptual stardom, if not return an old notion to an honorable pedestal. They treated "reason" not just as an idea that still mattered, but perhaps the proper cynosure of philosophy, rightly understood. Their voices exuded familiar revolutionary commitment: Listen to my big ideas because they may change your thinking about thinking *forever.*

Lakoff and Johnson delivered their goods in preachy language, particularly when taking swings at philosophy as a discipline. Their collaboration had first borne fruit in their influential work on metaphor—*Metaphors We Live By* (1980)—later expanded in *More than Cool Reason* (1989), then elaborated separately by the authors in Lakoff's *Women, Fire, and Dangerous Things* (1987) and *Moral Politics* (1996), and Johnson's *The Body in the Mind* (1987). *Philosophy in the Flesh* aimed to mine the gold of that corpus for the well-educated nonspecialist, to trumpet for the sentinels of lay culture that a Cartesian-size turn in philosophy had arrived (however anti-Cartesian its bent).

Lakoff, a distinguished professor of linguistics at the University of California, Berkeley, assisted by Johnson, head of the philosophy department at the University of Oregon, began with "three major findings of cognitive science": first, that the mind "is inherently embodied"; second, that thought "is mostly unconscious"; and third, that abstract concepts "are largely metaphorical."

"More than two millennia of a priori philosophical speculation about these aspects of reason are over," the two declared in their introduction, for these findings "are inconsistent with central parts of Western philosophy: They require a thorough rethinking of the most popular current approaches, namely, Anglo-American analytic philosophy and postmodernist philosophy." The best way to see why was to examine how the findings altered the concept of reason. "Reason," the authors stated, is still viewed as "the defining characteristic of human beings." It includes "not only our capacity for logical inference, but also our ability to conduct inquiry, to solve problems, to evaluate, to criticize, to deliberate about how we should act, and to reach an understanding of ourselves, other people, and the world."

Reason according to cognitive science, however, "is not disembodied, as the tradition has largely held, but arises from the nature of our brains, bodies, and bodily experience. . . . [T]he very structure of reason itself comes from the details of our embodiment. The same neural and cognitive mechanisms that allow us to perceive and move around also allow us to create our conceptual systems and modes of reason. Thus, to understand reason we must understand the details of our visual system, our motor system, and the general mechanisms of neural binding."

Reason, in short, was not independent of perception and bodily movement, and neural associations took place between perceptual and inferential acts. Our bodies and brains determined the kinds of categories we formed in making sense of experience. So, for instance, our spatial notions of "in front of" and "in back of" derived from our being creatures with fronts and backs who projected that distinction onto objects like cars and TVs. Reason was also "evolutionary, in that abstract reason built on and made use of forms of perceptual and motor inference present in 'lower' animals." That discovery utterly changes "our relation to other animals and . . . our conception of human beings as uniquely rational."

According to Lakoff and Johnson, reason was therefore not universal in the sense of being transcendent—it was "not part of the structure of the universe." That led some early readers to tag the pair as "relativist," which they denied. They acknowledged that reason might be widely or universally (if contingently) shared by humans because of our similar bodies, a position they call "embodied realism" as distinct from the philosophical tradition's "disembodied realism." As such, reason was not "completely conscious, but mostly unconscious." It was "not purely literal, but largely metaphorical and imaginative," not dispassionate but, rather, "emotionally engaged."

If all this was true—and *Philosophy in the Flesh* attempted to demonstrate it by applying "embodied realism" to classic metaphysical puzzles, such as time and causation, as well as the history of philosophy itself—much of our philosophical baggage from "major classical views of what a person is" went out the window. Goodbye to the Cartesian subject, with a mind independent of the body. So long to Kant's radically autonomous person, because reason didn't transcend the body. Adieu to the ideal utilitarian agent, since embodied humans didn't control most of their reasoning, let alone the part that maximizes self-interest. Equally dispensable was the fashionable image of the mind as purely computational and fungible software working on equally fungible hardware—because real embodied minds did not merely manipulate empty symbols.

It was a heady onslaught of ideas. For all the repetition and jargon that made the volume a homely "container" for marvelous ideas, they took the momentous insights associated with continental thinkers from Fontenelle to Derrida—the most important being that metaphor suffuses all supposedly abstract philosophical language—and explored them in a characteristically American, empirical spirit. Like Steven Pinker, who later on joined in their re-elevation of reason, they marshaled heaps of scientific and social-scientific data and schematized them to a degree that would have fatigued a lightly empirical concept reviser like Foucault and seemed ploddingly dull to a skeptical ironist like Derrida. Lakoff and Johnson's dissections of "primary metaphors"—paradigms like "Affection is Warmth" ("They greeted me warmly") or "Happy is Up" ("I'm feeling up today")—significantly illuminated how we form abstractions by grafting physical phenomena onto subjective experience. Whereas study of metaphor had remained a back alley of philosophy for decades, their work, and landmark anthologies like Andrew Ortony's

Metaphor and Thought, meant that no respectable philosopher or linguist could now ignore metaphor's upshot for epistemology and metaphysics.

Further, the authors rightly claimed that what insider cliques in analytic philosophy continued to view as prestigious work—piecemeal defining of truth conditions for abstract words as if they bore a literal rather than metaphorical pedigree—amounted to bankrupt stuff. Lakoff and Johnson were the Lewis and Clark of philosophy's Age of Metaphor, not always getting things right but endlessly clearing intellectual paths for others. That said, the repercussions they announced for "reason" suggested why *Philosophy in the Flesh,* despite its girth, failed to settle the brute matter of how to view reason. It should, for instance, have given Lakoff and Johnson pause that while they claimed "evidence from cognitive science shows that classical faculty psychology is wrong," the Canadian neurologist Donald Calne, in his own work, found reason as a "faculty" perfectly adequate. That's because he, a professional neurologist and amateur historian of ideas, unlike Lakoff and Johnson—two devotees of cognitive science—never forgot that "reason" and its cognates remained cultural terms whose delineation could "never exceed in precision" the official compromises of lexicographers.

Lakoff and Johnson, instead, believed concepts such as reason were "neural structures" and conceptual inference was simply "sensorimotor inference." They thus accepted materialist identification between words and concepts on the one hand and neurological matter on the other. Far from being radically new, of course, that flirting with mind-body identity dated back to Plato's *Phaedo.* Contrary to what they claimed, nothing in contemporary cognitive science or philosophy requires us to accept it. No less than Steven Rose, a leading neuroscientist, reminded us in *From Brains to Consciousness?: Essays on the New Sciences of the Mind* that "being able to map mental processes into physiological, anatomical and biochemical mechanisms" may tell us "how the brain/mind works," but it "will not be able to tell us what the mind is doing and why. These questions will have to be answered at a higher level of analysis, and using a different language, than that offered by the best of neuroscientific technology."

It was clear, however, that Lakoff and Johnson saw their work as analogous to the human genome project, with metaphor-soaked concepts ultimately to be neuronally coded and identified. Unless, however, neurologists find in gray matter something like the cloth name tags Mom used to sew into your Camp Kitcheewawa T-shirts ("This sliver of cerebellum holds Bobby Smith's conception of happiness"), the connections will depend on culturally driven associations. The authors might have spent more time with amateur etymologist Raymond Williams, whose entry on "Rational" in *Keywords* provided a judicious guide to the zigs and zags of reason and its oddball cousins (particularly "reasonable" and "rationalize"). The authors might also have acknowledged that the straw-man philosophical tradition they persisted in depicting as massively Cartesian and hostile to the body had been powerfully altered by pragmatism, Wittgenstein and deconstruction, so that many anti–a priori beliefs Lakoff and Johnson advanced might be regarded as articulated by the others, minus the neuronal chemistry. (The authors did offer Dewey and Merleau-Ponty appreciative bows, but ignored their focus on the social construction of concepts.)

For all their industry, Lakoff and Johnson displayed little energy for considering how their vision clashed with deeply held views of metaphorical genius as an individual gift. They slighted the creative side of metaphor, the ability of literary and scientific genius to reject clichéd associations and images. (Some years later, James Geary would offer a more accessible and sweeping account of metaphor for the general reader, miserably titled, after a cryptic phrase from Rimbaud, *I Is an Other: The Secret Life of Metaphor and How It Shapes the Way We See the World*.) In their final chapter, Lakoff and Johnson asserted that "we do not, for the most part, have control over how we conceptualize situations and reason about them," and "[w]e cannot freely change our conceptual systems by fiat." Newton and Mallarmé, Einstein and Yeats, would have demurred. Aristotle famously wrote that to be a master of metaphor was the greatest of all things, while Lakoff and Johnson thought of metaphor as producing our minds. The truth, Aristotle would have pointed out, lay in between. Finally, if the new reasoning about reason sometimes faltered because it failed to square with previous wisdom we still supported, it also lost a few revolutionary points for reiterating what had previously been said better. Did Lakoff and Johnson's message differ vastly from Roger Bacon's thirteenth-century insight that "[r]easoning draws a conclusion—but does not make the conclusion certain, unless the mind discovers it by the path of experience"? Or Wilde's intuition, expressed through Lord Henry in *The Picture of Dorian Gray*: "I can stand brute force, but brute reason is quite unbearable. . . . It is hitting below the intellect"?

Philosophical revolutionaries like Lakoff and Johnson resembled political ones in speaking too quickly for the rest of us. Science might solve various mysteries of neural causation, but it would be "culture" that decided how the numbers and chemistry hooked up with the words and concepts we know and love.

The mathematician normally found himself in a considerably stronger position vis-à-vis cultural forces than other intellectuals. His subjects didn't twist and shout depending on who was looking at them. And yet.

A key question for traditional philosophers had long been, "Why is there something rather than nothing?" Twentieth-century analytic philosophers found the question on the one hand too cosmic, and its component parts ("something" and "nothing") on the other too empirical. In America the Philosophical, part of the challenge not picked up by journalists, nonfiction writers, social scientists and philosophy professors was newly illuminated by a number (so to speak) of mathematicians, most prominently Harvard's Robert Kaplan in *The Nothing That Is*.

Kaplan caught the subject's fey quality. Nothingness, after all, happened. You just looked in your empty pocket. Or glanced at the glass in your life reduced from half full to nada. Nature adored a vacuum, and especially naming it. It was not for nothing—though it was presumably for something—that we had the words "nil," "naught" and "null." Yet zero posed problems as a name for this nothingness. If you added a few zeros to the balance in your account, you had more, not less. Listen to Gershwin and you started thinking, "I got plenty o' nuttin' / An' nuttin's plenty fo' me." Pretty quirky behavior for a cipher. It made you think someone ought, if not aught, to investigate. Kaplan, to his credit, believed we couldn't avoid the matter. So there he was, in an absolutely scintillating book, asking the reverse of a time-honored query: "Why is there nothing rather than something?"

The charm of his approach, aside from his droll colloquial style, came in his decision to zero in on zero as "a naturalist, collecting the wonderful variety of forms zero takes on—not only as a number but as a metaphor of despair or delight; as a nothing that is an actual something; as the progenitor of us all and as the riddle of riddles." He was, in short, that rare author interested in signifying nothing—even as he showed that one can't dispose of zero in *World Book* style. Yes, zero may conventionally be, as that encyclopedia told us, "the name of the digit 0 . . . used to indicate the absence of quantity." True, it was "needed in a positional numerical system" such as ours, in which the "place of a digit determines the digit's value." And no one would dispute that mathematics scholars continued to argue about its origins, citing the ancient Mayans and Babylonians, and the Hindus hundreds of years later, as precursors of the Europeans who took zero into full use in the seventeenth century. Similarly, etymologists leaned toward the *World Book*'s explanation that the word "zero" "probably came from *ziphirum,* a Latinized form of the Arabic word *sifr,*" itself "a translation of the Hindu word *sunya* (void or empty)." But that left out much. Listen to Kaplan on the subject: "What can be nothing one moment and something the next, yet disappears in the presence of anything? This sounds like one of those conundrums dear to nervous people at parties, but in fact is the puzzle at the heart of the Indian *sunya.* The answer lies in our always having mistranslated this word by 'void' or 'empty.' For the Hindus there is no unqualified nothingness. In the same spirit of our Law of the Conservation of Matter, substance for them cannot disappear but can only change its form or nature."

It stood as an example of one of Kaplan's fundamental beliefs: "If you look at zero you see nothing; but look through it and you will see the world." Kaplan's erudition tumbled forth from the opening chapter of his book. Starting with what he called "the vagaries of zero's infancy," the beginning of zero's career as "two wedges pressed into a wet lump of clay," Kaplan painstakingly outlined its development from absence to presence in different systems, through Babylonian, Greek and Roman figures, with all appropriate squiggles depicted. Kaplan explained everything quite precisely as he proceeded, while wonderfully collapsing the millennia between then and now. As he noted, a clay tablet back in Mesopotamia recorded this exchange between father and son:

"Where did you go?"

"Nowhere."

"Then why are you late?"

Kaplan sighed: "You realize that 5,000 years are like an evening gone." His early chapters stressed zero's humble origins, that it "evolved from a punctuation mark and long kept its supernumerary character—no more a number than a comma is a letter." Kaplan playfully asked, "What does it take for an immigrant to the Republic of Numbers to gain citizenship?," then gracefully showed that "for something to be a number it must socialize with the numbers already there, able at least to exchange civilities with the natives." Along the tour of zero's ascent that followed, one enjoyed an interlude about the "dark side of counting" among the Mayans (a culture of obsessive-compulsive calculators, according to Kaplan), the complications of counting boards and the impact of calculation for visions of the Apocalypse, and passages on the later European concern that zero was "the Devil himself." Gradually Kaplan explained how using zero aided the new age of trade and merchant transactions, while keeping his eye on its mathematical development and relations to the invention of exponents and calculus.

Finally, Kaplan took the tale of zero and nothingness deeper into issues of physics and culture, displaying his easy fluency between mathematics and the humanities. He touched on Sartre's *le néant*, the musings of Virginia Woolf, the relevance of Scandinavian wood, always gently seguing from them to mathematical topics like the empty set. In the end, Kaplan happily exhibited zero patience for false cockiness about his ideas or flat energy in his prose. Just as he delighted us with *en passant* anecdotes about the likes of nineteenth-century sultan Abdul Hamid II, who eliminated references to H_2O in local chemistry books for fear it stood for "Hamid the Second is Nothing!," he insistently maintained his modesty—and ours. For even while asserting that we've come to "know zero intimately in its mathematical, physical and psychological embodiments," Kaplan conceded that we remained, in regard to nonexistence, in a "nightmare" of uncertainty, where "images dodge and shift their shapes and return from directions you didn't even know were there."

Kaplan's work was not for the fainthearted or readers with attention deficit disorder. If anything, one would have wanted a pill or shot to prod attention *surplus* disorder—because the peculiar pleasures of *The Nothing That Is* required following Kaplan's exquisite explanations and descriptions slowly, even dutifully. Like Martin Gardner, Douglas Hofstadter and Pinker, similarly lustrous outsiders in America the Philosophical, Kaplan wrote prose both enormously accessible and routinely challenging—he'd prove that *The Nothing That Is* was no fluke by following it with the equally beguiling *Hidden Harmonies: The Lives and Times of the Pythagorean Theorem*, written with his wife, Ellen. Just when it seemed Kaplan could say nothing more about a topic, he took down—or is that put up?—the No Vacancy sign and opened another room of thought. We had all learned, by a certain age, that less was more—at least sometimes. Who knew that zero was quite so much? For taking up yet another beguiling task abandoned by professional philosophers, we could thank Kaplan for "nothing."

If Kaplan and peer mathematicians couldn't stop thinking about nothingness (notice how much more metaphysical the suffix makes it sound), his fellow "non-philosopher," neurologist Oliver Sacks, never stopped thinking about something: How much "something" did a person need to be recognizably human? Sacks, the literary pride of his field who kept mistaking synaptic systems for human beings and getting away with it, liked his forms of intelligence to come with the palpable texture of life.

In the kitchen of the West Village office where he worked with two assistants, Sacks, burly, with Kris Kringle features, caressed some of his beloved ferns (he owned up to being a card-carrying member of the American Fern Society) while showing them to a visitor. In the spare room where he was writing a book about Pingelap Islanders and other communities burdened by congenital color blindness, volumes on the palm-like cycads some blame for the condition abounded: *Cycads of the World, The Living Cycads, Cycads of Africa*. As man and thinker, Sacks won plaudits for the emotional empathy he brought to case studies of neurological conditions like those possessed by the people in one of his many books, *An Anthropologist on Mars*: a research scientist with Asperger's syndrome; a painter condemned to color blindness by an accident; a doctor with Tourette's syndrome.

Was Sacks a theoretician? A systematizer? Or a portraitist fascinated by the lives of his patients? Sacks always implied that the people who should be most challenged by the "neurologically challenged" are the rest of us. His empathetic, anecdotal and yet clinically thorough approach was suggested by the epigraph of *Anthropologist*: "Ask not what disease the person has, but rather what person the disease has."

Like Coles, whose doppelgänger he could seem in the world of science, Sacks put the emphasis on "person" in his long practice as a neurologist in New York, which began in 1965. Not everything that involved "intelligence" fascinated him. When, long before "Watson" aced *Jeopardy*, IBM's Deep Blue computer showed signs of a real "mind" in its losing battle with chess champion Garry Kasparov, he appeared underwhelmed.

"First, I'm not a chess player, and I don't know enough about chess," Sacks said genially. Still, Sacks sympathized with the interests of those sitting near him. "It is intriguing," he said, hands cupped behind his head, comfortable as could be in wire-rim glasses, green chinos, athletic shirt and running shoes. "I'm not indifferent to it. I think I'm probably ignorant or illiterate here." But as the wheels slowly spun about mechanical intelligence, his long pauses signaled rumination. He observed that the phenomenon of rich and complex "stereoscopic vision," which he "delights" in, nonetheless arises (like computer calculation) from simple mechanics. He noted that "one's computational powers, like one's motor powers, can certainly be felt as owned, personal and very much part of you." And yet he thought that if we someday have "mind and consciousness" in "artifacts," the artifacts will be quite different from Deep Blue. One feels that a chess champion, he remarked, "is living the life of the mind very intensely, whereas the computer, when it gives a performance, is more called into action."

Here, in mulling artificial intelligence, Sacks betrayed his abiding preference for the organic, the human, the humane: "I like to think very much in terms of a fertile complementareity between machines and us, and no sort of competition." Indeed, Sacks described his intellectual focus as less neurological than philosophical. Asked, for instance, whether it was only neurological abnormality that attracted his attention, as opposed to such other kinds of severe physiological anomaly like quadriplegia, he replied, "I think what I'm interested in is not the anomaly as such, as what is the richest, most interesting, most appropriate sort of life one can have under certain circumstances."

With many successful books behind him (the most famous being *The Man Who Mistook His Wife for a Hat*), and media celebrity since Robin Williams played him in the movie version of *Awakenings,* Oliver Sacks pretty much pursued his philosophical brand of science writing as he chose—his uniqueness among writerly thinkers could be confirmed by one of the hats he wore himself late in his career: designation as the first "Columbia University Artist." While he still saw patients, he described the balance between his doctoring and his writing as about "half and half." He lived (then) on City Island in the Bronx, where he could indulge his love of swimming. In fact, Sacks's many fans (he received a reported fifteen thousand letters a year) knew him as an accident-prone doctor, renowned for pulling this or that muscle and living to write about it, once relatively well and back in the water. The *New Yorker* writer Lawrence Weschler once described observing Sacks at sea as "like watching a porpoise."

A philosopher with a porpoise, that is. At seventy-seven, he was reading a biography of the family of Ludwig Wittgenstein, one of his "favorite philosophers." He was still not on Twitter or Facebook, still not using a computer.

THE CASUAL WISEMEN

While rigid taxonomists might protest the description of psychiatrists, political scientists or neurologists as philosophers, few would question the academic seriousness or intellect of these credentialed sorts. But does America the Philosophical include pop psychologists, spiritual healers, empowerment lecturers, slumming scholars, magazine moguls—idea salesmen sometimes derided as "gurus"? Some reflection on the species in general helps before pondering three of America's own.

The Sanskrit word *guru*, psychiatrist Anthony Storr explained in *Feet of Clay*, his study of the ilk, originally meant "one who brings light out of darkness." But in English, he continued, it had come to refer to the spiritual adviser of one sort or another who "provokes bad press because of his or her *own* dedication to obscurantism, supernaturalism, and worse." Throughout his sober, exacting, clear-eyed exercise in debunking rubbish, Storr made clear that he'd rarely met a guru he liked.

Many gurus, Storr reported, are "unscrupulous wielders of power" who "exploit their disciples emotionally, financially and sexually." Many are "entirely unworthy of veneration: false prophets, madmen, confidence tricksters." As children, Storr related, gurus tended "to have been rather isolated." As adults, gurus "seldom have close friends" and are "introverted and narcissistic." Gurus, he explained, also usually "go through a period of stress, sometimes amounting to a psychotic illness, which is brought to an end by the revelation of a new truth which dispels confusion, brings order and provides relief." Once they enter guruhood, they tend to be "intolerant of any kind of criticism" and "elitist and anti-democratic." Gurus "seldom discuss their ideas; they only impose them." All share "the apparent conviction that they know, and that their personal revelation applies to everyone." Gurus frequently claim "special powers of clairvoyant perception," suffer delusions that they are God or advance "absurd theories about the universe."

An ignoble crew, it seemed, until you realized that among the people Storr placed under his semantic tent, sharing space with the likes of Jonestown's Jim Jones and Branch Davidian loony David Koresh, were Jesus and Gandhi. They posed a problem Storr faced squarely in his nervy, smoothly synthesized study: How should we deal with "gurus whose holiness, lack of personal ambition and integrity are beyond question," who share unwelcome psychological proclivities with evil gurus while occasionally leaving the world a better place? Storr's sensible solution, as he conducted a biographical tour of alternately grotesque and admirable figures (among them Georgei Gurdjieff, Bhagwan Shree Rajneesh, Rudolf Steiner, Carl Jung, Sigmund Freud, Ignatius of Loyola and Jesus), was to argue that guruhood is almost always bad in itself, even if some gurus promote beliefs that—like Steiner's on progressive education, or Jung's on humankind's need for a religion replacement—prove useful.

That is, the positive aspects of gurus—their intensity, determination to transcend personal psychological crises, and frequent verbal and intellectual fluency—can't compensate for their vices: primarily an arrogant dogmatism that typically devolves into corruption and autocracy. Part of intellectual sophistication, Storr asserted, was the recognition that "no one knows in the sense that Gurdjieff or Rajneesh or Jung believed that they knew and were supposed to know by their disciples." He drove that point home with detailed descriptions of the worst of his players, Jones and Koresh. Tracing the rise of their paranoid delusions until the destruction of their communities (through the murder and mass suicide of more than nine hundred people at Jonestown, and the FBI siege of Ranch Apocalypse at Waco, Texas, that left eighty-six dead), Storr foreshadowed what he ultimately characterized as his main message: We should all "distrust characters who are both deeply self-absorbed and authoritarian."

That warning also applied to gurus of a less criminal and destructive nature, however charismatic. Gurdjieff (1866–1949), a Greek-Armenian original, claimed to carry imparted knowledge from mysterious Asian wisemen. He declared that all evil deeds "are controlled by the moon," and made it through occupied Paris in World War II by telling food shop creditors he'd been given an oil well by an American student. He was, to be sure, a warped masterpiece of personality (Robin Williams as Gurdjieff?). In turn, Bhagwan Shree Rajneesh, the Blessed One, placed a sign at the entrance hall of his original ashram that read "Shoes and minds to be left here."

Exactly the problem, Storr indicated. His crisp and graphic reportorial work, recording the sexual and other degradations Jones, Koresh and others imposed on their followers, corroborated his suspicions and warnings, while also confirming how far the normal judgment of acolytes goes astray. Yet as Storr departed exemplars of evil for gurus who retain respect from worldwide followers, his own asperity softened. He grinned at the "confidence-man trickery" of Gurdjieff (who lied constantly and bragged about it) while mocking his "incoherent" metaphysics. He respected the erudition of Rajneesh, who started out as an extremely well-read professor of philosophy in India, while regretting his decline into sexual decadence and dictatorial abuse. He credited the saintly Rudolf Steiner, the solipsistic Carl Jung and the dogmatic Sigmund Freud with contributing extremely valuable insights to world culture—such as Freud's analysis of religious belief as disguised infantile longing for a father's protection—while insisting that they count as gurus nonetheless. Along the way, he helpfully thumbnailed the theories of each of his thinkers.

Because Storr was a theoretician devoted to the philosophy of personality, his chief ambition in *Feet of Clay* narrowed into outlining the flimsiness of gurus while showing how standard psychiatric terms, such as "psychotic" and "schizophrenic," prove "woefully inadequate" in capturing their peculiar "problem-solving" delusions. Storr fulfilled that ambition by examining where gurus stand on the continuum between normal mental health and conditions such as manic-depressive illness. Departing from his profile approach, Storr systematically analyzed the concepts of sanity and insanity, chaos and order, and delusion and faith. In each of those areas, his bent was to resist rigidity in understanding psychological phenomena without abandoning the scientific method.

So he closed with a chapter titled "To Whom Shall We Turn?" The first part of the answer, he advised, was to know to whom we should not. All "authoritarian" and "paranoid" gurus, Storr warned, remain "potentially dangerous." Danger signs include the desire to "exercise personal control" over disciples' lives, excessive oratorical flourish, inaccessibility and self-absorption. The positive part of his answer was more direct: "If anyone is in urgent need of help or guidance, let him find someone who will listen rather than preach; someone who will encourage him to look inward and find out what he as a unique individual thinks and believes, rather than accepting some guru's dogma."

Storr's caveats suggested that America the Philosophical cannot and should not expand in any direction at all, and especially not toward intellectual charlatanism. At the same time, they offered crystal-clear value when applied to the domestic scene. For, as it happens—without ignoring some demon-like counterexamples in our history—Americans favored a kind of figure best understood as "guru lite." The charismatic wiseman or -woman less likely to walk people off a cliff than to steer them into a stadium at $50 a ticket. The well-groomed multicity performer inclined to attract stalkers more than followers. The canny businessman or -woman intent on extracting a subscription, or a book sale, for his or her wisdom. America the Philosophical includes such guru lites with their hearts on their sleeves, devoted to causes. We cannot profile all of them—the Tony Robbins or Marianne Williamson or Deepak Chopra fan will have to look elsewhere. But it's important to consider the role. For the casual wiseman in America, rhetorical magic might be expounded anywhere, from a bookstore signing to a hot tub party with cavorting young Playmates.

Robert Fulghum, the author of *All I Really Need to Know I Learned in Kindergarten* and other best-selling volumes of easy-to-grasp wisdom, stood as a star of the former type of event once his successful career took off. One thing he failed to learn in kindergarten, he admitted, was that people would try to promote him from big-name author to guru. ("I don't do messages. That really comes as a surprise to some people.") He also lacked the clairvoyance years back to know that his IBM officemate from decades earlier in Dallas—H. Ross Perot—would one day run for president. ("He gives away copies of my books.")

Relaxing in a fancy Peninsula Hotel suite in Manhattan to face the touring author's equivalent of rock groupies—stacks of books waiting to be signed—the mega-selling ruminator explained his high concept.

"I hate the things," he said, referring to author tours, "because usually they're so greed driven." But then the longtime Unitarian minister and art teacher, a Seattle resident for more than thirty years, got to thinking about Willie Nelson, Whoopi Goldberg and other artists who raised money for charity. So as promotion time neared for another book of musings—*Maybe (Maybe Not): Second Thoughts from a Secret Life*—he pitched a charity idea to his publisher. "Their initial attitude," he recalled, "was, 'Well, anything that'll keep him out there is great.'"

The idea became a raving success. The original count of

twenty-two cities rose to more than forty, and his philanthropic twist on traveling-author madness filled coffers for the ACLU, Habitat for Humanity and others. Fulghum sounded elated—he loved the idea of sticking his publisher "with the thought that it ought to keep doing good."

And would that publisher feel anything but gratitude to its bankable star if it could see him just then, an upbeat figure in white shirt and brilliant bowtie, making the supreme effort for his house? With his right hand wrapped in bandages due to carpal tunnel syndrome—revived by signing two thousand books a few days before—he instead "signed" little bookmarks with his still-functioning thumb and a Japanese stamp pad. "The thing is to keep it off my shirt," he said. "I got it all over my shirt yesterday." He smiled. If you were an ad agency hawking genial smiles to the nation, Robert Fulghum might have been your campaign poster guy. A onetime rodeo cowboy, ditchdigger and bartender, he still sounded a bit like his native Waco, looked like a Macy's Santa after a beard trim, and moved like a man who slept late in Seattle.

He owed his national reputation to *All I Really Need to Know*. It contained what the subtitle promised: uncommon thoughts on common things. Fulghum started with a brief homage to "The People's Publishing Company," that network of clippings on refrigerator doors and office bulletin boards that tells us what really moves folks. He'd contributed a short essay to the network that most of his friends called "The Thing About Kindergarten." The piece, one of his biweekly essays that appeared in a church newsletter for many years, said that he had picked up most of the wisdom anyone needed in life "not at the top of the graduate-school mountain but there in the sandpile at Sunday School."

The maxims stayed pretty simple. Play fair. Don't hit people. Share everything. Say you're sorry when you hurt somebody. Fulghum recalled that it made its photocopied way to kindergarten teachers across the country. New York literary agent Patricia van der Leun saw it, liked it and asked Fulghum if he had more material. After receiving a boxful, she snared him a $60,000 book contract.

All I Really Need to Know startled the publishing industry with its unabashed sentiment, childlike optimism and whimsical common sense. "Think what a better world it would be," Fulghum wrote, "if we all—the whole world—had cookies and milk about 3 o'clock every afternoon and then lay down with our blankies for a nap." He pondered such things as doing laundry, working an abacus, hometowns, heroes in news accounts,

old friends, crayons, playing hide-and-seek—all in hip, casual, fragmented sentences that confided he was talking out loud, not writing to
us. After it appeared, the book became the nonfiction hit of its decade,
occupying the No. 1 position on the *New York Times* nonfiction bestseller
list for ninety-six weeks.

His second and third books, with the easy-entry titles *Uh-oh* and
It Was on Fire When I Lay Down on It, also shot to No. 1, making him
a publishing Bigfoot with wares available in twenty-four languages in
ninety-three countries, and 10 million copies in print in the United
States. It was an amazing rise in a short time, but Fulghum insisted that
his head remained screwed on straight. "It's hard sometimes for people
to believe this," he said, "but I had the life I really wanted. I worked for
it. I paid for it. I made the mistakes that got me there. I don't want to
lose that life. People say, 'You still live in the same house?' I say, 'Yeah,
that's where I was happy.' And I still have the same wife. And my kids
still speak to me. And I play poker with the same guys."

His contentment, it seemed, ran deep, especially regarding his second wife, Lynn Edwards, a half-Japanese physician he met in 1972 as he
was about to enter a Zen Buddhist monastery in Japan. "My wife said
something I really like," he confided. "We were talking about all this
fame and fortune stuff. She said, 'If we ate off of solid-gold plates, the
food wouldn't taste any better, and I wouldn't love you any more.'"

Fulghum's own life hadn't always been so sanguine. His father drank
heavily and his mother became a religious zealot who disapproved of
his liberal attitudes. Only after much job hopping and a hippie phase
in California did Fulghum settle in Seattle. Four children from a first
marriage, including an adopted daughter, Molly, who is half-Senegalese,
kept his family life full.

To readers who knew just the name and the rep, Fulghum hovered
on the edges of culture consciousness as a lightweight pop star, but he
was far better educated than he let on in his books, with the University of Colorado, Baylor and Berkeley all under his belt. He believed
in simplicity, to be sure, but not simplemindedness. "Wittgenstein's my
hero," he explained. "As far as modern philosophers, he's the guy I really
read most. Him and Bertrand Russell. And as far as modern artists are
concerned, Duchamp, for the same reason. As far as physics, Richard
Feynman, again for the same reason. I like plain talk."

Fulghum was also "very much influenced by Buddhism. Buddha says
that the love of possessions leads to sorrow. And it's true." On the jacket

of *All I Really Need to Know,* the world learned that Fulghum's business card simply said "FULGHUM," reflecting his "open-ended notion" of what his occupation might be. With three tomes under his belt, the *Maybe (Maybe Not)* book jacket dubbed him a philosopher and essayist. "I use the term for two reasons," he said, denying that the shift indicated a taking on of airs. "One, because it's literally true. I'm one who likes to think about everything. But also because it's provocative." Indeed, he conceded that he hated when his books were placed in "self-help" sections rather than under "essays" or "biography." Still, he was committed to keeping his simple author's voice unspoiled. "I'm so concerned," he said, "that I'll be tempted to become literary or highfalutin that I have an editor in Seattle whom I pay . . . and she is the meanest-spirited high school teacher you've ever seen. Her job is to go after everything I write with an ax, and keep me from shifting into some other language or some other mode."

Maybe (Maybe Not), his most introspective book, complicated his image. How can you make a guru out of a man who offered a table of contradictory proverbs (e.g., "Out of sight, out of mind" vs. "Absence makes the heart grow fonder")? How could you call a man a Pollyanna who admitted, recalling family fibs to the youngins, that "the hamsters didn't die of old age," and even owned up to a suicide attempt twenty-five years before? To Fulghum fans, it might have proved as shocking as a delicate romance to Tom Clancy regulars. Yet the defining virtue of *Maybe (Maybe Not)* remained an indefatigable resiliency.

If Marx believed we should see the world as base and superstructure, and Sartre that we're all condemned to be free, Fulghum stood for glass warfare: the glass was always half full, not half empty. "People ask me if I'm an optimist or a pessimist," he said. "I say, I'm a realist. I'm trying to see the whole thing. That's what an artist wants to do." The world, nonetheless, is better than it used to be, when "women couldn't vote and children were working in factories." And he, after all, felt perfectly capable of slipping the guru and exploitation traps. When others projected the former on him, he resisted with a standard rebuke: "You haven't read my books if you think that's what I'm about." And he'd been just as quick to resist a suggested NBC sitcom on him, and the standard overexposure routine of T-shirts, lunch boxes and calendars. "I'd rather have someone write something I said in a journal they want to keep," he remarked, convincingly, "than to have it on a calendar they're going to throw away." His altruism burned strong: "It bothers me when people have great power and don't use it for good things." As late as his last book, he still seemed in musing mode: *What On Earth Have I Done?*, he called it.

If Fulghum represented the Jesus, Steiner, Gandhi, side-of-the-angels version of America's casual commercial philosopher, Paul Fussell, the well-established English literature scholar, embodied another type: the sardonic intellectual on a lark. Figuring that everyone else in America seemed to have a right to shoot his mouth off on big ideas, Fussell began, mid-career, a series of wry, top-of-the-head meditations on American life.

The first, *Class: A Guide Through the American Status System,* appeared when Fussell, winding up years teaching at Rutgers University in New Brunswick, New Jersey, still lived in tony nearby Princeton in a modest apartment on the town's main drag. Shortly to become the Donald T. Regan Professor of English at the University of Pennsylvania, he was a writer intent on monitoring the skirmishes of class struggle with tongue firmly in cheek. Fussell possessed articulable tastes the way some people have lint on their shirts—everywhere. In his apartment, many of his objects took the form of English collectibles: a poster welcoming Queen Elizabeth to Mexico, a nineteenth-century notice from the Savoy Theater, a British World War I enlistment notice to recalcitrants. "Anglophilia's going out now that the British are poor," he remarked, unapologetically, as he pointed out the bric-a-brac.

Those Anglophile leanings were not to everyone's taste. Some critics charged that *Class* catapulted Fussell to the status of America's leading snob. The jabs suggested he was a captious twit who probably took his own cloth napkin to McDonald's—a genteel ninny ready to wither others with a raised eyebrow, or to drop the news that someone's misshapen polyester sports jacket was a disgrace and their use of double negatives a blot on mankind. Fussell, they implied, would have dumped Marie Antoinette if she'd ordered the wrong kind of cake. But Fussell, said Paul Fussell, was a great kidder.

"There was a review in *Time* magazine which said as a criticism of the book that this is not to be taken seriously," related the cheery, verbally deft Californian, best known among scholars for his prizewinning book about literary modernism, *The Great War and Modern Memory.* "I would say, Of course not. The book pretends to be a solemn, straight-faced survey of the class situation in the United States. Actually, the book is an implicit send up of the anthropological or sociological certainties customary in those procedures." That aim did seem obvious. Without the slightest nod to sociological method or analytical rigor, Fussell divided America into nine social classes ranging from the bottom-out-of-sight (the destitute) to the top-out-of-sight (their houses can't be seen from the road), with uppers, middles and proles further subdivided between them. The criteria and principles he employed to distinguish them were a mix of familiar road signs, idiosyncratic biases and playful teases: "the money you've inherited, the danger of your job, the place you live, the way you look, the shape and surface of your driveway, the items on your front porch and in your living room, the sweetness of your drinks, the time you eat dinner, the stuff you buy from mail-order catalogues, the place you went to school and your reverence for it and the materials you read."

Desks were ranked in traditional class hierarchy—oak at the bottom, teak at the top. In dress, "to take any hat seriously is to descend." Among flowers, poinsettias were vulgar, rhododendrons upper. Compliments were middle class. The nerd pack—that plastic pen envelope worn in the breast pocket–was irrevocably lower. Bottles remained classier than cans on the archaism principle: older is higher. Mapped across these indicators and classes was a so-called category X that Fussell considered "the only escape from class." If you were in category X, according to Fussell, you'd "learned to avoid letting class bother you at all. To ignore it. Which meant in essence to develop so much personal dignity and security that you no longer needed the support and crutches of all those external signs: Xs can be artist or intellectual types (Joyce Carol Oates, Albert Einstein), happy-go-lucky sorts like Huckleberry Finn, or even successful criminals.

"Anybody who sort of gets away with it is a category X figure," said Fussell. "I call it a category because class to me is inherited. Category is something you earn." For the rest of us, though, class signs carry weight, and Fussell hunted them like helpless rabbits. Speech habits, the clearest indicator, sent him positively rattling off examples. "To pronounce the word 'exquisite' on the middle syllable," he said, "that is, ex-QUI-site, is usually a sign of cultural disadvantage." Similarly, "to call the green stuff that accumulates on brass a pa-TIN-a is also a sign of a misspent youth. It's PA-tin-a, as one could tell from a dictionary. To mispronounce the names of remote English composers like Purcell (calling him Pur-CELL) makes me ill, just the way it does when people call me Fus-SELL" instead of rhyming his name with Russell.

Some folks obviously missed the jokes. "It's done with a very solemn straight face, which is my mode of being funny," Fussell maintained. "I never laugh at my own jokes. I never tell people that they're funny. And I find that if you don't do that in this country, half the people miss what you're getting at. Because there's so little appreciation of irony here." Circumstantial evidence that Fussell didn't really want everybody rounded up and sent to separate stadiums came on his bathroom shelves. Sitting there were a flask of Aqua Velva lotion, a stick of Arrid Extra Dry and a can of Gillette Tropical Coconut shaving cream. No one that respectful of Madison Avenue could be a total elitist. "It's not my subject, it's my joke," he quipped, when asked if he would ever make "class" a lecture topic at the university. "What I wanted to do was to be funny, to be provocative, to invite people to look at a number of signals of class which I've been observing with great pleasure for years. And to sort of use the book as a springboard for a number of my own biases, such as the discomfiture of air travel and the fraudulence of any kind of advertising having to do with gourmet cuisine."

Many of the observations, especially those relating to locale, emerged as wildly casual. "One reason no civilized person could think of living near Tampa," he wrote, "is that during the 1970s this sign was visible there, advertising nearby Apollo Beach: 'Guy Lombardo Wants You as a Neighbor.'"

"That's very facetious," he admitted. "That's dishonest, too. I'll get hundreds of letters from Truth or Consequences, New Mexico (another ridiculed spot), objecting to this snobbery." Other class criteria like "high prole houses in the Middle West sporting a grass-green carpet on the front steps" he simply decided to "promote into inviolable truth."

"It's supposed to be ironic," he kept saying. "This is a game that anyone can play." How, though, did the author of *The Rhetorical World of Augustan Humanism* and *Theory of Prosody in Eighteenth-Century England* get lured into playing H. L. Mencken? According to Fussell, publishers requested that he expand a *New Republic* article he'd written about status within academe. He agreed to do it at fifty thousand words in order to cover "the extremely expensive bills" of his son at Christ Church, Oxford. "My thesis in the article," he said, "was that very much like religion in the sixteenth century, the university and college today is virtually immune to criticism. We need something like a Reformation. It's amazing what institutions of higher learning get away with in the matter of snobbery." The piece drew sharp letters. "I was taken to task," recalled Fussell, "largely by pathetic administrators of sad-sack Middle Western teachers' colleges which have been transformed by name only into universities. And they naturally feel very goosey and uncertain about what they're doing."

Asked how one researched nine social classes, he replied, "You don't. You just make it up. Actually, I made up these nine classes. I could have done fourteen or I could have done three. I made up nine because most people believe in three. I thought it would be funny to affect a certain mock scholarly refinement." Lighthearted about his handling of the subject, Fussell was definitely not blithe about the importance of "class" itself.

Fussell first became conscious of it, he said, as a child in Pasadena. His father was a corporation lawyer, his mother "a kind of clubwoman of the 1930s." "When everybody else was getting poorer," he recalled, "I began to notice that we were getting richer. When everybody else was losing his house on a mortgage foreclosure, we were building this immense mock Tudor house in Pasadena. It became clear to me that I came from a privileged oasis in society." His antennae for class friction stayed sharp while attending a public high school, earning his BA at Pomona College and his PhD at Harvard, then teaching at Rutgers. Recent events, he observed, had reminded him that class was no laughing matter. "I don't know a single soul whose son is in the Marine Corps," he noted. "They don't come from my class." So class is important: "It means the life or death of certain people. It's more than just a facetious idea." Having retired from Rutgers after twenty-eight years (he proudly displayed on his wall the commemorative scroll that misspelled his name), Fussell was using a Rockefeller humanities grant to work on his next book—a scholarly one, about the culture of the Second World War. As a visitor left his small corner of a clapboard house that is forever England, a gnawing question surfaced. When all was said and done, wasn't Fussell just an erudite cultural snob? "I would be offended with that," he said good-naturedly. "I'd like to be called a cultural elitist—with the proviso that I want everybody to be a cultural elitist. A snob is happy at his superiority to others. I'm unhappy about it."

Fussell kept up the effort to be a critic—not a scold or a snot, but a gadfly—a few years later in *Bad or, The Dumbing of America*, a screed against pretentious American mediocrity. As a scholar and historian, Fussell had specialized in excellence without pedantry, writing frequently for literary reviews such as the *Times Literary Supplement*. For grad students, he was a modern statue at the intersection of Educated Intellect and Experience of War, a professor who illuminated that street scene with the blunt intelligence of the platoon leader he was in World

War II. As a mass-market entertainer, Fussell tried to be an item he thoroughly understood: a matter of taste.

Bad marched to a similar, though flintier, different drummer than *Class*. Fussell explained that upper-case "BAD" was not just second-rate stuff no one considered good, such as a failing grade. That was just lower-case "bad." Upper-case "BAD," au contraire, was "something that many Americans can be persuaded is genuine, graceful, bright, or fascinating. . . . For a thing to be really BAD, it must exhibit elements of the pretentious, the overwrought, or the fraudulent." Atrocious food in Al's Diner was just bad. Atrocious food in a nouvelle-cuisine spot named Chez Al was BAD. A mathematician might summarize the equation as BAD equals "bad plus good PR." As Fussell observed, "A thing that is palpably bad doesn't stay bad very long before someone praises it and thus elevates it to BAD."

Once he'd nailed his theses to the reader's forehead (in a tone just short of Lutheran fury), Fussell moved on to "BADNESS" in, among other things, advertising, airlines, airports, architecture, banks, behavior, beliefs, films, food, hotels, naval missile firing, newspapers, objects, restaurants, signs and television. He swung his terrible swift sword this way and that. Airlines that advertised "spacious, wide-bodied jets"? He knew the "more spacious, the longer the line trying to get in the toilets." And those boring straight lines of modern architecture? They celebrated "the assumption that no one has sufficient experience or learning to enjoy the allusive exercise required by traditional architectural details, such as balustrades, crockets, finials, metopes, or triglyphs."

If that didn't madden the reader, Fussell attacked people who named their cat Clytemnestra. And "the whole state of Utah, a place famous for its ninnies." And those third-rate colleges and "universities" where you could expire trying "to find someone who's read anything but a best-seller, who has an iota of historical imagination, or who manifests curiosity about anything but money, sports, 'entertainment,' or hobbies." It was like following a cultured English tourist as he swerved between high and low on a day in Manhattan: examining medieval tomes at the Pierpont Morgan one moment, trying to get his mouth around a recalcitrant Sicilian slice the next. Thus "BAD language" smartly zapped such expressions as "interdisciplinary" or "Renaissance Man" in the best Orwellian style, while "BAD movies" rightly mocked blockbusters whose contents couldn't match their promotional budget.

Was Fussell being even slightly serious, or SERIOUS? Late in the book, his creeping counterattack on multiculturalism suggested polemic was eclipsing farce: "Actual American life as experienced by most people is so boring, uniform and devoid of significant soul, so isolated from traditions of the past and the resonances of European culture, that it demands to be 'raised' and misrepresented as something wonderful. BAD thus becomes an understandable reaction to the national emptiness and dullness."

Sure enough, the last chapter urged, though without real hope, a string of measures: "reinstall Latin in the high schools . . . speak and write English and other languages with some taste and subtlety . . . start a few sophisticated national newspapers." It sounded as if Fussell had failed to transmute into one of the category X people he had admired in *Class,* whose "personal dignity and security" permitted them to avoid letting matters of status bother them at all. And that he risked his bad beliefs suddenly going upper-case, which happened "when you get all sincere and pretentious and full of self-importance and proselytize to convey your unique wisdom to an inattentive world. . . . And when you do that to make money, you are so BAD that you may go to hell, a place where fires burn everlastingly to torment awful people like you (see Matthew 25:41)."

By comparison with authors like Fulghum and Fussell, Hugh Hefner's influence as a casual philosopher needed to be partly determined by the number of stapled centerfolds distributed, and corny party jokes repeated. But his "Playboy Philosophy" still looked like a belief system with plentiful adherents, to judge by the number of "Bunny" symbols one spotted in cars and bars.

On a bright spring morning in Los Angeles at Playboy Mansion West, Hefner, on time for a long-scheduled interview and slightly rosy-cheeked, explained why "I have a little color"—he'd been to Disneyland the day before. "Wonderful time, wonderful time," he assured.

Entering the oak-paneled library of his gray-stone, thirty-room Holmby Hills castle, the 1927 Gothic mansion that thousands of Bunnies (and more than five hundred Playmates) didn't build but certainly helped to keep operational, Hefner the senior citizen remained bouncy and good-humored, still clad in black velour jacket over purple pajamas in mid-afternoon, still fond of sitting over a coffee table topped with backgammon boards. After decades as America's most prominent swinging single, Hugh Hefner was in marriage number two at the time, to Kimberley Conrad, whom he wed when she was in her mid-twenties,

Hugh Hefner (1926–), founder of *Playboy* magazine, declared that a "*Playboy* Philosophy" came with the centerfolds, and published scores of articles outlining its tenets.

and with whom he had two sons. Hefner's first marriage lasted from 1949 to 1959, and produced two children, one of them Christie, the former CEO of Playboy Enterprises.

The married Hef drank caffeine-free Diet Pepsi instead of his old hard stuff—straight Pepsi on the rocks. And as a Father's Day poster boy, Hef seemed to be in step with the drill. Outside at the notorious Grotto, the recessed pool made from granite and Palo Verde rock where Hollywood celebs and Playmates of the Moment expanded the meaning of the buddy system, the plastic toys strewn about were the kind they sell in toy stores. As a visitor ascended the inclined driveway past the famous gate with talking boulder, an enormous Children at Play sign urged caution. Throughout the lush 5.35 acres of Hefner's bougainvillea-laced enclave, equally well graced with tropical foliage and satellite-dish downlinks, the exotic specimens drawing notice were roaming albino peacocks and crested cranes from Africa. The sounds heard while walking around weren't moans or squeals but birds yakking, squirrel monkeys and toucans going about their business, and some chatter from his two young boys, playing with the monkeys.

But he wouldn't have been Hef if the explanation for his strange change of life at the time—from King of the Libertines to Father's Day pinup—wasn't more open-minded than it seemed. He remained, after all, the legendary Chicagoan whose magazine, launched in December 1953, expressed his own vision of a Frontierland for men that didn't require cowboys or forts, a magazine that quickly became the publishing success story of the 1950s, and remains one of the most popular men's magazines in the world. "What I tried to say very early on," he explained, "when I got married right out of school like everybody else and it didn't work, is that the major cause of divorce is early marriage. A person ought to find out who he or she is before choosing a lifetime mate. When you get out of school, you should live as an independent adult for a while, away from home, and get some sense of who you are before settling down. Now, not everybody has to wait for forty years. I had a longer adolescence than most. I had a few advantages in my own particular position."

Then he beamed. "What's happened now is like coming home for me. I've managed to romanticize a marriage. Marriage is not romantic in America. It's not romantic in Western civilization. In Western civilization, romance is largely unrequited love—Romeo and Juliet, and people dying—or, when you get married, you transfer the romance to a mistress. Well, I've managed to romanticize marriage and children."

Was he, then, telling his readers that it was time to settle down? No. Rather, he said he was still arguing that "there's more than one moral way to live your life. It may be married, it may be single. When I was growing up, there was only one moral way for a good Protestant boy to live his life. That was to get married very early, and raise the family. That isn't always moral. And beyond that, there are many other options."

Some folks, of course, thought the central tenet of the Playboy philosophy was always to do whatever Hef was doing. Not true, he insisted. "What he's doing," Hef shot back, "is suggesting that there are many ways of living!" Indeed, as *Playboy* rolled along decade after decade, Hefner insisted that a distinction had to be made between changes in his own life and the ongoing commitment of *Playboy* to "Entertainment for Men" and personal freedom. "I don't think the morality of sex has much to do with whether you are married or single, or whether you're sleeping with one person or thirty people," Hefner declared, adding impromptu gloss to the "*Playboy* Philosophy" he published in the early 1960s at a length of roughly 250,000 words—the book-length compilations of it now sell for first-edition prices on Amazon.

"Married, single, straight, gay. What I said from the very beginning is that what we call sexual morality is the most 'immoral' morality. In every other area of morality, we define what is moral as what is good for people. Until we get to the subject of sex. Then we define morality by a bunch of 'Thou Shalt Nots' that are not necessarily good for people at all. They're hypocritical, hurtful. They destroy lives."

In short, he always believed in free choice in sexual matters. When he decided he wanted to marry Conrad, Hefner said, he weighed its effect on his business, but he "never saw it as a negative." People who thought his original message was that "you had to be single all your life" simply weren't reading what he wrote. "If I continued to live the life that I was living in the '70s," he added, "if I continued to just repeat that celebration of adventurous sexuality over and over again, I think some-place along the way it would have become rather pathetic. I mean, one might very well argue that it took too long as it was. And maybe it did. It's perfectly clear to me that there was an obsessive side to all of that because of the way I was raised. It also was obviously related to the fact that I had a rare opportunity. I was a very lucky fellow in a very special place. So that as a bachelor, I was able to live a lot of other guys' dreams. Well, it was my dream too."

"Now," he continued, "in the September years, looking back over all of that, with very few regrets, and a great deal of pleasure, I am in the best place that I've ever been. Because I've come full circle. I'm in a safe harbor, having ridden the waves, and able to savor the life, what I've managed to accomplish, that feeling of satisfaction, and a wonderful relationship with children."

Ages ago, Hefner signed up to do his autobiography for a six-figure sum. Yet Hefner, whose dedication to documenting his life and career is legend—he employed full-time staffers to maintain his archive of scrap-books and tapes, which tended to run more than a decade behind—kept missing his deadline, and eventually agreed to pay back his advance. "I think it was new management," he said, "and they were just trying to clear their books. And they were rightfully impatient. So I was glad to have that pressure off my back." Still, the obstacle to getting the book done was the very reason for doing it: the amazing, overflowing content of an American life that the London *Sunday Times* once ranked as one of the most influential of the twentieth century.

"That's part of the problem," he acknowledged. "I have so much research, and such a story to tell." He got "lost in the details of it all." Having worked first with a collaborator suggested by his publisher, and then with assistants of his own choosing, he was "doing it on my own. . . . [T]he facts will be important, but the feeling will be more important." Tentatively titled *Golden Dreams,* it begins with his 1985 stroke, moves to a prologue examining his feelings of reassessment after that, then goes back to his parents and childhood, and proceeds on.

Yet it was the life that came before and after that most challenged a chronicler. Born in Chicago on April 9, 1926, to Methodist parents who had moved to the Windy City from Nebraska, Hefner grew up propelled by editorial and artistic ambition. In high school, he worked as a cartoonist for the student paper. Following Army service from 1944 to 1946, he enrolled at the University of Illinois, became managing editor of the campus humor magazine and graduated in two and a half years. He also pursued graduate work in sociology at Northwestern, where he wrote a paper examining U.S. sex laws in the wake of the groundbreaking Kinsey Institute reports.

After graduation in the early 1950s, Hefner worked at different projects before finding his ticket to the top. He published a collection of satirical cartoons about Chicago, worked as the assistant personnel manager for a box company, served as a promotions copywriter for *Esquire,* and later worked as circulation manager for *Children's Activities* magazine. Finally, in 1953, with a personal investment of $600 and a total of $8,000 contributed by friends and acquaintances as stock ownership, he produced the first issue of *Playboy* (slated to be called "Stag Party" before a field and stream magazine protested). It was a 1950s product marked by the visual symbol of a rabbit in a tuxedo, and built around the surefire seller of Marilyn Monroe's famous nude calendar photo. Convinced that the world needed a sophisticated men's magazine with a postwar outlook, but uncertain whether his version would sell, Hefner didn't even put a cover date on it. Remarkably, the issue sold 51,000 copies of 70,250 printed, enabling Hefner to put out another one.

From that point on, *Playboy* zoomed forward with one of the most astounding growth rates in magazine history. Stressing "Entertainment for Men," promising its male readers a guide to classy urban life, eager to complement its nude photos with the best editorial copy money could buy, the formula was once described as sending "a message of freedom in an age of restriction." It worked beyond anyone's expectations. By its first anniversary, *Playboy* was selling 175,000 copies a month. By 1959, it was selling over 1 million—more than *Esquire*—and won recognition from some media commentators as a part of 1950s rebellion against American cultural puritanism, evidenced by such disparate phenomena as abstract expressionism in art, beat writing in literature and the provocative comedy of satirists like Lenny Bruce.

In the late 1950s, the previously withdrawn Hefner decided to become the personal symbol of his magazine's lifestyle, and he became an American icon, fabled for lavish (and presumably lascivious) parties at the forty-eight-room Chicago Playboy Mansion. At the same time, the publication regularly found itself in the eye of the storm. In court after court, *Playboy* battled federal and local governments to get its material to readers. And in the early 1960s, Hefner sought to give the magazine greater weight by publishing "The Playboy Philosophy," a lengthy series of editorials expounding his views on free speech, sexuality and other topics crucial to the magazine. Meanwhile, the magazine's huge success enabled Hefner, a self-confessed workaholic who fueled himself with Dexedrine, to expand the Playboy empire beyond magazines to twenty-three Playboy Clubs, resorts, hotels and casinos around the world (at the peak, 900,000 men were keyholders), foreign editions, TV and film production, a book club, a record label, an annual jazz festival and other projects. Hefner became world famous, flying around in the black Big Bunny DC-9-30 jet he acquired in 1970. By 1971, when Playboy Enterprises went public, Hefner was worth an estimated $157 million, and *Playboy*'s circulation had skyrocketed to 7 million copies a month. But Hefner's fame and *Playboy*'s prominence also drew trouble.

For several years in the 1970s, drug probes of the Playboy empire hung over Hefner, leading one of his closest assistants, Bobbi Arnstein, to commit suicide. The emerging feminist movement set *Playboy* in its sights, aided by Gloria Steinem's magazine exposé of what it was like to work as a Bunny. Increasingly unhappy in Chicago, and eager to enter the film business, Hefner moved his operation to the Los Angeles mansion in 1971. That decade, after Arnstein's death, proved the time of Hefner's most hard-core partying. But more bad luck followed. The advent of Ronald Reagan and the 1980s "conservative revolution" came just as *Playboy*'s image was suffering guilt by association from the murder of Playmate Dorothy Stratten, who had become the lover of director (and then Hefner friend) Peter Bogdanovich. With the permissive atmosphere of the 1960s and '70s gone, and the Meese Commission Report on Pornography on the way, the federal government tightened its scrutiny of *Playboy*.

Technical violations of British gaming laws caused Playboy to lose its club license in London. Poor management within Playboy Enterprises and Hefner's own waning interest in the business side combined to turn Playboy's planned Atlantic City casino into a debacle. Only with the appointment as his successor of daughter Christie, a Brandeis University graduate, did the bad news begin to come under control for Hefner. Still, when he thought back to his stroke in 1985, he was sure it followed from that "stress" of the early 1980s.

Asked why he decided to marry Conrad rather than any of scores of earlier girlfriends, Hefner laughed, turned behind him, grabbed a framed photo of the beautiful onetime Playmate of the Year, and held it up for his visitor. "Part of it's there," he said, his voice as tremulous as a teenager who couldn't believe his luck. But not all of it was there. "I was very romantic," he maintained of his promiscuous years, "and was involved in primary relationships most of my life, even while there were other relationships as well."

On March 8, 1985, however, he suffered what seemed a moderately severe stroke at the mansion, which initially left him partially paralyzed on his right side and unable to speak. Determined to recover while remaining at home—he told his doctor he thought he'd die if he went to the hospital—Hefner fought back so successfully that he emerged with virtually no trace of the event in his speech or movement. He told the makers of *Once Upon a Time*, a documentary about his life, that he "used that stroke" to reevaluate his life: "I said that this gives me permission to put down the luggage of my life." Nonetheless, he recalled, reflecting on falling for Conrad, "immediately before I met her, I had no thought of getting married. Always before, I used to think, This is wonderful, but I wonder what lies over the hill. Well, in this relationship, I felt that having lived the bachelor's life for all those years, I had a fair sense of the variations on a theme that lie over the hill, and felt, I don't think there was going to be anything better than what's going on here right now. And, within a very short period of time, I found myself ready. And the children were a totally unexpected bonus. I always felt prior to that that children were a natural outgrowth of being married, but that they didn't tend to enhance romance. I don't believe that anymore. The children are the most romantic part of it. I can't separate the one from the other."

"There are two major accomplishments in my life," he said. "One is the magazine and the changing of society through it. And the other is the life itself. The living of the life itself. Fitzgerald said there are no second acts in American life. Well, I'm living my third act, and making it the best of all. That's what I'm doing."

As it turned out, Hefner enjoyed fourth and fifth acts as well. Like the radically different Francis Fukuyama, he did an about-face. A few years later, he separated from Conrad and returned with a vengeance to the promiscuous lifestyle he and his magazine had promoted before. In the age of Viagra, Hefner took on a bevy of blond girlfriends, whom the magazine, true to tradition, endlessly featured in photos with him. Perhaps most comforting to his ego and philosophy, the early twenty-first century saw the magazine industry turn sharply back to his editorial ideas, years after dismissing his "girly" magazine devices as passé. So-called lad titles like *Maxim* and *Gear*, aimed at young, horny, high-testosterone men, took off as the hottest glossies in the business before all of them but *Maxim* crashed. Licensing fees from foreign editions, particularly in eastern Europe and Russia, helped soften the impact of recession and the general slippage of print publications. Playboy's *The Girls Next Door* reality-TV show turned into a huge success. As Hef kept partying into his eighties, it appeared that his "Playboy Philosophy," instead of petering out, had trickled down.

Then, in late 2010, eighty-four-year-old Hef found himself the object of ridicule, not to mention incredulity, when he announced on Twitter that he had proposed to twenty-four-year-old Playmate Crystal Harris. She, bursting into tears, had accepted. When comedian and host Ricky Gervais insulted Hef (as well as everyone else present) at the subsequent Golden Globes ceremony, comparing the octogenarian-in-love to "The Walking Dead," Hef—philosophically, you might say—shrugged it off, saying he "wasn't offended." Around the same time, he surprised many investors by successfully taking his Playboy empire private again.

Comedians might have had a field day with scheduled marriage number three, but to dismiss Hefner as a lightweight, intellectually or culturally, simply didn't fit the facts. To filmmaker Brigitte Berman, he was the title of her 2010 documentary—*Hugh Hefner: Playboy, Activist and Rebel*—a civil-rights hero. To historians Elizabeth Fraterrigo and Carrie Pitzulo in their respective scholarly volumes, *"Playboy" and the Making of the Good Life in Modern America* (2009) and *Bachelors and Bunnies: The Sexual Politics of* Playboy (2011), he was a transformative figure in American culture. To his most serious biographer, Steven Watts, professor of history at the University of Missouri, whose *Mr. Playboy: Hugh Hefner and the American Dream* (2007) treated his subject with great respect, Hef had, in regard to sex, consumerism, pop culture and, yes, women's rights, "profoundly altered American life and values." By late 2011, members of the Bertrand Russell Society—a group of philosophers devoted to study of the libertine Englishman universally regarded as one of the twentieth century's greatest thinkers—were considering Hefner for the organization's annual Bertrand Russell Award, in honor of his lifetime contribution to civil liberties.

Not everything, however, went smoothly for the high-octane octogenarian. In June 2011, Hefner had to announce that "[t]he wedding is off. Crystal has had a change of heart." She'd reportedly grown tired of Hef's lifestyle. He hadn't.

Indeed, on the eve of 2012, having watched Harris sell her 3.39-carat engagement ring at Christie's for $47,500, and also hold on to the pet pooch they had shared, Hef told *People* magazine: "I am clearly not meant to be married. Married life isn't for me."

Fast forward another year. On New Year's Eve 2012, Hef and his runaway bride—who apparently missed the old codger—got hitched after all at the Playboy Mansion. At 86 and 26, they'd matured.

THE PRINT JOURNALISTS

Time magazine once diagnosed newspaper columnist, author, thinker, professor-at-large and later Hefner hanger-on Max Lerner (1902–1992) as suffering from a "crush on America." Nearly twenty years after his death, Lerner's faint presence in repositories of print immortality suggested that the feeling was no longer reciprocated. Despite six thousand columns for the *New York Post*, wide syndication in his prime and scores of trenchant articles for *PM,* the *New Republic* and the *Nation* (of which he was briefly political editor in 1938), Lerner enjoyed no entry in Donald Paneth's *Encyclopedia of American Journalism* or many other reference works.

Despite his fifteen books, including *America as a Civilization* (1957), a masterly 1,036-page study that Henry Steele Commager thought

Max Lerner (1902–1992), journalist and professor, wrote *America as a Civilization* (1957), which praised "American dynamism."

earned the author his "place alongside Tocqueville and Bryce," Lerner got no article in such standard sources as Eric Foner and John Garraty's *The Reader's Companion to American History*. (There the entry on old rival Walter Lippmann added insult to injury, describing Lippmann as "unique among twentieth-century writers in combining a career as an editor and syndicated columnist with that of an intellectual.") If you turned to "L" in *Bartlett's Familiar Quotations*, there was just one line from Lerner—Alan Jay Lerner.

Was Lerner's low profile just a routine postmortem slump? Did Lerner's autumnal shenanigans at the Playboy Mansion, Esalen and similar drive-throughs of California sexuality kill his chances for inclusion in the establishment pantheon? Or was Lerner's dimmed reputation a cautionary tale for all intellectuals who succumb to the lure of journalistic commentary for big bucks—the Alsops of yesteryear, the George Wills and Michael Kinsleys of today? Lerner's eclipse may have indicated an inverse relationship between excessive ephemeral writing and sustained reputation, yet to judge him as less than a philosopher distorted his career from beginning to end.

Sanford Lakoff's *Max Lerner: Pilgrim in the Promised Land*, the first full biography, made a case for its subject as a cultural thinker. The author, a University of California, San Diego, political scientist and one-time Lerner student, monitored his hybrid scholar/satyr from Minsk cradle to American grave, and sought through mounds of accumulated detail to protect Lerner—a romantic-poetry buff—from going the way of Ozymandias.

Lakoff faced every literary biographer's toughest challenge—his subject's birth to early adulthood—by calling on an excerpt from Lerner's unpublished autobiography. Lerner's account of classic immigrant struggle—the twin siblings who didn't survive, the Ellis Island arrival at age five, the humiliations of poverty as his gentle, autodidactic father moved from garment work to a milk-delivery business in Bayonne, New Jersey, and New Haven, Connecticut—went a long way toward explaining his later outsize intellectual appetite. More germane in assessing Lerner's importance was evidence of his brilliance. Lerner entered Yale in 1919, a scholarship student from a New Haven high school. Unlike many journalists who parlay media experience into professorial posts despite inferior academic credentials, Lerner started as an impressive scholar, then gravitated toward the press. As an undergraduate, he won four prizes: three for scholarly achievement in English and German, and one for the best essay on patriotism. Still, as he approached graduation, a favorite teacher delivered blunt news: "You ought to know that, as a Jew, you'll never get a teaching post in literature in any Ivy League college."

Stymied after graduation in 1923, Lerner attended Yale Law School, but stayed just a term before souring on the subject. Around that time he read *The Theory of the Leisure Class* by Thorstein Veblen, whom he came to view as "the most considerable and creative mind America has yet produced." Fired up by the maverick economist's holistic belief that economics, psychology and the rest of life must be studied together, Lerner headed off to Washington University for a graduate fellowship in economics. Lakoff recounted the slow building of Lerner's academic career. Having impressed his MA thesis adviser, Isaac Lippincott, as "the most capable graduate student I have had," Lerner transferred to the Washington, D.C.-based PhD program of what's now the Brookings Institution, then boasting such faculty as Charles Beard, Carl Becker and Franz Boas. Again, Lerner proved so impressive that the school granted him a PhD solely "on the strength of the papers he had written." One professor wrote that in the general opinion of faculty and students at Brookings, Lerner was "the most brilliant student" they'd seen.

In overdocumenting his subject's academic excellence, Lakoff sought to compensate for the condescension Lerner's later journalistic career invited. Indeed, he showed that Lerner could match credentials with Lippmann, who traded mightily on his onetime philosophy assistantship with George Santayana at Harvard, then eschewed the academic career Lerner pursued. After receiving his PhD in 1927, Lerner quickly rose to managing editor of the *Encyclopaedia of the Social Sciences,* then drew teaching offers from Sarah Lawrence, Harvard and Williams College, where he became the first Jew appointed to the faculty. From that point on, Lerner combined careers as professor and political journalist.

Lakoff started to flesh out Lerner at that stage, converting him from walking CV to overachiever in both lust and work. Throughout Lerner's professional life, Lakoff explained, this wiry, five-foot-seven-inch man with the broad face, flat nose, and powerful pompadour felt unattractive. To compensate, he wooed "daughters of the conquerors": beautiful, non-Jewish establishment women. After an unfaithful twelve-year first marriage to fellow Brookings student Anita Marburg, he left her (and three young daughters) to marry one of Anita's Sarah Lawrence students, Edna Albers. Lakoff characterized the resulting nearly fifty-year marriage as passionate and happy, while adding that even after remarriage and three sons, Lerner "remained intent upon sexual conquest and adventure."

Over the sweep of his life, Lerner managed an affair with Elizabeth Taylor (she called him her "little professor") and more flings than his biographer could chronicle. Instead of trying, Lakoff aimed at establishing a parallel between Lerner's sexual energy and his prodigious capacity for academic and journalistic work. Lerner, he wrote, felt that "his erotic adventures and his efforts to gain literary celebrity were mutually reinforcing, as if the desire to court women and the desire to court readers arose from the same erotic impulse." Lerner's intellectual career, unlike his sexual one, underwent principled evolution rather than madcap expansion. Building on his early admiration for Veblen, Lerner came to feel around 1930 that "collectivism was destined to replace individualism" in the United States. At the same time, watching the New Deal era unfold, he began to consider Roosevelt's "level-headed American pragmatism" the best thing for both democracy and the part of capitalism worth retaining.

The 1930s saw Lerner build his two careers simultaneously, publishing articles in Ivy League law reviews and journals while also writing for the *New York Herald Tribune,* the *Nation* and the *New Republic.* During his year as a lecturer in Harvard's government department, Lerner was introduced by Harold Laski, already a friend, to another future friend, Felix Frankfurter. Years later, according to Lakoff, Frankfurter would lobby the president of Brandeis to improve Lerner's position and draw him away from the habits of mind that journalism "begets in its practitioners." For the most part, however, Frankfurter provided the sterling intellectual company that enabled Lerner to develop clear views on charged issues of the '30s: the New Deal, the Supreme Court's so-called judicial restraint, Roosevelt's court-packing scheme. Lerner's primary view, expressed in an influential 1933 law review article, was that "the Constitution had been made into a weapon for the defense of economic inequality and used against all attempts to modify property rights for the sake of economic democracy."

For almost fifty years, Lerner would continue to comment on the social issues of his time, both in short genres and in once-famous books such as *It Is Later Than You Think* (1938), a study of liberalism that popularized the title phrase. Like any biographer obligated to provide play-by-play of so prolonged an intellectual life, Lakoff struggled valiantly to capsulize Lerner's views. He recounted Lerner's prominence as a spokesman for Popular Frontism before World War II and his activism in favor of early U.S. involvement against fascism. (Lerner spent a day with Roosevelt at Hyde Park in 1941, talking philosophy and urging a tough stand toward Nazi Germany.) Lakoff showed Lerner becoming a "Walter Lippmann of the democratic Left" in the 1940s, suffering criticism for supporting our wartime alliance with the Soviet Union for too long (Walter Winchell referred to him as "Marx Lerner"), then suffering further criticism in the 1950s for becoming a "centrist liberal," backing pro-UN internationalism, collective security and containment. In the 1960s and '70s, Lerner became "the spokesman for liberal New York opinion" through his *New York Post* column. There he attacked the New Left and hippie values that offended him, and, in his seventies, began his celebration of "eros" with Hefner, whom he exalted as a great American "guilt killer." ("I teach him sex," Lerner joked, "and he teaches me politics.") Lerner's least attractive years proved to be the 1980s, when the columnist became more routinely centrist, denounced political correctness, clung to an image of priapic virility and obsessed over illness and immortality.

Amid his subject's almost suffocating avalanche of commentary, Lakoff rightly centered Lerner's claim for enduring importance as a thinker on his triumph, *America as a Civilization.* If, as various speakers once suggested at a Manhattan tribute to critic Alfred Kazin, that Jewish son of Yiddish-speaking immigrants invigorated the reading of American literature in *On Native Grounds* by thinking "with his whole body," Lerner achieved something similar for broad-based philosophizing about the U.S. Lakoff accurately described *America as a Civilization* as "a prodigious and extremely ambitious effort of synthesis, ranging over the country's social history, natural setting, literary and popular culture, economics, and politics, as well as its national character and style—all in an effort to define what was unique about the country and to analyze the factors that accounted for its development."

Lerner, writing in the Toynbee era that saw America as a marginal nation-state, insisted that America should be viewed as a new civilization, not a spinoff of European predecessors. He argued that American character comprised two key elements, thumbnailed by Lakoff as "self-reliance, coupled with endurance, friendliness, a democratic informality," and "a sharp aggressiveness, coupled with an organizing capacity, a genius for technology, a sense of bigness and power." Together, they'd fused into an American character that produced the "archetypical man of the West." Against an ugly view of American imperialism driven by hegemonic capitalism, Lerner maintained that America practiced "the imperialism of attraction," winning other people's hearts and feet through the appeal of ideas and accomplishments. As such a précis suggests, Lerner utterly unburdened himself in *America as a Civilization* of lingering radical impulses. He clearly decided, Lakoff wrote, that "radicals could not compete with liberal reformers in concrete programs." He became "Galbraithian" in that he "saw the managed economy of the affluent society as a reasonable approximation of the democratic collectivism he had earlier advocated."

Ultimately keeping to Veblen's evolutionary view of society, Lerner considered America a civilization protected from Rome's exhaustion by a central virtue: the "access" it provided to its elite structure, albeit often only after social battles. "In *America as a Civilization,*" wrote Lakoff, Lerner "rejected as incomplete all the formulaic explanations of America's success, such as the frontier, natural abundance, isolation, and ideology, both religious and secular. Instead, he argued that the key to understanding the civilization Americans had created is its special capacity for innovation and adaptation"—what he called "American dynamism." In sidestepping hints of reductionism in the genre of American intellectual history—whether Charles Beard's economic constitutionalism, Vernon Parrington's eternal battle between democracy and elitism, or Perry Miller's elaboration of the Puritan mind-set—Lerner teased out pragmatic veins in that genre and realigned it with American common sense.

Lakoff drew persuasive biographical conclusions from his assessment of *America as a Civilization* and its impact. Lerner, he observed, "must have known that defending liberal America would cost him the polemical niche he had carved out for himself," that he'd be accused of having sold out. Though historians like Samuel Eliot Morison were "unstinting in their praise," others complained that the book lacked edge. Lakoff himself, confirming that his allegiance to Lerner extended only so far, confessed his preference for the nervier views of his later teacher Louis Hartz about America's "liberal tradition." Hartz, in *The Liberal Tradition in America* (1955), argued that because Americans were spared feudalism and both absorbed and apotheosized a "Lockean ethos," they grew inoculated against extremist ideologies—a judgment Lerner remained too skeptical to share. Checkered responses, in any event, greeted Lerner's career as a whole. In the course of it, as Lakoff reported, Lerner drew praise from figures as diverse as Noel Coward, I. F. Stone, Charlie Chaplin, Felix Frankfurter and Hannah Arendt. At the same time, Lakoff recorded harsh criticisms of Lerner by journalist Sydney Harris, who skewered his style, and *Ramparts,* which mocked his "Slow Lerner" politics.

Nonetheless, Lerner wrote his one great book "less for contempo-raries than for the next generation," his biographer contended. And its vitality continues precisely because it transcended the narrow explanatory habit of overprofessionalized American historians. Somewhat inadver-tently, Lakoff rightly situated Lerner as the author of the best pragmatist intellectual history of the United States: a narrative that insisted twists of American history emerged from complex, intricate problems in real life, not from a script driven by one powerful idea. A consensus on the man seems more elusive. At times, Lerner came off as a sexist exploiter of women and a braggart. Men, on the other hand, he gently mentored. During his academic time at Williams, and twenty-five postwar years as a professor of American studies at Brandeis, he nurtured such students as James MacGregor Burns and Martin Peretz, both of whom remained close to him. At Lerner's memorial service, Peretz eulogized him as a "mixture of gaiety with gravitas, mischief with illumination."

Lakoff ended by urging future Americanists not to dismiss Lerner for his "eclecticism," not to make him pay a price "for being a general-ist," even if Lerner himself "had a nagging sense that he had not done enough important work, having put too much into newspaper journal-ism and not enough into more enduring forms of writing." That he never became Isaiah Berlin is clear. Lerner's own self-analysis helped explain why he suffered secondary status to Lippmann, whom he denounced in the 1930s as a "reactionary" but saluted upon Lippmann's death for giving political columnists "a sense of our intellectual role." Lippmann (1889–1974) surely wrote a greater number of important books, *Public Opinion* and *A Preface to Morals* among them. His application of Freud-ian ideas to politics and intense focus on mass opinion in political theory offered original perspectives Lerner rarely matched.

Yet Lakoff's biography, particularly the rich context it erected around the author of *America as a Civilization,* showed the gap in their reputations to be too great. Lerner's candor and ethnic authenticity con-trasted favorably with Lippmann's intellectual reticence, his infamous suppression of his Jewishness. Lerner's willingness to cross swords with power over decades shone beside Lippmann's lifelong campaign to be chief theoretician of the Establishment. Lerner's empathetic support for collective security, a phrase he popularized, appealed more than Lippmann's cold-fish realism about America's interests. Finally, Ler-ner's version of American exceptionalism's continued force in the early years of a century in which America the Philosophical's cultural impact on other countries seemed clear—even as America's economic power wanes—makes more sense than Lippmann's cosmopolitan allegiance to European models of explanation. If Lippmann remains the deeper thinker about liberal tradition, Lerner endures as the more authentic and philosophical Americanist, confronting his country, like Kazin, with all organs working.

A 1963 *New Yorker* cartoon, published during the newspaper strike that closed every New York daily except the *New York Post,* captures Lerner's plight on the sideline of culture. It shows a commuter car full of conservative businessmen, denied their usual paper, unhappily reading the *Post.* One grumbles, "Who *is* this Max Lerner?" Lakoff confronted the contemporary version of that question and answered it bluntly: a thinker worth remembering as both case study and exemplar of rude truths. Another answer was: the author of *America as a Civilization,* the intellectual history Dewey might have written if—strange thought—he'd been Max Lerner.

Lerner was hardly alone among intellectual journalists in turning, in the mature decades of his career, to increasingly philosophical work. Five years younger, I. F. Stone (1907–1989) had made his reputation as the indefatigable one-man show of leftist journalism. His weekly muckraking newsletter, published from 1953 to 1971, regularly broke stories by paying close attention to government documents and publications. At nearly eighty, he nonetheless broke what he considered his biggest cultural story: the undeserved praise heaped upon Socrates, Western philosophy's most admired founding father. Stone smelled a rat in Socrates, and not just in the middle of his name. (In Part 5 of this book, I also question Socrates's apotheosis, but from a different direction.)

Never one cowed by authority, Stone didn't care that Plato, Socrates's student, friend and publicity director, regarded the great Greek kibitzer as "the most righteous man of the whole age," establishing his traditional image as Western civilization's first intellectual saint and martyr for free thought. Or that the oracle at Delphi declared that no man was wiser, more generous, more just or more sensible than Socrates. Or that Aristotle described the Athenian trial and execution of Socrates at age seventy as a sin. According to Stone, radical journalist turned classicist, Socrates was a "snob" full of "immeasurable conceit" and "class prejudice," a man guilty of "gross simplification" in his philosophy, an irritating questioner who "never questioned slavery" and "neglected the affairs of his family and his city to engage in constant conversation."

Worse, wrote Stone, Socrates didn't give a damn about democracy, and condescended to politics in general. That inspired young Athenians fond of oligarchy, including some of Socrates's former students, to test the city's fragile democracy a few times too many. In Stone's view, Socrates's famous mission to enlighten others was just "an ego trip—an exercise in self-glorification for Socrates and of belittlement for the city's most respected leaders. He thus undermined the polis, defamed the men on whom it depended, and alienated the youth." We know where that led. In 399 B.C., three Athenian citizens charged Socrates with "corrupting the youth" and "introducing false gods." Socrates defended himself, but the jury of five hundred peers found him guilty by a vote of 280 to 220. By an even larger margin, they sentenced him to death. Although his friends arranged a plan for Socrates to escape, he refused, citing an obligation to the laws of Athens not to run, and drank the hemlock.

Stone, a deep believer in free speech, agreed that the execution remained "a black mark for Athens and the freedom it symbolized." Yet he sought "to give the Athenian side of the story, to mitigate the city's crime and thereby remove some of the stigma the trial left on democracy and Athens." Stone's conclusion was that while Socrates didn't quite deserve hemlock, one couldn't totally blame the Athenians who sentenced him. Was this a reasonable picture of a man Hegel and others compared to Jesus? In Stone's view, Socrates clashed with his fellow Athenians on three key issues. Most of Socrates's contemporaries, wrote Stone, thought themselves capable of self-rule. Socrates and all his followers looked down on democracy as rule by the "herd." He believed the herd needed a shepherd and argued for rule by "the one who knows"— by an expert or experts. Stone's Socrates also undermined Athenian democracy by arguing that (a) virtue was knowledge and (b) knowledge was almost unattainable. The combined position implied, according to Stone, that ordinary Athenians lacked the qualifications to govern themselves.

Third, Socrates failed to be "a good citizen," because he "preached and practiced withdrawal from the political life of the city." Following what Stone calls the "Three Earthquakes" that struck Athenian democracy—coups in 411 and 404 B.C. and a near coup in 401—such views no longer seemed a laughing matter. Stone offered further harsh judgments on Socrates. He accused the colorful, ever-ironic questioner of condemning people to death by declining an activist role in politics, of lacking compassion, of turning philosophy into a "wild goose chase," and even, in the end, of a "death wish." Although scholars traditionally see Plato's *Crito* as a profound explanation of why Socrates felt morally obligated not to evade the laws of Athens, Stone held that Socrates "did not reject escape because the Laws won the argument. He let the Laws win the argument because he did not want to escape."

Stone's certainties clashed with the doubt that hangs over much of our knowledge of ancient Greece. Every great modern Socrates scholar agrees that we can't conclusively establish Socrates's life and character from the mixed historical evidence. One of the most thorough, V. de Magalhães-Vilhena, whose eight hundred pages on the subject received an amazed nod from Stone in his footnotes, concluded that "it is quite clear that we do not possess a portrait of Socrates as he really was." Yet Stone offered his portrait with few qualifications, perhaps because many of his views, far from being fresh discoveries, were quite familiar from the scholarly literature.

The sophist Polycrates, six years after the trial, first made the argument that Athens, nervous after several coups, tried Socrates as an enemy of democracy. In modern times, translator R. E. Allen argued for it in a 1984 commentary on the *Apology*. In the name-calling category, Nietzsche long ago castigated Socrates as "decadent" and a "buffoon." Karl Popper, one of the twentieth century's major philosophers, notoriously attacked Plato, if not Socrates, as a forerunner of totalitarianism in *The Open Society and Its Enemies* (1945). In *Class Ideology and Ancient Political Theory* (1978), Neal and Ellen Wood indicted Socrates as a partisan of aristocracy. The list could go on.

All these arguments came with ammunition and sparked opposition fire that any subsequent writer might have addressed. Stone, while boasting of how many commentaries he'd read, found himself more drawn to his old journalistic principles: focus on primary sources. He wrote disdainfully that "the Socratic literature is mountainous; the evidence, meager." A reporter's "first step," he advised, was "to turn from these distant and often acrimonious debates and re-examine the basic documents themselves."

It may not have been the wisest move. By turning predominantly to the Socratic dialogues themselves, Stone failed to inform the reader of considerable opinion arrayed against many of his views, particularly when it came to blaming Socrates for positions possibly imposed on him by Plato. Popper, for instance, argued in *The Open Society* that Socrates opposed slavery and was fundamentally "a friend of democracy." His Socrates criticized democracy because he wanted to educate it. The classicist Richard Kraut, agreeing that Socrates was "a democrat of sorts," argued in *Socrates and the State*—a brilliant synthesis that analyzed many issues Stone shadowboxed with his left hand—for a Socrates who valued free speech, ridiculed class bias, did not condescend to the working class, thought all men capable of being experts and viewed his own work as contributory to the state.

Any reader of Plato could also see that Stone's conclusions about Socrates, charitably interpreted, at the very least faced challenges within the Platonic corpus. Stone insisted, for instance, that Socrates felt only an elitist contempt for working people, but ignored that Plato's *Republic* can be seen as a meritocratic, not aristocratic, vision. Similarly, a champion of Socrates could argue that Stone failed to acknowledge how children of the elite can be demoted if they fail to measure up; that Plato's women and slaves are capable of virtue; that Socrates sought to speak with the poor as well as the rich. Stone's go-it-alone posture obscured from the reader one reason for his interpretations—his bold choice of whom to believe on Socrates.

Only two full contemporary portraits of the older Socrates exist: those of Plato and Xenophon, the Athenian general. Xenophon's Socrates is an arrogant orator, extremely hostile to democracy and the lower classes. Much of Stone's interpretation depended on appealing to Xenophon's evidence over Plato's. Yet Xenophon didn't attend Socrates's trial, left Athens a good two years before it began and wrote about it much later. Plato, by contrast, attended the trial, knew Socrates well and specifically reported (in an odd aside for him) that he heard Socrates's speech.

Most scholars thus favor Plato's version of Socrates over Xenophon's. As A. E. Taylor wrote, "Xenophon's relations with [Socrates] seem not to have been close, and he has even been suspected of deriving much of his material from Plato's dialogues. His admitted deficiencies in imagination and capacity for thinking do not make him the more faithful exponent of a philosophical genius." Perhaps most damaging to Stone's conclusions, his book made almost no attempt to separate Socrates's views from those of Plato, even though doing so was a sine qua non for respectable discussion of their positions. On small matters of philosophical and factual accuracy, Stone frequently stumbled. Referring to the contract between state and citizen discussed by Socrates in the *Crito*, he called it "the first appearance of the social contract theory in secular literature." But "social contract theory" refers to pacts among free people to create a state, not those of citizens with a state, and arose long after Socrates. Stone also tended toward carelessness, misspelling important names.

The greatest irony of *The Trial of Socrates* was that Stone seemed blind to a time-honored interpretation of Socrates that fit his own career as a journalist—the notion that far from being an enemy of democracy, Socrates was simply a severe critic of it. Stone hardly explained to the reader that Athenian democracy, unlike our own, amounted to radical democracy, without checks and balances, without judicial review, without the core of individual rights that protects us against what John Stuart Mill later called "the tyranny of the majority." Instead, Stone wound up—bizarrely, given their opposed political leanings—as an ally of Allan Bloom, who had written about Socrates's "profoundly aristocratic or even monarchic" approach to social issues.

For all that, his foray as journalist into philosophy couldn't have been bolder. To take on classical philosophy's most controversial event at age eighty, despite failing eyesight, required fierce intellectual pride and remarkable chutzpah. In an era of growing sound bites, Stone, like Lerner, propelled himself beyond the confines of journalism.

Stone's style of aggressive political journalism, both from the left and into the world of big ideas, passed on by a kind of inside-the-Beltway inheritance to an Englishman, Christopher Hitchens (1949–2011), who, by the early twenty-first century, became an American citizen after decades of residence and work in Washington, D.C. On the schmooze map of that status-mad city overrun by journalists and politicos, Hitchens's spacious apartment in the swank Wyoming functioned as a station of the cross, a designated performance space for names in the news. Right-wingers and left-wingers, libertarians and ex-Marxists, government officials and wise-guy reporters—all came to Hitch's fabled salon-like dinners to cross swords without cameras, eager to hear the most controversial opinion journalist in America rocket his latest serves:

That "fascism with an Islamic face" must be crushed.

That "Pakistan is an enemy of everything the United States stands for."

That onetime leftist ally Noam Chomsky was guilty of "casuistry" (if not worse).

Given the volume of the self-anointed contrarian's outbursts in *Vanity Fair,* the *Atlantic* and elsewhere, opinion journalism in the Northeast sometimes seemed like Christopher Hitchens's world, with everyone else simply dropping in for brief stints. Within that everyone-reads-everyone clique, the combative ex-Marxist journalist, best known for his acerbic tone and caustically titled books about political enemies (*No One Left to Lie To* about Clinton; *The Missionary Position* about Mother Teresa), practiced the pull-no-punches style he recommended in his *Letters to a Young Contrarian,* a guide to freethinking intellectual independence for tyros in the trade.

"The whole excitement of trying to lead a life of the mind," said the portly smoker, chatting in his apartment over ginger ale and a succession of king-size Rothmans of London cigarettes on a slow Sunday afternoon, "is finding out what other people think, why they think, and how they think. You want to make them clash and see who wins, who has better points." He described his orchestrated social life—which took off in the early 1990s when he and *Vanity Fair* began hosting an alternate party to the yearly Washington correspondents' dinner—as "perfectly congruent" with the ideas expressed in his "contrarian" manual. "I love doing that. We do it quite a bit here." On one evening in the Hitchens living room that spectacularly overlooked a lively stretch of Connecticut Avenue near the Washington Hilton, dinner guests had huddled around the coffee table, lent dignity by a chess set and illuminated by small candles.

Sitting on a couch, Akbar Ahmed, the distinguished Pakistani scholar of Islam at American University, warned that his country's government could not shoot protesters in the home areas of many Pakistani military without serious repercussions. Grover Norquist, the controversial Republican political strategist partly responsible for President George W. Bush's outreach to American Muslims after 9/11, shrugged when Hitchens provocatively advised him that, according to rumor, enemies had a photo floating around of Norquist with Osama bin Laden. Within minutes, Hitchens scooted off to do the syndicated radio program of conservative talk-show host Laura Ingraham, his wife calling on the sloppily attired writer to "put on a jacket" as he closed the door.

Sure enough, an hour later, as his guests sat down to caprese salads, Hitchens returned with Ingraham in tow. As the night wound down, the congenitally anticlerical and atheistic Hitchens could be heard challenging Ingraham on her Christian beliefs, with Ingraham assuring Hitchens, "The gates are always open," if he wanted to emulate St. Augustine and switch sides.

"Grover has become a friend because of our common interest in opposing authoritarianism," Hitchens remarked afterward. "I called Akbar because I'm trying to improve Grover's profile with Muslims." As for Ingraham, Hitchens just reeled her in while the reeling was good: "I don't think she would expect anyone would invite her to a dinner to discuss theology. She said, 'I didn't come to do that.' What interests me about her is that she's tough. I like people who are tough. . . . I've always had the feeling that Washington can be so hollow at its core, so company-town-like, that you could try and have something like a salon as long as you didn't call it that."

In a departure for Hitchens, his manual, *Letters to a Young Contrarian*, subtitled *The Art of Mentoring*, eviscerated no famous contemporary enemy. Instead, taking German poet Rainer Maria Rilke's classic *Letters to a Young Poet* as a model, Hitchens offered a series of short letters to unnamed students and younger journalists who had asked him for advice. He began by mulling terms that might fit his trade—"dissident," "radical," "maverick," "loose cannon," "rebel," "angry young man," "gadfly," "curmudgeon" and more (though not "philosopher")—explaining why he admired the moral courage of writers such as Émile Zola. Hitchens urged the young would-be contrarian to examine his commitment to writing ("You must feel not that you want to but that you have to") and to living, as Walzer too had advocated, "at a slight acute angle to society." Radical critics, he urged, should discard the "idiotic" notion that consensus "is the highest good," and recognize "as a law of physics that heat is the chief, if not the only, source of light." Argument, he and good critics believed, was valuable for its own sake.

Hitchens went on to counsel young contrarians to avoid "invitations to passivity or acquiescence." It's helpful, he wrote, to remind yourself that you have only one life to live, to travel to challenging places, to expose yourself to morally charged environments like Bosnia, to see the twin evils of racism and religion. True to his beliefs, Hitchens described religiosity as "positively harmful," an "irreducibly servile and masochistic" mind-set. Along the way, the former Trotskyite addressed the phenomenon regular readers had wondered about for a while: Was this once celebrated tribune of the left still a leftist?

"I have not abandoned all the tenets of the left," Hitchens wrote, mentioning some he still supported, but asserted that he had "learned a good deal from the libertarian critique of this worldview." Perhaps for that reason, he'd been under fire from some old allies for beating the war drums against terrorism. E-mails informed him that he had been "excommunicated from the left." University of Pennsylvania economist

Edward S. Herman, a longtime Chomsky collaborator, depicted Hitchens as "rushing toward the vital center, maybe further to the right, with termination point still to be determined." Hitchens's response came forcefully in the *Atlantic*: "Members of the left, along with the far larger number of squishy 'progressives,' have grossly failed to live up to their responsibility to think; rather, they are merely reacting, substituting tired slogans for thought."

Asked to offer a mini review of his own guide, Hitchens replied, "It's a little bit impressionistic, a bit slight, and free associating, perhaps." He was glad it was coming out at a time when unpopular opinion appeared challenged by the country's circle-the-wagons unification against terrorism. While not sympathetic to every figure whose mouth had gotten him in trouble since September 11 (he called Bill Maher "a cheap, thuggish demagogue"), Hitchens said, "There's never going to be a time when dissent is what everyone reveres." Yet he hoped younger journalists would take to heart the importance of his manual's key matters: keeping to one's principles, staying uncompromised by sources, emulating the singular moral courage of his great hero, George Orwell.

"He's the gold standard for me," Hitchens said. Not because Orwell wrote faster, or more, or accomplished extraordinary feats, but because, Hitchens noted, he possessed distinctive intellectual and literary integrity. "Anyone could do what he did," Hitchens said, making it sound simple. "You just have to forbid yourself the lie. And forbid yourself the euphemism and neologism."

By 2011, battling esophageal cancer, his hair an on-or-off matter, he was still keeping to that pledge. *God Is Not Great* (2007), his best-selling tirade against religion, had elevated him to "author and thinker" as much as journalist—with typical Hitch panache, he quipped that the only criticism he'd accept of the book was that the title might be one word too long. *Arguably* (2011), a hefty collection of his essays and reviews, further reminded everyone of the many public issues he'd pugnaciously engaged.

In December 2011, the cancer killed him, triggering an immediate front-and-center obituary on the *New York Times* website, scores of appreciations by leading intellectuals and more than a thousand comments. Many of the latter lauded him for his lifelong commitment to a fundamental philosophical task—public persuasion through expertly chosen words.

It was hard to imagine any philosophy professor in America whose death would have set off such a cascade of thank yous from the well-educated.

THE BROADCASTERS

Recent tradition dictates that news broadcasters also be called journalists. When longtime CBS anchor Walter Cronkite died at the age of ninety-two, the *New York Times* and other arbiters of elite culture bade him farewell as virtually the central journalist of his age. In part, they did so because he'd earned his reportorial creds in both print and TV, and because he recalled an era when the sober, measured, judicious, mostly neutral and indisputably influential voice of the network news anchor approximated the voice of the people, expressing its commonsense "philosophy" or "take on things," as closely as any single human voice might in technology's modern age.

But in the first decade of the twenty-first century, loudmouth behavior and shifting standards made the issue of whether broadcasters added to a growing America the Philosophical a contentious one indeed. As noted at this book's outset, the "talk show" between Socrates and his interlocutors, which readers can still enter, bears some resemblance to what the phrase indicates today, but not a lot. Perhaps no one made the brief for that skeptical view of the contemporary genre more effectively than Howard Kurtz, host of CNN's *Reliable Sources,* the longest-running media criticism show on TV, and longtime media reporter for the *Washington Post* before joining Tina Brown's *Daily Beast.* The author of numerous well-reported critiques of how media, politics and business intertwine—among them *Media Circus, Spin Cycle, The Fortune Tellers* and *Reality Show*—he brought together the evidence in *Hot Air,* his own Baedeker of talk-show stars.

Kurtz served it up raw. There was blustery John McLaughlin of *The McLaughlin Group,* defending his weekly media circus by insisting, "Blurting is good! We want blurting!" And CNN's now departed Larry King, bragging to all that he didn't prepare for interviews. And the Washington screamfest producer whose job included shrieking, "Get mad! Get mad!" into the cohost's earpiece when a guest from Congress threatened to link more than three sentences together.

Could even DNA sampling detect any philosophy done on these premises? The syllogism was out, Shill-igism in—particularly by big-name Washington journalists giving speeches for a cause or their own bank accounts. Once upon a time, TV talk-show hosts like David Susskind had occasionally interviewed a guest such as Bertrand Russell. Now it was out with the dialectic, in with the hectic and septic. Or so it seemed.

"Anyone can say anything at any time with little fear of contradiction," reported Kurtz in his spirited expedition into America's growing oral cavity. "It is raw, it is real, and it is immensely popular. The gatekeepers of the elite media have been cast aside and the floodgates thrown open." The upshot, Kurtz thought, looked virtually all bad. "As the talk show culture has exploded," he warned, "the national conversation has been coarsened, cheapened, reduced to name-calling and finger-pointing and bumper-sticker sloganeering. Television has little time for context, subtlety or caveats. Seat-of-the-pants judgments—up or down, yes or no, who won and who lost and committed the outrage of the week—have become a driving force."

Washington journalist Jim Fallows's earlier book *Breaking the News* had made similar points about the plummeting quality of the republic's rhetoric, even using some of the same quotes. So had Neil Postman's *Amusing Ourselves to Death: Public Discourse in the Age of Show Business*, reacting to TV culture as far back as 1985, before the explosion of the Internet. Postman, an NYU communications theorist, lamented that while "America was founded by intellectuals," we now lived in a culture where "all public discourse takes the form of entertainment," degrading the way we discuss news, politics, education, science, sports, religion and commerce. The typical TV discussion, he asserted, permitted "no arguments or counterarguments, no scrutiny of assumptions, no explanations, no elaborations, no definitions." It left us with only "marginal propositional content" in our discourse and "getting sillier by the minute."

Kurtz's portrait, offering lively, sassy fun and pulling one as far inside America's house of hot air as one could get without forming a capital gang of one's own, looked like the messenger delivering Postman's prophecy. Too accomplished at the star reporter's task of expertly describing scenes, getting off tart lines and keeping the play-by-play going to sit back, take a deep breath and think in an academic way about the larger implication of Talk Nation, Kurtz understandably didn't provide a scholarly critique of the culture he covered.

Yet the breadth of Kurtz's reportage and his incisive opinions formed a philosophical argument of sorts, an act of persuasion about a broadcast culture *of* persuasion. He zoomed in on "Daytime Dysfunction"; Larry King as the "King of Schmooze"; "politicized hosts"; "Radio Rebels" such as Howard Stern and Don Imus; *Meet the Press* and the Sunday-morning political shows; "The Rush Hour" of Rush Limbaugh; the journalists' gravy-train circuit of speeches for big fees; the political influence of talk radio; the revolving door between media and politics; and his own forays into TV and radio. He exposed the depths of the fakery, commercial greed and "coziness" between journalists and politicians at every level of talk media, such as the practice of taking what Michael Kinsley called Washington's "televised journalistic gasbaggery" on the road to trade group conventions for even more lucrative food fights in public.

Kurtz expertly employed the old *Spy* magazine device of slitting many subjects to death with brief adjectival prefaces: "onetime sex lecturer" McLaughlin, or "onetime food-stamp recipient" Sally Jessy Raphael. Noting that "the issue of journalists taking money from interest groups would seem a legitimate subject for public debate," he emphasized the defensiveness of honcho Washington journalists on the topic by listing, staccato style, their responses to his question about their paid speaking engagements. Some examples?

"I'm not an elected official," said Fred Barnes.

"I'm a private citizen," said Chris Wallace.

"I'm not an elected official," said Gloria Borger.

"I'm not going to disclose it," said Al Hunt.

"I don't exercise the power of the state," said George Will.

Kurtz also reported a telling feature of the scene: the rampant lack of mutual respect that lurked just beneath the pushy, ebullient personas exhibited by on-air folks. Sometimes it emerged in the asperity talkmeisters unloaded at one another. "Fred's never let talking about something he knows nothing about bother him," said Kinsley of chat-fest colleague Barnes. "Kinsley is symbolic of everything we loathe and despise," said conservative Mary Matalin. "He's a hypocrite and he's a fraud. He criticizes other people for 'spin' and then he becomes Mr. Showbiz, Mr. Sound Bite."

But it also emerged through confession, as by former McLaughlin group member Jack Germond. "I am not comfortable with any of this," said Germond, "but I do it for the money. When you get to your mid-forties, either you become an editor or you have to find a way to become a mini-conglomerate if you want to have control of your schedule. If you want to make enough money, you have to do television. If I didn't have to pay alimony, I wouldn't do it."

That piling on of detail about hot-air America, what Kurtz called the "insular and self-serving world of talk-show journalism," accomplished its task of downsizing the glory attached to the enterprise. Inadvertently, however, it also corroborated a larger truth about America the Philosophical, equally overlooked by Postman and Kurtz. While each individual broadcaster fell short of an old ideal of the philosopher/persuader who takes on all the "on-the-one-hand, on-the-other-hand" himself, broadcast culture itself teemed with arguments on almost every side of every issue. Everyone involved seemed to recognize that, across America's fruited plains of freewheeling opinion and argument, *someone* would take care of the other side of the argument. That in itself appeared to liberate everyone to be one-sided and polemical.

As the Fox News era of hell-bent partisanship began, that mind-set seemed only to expand, with talk-show hosts such as MSNBC's Keith Olbermann and Rachel Maddow taken as balancing, in a big-media way, Fox's Glenn Beck or Bill O'Reilly. America the Philosophical, in that cable-TV respect, tracked the adversarial paradigm that sustained American law: run a system in which every side of an argument gets maximum focused support, and a wide ideological marketplace will result.

To be sure, the avalanche of "pointless punditry" Kurtz feared might be overtaking the country betrayed the author's intense inside-the-Beltway perspective. Most educated professionals outside Washington paid little or no attention to the capital's local industry of political chat shows, and made no decisions based on them. His concerns only came to pass as cable created national figures such as Olbermann and Beck. Even with that eventuality, Kurtz's Paul Revere–ish tone, applied then or now, ignored one dirty little secret of class-difference America that Fussell might have flagged, and that Susan Jacoby had also missed: despite media pandering to mass America and its dollars by shoveling endless trash TV and music toward them, most well-educated professional Americans—the people running the country—watched little talk TV, listened to little talk radio beyond NPR, and made their decisions based on the quality news products and magazines they read.

Only a few characters came out heroes—or survivors—on Kurtz's scorecard. Brian Lamb, the founder and owner of C-SPAN, stood tall as a decent, principled defender of sensible coverage. Lamb reminded one that broadcast culture remained, by definition, "broad," and that Kurtz's chosen territory and project excluded much by design. The nation's academic, legal and policy worlds, full of complex argument, still exhaled "serious air," as did *Fresh Air,* the NPR show hosted by Terry Gross. The same went for scores of other shows run by radio and TV professionals—*The Charlie Rose Show* among them—that imposed a higher set of conversational standards on themselves than did Kurtz's crew.

But the contribution to America the Philosophical by broadcasters could best be documented by two examples. The first was the TV veteran and alumnus who came closest to incarnating the image of the philosopher-broadcaster, Bill Moyers.

On one spring day in Manhattan, you could find him just above the D'Agostino supermarket at Ninth Avenue and West 57th Street, on the second floor of a building devoted mainly to television, in an office cramped by more books, one suspected, than complicated the ambitions of any other TV personality in America.

Hardcovers and paperbacks, impassioned polemics and academic mumbo jumbo, pressed together on packed shelves worthy of an excellent neighborhood library. Beneath them, typed tags like "Journalism and the Media Environment" identified his library's sections. A framed passage from Dostoevsky's *The Brothers Karamazov* contributed to the literary air, and seemed to gaze down at the five chairs pulled up around his desk: "And even if we are occupied with important things, even if we attain honor or fall into misfortune, still let us remember how good it was once here when we were all together; united by a good and kind feeling, which made us better perhaps than we are."

"I think what intrigues me," said Moyers, TV's iconic humanist, after slipping behind his crowded desk, "is the connection between things. When I was thinking about being in religious teaching for a calling, I read everything I could about religion. And when I thought about journalism, I read everything I could about journalism. And government and politics, everything about government and politics." The books, artifacts of a pensive man, competed for office space with booty from another world—that medium often embarrassed by traces of intellect, by strong emotions not directed at destroying anything.

His many golden Emmys—more than thirty by 2010—stood perched behind him, their aligned wingspans suggesting an exaltation of angels always at his back. Other awards for television work—the RFK prize, the Peabodys—lay around everywhere, easily mistaken for paperweights or space dividers. A yellowed *Wall Street Journal* clip on the door announced, "Some Ideas May Be Too Weird for TV, But Not Very Many." It was far easier, one imagined, for this gently smiling alumnus of Southwestern Baptist Theological Seminary to take credit for a book than for a TV show. Yet there, too, he was modest. The *New York Times* might have described one of his bestsellers, *Healing and the Mind*—a companion volume to his documentary series about alternative approaches to health—as "by Bill Moyers," but by Moyers's request that designation didn't appear on the book, because television's embodiment of conscience declined to take the credit.

"I'm not the author of *Healing and the Mind*," explained Moyers. "I know that, and I've been saying that all along. I wasn't the author of *Joseph Campbell and the Power of Myth*, which was over a year on the bestseller list, or *A World of Ideas*, which became a bestseller." Each, he said, was a "collaborative effort in which I am the facilitator." You expected that kind of honesty from Moyers because he bore public TV's most honorable CV, caused normally earthy guests to turn Socratic and wise, and was the gadfly constantly accosted by ordinary people—those viewers network bosses thought weren't interested—and thanked for an interview with poet Archibald MacLeish, or his mesmerizing hours with Campbell.

Go back to the beginning, and you found an Oklahoma boy, raised in Texas, starting out as a sixteen-year-old cub reporter at the *Marshall News Messenger* while listening to teachers who "turned me on to poetry as music for the human ear, and prose as a revelation of this inner working of your inner mind." Skip forward through the University of Texas to the Kennedy administration, and he was deputy director of the Peace Corps while still in his twenties, special assistant to President Lyndon B. Johnson from 1963 to 1967.

But it was only when he went to television, after a brief turn as publisher of *Newsday*, that his distinctive profile emerged on the American scene. "I was thirty-seven," he recalled, "already formed. Or let me say that the great advantage was I hadn't been deformed by network experience."

With *Bill Moyers Journal*, and regular analysis and documentaries for CBS, he established a reputation for literacy in a medium galloping

Bill Moyers (1934–), over a distinguished career in both network and public television, put
notable thinkers such as Joseph
Campbell and Martha Nuss-
baum on the air.

toward pictures. After he founded his own production company, Public
Affairs Television, in 1986 with a $5 million seed grant from the MacAr-
thur Foundation, he began to produce, with his wife, Judith Davidson,
the unique programming that made him a household conscience. Unlike
TV journalists who competed fiercely to work within established agendas of coverage, Moyers repeatedly followed his own inklings in seizing
new territory for television.

"It's the thing that I'm most in wonder about myself," he said, his
expression suggesting genuine puzzlement. "There's an intuition down
there that seems often ahead of the curve." With so many successful
documentaries under his belt, Moyers seemed to be the quintessential
bankable enterprise, both commercially and critically, facing no obstacles but his own uncertainty about the next challenge. Not so. For one
thing, he pointed out, not everyone liked him. "Part of my image," he
said, "is, 'Geez, I wish he weren't so solemn and so sober, and so square,
and so earnest.'" Then there are the "right-wingers who loathe the very
seat I sit on in a show. And the commercial broadcasters who think I'm
pious, and don't appreciate that."

And those were just the enemies. Even friendly folk had problems with Moyers—because, after all, he was in television, and yet he kept doing all those talking heads.

"I am sometimes tempted to tie rockets onto my subjects' earlobes," joked Moyers, "because the urge for picture is the sorcerer's apprentice in this business. Some producer or I am always saying, 'Well, how can we illustrate that?' But truthfully it's never been a serious conflict for me, because there's no more interesting production value to me than a human face. I come out of a tradition that says, 'In the beginning was the word, and the word was made flesh.' So to me, a human being is the incarnation of an idea."

"Now, my audience may have a problem with that sometimes," he conceded, "or my good and dear friends in public television, who also are part of a professional culture thirsting for visual exclamation points." He paused. "I will be extinct one day because it's not a problem for me. . . . But for the doers and shakers of this industry, Moyers is a brontosaurus."

Extinct? The man named in a poll of TV critics as one of the ten journalists who'd had the most influence on TV news? The winner of Columbia's Gold Baton, the Eric Barnouw Award, the James Madison Award, the Elmer Holmes Bobst Award and, probably someday, the award for most TV awards?

"I can't really do what I want," he remarked, explaining that the "skewered system" of public television, with hundreds of stations around the country, "makes it impossible to create a consensus at any given moment to commit to an ongoing series." If he "could do one thing above all," he said, it would be to continue his *World of Ideas* series on a regular basis. But with those hundreds of stations operating with separate brains, his search for funding and the right mix of airtime remained a constant headache: "To get their attention at any given time is almost impossible. . . . I don't have an ongoing critical mass of funds, or commitment for those funds, to do anything. I have to start over every time I set out. I long, for instance, to do a series of regular, weekly programs about religion. I cannot get anybody in the foundation world, the corporate world or public broadcasting to share that vision with me. . . . I have about ten to fifteen proposals working simultaneously all the time. It takes ten letters to get one phone call returned, and thirty phone calls to get one visit."

And yet, when someone in liberal government or journalism sought that magic public commodity—"credibility"—the call often went out to Moyers. President Jimmy Carter, he confided, offered him the position of secretary of education or chief of staff. He declined. President Clinton asked him down to Little Rock after his first election, and questioned him closely about White House operations, but didn't offer a job. Later in Clinton's transition, Moyers said, someone did call to feel him out about an administration job, but he said no again. Every once in a while, his name was floated for the presidency of a network news operation. Moyers found that ironic because, he related, young people who worked with him often couldn't get hired by the networks.

"That's the sad reality," he said. "Young people come in here and say, 'I want to try to do in television what you've done.' And I try to give apprenticeships to a lot of young people. But they often get hurt by it. . . . The networks say, Oh, you've been over there with Moyers. . . . I had one caller this morning who told me she got turned down at one of the networks because they said, 'Well, you can't do glitz. You've been working with Bill.' They admire me, but it's not an advantage to work with me if your ambition is to make money in commercial television."

Indeed, he worried that "the next generation is going to be all producers," all "bright hotshots who know how to bring pictures together, but little about telling stories with historical credibility." Bureaucratic positions didn't excite Moyers anyway, because, he said, he remained mostly "a news hound. . . . I'd rather be hiring Bill Moyers to do what Moyers does best—produce programs, analyze, report and interpret."

Listening to Moyers for an afternoon, hearing him tackle subjects imposed on him, you believed him that he was an assignment editor at heart, and a reporter devoted to keeping his finger on the country's pulse. If his projects seemed philosophical, they were so, he said, mainly in the sense that they provoked thought through old-fashioned reporting. He characterized his mandate as the one enunciated by Benjamin Harris in *Publick Occurrences Both Forreign and Domestick,* the first American newspaper: "To give an account of such considerable things as come to his attention."

Approaching new challenges casually, Moyers found that his next project often depended on serendipity: a book falling into his lap, the reading of a review, a conversation. Because he believed "narcissism is the poison of television," he didn't do a lot of "first-person-singular thinking." He tried to keep his attention focused outward, to honor his odd broadcasting niche by continuing to produce quality work.

"It's a paradox," he mused. "You almost have to be marginal to have impact. I. F. Stone once said to me, 'You only need five thousand readers if they're the right five thousand readers.' In other words, you almost have to be out on the margin to have your singularity fulfilled. And yet to be out there means you're disenfranchised from trying it in the mainstream."

Sometime in the future, the "by Bill Moyers" problem might no longer be an issue. "There's a part of me that really wishes I were a writer," he said, "so that more of what I think, and believe, and have found, would emerge than emerges through secondary sources. I'll do that someday. . . . I may have some reflections on the medium. I don't know. I really don't know."

Until recently, it almost came to pass. We saw more of Moyers on the page, less on the screen. *Moyers on Democracy* (2008), a collection of his speeches, led Studs Terkel to call Moyers "my North Star," citing his thoughtfulness about America and its ideals. As the pro bono president of the Schumann Center for Media and Democracy, the winner of the Lifetime Achievement Award from the National Academy of Television Arts and Sciences looked more and more, from the outside, like a writer and thinker.

In early 2011, fate even kicked in to lend him a setting true to his evolving philosophical bent. At the invitation of Kathleen Hall Jamieson, head of the spanking-new Annenberg Public Policy Center, Moyers found himself speaking to hundreds in the center's "Agora," that public place whose name an irrepressible commentator named Socrates would have recognized.

For more than an hour, following Jamieson's praise for him as a man who always asked, "Will it make a better world?," who had always taken on "people in power," Moyers watched video clips of himself on a giant screen, and sought to explain the principles by which he had run his career.

He joked that his service in both journalism and government made everything he said "twice as hard to believe." Watching an old clip of himself, then in LBJ's administration, carefully answering a question from Dan Rather, he observed, "There's always tension between people who want to know the truth and people who don't want to disclose the truth." At that time, he said, his rule with journalists was, "Tell the truth if you can, but if you can't tell the truth, don't tell a lie."

As his true career developed in journalism, however, Moyers came to deeply appreciate that "news is what people want to keep hidden," and that "the passion of a journalist must be for the facts." He liked a line, he confided, spoken by the photographer in Tom Stoppard's play about journalism, *Night and Day*: "People do awful things to one another, but they do them more often in the dark." Offering a thought one could have imagined Socrates expressing if he'd been asked, "Why are you a philosopher?," Moyers observed, "I'm a journalist because I don't know the answers." That accounted for his tough reporting, the "hard-hitting documentaries." What is "important for journalists," he told the rapt audience, "is not to be close to power, but to get close to truth."

At the end of the Q and A, partly on that principle, one suspected, he invited his wife of fifty-six years, Judith Moyers—the president and CEO for decades of their production company—to join him at the podium, where she added her own pungent thoughts: that whether one is doing a television piece or writing an article, or developing almost any another project, the person reacting is likely to ask two questions: "So what?" and "What does this have to do with me?" And if you can't answer those questions, Judith Moyers advised, "you need to look back at what you've done."

The truth was, they'd done almost everything together.

If, in Bill Moyers's voice that earlier day in the office, one heard the wistfulness of someone who perhaps wondered whether he'd have been better off following a different trajectory, his day in the "Agora" helped explain why he'd pursued the career he did: the chance to use the journalistic skills and media savvy he'd acquired to channel not just political facts but the big ideas that appealed to his philosopher side.

It also explained why, sure enough, after one of those big grants came through, he returned to TV in 2012 with a new show, *Moyers & Company*. He aimed once again to do what he did better than anyone else: shepherd thoughtful conversation onto a medium ever more resistant to it.

No collaboration, however, equaled the success Moyers achieved with his greatest hit of "highbrow" philosophical broadcasting: Joseph Campbell. That singular mythologist established his scholarship first, then rose to national fame thanks to Moyers's spotlight. Campbell graced his own years as a broadcaster with the virtue one might expect in a great scholar closer to history's conventional view of a philosopher: an almost all-consuming concentration on his personal vision of his subject.

"It's an inexhaustible field," Campbell explained one afternoon in his longtime Greenwich Village apartment, his conversation a brisk pidgin of local slang and casual divinity dropping. In the new Hawaii home to which he was slowly moving his books and work, he said, he still ran across fresh "creation" variants all the time. In one sense, he suggested, if you'd heard one creation myth, you'd heard them all. But not in quite the same detail as America's greatest myth man. Reminiscing, the feisty mythologist, then almost eighty, could spin off versions of the forbidden-fruit story of Togo's Bassari tribe; the Pima of Arizona's "Song of the World"; the "Out of One, the Many" legend from the Brihadaranyaka Upanishad; or even that more familiar tale that resembles them all—the Old Testament account of how God created the world.

The feat of memory fell short of the astonishing because, as Campbell once wrote, mythology is everywhere the same "beneath its varieties of costume." The great deluge, the land of the dead, the virgin birth and the resurrected hero—all "have a world-wide distribution," he once noted. "If you get the point of mythology," said Campbell, "and see that what's being talked about over here is what's being talked about over there, too, you don't have to quarrel about the vocabularies."

Few critics could have won a quarrel with Campbell anyway. Unlike Thomas Bulfinch, the Victorian popularizer who recast Greek myths into quaint fairy tales, Campbell spent fifty years mastering the sweep of world mythology. His major work, the four-volume *The Masks of God* (1968), was one of the most thorough explorations of myth ever published. His earlier book, *The Hero with a Thousand Faces* (1949), examined the archetype of the hero through such figures as Apollo and the Frog King, sold hundreds of thousands of copies and reportedly inspired George Lucas's *Star Wars* series. As a professor at Sarah Lawrence College from 1934 to 1972, Campbell built his course on comparative mythology into the most popular on campus, sparking similar courses elsewhere. He lectured widely and drew fourteen thousand letters after his first TV appearances with Moyers. *Time* magazine once commented that his writings carried "extraordinary weight, not only among scholars, but among a wide range of other people."

"Do I ever get fed up?" he asked, referring to the endless twists on mythic themes he encountered. "No. There's always some wrinkle. And I'm having a ball." His most recent book at the time, *The Way of the Animal Powers,* traced the mythic stirrings of the earliest hunters and gatherers amid a splashy format of hundreds of illustrations and photographs. For the subsequent volume, which dealt with planter cultures, he was already working on a "fantastic" Iroquois creation myth. "I've read it before," he said, "but it's so alive. These people were terrific storytellers." In fact, Campbell regretted that so many people equated mythology with Greek mythology, and ignored such key sources as the Plains Indians. "They're closer to the land," he said of the latter. "They're closer to general humanity."

As a TV broadcaster, Campbell projected, by association with his subject, the air of a wise man whose connections reached deep into the past—an impression he didn't mind stoking. He liked to credit his start in the myth business to seeing Buffalo Bill. "He was right off the Plains," said Campbell, recalling his visit to the famous cowboy's show around 1912. "They would come in and set up their tepees, and the lights would go down. And they'd do dances, and a stagecoach would come in, and they'd raid the stagecoach and shoot it—oh, it was great!" The experience convinced an Irish Catholic boy he had Indian blood. "Finding out about Santa Claus was nothing," remarked Campbell, noting Santa's Germanic and Christian elements. "But finding out that I could never be an Indian was something else."

Making do as he grew up in Manhattan and suburban New Rochelle, New York, he visited Indian museum exhibits, read Indian books in the local library and talked sign language with a scholarly adult who understood it. "I was just into it," said Campbell. "All the way." His prep-school days in Connecticut introduced him to Polynesian legends. Later he studied Arthurian tales at Columbia University, medieval philology and Provençal at the University of Paris, and Sanskrit and Hinduism at the University of Munich. Raised as a Roman Catholic, Campbell started "thinking about that mythology without losing it. It was a wonderful lesson—Santa Claus, part two." But when Campbell returned to the United States just before the 1929 crash, he needed a real-life Santa. He had no job, a passion for his subject and a few thousand dollars saved from playing in a college jazz band. Making the biggest decision of his life, he dropped his studies for a Columbia PhD, headed up to a country shanty near Woodstock, New York, and did nothing but read and take notes on his subject for five years.

"I just wanted it," explained Campbell of his erudition in mythology, and after years of immense discipline, he got it. He hadn't seen a movie in twenty years until Lucas screened the original *Star Wars* trilogy for him. The years, though, brought frequent encounters with artists, whom he considered the chief beneficiaries of myth. He met many through his wife of more than four decades, choreographer and native Hawaiian Jean Erdman, and his late friend John Steinbeck included traces of him in his novels *Cannery Row* and *In Dubious Battle*. The erudition, naturally, brought him face-to-face with the big questions pondered by mythologists since the seventeenth century: What was myth? What were its functions? How did it relate to dreams, psychology, religion, literature, philosophy, art? Did it matter at all in the modern world?

According to University of Chicago historian of religion Mircea Eliade, like Campbell one of the world's great experts on mythological theory, modern Western traditions treated myth as a "fable," "invention" or "fiction" until this century. Most contemporary scholars, however, agreed that myths were best understood, at least within their own societies, as true tales of a sacred beginning or creation. They involved supernatural beings and served as models of human actions. Also, modern scholars recognized that mythological knowledge served as a model for human behavior, and typically required that one ritually retell the myth or perform some ceremony attached to it.

Campbell generally agreed. He said he wanted to persuade readers and viewers of the facts about myth, an opportunity that becoming a broadcaster expanded beyond expectation: "My feeling about myself is, I'm a historian, not a sociologist. I put down what I find in the material." And yet, in *The Hero with a Thousand Faces,* he noted that his subject had been variously interpreted as a kind of primitive science or philosophy, as prehistoric poetry misunderstood by subsequent ages, as a kind of allegory that shapes individuals into community members, as a group dream, and as God's revelation to his children. "Mythology," he concluded, "is all of these." Campbell, however, did generally adhere to one of Swiss psychologist Carl Jung's fundamental tenets: that all people connect to a collective unconscious from which certain basic ideas spring into their dreams or myths. For Campbell, dream was "the personalized myth, myth, the depersonalized dream." Mythology was not a statement of fact, but rather the "material of the muses," and thus ultimately poetic, metaphoric and mysterious.

Campbell conceded that he worked both the psychological and historical sides of the street in mythology. "I see mythology as biologically grounded," he said. According to Campbell, however, most academic experts on mythology favored a sociological approach that stressed historical differences. That prompted them to neglect the psychological implications of myth's worldwide similarity: "They will tell you, in all seriousness, 'The people in the Congo have five fingers on their right hand,'" he gibed. "If I say, 'Well, the people in Alaska have five fingers on their right hand,' I'm called a generalist. And if I say that the people in the caves in 30,000 B.C. had five fingers on their right hand, I'm a mystic."

According to Campbell, myth's psychological base guaranteed its continuing importance in human affairs. Part of Israel's claim in the Mideast, he remarked, was the claim of a "mythological donation" of land. But for myth to remain alive within a society, he contended, it must be consistent with that society's current scientific thought. "Elijah, Jesus and Mary have all ascended to Heaven," he said, citing what he considered a myth hard to square with Western science. "But at the speed of light, they wouldn't be out of the galaxy yet. What are you going to do with that?"

Nonetheless, Campbell got along fine with most religious leaders and scholars. The better educated, he said, realized that sacred texts needn't be defended as literally true, and that "spiritual truths are taught through religious images." Although critics tended to emphasize Campbell's lifelong interest in the uniformity of myths, he came to appreciate their differences, too. A visit to India, for example, made him realize how Western he was. "The grounding Western myth for me is the Arthurian version of the Grail," explained Campbell. He recited a particularly deft summary of it, a sentence from a fifteenth-century version of the quest for the Grail. " 'They thought it would be a disgrace to go forth in the group,' " he quoted from memory. " 'Each entered the forest at a point that he had chosen, where it was darkest and there was no way or path.' "

"That's the West," said the still-cocky intellectual adventurer with a laugh. "Your own track, kid, and not what your guru tells you."

PART 3

THE RISING OUTSIDERS

AFRICAN AMERICANS

America the Philosophical always included African American philosophers. That might seem clear today, but as the stories of Johnny Washington, Lucius Outlaw and Leonard Harris in Part 1 indicated, the recognition came slowly to many practitioners and observers of a discipline—better understood as an activity—traditionally depicted as lily white. (Only one percent or so of professional philosophers in the United States are black.) Today prominent black philosophers such as Cornel West and Kwame Anthony Appiah teach at Princeton University, a cornerstone of the American establishment. Appiah, Ghanaian by birth, is already, in his fifties, a past president of the American Philosophical Association. Previously slighted black thinkers such as Alain Locke increasingly get a place in histories and syllabi. The growing self-confidence and stature of black women philosophers jumped forward with the founding, in 2008, of the Collegium of Black Women Philosophers. In 2009, one of them, Michele Moody-Adams—who earned her PhD under John Rawls with a dissertation on David Hume—became the first African American dean of Columbia College, and the vice president for undergraduate education at Columbia University, though she later resigned in an internal power struggle.

The marginalization of black philosophers from the rest of the "profession," however, stretches back as far as ancient Greece and Africa. To understand the place of African American philosophy in the U.S.—why some of its practitioners still label their conferences "Philosophy Born of Struggle"—it's helpful to attempt the long view. Among the many lively disputes roiling the intellectual world "outside" hidebound philosophy departments in recent years, one of the liveliest involved whether Africans took part in the creation of Western philosophy.

The debates came to life with the publication of *Black Athena:*

The Afroasiatic Roots of Classical Civilization (1987) by Martin Bernal, a Cornell University sinologist. Bernal, a leading advocate of the view that Greece owed a significant debt to black Africa for key elements of "Western civilization"—philosophy, science and democracy—argued that racist nineteenth-century scholars downplayed Egyptian influences on Greek culture, creating a false image of Greek civilization as a kind of virgin birth. Unlike more radical Afrocentrists, Bernal recognized that many of his claims depended on inferences rather than knockdown proof. He urged "scholars of antiquity to speak of competitive plausibilities rather than history," contending that they "have been so thoroughly imbued with conventional preconceptions and patterns of thought that they are extremely unlikely to be able to question its basic premises."

His theses led to heated exchanges once Mary Lefkowitz, professor of classics at Wellesley, confronted them. She reviewed Bernal's book along with others on related subjects in the *New Republic*. Although she regarded Bernal's book as off base, and would later deem it a "work of fiction," she ended up more troubled by so-called extreme Afrocentrists—writers certain that Socrates and Cleopatra were black, that the Greeks stole philosophy from the Egyptians, that racist classicists purposely ignore African primacy, that a "melanin" theory of human behavior makes sense. Lefkowitz confronted such claims as that Egypt "had actually invaded Greece during the second millennium BC and that there was a large component of Egyptian vocabulary in ancient Greek." *Stolen Legacy*, by George G. M. James, in print nearly forty years, argued that "Aristotle took his ideas about the soul from *The Egyptian Book of the Dead*." *Africa: Mother of Western Civilization*, by Yosef A. A. ben-Jochannan (1971), "charged that Aristotle had stolen his philosophy from works by Egyptians in the library of Alexandria" and even "put his name on them." The *New Republic* lent some incendiary verve to matters by coming up with a flamboyant cover—the bust of a Greek philosopher wearing a Malcolm X cap, with highlights in purple.

An even more provocative introduction for Lefkowitz to Afrocentric perspectives on philosophy came the next year. Ben-Jochannan himself, described in campus publicity as a "distinguished Egyptologist," visited Wellesley to give the school's annual Martin Luther King Jr. Memorial Lecture. In it, he claimed that Aristotle accompanied Alexander the Great to Egypt, stole books from the famous library of Alexandria (the ancient world's greatest), and based his philosophy upon them. Lefkowitz pointed out in the question-and-answer session that Aristotle died two decades before the library of Alexandria was built, and, as she later put it, "no ancient writer records that Aristotle ever went to Egypt."

The lecturer was not amused. He declared that he resented Lefkowitz's tone. Nor did it help when ben-Jochannan suggested that the dates of Aristotle's death and the library's construction were uncertain. Lefkowitz's husband, the distinguished British classicist Hugh Lloyd-Jones, responded, "Rubbish." Some students in attendance went to see Lefkowitz after the talk and accused her of racism. Lefkowitz's colleague Anthony Martin later charged the pair with "insulting" ben-Jochannan. Before long, the issue of whether Lefkowitz and her husband had been rude to a visiting speaker threatened to eclipse the factual issue. Meanwhile, Lefkowitz's dean observed, "Each of us has a different and equally valid view of history."

Troubled that her dean and some students would argue that hard historical facts in her field were really subjective matters, Lefkowitz produced *Not Out of Africa*. In its introduction, she declared that she had "only the highest respect for the advanced civilization and accomplishments of ancient Egypt." But she aimed to set certain things straight. "The ancient Egypt described by Afrocentrists," Lefkowitz wrote, "is a fiction." Moreover, "virtually all the claims made by Afrocentrists can be shown to be without substance."

One by one, Lefkowitz subjected the Afrocentric claims to counter-evidence. Ancient Egyptians, she noted, while darker than Europeans, were not mainly African in physiognomy. Evidence showed that they distinguished themselves from Nubian blacks to the south, whom the Greeks called Ethiopians. For Cleopatra to be black, Lefkowitz pointed out, we needed to explain away Egyptian sculpture and coinage, which show Cleopatra with straight hair and a hooked nose. We also know that three of Cleopatra's four grandparents were Macedonian and Ptolemaic Greeks, famous for their ideas of racial purity and refusal to intermarry with Egyptians. The claim that Cleopatra was black, Lefkowitz implied, was as unlikely as Louis Farrakhan's notion that Napoleon cut off the nose of the Sphinx to hide its African features. Cleopatra, Lefkowitz later wrote, "regarded herself as a Macedonian Greek Pharaoh."

The case for a black Socrates, she argued, was no better. If Socrates was black—a claim that rested on nothing, Lefkowitz argued, but traditional depiction of him with a snub nose—why didn't that come up in any of the voluminous material about him, such as Plato's dialogues? Why didn't Aristophanes mention it in his no-holds-barred satire of

Socrates? And how should we massage the fact that Athens in the era of Socrates, an Athenian citizen, did not permit Greeks from other city-states to become citizens?

Last, and most boldly, Lefkowitz argued that selected ancient Greeks, such as Herodotus and Diodorus—often quoted to support the Afrocentrist perspective—were mistaken in assessing the degree of Greek indebtedness to Egypt. Modern archaeological evidence such as deciphered hieroglyphics, Lefkowitz reported, did not support such claims. Nor did it support the Afrocentrist notion of an ancient "Egyptian Mystery System" from which the Greeks plagiarized their philosophy, as though ancient Greek philosophy remained a univocal thing from Thales to Aristotle. That canard, Lefkowitz maintained, could be traced back to an eighteenth-century novel titled *Sethos* (1731) by the French abbé Jean Terrasson, whose musings influenced the Freemasons and entered their rituals.

On the whole, Lefkowitz declared her main objective to be opposing a new academic ethos under which, she wrote, history is "a form of fiction that can and should be written differently by each nation and ethnic group." Afrocentrism "not only teaches what is untrue," Lefkowitz insisted. "It encourages students to ignore chronology, to forget about looking for material evidence, to select only those facts that are convenient, and to invent facts whenever useful or necessary." In an era when extreme Afrocentrism had entered the curriculum in the Oregon school system and elsewhere, Lefkowitz saw it as a cynical effort to build intellectual self-esteem among blacks by offering them a larger piece of the world cultural pie. But once her book started to draw attention, she did not get off lightly.

Black historian Wilson Jeremiah Moses labeled her "an obscure drudge in the academic backwaters of a classics department." Her colleague Anthony Martin dubbed her a "national leader of the Jewish onslaught against Afrocentrism in general, and me in particular." Khalid Muhammad, formerly of the Nation of Islam, railed against her in 1997 as "Left-o-witch," a "hook-nosed, lox-eating, bagel-eating . . . so-called Jew."

Survivors of scholarly controversies, of course, often exhibit serious scars from infighting. Lefkowitz wound up sued, assailed by Afrocentrists, and battling breast cancer at the same time—a sufficiently cautionary tale that she later published a memoir of her experiences, *History Lesson: A Race Odyssey.*

"Was it worth it?" she asked. Her answer was "Yes," despite the political correctness and collegial wimpiness she endured. ("I couldn't take sides because it wasn't my field," one colleague explained.) Much of *History Lesson* recounted Lefkowitz's effort, in her review, lectures and *Not Out of Africa*, to bring the known historical record to bear on Afrocentrist assertions. As she narrated the tale from retirement, Lefkowitz stressed that her prime concern remained a core scholarly one: making sure professors taught facts about the ancient world, not "plausibilities." Truth, she asserted, was "not impossible to know," and she believed it to be the "particular duty" of academics to "look for it."

Still, one can understand why the Lefkowitz brouhaha rubbed some blacks in America the Philosophical the wrong way. To be sure, Lefkowitz reminded all in *History Lesson* that she'd "never said" that "Africa had no history, that ancient Egypt hadn't had a high civilization long before the Greeks, or that the ancient Egyptians had not been capable of profound thought." She said she never wanted racial factors to come into the discussion, and regretted that they did. But the peculiarities of classical scholarship made Lefkowitz's task challenging.

On the one hand, she repeatedly insisted that certain truths about Greek culture were known and not open to rival interpretation. To wit, Greek philosophy did not and could not have come from Egyptian philosophy. She repeated that Egyptians were not black (though they weren't lily white), and they distinguished black people to their south as different from themselves. There was no evidence, archaeological or linguistic, that Egypt invaded Greece in the second millennium B.C.

At the same time, Lefkowitz more than once conceded the fragility of our access to ancient culture: "The evidence is often incomplete. The cultures are remote and difficult to understand. The ancient languages take years to learn properly. We can never know what happened then with the kind of precision we can now bring to bear on current events." In light of those admissions, it was not always easy for the non-classicist to reconcile Lefkowitz's crisp certainties with her intermittent concessions. She followed the admission above, for instance, with the remark, "Getting it 90-percent right is surely better than (say) 10 percent or even none."

Yet when evidence is incomplete, can one assign percentages for probable rightness? Some of Lefkowitz's certainties about the nontransference of philosophy from Egypt to Greece depended, for example, on a particular notion of philosophy—its character as abstract and non-theological discourse—that not all interested parties would accept. She admitted, in places, that the Egyptians might have mulled over some concepts very similar to those of the Greeks.

Similarly, Lefkowitz stated, "The only way one can learn about the ancient world is by studying its surviving texts and artifacts. We have no other choice." But that was a tricky claim. Selwyn R. Cudjoe, a member of Wellesley's Africana studies department who condemned anti-Semitism and worked with Lefkowitz to arrange civil on-campus discussions about Bernal's work, published a *Boston Globe* op-ed blasting Lefkowitz's *Not Out of Africa* views. He complained that she seemed to believe "all knowledge can be reduced to texts." And yet philosophy in ancient times was at least partly an oral activity. Lefkowitz still boasted the stronger position on Greek philosophy's origins based on textual evidence. Yet the sternness of her implied judgment that the Greeks could not have absorbed philosophical notions from Egyptians with whom they interacted tested common sense. Meanwhile, the complexity of the scholarly issues raised by Bernal's work, distinguishable from those of less precise Afrocentrists, continued to play out in subsequent scholarship, such as *Black Athena Revisited* (1996), a collection of critical essays edited by Lefkowitz and Guy MacLean Rogers; and *Black Athena Writes Back* (2001), in which Bernal replied to his critics.

True or false, the fierce rejection of claims that Africans might have taken part in Western philosophy's creation stiffly reminded both Africans and African Americans of their exclusion from the canon much later as well. For even by the 1990s, when multiculturalism became all the rage in American academe, one could make a rueful observation: the unexamined discipline was still philosophy. Everywhere else you looked, literary studies were doing the "Canon Twist," switching teachable partners (out went Joseph Conrad, in came Chinua Achebe), showing that breaking up with old syllabi wasn't hard to do. But philosophy simply lumbered on, slow-dancing with itself. No analogue to Zora Neale Hurston disturbed the white-boys' club of Russell, Wittgenstein and other familiar members. No doppelgänger of Harriet Jacobs crowded the space of nineteenth-century stars like Nietzsche and John Stuart Mill. No eighteenth-century confessor on the order of ex-slave turned memoirist Olaudah Equiano diversified the lineup of the Enlightenment.

As University of Texas philosophers Robert C. Solomon and Kathleen M. Higgins grumbled in their against-the-grain anthology of essays, *From Africa to Zen: An Invitation to World Philosophy*: "Even a casual review of the standard course offerings and dissertation topics demonstrates an embarrassing one-dimensionality, stretching through time from Socrates to Sartre or Quine with nary a mention of Confucius or Nagarjuna. There is no mention of African philosophy or any African philosopher (except Augustine, whose origins are conveniently ignored), and no Latin American philosophy."

That barren landscape made the liftoff of an article entitled "Race and the Modern Philosophy Course" in a 1990s issue of the journal *Teaching Philosophy* even more entertaining to watch. Two Villanova University scholars, John Immerwahr and Michael Burke, examined that virtual fossil, the widely taught "early modern philosophy course." It had, they acknowledged, "traditionally been a review of the thoughts of seven European white males (Descartes, Leibniz, Spinoza, Locke, Berkeley, Hume, and Kant) on epistemology, metaphysics, the evil demon, the tree in the quad, the billiard balls."

And what a crew of white males at that! Like Edward Said, focusing in *Culture and Imperialism* on the Antiguan slaveholding of *Mansfield Park*'s Thomas Bertram, Immerwahr and Burke zeroed in on facts typically hidden behind long-standing protective images. John Locke, for instance, "invested a large sum of his own money in the Royal African Company, an enterprise specifically devoted to trading in slaves for sale to the plantations in America. . . . As unofficial secretary to the Lord Proprietors of Carolina . . . Locke appears to have authored (or co-authored) the 'Fundamental Constitutions of Carolina,' which provide that 'every freeman of Carolina shall have absolute power and authority over his negro slave of what opinion or religion soever.'" George Berkeley "owned slaves when he lived in Rhode Island," Immerwahr and Burke pointed out, "and defended the practice of slavery." David Hume opposed slavery but "was a committed racist who held that 'the negroes' were 'naturally inferior to the whites.'"

Setting aside the explosive question of whether standard early modern philosophy courses *should* be diversified, the two authors took on the grunt work of examining how a diversified course could represent "precisely the time when Europeans confronted other cultures and races and were forced to incorporate them into their world views."

"We are unaware," they asserted, "of any significant texts from this period written by philosophers of color. The only possible approach is to talk about racial issues as they relate to the context and writings of white European philosophers." Scholars of Chinese, Persian or Indian philosophy wouldn't have agreed. Immerwahr and Burke's tone of resignation, alas, sounded like an unfortunate echo of the most quoted challenge to multiculturalism of that era, Saul Bellow's acerbic line, "Show me the Tolstoy of the Zulus and I'll read him." To be fair, the two authors plainly had in mind philosophers of color who lived within traditional European or American precincts of philosophy. They just couldn't find a black Kant who took clockwork walks around Königsberg.

Yet even there, it seemed, a good reminder lurked that the habit of not looking often leads to a failure to find. Why hadn't the pair given a glance to the little-known but not wholly obscure Anton Wilhelm Amo (ca.1703–ca.1759), the African philosopher whom Archibald Laud-Hammond had discussed at the African American Philosophers Conference in Charlotte? Amo had been adopted as a child and raised by the Duke of Brunswick-Wolfenbüttel. He received his doctorate in philosophy from the University of Wittenberg in 1734 and taught for a decade at the University of Halle, where a statue of him still stands. Reportedly a master of six languages, he published, in Latin, the aforementioned *Treatise on the Art of Philosophising Soberly and Accurately,* and also supposedly wrote that now lost manuscript on the rights of black people in Europe. Surely, the serendipity of his surname alone should have counted for something.

But regardless of the oversight in Immerwahr and Burke's investigative reporting, the two directed welcome attention to eye-opening material. To examine European treatment of Native Americans, for example, they suggested that philosophers teach the great public debates that took place in 1550 and 1551 in Valladolid, Spain, between Bartolomé de Las Casas, the Spanish missionary and historian who became the first European intellectual to oppose the enslavement of Indians in the New World, and Juan Ginés de Sepúlveda, the influential Spanish court scholar. Their debates addressed the question "How can conquests, discoveries, and settlements be made to accord with justice and reason?" Sepúlveda, an Aristotelian, had argued in his treatise (*Concerning the Just Cause of the War Against the Indians*) that Indians "are inferior to the Spaniards just as children are to adults, women to men, and, indeed, one might even say, as apes are to men." Las Casas, who campaigned for decades against Spanish oppression of the Indians and predicted that God would punish Spain for its sins, countered that Indians were rational beings, "not demented or mistakes of nature, nor lacking in sufficient reason to govern themselves."

According to the authors, "Charles V, the Holy Roman Emperor and the strongest ruler in Europe at the time, suspended all overseas conquests pending the outcome of this debate." But with slavery already a fait accompli in the Americas, Sepúlveda's views eventually prevailed. Immerwahr and Burke urged teachers to include in their revamped early modern philosophy courses a showing of *The Mission,* the Robert De Niro–Jeremy Irons film that dramatizes, Hollywood-epic style, some of these conflicts.

Elsewhere in the article, Immerwahr and Burke asked philosophers to probe the relationship between racism and British empiricism, a staple of such courses, by confronting students with some of the worst inductive arguments of the great white men, such as a notorious Hume footnote claiming that "there never was a civilized nation of any other complexion than white." They also invited new attention to forgotten figures such as James Beattie (1735–1803), a precursor of anti-Eurocentrism in his *Essay on the Nature and Immutability of Truth* (1770): "That every practice and sentiment is barbarous, which is not according to the usages of modern Europe, seems to be a fundamental maxim with many of our critics and philosophers."

No wonder, then, that in the United States in particular, when historic forces made it possible for African American thinkers to come to notice, it happened with passion and even righteousness. After all, as Lucius Outlaw pointed out, hadn't the very first American thinker to use the word "pragmatism" in the nineteenth century been none other than Martin Delany (1812–1885), the journalist and physician often seen as the first writer to clearly articulate black nationalism?

By the last third of the twentieth century, the move to establish black thinkers had taken on steam. One example came in *Black Messiahs and Uncle Toms: Social and Literary Manipulations of a Religious Myth* by Wilson Jeremiah Moses, that stern critic of Lefkowitz. Solidly researched, tightly written and magisterial in its synthesis of earlier scholarship, the book told the story of black nationalism and messianism in America with an unsentimental bluntness worthy of Ralph Ellison. A history professor at Pennsylvania State University, Moses examined the movement's investment in redemption, its internal myths and outsize leaders, with a force that left false images strewn along the wayside.

As Moses defined it, messianism was the belief that a person or group had "a manifest destiny or a God-given role to assert the providential goals of history and to bring about the kingdom of God on earth." It's a form of utopianism that implies faith in man's perfectability, a willingness to serve as conscience for the rest of humanity, "sometimes as a suffering servant or a sacrificial lamb, sometimes as an avenging angel."

Moses acknowledged and shared the standard view that the United

States "appropriated to itself from its earliest history a messianic role," an impulse dating back to John Winthrop's claim that the Massachusetts Bay Colony's covenant with God would make it a citadel of perfection. Moses's singular contribution was to demonstrate not just that messianism suffuses African American social thought, but how such thought triumphed most when it appealed to American moral ideals.

Examining such landmark nineteenth-century black activists as David Walker (1785–1830) and Henry Highland Garnet (1815–1882) as well as contemporary figures, Moses showed how the righteousness of the black cause proved a key element in nineteenth-century black polemics, as well as in American liberal thought about blacks—it established a moral core in black messianism even as more aggressive, confrontational attitudes developed. Moses stated matters plainly: the black messianic tradition had always experienced internal friction between "Uncle Tomism and Nat Turnerism." By the first, Moses didn't mean the contemporary misunderstanding of Harriet Beecher Stowe's Uncle Tom as a symbol of "racial treason." He argued, rather, that Stowe's Uncle Tom was meant to be a Christian hero, that he stood for "the qualities of kindliness, patience, humility, and great-hearted altruism," virtues that Stowe believed would make the African people, post-slavery, "an elevated and cultivated race."

By "Nat Turnerism," so called for the leader of the most famous antebellum slave revolt, Moses meant the determination to aggressively confront white domination first voiced in David Walker's fiery *Appeal* (1829). As Moses pointed out, the tension between the two prominently figured in the rivalry between what he called "Martinism and Malcolmism," particularly in the gestures that both Martin Luther King Jr. and Malcolm X made toward each other in the last years of their lives.

In exploring that historic conflict within black messianism, Moses synthesized the beliefs of multiple crucial thinkers, unpacking traditional models of black leadership and thought from the disciplined humility of Booker T. Washington to the antiwhite chauvinism of Marcus Garvey. Garvey's approach led to nasty personal exchanges with the great, broad-minded sociologist W. E. B. Du Bois, who might be added to the list of great African American philosophers if the enormous empirical power of his work on black "double consciousness" in classics such as *The Souls of Black Folk* didn't make it seem as if "sociologist" was (and needed to remain) part of his given name. At the same time, Moses explained much about the positions of intellectuals at the heart of black studies such as E. Franklin Frazier, Melville Herskovits and others. He usefully called attention to how, in order to prick the American conscience, early black American thinkers employed the rhetorical device of the jeremiad—a lamentation over some present tragedy, with warnings of worse to come. Black writers, he wrote, "showed a clever ability to play on the belief that America as a whole was a chosen nation with a covenantal duty to deal justly with the blacks." At the same time, Moses did not ignore shabbier forms of black messianism, skewering the "charismatic charlatanry" of figures such as Father Divine. He evinced remarkable evenhandedness throughout the book, plainly rejecting any lurch toward either Turnerism or Tomism, while warning that the lack of a moral brake formed a large problem with the modern black messianic tradition: a secularization that threatened to cause black politics to lose its "traditional missionary and moral character."

Such scholarship increasingly opened the gates to recognition of the largely ignored role of black thinkers and writers in America the Philosophical. With the empowerment of scholars such as Henry Louis Gates at publishing houses like Basic Civitas and Amistad, and a new appetite among university press publishers for works from the African American tradition, worthy nineteenth-century thinkers and writers such as Douglass, Martin Delany, David Walker, Anna Julia Cooper, Frances Ellen Watkins Harper and others were brought back into print, spurring still more secondary work. Yet with the exception of Douglass's impact on abolitionism, no phenomenon so powerfully drove the point home—the importance of black thought to an accurate view of America's philosophical landscape—than "the Harlem Renaissance," expertly captured by George Hutchinson in his definitive history, *The Harlem Renaissance in Black and White.*

At its core, the phrase referred to the unprecedented accomplishment of black writers, painters and intellectuals in the 1920s, among them Langston Hughes, Jean Toomer, Claude McKay, Jessie Fauset, James Weldon Johnson, Nella Larsen, Countee Cullen, Aaron Douglas, Du Bois and Locke. During that period, modernism filled the air in New York City, as jazz and blues filled the clubs. Young artists threatened the genteel complacencies of traditional American culture. The presence in Manhattan of important black political organizations such as the NAACP and the Urban League, which made Harlem the symbolic black capital of the United States, helped prod the awakening. Both groups encouraged black artists through their respective publications, the *Crisis* and *Opportunity,* and emphasized their importance to racial progress.

If that extraordinary flowering of black poetry, fiction, painting, criticism and music in 1920s Manhattan remained the most challenging moment in American cultural history, it was because, in its complex mix of ideologies, personalities and manifestos, it put into play almost every aesthetic and political issue raised by African American life in the United States. Under such prodding, both black and white artists rethought American culture. For the first time, America's black and white artists seriously mulled their common traditions, even if the idea of a "movement" that could reconcile viewpoints of its prickly individualists has always been more a convenience than a realistic historical view.

Philadelphia-born philosopher Alain Locke (1886–1954) came to be designated the Renaissance's chief ideologist. (He preferred the word "midwife.") His groundbreaking anthology, *The New Negro* (1925), articulated how African American art would provide the vehicle by which "race proud" yet patriotic blacks assimilated into mainstream American life. Still, that very aim proved controversial, criticized as too deferential to white America's desire for black exoticism, primitivism and obeisance. Du Bois complained that too much Harlem Renaissance literature was "written for the benefit of white people." Harold Cruse criticized the "cultural paternalism" of the Harlem Renaissance in his trenchant book *The Crisis of the Negro Intellectual.* David Levering Lewis's later volume on the Renaissance offered the acerbic title *When Harlem Was in Vogue.*

Debates about the pros and cons of Locke's role continue today. As critics and scholars such as Nathan Huggins and Lewis helped us recognize, the Harlem Renaissance's genius rested not in its coherence, but in the panoply of possibilities it presented for black life and art. It comprised Langston Hughes's resistance to sublimating black art to black politics, Du Bois's encouragement of it and the determination of a writer like Zora Neale Hurston to pursue her own projects, such as the recovery of folk culture for fiction.

The great service of Hutchinson's comprehensive study was its willingness to acknowledge the many inconsistent philosophical and institutional influences on those who brought the Renaissance to life: all the "pragmatist philosophers, Boasian anthropologists, socialist theorists, and new journalists" in the background. Chairman of the American Studies Program at the University of Tennessee at Knoxville, Hutchinson went back to the journals and books that the players were reading at the time, producing a landmark—the most multi-shaded portrait of the period's cultural politics that we've had. In contrast to experts on the period who turned sardonic or hostile toward its key white figures—from writer and photographer Carl Van Vechten to anthropologist Franz Boas—Hutchinson sized them up squarely, outlining and explaining their contributions. That served his chief purpose of challenging "assumed oppositions between American and African American cultural nationalisms." Hutchinson's strategy to downplay racial issues in turn heightened the focus on the illuminating modernist matrix from which the Renaissance emerged. Even more welcome was his refusal to be scared off by the multilayered "interracial dynamics" that produced his book's too often caricatured subject. As a result, Hutchinson succeeded in showing that "the Harlem Renaissance writers were less concerned with proving their humanity than with demonstrating their Americanness, in the process challenging their white kinfolk to remake themselves and their concepts of America." By explicating a wide range of the pragmatist literature, criticism and art that propelled the Renaissance, he rendered that overarching interpretation more credible.

"The Harlem Renaissance program of using the arts to advance freedom and equality," Hutchinson wrote, "derived not from a desire to prove that blacks could reason and write, as has often been charged, but from a belief in the central role of aesthetic experience in the achievement of new forms of solidarity and understanding. . . . The Harlem Renaissance was in fact a striking experiment in cultural pluralism." In that respect, Hutchinson agreed with other modern scholars who rejected the old tendency to treat white America and black America as separate cultures.

No one advocated the pluralism implied by such scholarship more than Locke. The appearance in 2008, from a distinguished university press (Chicago), of the first comprehensive biography of him—*Alain L. Locke: The Biography of a Philosopher,* by Leonard Harris and Charles Molesworth—counted as yet another mark of African American thinkers finding their place in a philosophical world that once shunned them.

When Locke wrote home to his mother shortly after beginning undergraduate life at Harvard, his resistance to in-group racial solidarity couldn't have been more obvious. According to Harris and Molesworth in their incisive biography of the man they call "the most influential African American intellectual born between W. E. B. Du Bois and Martin Luther King, Jr.," Locke complained that he couldn't understand how his few black student peers "come up here in a broad-minded place like this and stick together like they were in the heart of Africa."

Alain Locke (1886–1954), regarded as the
"father of the Harlem Renaissance," was the
first African American Rhodes Scholar.

Raised only four blocks from centrally located Rittenhouse Square
as a member of Philadelphia's free black elite—a community that, the
authors write, "did not look with special indulgence on lower class people from any race"—Locke regarded many of his Harvard classmates
as "coarse," a flaw he believed his fellow black students compounded by
their separatism. "[By] common consent," Locke wrote to his mother
about dining-room habits at Harvard, black students had "unanimously
chosen to occupy a separate table together. Now what do you think
of that? It's the same old lifelong criticism I shall be making against
our people." Like many a philosopher, Locke knew himself well. He
understood that his future work would celebrate cultural pluralism,
both philosophically and personally. That corpus now gets credited, in
African American thought, for undergirding what came to be called
"multiculturalism."

From his early postgraduate studies in Oxford and Berlin to his
embrace of the Baha'i faith, this first African American Rhodes Scholar,
well known for his vast collection of African art and always an intellectual player during his decades (from 1912 on) as head of Howard Uni-

versity's philosophy department, more or less created the image of the black cosmopolitan emulated by African Americans from jazz artists to professors. Yet how did such an elitist aesthete, fond of fine things like personalized stationery, sufficiently enamored of French literature that he changed his name from Allen to "Alain," also become the famous catalytic editor of that *New Negro* anthology, so crucial in establishing the "Renaissance" as an epochal moment in American cultural history and stirring renewed respect for black folk culture?

Harris, a philosopher at Purdue University regarded as the top expert on Locke's thought, and Molesworth, a literature scholar at Queens College, traced the causes in their long-overdue examination of a thinker for whom schools, prizes and societies across America have often been named. Why did it take so long for a definitive biography of Locke to appear, when works on comparable black intellectuals abounded? Locke scholar Russell J. Linnemann had once offered a celebratory explanation. Noting Locke's extraordinary interests in "anthropology, art, music, literature, education, political theory, sociology and African studies," Linnemann speculated that few "potential biographers" possessed the "intellectual breadth" to "fulfill the task properly."

Yet Harris and Molesworth also drew back the curtain on other factors. Perhaps the largest was Locke's predominantly closeted gay life, though people of any acuity in his milieu understood his sexuality. It was an orientation that created tensions between Locke and homophobic parts of conservative black culture, while also moving some supporters to urge keeping his life under the biographical radar. Entries on him in such standard reference works as *The Oxford Companion to African American Literature* and *Africana: Arts and Letters,* for instance, do not mention his homosexuality.

Harris, in a courageous 2001 essay titled " 'Outing' Alain L. Locke," accused some Locke scholars of merely mentioning Locke's gay life in passing, inaccurately leading readers to believe that "Locke's sexuality was irrelevant to his intellectual and personal history." Harris and Molesworth closed that gap, not by going into Locke's intimacies with the detail of Harris's essay, but by explaining how they shaped the philosopher's prodigious aesthetic sensibilities.

The third important obstacle to a Locke biography was its subject's personality. Harris and Molesworth's adjectives for their subject, such as "aloof" and "elitist," confirmed that Locke, even in their view, "did not suffer fools gladly," and was always more respected than loved.

Harris and Molesworth's book thus unfolded as no crowning of unrecognized philosophical royalty, but a critical, contextualized understanding of a singular thinker who did not fit, for many, the stereotype of a black intellectual. As Harris had written elsewhere, Locke never operated as a black activist with a political solution for every problem. He refused to be either a black Christian or a foundationalist with simplistic answers to epistemological questions. He couldn't be typed as a family man like Du Bois, or a "poor black man who works by candlelight to become successful."

Rather, Locke showed that a black philosopher in America might be just as idiosyncratic and singular as a white one. He struck most as an erudite genius and elegant networker whose championship of African American work in theater, sculpture, painting, literature and music helped the glow of the Renaissance become a permanent spotlight on African American art as included in American culture. Still, the difficulty of fitting an African American philosopher into America's mostly palefaced philosophical establishment even in the middle of the twentieth century could be seen in the story of a much lesser known acquaintance of Locke's.

William Fontaine (1909–1968), the only African American philosopher at a first rank university when appointed at the University of Pennsylvania in 1947, broke ground by that accomplishment alone. A lanky man from modest circumstances, he bore credentials and manners pleasing to a white professional class whose previous racial barriers he broke. In the eyes of white thinkers eager to bring him under their wing, he was a proud man full of promise, whose bonds to historic African American culture involved periods of uncertainty and friction. Perhaps most poignantly, this professional first-of-his-kind black man stood accused at least once, by the prominent African American intellectual E. Franklin Frazier, of being a black man "trying to act white"—a "wuzzlehead," in the slur of the era.

How Bruce Kuklick, the Penn historian best known for his accounts of American philosophers and intellectuals, came to write a biography of Fontaine was as good a story as the life itself. Commissioned by the American Academy of Arts and Sciences to produce an essay about post–World War II American philosophy, Kuklick found himself in 2002 exploring Penn's archives. A staffer persuaded him to look at the papers of Fontaine, who had taught at Penn for two decades. They filled "one small box of correspondence." Kuklick remembered taking a lecture course as a 1960s Penn undergraduate from Fontaine, but was stunned to discover that Fontaine had written a graduate school recommendation for him years ago, something Kuklick had forgotten.

That startling surprise "summoned" Kuklick to explore the life of this largely forgotten ceiling shatterer, and Kuklick "became absorbed in his compelling life story." *Black Philosopher, White Academy* did credit to both the author's investigative skills and his passion for the tale. Bringing back successful figures heavily documented in public records was a common enough academic project. Resurrecting Fontaine, who, Kuklick concedes, "did not achieve the public eminence of someone such as Du Bois," constituted a more remarkable achievement.

Born and raised in the poor, segregated West End neighborhood of Chester, Pennsylvania, the second of fourteen children, Fontaine attended Chester High, where he played violin and excelled at Latin, then graduated first in his class from Lincoln University in 1930. In his early years as an academic—pursuing a PhD in philosophy at Penn, teaching Latin at Lincoln, and then philosophy at Southern University and Morgan State—Fontaine exhibited enormous interest in both African American literary and intellectual history and philosophy's standard canon.

In the latter vein, Kuklick reported, Fontaine steeped himself in everything from the modern, rarefied analytic epistemology of Harvard's C. I. Lewis to the sociology of knowledge of German thinker Karl Mannheim. In the former, he celebrated the aesthetic accomplishments of the Harlem Renaissance, even sketching out a play and beginning an acquaintance with Locke.

Fontaine seemed unlikely to be coopted by mid-twentieth-century academic philosophy's hyperanalytic artificiality, which largely removed it from public significance. In 1936, he earned his PhD with a thesis comparing Boethius and the rebellious Giordano Bruno. But something changed, Kuklick explained. After being drafted into the segregated U.S. Army of World War II, Fontaine taught at a military installation. There he came under the influence of a sergeant named Nelson Goodman, a future Penn and Harvard analytic philosopher. Once Goodman engineered Fontaine's groundbreaking, ongoing appointment at Penn in 1947—a kind of "tenure without tenure" for most of Fontaine's career due to Fontaine's tuberculosis and meager record of publication—the younger man morphed into a different kind of intellectual. At Penn, his earlier devotion to African American culture evolved in a direction that emphasized the entanglement of black and white history, and perhaps smoothed edges that might have hurt him at Penn.

"[T]he Negro does not think in a vacuum," Fontaine wrote. "Standards of the total culture and the desire for status affect his thinking." Kuklick wrote that Fontaine "had learned to mingle deference with gentility.... [H]e had matured into a demure scholar who could behave himself in an upper middle-class white environment." Kuklick's research showed that "The Mind and Thought of the Negro," Fontaine's most significant publication, "was the only article Fontaine *never* mentioned" in the resumes he prepared for Penn during the next twenty years.

According to Kuklick, Fontaine at Penn—despite regularly having "coffee together" with a student named Martin Luther King near campus (King also took philosophy courses at Penn)—"published essays from which philosophers could draw no social implications." When Penn's public relations people asked whom he favored as philosophers, Fontaine mentioned not Locke or Du Bois, but white philosophers such as Goodman and Lewis.

Kuklick recognized that his pioneering portrait depended on scanty materials. Despite that, he stayed resolutely fair to his subject. He noted, for instance, that Fontaine's interest in African American issues revived in the early 1960s. And while he candidly assessed Fontaine's light scholarly production, he also ascribed "more than outstanding merit" to what his imperfect subject did publish on African American culture. Similarly, he reported the great admiration still felt for Fontaine by many former students. And so if, as Kuklick observed, Fontaine ended up a "liberal, internationalist Cold Warrior" and inveigher "against the black power movement" for asserting "a special culture untouched by white America," he also found a home in the "intellectual forefront of the burgeoning civil rights movement" and engaged forcefully in pan-African issues. Reflecting on Fontaine's life, Kuklick divided blame for his subject's failure to achieve great stature.

Always "a bit standoffish," Fontaine struck Penn students such as future novelist John Edgar Wideman as "aloof." Fontaine's only book, *Reflections on Segregation, Desegregation, Power, and Morals* (1967), Kuklick opined, combined "long-simmering anger" and "a breakdown of control" over his material. At the same time, Kuklick also indicted Fontaine's discipline—academic philosophy—for his truncated achievement. It had, this leading historian of the field declared, "no time for what he did well and dismissed his mainstream philosophical work."

Fontaine's "immersion in white institutions," Kuklick concluded, "came with a penalty."

Fontaine's onetime coffee mate, Martin Luther King Jr., showed what could happen on America's political stage if one abandoned the deference to established ways that marked Fontaine in his career. In academic philosophy, it was Cornel West, decades later, who became the black philosopher most flamboyantly committed to ditching deference in making his way.

Called the "preeminent African-American intellectual of our generation" by Henry Louis Gates Jr., Harvard's longtime director of African American Studies, West had already published, by the age of forty, eight books, including *Prophesy Deliverance! An Afro-American Revolutionary Christianity, The American Evasion of Philosophy, The Ethical Dimensions of Marxist Thought* and *Race Matters* (Beacon Press), his first work with a major trade house. As a fast-talking, precociously erudite seventeen-year-old out of Sacramento, California, West blazed his way

Cornel West (1953–) and Michael Eric Dyson (1958–), philosophers and public intellectuals seen here with the Rev. Jesse Jackson, kept alive the link between black social thought and activism, regularly appearing on radio and TV talk shows.

through Harvard magna cum laude in three years, earned his Princeton philosophy doctorate soon after, then taught at Yale, Union Theological Seminary and the University of Paris before settling in as a professor of religion and head of Princeton's African-American Studies program in 1988. Nonetheless, he talked of still watching ten empty cabs pass him at East Sixtieth Street and Park Avenue as he waited, increasingly late for a Manhattan appointment to be photographed for the cover of *Race Matters.*

The book essentially accomplished the mainstreaming of West. In *Time,* under the heading "Philosopher with a Mission," the magazine announced that "with his new, hot-selling book on race, Cornel West could become the most important black intellectual of the 1990s." That same year, the *New York Observer* suggested that "Princeton's Racial Tightrope Walker," described as "a man on fire," might be preparing "to play a more central role in leading the black freedom struggle."

His publisher sent him on a fourteen-city tour, the speaking invitations flooded in, and the paperback rights to *Race Matters* sold fast for $175,000. West was next reported to be splitting a $100,000 advance with Michael Lerner, editor of the progressive Jewish magazine *Tikkun,* for a volume on black-Jewish relations. In the wake of *Race Matters*—released one year after the riots in Los Angeles—elements of the Cornel West phenomenon, like the jazz improvisations he loved, finally seemed to have found their right media arrangement.

West's preacherly charisma, honed in 150 speeches a year to church and other community groups, turned podiums into pulpits as West built bridges between African American intellectual life and the everyday reality of what he liked to call, borrowing affectionately from Sly Stone, "everyday people." He adopted a regular stylish uniform of dark three-piece suits, with gold watch and chain in the vest pocket, a sartorial code intentionally borrowed from the great Du Bois to emphasize the dignity and seriousness of his calling. He showed a willingness to criticize both left and right, black and white, as he tried to articulate a "politics of conversion" that invested black liberation with Christian love.

American media, which typically simplify intellectuals as they elevate them to fame, began to construct West's pigeonholes. The *Los Angeles Times* declared that he married "the moral traditions of the black church with the radical impatience of the Black Panthers." According to the *New York Times,* he was "a young, hip black man in an old, white academy; a believing Christian in a secular society; a progressive socialist in the age of triumphant capitalism; a cosmopolitan public intellectual among academic specialists." West responded to the spotlight and those categories appropriately. As a self-declared pragmatist, he kept his beliefs flexible. His biography and writings indicated a man in whom scholarly caution and a taste for abstraction clashed with the preacher/activist's straight talk.

Born in Tulsa, Oklahoma, the grandson of a self-educated Baptist preacher, West grew up in a working-class black neighborhood of Sacramento. His critical side surfaced early when he hit a teacher who tried to force him to recite the Pledge of Allegiance—his protest of the second-class treatment of blacks. The action landed him a suspension for six months. Student-body president of both his junior and senior high schools, track star, all-star second baseman, first-chair violinist in the school orchestra, West also shaped himself as a competitive sampler of ideas. He drew on the Christianity of his church, the militant nationalism of the local Black Panthers, the committed nonviolent activism of Martin Luther King Jr. (West cried, at age ten, after he heard Dr. King speak in Sacramento), the sheer love for black fans exhibited by athletes like Willie Mays and performers like James Brown.

Making his first trip east to attend Harvard in 1970, West washed dishes and cleaned toilets to support himself, took heavy course loads to speed himself through, and acquired a reputation as a fierce dancer and activist: he helped support the 1972 takeover of Harvard's Massachusetts Hall to protest the school's investments in South Africa. In his introduction to *The Ethical Dimensions of Marxist Thought,* his clearest self-assessment as a thinker, West credited his "close-knit family and overlapping communities of church and friends" for providing him with "existential and ethical equipment to confront the crises, terrors and horrors of life . . . a Christian ethic of love-informed service to others, ego-deflating humility about oneself . . . and politically engaged struggle for social betterment. This Christian outlook, as exemplified in our time by Martin Luther King Jr., serves as the basis for my life vocation."

Those early convictions governed his seemingly centrist take on racial issues in *Race Matters.* In his introduction there, he faulted liberals for the "simplistic" notion that "more government can solve racial problems," for their reluctance "to exercise principled criticism of black people." He faulted conservatives for thinking that the "moral behavior of poor black urban dwellers" is at the heart of racial trouble, for highlighting "immoral actions while ignoring public responsibility for the immoral circumstances that haunt our fellow citizens."

Yet West dismissed both political labels. Liberals and conservatives, he wrote, failed to see "that the presence and predicaments of black people are neither additions to nor defections from American life, but rather constitutive elements of that life." Ranging beyond those categories, West saw a country where black "nihilism," a "pervasive spiritual impoverishment" spurred by white racism and the economic woes of recent decades, was everywhere. In West's view, much of black society was worse off than thirty years before, because of drugs and a coldhearted "market culture" whose selfishness had slowly destroyed institutions that previously had kept black society resilient: the church, the family and black solidarity itself. West believed that only black self-love could stop "the profound sense of psychological depression, personal worthlessness, and social despair so widespread in black America."

A variety of leitmotifs ran through *Race Matters*. West relentlessly lamented the "paucity of courageous leaders" among blacks. He found too many black leaders "hungry for status" and lacking in "authentic anger" or "genuine humility." He deeply believed that America had been "historically weak-willed in ensuring racial justice," and that therefore affirmative action couldn't be abandoned or else discrimination "would return with a vengeance." He believed "black murderers and rapists should go to jail," but warned that rampant black nihilism "contributes to criminal behavior." His recurrent attack on the "market values of profit-hungry corporations" reflected a side of West that mass media played down: his conviction, as he wrote in *The Ethical Dimensions of Marxist Thought*, that Marxist thought still helps in analyzing society.

At the same time, West described himself as "a non-Marxist socialist" because his Christian perspective "embraces depths of despair, layers of dread, encounters with the sheer absurdity of the human condition, and ungrounded leaps of faith alien to the Marxist tradition." Throughout *Race Matters*, sharp opinions abounded. Afrocentrism he regarded as "gallant but misguided." Black intellectual life was "a rather depressing scene," suffocated by "mediocrity." The best of black culture refused "to put whites or Jews on a pedestal or in the gutter." Black sexuality was "a taboo subject in America" because it was "a form of black power over which whites have little control." The Los Angeles disturbances of April 1992 were "neither a race riot nor a class rebellion" but a "display of justified social rage."

As West's star rose, not everyone applauded. Black conservatives Shelby Steele and Stanley Crouch both criticized West. Steele wrote that he avoided "most of the difficult issues" in his book, and Crouch accused him of failing to condemn the "anarchic opportunism" that went on in Los Angeles. A recurrent criticism was that West tried to please too many different people, that his formulations ended up too vague. Some saw that as evidence of his real-world political ambition.

Exaggeration also tended to surface regularly in West's writing. Regarding the Los Angeles disturbances, for instance, he spoke of the "astonishing disappearance of the event from public dialogue." In fact, it continued to draw significant media discussion, which partly accounted for West's rise to prominence. But perhaps the greatest obstacle to West's winning of more readers remained his aim of replacing what he called the "pitfalls of racial reasoning" with moral reasoning. West often talked of "broad redistributive measures" in regard to wealth as though they were morally unproblematic. Yet every redistribution was a taking from someone. If West truly wanted to become a "race-transcending prophet," he needed to persuade whites (who still had most of the money) that it was morally right for their earned income to be redistributed to blacks who didn't earn it. That, as ever, remained one of the yawning gaps between the right and the left.

Du Bois had famously remarked on the "double consciousness" borne by every black American, the sense of always having to look at oneself through the eyes of whites as well. Just as many socialists made little effort to understand why capitalists think as they do (and vice versa), so many black intellectuals still made little effort to understand why whites thought what they did about blacks, and to change that thinking where appropriate. West, however, was not among them. It is doubtful that any intellectual of his generation possessed quite his exhilarating appetite for ideological battle, his enthusiasm for new knowledge and his generous response to criticism. Although he railed at the state of black life—"too much poverty and too little self-love"—West's rejection of polarization between whites and blacks acknowledged the positive truth that amid all the ugliness tracked by the media, there had never been so many friendships between American blacks and whites, so many romances, so much normal, decent communication. Not long down the road would come the first black president, who perhaps read, in *Race Matters,* West's declaration that "[t]he time is past for black political and intellectual leaders to pose as the voice of black America. . . . The days of brokering for the black turf—of posing as the Head Negro in Charge (H.N.I.C.)—are over."

The implication in that announcement that revolutionary airs belonged to the past, that a certain calm normality now attended the still fraught matter of where black thinkers resided in America, received a kind of corroboration in West's continued cultural mainstreaming, his advising of presidential candidates from Bill Bradley to, at least early on, Obama, his instantiation as an academic object of study in tomes such as *Cornel West: A Critical Reader*. By 2011, he appeared regularly on *Real Time with Bill Maher*, trading one-liners with actor Matthew Perry, guffawing at the host's monologues on masturbation, but also kicking in with scholarly high seriousness when the need arose. At the same time, West did not muffle his radical critique of mainstream politics and of President Obama for disappointing campaign supporters such as West. In stinging remarks that broadcast his disenchantment with Obama's tendency to compromise progressive agenda items in order to work with Republicans, he called Obama "a white man with black skin" and charged on MSNBC that Obama had "a predilection much more towards upper- and middle-class white brothers and Jewish brothers and a certain distance from free black men who will tell him the truth." In late October 2011, West was arrested twice during protests against police stop-and-frisk practices—once as part of "Occupy Washington, D.C." and the second time in Harlem. Toward the end of that year, he announced he would leave Princeton University to return to Union Theological Seminary—at a lower salary—in order to better combine his activist and intellectual missions.

A less confrontational corroboration of the arrival of the black philosopher in the main arena of American philosophy came in the sparkling career of Kwame Anthony Appiah.

As a personality, Appiah came across as the anti-West, closer to Barack Obama's controlled coolness than West's often histrionic agitation. To West's showy adoption of hip-hop rhetoric, intonation and rhymes on panels occupied by timorous scholars who could barely be heard, Appiah opposed elegant, soft-spoken niceties. In contrast with West's "I-am-at-one-with-the people" style, Appiah—like Alain Locke, gay but not politically crusaderish on the subject—evinced an aloof, almost elitist air. And yet no one at the beginning of the twenty-first century enjoyed a more successful establishment career in philosophy than Anthony Appiah.

Chatting in the immaculate Chelsea loft he shared with partner Henry Finder, the deputy editor at the *New Yorker* who had previously been an editor at *Transition*, a journal published by Henry Louis Gates and Wole Soyinka at Harvard, Appiah sat surrounded by the artifacts of a brilliant, privileged, cosmopolitan life. Terra-cotta artworks from Ghana, collected by his English mother. Russian icons inherited from her diplomat father, once Britain's ambassador to Russia. Art objects from other African countries that kept vibrantly present the continent of his Ghanaian father, Joseph Appiah, a London-educated barrister who fought for his nation's independence.

A coffee table displayed evidence of Appiah's success as public intellectual: recent issues of the *New York Review of Books* and the *New York Times Magazine,* both with cover pieces adapted from his recent book, *Cosmopolitanism: Ethics in a World of Strangers.* In a few hours, the British-born Appiah (pronounced AH-pee-uh), spiffy in a blue pinstriped suit, would head off for a meeting as a board member of the American Academy in Berlin—one of several establishment power posts that he juggled.

But also suddenly on his to-do list was a fast trip to Newark Liberty International Airport to buy a British Airways ticket to Ghana, the country where he grew up, and to which he would be returning soon for his mother's eighty-fifth birthday. It turned out that one couldn't buy a British Airways ticket to Africa over the phone, even if one was arguably the English-speaking world's most prestigious thinker about African philosophy. Appiah's expression indicated, almost with relief, that his success didn't protect him from such indignities of our "globalized" world.

At age fifty-one a settled and super-connected player in elite academe and media, he appeared to take the inconvenience in stride, his acceptance perhaps part of gratitude for his charmed, highly accomplished academic life: a University of Cambridge education (PhD, 1982); teaching posts at Yale, Cornell, Duke and Harvard before Princeton; international acclaim for his breakout book, *In My Father's House: Africa in the Philosophy of Culture* (1992); early mentoring from Henry Louis Gates Jr., then partnership with the energetic Harvard scholar in such book projects as the *Africana* encyclopedia (1999). In *Cosmopolitanism* (2006), Appiah expanded the thinking of his previous book, *The Ethics of Identity* (2005).

There he had urged readers to understand how "identities" (religious, national, sexual), like "races," are social constructs that, properly managed, can lead to cooperation, not confrontation. In his new book, Appiah argued that cosmopolitanism's central idea was simple: "Everybody matters." From that premise one could build a universalist worldview that abandoned tribalism and extended beyond mere tolerance. Rather than seeking "agreement" with everyone, Appiah suggested, we ought to "get used to one another" before possibly rising to the next level of sympathetic engagement. Ideally, cosmopolitanism amounts to "universality plus difference."

Appiah described his idea as "rooted cosmopolitanism," a jab at the "rootless cosmopolitanism" Hitler used as an epithet against Jews and others. That charge, Appiah said, implies that someone "open to the rest of the world couldn't be fully loyal to his home country. . . . It's the mistake of thinking . . . you can only be loyal to one thing."

"But look," he elaborated. "We have families. We have communities. We have churches, synagogues and temples. . . . Can't we be loyal to all of them?" Appiah said he learned the lesson early from his father, imprisoned three times for his political activities. "In a message he left for me and my sisters," Appiah recalled, "the first thing he said was, 'Remember always that you are citizens of the world.' He thought it evident that you could be loyal to humanity, loyal to God, loyal to Africa." Although Appiah's own upper-class British accent and background might suggest that the "cosmopolitan" outlook was available only to the well traveled and educated, he rejected that.

In his view, cosmopolitanism was more a matter of "temperament" than education, verbal skill, upper-class origin or travel. A humble immigrant might possess it, an insular CEO might not. Mere "habits of living together" in a mixed city, Appiah believed, fanned the feeling, including the good-natured way cabbies asked where a passenger was from, and vice versa. (Appiah said strangers sometimes assumed he was Indian, even talking to him in Hindi, "a language I don't know a single word of.")

Cities like New York and Philadelphia, he observed, "are places where you can practice living together with difference and see that it can be made to work." He cited the difference between Muslims and Jews on the one hand and Christians on the other over whether God sent his only son into the world two thousand years ago. "Nevertheless," Appiah remarked, "in London and New York people who disagree about this say hi to one another every morning in groceries." Asked about his own identity—one Web page pegged him as a "Ghanaian," another as an "American born in Britain"—he took pride in his new American citizenship while cautioning about deducing too much from it.

"When I became an American," Appiah said, "I was moved by the process." He felt "a kind of responsibility" to think about America's place and behavior in the world. At the same time, his family's extraordinary interconnections made him wary of reductivism. His aunt, a Christian, married a Lebanese Muslim. His elder sister "is married to a Norwegian, she lives in Namibia, she travels on a British passport and she's probably entitled to Norwegian citizenship. . . . Her sons have Norwegian and British citizenship, but right of residence in Namibia."

It was, Appiah implied, not a crazy but a lovely mixed-up world. "For me," he said evenly, "a passport is a travel document. It's not a statement about my soul."

And so as Appiah's success within the formal structure of American academic philosophy also allowed him the breathing room to address a broader public—he soon added the presidency of the PEN American Center to his administrative achievements—one could see how black philosophy's greater institutional rooting in West's generation contributed to a broad flowering both inside and outside the profession, and among younger aspirants.

In the footsteps of West, and on the borderline between philosophy broadly conceived and cultural talk widely dispensed, came Michael Eric Dyson (1958–). Like the five-years-older West, Dyson had gotten his first taste of broad media fame in the mid-1990s. A *New Yorker* magazine article by Michael Bérúbe, "The New Black Intellectuals," celebrated the young scholar, then at the University of North Carolina, along with such figures as West and Gates. Fast on its heels came a cover story in the *Atlantic,* "The New Intellectuals," which added a further story line: that black intellectuals had replaced white intellectuals—particularly the old Jewish ones, such as Irving Howe and Daniel Bell of the so-called New York school—as the quintessential public thinkers of their time. But then a less flattering take came down, one that angered many black intellectuals: a cover piece in the *New Republic* by the magazine's literary editor, Leon Wieseltier, "The Decline of the Black Intellectual."

Wieseltier's article, which focused only on West, described West's books as "almost completely worthless." It riled Dyson, who, talking over a breakfast of eggs and toast at the Down Home Grill in Philadelphia, saw it as indicative of an enduring bad strain in how the American intellectual establishment saw black thought.

"There's been a whole tradition with African American culture that there's only been one allowed," asserted Dyson, a fast-talking Detroit native whose own catapulting to wider media attention owed most to his *Making Malcolm: The Myth and Meaning of Malcolm X.* "That's the pernicious nature of the Leon Wieseltier article.... First, it talks of the decline of the black intellectual, but it has one black intellectual in mind. How racist and how presumptuous and how idiotic to suggest that Cornel West *is* black intellectuals, even if he's conceded to be a premier figure with extraordinary talent, which he is. I think that does a disservice to the enormous combativeness and range of voices within African American culture.... They wouldn't say 'The Decline of the White Intellectual' because Lionel Trilling had a bad book."

"You want to talk about a subtext?" Dyson continued. "It's 'All these black people getting this praise don't really deserve it.' The clear sign to African American intellectuals was, 'You're getting too uppity.' It's the same old uppity-nigger syndrome. It says the Head Nigger in Charge, if you will, the one getting the most visibility, ain't really nothin'. If he's nothin', then by definition, none of them are anything."

The words came fast. They sounded fiery. But Dyson delivered them in the same smart, friendly, efficient style that would go on to make him one of the crown princes of cable media when CNN or other networks sought a fast-talking, available black intellectual.

Dyson increasingly enjoyed access to national media, writing pieces for the *New York Times,* the *Washington Post,* the *Nation,* and *Rolling Stone,* getting invited on *Oprah* and other talk shows. It made Dyson, whose academic peregrinations would take him from Brown to North Carolina to the University of Pennsylvania and Georgetown University, both pleased and cautious.

"It's affirming, of course," he said, "but it also feels awkward. I think of myself as a Trojan horse. I don't have an earring in my nose or ear. I don't have my hair combed back in a ponytail, or rough-hewn. I look like an insider. But there's a whole lot of Negroes inside of me. There's a whole lot of black men inside of me. And when I get in somewhere, I let them out."

Swinging between street talk and academese in his public appearances as it suited the moment, Dyson apologized for neither style. The son of an automobile worker and a paraprofessional in the school system, he saw one key turning point of his life as the gift made to him by a generous neighbor when he was fourteen: a set of the Harvard Classics.

"I was reading *Two Years Before the Mast,*" he said, playfully, "and also getting my Smokey Robinson." After graduating from high school at eighteen, Dyson became a teenage father and worked in maintenance and car sales, at one point getting fired about a month before his son was born, which forced him onto welfare. At twenty-one, his first marriage dissolved. Licensed as a Baptist minister by his pastor, he started studying religion and philosophy at Knoxville College in Tennessee, later graduating from Carson-Newman in Jefferson City, Tennessee.

His leap to the academic big time came with a graduate fellowship to Princeton University's religion department in 1985, which led to interim teaching posts until he received his doctorate in 1993. After a brief time at Brown, and the publication of his first book, *Reflecting Black: African-American Cultural Criticism,* Dyson moved to Chapel Hill to run the Institute of African American Research and serve as a professor of communication studies.

"I have to constantly negotiate the tension between past neighborhood and present neighborhood," Dyson said. He was plainly comfortable with the task. The smooth, nuanced take he offered in *Making Malcolm* aimed at articulating the lasting legacy of Malcolm X without losing the slain black leader's rage, flattering his acolytes or ignoring his flaws.

"My point was," Dyson explained, "that Malcolm is an extraordinary prism through which to view the landscape of American popular culture, especially in African American society." Dyson wanted "not to simply celebrate him by imitating or heroizing him, but to criticize him, to figure out what was good, what was bad, what was helpful, what was not helpful."

Like his table talk, Dyson's writing bore a signature: a willingness to see both sides of an issue while still taking a stand on them. In *Making Malcolm,* for instance, Dyson criticized Malcolm X's longtime hostility to women, but appreciated that "in the latter part of his life, he began to see that you can't just dump on women. . . . Any measure of the integrity of a culture is measured by how it treats its women." (It came as no surprise when Dyson later published a book—criticized by some academic peers as an example of his pandering to mass-market tastes—titled *Why I Love Black Women.*)

Similarly, while he recommended Martin Luther King Jr. to students if they wanted to see "a real revolutionary," he argued strongly that "King was able to be good because Malcolm was perceived as bad." Dyson believed that Malcolm X's nationalist fervor and rejection of nonviolence—his suggestion that "we've got to stop singing and start swinging"—spurred white America to respond to King's more acceptable approach to civil rights. "Martin became a hero," Dyson said, "by not being Malcolm."

As Dyson's name brand grew, he published prolifically, seeking to operate as a cultural commentator while not losing his academic cred. *Holler If You Hear Me* (2001), his meditation on rapper Tupac Shakur, brought him a whole new audience—the publisher identified him on the book cover as a "hip-hop intellectual." *Open Mike: Reflections on Philosophy, Race, Sex, Culture, and Religion* (2003), a thick collection of occasional pieces, suggested that almost everything that came out of his mouth needed to be in print.

At the same time, *The Michael Eric Dyson Reader,* geared to a more academic audience, and edited by the highly credentialed black historian Robin D. G. Kelley, demonstrated that Dyson still maintained the respect of many of his philosophical peers. West continued to gift him with coruscating blurbs, calling Dyson "the most talented and articulate intellectual of his generation," as well as "the most talented rhetorical acrobat in the academy." Steven Nadler, a distinguished professor of philosophy at the University of Wisconsin and noted Spinoza scholar, observed, "If any one person is continuing Du Bois's idea of the engaged public intellectual on African-American issues, it's Michael Eric Dyson."

For his part, Kelley, in a spirited introduction to the *Reader,* playfully wrote of Dyson, "It was as if W. E. B. Du Bois and Fab Five Freddy had been merged together in some Frankensteinian Experiment." Kelley acknowledged that in the often competitive and jealous byways of "blackademe," some criticized Dyson as a "race hustler" and "charlatan," complaining that "Dyson doesn't do his work and just slides by on his quick wit and glib tongue." Kelley rejected the charge, writing that "beneath the surface of [Dyson's] wit and humor one finds intellectual depth, scholarly integrity, and a startling level of erudition."

One way Dyson handled his own prominence, he explained that day over breakfast, was to try to extend it to other black thinkers by dropping their names with producers and editors. There was a particular desire by TV types, Dyson noted, "to crown those few voices who speak for the people. One of the things we should be saying is that there's no such a voice."

Dyson added that there was an even flintier message to pass on. "We have to say," he emphasized, "I'm not the smartest one, I'm not the only one, I'm not the first one."

Nor were any of the now prominent African American philosophers likely to be the last one. Everywhere one looked in prestige academe of the early twenty-first century, positive signs emerged. At Princeton, the talented young scholar Eddie S. Glaude Jr., mentored by West, published *In a Shade of Blue: Pragmatism and the Politics of Black America* (2007), taking a core strain of American thought once largely separate from black philosophy and applying it to issues of African American life.

At Harvard, the young philosopher Tommie Shelby, encouraged as an undergraduate at all-black Florida A&M University by Cornel West to keep truckin' in the field, published *We Who Are Dark: The Philosophical Foundations of Black Solidarity* (2005), which won *New York Magazine*'s award for best academic book of that year. The innovative Temple University scholar Lewis R. Gordon continued to expand another previously color-free area of philosophy with books such as *Existentia Africana: Understanding African Existential Thought* and *Existence in Black: An Anthology of Black Existential Philosophy*. At Northwestern University, Charles W. Mills, the John Evans Professor of Moral and Intellectual Philosophy, boldly brought issues of "critical theory"—race, gender, class—to the largely abstract area of social contract theory revived by Rawls and Nozick. At Penn State University, the arrival of Robert Bernasconi, whose mentoring of young black graduate students of philosophy at the University of Memphis accounted for an impressive number of younger scholars in the field, and the energetic young black philosopher Paul Taylor, indicated that the school, traditionally a powerhouse in producing philosophy PhDs, regarded African American philosophy as a pillar of its commitment to the subject. And at Duquesne University in Pittsburgh, scholar George Yancy emerged through multiple books and his coeditorship of the APA *Newsletter on Philosophy and the Black Experience* as the profession's foremost monitor of how blacks were faring in their mainly white discipline.

Now if someone could just find that lost manuscript by Amo.

Why have women philosophers in America experienced such difficulty? Because women thinkers *everywhere* have faced harassment and obstacles. The problems dated as far back as Hypatia, the mysterious Neoplatonic thinker usually described, according to Polish classical scholar Maria Dzielska in her *Hypatia of Alexandria,* as "that beautiful young pagan philosopher who was torn to pieces by monks (or, more generally, by Christians) in Alexandria in 415."

Almost from the moment she came asunder, Hypatia turned into the icon and poster woman of poets, philosophers and others eager to make her a symbol of the death of classical culture, the rise of repressive Christianity, the precariousness of women's intellectual freedom, and other historical motifs. Already in the fifth century, church historian Socrates Scholasticus declared that "she surpassed all the philosophers of her time." By the late Byzantine era, "Hypatia" functioned as a ready-made appellation for any erudite and sagacious woman. Reexamined centuries later by Enlightenment figures, Hypatia—by then more a legend than a person—plainly belonged to history. Voltaire presented her as a martyr to, in Dzielska's phrase, "the Hellenic gods, the laws of rational Nature, and the capacities of the human mind free of imposed dogmas." Gibbon depicted her as "in the bloom of beauty" when she met her death, a flesh-and-blood confirmation of his belief that Christianity destroyed the Roman Empire. In the mid-nineteenth century, poet Charles Leconte de Lisle inaugurated the compliment most commonly attached to her: "the spirit of Plato and the body of Aphrodite." Even today, the foremost feminist journal of philosophy honors Hypatia by taking her name.

All a marvelous achievement for a woman whose birth date is unknown, whose books (and their titles) remain lost, and whose entire life, personality and philosophy come to us through the references and allusions of others. The scarce sources on Hypatia, Dzielska noted, discouraged scholarly attention to her, as though even the most skeptical scholars didn't want to ruin a good story on thin grounds. Like many modern classicists, however, Dzielska preferred the best Holmesian surmise about a murky historical figure to sentimental myth. In her view, many flashy aspects of Hypatia's life appear more classic Hollywood than classical fact (and, naturally, Hollywood finally got to Hypatia in *Agora,* starring Rachel Weisz).

Hypatia, we learned from Dzielska, was almost certainly sixty or older at the time of her death—an unlikely object of sadistic lust for predatory Christians. Contrary to the long-standing view that Hypatia vehemently rejected Christianity and threatened it with her own radical Hellenism, Dzielska asserted that she displayed an ecumenical openness toward students of different beliefs, some of whom advanced to high ecclesiastical posts, and was never "an active, devoted pagan." In fact, Dzielska argued, Hypatia "sympathized with Christianity." Further, her philosophical methods aimed at religious experience, the "most ineffable of ineffable things," in her student Synesius's words. Several scholars believe Hypatia's life provided some biographical elements for the story of St. Catherine of Alexandria. Thus Hypatia's murder by Cyril, the fanatical Christian patriarch whom Dzielska (agreeing with tradition) blamed for her death, owed more to her general support for Orestes, the civil leader in Alexandria and Cyril's rival, than to any anti-Christian activism on her part. Finally, Dzielska warned, using Hypatia as a marker for the end of ancient Greece's hold over Mediterranean culture clashes with much existing evidence. "Pagan religiosity did not expire with Hypatia," wrote Dzielska, "and neither did mathematics and Greek philosophy."

In the style of much classical scholarship on uncertain subjects, Dzielska, in a manner that would please Bernal, frequently adopted the voice of the prudent risk taker. Based on combined shreds of evidence, Hypatia's father "must have been born around 335," certain Ptolemaic texts "were probably prepared for publication by Hypatia," and so on. Much of Dzielska's judgment rested on the 156 extant letters of Synesius, and the history by Socrates Scholasticus. In drawing on them, Dzielska operated conservatively, avoiding speculations that might only add to the hazy portrait she sought to undermine.

That said, who could be shocked that the most directly detailed event in Hypatia's life was her grisly death? Socrates Scholasticus stated that "they threw her out of her carriage and dragged her to the church called Caesarion. They stripped off her clothes and then killed her with broken bits of pottery. When they had torn her body limb from limb, they took it to a place called Cinarion and burned it."

Dzielska did not sensationalize the available material, but she also never addressed a provocative thought suggested by her study: that a "survival of the sensational" principle may well govern a fair amount of what we retain from classical antiquity. Whether Hypatia's enduring fame fits into that pattern is open to question. Yet it should surprise no current media critic or scholar that we probably know of antiquity's greatest woman thinker because of one and one thing only—that men killed her in the most gruesome murder case of her time.

Women philosophers, and scholars devoted to making sense of philosophy by women before the modern age, understandably mix reportage with stinging criticism, since just knowing the historic facts about women in philosophy remains challenging. One groundbreaking book that helped to put matters in perspective was *The Man of Reason: "Male" and "Female" in Western Philosophy*, by the Australian philosopher Genevieve Lloyd.

Lloyd argued that male characteristics have always colored the notion of rationality, the Holy Grail of modern Western philosophers. If there was a model of the woman Lloyd sought to save, it was Katherine Hilbery, the heroine of Virginia Woolf's novel *Night and Day*, who wanted to trade up from the sensuous confusions of everyday female life by indulging in the supposedly higher realms of the abstract—in Katherine's case, mathematics. Don't run scared, countered Lloyd. The whole business amounted to a historical ruse.

Starting with Greek theories of knowledge, Lloyd panned for incriminating evidence in the works of the chief macho men of the Western philosophical tradition, and she found some gold early on. "From the beginnings of philosophical thought," Lloyd wrote, "femaleness was symbolically associated with what Reason supposedly left behind—the dark powers of the earth goddesses, immersion in unknown forces associated with mysterious female powers." Thus the Pythagoreans made maleness clearly superior to femaleness in their "table of opposites." The former was "associated with a clear determinate mode of thought, femaleness with the vague and indeterminate."

The associations, argued Lloyd, stuck in the culture. And like lots of first impressions, they seemed unfair. "Female" got packed away with such fun adjectives as irrational, disorderly, material, negative, static, unknowable, complementary, passive, personal, particular, subjective, partial, warm and touchy-feely (or the Latin equivalent). "Male" meanwhile got to hang out with rational, orderly, abstract, positive, active, knowable, essential, dominant, distant, universal, objective, impartial, cold and achieving—the achievement being, in part, the act of transcending the condition of being female. For Lloyd as for other feminist critics, the quintessential sexist philosopher was Francis Bacon (1561–1626)—he of the "knowledge is power" adage. Bacon personified Nature and bid man, in one sexual metaphor after another, to aggressively master the lady. In identifying knowledge with the control of Nature, Bacon spoke of the latter as "a nuptial couch for the mind" and of science as "a chaste and lawful marriage between Mind and Nature." In one work, Bacon informs the reader that he will bind Nature "to your service and make her your slave."

But as Lloyd subsequently examined one modern philosopher after another, she was forced to concede that their contributions to the tradition in question were largely inadvertent. Descartes, for instance, turned out to be guilty of no crime except exalting the abstract aspect of Reason, and thus reinforcing biases already in the culture. David Hume, she admitted, believed that Reason "ought to be nothing but the slave of the passions, pretending to no other office but to serve and obey them." And by the time she got to Immanuel Kant, Lloyd had stretched her thesis thin. The German philosopher, after all, founded his entire moral philosophy on the concept of principles applicable to all rational beings, and not necessarily even human beings—he'd have admitted a rational Martian into his scheme.

Yet other champions of women thinkers lent support to Lloyd's general approach, making clear the handicaps women faced over most of Western (let alone Eastern) history. In *The Creation of Feminist Consciousness: From the Middle Ages to Eighteen-seventy,* Gerda Lerner, past president of the Organization of American Historians and author of *The Creation of Patriarchy* (1986)—a landmark book in women's studies—provided a sharp account of how women intellectuals have fared.

If *The Creation of Patriarchy,* described by one journal as possibly "the most important work in feminist theory to appear in our generation," examined how ancient man established the notion that men should control women, *The Creation of Feminist Consciousness,* a long-awaited sequel by this senior professor emerita at the University of Wisconsin–Madison, traced how female thinkers rebelled against that belief. For Lerner herself, the spirit of rebellion burned for a long time. Born in

Austria, she began distributing underground anti-Nazi newspapers as a teenager. The Nazis jailed her at seventeen (along with her mother) to blackmail her businessman father. Terrified that she would miss a comprehensive exam necessary for going to college, Lerner begged the guards to let her take the test, scrawling her appeals on toilet paper. To keep active, she taught her cell mates, sometimes as many as six in a space meant for one person.

Released after her father had signed away his belongings, Lerner showed up for the test and defiantly insisted that she be allowed to eat during the exam because she'd been starved in prison. The officials let her take the test while eating a roll, and Lerner graduated. In a newspaper interview, Lerner credited jail time with teaching her "basic courage."

Lerner proved her mettle anew in 1939. Leaving her émigré family behind in Europe, she arrived in the United States at age nineteen with five dollars in her pocket, supporting herself as a waitress and domestic. Within two years, she married film editor Carl Lerner and became a housewife and mother. Only at age thirty-eight did she begin to take history courses. Ten years later, she received her doctorate from Columbia. During her graduate training, Lerner once recalled, she didn't have a single female teacher. No one discussed women's history. Instead, she learned that "one-half the human race is doing everything significant, and the other half doesn't exist. I asked myself how this checked against my own life experience."

The Creation of Feminist Consciousness reflected the crusading research and ideological spin one might expect from such a survivor, drawing attention to neglected women intellectuals. Lerner properly insisted that patriarchy hindered women and focused on the raw deal given women thinkers. During the early modern West, for instance, she compared the difficulties of the put-upon female thinker with the putatively ideal niche of "the male thinker, whose authority was unquestioned, whose right to his own experience was taken as a given and who could develop his own thought standing in discourse with the great thinkers behind him." She blamed men for every hitch in feminism's tardy rise, refusing to fault women for their centuries-long failure to investigate predecessors—a task Lerner and her academic progeny are now accomplishing. Lerner contended that "women were denied knowledge of their history, and thus each woman had to argue as though no woman before her had ever thought or written. Women had to use their energy to reinvent the wheel, over and over again."

The Creation of Feminist Consciousness thus mixed two disparate elements: a welcome survey of feminist intellectuals and their struggle, and a debatable, understandably bitter set of explanations for their secondary status. In her introduction, Lerner defined feminist consciousness as "the awareness of women that they belong to a subordinate group; that they have suffered wrongs as a group; that their condition of subordination is not natural; . . . that they must join with other women to remedy these wrongs; and finally, that they must and can provide an alternate vision of societal organization."

As Lerner traced the rise of that consciousness, her chief feat was reportorial: demonstrating that significant feminist intellectual activity existed before the nineteenth century. Lerner commented on a millennium of feminist thinkers, some already well known. She pondered Hildegard of Bingen (1098–1179), the Rhineland nun self-anointed as "God's little trumpet" (like Hypatia now portrayed on film, in Margarethe von Trotta's *Vision*) and Christine de Pizan (1363–c. 1430), widely regarded as the first European woman to earn her living by writing. She also gave time to less familiar figures, such as Elizabeth Elstob (1683–1756), a great scholar of Anglo-Saxon.

In presenting them, Lerner repeatedly stressed key historical themes: the "disadvantaging of women in gaining access to education," the need for women to "authorize themselves to speak and write," the "waste of talent and insight," and the misogyny in the Bible. Lerner also emphasized that feminist consciousness depends on "the ability of a sizable group of women to live outside of marriage in economic interdependence" and on social changes that allow large groups of women to skip childbearing. Much of Lerner's intriguing information hit home, yet several of her analytical observations also stirred traditional questions over how best to explain the intellectual marginalization of women over the centuries. While Lerner insisted, for instance, that women were "almost universally educationally disadvantaged," she also provided repeated examples of basic education of women throughout the ages: girls in Sparta, young women under the powerful medieval abbesses, Virginia Woolf's tradition of "educated daughters of educated men." Of Hildegard, Lerner wrote, "Undoubtedly, she was a model for others." Yet Lerner's main complaint seemed to be that Hildegard did not prove to be a model for a *sufficient* number of others. According to Lerner, "one can safely say that up to 1700 there are fewer than 300 learned women in Western Europe known to historians."

Given the high number of women with basic education, it was not entirely clear why more women didn't continue on to higher achievement in philosophy and other areas of literate culture, even given familial pressures. When one added the number of educated nuns, patriarchy didn't provide a clear-cut reason.

Lerner also contended that in both America and Europe, women had to battle men to conquer every level of institutional learning. "Resistance by individual men and by male-controlled establishments," she wrote, "was relentless and unwavering." She spoke of "the constant barrage of discouragement every intellectually active woman faced." Yet, there too, her own book cited example after example (usually in passing) of men encouraging learned women, such as Montaigne's mentoring of Marie de Gournay. Without the endorsement of Bernard of Clairvaux and Frederick Barbarossa, Hildegard herself would have been a much littler trumpet.

Lerner's lack of evenhandedness showed most strikingly in the different approaches she took to what one might call the "off-peak" thoughts of premodern male and female thinkers. She condescended to Aristotle, appropriately, for assuming (as was common in his time) that women were naturally inferior to men. At the same time, she raved about the "genius" and "originality" of Hildegard despite the latter's peculiar notion of reproduction: "If one or the other partner is lacking in love, the offspring will either be a girl or an embittered boy."

Lerner's deeply empathetic approach to female thinkers, which she called "compensatory" women's history in a 1976 essay, foretold her conclusion that "the hegemony of patriarchal thought in Western civilization is not due to its superiority in content, form and achievement over all other thought; it is built upon the systematic silencing of other voices." Whether or not that claim was true in its broad form—we might continue to believe that if a woman had formulated a theory as powerful as those of Aristotle or Newton, she'd have gotten the attention she deserved—Lerner solidly outlined its truth in a myriad smaller regards.

That disregard of women thinkers continued into the early modern period. (Immerwahr and Burke, occupied with race, couldn't devote much attention to the total absence of women in the early modern philosophy course.) Nancy Tuana, a Penn State philosopher who edited her university press's series of "Feminist Interpretations" of great philosophers—a momentous achievement in bringing women's perspectives into the history of philosophy—observed, at a Princeton conference on analytic distortions of philosophical history, some of the consequences wrought by suppression of women. The marginalization of female philosophers such as Princess Elisabeth, Descartes's famous correspondent, led later commentators to denigrate the importance of emotions in his thought, not to mention in philosophy generally. (The work of philosophers Robert C. Solomon and Martha Nussbaum, among others, has helped correct that mistake.)

Tuana pointed out that women philosophers, to the extent they existed in standard histories at all, disappeared from them between the seventeenth and nineteenth centuries, a process documented by Eileen O'Neill of the University of Massachusetts at Amherst, a leading scholar of women thinkers in the early modern period. How would the history of philosophy look, Tuana asked, if we took seriously what women produced in salons and convents, as John J. Conley remarkably did in his fresh-thinking book, *The Suspicion of Virtue: Women Philosophers in Neoclassical France* (2002), which reintroduced us to such fascinating figures as Madame de Sablé, Madame Deshoulières and Madame de Maintenon. Thankfully, a number of American women philosophers with a historical bent, most notably Mary Ellen Waithe of Cleveland State University in her four-volume *A History of Women Philosophers*, have taken up the task of recovering the past. Meanwhile others, such as British scholar Beverley Clack in her astonishing anthology, *Misogyny in the Western Philosophical Tradition: A Reader*, documented the attitudes women philosophers had encountered even from their most esteemed male peers. (Aquinas, for instance, described woman as a "misbegotten male," and Schopenhauer dismissed women as "big children their whole life long.")

In an American context, this unhappy story is reflected in statistics, early and recent. In 1901, a year after its founding, the APA included all of ten women. In 2008, 21 percent of employed philosophers in the U.S. were women, compared with 41 percent in the humanities generally, and women earned only about 27 percent of philosophy PhDs over the past fifteen to twenty years. A well-known article by MIT professor Sally Haslanger found that only 2.36 percent of articles in top philosophy journals deal with feminist issues, even though the Society for Women in Philosophy, the profession's main organization for women, will celebrate its twenty-fifth anniversary in 2012.

The historical story is best picked up by focusing on two nineteenth-century women both celebrated in intellectual history, yet oddly missing from philosophy department curricula: Margaret Fuller (1810–1850) and Jane Addams (1860–1935). In *Pragmatism and Feminism,*

Purdue philosophy professor Charlene Haddock Seigfried spoke of the price to pragmatism of a canon that long excluded such thinkers. To be seminal, she noted, one needn't be an inseminator. In one passage, she made her point by referring to the business-as-usual exclusion of Fuller from another American movement in philosophy, Transcendentalism, in Morton White's standard work, *Documents in the History of American Philosophy: From Jonathan Edwards to John Dewey*. Seigfried wrote, "The status of George Ripley and Theodore Parker is raised, for instance, by their being included as Transcendentalists along with Ralph Waldo Emerson and Samuel Taylor Coleridge. Margaret Fuller is not included, thereby diminishing her intellectual reputation."

The "Fuller Brush-off" in American intellectual history—denying Margaret Fuller's philosophical centrality to Transcendentalism—is indeed a vexed affair. For one thing, Transcendentalism as a rubric for a set of New England thinkers from about 1830 to the early 1850s—they included Ralph Waldo Emerson, Bronson Alcott, Ripley, *and* Margaret Fuller—remains a case of outsiders placing a tag on insiders, who at first resist the tag, then embrace or try to make sense of it after it enters public consciousness. That is, there's a Marxist aspect to the original coining, as Philip F. Gura's lucid *American Transcendentalism: A History* instructs—a version, that is, of Groucho's wish not to be a member of any club that would admit him.

The Transcendentalists initially were "called the 'club of the like-minded,'" Fuller's close friend James Freeman Clarke reported, "because no two of us thought alike." Orestes Brownson, an "erstwhile member" according to Gura, seconded the observation: "No single term can describe them. Nothing can be more unjust to them, or more likely to mislead the public, than to lump them all together, and predicate the same things of them all." Nonetheless, Transcendentalism became a cutting-edge intellectual movement with which to be associated. That made rather shabby the dismissive treatment of Fuller as one of its shapers, a syndrome that began after her tragic 1850 death at age forty in a shipwreck off Fire Island.

Fuller's most famous work, *Woman in the Nineteenth Century* (1845), teemed with arguments and examples, and became an urtext for later nineteenth-century feminists. It indisputably applied Emerson's "enshrinement of the self-reliant individual," in Gura's phrase, to women. Fuller famously asserted, "What woman needs is not as a woman to act or rule, but as a nature to grow, as an intellect to discern, as a soul to live freely and unimpeded, to unfold such powers as were given her when we left our common home."

Fuller also served as inaugural editor of the *Dial,* Transcendentalism's most important publication. The later nineteenth-century feminist Caroline Dall concluded, in the 1880s, that "what is meant by Transcendentalism perished with Margaret Fuller." Yet many scholars still dismissed Fuller as a thinker until recently. A thoroughly condescending assessment, an aberration for that usually spot-on scholar, came from V. L. Parrington in his classic three-volume *Main Currents in American Thought* (1927), which won the Pulitzer Prize for history in 1928. To Parrington, Fuller, despite a classical education almost as rigorous as John Stuart Mill's, and despite Emerson's sky-high praise of her abilities, "wrote nothing that bears the mark of high distinction either in thought or style. Impatient of organization and inadequately disciplined, she threw off her work impulsively, not pausing to shape it to enduring form."

"Perhaps," Parrington wrote, "it was a mistake to force her into the rigid groove of classical learning when she should have been playing with her dolls." Yes, he actually wrote that, and it gets worse. Fuller's "intense emotions" inevitably "quickened her mind and distorted it." Her "ardent nature was the victim of disastrous frustrations, rendered the more acute by premature development. If she had married earlier, as Harriet Beecher did, and her excessive energy had been turned into domestic channels, her life must have been less tragic, whatever the effect might have been on her intellectual development."

Then comes Parrington's coup de grâce against this "most hectic" of Transcendentalism's "expounders": the "intellectual foundations of her Transcendentalism were so slight in comparison with the equipment of Frederic Hedge and Theodore Parker as scarcely to justify her pretensions to their fellowship. But what she lacked in knowledge of Kant and Fichte she made up in enthusiasm, and none questioned her right to speak for the group."

Anyone familiar with Fuller's writings knows the falsity of Parrington's judgments. Decades past second-wave feminism, it can irritate to confront the prejudices of faded sexist scholars again. Such derision made it easy, though, for even better-intentioned sorts to reject Fuller as a thinker. Elizabeth Flower and Murray G. Murphey, in their two-volume *A History of Philosophy in America,* mention Fuller as a member of the Transcendentalist "movement," but refer to her only one more time, when they quote a letter to her from Emerson. Neither *The Encyclopedia of Philosophy* (1967) nor *The Routledge Encyclopedia of Philosophy* (1998), two authoritative reference works in the field, include an article on Fuller.

Of course, as a writer and women's rights thinker, Fuller survived and transcended her trashing by Parrington and others. Markers of her classic stature included her Viking Portable edition, a six-volume edition of her letters, scores of monographs, and a regular place on syllabi outside philosophy departments. Her rightful stature as a Transcendentalist thinker, however, didn't come into clear focus until the appearance of two superlative acts of scholarship: Gura's astute, readable, fair-minded history for a general audience; and Charles Capper's completion of his monumental and definitive two-volume biography, *Margaret Fuller: An American Romantic Life: The Public Years.*

"After the end of the 19th century," conceded Capper, "Fuller virtually disappeared from public memory, except as an also-ran in the 'idyll' of Transcendentalism." She was "mostly mocked by modernist critics." Capper called that "deeply ironic," complaining, "If America had a modernist forerunner before the 20th century, it was surely Margaret Fuller." He and Gura corroborated that. Gura did his part for the "brilliant and mercurial" Fuller by repeatedly rejecting the notion that her later activities, after she left Boston and began a new career as literary critic for the *New York Herald Tribune*, represented a conceptual abandonment of her Transcendental sympathies. To Gura, Ripley "provided as good a definition of Transcendentalism as any in the movement ever wrote." Ripley stated that Transcendentalists "believe in an order of truths which transcends the sphere of the external senses. Their leading idea is the supremacy of mind over matter. Hence they maintain that the truth of religion does not depend on tradition, or on historical facts, but has an unerring witness in the soul."

That soul, Ripley declared, enjoys "absolute independence and right to interpret the meaning of life, untrammeled by traditions and conventions." By the very attention he devoted to Fuller's activities that scholars once saw as irrelevant to Transcendental thinking—her passionate journalism about prisoners, prostitutes and class and racial inequality in New York; her commitment to the Italian revolutionary struggle; even her battle for a private life in which something "sweet" might balance pure intellectual achievement—Gura legitimized them as expressions of Transcendentalist engagement.

Capper, the foremost expert on Fuller, put even more of a shoulder behind Fuller's philosophical restoration. He demonstrated that she "reconfigured" Transcendentalism, advancing "a vitalist reformulation of the Transcendental alchemy that Emerson had presented." She did that by expanding its masculine, introspective tropes, its exaltation of the Imperial Self, in a cosmopolitan direction and toward freedom for women too. Capper championed *Woman in the Nineteenth Century* as "a philosophical text founded on a particular liberal Romantic ideology of inward and outward freedom" whose "central argument is not one of women's rights" but "a transcendent ideal of manhood and womanhood measured against the opinions and actions of men and women." Like Gura, he portrayed Fuller, who mastered Italian, French and German during her extraordinary education, grappling with the complex ideas of Fourier, Swedenborg, Goethe and others in her work—hardly the performance of Parrington's "tragic" failure.

A long tradition had existed of punishing Margaret Fuller for her high self-regard and alleged pomposity. The exchange most famously used against her remains her declaration, "I accept the universe!" and Thomas Carlyle's retort, "My God, she'd better." But Capper's astonishingly comprehensive play-by-play of Fuller's life and work, and Gura's smooth integration of both in interweaving the major and minor Transcendentalists, indicated that the tradition owes more to the kind of hostility exemplified by Parrington than to Fuller's personality. "We accept Margaret Fuller!" historians of Transcendentalism had finally declared. After that only the philosophy academics were missing in action.

A similar tale could be told of Jane Addams. In Louis Menand's *Pragmatism: A Reader*, the most widely used anthology of writings from the line of thinkers said to represent America's chief contribution to philosophy, she was the only woman among the usual suspects—Charles Sanders Peirce, William James, Oliver Wendell Holmes, John Dewey and George Herbert Mead—presented as the "First Generation." Remembered chiefly as America's social worker supreme, the saintly cofounder of Hull House in 1889, Addams won the 1931 Nobel Peace Prize. And showing how, as Lerner's dictum suggested, the rise of women philosophers begat a restoration of earlier women philosophers to appropriate stature, Jean Bethke Elshtain, herself a leading contemporary political philosopher, fueled Addams's reascension with her *Jane Addams and the Dream of American Democracy* and companion volume, *The Jane Addams Reader* (2001), both complementing the University of

Illinois Press's republication of Addams's own books in handsome new paperback editions.

Coming only a few years after the journalist Gioia Diliberto's eye-opening trade biography, *A Useful Woman: The Early Life of Jane Addams,* Elshtain's enlightening meditation, more admiring commentary than biography, left no doubt that Addams, "America's best-known and most widely hailed female public figure at her death," should once again rank as a household name in cerebral households. In the Vintage anthology, she merited a mere 15 pages of 522. And the minimization did not stop there. Tellingly, in the volume's introduction, Menand largely skipped over her, jumping from Dewey to Mead as he systematically provided brief introductions to the key ideas of everyone but Addams in the "First Generation" section. Even though Menand briefly acknowledged that Dewey's influential emphasis on "learning by doing" in education may have been "partly formulated" by Addams, the second and final time he mentioned Addams he whizzed right past her. ("The implication is that after the generation of Peirce, James, Holmes, Dewey, Addams, and Mead, pragmatism went into eclipse.")

An odd narrative move, but actually an explicable one, more likely a reflex than a pointed exclusion. The standard view, after all, has been that Addams exemplified pragmatism more than she theorized it. And in a discipline cursed by ossified syllabi and glacial stumbling toward new perspectives, violating the "White Guys" portrait of nineteenth-century American pragmatism required revolutionary edge, like getting cookie-cutter assistant professors of early modern philosophy to question the lineup of "Rationalists" (Descartes, Spinoza and Leibniz) and "Empiricists" (Locke, Berkeley and Hume), or classicists to ignore Plato's slanted opinions on which ancients count as philosophers rather than rhetoricians.

Arguably—and Menand suggested this in his history, *The Metaphysical Club*—if pragmatism remained best understood as the kindred perspectives toward truth, certainty and inquiry that emerged among a handful of white, male nineteenth-century American theorists who knew and shared ideas with one another, the standard view stays accurate, however inconvenient it may be in the age of tenured radicals. Yet the broader characterization of pragmatism sparked by Rorty in philosophy, egged on by Posner in law and attested to by an array of cross-disciplinary scholars in collections like *The Revival of Pragmatism,* challenged the traditional lineup. After all, the term's rebirth has come as a designation for thinkers identified by philosophical allegiance and practice rather than membership cards in a club.

Should Benjamin Franklin be included as a proto-pragmatist, given his commitment to experience, experimentation and community inquiry long before Peirce? Does Franklin, whatever his aversion to tiresome treatise writing, confirm his pragmatist ethos by writing in 1784 that "perhaps for Fifty Years past no one has ever heard a dogmatical Expression escape me"? (We should remember here that professors constructed the "existentialist" canon backward from Sartre to Kierkegaard, honoring the latter's grudging admission that life must be understood backward, even though he didn't think it could be understood at all.) Should the nineteenth-century African American thinker Martin Delany be admitted, given his declaration in *The Condition, Elevation, Emigration, and Destiny of the Colored People of the United States* that "[e]xperience has taught us that speculations are not enough; that the *practical* application of principles adduced, the thing carried out, is the only true and proper course to pursue"? Isn't the reason Addams made Menand's anthology at all her family resemblance to the stalwarts?

She insisted, after all, in the very excerpt included there, that the "ideal and developed settlement would attempt to test the value of human knowledge by action." Didn't she deserve a piece of the action for solving all those practical problems with immigrants in an experimental way, and not just for palling around with Dewey? Surprisingly, in light of Elshtain's ambitions for her heroine, the University of Chicago professor of social and political ethics barely touched on Addams's pragmatist or philosophical credentials—the *p* word didn't make Elshtain's index, and Dewey gets only a passing reference on page 216. Elshtain was after other game: immortalizing Addams as a significant progressive, or tribune of democracy, and she advanced her cause gracefully, drawing the reader into her own attachment to Addams. Elshtain reminded us of the fresh eye Addams brought to political assumptions when we heard again about Addams's notion of "public housekeeping," by which women extended the care they exercised on domestic terrain to the public sphere. That idea flintily clashed with the "tragedy of the commons"—the belief that individuals will naturally invest little energy in public spaces—that so many political scientists take as stern psychological reality.

But the new spotlight Elshtain shone on Addams also made her subject's return to center stage an occasion to ask questions important to philosophers, feminists and intellectual historians. Was Jane Addams a significant pragmatist, or the Queen of Pragmatist Tokens, added to teaching texts to ease embarrassment at the *p* group's homogeneity? If the former—despite the supposed paucity of her "theoretical" texts, her scant interest in epistemology and her proclivity for solving social problems in concrete ways—did that call for reassessing criteria for who counts as a major pragmatist philosopher?

Much of the critical commentary spurred by Elshtain's book, despite the author's own limited enthusiasm for pure biography, understandably zeroed in on Addams as complex personality and remarkable innovator. As much an impresario as Franklin himself, she started Chicago's first playground, first kindergarten, and more. Her pacifism in World War I, her long personal partnership with Mary Rozet Smith, her ability to deliver "compassion without condescension" (in Walter Lippmann's much-cited phrase) all made better copy than her status as philosopher. Elshtain surveyed contemporary views of Addams as a thinker only in her first chapter and a long footnote. She quoted the University of Rochester historian Robert Westbrook: "It is difficult to say whether Dewey influenced Jane Addams or Jane Addams influenced Dewey." Plainly, Westbrook and others have agreed, they influenced each other. Elshtain just as clearly wanted Addams to be accepted as a crucial thinker—of some pedigree—about democracy.

But once again it was Seigfried, in *Pragmatism and Feminism,* who rightly understood that establishing Addams as a pragmatist philosopher might fuel the larger aim, thus challenging the criteria by which male philosophy professors traditionally bestowed that cachet (e.g., excessive attention to the theory of knowledge). Seigfried straightforwardly credited Addams with "original (albeit mostly unacknowledged) contributions to the initial formulation of pragmatism." She cited the University of Nebraska sociologist Mary Jo Deegan's assertion that it was out of the "collegial contacts and intellectual exchanges" of Dewey and Mead with Addams "that Chicago pragmatism was born."

To Seigfried, the taxonomic issues partly resulted from familiar academic dissing: "In the patriarchal records, the philosophers relegate Addams to sociology, while sociologists relegate her to amateur reformism, at best to the status of a social worker." Yet even Seigfried's spare examples demonstrate the degree to which Addams fired Dewey's imagination with her tactile experience of "reciprocal" learning among the different classes and ethnicities of Hull House. On the fortieth anniversary of Hull House, Dewey declared that Addams had "reminded us that democracy is not a form but a way of living together and working together." He and Addams would have welcomed the same description of knowledge itself.

So, in recent years, mulling Jane Addams, instead of just Hulling her—like thinking in fresh ways about Franklin, or Delany, or a contemporary maverick such as Robert Coles—revealed that pragmatism's tent in American intellectual life always stretched much further than philosophy professors or standard anthologies acknowledged. Today, philosophers increasingly recognize that persuasive storytelling, the genre in which Addams and Coles excel, may count as effective philosophical argument. The story of Jane Addams drove that point home. Coming to the twentieth century, one could say the story of Ayn Rand extended it to the bestseller list.

Love her or leave her, Ayn Rand (1905–1982) spunkily agitated within American literary and intellectual life for forty years, a rude, self-styled "radical for capitalism" unwilling to sit down and shut up even when assaulted by hisses from the leftish crowd that predominated in American literary culture during most of her career. From the success of her massive novels *The Fountainhead* (1943) and *Atlas Shrugged* (1957) to the six-foot-high dollar sign that marked her coffin, Rand proselytized her vision of man "as a heroic being, with his own happiness as the moral purpose of his life, with productive achievement as his noblest activity, and reason as his only absolute." The ironic title of Barbara Branden's biography, *The Passion of Ayn Rand,* played on that last belief, for no one was better equipped than Branden—a close Rand friend for nineteen years—to expose the turbulent emotions of the writer who exalted reason as the sole standard of human behavior.

Branden wrote of Rand's hatred for the Bolshevik revolution that destroyed her Jewish family in St. Petersburg, Russia, her dependence on altruistic relatives when she came to the United States as a young woman, and her rationalization of her affair with Branden's then husband, Nathaniel (her chief disciple), as an act of supreme rational morality. She repeatedly showed that real life turned Rand, as it does most ideologues, into a hypocrite. Indeed, the details of Rand's life were so entertaining—how she got her first Hollywood job from director Cecil B. DeMille; how she liked to be called "Fluff" by actor Frank O'Connor,

Ayn Rand (1905–1982), the
Russian-born libertarian novelist and philosopher, produced
many public disciples, from
Alan Greenspan to Representative Paul Ryan, who asked his
staff to read *Atlas Shrugged.*

the passive husband whom she insisted was both brilliant and "a hero"—
that Branden's insider information focused attention on how a thinker's
personal struggles and beliefs go together.

Shortly after Alice Rosenbaum, daughter of a Russian-Jewish phar-
macist father and a highly opinionated homemaker mother, came to
the United States at age twenty-one, she moved to Hollywood, where
a chance encounter with DeMille led to scriptwriting for his studio,
and a meeting with O'Connor, whom she married in 1929. To pursue
her ambition to become a great writer, she chose a new name, taking
"Ayn" from a Finnish writer she'd never read and "Rand" from her typewriter. The public career began with the success of her play *The Night of
January 16th,* which enjoyed a long run on Broadway in 1935. Two short
novels, *We the Living* (1936) and *Anthem* (1938), followed, but it was *The
Fountainhead* that made Rand a singular literary figure and presence. For
Rand, the "hero"—a person of uncompromising moral independence and
enlightened self-interest—became central to her understanding of ethical life. Her *Fountainhead* protagonist, Howard Roark, more than filled

the bill. A brilliant architect modeled partly on Frank Lloyd Wright, he loathes mediocrity and never compromises his genius, regardless of the consequences for his career and love life. The 1949 film version, starring Gary Cooper, only reinforced Roark as an icon of American individualism, particularly for young readers, and Rand as that concept's chief booster and ideologue in the literary world.

Perhaps the most famous young acolyte of Rand was former Federal Reserve Board chairman Alan Greenspan, who once sat at her feet as part of a group of young admirers she sarcastically dubbed her "collective." Rand described him as a "disciple," and Greenspan invited her to attend his swearing-in as chair of the Council of Economic Advisers in 1974. "Ayn Rand was instrumental in significantly broadening the scope of my thinking," Greenspan told Barbara Branden, "and was clearly a major contributor to my intellectual development, for which I remain profoundly grateful to this day."

But it was Nathaniel Branden, one of her young readers and admirers, who caused the most sensational upheavals in her life after she met him in 1950. A UCLA student, Branden and his soon-to-be wife, Barbara Weidman, became members of Rand's inner circle, first in Los Angeles, then in New York, where Rand and the Brandens moved the next year. By 1955, Rand and Branden—twenty-five years her junior—were in a full-scale sexual affair for which they requested and received grudging permission from their spouses. The affair plainly catalyzed Rand's work. In 1957, Rand finally finished *Atlas Shrugged*, a more overtly philosophical novel than *The Fountainhead*, after twelve years of work. A critique of collectivism that permitted Rand to imagine her ideal man, John Galt, a paragon of moralism and supreme intellectual self-confidence, it solidified her reputation as a spokeswoman for what she later termed "the virtue of selfishness," the incoherence of self-sacrifice, the appropriateness of minimal government, and other out-of-the-mainstream beliefs at the core of her philosophy, which she came to call "Objectivism." It so impressed a young southern businessman named Ted Turner that he bought cryptic billboard signs across the South asking, "Who is John Galt?"

Meanwhile, Rand announced that Branden was her "intellectual heir." For the next decade, their intellectual enterprise flourished as Rand grew more autocratic, breaking with one follower after another. At the same time, her sexual affair with Branden faded, though Rand sought to rekindle it. The moment of truth came in 1968, when Rand learned that Branden, separated by then from his wife, had been engaged for years in yet another affair. In a scene famous to all Randians, she furiously excommunicated him, cursed him and slapped him multiple times. Rand rendered Branden a nonperson in all subsequent official "Objectivist" publications and activities.

For decades since, it has often seemed impossible for both insiders and outsiders to separate three issues: her stature in the culture, the soap opera and schisms that followed from that cataclysmic break of Objectivism's founder and anointed heir, and the independent merit of her philosophical ideas. To be sure, her staying power in the world of ideas is now undisputed, with supporters emphasizing her quality and sheer facts on the ground confirming her influence.

To Allan Gotthelf, former head of the Ayn Rand Society and emeritus professor of philosophy at the College of New Jersey, she's "one of the most important thinkers of the 20th century." To Canadian journalist Jeff Walker, author of *The Ayn Rand Cult,* she's a "pop philosopher" and icon of a movement of true believers whose cult "is alive and well on planet Earth." To Mimi Gladstein, University of Texas literature scholar and coeditor of *Feminist Interpretations of Ayn Rand,* she's "an extremely courageous thinker and writer who basically went against the mainstream of American literature and philosophy." To Showtime producers, whose film version of Branden's book (Helen Mirren as Rand, Peter Fonda as O'Connor) appeared a few years back, she was an occasionally unclad woman of a certain age, an intense Lady Svengali with a thick Russian accent and archly perched cigarette who sprinkled aperçus ("Lesser people could never accept this") as she stormed about her house and carpets in torrid love scenes with Branden. ("Far worse than the book," said Gotthelf at the time. "It portrays her as a kind of pathetic neurotic.")

Without doubt, her texts, quasi-sacred for believers, endure. Rand's books have sold more than 30 million copies around the world, and still sell some 400,000 copies annually, according to the Ayn Rand Institute in Irvine, California, the headquarters of official Rand studies. "Though her philosophy is dismissed by the academic establishment and her novels deprecated by belles-lettres critics," wrote Gladstein in a 1995 article on Rand for *The Oxford Companion to Women's Writing in the United States,* "her ideas have wide-ranging influence. A 1991 survey by the Library of Congress found *Atlas Shrugged* second only to the Bible in a list of books that most influenced readers' lives."

Nineteen ninety-five also saw the publication of the first scholarly study of Rand published by a respected university press, *Ayn Rand: The*

Russian Radical (Penn State) by Chris Matthew Sciabarra, a political scientist. That book spurred debate with its novel claim that Rand, who came to the United States in 1926, is best understood as a thinker whose roots in Russian philosophy and Marxism's dialectical tradition account for the unique syntheses of her later work. Since then, scholarly interest in her has significantly spiked, if not boomed, fanned by the wide theatrical distribution of *Ayn Rand: A Sense of Life,* a 1997 Oscar-nominated documentary approved by the Ayn Rand Institute, and such studies as *What Art Is: The Esthetic Theory of Ayn Rand* by Louis Torres and Michelle Marder Kamhi. The *Chronicle of Higher Education,* in an overview of Rand's place in academe, reported many more books on Rand's thought on the way (including a study by Gotthelf), as well as a journal devoted to Randian literary studies.

In a nod to Rand's rising academic profile—leading reference works on twentieth-century literature and philosophy frequently ignored Rand in the past—she received an entry in Routledge's recent ten-volume *Encyclopedia of Philosophy.* The Twayne's Masterworks Studies Series, a further barometer of academic credibility, published volumes on *The Fountainhead* and *Atlas Shrugged.* The U.S. Post Office issued an Ayn Rand stamp in its literary arts series, making her only the sixteenth American author so honored. Gene Bell-Villada, chair of the Williams College romance languages department and author of *The Pianist Who Liked Ayn Rand*, a volume of short fiction whose title novella examines a Chicano jazz pianist who reads all of Rand to win the heart of a sorority sister, arranged a session on Rand for a December annual meeting of the Modern Language Association, often mocked for its politically correct panels.

On the soap opera front, Nathaniel Branden went on to publish nineteen books and become a founder of the "self-esteem" movement in psychology. His side of the story appeared in a memoir, *My Years with Ayn Rand.* Leonard Peikoff, a cousin of Barbara Branden, replaced Nathaniel Branden as Rand's chief confidant, and became executor of her estate, director of the institute and preserver of her official message. Both Rand until her death, and Peikoff afterward, continued to shun and discard adherents who took too independent a line on Rand's thought.

One noted heretic, David Kelly, founded his own Institute for Objectivist Studies in Poughkeepsie, New York. For the most part, the progeny fight. Gotthelf, who knew Rand personally, says Walker's book is "a farce, just unspeakable trash," that Sciabarra's is "an embarrassment," and that Gladstein's coedited volume contains much "nonsense." Walker calls Peikoff "a lunatic . . . a cartoon character," Branden "a total creep," and writes that Sciabarra's book is "precisely the kind of academic exercise" that would have drawn Rand's contempt. Sciabarra returns the compliment by remarking that the sole virtue of Walker's book is the way it "takes all the gossip and puts it in one place." Gladstein, who explains that many reference works wouldn't contain mentions of Rand if she hadn't consented to write them, notes that Rand refused to speak even with her, a snub repeated by Peikoff.

According to Sciabarra, at the New York ceremony for the new Rand stamp Peikoff, Kelly and others politely ignored one another. "It will take the death of everyone who knew Rand personally," Sciabarra added, "for this to go away."

Finally, there's her philosophy. "I am haunted by a quotation from Friedrich Nietzsche," Rand once told a *Time* magazine reporter, explaining her withdrawal from punditry to focus on philosophy. "It is not my function to be a flyswatter." And she meant it, always thinking big. "I did not want, intend or expect to be the only philosophical defender of man's rights in the country of man's rights," she declared with typical grandiosity when she closed down her regular newsletter in 1976. "But if I am, I am."

At the centenary of her birth in 2005, the occasion was marked around the country—a country whose administration at that time vigorously embraced some of Rand's once iconoclastic ideas about human freedom—by special events, including a symposium sponsored by Republican congressmen at the Library of Congress. A new illustrated biography by Jeffrey Britting, archivist of the Ayn Rand Institute, also appeared. "One of the great urban myths," wrote Britting, "is the notion that Ayn Rand was a dictator of people's tastes." Britting saw her as a "generous" and "fiery" philosopher devoted to argument, dialogue and explanation of her ideas, whose greatest legacy remained her "ability to dramatize ideas." He admitted, of course, that "vigorous debates about details and specifics of her philosophy" continued.

And so they might. Rand's beliefs, including her core trust in the "supremacy of reason," permeated her philosophical novels, but she also expressed them in traditional nonfiction form, as in the essays gathered in *Philosophy: Who Needs It.* "For some 200 years," she proclaimed there, "under the influence of Immanuel Kant, the dominant trend of philosophy has been directed to a single goal: the destruction of man's mind, of his confidence in the power of reason." Thus, she counseled, we must continue to fight "the profoundly Kantian hatred of the innocent, the strong, the able, the successful, the virtuous, the confident, the happy." That alleged sentiment expresses itself in "mawkish concern with and compassion for the feeble, the flawed, the suffering, the guilty."

Only philosophy, she warned, "can provide you with these weapons." Yet while Rand described philosophy as a tool, she more often used it as a kind of "Good Headkeeping" seal: a prestigious cultural label to place on her arbitrary beliefs. For Rand, respect for reason created not an "open mind" but an "active mind" that rejected the tendency of modern intellectuals to fear certainty. Such an "active mind" quickly realizes that "altruism," Rand's bête noire, is a dispensable "tribal" notion. To be fair, by altruism Rand did not mean "kindness, good will or respect for the rights of others"—three things she claims altruism makes impossible. Instead, she meant the principle "that man has no right to exist for his own sake, that service to others is the only justification of his existence and that self-sacrifice is his highest moral duty, virtue and value." Since self-sacrifice meant to her "self-immolation," and reason dictates that man choose a morality that sustains his life, reason and altruism were "incompatible."

Yet despite Rand's rantings against "mysticism"—"the acceptance of allegations without evidence or proof"—she never argued when she could name-call. B. F. Skinner's *Beyond Freedom and Dignity* was a "worthless, insignificant book," and Emerson "a little mind." To her, "nothing is self-evident except the material of sensory perception," a claim long put in question by philosophers arguing from illusion, dreams and other counterexamples. Her analytical style, she announced, was to "attach clear, specific meanings to words." But, as Wittgenstein showed, words rarely have such clear meanings. Most philosophers handle these land mines carefully. Rand simply sauntered over them like a queen touring her estate. In doing so, she interpreted every philosophical doctrine opposed to hers as a "rationalization" for psychological weakness, and uncritically adopted historical clichés.

For instance, the "low wages and harsh living conditions" of early capitalism, she asserted, "were all that the national economies of the time could afford." The owners, presumably, could not rationally take less profit. Moreover, contradictions sometimes came in the same sentence: "Nature does not give man any automatic guarantee of the truth of his judgments (and this is a metaphysically given fact, which must be accepted)." Her claim that Kant believed we owe moral duty only to others, not oneself, utterly distorted his work, as shown in a 1952 article by the scholar Julius Ebbinghaus.

For all that, Rand's influence continued to show the trickle-down impact, even amid the 2008 economic catastrophe that many laid at the feet of Alan Greenspan and the laissez-faire Wall Street he spawned, of a woman philosopher in America the Philosophical. In 2011, newly powerful U.S. Congressman Paul Ryan assigned his staffers to read *Atlas Shrugged*. The same year, a $20 million film version of the novel, produced by businessman and Rand admirer John Aglialoro (who made it himself when he couldn't get a studio to take it on), proved so popular that it played for weeks in national multiplexes usually open only to Hollywood product. It's doubtful that any of Rand's tribunes would have felt the need to stamp a book about her with a title such as the one scholar Elisabeth Young-Bruehl chose for her testament to a more academically respected member of America's female philosophical firmament, whose stature she sought to solidify.

In *Why Arendt Matters,* a staunchly devotional brief for her former teacher's ongoing relevance, Young-Bruehl understandably complained that despite writing "more than a dozen dense volumes," several "masterpieces of political analysis," and posthumously becoming "the subject of hundreds of books and articles," Hannah Arendt (1906–1975) lived on "in newspeak through just four words": *the banality of evil.* Young-Bruehl lamented, at her book's outset, "This is the sound bite by which Hannah Arendt has become popularly known." What, the noted psychoanalyst asked, "do people make of it when, every time some especially appalling, hard-to-fathom mass crime takes place, 'the banality of evil' turns up in their morning papers or jumps out of the mouths of TV pundits?"

Having taken her PhD with Arendt at the New School, then written the best biography of her adviser—*Hannah Arendt: For Love of the World*—Young-Bruehl grieved at how the Week in Review section of the *New York Times* juxtaposed photos of Adolf Eichmann and Saddam Hussein at their respective trials with the caption "From Banality to Audacity." It accompanied a story in which Arendt's phrase "was predictably and reverently invoked—and completely misunderstood." Young-Bruehl didn't blame her subject's ontological transformation into sound-bite fodder on male suppression. But it appeared to add insult to posthumous injury.

A decade before, Arendt had suffered the sting of another refugee European scholar turned professor in the U.S., MIT's Elzbieta Ettinger. Young-Bruehl loyally bristled at Ettinger's highly controversial book, *Hannah Arendt/Martin Heidegger*, about Arendt's lifelong relationship with Heidegger (1889–1976), her lover for four years in the 1920s when he taught Arendt at Marburg. "Ettinger," wrote Young-Bruehl, "projected a naïve and helpless Jewish schoolgirl and a charming but ruthless married Catholic professor playing out a drama of passionate recklessness and betrayal, followed by slavish loyalty on the part of the betrayed mistress." Young-Bruehl labeled that version a "fantasy."

But in the commentary that ensued and continues to this day, it stood not as fantasy but one of many possible interpretations of Arendt's behavior. Arendt's stature as a thinker after Ettinger's book, as well as after the German publication four years later of the extant Heidegger-Arendt correspondence, could not easily be isolated from the choices she made about Heidegger. It's a tale that spoke volumes about the ultimate American philosophical caste of a German-Jewish thinker fiercely loyal to her German mentor, and one that continues to divide those familiar with both Arendt and Heidegger. For Arendt's attitudes toward Heidegger never fit well with her other thoughts and commitments.

As a Jewish schoolgirl in Königsberg, the Prussian hometown she shared with no less a rationalist precursor than Kant, Arendt operated under strict instructions from her mother. If a teacher uttered an anti-Semitic remark, she was to stand up immediately, leave class and go home. Her mother, Arendt explained, "always insisted that I not humble myself."

Some sixty years later, as a world-renowned "political theorist" (she preferred the description in later life to "philosopher"), living in an apartment on Manhattan's Riverside Drive, Arendt remained under the eye of Martha Arendt. Mother peered out from one of three photos on her desk. The others watching were her second husband, Heinrich Blücher, and her first philosophy professor, Martin Heidegger.

It was the Heidegger portrait that would have nettled Arendt's mother. After several decades of courageous scholarship by Hugo Ott, Victor Farias and Emmanuel Faye in Europe, and related work by American scholars Thomas Sheehan, Richard Wolin, Tom Rockmore and others, no sensible observer today doubts that Heidegger, the most celebrated figure in twentieth-century German philosophy, lied his inauthentic head off after the war about his relation to the Nazis. Far from being a reluctant sympathizer for a brief period in the early 1930s, as he sought to convince his denazification committee, Heidegger had been an enthusiastic believer in National Socialism's "inner truth and greatness." He hoped to become Führer of the German university system, to play philosopher-king to Hitler's *Führerstaat*—aiming, in the words of philosopher Otto Pöggeler, *den Führer führen*—"to lead the leader."

The explosion of research on Heidegger's Nazi activities also undermined a second, fallback position for Heidegger's many acolytes: that Heidegger may have enthusiastically backed Nazism, but those politics have little to do with his most profound philosophical beliefs about "Being," "authenticity," "technological culture" and other characteristic concerns. On the contrary, it's increasingly clear why Theodor Adorno described Heidegger's anti-public, anti-democratic, anti-pluralistic philosophy as "fascist down to its most intimate components," why Karl Jaspers denounced it as "unfree, dictatorial and incapable of communication," and why Heidegger himself, in a 1936 conversation with his former student Karl Löwith, agreed "without reservation" that "his partisanship for National Socialism lay in the essence of his philosophy."

All that bad archival news made it more awkward than ever, for admirers of Arendt, that Heidegger remained a dominant influence on her life and thought. Their passionate four-year love affair began when she was an eighteen-year-old first-year student of his at Marburg, and he was a married thirty-five-year-old junior professor with two children. Arendt cared about no intellectual process so much as "understanding," but understanding her lifelong behavior toward Heidegger, which lasted—after a seventeen-year break between 1933 and 1950—until her death in 1975, is not easy.

How could a brilliant, imperious, self-aware Jewish intellectual, who worked for both the German Zionist Organization and the Paris branch of Youth Aliyah, remain so smitten? How could a refugee who fled Germany with her mother in 1933, wrote forcefully about the need for antitotalitarian political action, and took it as a fundamental credo that "when one is attacked as a Jew, one must defend oneself as a Jew," stay powerfully devoted to a mentor who betrayed Jewish colleagues (including *his* august teacher, Edmund Husserl), promoted approval of the Nazi agenda for Germany as rector of Freiburg University in 1933, remained with a viciously anti-Semitic wife for decades, and never repented?

Answers had long been frustrated by the unavailability to scholars of the Heidegger-Arendt correspondence. Young-Bruehl, who first reported the romance in her groundbreaking 1982 biography of Arendt, noted more than once that she could not obtain access. Neither could Hugo Ott, the German economic historian whose 1988 probe, *Martin Heidegger: A Political Life,* supplied the strongest documentation for the fervor and tawdriness of Heidegger's cooperation with National Socialism.

Yet Ettinger, author of a Rosa Luxemburg biography, managed to read the letters, having asked permission in order to help her write an Arendt biography. (Due to copyright restrictions, she quoted Arendt directly while paraphrasing Heidegger.) She came up with startling excerpts, as well as an explosive interpretation. Heidegger, it seemed clear, may never have been able to put his finger squarely on "Being," but he could always make time for Arendt. As for Arendt's all-too-human condition of eternal loyalty, it was simply the banality of romantic obsession. Ettinger's crucial claim, stripped of academic diction, was that Arendt never overcame her schoolgirl crush on Heidegger, even after World War II, when it grew intertwined with her expatriate obeisance to the majesty of German philosophy and Heidegger as its living king. In consequence, Ettinger asserted, Arendt agreed to serve as Heidegger's "goodwill ambassador to the world at large," supervising his translations, refurbishing his reputation, exonerating him before the world philosophical community. She became Heidegger's willing dupe.

That, Ettinger suggested, was reprehensible. Arendt, she wrote, "went to extraordinary pains to minimize and justify Heidegger's contribution and support of the Third Reich," blaming everything on his rabidly anti-Semitic wife, Elfride. Like other apologists for Heidegger, contended Ettinger, Arendt "endeavoured to portray him as a helpless victim of [Elfride's] sinister obsession." But Heidegger, Ettinger insisted, "was never a tool in the hands of his wife or anyone else." Arendt blamed Elfride because "the women were jealous of each other" and because "Arendt never ceased to believe that she was *the* woman in Heidegger's life." Arendt strove to protect "the special role that she believed she played in his life, the spiritual kinship that she believed he shared with no one else." Arendt "was convinced that she alone could understand the depth of his soul . . . that she was his muse and healer."

All that intensity, Ettinger argued, began in old-fashioned romantic loopiness. In an unsent note to Heidegger that she wrote at age fifty-four, Arendt declared that he was the man "to whom I remained faithful and unfaithful, and both in love." In their earlier years, when, according to Ettinger, Arendt "idealized Heidegger beyond measure," Arendt wrote to him, "I would have lost my right to live had I lost my love for you."

Elsewhere, she promised, "I will love you more after death." For those who found it hard to think of Arendt and Heidegger doing more than rubbing foreheads together, Ettinger quoted Arendt's announcement of a more sensuous gesture: "I kiss your brow and your eyes."

After Ursula Ludz's edition of the correspondence was published in German in 1999 (and in English translation in 2004), we got to hear some of Heidegger's reciprocal ardor. From the frenzy of his first note in February 1925 ("Dear Miss Arendt! I must come to see you this evening and speak to your heart"), Heidegger is a Black Forest existentialist in heat. Always furtive, he orders Arendt to "Destroy this note!" after arranging one tryst. Their passion for each other can't be doubted. Even in their final years, Heidegger expressed the wish that he could run his fingers through her hair. His repeatedly expressed longing for Arendt often took Hallmark form ("I would have liked to wander with you for nights on end"). After their postwar reconciliation, it devolved into an attempt to mythologize their early meetings, but unquestionably stayed powerful. In turn, if Arendt's later love seems inseparable from reverence for Heidegger's philosophical majesty, it also suggests a carnal aspiration perhaps peculiar to philosophers: the wish to once again sit at the master's feet, or by his side in a seminar.

Ettinger asserted that Arendt's husband, Heinrich Blücher, "never fully understood, as their postwar letters make clear, the depth of her bond with the philosopher. He erroneously considered her affair with Heidegger as ended." Heidegger, for his part, is shown by Ettinger to have been passionately in love with Arendt in their prewar days, so much so that the world-champion obscurantist wrote her intelligible prose (love letters notable, Ettinger sniffed, for their platitudes). Ettinger described his sixteen letters to her in 1950, after their mature reconciliation, as "warm, elegant, romantic, even seductive." In Ettinger's recap, Heidegger wondered "what was more beautiful: Hannah's letter or her picture." He dreamed, she reported, "about her living nearby." By 1952, Arendt was expressing the conviction that "nothing has changed between us."

At the same time, Ettinger explained, Heidegger continued until the last years of their relationship to treat Arendt as a student rather than a fellow philosopher and author. He couldn't stand her growing world prominence after the publication of *The Origins of Totalitarianism* (1951), a reaction Arendt at first accommodated. She wrote to Blücher in the 1950s, "As you know, I am quite ready to behave toward Heidegger as though I have never written a word and will never write one. And this is the unspoken *conditio sine qua non* of the whole affair."

Ettinger argued that Arendt's correspondence with Karl Jaspers, the other major German philosopher with whom she maintained a lifelong relationship—in their case, of mutual friendship and respect rather than romance—shows that Arendt knew she was functioning as Heidegger's apologist in the West. In a 1951 letter, Arendt admitted to having a "bad conscience." In the latter part of her book, Ettinger detailed how both Jaspers (whose Jewish wife received shabby treatment from Heidegger before the war) and Arendt struggled over how to treat Heidegger in later life.

Jaspers finally urged Arendt to break with their old friend. Arendt refused. After Arendt smoothed rough patches in the 1950s and '60s by a visit to Heidegger in 1967, she visited him and his wife once a year, even trying to help him peddle the manuscript of *Being and Time* when he needed money. Heidegger wrote that he would have preferred for her to visit him *twice* a year. Arendt died in December 1975, four months after her last visit to him. Heidegger died five months later.

Sizing up the drama, Ettinger expressed contempt for Heidegger and was dismissive of both Arendt and Jaspers. Heidegger, she commented, "reinforced the 'slavish' streak" in Arendt. Arendt and Jaspers "were seriously involved in questions of ethics and morality, but their theories failed them when it came to Martin Heidegger." After Arendt's 1950 meeting with Heidegger, Ettinger asserted, his former student-lover simply "did what she could to whitewash his Nazi past."

Ettinger's version both reflected and clashed with the standard Arendt-Heidegger story, the one sketched by Young-Bruehl in her biography. According to that book, Arendt and Heidegger conducted a student-teacher affair, an "illicit and impossible love," with Arendt continuing to rush to him whenever he summoned her even after she left Marburg for Heidelberg (and Jaspers) to do her dissertation on St. Augustine. After Arendt fled Germany for Paris in 1933, the seventeen-year break ensued.

Young-Bruehl pointed out that in a 1946 *Partisan Review* article, Arendt described Heidegger as a philosopher of "absolute egoism," compared him unfavorably to Jaspers and faulted Heidegger so much for his betrayal of Husserl that she labeled him "a potential murderer" of his mentor. In 1950, however, when she and Heidegger had their first postwar meeting (Ettinger noted that Elfride was not present), Heidegger convinced Arendt that claims about his enthusiastic Nazism were slander. Their friendship resumed, and Arendt thereafter undertook her role in promoting Heidegger's work. As Richard Wolin characterized matters, Arendt saw Heidegger's Nazism as more "a character flaw" than a manifestation of inner evil. In the *Partisan Review* article, she ascribed his "complete irresponsibility . . . partly to the delusion of genius, partly to desperation."

In a 1969 address, "Martin Heidegger at 80," Arendt also blamed Heidegger for thinking, like Plato and too many philosophers, that philosophy could take place in a separate realm from politics, leading to "what the French call a *deformation professionelle.*" On the standard view, their relationship continued (without ardor) despite Arendt's sharp criticism of Heidegger's activities, her condescension toward his judgment, even her contempt for his character. (Young-Bruehl noted way back, as did Ettinger, that Arendt once described Heidegger as a man who "lies notoriously always and everywhere, and whenever he can.")

The achievement of Ettinger's book lay in its documentation of Arendt's emotional bond with Heidegger. Its weakness rested in its deemphasis of all the factors in Arendt's loyalty more intellectually complicated than romantic bondage, and in its condescension toward Arendt herself, a woman who struck no one who knew her as shy, deferential, lovesick or easily manipulable. Something too automatic clung to Ettinger's diagnosis, as if the Heidegger-Arendt affair began as run-of-the-mill sexual harassment (of the "consensual" type), with Arendt playing out the part of damaged abusee. It didn't entirely compute.

To be sure, Heidegger, whatever his sins, represented a kind of cultural home to Arendt, perhaps even more strongly after she became an American and a New Yorker. "If I can be said to have come from anywhere," she wrote in a 1964 letter to the great Jewish scholar Gershom Scholem, who had rebuked her for her allegedly unsympathetic attitude toward the Jewish people in *Eichmann in Jerusalem* (1963), "it is from the tradition of German philosophy." To walk out on Heidegger, as her mother once urged she do at the voicing of anti-Semitic remarks, would have been to leave her own intellectual temple. It's no surprise she kept his photo nearby.

Moreover, Heidegger's own intense, virtually religious sense of philosophical mission and seriousness, the deeply subjective, self-reflective demands of *"passionate* thinking" she saw him place on himself, plainly struck a chord in Arendt and influenced her own view of what marked philosophical thinking. She, too, always placed philosophy on a lofty plane, wove stark binary distinctions throughout her work (the *vita activa* and the *vita contemplativa,* the public and the private, the political and the social), and didn't like, in principle, to mix matters of the flesh and thought. For Arendt, Ettinger acknowledged, "there was no place in the life of the spirit for matters of the flesh."

It's also possible to accept Ettinger's innuendo throughout the book that Arendt vigorously exploited her American status as agent for high European philosophical culture, the imprimatur she got from her pedigree as a personal associate of Heidegger and Jaspers. In his memoir *The Truants,* William Barrett, the celebrant of 1950s existentialism (*Irrational Man*) who translated Arendt's first *Partisan Review* article, recalled that "she was always conscious of coming from elsewhere—of speaking for something older and deeper that she understood as European culture, something she guarded at her center." Her pride in the status of German Jews before the Nazis, the "almost complete" assimilation of Jewish and non-Jewish German intellectuals at the time, particularly struck him: "She harbored a nostalgia for that condition and that period." Some scholars thought Arendt made "quiet appropriations" from Heidegger in her work. Fair or not, Arendt surely profited, and legitimately, from prestige by association.

But where Ettinger's interpretation fell most short was in the area she also mined most: the purely human. Despite manifold evidence that Arendt viewed Heidegger as a severely flawed man, even a fool when it came to politics, Ettinger insisted that Heidegger was simply evil, calculating and unscrupulous, a dangerous political climber, and she therefore could not excuse Arendt's charity toward him. The years since Ettinger's book appeared have seen more evidence come to light to support her view than Arendt's. While the American and British political theorists Mark Lilla and Alan Ryan savaged Ettinger's book, the former endorsing the latter's judgment that the book was "a disgrace," the 1999 publication in German of Ludz's edition of the Arendt-Heidegger letters supported, in large part, Ettinger's slant.

Moreover, the 2005 French publication of Emmanuel Faye's controversial *Heidegger, l'introduction du nazisme dans le philosophie,* which drew on previous unpublished 1930s writings of Heidegger to argue that he overtly sought to shepherd Nazi ideas and vocabulary into his philosophical work, made Ettinger's unsentimental take on Heidegger all the stronger.

Still, Ettinger's stance showed no deference to Arendt's arguably privileged perspective—that she, an immensely savvy, down-to-earth, cosmopolitan judge of people, knew Heidegger the man for decades, whereas Ettinger knew him only as a distant cultural titan. Arendt had been lucky to escape to the United States from France in 1941 and become an American citizen in 1950. Ettinger, some two decades younger, was a Warsaw native who survived the Holocaust, worked with the Polish resistance and endured interrogations and blacklisting under Communist Polish rule until her own escape to the West in the 1960s. Wasn't it also possible that Arendt's gentler handling of Heidegger reflected her ability, as an émigré long ensconced among the victorious Americans, to forgive the unsavory side of her first great love?

The view of Heidegger as weak and foolish—regarding his wife, regarding Realpolitik, regarding how others saw him—surfaces repeatedly throughout Arendt's writings. Ettinger herself quotes Jaspers's telling remark to Arendt on her first visit with him after the war in 1949: "Poor Heidegger. Here we are sitting, the two best friends he has, and we see right through him."

It's plain from evidence with which Ettinger was familiar that Arendt thought of Heidegger as a dupe when it came to the Nazis: a judgment she probably would have kept to even if she'd seen the new evidence of his activities that emerged in the last thirty-five years. We know from her last work, *The Life of the Mind,* that she considered Heidegger exceedingly unworldly. In her 1953 notebook entry later published as "Heidegger the Fox," she wrote directly about Heidegger as "so lacking in slyness" that he got caught in one trap after another.

That entry makes it clear that it was also Heidegger, among others, she was thinking of in her famous 1964 interview on German TV, when asked about her first postwar visit to Germany. Speaking of prewar intellectual friends who had proved disloyal, she said, "They were not all murderers. There were people who fell into their own trap, as I would say today. Nor did they desire what came later. Thus it seemed to me that there should be a basis of communication precisely in the abyss of Auschwitz. And that was true in many personal relations. . . . Somehow things were set straight again with a lot of people."

Given that she famously detested self-protecting intellectuals as a class by the time she fled Germany for Paris, Arendt, if she was to forgive Heidegger after the war, would have had to see him as different from the street-smart intellectual careerists she loathed. It is certainly possible, as Ettinger believed, that love blinded Arendt to decency when it came to Heidegger. There's no question, in the light of Emmanuel Faye's scholarship, that Ettinger's view of Heidegger's involvement with Nazism got things more right than Arendt's.

But in light of everything we know about Arendt and her work—her "genius for friendship," her concrete acts of kindness over the years, her refugee shrewdness about people's characters, her no-nonsense recognition of man's weakness before temptation, her belief that one must act politically and communicate with others to solve social problems—it's far more likely that decency, and a unique understanding of Heidegger's moral flaws, made it possible for her to continue to love a part of him while regretting the rest. Ettinger's book implied that, knowing what we know now, we should respect Arendt less. It is just as possible to come away from the Heidegger-Arendt *pas de deux* respecting Arendt more.

One could therefore sympathize with Young-Bruehl's effort, in *Why Arendt Matters*, to promote Arendt's relevance today. She did so by persuasively suggesting that Arendt's ideas inform such modern political phenomena as Poland's Solidarity movement and South Africa's Truth and Reconciliation Commission, and anticipated current issues of globalization. She also highlighted that relevance by speculating on what her mentor would have thought about events since her death. Dissecting *The Origins of Totalitarianism* (1951), a veritable "field manual" for identifying an enemy, Young-Bruehl suggested that Arendt would have "taken the measure of Slobodan Milosevic's government from his talk about 'Greater Serbia,' a phrase he obviously and purposefully modeled on Hitler's 'Greater Germany,'" and, after 9/11, "gone straight to her writing table to protest that the World Trade Center was not Pearl Harbor and that 'war on terror' was a meaningless phrase." At the same time, the author acknowledged, "Neither I, her biographer, nor anyone else should presume to know what Hannah Arendt would have thought about any event, trend, idea, person, or group that she did not look upon with her own fiercely observant eyes and the eyes of her uniquely and inimitably brilliant mind."

The last statement evinced Young-Bruehl's reverential respect for her teacher, but who could object to that? Some powerful attachment, after all, must fuel projects in which one thinker exalts another. Young-Bruehl repeatedly and successfully unpacked Arendt's views on action, power, forgiveness, judgment, radical evil, revolution and the human condition itself. Arendt's phrasemaking and popularization of notions such as "totalitarianism" developed, Young-Bruehl explained, because she "wanted thoughts and words adequate to the new world and able to dissolve clichés, reject thoughtlessly received ideas, break down hackneyed analyses, expose lies and bureaucratic double talk, help people withdraw from their addiction to propagandistic images."

If Arendt's ambition and life story helped frame the peculiar challenges that an old-world philosopher faced in winning the attention and respect of Americans, the ambition of a far more journalistic American figure—fifteen years Arendt's junior—took her right to the cusp of functioning as philosopher to a great segment of readerly American women.

Was feminist icon Betty Friedan (1921–2006) mainly a midwife of the ideas of European feminists such as Simone de Beauvoir, a notion that took on steam when some Beauvoir scholars accused her of conceptual plagiarism? The image amounted to reductionism for anyone who had actually read Friedan, or talked with her over the years.

Answering the phone one special day, Friedan sounded every bit as brusque as her reputation.

"Whaddya want?" snarled the curmudgeonly activist and author whose central work, *The Feminine Mystique* (1963), launched the American women's movement in the 1960s with its picture of domestic femininity as a "comfortable concentration camp."

Oh, just wanted to wish you a happy eightieth birthday, her caller said, and talk a bit about the milestone.

"Well, it's happening," she said, warming up a mite.

"Actually," said Friedan, just returned from a conference with European women leaders in Bellagio, Italy, "having this birthday, I was thinking, 'What have I done with my life?' And the answer came pretty easily: I have three wonderful kids, nine grandchildren, I've written six books, and I started a wonderful revolution."

Yes, Friedan made clear, she felt pretty good. As she did about the "movement" she spearheaded. "It's awesome. Awesome. A-W-E-S-O-M-E," announced the cofounder of the National Organization for Women, spelling out the word. "Where was I? Oh, the International Conference in Beijing, and I see some women in chadors marching. I couldn't tell from their signs what they were marching for. It was probably something I wouldn't agree with at all. But I was so happy to see them marching. They'll never be the same again once they learn to march for what they want. You know, I helped make that happen."

Almost half a century after the publication of *The Feminine Mystique*, Friedan's influence on modern feminist consciousness remains powerful because of her book's widely recognized spurring of what historians call the "second wave" of American feminism, and her feisty, indefatigable activism in the decades that followed. "She was a towering figure," observed Judith Hennessee, author of *Betty Friedan: Her Life,* "honored and feared, loved and reviled, who had a reputation for outrageous behavior." Daniel Horowitz, an intellectual historian at Smith College and author of *Betty Friedan and the Making of* The Feminine Mystique: *The American Left, the Cold War, and Modern Feminism,* agreed: "As much as any book written in the middle of the 20th century, *The Feminine Mystique* helped transform the course of America's political and social history."

Much of Friedan's life story became familiar to generations that read *The Feminine Mystique,* since the book arose out of her own experience. Born in Peoria, Illinois, Betty Goldstein attended Smith College and studied psychology for a year at the University of California, Berkeley, before dropping out in 1943 to become a union journalist—she spent years writing for the *Federated Press* and the *UE News,* the newsletter of the United Electrical, Radio, and Machine Workers. It was a part of her life that Friedan spent much of her later career playing down, an action Horowitz spotlighted in arguing for her powerful roots in an older leftist tradition.

She lost one of her jobs to a returning GI as employers fired women to make room for World War II veterans. After marrying Carl Friedan in 1947, she turned to freelance writing for women's magazines—a job compatible with raising a family—and turned out articles such as "I Was Afraid to Have a Baby."

"Honestly," Friedan said at eighty, reflecting on women's magazines, "I don't think they've changed that much. I looked at them a while back and I was quite amazed at what I saw. Even though the great majority of American women are now working outside the home and there's been more and more education and sophistication, women's magazines seem to me directed at the lowest common denominator."

In 1957, Friedan surveyed her Smith College classmates and found many of them deeply troubled about their lives as housewives, struggling to express what she later famously described as "a problem that has no name." Friedan sympathized, but found that editors of women's magazines weren't interested in sharp social criticism of feminine norms. So *The Feminine Mystique* began to jell. Asked about her contributions to feminism, Friedan said the book "remains the most important thing." Its advocacy of both motherhood and work outside the home made it provocative but acceptable to men and women, and its bestseller status shot Friedan to national prominence, bolstered further by her cofounding NOW in 1966.

But from the late 1960s to the publication of her next book, *The Second Stage* (1981), Friedan also grew controversial. Some younger feminists, such as Shulamith Firestone, took far more critical stands toward patriarchal American society, deriding Friedan as a moderate liberal too invested in gradualist reform, too timid about shaking up male-dominated social structures, too focused on the concerns of white middle-class women. It didn't help when Friedan, never a shrinking violet in such disputes, denounced lesbians within NOW as a "lavender menace" and declared in *The Second Stage* that a "sexual war against men" was "self-defeating," that motherhood and heterosexuality remained "the life-serving core of feminine identity."

Looking back, Friedan declined to reopen the battles: "They made their contribution, but it didn't undo what I did. . . . By now, you know, I'm appreciated for what I am. There are these clichés or stereotypes about man-hating feminists. Well, I'm obviously not that." In any case, she asked, "Why would you think that all women leaders, or all feminists, would agree? You don't expect all men to agree about everything. It was an enormous movement, and there were lots of different voices."

Friedan did concede that her own bristly personality helped to fan flames: "I am hot-tempered, there's no doubt about that. I'm no angel. I'm passionate, but that's good. I was able to be fairly effective on behalf of a cause that I thought important." In her biography, Hennessee described Friedan as "a woman of profound contradictions" with "a first-class mind and a second-class temperament." She also offered a further overarching assessment: "She was a woman who yearned for a happy marriage and family life, yet urged others to fulfill themselves outside the family. A conventional woman who shook male-female relationships to the core. A reformer who started a revolution. A revolutionary who wanted to be part of the Establishment. An elitist who fought for working women; a class snob who fought for equality; a humanitarian who treated individuals, particularly women, badly. She was a feminist who preferred men, became girlish and flirtatious in their company, and deferred to them—and did not even like most women."

Friedan, asked about Hennessee's book, said she'd never read it. But she made clear she disagreed with many of the ways she'd been situated in feminist history. (Her memoir, *Life So Far,* offered her own perspective.) One example she mentioned was the tendency of younger feminists to see her as having adapted the perspective of Beauvoir, in her classic, *The Second Sex,* to American women.

"That was not an influence on me," Friedan insisted, adding that the perspectives on women in her book that paralleled Beauvoir's observations were natural, given women's roles in both societies, rather than derivative. "I was originally going to be a psychologist. I had very good training in psychology," she said. The notion that *The Second Sex* significantly influenced her, Friedan reiterated, just "isn't true. When I read *The Second Sex,* I was kind of appalled. . . . My feminism—it's all on the record—arose out of my own experience."

At eighty, Friedan reported, she was "in great shape." She enjoyed being frequently stopped in the street by "women of all ages who say, 'You changed my life.'" Asked what the biggest misconception was when people first met her, she replied, "They're always surprised that I'm not as much of a battle-ax as they expect." She divided her time between "a beautiful apartment near the Washington Hilton" in D.C. and her longtime house in Sag Harbor, New York, where she summered. At the time of her memoir's publication she'd had quite a public battle with her ex-husband Carl (they divorced in 1969) over who might have hit whom during their marriage. But "we're good friends now," she said. "We were married twenty-odd years, had three terrific kids, lots of good times and adventures and houses. . . . He's the father of my kids—he's a good guy."

Did she read any books by younger feminist thinkers? "You know," she replied with a merry cackle, "enough is enough already. It's slightly boring." Was she working on another book herself? "I don't want to do something serious," Friedan confided. "I'm sick of serious writing. I'm thinking of writing a detective story. So I've been looking for a course, a seminar, a workshop, to jump-start me in how to write a mystery story. . . . I always have to have some project. I thought, Oh well, I've got to do something completely new, but I'm not exactly going to take up ceramics."

Her caller suggested that making the sleuth a man would be a kind of new step. The rebuke came quick. "No, no, no!" she shot back. "Obviously, I'm going to have a woman detective."

Friedan's "genre restlessness" late in life, the need to get away from philosophy "by treatise," was an American philosophical bent in both men and women. But it surfaced more powerfully in women thinkers, perhaps because their entreé to the professionalized world of philosophical-treatise writing remained largely obstructed anyway.

Probably no American woman thinker of the twentieth century so exemplified the inclination as Susan Sontag. Many reasonably well-educated professionals, if asked by a reporter during the height of her career to give the name of an American woman philosopher, might have cited her. It would have been an appropriate answer. No woman thinker more represented the peculiar nature of the American activity, in the liberating, expansive form that Rorty had articulated, than Sontag, who had known Rorty at the University of Chicago. For like a much artsier, terribly more famous and unquestionably more diva-like Rorty, she too believed that philosophy, persuasion, the reaching of that intersubjective agreement called truth, was often accomplished best by storytelling, by narrative. Ironically, the story of her own life came to look inextricable from the unfolding of philosophy in American life. Everything about her—her intellectual dazzle, her pop-cultural flair, her confidence—proved as outsize as the country she called home. She demonstrated that once on a rainy Friday afternoon in Manhattan.

In a nearly empty screening room at New York's Public Theater, Sontag hunched down, waiting for the beginning of Nagisa Oshima's *Hakuchu no Torima* ("Violence at Noon"). Only a handful of other cineastes shared the countdown to that middle work by Japan's Godard. According to the de rigueur plot summary passed out at the entrance, it was the story of "a village schoolteacher who tries to organize a collective farm," but fails when "a flood wipes out the commune." After an idealistic young woman named Shino survives an attempt to hang herself, a passing farmhand rapes her. The rapist later marries the schoolteacher.

Then the schoolteacher and Shino try to commit suicide.

Shino screws it up again.

"Looks grim," Sontag remarked to her companion for the afternoon.

Within moments, the film began, but it didn't follow the plot summary. Sontag's pique built as the film scooted off in its own direction. This may have been Japanese New Wave, but a text was a text. Finally, after ten minutes, Sontag stood up and announced, to no one in particular, "This is not the first reel!"

A frustrated look on her face, she cut across the empty aisle to the door, signaling and then dispatching an assistant to fetch the theater's film program coordinator. A few minutes later, he entered and tried to put Sontag at ease.

"Susan," he whispered, in a tone of mingled respect and fear, "Oshima has seen this print. This is *definitely* the first reel." As it turned out, an SOS had been rushed to a cineaste in Ohio to determine exactly that. Eventually, the movie circled round to that deceptive text. Asked later whether, given his terminally au courant audiences, he'd ever seen anyone question the order of reels in a previously unseen film, the coordinator paused—his mood, one surmised again, a mixture of respect and fear—and replied, "Frankly, no. That has never happened before."

No one ever accused Sontag of timidity. Not when she got her legendary fast start in school by starting third grade at age six (because she could already read and write). Not when, at age seventeen, and just a junior at the University of Chicago, she married twenty-eight-year-old instructor and future sociologist Philip Rieff ten days after they met. And certainly not when she published her notorious essay, "Notes on Camp," an apotheosis (in Sontag's phrase) of the "sensibility of failed seriousness," and the media made the thirty-one-year-old freelance writer a star—the "Natalie Wood of the U.S. avant-garde," in one memorable if ephemeral formulation.

"I don't feel like a living legend to myself," she said facetiously on one occasion in her home at the time—a duplex apartment near Manhattan's Holland Tunnel—"but what can I do?"

Yet for nearly half a century, Susan Sontag exemplified the intellectual as clip file, a career lived in headlines, a name frequently nestled between Socrates and Sophocles in quality indexes everywhere. Journalists deferred to her as a philosopher and philosophers sometimes disparaged her as a journalist. An aspiring Nietzsche, she commanded a niche.

By mid-career, in the late 1980s, she had directed four movies, published five collections of essays, one volume of stories and two novels, fought cancer to a standstill (though it would return and return), won a variety of fellowships and prizes, become president of the PEN American Center, and remained a good mother to her son, the writer David Rieff.

In 1975, while writing her prizewinning book *On Photography* (1977), she confronted the cancer that would lead to five operations, a mastectomy, chemotherapy and *Illness as Metaphor* (1978). The latter book assailed the cultural tradition of linking cancer and tuberculosis to stereotypes of personal character, which Sontag blamed for creating passivity in patients. Then came *AIDS and Its Metaphors.*

Originally intended as a four-or-five-page appendix to *Illness as Metaphor*, it took off in its author's hands. The book extended the argument of the earlier volume that diseases are physical, not spiritual or cultural, and should be treated that way. Sontag attacked the military, plague and developmental metaphors we attached to AIDS, and the attempt of the right to use it as a club to beat down the values of the 1960s and announce the apocalypse. *Newsday* credited the book with "precision, clarity" and "wide-ranging learning," but the *New York Times Book Review* rejected its thesis, concluding that "the disease itself, and not the way we talk about it, is the true source of its horror." Randy Shilts (*And the Band Played On*), then regarded as the leading journalistic expert on AIDS, welcomed the book in the *San Francisco Chronicle*, but also called it "ultimately unsatisfying," writing that Sontag wasn't "always accurate" in describing the AIDS myths she discussed and that she engaged in "cursory" analysis.

"I'm disappointed that the book is getting a one-dimensional reading," she told a San Francisco crowd when quizzed on the reviews. To *Newsday*, she complained, "I don't know why the early reviews are all by science writers. It's not really about AIDS. It's about what we think about AIDS."

"I know about AIDS humanely," she acknowledged to *USA Today*. "But when I sit down, I can't be Randy Shilts. I'm a literary writer. I wrote about what I can." Once again, Sontag was controversial, well attended to, and duking it out in public. Hers was an impressive track record, and, in many ways, an unlikely one.

Born in New York City on January 16, 1933, and raised mostly in Tucson and Los Angeles, Sontag stood for the proposition—among countless others in American life—that Valley girls turn out in the strangest ways. Her father, a businessman named Jack Rosenblatt, and her mother, Mildred Jacobsen, an occasional schoolteacher, were old hands working in the Tianjin fur trade when Sontag was conceived: "Gatsby and Daisy inside the British concession," as Sontag once put it.

Medically cautious, her mother decided to give birth in New York, where Susan remained, raised in part by relatives. (Her first public school lie, she once confided, was claiming to have been born in China.) When she was five and living with her grandparents, her father died of tuberculosis in China, at the age of thirty-three. Her mother subsequently married Nathan Sontag, a traveling salesman who at one time sold clocks with advertising slogans on them. The Sontags were suburban, middle-class, assimilated Jews from a family that had been here "one hundred years." Susan's younger sister, Judith, later became the manager of a department store in Hawaii.

As a teenager in then-rural Canoga Park (outside Los Angeles), where her family moved when she turned thirteen, Sontag read European fiction, the British socialists Sidney and Beatrice Webb, and the cutting-edge newspaper *PM*. Her parents regarded her, she once recalled, "as something of an oddity." She attended Eisenstein films at

Susan Sontag (1933–2004) wished late in life to be recognized as a novelist rather than a cultural critic or philosopher, but she continued to publish incisive essays and nonfiction books on timely cultural ideas.

the American-Soviet Friendship Society, bought copies of the *Partisan Review* at Hollywood and Vine. At age fourteen, she boldly set off to visit Thomas Mann at his California home. She graduated from North Hollywood High School at fifteen, briefly attended Berkeley, then transferred to the University of Chicago.

She received her BA from the University of Chicago in 1951, at age eighteen, and gave birth at nineteen to David. Later she did graduate work in philosophy at Harvard and Oxford, spent part of a year at the Sorbonne, and taught during the 1950s and early '60s: a year of English at the University of Connecticut, two years at Harvard in philosophy and the humanities, a year each in philosophy at Sarah Lawrence and CCNY, four years at Columbia as an instructor in the religion department. During her marriage to Rieff, they collaborated on what became his first book, *Freud: The Mind of the Moralist* (1959). The marriage lasted nine years, ending in divorce in 1959. Sontag received custody of David. That same year, she also worked briefly as an editor at *Commentary*.

Exactly how she became a star is, like Sartre's ascension as the "pope of existentialism" in 1947, a part of intellectual PR history. Sontag, like Sartre, became a mass-cultural figure in America largely due to *Time* magazine. In its December 11, 1964, issue, it ballyhooed her radical *Partisan Review* essay, "Notes on 'Camp.'" As Nora Ephron later put it, *Time* "wrote about camp and Miss Sontag as if the two were symbiotic." Sontag ascended as the "Queen of Camp." *Vogue* decided that "People Are Talking About . . . Susan Sontag." Sontag (naively, she said later) cooperated, and so there she was, staring out from the pages of *Mademoiselle* one month, then hanging on the arm of Warren Beatty in Earl Wilson's gossip column another. The dark good looks and rarefied suggestions of sensuality helped.

"She burst from nowhere amid something like a ticker-tape parade," wrote Eliot Fremont-Smith in the *New York Times*. His colleague Herbert Mitgang called her a "literary pin-up." Reviewers picked up the tempo, sometimes embarrassingly. "The lady swings," raved Benjamin DeMott, reviewing *Against Interpretation* in the *Times*. "She digs the Supremes. She catches the major Happenings and the best of the kinky flicks."

By her mid-fifties, Sontag no longer fit the image of Cher with a brain transplant from Dorothy Parker, but she looked healthy enough to pass, happily, as a mere outside expert on a disease she had temporarily beaten. Warm, funny, down-to-earth, imperious, lightning quick, maternal, supercilious—she remained a cultural icon. In a popular movie of the decade, *Bull Durham*, Kevin Costner's character suddenly demonstrated his hidden wattage by announcing to Susan Sarandon's teacher-groupie character that Sontag's novels "are self-indulgent, overrated crap." A few years before, in *The Decline of the American Empire*, a Canadian movie about academics, a character declared that the woman he most wanted to sleep with was Susan Sontag. (Sontag, who saw the movie, told *Time*, "It was like somebody threw a spitball at me in the theater.")

"I can't take it altogether seriously," she sighed about the *Bull Durham* reference, "because I know where these things come from. They come from all-night script conferences of people who've had too much coke. The main thing is, I can only speak for myself. I don't think it's possible for me to take in too much of what is said or written about me. I know it isn't all negative. Some of it's very flattering. But what I'm aiming at is much more ambitious."

"I want to be a really good writer," she said. "That's a full-time job. And whatever is said about me now, if I live long enough, won't be said about me in five years. So all I have to do is live a little longer, and do some more work, and the image will shift."

Still, she stood at mid-career as a staple of cultural history, a name to which familiar phrases attached. And familiar phrases naturally irritated. To some, she was the Happy Highbrow in an era that gave America the Happy Hooker, the person who told an interviewer in 1967 that she'd read a book a day for fifteen years. To others, because of the camp essay (with its attention to mass entertainment figures, then largely off-limits to intellectual analysis), she was still a pop-cultural slummer—an image that clashed sharply with her midlife high seriousness.

"I'm often viewed as someone who says that popular culture is the same as high culture," she acknowledged. "Well, there is no one in the world, Allan Bloom included, who is more of a defender of high culture than I am." She thought "one probably has to be quite conservative culturally now. Just try and hang on to the best things. . . . Because, simply, the enterprise of defending seriousness is in question."

"Of course," she added, "I can lighten up like anyone else. . . . But if I make one or two jolly references in passing to something in popular culture, I'm pilloried by a lot of jealous academics and uncomprehending opinion makers. . . . I don't feel any compulsion to offer some well-balanced image. I don't feel any compulsion to offer an image at all."

Nonetheless, she projected several. Just as Sartre and Beauvoir defined, for a generation of intellectuals, love in the age of existentialism, Sontag incarnated for many the last temptation for the academicized egghead and writer—life as a free cerebral spirit, unburdened by deans, term papers and committee meetings. To many, she was the last bohemian public intellectual. In mid-career, before the cell-phone age exploded, she still operated without an answering machine, word processor, business card or car. Kidded about it, she retorted, "Oh, c'mon. I'm just trying to keep things simple." She owned no TV, determined to concentrate on reading. "It's my TV," she once quipped. She regularly declined to teach.

To Russell Jacoby, whose book *The Last Intellectuals* scorned the academization of intellectuals, Sontag represented "a dying species" in her refusal, as she put it, to "seek institutional cover." Steve Wasserman, a longtime friend and editor, said Sontag believed it was more important "for the life of the mind" to go to a rock club one night, "to the Met the next night, to hang out someplace else the following night, than to go to faculty meetings."

"Some pioneers invent niches," commented Todd Gitlin, author of *The Sixties* and many other books, "and in a sense, she has. After the fact, you look at her and say, 'It's a great success.' I honor her for having worked out a way of living in the open without shelter. Unemployment is a hard job to find. I tried to do it and couldn't."

Sontag pulled it off, but not easily. When she received her first cancer diagnosis, she had no medical insurance—editor Robert Silvers of the *New York Review of Books* raised money from friends. She made only modest royalties from her books. At one point, she was forced out of her two-story apartment in a Gramercy Park brownstone when the rent shot up. Her jet-black hair turned white and she dyed it, leaving a dramatic wing, like a blank sheet of paper shooting off her temple. Somehow, she pushed on, postponing many chores until Fridays to preserve the other days for writing. When Sontag wasn't working, her New York life seemed a festive dance of reasonably priced stimuli: screenings, reading, consultations with her publisher, breakfasts with David and visiting culturati. She also adored traveling, joking that "I'm sufficiently primitive to not believe in the reality of any place that I haven't been in."

Sontag often got melted down by the reference book industry, particularly the quotation books. Her most famous lines, such as "Interpretation is the revenge of the intellect upon art," and her later-repudiated "The white race is the cancer of history," pursued her like implacable ex-lovers, determined to shame her in the present. Sontag recognized that some critics cited her gift for aphorisms, then pounced, dismissing her as a sloganeer: "It's always the same three [aphorisms], and they're always twenty-five years old. . . . I think it's grotesque to be saddled forever with two or three high-spirited formulations when I was at the beginning of my writing life."

She said she rewrote her essays "five, ten, fifteen times," sometimes devoting a year to one. "It's true I have a weakness for aphorism. It's something that just happens—they come out of my mouth like birds. But they function in context. . . . It's just the way I think. My idea is to turn soup into bouillon cubes. . . . I'm not trying to do stunts of any kind. I'm not exhibitionistic as a writer."

Undoubtedly, the phrasemaking helped Sontag endure at the top of the culture charts, though a career as long and electrified as hers quickly outran simple explanation. One of the cheekiest ponderings of Sontag's ascent came in *Making It,* the memoir by former *Commentary* editor Norman Podhoretz. Podhoretz argued that American culture carved out the position of "dark lady of American letters" for Mary McCarthy in the 1930s. The job required a "clever, learned, good-looking" woman, "capable of writing family type criticism as well as fiction with a strong sense of naughtiness." With McCarthy promoted by the mid-1960s to "Grande Dame," Podhoretz claimed, critics took Sontag's early writings as an "implicit" application for the job, and hired her.

She maintained her post, so reactions swirled around her. If not quite, as Auden said of Freud, a "whole climate of opinion," she proved to be more than a passing storm. John Updike offhandedly described her as "our glamorous camp follower of the French avant garde." Irving Howe noted how she pronounced America to be a "doomed country" with "the most brutal system of slavery in modern times." He cited her as an example of fuzzy thinking in the late 1960s. Alexander Cockburn, irked by her move toward the political center, wrote that Sontag "tries sometimes to contrive" a "sense of martyrdom amid her evident prosperity."

As for the scholars who wrote on specific topics treated by Sontag, W. J. T. Mitchell backhandedly credited her book *On Photography* with giving "eloquent expression" to a view he rejected: "that images have a power in our world undreamed of by the ancient idolators." Harvard's Stanley Cavell similarly dismissed her.

American academic philosophers largely ignored Sontag's work. The *Philosopher's Index* showed not a single treatment of her work in the decade following 1966—the year *Against Interpretation* appeared. Many major thinkers—Rorty, Quine, Davidson—didn't comment on her thought. Danto, an exception, argued that interpretation is central to understanding a work of art, and labeled Sontag's position "anti-intellectual." Yet the importance of Sontag's early essays for 1960s culture and her prime place in the left/right politics of the era remain undisputed.

Her political symbolism dated back to 1960, when she visited Cuba for three months and later characterized Fidel Castro and Che Guevara as "heroes and cherished models." In May 1968, like other American intellectuals before her, she accepted an invitation to North Vietnam. Although Sontag returned with a complicated view, she wrote that North Vietnam enjoyed a "genuine substantive democracy, much of the time." The trip alone, like so many of her public gestures, made a splash.

Even later, intellectual right-wingers often thought of her as their Jane Fonda. But for savvier politicos, Sontag's image took a sharp turn after February 1982, when she addressed a meeting at New York City's Town Hall called to express support for Polish Solidarity on the left. Sontag (she later admitted) purposely provoked the audience by stating that "the principal lesson" to be learned from Poland was "the utter villainy of the communist system." Alluding to the left's intellectual insularity, she asked, "Can it be that our enemies were right?" Communism, she concluded, "is fascism—successful fascism, if you will . . . fascism with a human face."

Many audience members booed, and the press headlined her remarks, as unexpected as a Republican conversion by the Rev. Jesse Jackson. Historian and columnist Garry Wills attacked her thinking as simplistic. Editor Philip Pochoda, in print, suggested Sontag risked becoming "Norman Podhoretz with a human face."

The chief expression of her politics later came in her role as president of the PEN American Center, where she practiced what she called "the most difficult of the ethical arts"—cultural diplomacy amid the "unclassifiable, unruly, impossible organization of writers" that constituted PEN. In September 1988, at the group's fifty-second International Congress in Seoul, she delivered a trenchant address that could stand as her manifesto.

Decrying "conformist tendencies" among writers, the "desire to be on good terms with power," she offered instead the duty "to speak truth to power." Sontag ran through the clichés of authoritarianism—that "freedom is a luxury" in dangerous times, that "irresponsible activism" must yield to "loyal opposition"—and rejected them as "moral blackmail." When order and freedom conflict, she declared, or a short-term practical goal clashes with long-term principle, "[t]here will always be more than enough people to defend the cause of Realpolitik," she said. Sontag urged every writer to resist being a "grateful houseguest," "docile" government supporter or even "dissident."

"It is already a great deal," she concluded, "for writers to be 'unofficial.'"

Watching Sontag do her duty in Korea, at that time still an authoritarian state, one saw the blend of high intellect and common touch emerge in scores of moments. After French poet René Tavernier jabbed her in his own speech, she gushed, nonetheless, at how his "French is so gorgeous." When Korean translators obviously truncated her remarks, she deadpanned, "Korean seems to be briefer than English." At sessions during the week, Sontag was always the one who noticed and spoke up when someone failed to speak into the mike. She skipped the highly regimented trip to Olympic Stadium ("There's never any evening event that can't be avoided"), preferring a night of barhopping. At the National Museum, sweeping past the celadon pottery and Buddhas, she found herself reminded of Hollywood's Sabu, climbing up a statue to steal the jewels. Then she advanced to the notion that a museum is a "desacralizing location."

Bounding through Insadong, Seoul's antiques district, Sontag the bibliophile came alive. Passing a building with a British architectural facade, she commented, "It's like Foyles" (the enormous London bookstore). Heading back, she bragged of a "God-given talent" for dealing with cabs, proud of having already whittled down several fares to the hotel to only 8,000 won. In a purple punk jacket, black pants and white sneakers, strewing quips right and left, she was anything but the intimidating figure who once prompted a magazine writer to begin his profile of her with "Getting to meet her is a bit like trying to meet Joan of Arc on her day off."

Sontag could ask a companion, "Have you ever been to Asia?," get her answer, ask follow-up questions, get more answers, then ask the same person exactly the same questions the next day. Told gingerly that she was going over plowed territory, she said, "Oh, I'm sorry. I'm really sorry. Sensory overload." Reaching Seoul's sprawling central plaza by the Lotte Hotel, she threw up her arms and crowed to her son, David, and company, "This is it! You're in the center of the economic miracle." At dinner, alert to a dinner mate's bad stomach, she leaned over and said, "Oh, you can eat this. The rice will be okay for you."

At the same time, Sontag could be intense, persnickety and unyielding if an official PEN letter failed to reflect some precise distinction she considered important to the occasion. Overhearing her colleagues fret about shopping time, she cracked with slight hauteur, "All these people worry about their clothes. I haven't even bought a piece of gum."

Sontag's constant seesawing between calculated plans and spontaneous impulses suggested that her lifelong emphasis on the immediacy of experience was visceral, not feigned. One moment, she could remark, "What I know about Korea you can fit in a thimble and still have room for a finger." An hour later, discussing PEN politics at the Robang Coffee Shop, she'd insist her group's Korean strategy was unquestionably correct. Hypocritical? No. One concluded that this thinker ditched Emerson's hobgoblin of foolish consistency before puberty.

Months later, at a PEN panel in New York, one saw the same forceful mix. When speakers from the audience apologized for their lack of expertise, she reminded them, "We're all just readers here." As in Seoul, she quietly monitored mike efficiency. She pointed a latecomer to an open seat, then commented on the place of commas in Dickinson's poetry. That organic relation to the everyday deflated the Joan of Arc persona. Asked by a reporter whether she cooked, she replied, "I heat." Fooling around with the rumbling PEN copier, she cracked, "This thing is becoming a dryer."

One oddity about Sontag was that the writing she cared about most, her fiction, caught the sternest criticism early in her career for its supposed distance from the concrete. Her first novel, *The Benefactor* (1963), presented a sixtyish actor named Hippolyte who seeks to repeat his strange dreams in life. In *Partisan Review,* of all places, critic Tony Tanner described the narrative as "tiresome." Her second, *Death Kit* (1967), focused on a businessman who isn't sure whether he has committed a murder. Gore Vidal accused Sontag of "a perfect absence of humor" and excessive "literary borrowings" from European modernists. Tanner labeled the book "a rumination without a view."

But Sontag's fiction became less mannered. Her short story collection, *I, etcetera* (1978), drew good reviews. Her story "The Way We Live Now" opened *The Best American Short Stories 1987,* edited by Ann Beattie. When critic Frederick Karl wrote that "her fictions are a gloss on her critical ideas," Sontag replied, "I've certainly never written fiction in order to illustrate any idea that I've had as an essayist."

"I have the impression that I've just begun to be a writer," she said, "that I can do much better. And it certainly doesn't have any relation to these labels about what I am, or what I'm seen as in the culture, or what my 'career' is."

"I'm a producer of texts," she offered as a half-baked definition, noting that she faced some familiar writerly obstacles: "I worry too much. I'm too anxious, and I'm too easily distracted, perhaps. I'm not a very prolific writer. But I think every day I do something that makes it more possible to write, even if I'm not actually writing."

Indeed, Sontag believed that her literary reputation suffered in a predictable way because of America's anti-intellectualism. She regretted the difference in cultural preconceptions between America and Europe.

"The notion of an intellectual in most Americans' minds is so impoverished," she asserted, "that it's separated from that of a writer." Almost all European writers, she remarked, have been intellectuals by American standards: "Nobody would say, 'Now, Mr. Gide, what do you think about your intellectual career?' It would be a meaningless question."

"Even 'intellectual,'" she continued, "is too grandiose a word. For American writers simply to avow that they have the education, or the cultivation, that they very often have, is something that isn't done—they're like politicians who want to adopt a folksy accent."

"I think the so-called minimalists," she said, "are the first visible group of people, as opposed to single instances, who have taken this lesson to heart. European writers—or South American writers—can say that I'm influenced by so-and-so, I admire so-and-so. . . . Everyone in America wants to say, 'Oh, I'm not interested, not influenced by Borges or Calvino. I mean, I'm influenced by the Three Stooges, or, you know, Sgt. Bilko.' It's always to get down there, to be a good ol' boy, or good ol' girl."

Meanwhile, Sontag monitored her own accomplishments—and reputation—carefully. She frequently told reporters that she was "not a journalist or reviewer." She similarly resisted being seen as a philosopher without institutional portfolio. Sontag counted herself a writer who enjoyed reading philosophy but formulated beliefs in the aphoristic tradition of Nietzsche.

At Sontag's apartment, one saw no evidence to undermine the claim—no bust of Plato, no print of Raphael's *The School of Athens,* no *New Yorker* cartoon like the one in which a porter asks a bespectacled student, "You have a PhD in philosophy too?"—all staples of the office doors of philosophy fanatics.

Instead, her home offered small comforts and no coy messages. The orange-tiled back patio looked out on a path of foliage, a bit incongruous so close to the Holland Tunnel. A modest shell collection and antique maps of Italy ("Piante Della Grotte Vaticane") also fought the urban gloom. In the background, Sontag tried desperately to get her phone fixed. "You know," she barked into the receiver, "I'm just getting the runaround now. I called on this three days ago." Minutes later, over the same recalcitrant instrument, she practiced the difficult art of crafting a book blurb for a friend's forthcoming tome ("shrewd, independent, unsentimental").

A browse through the apartment revealed concert notices on the fridge, no rug on the wood floor, and the fabled books—a few of them. The main reading room offered a long wooden refectory table with bench and wooden chair, a black leather recliner, a Nikko AM/FM stereo tuner NT-790 with NA-890 integrated stereo amplifier and Celestron speakers, and nine shelves of books on each wall, stretching some sixteen feet high. Atop the table lay a mix of reading matter: *The Colloquies of Erasmus,* newspaper clippings from the *Times, Village Voice* and various mainstream magazines. A Tower Records bag rested in a corner with thirteen new albums. The record bins teemed with classical albums, the few popular items betraying a certain age: Cream, the Supremes, Springsteen.

Sontag's blurb writing over ("That's what's to go off to all the ships at sea," she told the caller), she resisted any self-definition narrower than "writer." In her twenties, she conceded, she expected to remain a philosophy teacher, concentrating on Greek and German philosophy, as well as aesthetics: "Actually, I taught everything. I even taught a logic course, for which I was singularly ill-fitted. I mean, I was always one lesson ahead of my students. I used to joke that I was once the youngest instructor in America, and then I ended up being the oldest, simply because I never wrote my dissertation. So I was never promoted. I was always either an instructor or a lecturer."

"It wasn't as if my dream was to be a professor of philosophy," she went on. "Teaching philosophy was as natural as breathing. This was what interested me, and this was an absolutely sublime way to make a living. It's not that I gave up a goal—I sacrificed a vocation."

Sontag said she stopped teaching because she "couldn't keep up. I couldn't be a writer, too. I take them both too seriously. . . . If I had gone on being an academic, I would have become a part-time writer." Yet while philosophy was the only subject she'd want to teach, she didn't align herself with particular positions in the field: "I don't have that temperament. I don't think of myself as a member of a school or camp." She said she had never "met a label that did anything for me."

In conversation, Sontag tenaciously held to the anti-interpretive, pro-experience sensibility expressed in her early work, resisting the vocabulary of philosophic movements. "You see," she said, "you want to put a jargon on it. I don't. I agree, I don't agree. I'm open, I'm not open. This is what I do all my life. I look at painting. I listen to music, I read, I'm open in every minute, I'm open to you, I'm open to whatever happens to me. It's not something I want to declare as a principle. It goes without saying."

When she heard the jargon of semiotic or deconstructionist schools, she confided, "I feel something in my own head go dead. I'm not saying it's of no use to other people, but it's of no use to me." That was one reason, she said, she "stopped reading criticism." To her, *Against Interpretation* fundamentally "wasn't a work of philosophy. It was a manifesto, just like the Surrealist manifestos. I have a lot more in common with André Breton than I do with American philosophy. I'm not in that game. I'm in the game of Breton or Nietzsche."

Saying it, of course, didn't make it so. More accurately, she had made the Breton-Nietzsche game part of American philosophy. But that adamant go-it-alone ideal informed all Sontag's work, just as a Whitmanesque sense of being at peace with evolving self-contradiction did. Despite writing two books about metaphors in common thinking, she hadn't read contemporary philosophical literature on metaphor. At the beginning of *AIDS and Its Metaphors,* she simply invoked Aristotle's traditional notion.

Asked about a contemporary study of metaphor such as Lakoff and Johnson's *Metaphors We Live By,* she replied, "I don't know anything about it. . . . I'm someone who's mainly read the classics. I never heard of these people. . . . I've never read a book about metaphor and I don't know those names. . . . I started from Aristotle. You must understand that the two most important writers in my thinking life are Plato and Aristotle."

"I don't keep up," she elaborated. "I'd much rather reread Kant or Nietzsche or Spinoza or Hume or Wittgenstein or somebody. . . . I don't *read* secondary literature. I read philosophy. . . . I meant it quite literally—that's what I meant by metaphor. I meant what I said I meant."

But how does one decide the difference between primary works and secondary works? Sontag's hostility to methodological questions flared. "*I don't read secondary works,*" she reiterated. Still, she was asked, "How do you decide, primary versus secondary?"

"I know."

"You just know?"

"Well, sure," she said. "It would take you a couple of days to go through this library. It's a great private library. I'm interested in doing my own thing. But I'm surrounded by ten thousand books. C'mon, I'm working in one of the best private libraries in the world—my own. *Don't you understand?* Don't think that I'm just going my own way. I have this incredible keyboard here. I'm not doing research. It's in my head. These books are all in my head. I've read these books. When I wrote *Illness as Metaphor,* I didn't look anything up. I quote it more or less from memory, and then I check the quotations to see if they're accurate. I don't do any research. The quotes come because they're in my head."

"You read and then sit down?"

"No, I don't. I was trying to say it the other way around. I don't read and read and read. I sit down and the books are already in my head. Don't you understand? I wasn't doing reading. I remembered it from all the books I've read."

In the impatience, the near fury just below the surface of Sontag's remarks, one could hear the thinker determined to be an artist in thought, opposed to acknowledging drudge work behind the curtain, any need for rehearsal or workmanlike preparation. One recalled Sontag's essay on the Nobel Prize–winning philosophical novelist Elias Canetti and his famous character Kien in *Auto-da-Fé*, a bibliophile whose obsession, Sontag wrote, "is to put the books inside one's head: the real library is just a mnemonic system. Thus Canetti has Kien sitting at his desk and composing a learned article without turning a single page of his books, except in his head."

Life imitating art imitating life.

How much did she actually read?

"Oh, ten to twenty books a week. Well, a lot of it's rereading. I don't have to lock myself in my room. This is what I do. That's what I've done all my life. I am gifted with, you know, almost lightning—I mean, I can almost read a page at a glance. I reread these books over and over again."

Sontag's resistance to imposed academic models turned an ongoing interview into a nonstop debate, with chess clocks running. Another query also irritated her: whether the aphoristic tradition she admired didn't force one to write less than the truth. The mere suggestion, she replied, was an insult.

"If I think there is a counterargument to what I'm saying," she declared, "I take account of it, and anything else would be an intellectual disgrace. I'm shocked by your question. I'm not a polemicist in that sense at all. I'm interested in the truth. Haven't you noticed?"

"I have."

"But for God's sake," she continued, "it's as if you're asking if I'd perjure myself. If I'm aware of counterevidence, or counterarguments, would I suppress them, would I ignore them? I'm sorry, but that is the equivalent of perjury. It's shocking."

The conversation turned to a statement in *Illness as Metaphor*: "As death is now an offensively meaningless event . . . ," a viewpoint Sontag attributed to society. "Many writers would be afraid to make such a strong statement," she was told.

"*Excuse me,*" she said, her voice rising, "but I don't know who these other writers are. Do you know whom I'm measuring myself against? Who my standards are? If you had Nietzsche sitting in front of you—and I'm not saying I'm Nietzsche, far from it—would you say, I wonder if you could explain to me here, Nietzsche, why you appear obliged to make these incredible generalizations about our culture? I mean, don't you realize that this isn't just this, but it's also that? I mean, *excuse me.* What namby-pamby writers are you thinking of?"

She simmered down—a bit. "If you're going to tell me that some-one else wouldn't do it," she continued, "then I'm afraid I must answer impertinently, Someone else isn't me. *This is what I do,* and there is a great tradition of doing it. And I may be the least talented and most insignificant member of this tradition, but it is *my* tradition. And I do not see why I have to deal with the namby-pamby writer who wouldn't do what I am doing when I have Friedrich Nietzsche as a model. And why I have to be put on the defensive for making bold statements of whose truth I am *profoundly* convinced. And I believe it is very impor-tant to say these truths. These are the sort of truths that make a differ-ence. I've done a lot of work and I've earned the right to do this."

"Strong formulations like yours—"

"*You have to earn the right,*" she interrupted. "Earn the right to talk that way, by your own depth and eloquence. It's not a theoretical mat-ter. It's not a competition between two views, one of which says, Strong formulation. No, it is something you can do as an individual if you've got the stuff. It's not theoretical. It's not two views about what writing is. You see, you keep theorizing and I won't theorize about it. I think all those theories are just rationalizations of one's temperament. *Earn* the right to make strong formulations. Don't worry about the theory that justifies strong formulations. *Be* a person who can do it and you'll know if you can.

"I've told you in every eloquent way that I can," she wound down, "that the academic model of discourse is not my model, even though I live surrounded by university press books."

But how did one settle the question of which model of discourse gets closer to the truth?

"I'm not interested in settling the question!" she shouted.

"But I am."

"Then *excuse me,* you're wasting my time. For heaven's sake, that's like asking a Montaigne to be Thomas Aquinas. You go see Montaigne, who writes essays, and you want to know why he's not working on the *Summa Theologica!*"

"Because it helps you to understand why he's not working on the *Summa Theologica.*"

"But I'm definitely with Montaigne, okay? In fact, I could be, like Montaigne, fascinated by the *Summa Theologica,* thinking about Aqui-nas. I might prefer reading Aquinas compared to some other essayist. But it's certainly not what I'm doing."

"You see, you still think of me as a renegade or rogue member of the American philosophical establishment," she declared. "Whereas I'm really defrocked—self-defrocked. And my models *always* were elsewhere . . . it was always, if you will, Montaigne and Nietzsche for me."

Indeed, she added, if she'd been an academic, "I would have been influenced by the very thing you're talking about: the countermodel, the counterexample. I *would* have been more prudent, in ways that wouldn't be particularly interesting."

"One does have to protect one's edge," she remarked. "The right to be reckless. It's not that I want to be reckless. I want to be wisdom itself. I'm not interested in provocation for itself. Not at all. I'd love to be utterly convincing and utterly wise. But I know that it's a big, complicated world out there and it may be that one just does have to be more marginal. I would like to be marginal. It's okay."

Sontag caught her breath as she finally, belatedly, got ready to leave for a meeting. "It's not a question of success," she said. "It's a question of fire. Of *passion*."

Her fire burned for years afterward. And her commitment to the grand observation increasingly came together with the only form that could absorb and reflect the kaleidoscope of life she fed off—the novel. The big breakthrough came with her first wholly successful work in that genre, *The Volcano Lover: A Romance*. In that complex performance, which deserved the dual critical and commercial success of books such as Umberto Eco's *The Name of the Rose* and A. S. Byatt's *Possession*, Sontag got all her sainted influences to mingle nicely together.

The Volcano Lover told the story—yes, there was a story—of one of history's most heavy-breathing romances. In the late eighteenth century, Sir William Hamilton, a renowned art collector and expert on the Vesuvius volcano, served as British envoy to the Kingdom of the Two Sicilies in Naples. His second wife, Emma Hamilton, thirty-three years his junior, was a blacksmith's daughter whose remarkable beauty and acting ability aided her rise in status after they married. At the turn of the nineteenth century, Lord Horatio Nelson, the famous British admiral, came into their lives, helping to rescue them and the Bourbons of Naples from the Republican revolution of 1799. Nelson and Emma Hamilton soon commenced a fervent and flagrant affair.

The reputations of all three eventually suffered when Nelson presided over the brutal restoration of the Bourbons, ordering many of the

Neapolitan elite executed as Republican sympathizers. Civilized Europe, in Sontag's words, came to view Hamilton as "a famous cuckold," his wife as a "vulgarian" and Nelson as a corrupted hero, "part Lawrence of Arabia, self-appointed rescuer of incompetent native rulers; part Mark Antony, self-destructive lover of his own ruin."

The story itself, which Sontag unfolded from about 1765 to 1805, was famously rich—Hollywood produced it with Vivien Leigh and Laurence Olivier in *That Hamilton Woman* (1941). But Sontag's approach and trompe l'oeil wizardry far removed *The Volcano Lover* from standard historical fiction. Moving back and forth (until the very end) between the canny voice of an omniscient present-day narrator and a more stately voice suited to the time, the book flowed with meditations on the status of women, the nature of collecting, the allure of fragrance, the authority of beauty, the importance of irony and scores of other topics that Sontag deftly integrated with subtle psychological analyses of her players. At the same time, *The Volcano Lover* offered shrewd new dramatic forms for the mix of cultural elitism and human compassion that informed all of Sontag's criticism.

Sontag's chief triumph in *The Volcano Lover* was her ability to hit so many novelistic bull's-eyes without a stray shot, to wed traditional storytelling with the quirky modern sensibility that dominated her earlier fiction. As sage thoughts unfolded, we also thoroughly entered the main characters despite the third-person narration. William's self-image as "an envoy of decorum and reason" became palpable from sharing his psychology over the decades—the same alchemy occurred with one's intimate grasp of Emma's plebeian enthusiasms and Nelson's insatiable appetite for attention. Even Sontag's brief portrait of the thirty-seven-year-old Goethe, visiting Naples on his Italian journey, bristled with freshness (if not strict accuracy), capturing the immortal poet as impossible dinner guest, the authentic genius whose "every gesture is a reproach" because "he reminds the revelers of the existence of another, more serious way of experiencing."

"He is pretentious, overbearing, humorless, aggressive, condescending," Sir William thinks. "A monster of egotism. Alas, he's also the real thing."

If one detected a trace of displaced autobiography there, it was no accident. *The Volcano Lover* also functioned as a well-disguised exercise in memoir by a woman whose self-importance and ironic humor existed in a powerful balance, stabilized by the fact that she, too, was the real thing. True to her self-image as someone who collected the world's best literature in her head, who listened, retained and free-associated while others furiously scribbled notes, Sontag—that is, her narrator—projected some of it onto William, the professional collector: "The Cavaliere had a prodigious memory. He wrote few things down. It was all in his head . . . a prodigious profusion."

In fact, the recurring passages about collecting illuminated Sontag's own aggressive posture over the years in works like *On Photography* and *Illness as Metaphor*—she too, like William, had been a "volcano lover," a votary of the bold: "For the collector to show off his collection is not bad manners. Indeed, the collector, like the imposter, has no existence unless he goes public, unless he shows what he is or has decided to be. Unless he puts his passions on display."

As she dwelt on the matter, it was plain that Sontag used Hamilton's avocation as an opportunity to mull her own life, in which she'd acquired the enormous personal library and an unusually sure sense of its contents. Her continuing observations ("Every collector is also an accomplice of the ideal of destruction"; "The list is itself a collection, a sublimated collection") provocatively linked up with the acquisitive way the Hamiltons and Nelson viewed one another, as beloved entities that brought completion. Consistent with her apotheosis of the aphorist, *The Volcano Lover* predictably honored such classical models as La Bruyère and La Rochefoucauld, and contemporary favorites of the author like the Romanian E. M. Cioran. Among her many lovely efforts were these: "Living abroad facilitates treating life as a spectacle"; "When the right person does the wrong thing, it's the right thing"; "A man who has to admire in order to desire is likely to have led a modest sexual life."

But that was only one way in which the style of *The Volcano Lover* set it apart. Sontag utterly reinvented her prose style there, concocting a kind of chamber music studded by jazz riffs, with a subtheme from *Tosca*. Paragraphs often began with stark, modern, verbless phrases—the topic sentence as stage direction ("The Cavaliere in the room where he takes breakfast"). They then curved into Nabokovian cascades of many clauses, or pithy, contemporary bulletins. She dared a sentence like "&c, &c, &c, concludes the Cavaliere" as readily as she sculpted the most Augustan construction. Her vocabulary mixed up-to-date American acronyms (PMS) with delightful recherché diction: melismas, tramontana, gouaches, intaglios.

And yet *The Volcano Lover* emerged a great novel, not a perfect one. The brief prologue confused more than it invited. Sontag's catholic frame of reference too often jarred sentences out of their immediate mood ("Servants were everywhere, making everything possible, but, like the black figures in Noh plays who enter the stage to adjust a character's massive costume or furnish a prop, servants didn't count"). And for all Sontag's exaltation of literature over journalism, she occasionally suffered from journalistic weakness of the will when an opportunity for glib wordplay arose. Remarking that "the future is another country," or having Goethe reflect that if the English didn't exist, "nobody would ever have invented them," caught her trying too hard, tempted into a kind of Olympian copywriting.

Such cavils, though, were pebbles at the foot of a mountain. *The Volcano Lover* repeatedly scaled heights of complex thought, passion and expression that few American writers ever approached, while reimagining a majestic love story in dazzling style. That visit to Thomas Mann at his California home when she was fourteen had lent a literary grandeur to her teenage life. Many decades later, she'd finally written a novel he'd have celebrated. When some years later she achieved the peak of her career as a fiction writer—the National Book Award for *In America,* a novel troubled by unresolved allegations of misused material that not a few critics thought weaker than *The Volcano Lover*—some critical consensus held that it was overdue recognition of the masterful prior book that had been allowed to slip by without proper honor.

Her rise to novelistic master, combined with fleshing out of further multiple dimensions, served to position Sontag as an inimitable American thinker and intellectual influence as she entered the last decade of her life. The gradual exposure and acknowledgment of her bisexuality, in biographies such as Carl Rollyson and Lisa Paddock's *Susan Sontag: The Making of an Icon,* and in some interviews of her own, loosened the hermetic wrap she'd long placed around her personal life.

That made Sontag and her career, as evidenced in as recent a book as *The Scandal of Susan Sontag* (2009), material for serious rumination in yet another area of American philosophy typically pursued more outside philosophy departments than within—gender studies. The possibility at least existed that future intellectuals would read Sontag differently—as Edmund White implies we read Proust differently when we factor in his sexuality—because the Rollyson-Paddock book, whatever its quality, shone light in places its subject preferred to keep dark.

In her final years, however, Sontag made plain that more important issues occupied her when she returned to nonfiction. At the cluttered

kitchen table of her Chelsea apartment, just as book-packed as her earlier place by the Holland Tunnel, Sontag, still embedded in the controversies of her times, wanted to talk war, not sexuality.

"It was a siege," she said matter-of-factly of what you might call
"her war": Sarajevo, Bosnia, in the mid-1990s. "There was no electricity. There was no running water. There was no heat. . . . You were in
the middle of it, constant bombardment, bullets whizzing past your
head—bang, bang, bang. . . . And you didn't see how it was represented.
You didn't watch television. You didn't read the newspapers." It was a
conflict that Sontag witnessed during fourteen trips she made to Sarajevo over two and a half years.

Mulling over the experience—the gap between the war you watch
face-to-face and "our camera-mediated knowledge of war"—stirred her
to write her last profound work of philosophical analysis, *Regarding the
Pain of Others,* a meditation on war and its images published just days
before America's attack on Iraq. A *New Yorker* excerpt from it won Sontag a George Polk Award for Criticism. The issue it addressed was "gro-
tesquely and painfully topical," she said, acknowledging that all wars
resemble one another, but insisting that their differences and justifications must be understood as well.

It was coming back from Sarajevo to Manhattan, "talking to people
whose ideas about war all came from the representations," that returned
her to the long-essay form, twenty-five years after *On Photography,* after
those years devoted to writing *The Volcano Lover* and *In America.*

"I never promised never to write another essay," Sontag joked, with
that mix of seriousness and pitch-perfect colloquial voice. "This is a
book about war . . . [and] how you think about things that are terrible
and that aren't happening to you." A modest 126 pages, it began with
Virginia Woolf's reflections on photographs, then examined whether
war photos produce common reactions, and the photos' relation to
words about war.

Photos, she argued, become "a compact form for memorizing,"
and continue to haunt us, but remain chiefly illustrative. Understanding what they show requires turning elsewhere—to words that range
from captions to full-length narrative histories. "The problem is not that
people remember through photographs," she maintained, "but that they
remember only the photographs." That, unfortunately, eclipses other
forms of understanding. Pictures are not worth a thousand words, she
suggested, but rather invite at least that many.

The overriding point of her essay, she explained, nursing her espresso, was straightforward: "All pictures are in a context, and a setting. No pictures speak for themselves." Although graphic war photos might turn someone against war, they could, in another person, "just as well stimulate a desire to go on with war and avenge the deaths. Pictures don't come naked—they come wrapped." Thus war images "cannot be more than an invitation to pay attention, to reflect, to learn, to examine the rationalizations for mass suffering offered by established parties." If that sounded not quite in line with *Against Interpretation*, and closer to the pro-interpretation platform of Arthur Danto than one would ever expect of Sontag, well, she, like Whitman, contained multitudes.

As always in her essays, Sontag drew from an array of historical examples. They included Mathew Brady's Civil War photography as well as German pacifist Ernst Friedrich's controversial volume from the First World War, *War Against War!* (1924), which displayed previously unpublishable photos of men with their faces shot away ("The most horrible pictures I've ever seen in my life," Sontag confided). In the book, Sontag snapped out ideas the way photojournalists snap a subject from multiple angles. How did voyeurism or shame figure into our "appetite for pictures showing bodies in pain"? Do such pictures teach us anything? Do privileged Western viewers of war develop a spectator theory in which all harsh reality is simply spectacle?

Sontag acknowledged the tensions in her text: "It's trying to climb about seven different trees at the same time," she said. An old image then re-seized her, one both she and her visitor had heard before. "It's like a bouillon cube," she joked of the book's condensation of many ideas. "You have to sort of add water and serve." Add the still-bubbling runoff at the time of "Operation Iraqi Freedom," and her opinions came to a fine boil.

She criticized U.S. media for largely suppressing photos of Iraqi war casualties: "The fact is that gruesome pictures of civilian casualties are being featured in all the media everywhere in the world except the United States and to some extent England." The blame, she felt, lay with editors and producers at home, more eager not to offend customers by failing to seem "supportive" of the military than to inform readers or viewers. "When institutions raise the standard of what's in good taste or bad taste," she acidly remarked, "my antennae go up. I just think that's a mask for something else."

Should American media show graphic photos of carnage when the country is at war?

"The short answer is yes," she replied. "I think we should show the faces, show the reality of war."

A few hours bivouacked in Sontag's place was enough to see how the 2003 war impinged on her life, her thoughts, almost her every moment. Forty e-mails a day came in, and ten calls daily, from journalists seeking comment. Regarding the war itself, Sontag said, "I consider myself an American patriot," but she strongly opposed it: "My way of supporting the troops would have been not to send them." She remained unconvinced about Saddam Hussein's possession of, and intention to use, weapons of mass destruction, a skepticism that subsequent history ratified. Nor did she think that issue provided the Bush administration's real motivation for the war. She presciently dismissed Hussein's alleged link with al-Qaeda.

At the same time, Sontag observed that reading the signs at a Manhattan antiwar rally reminded her that she was not a pacifist. On some occasions, she thought, military force was "a desirable alternative. . . . I'm absolutely in favor of military intervention to stop genocide."

Such distinctions, Sontag argued, couldn't be communicated by photos. That was one reason her book didn't contain any. "I didn't want it to have photographs, because I really wanted it to be an argument, for people to think," she explained. "Photographs do not make the distinction between War is hell and This war didn't have to happen. For that, you need words."

The confidence, the wit, the panache, the authority—all made it hard to believe when Sontag succumbed to her final bout with cancer in 2004, a battle recorded by her son, David, in his moving rumination about it, *Swimming in a Sea of Death.* After that third struggle with cancer, Rieff recalled, he received condolence letters from old friends of hers notable for emphatically expressing, in addition to their sorrow, "their disbelief that she had not lived."

Sontag, indeed, made one feel she was too smart to die. She would, many figured, find a way around it.

Sontag first faced cancer in 1975 at age forty-two—stage IV breast cancer that led to a radical mastectomy, remission, survival, and *Illness as Metaphor.* Then, in 1998, came uterine sarcoma, which brought more surgery, chemotherapy—and survival again. The third brutal diagnosis, in early 2004, proved worse: myelodysplastic syndrome, sometimes called "smoldering leukemia," a "lethal form of blood cancer." Her death, in Memorial Sloan-Kettering Cancer Center in New York, came later that year, after "excruciating pain" and Sontag's effort to survive once more through a bone-marrow transplant and experimental drugs.

Swimming in a Sea of Death avoided a clinical account of Sontag's last battle. Rather, it became an extended meditation, in a sober, heartfelt tone, on the struggle and Rieff's and his mother's attitudes toward it. Watching Sontag die from a distance through her son's eyes, seeing her strategize against the dying of the light, reminded one of what made her so impressive, and colored in some of the most deeply personal aspects of her ambition and fighting spirit.

"No one I have ever known," wrote Rieff, "loved life so unambivalently." *Avidity* was the word he thought best described her personality. Very simply, he recalled, "There was nothing she did not want to see or do or try to know." Sontag confided that she'd have liked to live to one hundred, if only to complete her planned projects, "the work" that "had to be served."

Rieff believed that she'd gladly have accepted "an immortality that consisted of nothing but consciousness," the "science-fiction immortality of the disembodied head."

Because Sontag, Rieff wrote, "lived her life as if stocking a library"— she "wanted to absorb," not "be absorbed." In addition to her indefatigable reading, she made "lists of restaurants and books, quotations and facts, writing projects and travel schedules," and took in any information available.

Still a "rock-hard" atheist at her death, Sontag, Rieff observed, remained "loyal to the activity of acquiring information as one is loyal to a faith. Therein lay my mother's most deep-seated conviction about herself—her belief in her ability to take in and understand facts and then to face them."

That bent, Rieff said, explained how she confronted her three cancers. In her 1970s battle against breast cancer, she became the "straight-A student." She opted for a radical "Halsted" mastectomy—a brutal operation that removes "most of the muscle of the chest wall and lymph nodes in the armpits"—because she insisted it would improve her "slim" chances. In her final illness, she submitted to the bone-marrow transplant for the same reason.

She "believed in her own will," Rieff writes, "and, grandiose though it may seem, in her own star." He respected that, because "everything my mother accomplished . . . was undergirded by that belief." At the same time, Rieff conceded, his mother considered herself a "lucky person," someone who had "a good chance at being the exception in whatever situation she found herself in." Just after his mother received her third diagnosis of cancer, Rieff recalled, she told him, "This time I don't feel special." He adds, "Of course, none of us are special."

Rieff's memoir offered more feelings about his mother's death than facts about their relationship, but some of the latter inevitably appeared, helping one understand his continuing regrets. He explained that "neither of us had ever been physically demonstrative with the other," a habit that didn't change in the early part of her illness, when he sometimes felt "unable to say anything that mattered, let alone touch her."

To Rieff's credit, he knew that "the guilt comes no matter what you have or haven't done." In *Swimming in a Sea of Death*, he certainly offered sharp insights into his mother that mattered: her "astonishing mix of gallantry and pedantry," her tendency to be "divalike and unstoical about trivial things," her refuge in streety humor, as when she joked that she wanted to live as long as possible "just to see how stupid it gets."

After she died, the death kits delivered by obituary and appreciation writers sounded predictable. The scribes took a few of the most famous aphorisms from column A (e.g., "The white race is the cancer of human history"), a selection of books from column B (e.g., *On Photography*, *The Volcano Lover*), some immortal moments of media controversy from column C (e.g., her *New Yorker* declaration that the 9/11 hijackers "were not cowards"), then snapped them into place with the most famous self-descriptions from column D (e.g., "zealot of seriousness" and "obsessed moralist"). They colored in personal details: beautiful and precocious when young, fierce anti-cancer battler when old, reclusive Garbo when it came to soul-bearing intimacies, devout Luddite in the face of newfangled technologies like TV.

They ascribed to her enduring beliefs that supposedly changed American culture: that critical interpretation of art obstructs its "incantatory, magical" power, that "[i]n America, the photographer is not simply the person who records the past, but the one who invents it." Finally, they embalmed her in the clichés of her clip file: She cared most about her fiction, but would be remembered as a critic—she remained, most importantly, an "evangelist of the new." She counted as heterosexual because she married once, and, oh yes, she read more than anyone else.

One imagined her perched cross-legged on a couch at some cloud café over Sarajevo (the renowned Sontag loyalty continuing after death), reading all the pieces on her, shaking her head. To be sure, she'd find some hard to accept, because they emphasized the feats that made her famous rather than the characteristics that made her Susan Sontag. Too many people who sized her up committed the unpardonable intellectual sin in her book: parroting familiar clichés rather than thinking, reading and analyzing for themselves.

The most infuriating postmortem slap would have been the *New York Times*'s inability to nail her right—she'd have despised the doubly wrong headline on the appreciation "A Rigorous Intellectual Dressed in Glamour." That imperious expression would have taken hold of her face, the one that appeared when she prepared to set someone straight. Her philosophical bent, like that of Rorty and the country she embodied, had always pointed her precisely away from mock pseudo-technical "rigor," the mantra for decades of the European positivists whose scientism and piecemeal argumentation she rejected. The "dressed in glamour" image, absurd for a woman who attired herself like an artist rather than one of the *Times*'s fawned-upon Manhattan society dames, reflected the need of male editors to sexualize her (and heterosexualize her) and stress her looks because she'd been beautiful when young.

"She brought to the world of ideas not just an Olympian rigor," wrote the appreciation's author, "but a glamour and sexiness it had seldom seen before." Forced to read that parallel misjudgment, and the false active verb "brought," which pinned the blame on her, the waspish Sontag might well have replied that stiffening on the part of male editors was no reason to impute rigor to her. So, too, the *Times*'s blithe announcement, "Her reputation rests on her nonfiction," would rightly have incensed her, being so out of date. Having striven for years to produce fiction worthy of the literary greats she admired, she'd won not just the National Book Award for fiction, but the Jerusalem Prize for Literature, Spain's Prince of Asturias Award for Letters and the Friedenspreis (Peace Prize) of the German Booksellers Association. None of those prizes came for early essays like "Notes on Camp." If Sontag had lived for another decade, the esteem in which many international critics held her might have won her the Nobel Prize for Literature.

Why, then, did the cliché persist that she remained primarily a critic? Why couldn't the writers of appreciations—praising her for always thinking for herself—do so themselves? Sontag understood the syndrome: the problem harked back to the point Sontag had made in her apartment years before. The American media establishment, unlike its European counterpart, didn't know how to draw appropriate lines when it came to philosophy and literature. It didn't permit American writers to be intellectuals and literary novelists at the same time. That privilege remained restricted to non-Americans—Milan Kundera, Jorge Luis Borges, Yukio Mishima.

Not every appreciator got Sontag wrong. She'd have loved Paul Levy's salute in the *Independent* that she ended up "an artist among artists." The wisest take on Sontag's writerly evolution came from her longtime friend Wasserman, then literary editor of the *Los Angeles Times.* Sontag, he observed during an interview on National Public Radio's *Talk of the Nation,* in some ways "had outgrown her essays, and found that the conceit of fiction enabled her to inhabit multiple voices and to argue multiple ideas without ever having to come to a single position." She'd become uneasy, Wasserman suggested, with "the idea that in a particular essay the author had to be, as it were, hostage to a particular point of view—she found it confining, and the fiction gave a much more capacious arena to explore the literary dimension which was her first and true and enduring love."

Too many "appreciators," in short, failed to notice that her evolution back to literature extended rather than contradicted the aesthetic and philosophical notions of the early essays they wanted to preserve and petrify. Like Rorty, she reflected, in the end, a brash writerly independence, a respect for this world of multiple persuasive narratives, and a welcome to other thinkers that mirrored the openness of her country.

The Sarajevans named a street after her. The best her peers in America the Philosophical might have done was to emulate her. To write articles for publications, read by other than professional peers, that said absolutely what they thought. To pay no attention to whether those writings would block their ability to cling to the same institutional home all their lives. To hone the sentences to so fine a form that some of them might stand up and saunter away from their paragraphs, looking for a new home—perhaps a book of quotations, or the marble wall of an august hall of learning. Best of all, to write a novel, philosophically inclined, with all the uncertain certainty that would demand. The last tribute would behoove the bearer to add, as final touch, a simple phrase at the spot where dedications go: "For Susan Sontag."

Sontag's career created a niche in American life for writerly women intellectuals bold enough to emulate her juxtaposition of high and low, her enthusiasm for art, her openness to journalism, her ability to make a splash. Few did it as brazenly and lastingly as Camille Paglia (1947–), though it seemed, in the first decade of the twenty-first century, that her chances of equaling Sontag's philosophical impact were slim. Close to the time of her launch into the national philosophical arena, however, Paglia's possibilities seemed large.

On a lazy Friday afternoon in her corner office at Philadelphia's University of the Arts, the steel-plated Madonna of American intellectual life dropkicked verbal grenades. Quickly regarded as the world's flashiest new big-mouth scholar after her first book, *Sexual Personae,* became its decade's most controversial work of cultural criticism, she made racetrack announcers sound like Parkinson's patients. "I am the most obnoxious woman in world history!" the middle-aged humanities professor had warned over the phone. Who could argue? Did Cleopatra's eyes bulge like that? Could Emma Goldman spit out apostasy this fast? Up front, Paglia's mouth ran like an Uzi with the latch stuck on "fire," splattering intense, madcap, spiraling maxims of cultural heresy, personal revelation and high-strung free association.

"No woman has ever been freer than I am as a woman in America," Paglia declared. "I appear out of nowhere, like Athena." And the bulging eyes? "My passion has always been a problem," she admitted. "I'm just too intense." Friendly icons on the walls and dividers by her desk provided psychological support: Madonna, the Marquis de Sade, scandal girl Christine Keeler. A sign above her desk—"I Don't Have PMS, I'm Just Naturally Bitchy"—contributed to the mood music. Arms flailing, short grayish hair hardly mussed, she was coiled, gassed and ready to talk at the speed of sound. And talk.

Within a few hours of rat-a-tat conversation, Paglia had confessed to punching out an oaf who urinated on her at a concert, conceded a taste for car mechanics, described herself sexually as "a mad nun, like Teresa of Ávila," dismissed dolls as "humanoid rubber" (she liked swords as a kid) and remarked, "I could have made a fortune as a dominatrix."

She believed "civilization has been the creation of men." She was "pro-pornography," "pro-prostitution" and pro–legalization of drugs. She considered most academics "a bunch of coconuts," a crew "generally depressed and disappointed." She wanted to "bombshell the whole humanities curriculum." She derided American lesbians as "too politicized and doctrinaire," adding that "the best lesbians are the ones created by men."

Apropos of her own status, Paglia called *Sexual Personae* "the funniest academic book ever written." She felt confident that "when people look back at the twentieth century, at nonfiction books by women, it's going to be Jane Harrison, Simone de Beauvoir, and Paglia. . . . Susan Sontag will be a footnote."

Was this really taking place in Philadelphia? Where meek writers and intellectuals feel hip if they lunch once a month in New York? Who was Camille Paglia, and why was she saying those things?

The rhubarb began when Paglia published *Sexual Personae,* her 718-page first book, subtitled *Art and Decadence from Nefertiti to Emily Dickinson.* For two decades, academics hadn't paid any attention to Paglia, a State University of New York at Binghamton valedictorian who received her Yale doctorate in English under literary theorist Harold Bloom. As she taught at Bennington and Wesleyan, and talked of reforming criticism, seven major publishers rejected her decade-in-the-making book.

When it finally arrived, its bold claims flabbergasted readers accustomed to the endless "howevers" of academic books. "If civilization had been left in female hands," Paglia wrote in the one sentence heard round the intellectual world, "we would still be living in grass huts." Bluntly describing her method as "sensationalism," Paglia made more outrageous statements in her first twenty pages than most academics dare in a lifetime. Critic and scholar Walter Kendrick, in the *Village Voice,* commented that *Sexual Personae*'s beginning read "like the inventory of an unusually cerebral fortune-cookie mill: a cosmic claim in every sentence, all in the oracular mode." Believing that there's "truth in sexual stereotypes," Paglia asserted that "men invented culture as a defense against female nature." She wrote that "modern feminism's most naive formulation is its assertion that rape is a crime of violence but not of sex." Feminism, she complained, saw "every hierarchy as repressive, a social fiction; every negative about woman [as] a male lie designed to keep her in her place."

Asked to summarize her root thesis in a few sentences, Paglia replied, "That sex is an extremely complex, dark power. There's a perpetual sex war going on that's not going to be solved by women getting political equality with men, because the sexual problem is not a political problem. . . . It precedes politics. I say that everything in the West—intellect, art, political structures, and so on—are all attempted Apollonian containments of this enormous, Dionysian force that is sex, which is barbaric and immoral. And the idea that love is a wonderful, redeeming, transformative theory is wrong." Paglia's beliefs drove her to other radical views on culture. "Pornography and art are inseparable," Paglia wrote in *Sexual Personae,* adding in conversation that pornography is "a fundamental creative principle of high art itself. It's at the heart of imagination. It's all over *Hamlet*."

"Judeo-Christianity," she asserted in the book, "never did defeat paganism." A self-styled "advocate of aestheticism and Decadence," Paglia saw male homosexuality as "the most valorous of attempts to evade the femme fatale and to defeat nature." In one of her wildest passages, she contended that the "male projection of erection and ejaculation is the paradigm for all cultural projection and conceptualization."

Paglia also spritzed her water gun into bloodshot academic eyes through bold handling of venerable artistic reputations. She enjoyed raves for her rough treatment of that ostensibly sedate recluse, poet Emily Dickinson, labeling her an "autoerotic sadist" and "Amherst's Madame de Sade," a spiritual kin to "a homosexual cultist draping himself in black leather and chains," evocative slave to a "sweet tooth for sadomasochistic horror."

The Broad Street acolyte of the Marquis de Sade—Paglia liked the old social philosopher undone by a few fetishes—also zapped Mark Twain for his phony folksiness, described Donatello's *David* as "a frozen wet dream," and announced, "There is no female Mozart because there is no female Jack the Ripper."

As if all that weren't enough to make scholars blush, Paglia yoked together high and pop culture with more pizazz than anyone since Sontag twenty-five years before. Lord Byron and Elvis, Heinrich von Kleist and Bob Dylan, Cary Grant and Dorian Gray—first she engaged them, then she performed the wedding. Critical responses to the book absolutely sizzled.

"Reading Camille Paglia's book is a bit like being mugged," wrote Alan Bold in the *Times* of London, "as it relentlessly pursues its ambition to assault the emotions, batter the brain and aim a kick at the groin." *Washington Post* reviewer Lillian Faderman speculated, "Feminists may find *Sexual Personae* the book they most love to hate." Hilary Mantel in the London *Evening Standard* predicted, "This book will upset almost everyone, though homosexuals, neo-Nazis and pornography salesmen will dislike it less than most."

Across the English-speaking world, reviewers responded giddily to Paglia's brash prose and critical cartwheeling. Jonathan Keates, in the *Observer*, called the book "ceaselessly entertaining." Anthony Burgess, in the *Independent*, found that "each sentence jabs like a needle." Basil Miller of the *Irish Times* judged the style "delighting and infuriating." Here at home, Mark Edmundson, in the *Nation*, described *Sexual*

Personae as "a red comet in a smog-filled sky," and a Nashville reviewer wrote that "Paglia may well turn out to be the most outrageous and fun culture critic since Marshall McLuhan."

At the same time, stinging scholarly rebukes multiplied. Harvard's Helen Vendler attacked Paglia's style in the *New York Review of Books*, writing that "her sentences . . . lie on the page like so many repellent atoms, incapable of forming a molecular structure." Feminist critic Anne Neville concluded that Paglia was "a happy apologist for ensconced male-bias academic prejudice." In England, John Kemp, in the *Literary Review*, said she was "set to become the Ken Russell of literary criticism; an operatic vulgarian."

"Many of the reviews," commented Paglia, "are Rorschach tests of the reviewer. What people react to is what I'm uncovering in their own repressions." She pointed out that after the first chapter's startling claims, the book settled down to a scholarly tour of great Western art, from ancient Egypt to nineteenth-century New England. Paganism's battle against the Judeo-Christian tradition partly expressed itself, she argued, in such sexual personae as the "beautiful boy" in Oscar Wilde's *Dorian Gray.*

The impresario behind this bombshell production lived alone at the time in Swarthmore, Pennsylvania, in a two-room apartment, "jammed as a ship's cabin." She knew few people there, which suited her fine. Her background didn't do much to explain her hyperconfidence, not to say hypomania. Born in Endicott, New York, she grew up with a mother who worked in banking and a father who taught French at Le Moyne College in Syracuse. She stayed in close touch with a younger sister, Lenora, who worked in art conservation, and her large extended family. Paglia called herself a "total phone queen," though her scholarly fanaticism initially made her stingy about personal appearances.

Back then, she explained that she was hard at work revising volume 2 of *Sexual Personae,* which would target pop culture. Paglia adapted an old Brooke Shields advertising line in explaining her life, saying, "Nothing comes between me and my work." But volume 2 never appeared. "I'm a feminist," she said, "but it's a prewar idea of feminism, based on self-reliance, independence and not blaming other people for your problems." Her heroines, she confided, were old "battle-ax academics."

"I have no interest in getting married," she reported matter-of-factly, at the time being cagey about her sexuality—she later came out as gay. "I am just so interested in myself. When I look at other people, it puzzles me. What is it they're doing when they form dyads? Apparently, they need consolation, they need support, they need someone to tell them they're doing fine. They need nurturing. I don't need that."

Nor did she need a backup generator. After hours of Paglia yapping loudly and entertainingly at the Astral Plane restaurant, turning it into a lecture hall with specials, she began to seem more like Ayn Rand at the Improv—a libertarian with a sense of humor. "I think I'm very close to that," she said, with the caveat that she rejected Rand's "humorless" world. "My obligation as a woman," she added, "is to develop my talents to the max, to the utmost. I don't want anyone to waste my time."

Those who watched Paglia's career closely in subsequent years sometimes felt that no one did that to her as much as herself. As her media profile increased, Paglia caught the bug and started to appear more in media (she became a contributing editor at *Interview* magazine) and publish less sustained work. Instead of the second book of *Sexual Personae*, she published two volumes of short pieces, *Sex, Art, and American Culture* and *Vamps and Tramps: New Essays*, and a study of Alfred Hitchcock, *The Birds*. For six years, she took on a column at Salon.com. By the time of *Break, Blow, Burn: Camille Paglia Reads Forty-three of the World's Best Poems* (2005) she was, as that title indicated, attempting to transform herself into a brand. But though her publicist on that book, with its multi-page ruminations on single-page poems, described Paglia as "America's premier intellectual provocateur and cultural critic," there was little evidence that anyone else agreed. By 2010, Paglia had become more selective in her major media appearances, though her voice remained strong. Pooh-poohing, in the *Wall Street Journal*, the possibility of women soon having "a Viagra of their own," Paglia argued that medicine couldn't repair a desexualized modern environment stifled by middle-class values: "Contemporary moms have become virtuoso super-managers of a complex operation focused on the care and transport of children. It's not so easy to snap over from Apollonian control to Dionysian delirium."

Amid all the media air sucked in by Sontag and Paglia, one could argue that the American woman philosopher who'd drawn the short end of the stick—at least in regard to broad societal fame—was Martha Nussbaum (1947–), often and understandably seen within academe as the most prestigious female philosopher in America.

The reputation came from a mix of proximity to power, impressive analytical clarity and nonstop publication. Nussbaum had begun her teaching career in the Harvard philosophy and classics departments in the 1970s and early '80s. After she failed to get tenure in a controversial situation—some felt it reflected personal issues more than scholarly ones, and Nussbaum herself later spoke of a history of "discrimination" and "sexual harassment" in her career at Harvard—she landed at Brown University, and proceeded to publish prominently and often. She built a reputation as both a preeminent classical scholar and pioneer—at least among analytic philosophers—in exploring the virtues of literature for philosophy.

Nussbaum regarded herself as an Aristotelian, a supporter of moral universalism, a firm opponent of various sorts of relativism and a believer in politics as the means by which we create communities whose members can live fulfilled lives. At the core of *The Fragility of Goodness* (1986), her concern with ethics melded with her literary bent to advance the idea that great literary works should be understood as works of moral philosophy. In *Love's Knowledge* (1990), she drew on the Stoics and Epicureans she knew best to argue for a return to respecting emotions as forms of rational insight. (She even accepted the tag of "neo-Stoic" in elaborating that position.)

From that bare description, it might sound as if Nussbaum was headed up the same path as Sontag, with her attention to literature likely to break her out into greater renown in American cultural life. But Nussbaum, as a philosopher, proved to be the anti-Sontag in key respects. Whereas Sontag tried to disabuse others from seeing her as a philosopher (usually unsuccessfully), Nussbaum repeatedly instructed readers, even in passages stressing the way India's teeming humanity had moved her to lifelong engagement with it, that she was one. ("This is a philosophical project," she reminded readers of *Women and Human Development,* moments after explaining her determination to "focus throughout on the case of India," and its aim was "to develop a particular type of normative philosophical theory.")

Whereas Sontag decided to move away from academic models in her life, career, prose and projects, Nussbaum forcefully embraced academic life and writing with extraordinary commitment and energy. Virtually no one appeared on more APA and other academic panels. Virtually no one arranged to give more academic lectures. Virtually no one thanked more fellow academics in her acknowledgments. Virtually no one pumped out more university press books. Virtually no one received more honorary degrees—thirty-three, by 2011, from institutions as far-flung as the University of Haifa and Grinnell College.

Cultivating Humanity: A Classical Defense of Reform in Liberal Education (1997) drew on the critical spirit of Socrates and Seneca, celebrating the new cross-cultural diversity in curricula, faculty and students as a fine step to making graduates well-trained cosmopolitan minds, ready for world citizenship. In *Sex and Social Justice* (1999), Nussbaum began to expound on feminist lessons of her involvement, beginning in 1986, with UN international development work, arguing for a universalist conception of people's needs, abilities and dignity fitted to different cultures around the world, in both developed and developing countries.

A more domestically focused examination of American laws on sex came in *Hiding from Humanity: Disgust, Shame, and the Law* (2004). By then, Nussbaum was the Ernst Freund Distinguished Service Professor of Law and Ethics at the University of Chicago's philosophy department, law school and divinity school. Reacting in part to Supreme Court Justice Antonin Scalia's notion that "disgust" over activities such as same-sex marriage justifies laws against them—a position familiar in Anglo-American jurisprudential literature from Lord Patrick Devlin's advancement of that position when England's Wolfenden Report sought to decriminalize consensual homosexual acts—Nussbaum counterargued that shame and disgust should never drive the criminal law. She maintained that both project an unrealistic view of "human perfection," and stem from "impossible aspirations to purity that are just not in line with human life as we know it."

Three years later, swinging back to her internationalist side, Nussbaum published her most sociological book yet, *The Clash Within: Democracy, Religious Violence, and India's Future* (2007). A study of the Hindu right, it warned of that group's threat to democratic tolerance in India, where she'd done considerable volunteer development work.

Even in her private life, Nussbaum in mid-career kept things on campus, allied to high academic prestige—her politics and social positions reflected full-blown rejection of some of the family values with which she'd grown up. Though born in New York City, Martha Craven had been raised chiefly on Philadelphia's Main Line, amid what she called the "East Coast WASP elite . . . very sterile, very preoccupied with money and status." Her father, George Craven, a Philadelphia lawyer, held conservative and aristocratic beliefs, as well as some racist ones, that she totally repudiated. After attending the Baldwin School in Bryn Mawr, which awakened her interest in acting and literature, she attended and graduated from New York University in 1969 with a BA in theater and classics. Moving on to graduate school at Harvard, she earned a PhD under the classics scholar G. E. L. Owen in 1975. Her marriage to Alan Nussbaum, whom she divorced in 1987, involved conversion to Reform Judaism (she added a bat mitzvah in 2008) and produced her only child, Rachel, a historian.

In the 1980s, she became the partner of the distinguished Harvard and Oxford economist Amartya Sen, a relationship that exerted an enormous effect on her intellectual direction. Later, she formed a multi-year partnership with former University of Chicago legal thinker Cass Sunstein, who became head of President Obama's Office of Information and Regulatory Affairs while on leave from his new professorship at Harvard Law School. That relationship ended, and Sunstein married the author and Harvard human rights professor Samantha Power, who joined President Obama's National Security Council as a key adviser on humanitarian intervention.

Those relationships reflected and doubtless contributed to a further expansion of Nussbaum's academic tilt to the areas of law, politics and social policy. Sen had become known in the 1970s for what was called, in economics, the "capabilities" approach to justice. Instead of focusing, like Rawls and Nozick, on mainly distributional approaches to justice, Sen believed that real-life justice theory required us to look at whether and how social schemes make it possible for real people, especially the most disadvantaged, to live fulfilling lives. Nussbaum found the approach eye-opening. In 1993, Nussbaum coedited with Sen a collection of essays, *The Quality of Life*. By 2000, she was articulating her own version of it in *Women and Human Development: The Capabilities Approach*.

Promising a "much more compendious and scholastic book on capabilities" down the line, she explained that her eight years of going to Helsinki's World Institute for Development Economics Research for a month every summer had "transformed my work, making me aware of urgent problems and convincing me that philosophy had a contribution to make toward their solution." Her feminist articulation of the capabilities approach, she stated at the outset, grew out of the reality that "women in much of the world lack support for fundamental functions of a 'human life,'" and, as a result, "unequal social and political circumstances give women unequal human capabilities." By human capabilities, she meant "what people are actually able to do and to be" in a given society, and she insisted on a Kantian principle of treating each person as an end, not a means for others, and so entitled to a certain threshold level of such capabilities.

As she became involved with real-world workers through participation with Sen in United Nations projects and policy making, her work became less classically philosophical and more sociological and policy oriented. At the same time, Nussbaum expanded her official academic portfolio. At the University of Chicago, her official title became Professor of Philosophy, Law, and Religion. Indeed, when she issued a statement in 2008 explaining why she had turned down offers from Harvard and Brown, her chief reason was that she found Chicago, whose schools operated on one calendar (unlike, for instance, Harvard's), much more conducive to her interdisciplinary teaching, because giving a course "five or more different course numbers" solved all pedagogical problems.

None of that, however, did much for her influence on the broader culture outside academe. Unlike Rorty, Rawls or Danto, she was not identified by the general intellectual public with any signature philosophical ideas or arguments. While one could see that as an asset—Nussbaum had, to her credit, resisted vulgarization of her work—it also meant that few people outside of universities paid much attention to it. Though Nussbaum, like a handful of leading philosophers, got her share of invitations to do "mass-media intellectual writing," notably for the *New Republic* and the *New York Review of Books,* nothing she wrote there, with the exception of a celebrated attack on the opacity of gender theorist Judith Butler, created media heat.

True to her establishment, analytic credentials in philosophy, Nussbaum tended, for better or worse (and usually for both), to write like a computer programmed to argue: there were seven reasons on this side of the matter, eight on the other. While always clear, Nussbaum's writing lacked the flash and overstatement of Paglia, the imaginative daring and lapidary style of Sontag.

That showed in one of her atypical forays into trade publishing, *Poetic Justice: The Literary Imagination and Public Life.* Though Nussbaum had celebrated the blessings of literature in *Love's Knowledge,* *Poetic Justice* marked her first attempt to explain why synergies between law and literature attracted her. She argued that judges and public policy types too often analyzed life in the formal, bloodless style of economists, and that they would do better at "public reasoning" if they approached it as readers do novels, with openness to concrete realities. It was a worthy message, amply elaborated, especially given that judges in contemporary America (following the defeat of Robert Bork as a Supreme Court nominee and stretching to Sonia Sotomayor's need to mute signs of "empathy" in her 2009 hearings) were increasingly expected by congressional officials to claim that they operated, in Chief Justice Roberts's influential metaphor (later violated by him) like "umpires."

Unfortunately, in Nussbaum's book it was also a familiar notion, wanly delivered. Although Nussbaum's heart was always in the right place, and her analysis straightforward and precise, her prose too often plodded along with the verve of a textbook. At one point in *Poetic Justice,* she explained that the novel "constructs a paradigm of a style of ethical reasoning that is context-specific without being relativistic, in which we get potentially universalizable concrete prescriptions by bringing a general idea of human flourishing to bear on a concrete situation which we are invited to enter through the imagination." The motto seemed to be, "Let *Poetic Justice* be done, and bland abstract vocabulary honored, even if the heavens—and everyone else—fall asleep."

In Nussbaum's view, literary imagination amounted to "an essential ingredient" for getting us "to concern ourselves with the good of other people." To show that, she examined Dickens's *Hard Times,* which centers on Thomas Gradgrind, a fanatical utilitarian in the industrial city of Coketown. Gradgrind, a teacher, believes imaginative literature subverts clarity and distracts attention from the facts that allow political economy to capture life's complexities in "tabular form." Accordingly, Gradgrind raises his two children, Louisa and Tom, to reject the imaginative. He manipulates their lives, marrying Louisa off to brother Tom's thirty-year-old boss. Only when his stage managing backfires does Gradgrind realize the distorted nature of his thinking.

In assessing the book, Nussbaum repeatedly abjured any hostility to formalist reasoning. The "literary imagination," she said, "is not meant to displace moral and political theory." Rather, Nussbaum believed that "economic science should be built on data of the sort that novels such as Dickens' reveal to the imagination." Novels reflected people's individuality, the importance of understanding them from within (a point she developed with E. M. Forster's "gay" novel, *Maurice,* and Richard Wright's *Native Son*). Drawing on those insights, and her own acceptance of Stoic tenets along the same line, Nussbaum argued that emotion is a kind of perception or belief and therefore essential to rationality. A person able to think both abstractly and emotionally, she concluded, will come closest to fulfilling the ideal of Adam Smith's "judicious spectator." Such a person would also fulfill Whitman's ideal of the "poet as judge," a second Nussbaum model of the public policy sage who combines abstract reasoning ability and empathetic openness to all.

Oddly, though, given Nussbaum's apotheosis of literature, her lackluster prose ignored the stylistic lessons she insisted on philosophically: the importance of lively, metaphoric detail; the art of making points by telling stories; the power of light, entertaining word choices. Instead, Nussbaum wrote as if ordered to output a starchy, humorless diction. It suggested an academicism so unrelenting that it threatened to suffocate the message it should have propelled.

Every Nussbaum sentence, it sometimes seemed, began, "I shall focus," or "I shall argue," or "I shall emphasize," or "What I am about to say here," or "I have spoken," or "I have said," or "I must now insist again," as if the schoolmarmish signposting that high school English teachers urge on rambling students, dubbed "academic mumblespeak" by one wag, doubled as a prose virtue. (The English critic Geoff Dyer would later excoriate precisely that academic tic, targeting the art historian Michael Fried, in launching his regular column in the *New York Times Book Review*.)

Nussbaum's flat analyses of *Hard Times* sometimes read like parodies by Tom Stoppard or David Lodge: "This story puts before us characters—men and women in some ways like ourselves. It represents these characters as very distinct one from another, endowing them with physical and moral attributes that make it possible for us to distinguish everyone from every other. We are made to attend to their ways of moving and talking, the shapes of their bodies, the expressions on their faces, the sentiments of their hearts. The inner life of each is displayed as having psychological depth and complexity. We see that as humans they share certain common problems and common hope—and yet, as well, that each confronts these in his or her own way, in his or her concrete circumstances with the resources of his or her history."

Nussbaum's message, translated into sweaty Americanese, might have aided readers bamboozled by legal fictions like a judge's supposed ability to operate as mere umpire. But if she hoped to win general readers, she needed to abandon the professorial dialect of her books, and get imaginatively reconnected with American, as opposed to philosophy department, English.

That limp prose frustrated an admirer of her moral choices, for one could only applaud Nussbaum's energetic efforts to ditch the armchair routines of her early training in analytic philosophy to become a philosopher-activist who, as she detailed in *Women and Human Development*, found herself "going around with credit-union collectors in the slums of Kolaba in the hundred-degree heat, visiting a squatters' settlement in Trivandrum in the thick March humidity, seeing the daily operations of the Self-Employed Women's Association (SEWA) bank and union."

Even, however, in a book devoted to such palpable reality, Nussbaum's high-professorial voice endured: "I shall argue that the problem of preference-deformation makes a welfarist approach unacceptable as the basis for a normative theory of political principles; we need a substantive account of central political goods, of the sort the capabilities approach gives us." As recently as her filmed moments in Astra Taylor's ambitious 2008 documentary *Examined Life*, which sought to get philosophers out "in the street" on "excursions" with the filmmaker, Nussbaum, explaining her core ideas during a stroll by the Chicago lakeside, stood her ground about the need for abstract reasoning, however much "we always have to keep testing our abstract theories against the real world."

"Theories of justice," Nussbaum advised, "need to be abstract because if we remain immersed in the prejudices of our immediate time and place, we may create theoretical structures that are unfair to people in other places. So we need to rise above the details of our immediate situation and create theories that have the power to cover many different times and places."

Perhaps. But she seemed not to appreciate that concreteness need not produce unfairness. Didn't enduring literature show that all the time, by expressing universal ideas of love and beauty and goodness through specific characters and events? Asked by the *New York Times* "about the state of ideas in America," Nussbaum had once remarked, "There's just something about our public culture that's not that friendly to philosophy." If that was so, it might have been an American antipathy to philosophy stripped of the imagery that, by contrast, James so colorfully brought to his own writing. Nussbaum paid a price for emulating the bloodless style of her former teacher and colleague Rawls, for Rawlsian abstraction had its limits in an America that demanded facts, vitamins, fireworks and color in its thinky prose. That price was to remain queen of a limited demesne: the minor state known as the Republic of the American Philosophical Association.

Christina Sommers, by contrast, exemplified a principle that illuminated Nussbaum's important but limited role in America the Philosophical: one needed fifteen minutes of fame to smooth the path to years of lesser, but still tangible media attention—one needed the book everyone talked about for a season, the personal controversy that exploded *something*, and especially if you were a woman. It happened for Sommers when the forty-three-year-old associate professor of philosophy at Clark University in Worcester, Massachusetts, published *Who Stole Feminism?: How Women Have Betrayed Women.*

Sommers's views could be thumbnailed easily for the media, though "fingered-in-the-eye" might have been a more appropriate digital metaphor. In her view, most feminist-sponsored research teemed with errors. Those errors crept into textbooks and educational materials with disastrous effect. "Equity feminism," the traditional, sensible proposition that men and women should be treated equally, had been abandoned by too many younger American feminists for "gender feminism," the belief that America's "sex/gender" system still produces massive male domination of women and harmful "male" values such as cruelty and violence, and must be fought at every turn.

For Sommers, radical "gender feminists" wanted to replace the goal of equality between men and women with nutty, gynocentric philosophies tied to far more preferable female characteristics, and tended to revile and punish women who disagreed with them. Such radical gender feminists—targets in the book included Gloria Steinem, Naomi Wolf, Susan Faludi, Marilyn French and Catherine MacKinnon—also self-dramatized themselves, acting as though they were resistance fighters opposing a Holocaust-like tragedy. Sommers argued that they did not remotely represent the views of most American women, but nonetheless claimed significant ground in the academic world. The name-calling began almost immediately.

University of Illinois philosopher Sandra Lee Bartky, an old nemesis, dismissed Sommers as "a right-wing ideologue" who "masquerades as a feminist." Anne Bryant, executive director of the American Association of University Women, a chief Sommers target, saw Sommers's work as "full of hyperbole" and accused her of wanting to be "the Rush Limbaugh of academia." Deirdre English, former editor of *Mother Jones,* charged Sommers with "striking an ostentatiously girlish pose" in her book.

"I must say I was a little taken aback," said Sommers of the salvos that greeted her first book. She pondered them in the downstairs den of the home she shared with her husband, Brandeis University philosopher Fred Sommers, in a Boston suburb. Already packed and ready to hit the airport in an hour for another Washington talk show, she was amiable but focused—a breaking highbrow star, clearly up to the organizational demands of her fifteen minutes.

"Alan Kors [the University of Pennsylvania historian] is a friend of mine," Sommers remarked, "and he said honest feminists will find many good things in this book, and you will get some good reviews from honest feminists. So I thought that, yeah, they might whine about how I characterized the conferences, but they would be impressed with the thoroughness of the research and the exposé."

Instead, Sommers faced a tumultuous entrée into the publishing world, gifted with every first-time author's dream launching pad: a full-scale literary brouhaha. READ THE BOOK THAT SPARKED THE CONTROVERSY! screamed the ad in the *New York Times,* illustrated with reproduced headlines from the *New York Post* ("A P.C. Hatchet Job at the *Times Book Review*"), the *New York Daily News* and the *Washington Post.* The references were to the year's most controversial book review, a slam of *Who Stole Feminism?* in the *Times Book Review* by University of Pennsylvania English professor Nina Auerbach.

Auerbach described Sommers as a "muddled writer" who operated "in a vacuum." Dubbing Sommers "a wallflower at feminist conferences," she added, "In revenge, she attends them obsessively, writes down all the stupid things she hears and now has spewed them back." Auerbach judged Sommers's book "overwrought and underargued," with "a lack of solid research."

It soon emerged, however, that Auerbach, though unnamed in the book, had been a speaker at the City University of New York Graduate Center conference that Sommers ridiculed in the opening chapter of her book. To make matters worse, Auerbach was also the professor in a Penn course described by Sommers on page 237 of *Who Stole Feminism?,* in which Sommers's stepson was chided by his instructor for expressing the opinion that vocational opportunities for women are wider today than they were for Jane Eyre.

Hilton Kramer, the former chief *New York Times* art critic who later founded the *New Criterion,* savaged the review as a "deliberate attempt to annihilate an important new book on feminist politics" because the book was "very much at odds with the *Times'* own political line." Howard Kurtz, at the time media critic of the *Washington Post,* looked into the glaring conflict of interest.

Auerbach acknowledged to him that she was one of the conference speakers whom Sommers depicted as "prone to self-dramatization and chronically offended." She similarly conceded it was probably one of her teaching assistants who upbraided Sommers's stepson. But she still "dismissed Sommers' complaint," according to Kurtz, saying of her presence in the book, "There's nothing even subliminally I could take as me."

Whatever the case, the controversy had the usual effect: talk-show invites, interview requests and extra attention for the book. Most of *Who Stole Feminism?* consisted not of theorizing, but of investigative reporting into feminist research. Sommers attributed the latter's weakness to a mixture of sloppiness, bias and "gender warrior" mentality.

One of Sommers's chief targets was the widely published claim, endorsed in print by both Naomi Wolf and Gloria Steinem, that 150,000 American women died of anorexia nervosa each year. Sommers went back to the National Center for Health Statistics and discovered that the 150,000 figure applied to sufferers of the disease, and that the number of deaths is usually one hundred or fewer.

Another Sommers target was the claim, originally made by the president of the National Women's Studies Association, that, "[a]ccording to the last March of Dimes report, domestic violence (against pregnant women) is now responsible for more birth defects than all other causes combined." Sommers tracked the claim back to the March of Dimes, which denied it. It turned out the master of ceremonies at a nurses' convention had misstated the actual finding in the March of Dimes report—that more women are screened for birth defects than are screened for domestic violence.

In the meantime, the factoid had entered all sorts of government and media publications. Sommers similarly examined and rejected what she found to be false data on date rape, gender bias in education, domestic violence on Super Bowl Sunday (that it spikes 40 percent!) and self-esteem among young women. "I did not know that the information was this unreliable," she said, explaining that the shoddiness of feminist research occupied a larger part of her book than she ever anticipated: "I thought at first that it was a quirk that I found out that the anorexia statistic was wrong. I just knew that it couldn't be 150,000 because I'd always carried around in my head the statistic that it used to be 50,000 dead for car accidents. They taught us that in tenth grade, driver's ed or something. I thought, three more times than car accidents?"

After coming upon the March of Dimes screwup, she continued, "I began to check everything. And in every case that I looked into of women's victimization—of information produced by a feminist research center or a feminist researcher—it was unreliable. It began to be like shooting fish in a barrel."

Still, she started the book as a philosopher, not a would-be Seymour

Hersh. She admitted that a strong ideological agenda also ran through *Who Stole Feminism?* In it, Sommers announced early on that she was "a feminist who does not like what feminism has become." She rejected the vocabulary of women's victimization, and argued that equity feminism was feminism enough for many women—a view her discoveries regarding shoddy feminist research made more palatable.

"I consider myself a whistle-blower," she said. "I'm really trying to draw people's attention to serious corruption in scholarship, in information, in journalism, and also a betrayal of the first principles of feminism—so I give pictures, I give anecdotes. I don't think it takes a treatise to talk about simple principles of equity. They're so familiar."

Asked about the criticism that she did not articulate any overarching philosophy of feminism, she replied, "I don't know that we need feminist theory to explain why constitutional principles of equality and fairness apply to women as well as men." Nor, she believed, was that the only criterion by which to judge someone's feminist credentials. "I'm doing a lot for women," she asserted. "I'm telling the truth about women's research. I think they are doing dreadful things to young women, poisoning their minds, filling them with propaganda, lying with statistics. . . . I think that's the crisis for women in America right now: the epidemic of misinformation."

Auerbach's blast aside, reviews of *Who Stole Feminism?* were mixed, combining respect for Sommers's good points with doubts about the accuracy of her overall view of contemporary feminism. In the *New Republic,* for instance, Jean Elshtain praised Sommers's "journalistic stubbornness" and "energy" but criticized her resistance to any feminism that aspired to more than equity. She found Sommers "trapped in too sharp and severe a contrast between the bad new and the good old." Similarly, in *Newsday* and the *Washington Post,* respectively, feminist authors Susan Jacoby and Deirdre English found merit in Sommers's investigative work but pooh-poohed her alleged view that all important feminist battles have been won.

Though one Toronto critic described Sommers as "a martyr for the neo-con cause," Sommers saw that reaction as sad confirmation of feminism's polarization. In fact, she said, "I only identify with conservatives on certain cultural issues." She mentioned that ultraconservatives told her she wasn't "hard enough," given her admiration of all sorts of activists who do in-the-trenches social work. Sommers ultimately saw herself as "more of a humanist, I suppose, than a feminist. I don't consider being a woman being a member of a group, or a tribe or a class." If her beliefs in freedom of speech and high scholarly standards were "right-wing" ideas, she said, "I find that hard to understand, and very disorienting politically."

Indeed, Sommers's background seemed less than ideal for a potential Valkyrie of the right. Her mother had been a classic ACLU liberal. As a high school student in Los Angeles, Sommers protested against the Vietnam War, hung out at UCLA with Students for a Democratic Society, and palled around with Miriam Simos, who later became the "witch" Starhawk, a decidedly nonconservative thinker. As an undergraduate at New York University, Sommers spent her junior year in Paris and attended the lectures of the anti-establishment philosopher Michel Foucault, whose work Sommers (unlike Paglia) still respected.

As a PhD student at Brandeis in the 1970s, she worked on animal rights. It was only later, she explains, after venturing out of her own area to present a philosophical paper on the family, that she noticed "gender feminists" reacting like members of a sect rather than as philosophers. So she began to dig into feminist literature.

"The problem," said Fred Sommers, dropping by the conversation for a moment, "is that Christina is being pulled over to the right because the center's not there. I don't know where the center is." A logician with a genial manner, he found the intensity of his wife's feminist opponents disturbing. "I worry about her," he said. "She attracts so much hostility from these women. She's under strain and pressure. As she put it someplace, they're in 'constant agitated communication.' You can watch the e-mails, the bulletin boards. . . . But she stands up very well under it."

That she did. Exuding the snap and efficiency of a Manhattan businesswoman, Sommers was no slouch herself in the sarcasm department. She let a visitor know she was happy to debate one and all: "Anybody can come, they can bring placards, I have no rules. They can hiss, which they like to do. Although I've heard that that marginalizes people with lisps, so they're not hissing anymore."

Sommers's controversy highlighted yet another dimension of how women affected America the Philosophical: they brought not just themselves and their alternate physiology to philosophical concerns, but fresh topics—different emphases on which concepts matter in life and which don't. Like white male thinkers outside philosophy and African American thinkers both in and out of the field, women thinkers outside of philosophy "proper," feminist and not-so-self-defined, made America a philosophical hotspot by zeroing in on ideas that epistemologically obsessed white male philosophy professors largely ignored.

One example of that was the concept of beauty, which by the late twentieth century had fallen on hard times despite being the junior member of a threesome—with Truth and Goodness—that boasted a rather hallowed philosophical history. In an early, little-known dialogue entitled "Greater Hippias," Plato assigned Socrates—his mentor, literary protagonist and sometime mouthpiece—the task of harassing the pompous thinker of the title. By the end, Hippias grudgingly acknowledged that while we apply the term "beautiful" to objects as different as a person, a horse and a pot, we can't easily articulate what quality such objects hold in common. The best we can do, Socrates concluded, is concede that beauty is a "difficult" concept to grasp.

Normally, one Platonic dialogue sufficed to launch a concept into philosophical orbit, guaranteeing scrutiny for centuries. But the founder of post-Socratic thought also gave a leading role to beauty in his masterpiece, "Symposium," and riffed about it in "Phaedrus," "Philebus," "Gorgias," "Lysis" and "Republic." With that kind of send-off, the junior member of the threesome received almost as much attention from serious thinkers, for nearly two millennia, as its senior partners. Aristotle identified beauty with order, symmetry and definiteness. Plotinus regarded it as an ideal, beyond sense perception. Augustine saw beauty as regularity and simplicity. Aquinas defined it as "that which pleases upon being seen," because of its perfection, proportion, and clarity.

Then something happened during the seventeenth century, a conceptual turn in Western culture: people started to view beauty as subjective rather than objective. The English poet Thomas Overbury foreshadowed the fragile, relativist intuition when he tossed out a familiar phrase and thought in a poem, circa 1613: "All the carnall beauty of my wife / Is but skin-deep." Frances Hutcheson's influential 1725 treatise on beauty noted that "the word beauty is taken for the idea raised in us." By later in the eighteenth century, Voltaire, in his *Philosophical Dictionary,* could laughingly pass along the tale of a thinker who, having discovered that the English, French and others disagreed about the beautiful, saved himself the trouble of composing a treatise on beauty.

From that point on, despite influential works by major figures such as Kant and Santayana, and an ebb and flow of studies about beauty, the subject failed to recover its central importance to intellectuals. Until, it seemed, a flurry of books that began with Naomi Wolf's popular success, *The Beauty Myth*, and continued through such academic studies as Francette Pacteau's *The Symptom of Beauty*, James McAllister's *Beauty and Revolution in Science*, Eddy Zemach's *Real Beauty* and *Uncontrollable Beauty*, a lively anthology of articles by artists, critics and philosophers that drew attention to the topic in the context of visual art and won attention from the *New York Times*. The *Chronicle of Higher Education* reported that thinkers across disciplines increasingly saw "beauty" as a crucial notion in the age of multicultural questioning of standards and tastes, rather than a musty one irrelevant to twentieth-century sensibility.

One book that formed a kind of bridge between the feminist concerns raised by Wolf and questioned by Sommers, and the historic question of personal beauty, was Ellen Zetzel Lambert's *The Face of Love: Feminism and the Beauty Question*. Did beauty matter? For Lambert, then a fifty-five-year-old child of the feminist '60s and English teacher at Manhattan's tony Dalton School, the answer seemed clear.

"As a committed feminist," she wrote in the preface to her idiosyncratic and alluring book, "I've felt embarrassed that the beauty question *should* still matter to me. For we have thought and I have believed that women's traditional concern for their appearances was a part, and perhaps the most pernicious part, of the patriarchal legacy that demanded a subordination of her own self to masculine imperatives."

Far from being an issue women should ponder, the beauty question, for most of Lambert's adult life, was a "man's question," best seen as "one of the ways in which men have forced women to define themselves in terms of their desirability to others." *The Face of Love* marked Lambert's abandonment of that position, her recognition that some feminists "have shortchanged or oversimplified the question of appearances, and made taboo an issue that deserves to be explored in an open, nonjudgmental context." If sex was okay for feminist discussion, Lambert pointed out, why not beauty?

Moved by the trauma of her own mastectomy, broadened by her kinship with eighteenth- and nineteenth-century women novelists, put on notice by the odd fascination she felt for photo albums that recorded her youth, Lambert made palpable and moving to readers what she plainly experienced as a middle-aged woman: a secular revelation that beauty is very deep indeed, as deep as we're capable of making it. *The Face of Love*—a wonderful phrase for the notion of beauty Lambert slowly unfolded—began with Lambert's reflection on photos of her as a little girl, a child whose dark-haired beauty seemed to disappear after her mother died of cancer two months before her seventh birthday.

As she approached adolescence, Lambert felt ugly: "My face was too thin, my eyes too close together, my nose too long, my breasts (when they came) too small, my hips too large." Only later, when she became a mother herself, did she understand her self-image at that time: "[H]ow could the very features of my face not look 'wrong' when, in the most fundamental way possible, my whole life had gone wrong?" For the adult Lambert—writer, literary critic, survivor of mastectomy—that early attitude expressed a truth that much else corroborated. The importance of one's appearance had to be defended, she believed, "not as an appendage to the self, but as the very expression of the self—a self informed by the knowledge of its essential lovability."

The idea of beauty as "the face of love," she acknowledged, originally came to her as a misremembered line from Castiglione's classic, *The Book of the Courtier*, in which wise Bembo defends a version of Plato's connection between outer beauty and inner virtue. Lambert, unabashedly, interpreted the concept her way. To see "beauty as the face of love," she wrote, was "to affirm that the beautiful face is the one itself informed, or animated, by love." The face of love "is the face of one who loves. We need not, then, wait upon the lover to pronounce our beauty; we are, so to speak, the custodians of our own beauty, as our appearance (whether or not anyone is there to see it) is the expression of our identity."

Lambert, a sophisticated Bryn Mawr College graduate, Class of '62, understood the tradition within feminism she was pushing against in embracing concern with beauty and appearance as a potentially uplifting experience for a woman. Mary Wollstonecraft, the pioneering British feminist, had written in the late eighteenth century, "Taught from infancy that beauty is woman's sceptre, the mind shapes itself to the body, and, roaming round its gilt cage, only seeks to adorn its prison." Two centuries later, Lambert conceded, her own contemporary Susan Brownmiller had reiterated the protest against women's concern for appearance: "Appearance, not accomplishment, is the feminine demonstration of desirability and worth. . . . Because she is forced to concentrate on the minutiae of her bodily parts, a woman is never free of self-consciousness. She is never quite satisfied, and never secure, for desperate, unending absorption in the drive for a perfect appearance—call it feminine vanity—is the ultimate restriction on freedom of mind."

Lambert, however, ably insisted—in a voice of warm solidarity rather than ideological condescension—that beauty mattered "*precisely as a feminist issue.*" It was, she argued, "a very basic need for an adult, as for a child, to be loved *in the body,* and as feminists we are mistaken to deny the validity of that need." Thus she saw feminist scholar Carolyn Heilbrun's counsel to older women, in *Writing a Woman's Life,* "to ignore one's appearance and reach out, as it were, from behind it to attract and spellbind," as defeatist rather than wise. Better, Lambert suggested, to "redefine appearances" so women could speak to the world "*through* our bodies rather than from 'behind' them."

Lambert's greatest feat in *The Face of Love,* however, was her ability to make those overarching themes compelling and concrete. In a chapter entitled "The Woman of Parts," Lambert skillfully analyzed the literary conceit of a beautiful woman as a combination of ideal parts, a notion most stark in Orlando's description of Rosalind in Shakespeare's *As You Like It* ("Helen's cheek, but not her heart / Cleopatra's majesty / Atalanta's better part"). Lambert found many examples to ponder, from Samuel Richardson's *Clarissa* to Paddy Chayefsky's *Marty,* and her graceful interpretations of heroine portraiture set the stage for her book's finest sections.

The first of those was her articulation, over several chapters, of how England's great women novelists of the nineteenth century understood beauty in their own lives, and in those of their leading characters. Lambert's probes into such overly analyzed figures as Jane Austen's Anne Elliot in *Persuasion,* and Charlotte Brontë's Jane Eyre, and into such real-life drama as Elizabeth Gaskill's empathy for Brontë, yielded new insights. Lambert's second triumph came immediately afterward, as she shifted from literature to what she called "Two Mastectomy Narratives."

The first was the riveting story of how the novelist Fanny Burney, in her late fifties, underwent the surgical excision of her right breast in 1811 without anesthesia, an ordeal described in a long letter by the writer. The other was Lambert's own memoir. Together, they gave a different tilt to that inevitable mention in Western treatises on beauty, Lambert noted, of the painter Zeuxis, "who selected the best features of five different maidens of his native Croton as models for his painting of Helen of Troy." Woman—just the sum of her parts.

If Lambert's brief against such people chopping reevaluated the venerable notion of personal beauty from a stance of richly rethought feminism—showing how the activity of women in America the Philosophical made a difference not just to topics, but to approaches—Harvard psychologist Nancy Etcoff brilliantly illuminated the subject from another, flintier perch of modernity in *Survival of the Prettiest.*

Who could be surprised that women of vastly different intellectual stripes, forced to grapple with beauty's enormous role in their lives, might want to think about it more than men? Etcoff's book jacket boasted the only blurb ever seen on a scientific tome by model Cindy Crawford (a former valedictorian, mind you): "Although I did not enjoy being called a 'genetic freak,' I did find Nancy Etcoff's book thought-provoking and a good read—yes, we can read too."

According to Etcoff, the most unerring clue to the victor in a presidential election for the past one hundred years has been the candidate's greater height. She could cite survey after survey showing that prettier people were "more likely to get hired," more likely to be given generous personal space in public encounters, more likely to be treated altruistically by others. In that respect, Etcoff reported, "good-looking adults are more likely to get away with anything from shoplifting to cheating on exams to committing serious crimes," for while people say "pretty is as pretty does," she added, "what pretty does is often seen in a forgiving light." *Survival of the Prettiest* proved a smart, snappy brief for how modern science, especially fashionable evolutionary psychology, explained virtually all our psychological behavior in regard to beauty.

Etcoff's book grew out of the author's research on how the brain responds to beauty. A first task was to confront the notion, common in late-twentieth-century Western culture, that beauty is relative, "in the eye of the beholder." The chief popularizer of that idea in middlebrow American culture, according to Etcoff, was Wolf in *The Beauty Myth*. Wolf had argued, Etcoff wrote, that "beauty as an objective and universal entity does not exist," but is simply "a convenient fiction used by multibillion-dollar industries that create images of beauty and peddle them as opium for the female masses."

Etcoff's other goal was mainly methodological: to take a concept pondered more by philosophers and poets than by scientists or social scientists (though somewhat abandoned even by the former crew in this century) and bring cognitive psychology and the social sciences to bear on it. "The politics of beauty needs a fresh forum," wrote Etcoff, "free from the attacks of the beauty bashers, as well as the unthinking reverence of beauty worshipers. . . . The idea that beauty is unimportant or a cultural construct is the real beauty myth." Some intellectuals might disdain beauty, she added, but "nobody has stopped looking at it, and no one has stopped enjoying the sight."

Etcoff combined a chatty style and heavy-duty delivery of research findings. She saw "a core reality to beauty that exists buried within the cultural constructs and the myths. All cultures are beauty cultures, and everywhere beauty has been a powerful and subversive force, provoking emotion, riveting attention, and directing action." That belief helped Etcoff finesse the traditional uncertainty among aestheticians over whether beauty is intrinsic to an object, explicable in the mathematical ratios or definitions of symmetry that fascinated classical and Renaissance writers on the concept, or, rather, "the pleasure an object evokes in the beholder," the more recent view.

It also gave her a handle on the tricky issue of whether beauty rests on universal perceptual norms, or culturally variant ones. Etcoff gladly acknowledged that "our bodies reflect not only Darwinian forces which impel us to reproduce, but cultural ones, and social ones." She recalled how colleagues informed Darwin that the Chinese found prominent Western noses "hideous," and the first samurai sent to the United States after centuries of isolation expressed dismay that Western women had "dogs' eyes."

Regardless of how nature/nurture debates turned out, Etcoff contended, the important point established by modern science was that our bodies respond to beauty "viscerally," a truth corroborated by the way "our names for beauty are synonymous with physical cataclysms and bodily obliteration—breathtaking, *femme fatale*, knockout, drop-dead gorgeous, bombshell, stunner, and ravishing. We experience beauty not as rational contemplation, but as a response to physical urgency." Etcoff's initial agenda was statistical and anecdotal, to drive home beauty's impact on our lives. She cited the reported 696,904 Americans who underwent voluntary aesthetic surgery in a recent year, the 1,484 tubes of lipstick sold every minute in America, the prime regret once expressed by Eleanor Roosevelt—she would have liked to be prettier.

More significant for Etcoff, however, was elaborating evolutionary biology's belief that human beauty "may be in the adaptations of the beholder." Biologists, she wrote, "argue that at root the quest for beauty is driven by the genes pressing to be passed on and making their habitat as inviting for visitors as possible." So her book teemed with evolutionary explanations for what strikes us as beautiful: for instance, the way good skin indicates the potential mate's freedom from debilitating diseases and parasites. Drawing on her own research, Etcoff asserted that "detection for beauty is hard-wired, governed by circuits created by natural selection," and so "beauty's frisson is demonstrated in the brain—arousal and riveted attention are detected in our electrophysiology as we gaze at a beautiful woman."

With that kind of confidence, *Survival of the Prettiest* regularly threw one-two punches at the reader like: "Even in the animal world females can be lured by males with big gifts and good territories. Female scorpionflies will not even look at a male unless his gift, a tasty bit of insect protein, is at least sixteen square millimeters." Or: "Females prefer flamboyance to subtlety. Female swordtail fish like males with long swords (colored extensions of the caudal fins), female swallows and widowbirds prefer males with long tails, and so on."

Of course, not every Etcoff extrapolation from creepy, crawly, buzzy creatures to "us" came over well. Female scorpionflies, unlike Mimi in *La Bohème* and her many kindred spirits, probably couldn't articulate the romantic and sexual appeal of the impoverished artistic male. Nor could Amy Winehouse–like swallows and widowbirds explain why Alanis Morissette–like human females might prefer folkie mates with subtle tails—or just torn jeans and flannel shirts. The existence of such preferences among female humans suggested that species-to-species analogies could be simplistic, especially in estimating the intellectual element in human judgments of beauty. Evolutionary biologists explained such data in only one way—as a survival instinct.

The bulk of *Survival of the Prettiest,* however, and its gorgeous batch of data, permitted an overview of human attractiveness as well as the concept of beauty itself. Etcoff inspected smooth skin, underarm hair, makeup, symmetrical features, body odor, moles, fetishism over blondes, genitalia, breasts, pecs, high fashion (it "increases our mate value"), high heels, "lookism" as a kind of discrimination, and the beauty instincts of infants. Along the way, she also insightfully discussed the physics and mathematics of beauty—that oddity of intellectual history that led St. Augustine to declare equilateral triangles more beautiful than scalene ones, and later thinkers to determine that beauty required "that the height of the ear and the nose be equal, that the distance between the eyes equal the width of the nose, that the width of the mouth be one and a half times as wide as the nose, and that the inclination of the nose bridge parallel the axis of the ear." Etcoff, remarking that "the passion to quantify beauty is not easily quelled," concluded that scientists today believe no math formula "captures the beauty of the human face as a whole."

Somehow, Spinoza, Kant, and John Stuart Mill never got around to the topic in such exquisite detail. In her enthusiasm over beauty, Etcoff suggested that concepts considered crucial by women thinkers might catch on more broadly as objects of philosophical thought, that the

twists women thinkers could bring to subjects formerly dominated by
men demanded attention. One salient example in political theory was
Jean Bethke Elshtain, who marched to a different drummer than many
in her field.

An ethics professor at the University of Chicago who grew up in a small
Colorado town, Elshtain achieved escape velocity from the nether-
sphere of secondary academics through bold books (*Women and War;
Public Man, Private Woman*). They reexamined ossified issues in politi-
cal thought as her energetic criticism for opinion journals (notably the
New Republic) avoided the crayon appeal of primary ideological colors.

In one of those books, *Democracy on Trial*, Elshtain warned that our
own system was in danger, and not because one party was always in and
the other supposedly out of the electorate's good graces. It was, pure and
simple, because we were getting too hostile toward one another.

"We citizens of the United States," Elshtain wrote in her preface,
"are told by the young and the angry and the old, who should know better, that it is no longer possible for us to speak to one another; that we,
quite literally, inhabit our own little islands of bristling difference where
we comport with those just like ourselves: no outsiders are welcome."
Whether it was radicals on both sides of abortion who demonized their
opponents, or Young Turk party hacks in both major parties committed
to the politics of hate, Elshtain saw a separatist virus infecting American
democracy even before Barack Obama tried to squelch it.

"It is not," she suggested, "political rebellion, but what Nietzsche
might have considered the pernicious corrosion of resentment. . . . The
language of opposition now appears as a cascading series of manifestos
that tell us we cannot live together; we cannot work together; we are not
in this together; we are not Americans who have something in common,
but racial, ethnic, gender, or sexually identified clans who demand to be
'recognized' only or exclusively as 'different.'"

In opposing further atomization, Elshtain stressed Tocqueville's
belief that democracy couldn't flourish if it existed only on paper.
Democracy, she reminded, "requires laws, constitutions, and authoritative institutions . . . but it also depends on what might be called democratic dispositions. These include a preparedness to work with others
different from oneself toward shared ends; a combination of strong
convictions with a readiness to compromise in the recognition that one
can't always get everything one wants; and a sense of individuality and a

commitment to civic goods that are not the possession of one person or of one group alone."

True to her reputation as a thinker resistant to shibboleths from right or left, Elshtain found that a mix of dogmatism and inconsistency pervaded the political landscape. She remarked on "the irony of liberals seeking ways to tame the logic of the market in economic life even as they celebrate a nearly untrammeled laissez-faire in cultural and sexual life." But she also tweaked conservatives who "argue for constraints and controls in the cultural and sexual sphere but embrace a nearly unconstrained market."

Most often, Elshtain sided with antigovernment sentiment, criticizing welfare programs, special-interest campaigns that translated "wants" into "rights" (thus spurring resentment), judicial preemption of citizens' prerogatives and utopian engineering of any variety (though primarily "the Marxist dream that one glorious day politics will come to an end, absorbed into administration in the classless society").

In urging us to abandon the nastiness she saw in so much political debate, Elshtain commented on everyday policy issues from gay rights to educational standards to protections for battered women. Her aim, however, was not so much to lobby for specific policies as to push good, civic-minded "individualism" over "bad individualism," to promote the spirit of "solidarity" that the Vatican preached over cynical "egoism." As Elshtain crisply put it, "compromise is not a mediocre way to do politics." She endorsed the centrality of deliberation to democracy advanced by such other academic theorists as James Fishkin, Michael Walzer and Michael Sandel, as well as the desire for a renewed sense of civic "community" that united many contemporary political thinkers.

To achieve such goals, Elshtain argued, we needed to avoid collapsing the distinction between the "public" and "private" in modern life. Americans had to end the "politics of displacement" by which "private identity takes precedence over public ends or purposes." In such a situation, one's "private identity becomes who and what one is in public, and public life is about confirming that identity. The citizen gives way before the aggrieved member of a self-defined or contained group."

The result was that every aspect of one's identity turned into a public assertion of "right" and created "a world of triumphalist I's," caring only about themselves. Faced with the 1970s feminist slogan "The personal is political," Elshtain preferred novelist Milan Kundera's view that anyone "who was the same in both public and intimate life would be a monster."

If *Democracy on Trial* ended up more *cri de coeur* than scholarly masterwork, Elshtain still counted as a fine counterweight to the phalanxes of male political philosophers who had long dominated the subject. Her treasured staple of American political mythology—the friendly good-will of the traditional town meeting—indicated that she, like other women thinkers, built bridges to male-dominated traditions of American philosophy as much as they challenged them. And no one woman philosopher—or group of women philosophers—illustrated that truth more than the African American women philosophers who came together in October 2008 as never before. It happened in Nashville.

Participants had journeyed from all over to get to Vanderbilt University's Bishop Joseph Johnson Black Cultural Center, a comfortable place that typically brought African Americans together to talk about things white colleagues might also find interesting. Qrescent Mali Mason, a third-year grad student in philosophy at Temple University, had snared a $138 discount fare and made it down to the "Athens of the South" (which features, in the downtown area, its own full-scale Parthenon). Lina Buffington, who earned her PhD in philosophy at Emory University and then went to work for a nonprofit, came to give a talk on how she applied her research on philosophers Wilhelm Dilthey, Jean-Paul Sartre and John Dewey to help young blacks stay in college. Jameliah Shorter, a sophomore philosophy and religion major at Paine College in Augusta, Georgia, asked her mother to drive her eight hours through rough mountain roads to attend.

And Joyce Mitchell Cook—well, what would it have been without her? A 1955 Bryn Mawr grad and the first African American woman to earn a PhD in philosophy (Yale, 1965), Cook basked in the warmth of younger women who wouldn't have to face all the obstacles she did, such as whole rooms of Yale's main library she wasn't allowed to enter.

None of them wanted to miss the inaugural meeting of the Collegium of Black Women Philosophers—the first academic conference of black women in the sole humanities discipline that has been, according to white Vanderbilt philosophy professor Kelly Oliver, "the most resistant to opening itself not only to women and philosophers of color, but also to issues of race and gender."

"It's extraordinary to be here," keynoter Anita Allen, distinguished professor of philosophy and law at the University of Pennsylvania, told the audience, "because it is an extraordinary event. I couldn't have imagined it five years ago."

"This is historic," agreed Lucius Outlaw, professor of philosophy and associate provost at Vanderbilt, who urged the women to "keep on keepin' on."

The Collegium's prime mover was Kathryn T. Gines, an assistant professor of Africana and diaspora studies at Vanderbilt with a secondary appointment in philosophy. A graduate of Atlanta's historic Spelman College, the liberal arts school that produced more black women who have earned a PhD in philosophy than anyplace else, Gines said, apropos of founding the Collegium, that one "motivation was just identifying how many other black women are out there." But she also wanted to have "a network among us, so that we can mentor and support one another."

You could understand why. The American Philosophical Association, based at the University of Delaware in Newark, comprised about eleven thousand members, most of them philosophy professors or grad students, but it did not count how many members were women or from particular ethnicities. Gines, who launched the Collegium by shooting off hundreds of e-mails, identified only twenty-nine black women philosophy professors in the United States. An hour after the conference began at nine a.m. on a Friday, almost all were present, part of an unprecedented, for philosophy, reverse-mirror audience—forty-one black women, three black men, and one white male (an Italian-surnamed reporter of philosophy events, scribbling numbers and other observations into his notebook).

In welcoming black woman philosophers from around the country, Gines mixed her thanks for the Collegium's sponsors—which included the barely represented Vanderbilt philosophy department (apart from workshop presenters Oliver and José Medina)—with an explanation that she meant the conference to be "not just a reaction" to the painfully low number of black women in the discipline, but "a positive place." And it was. A positively eye-opening place. Could you wonder why Jacqueline Scott, a recently tenured Spelman alumna at Chicago's Loyola University, recalled that she'd asked herself when she entered graduate school, "What am I doing in this field?"

The balance shifted at times over the two days. One professor later on opening day brought a mix of black and white students. A couple of white grad students and junior faculty and the chair of the philosophy department (which cosponsored the event) showed up for Anita Allen's keynote speech. But several senior white male philosophy professors never came. Asked why, Oliver, who attended multiple sessions and co-conducted a workshop for the Collegium, replied, "That's a good question."

"Historically, philosophy has primarily been the domain of white men," Oliver commented, as well as an enterprise that sees itself as "trying to discern what is universal about experience. "Ironically," she continued, white males "have usually bracketed out consideration of race and gender and taken their perspectives unwittingly as universals." But, she pointed out, "those so-called universal perspectives haven't been universal at all. They've just been disguised white male privileged perspectives" that leave little room for other viewpoints. Oliver also thought market pressures such as multiculturalism had made philosophers "more protective and defensive," inclined "to make a kind of suicidal stance by entrenching what they take to be their standards and universals, rather than opening up to others and speaking to a larger kind of public."

In the Collegium's eight papers and addresses, one could see how black female perspectives shook up conventional notions even when some presenters analyzed standard figures and texts and adopted opaque vocabularies. Several rocked the room with high theory, stark relevance and laughs born of solidarity, a mix one rarely saw at mainstream philosophy sessions.

Scott, a Nietzsche scholar, launched things with an examination of her German thinker's "thin" notion of race in "The Price of the Ticket: A Genealogy and Revaluation of Race." It set off two days of feisty back-and-forth that often touched on her introspective graduate school query about whether she belonged in the field, one it seemed almost everyone in the room had asked herself. Their answers differed. Some emphasized mastering the discipline and its tradition. Others acknowledged that they deferred to that tradition in not always comfortable ways. But a critical mass plainly aimed to alter the subject's ossified corpus, its hermetic irrelevance to much contemporary intellectual life, its bad faith in remaining a largely whites-only field.

Scott immediately galvanized the room by linking Nietzsche—a thinker enthusiastically studied by the minority of philosophers who teach continental philosophy but largely ignored by the field's pseudo-scientific analytic epistemologists—to two black writers white philosophers hardly ever discuss, W. E. B. Du Bois and James Baldwin. Provocatively, Scott maintained that many theorists of color wanted to eliminate "race" as a category. She, by contrast, urged them not to "throw the baby out with the bathwater." Rather, she suggested they try on Nietzsche's "thin" and "multifarious" view of race, which avoided antiquated biological rigidities and held that, she explained, "[w]e are all contaminated. We are all of mixed race."

Reactions came fast when she finished. Wasn't a thicker view of race the fault of "sick people" who had instituted the "one drop" theory for blacks? Why did some blacks attack Tiger Woods for describing himself as "multiethnic"? A questioner suggested that a "thinner" view of race could allow "blackness" to "cover more territory." Allen, the University of Pennsylvania professor of philosophy and law, wondered how "thinned out" blacks who accepted "dynamic, malleable, artistic notions of race" would deal with racial slurs.

Scott's paper resembled a mainstream philosophy talk in a number of respects. She, like others present, had unquestionably internalized some norms of the discipline. Her paper dealt with a great white male figure in the canon. Her presentation kept, stylistically, to convention—no laptop to be fiddled with, no PowerPoint outlines, no background poster of Friedrich for scenery. Visuals at a philosophy conference? Not a chance. Black woman philosophers, like the rest, walked up to a lectern and talked.

But in other key ways, Scott's session felt different. Philosophy, as Scott remarked, "often doesn't do a good job of engaging the real world." Here, though, people kept offering examples, such as Woods, from that world. Another difference: laughter kept breaking out, as when one commentator sternly observed of racists, "It's them who need to thin out!"

Later papers also demonstrated, sometimes with extraordinary force, the fresh light shone on topics by speakers other than what Donna-Dale Marcano, an assistant professor of philosophy at Trinity College, called the "white young boys" who populate philosophy. Sybol Cook Anderson, an assistant professor of philosophy at St. Mary's College of Maryland who, at age forty-two, earned her PhD in philosophy at Johns Hopkins with a dissertation on Hegel's theory of recognition, riveted listeners with her struggle to understand a classic philosopher who would have viewed her as doubly inferior for being both black and a woman. (Among Hegel's helpful views in this area: the difference between men and women is like the difference between animals and plants, and non-Europeans can't rise to the same level of "spirit" as Europeans.) She explored how she "confronted" Hegel's racism without "excusing it."

"What can a racist and sexist have to say to us about difference?" Anderson asked. Much, she thought, though she'd accepted that Hegel's worst writings were not a matter of his having "a bad day." For Anderson, "We don't have to be stopped by Hegel when we can use Hegel to correct Hegel."

Yet it was Marcano, in her "Re-Reading Plato's Symposium Through the Lens of a Black Woman," who most electrifyingly stirred two opposed impulses in the auditorium: a bent for natural, no-holds-barred talk in the vernacular, versus a sense of traditional philosophy's propriety, its dignity, what you might even call its noncorporeal decorum and chastity.

Stating that a black woman might be conventionally viewed as "least likely to be considered the conveyor of philosophical wisdom," she likened the black woman to, in Plato's famous dialogue, Alcibiades, the dashingly handsome political leader who admits in *Symposium* to a failed attempt to seduce Socrates. According to Marcano, Alcibiades challenged the traditional white male philosopher's reverence for Socrates, the endless questioner and pursuer of abstract and eternal truths "who never reveals himself" and "refuses to be human." In elaborating on what she meant, Marcano got personal. From her earliest days as a student, she confided, philosophy aroused her physically.

"I blushed like someone was whispering sweet nothings in my ear," Marcano exclaimed to oohs and aahs, and a few looks of disapproval. "I really thought I was having an orgasm. I was in heat." But academic philosophy, in its relation to black women, "refuses to know us as its lover." Stay in the field long enough, Marcano warned, and "somehow your body drops out."

That's why, she continued, as both laughs and head shaking grew, she saw Plato's *Symposium* not as an apotheosis of Plato the thinker over Alcibiades the sensualist, but as a dialogue that forces the reader to confront different activities in life, and perhaps choose allegiances. Reading *Symposium* properly, Marcano advised, meant "removing the glasses where Socrates is already the hero"—questioning whether Alcibiades, rather than Socrates, might be the hero of the tale. Marcano contended that black women, in the manner of Alcibiades, should barge into philosophy "raucous, loud, and drunk, with wine and eros, so that our presence can never be suppressed."

The mix of reactions, like the wide assortment of voices and approaches at the Collegium, undermined any notion that black women in philosophy spoke monolithically. Wasn't Marcano self-defeatingly projecting images of black female sexuality at odds with the event's cerebral ethos? Or was she seeing elephants in a room where Socrates could see only capital *L* Love? The diverse responses to Marcano's talk also raised the issue implied in the title of Scott's paper: What was "the price of the ticket" for black women winning their place in philosophy?

Would they also have to adopt the worst artificial language games of the mainstream discipline—the hesitant, Anglophilic diction ("I think, perhaps, that what I want to say here is . . .") aimed at implying that one studied at both Oxford or Cambridge, and is terribly thoughtful? Or the opaque jargon, the pathetic ventriloquism, that always demanded an authoritative citation instead of straight talk? The Collegium offered moments of such fealty to tradition, too. One speaker stated, apropos of a late French "master of thought," that "Lévinas has the best articulation of an alterity that gets to be an alterity"—a thought cryptic enough to leave many uncertain of the claim.

Outside the formal sessions, amid occasionally depressing war stories—Blanche Curry of Fayetteville State cited a student who remarked to her, "This was a real good class. Who wrote the syllabus?"—almost everyone lauded the University of Memphis graduate program long led by professor Robert Bernasconi as the country's best at helping to make philosophy diverse. Before moving on to Penn State, Bernasconi had visited historically black colleges like Spelman to recruit black women into graduate study of philosophy at Memphis. One result: Memphis had awarded five philosophy PhDs to black women since 2003, and seven more women were currently in the program. Other proactive schools included Temple, where black philosophers Lewis Gordon and Paul Taylor, before he moved to Penn State, had put out a welcome mat. Qrescent Mali Mason, also a Spelman alum, knew about that. After accepting her, Gordon invited Mason to visit Temple at the school's expense. He took her out to lunch, introduced her to people in the department. "The sense was," Mason recalled, "we want you here . . . we want to build the kind of department that supports black people." Was the Collegium worth the trip? Said Mason, "It definitely has alleviated that feeling of, 'When I get out, is anyone going to want me? Am I just going to have this PhD and not be able to do anything with it?'"

At the close of the conference, Gines declared an open-mike session and invited participants to share their thoughts about how to institutionalize the gains of their first meeting. "We've got to write ourselves into the discourse," Marcano remarked. "Someone will find us." Good cheer ruled. After Lucius Outlaw spoke, Gines remarked, "I have a slight hesitation about giving a man the last word at this conference, so if anyone has something, even for thirty seconds . . ."

They did. For far more than thirty seconds. Scott raised the idea of having the Collegium regularly in different cities. "I love the notion of Paris," she announced with a big smile, making plain that the Collegium's tug-of-war between tradition and a bold new path would continue. And Allen's sum up stirred laughs: "If forty white men can start the APA, then twenty-nine black women can start this."

Talking about her career in the beautifully appointed University of Pennsylvania office that marked her status as Henry R. Silverman Professor of Law and Philosophy, Allen set out the not-so-funny realities of a black woman's path in philosophy. She recalled an extraordinary remark made by one of her white male University of Michigan philoso-

Anita Allen (1953–), one of the few African American women in academic philosophy, became a professor of law and philosophy at the University of Pennsylvania and supported the efforts of younger black women philosophers to organize within the field.

phy professors in the 1970s when she was in graduate school seeking a PhD in philosophy. At the time, the field lacked a single black woman professor.

" 'Anita,' he told me," Allen recalled between the good-natured laughs that punctuated the seriousness of what she was saying, " 'you will have to pee on the floor of the American Philosophical Association convention to not get a job in philosophy.' "

Was she offended?

"I thought," she continued, "well, maybe they're right." The notion helped ease her growing concern—the same sort Jacqueline Scott had alluded to—that she might be heading up an impossible path. Now, in contrast, she radiated the confidence you'd expect from someone many peers considered the most prominent black woman philosophy professor in the country, as well as one of the nation's top law professors.

A nationally known thinker on privacy and ethics who earned her Harvard law degree five years after taking her Michigan PhD in 1979, Allen was the author of several books, including *Why Privacy Isn't Everything* (2003), *The New Ethics* (2004) and a casebook of her own, *Privacy Law and Society* (2007). She'd also published scores of articles on such pressing legal and philosophical issues as affirmative action and reproductive rights. On any given week, she might be shooting off to some distant city for a lecture or panel.

She'd held visiting professorships at Harvard, Yale, Princeton and other elite institutions. She'd written a monthly column, "The Moralist," for the *Newark Star-Ledger,* and appeared frequently on TV as a commentator. Her twenty-seven-page CV teemed with fellowships, awards, publications, presentations and public service activities. In 2010, President Obama would name her to his Commission for the Study of Bioethical Issues. And, in 2011, she published *Unpopular Privacy: What Must We Hide?* (Oxford University Press), consolidating her reputation as a top expert in the field. If anyone in academe had arrived, it was Anita Allen.

Still, she recounted in stinging detail how tough it could be, as a black Army brat raised on bases from Georgia to Hawaii, to feel comfortable in philosophy, given its absurdly small number of black women. That partly explained why she decided to move to legal academe and express her philosophical interests from there, while maintaining a secondary appointment in philosophy.

"I'm in a livelier, more hands-on world," Allen explained, offering a sharp, chilly view of the discipline with which she fell in love as an adolescent. "I have not been able to encourage other people like me to go into philosophy because I don't think it has enough to offer them. The salaries aren't that great, the prestige isn't that great, the ability to interact with the world isn't that great, the career options aren't that great, the methodologies are narrow."

"Why would you do that," she asked, "when you could be in an African American studies department, a law school, a history department, and have so many more people to interact with who are more like you, a place where so many more methods are acceptable, so many more topics are going to be written about? Why would you close yourself off in philosophy? I feel that philosophy is hoisting itself by its own petard. Its unwillingness to be more inclusive in terms of issues, methods, demographics, means that it's losing out on a lot of vibrancy, a lot of intellectual power."

Despite delight at the birth of the Collegium, the existence finally of a "critical mass" of black women philosophers, she admitted that philosophy still felt to her "like an isolated profession."

"I don't think I would encourage a black woman who has big ideas necessarily to go into philosophy," Allen said. "Why? What's the point? Go out and win the Pulitzer Prize! Don't worry about academic philosophy. On the other hand, I would like to see that world open up to more women and women of color."

If Allen sounded like a person who fell out of love with philosophy as a malformed academic discipline, if not with the enterprise itself, the field could only blame itself. She could not have started off more enamored. Born in Port Townsend, Washington, one of six children of a career Army man and a "stay-at-home" mother—both high school dropouts from segregated Atlanta—Allen described herself as a "very quiet, pensive child." Because libraries on Army bases always contained "Great Books," she lost herself in them, reading philosophers such as Sartre and Plato as a teen. Allen credited growing up on bases for a "multicultural" environment that made her believe "there were no racial barriers to my being what I wanted to be."

A teacher at Baker High School, the Columbus, Georgia, alma mater she shares with Newt Gingrich, directed her to New College in Sarasota, Florida, an intensely intellectual experimental college. There she met Paul Castellitto, a "nice Catholic Italian boy from New York," who became her boyfriend sophomore year, an enduring friend, and her husband in 1985 after a short marriage to artist Michael Kelly Williams ended. (Allen and Castellitto, a retired white-collar defense lawyer, live outside Philadelphia with their two children.)

It was at New College that Allen lost her religious faith and dove headfirst into philosophy. Her faculty mentor steered her toward analytic philosophy and its problems of logic and language. She wrote her senior thesis on Rudolf Carnap, a key figure in the so-called Vienna Circle who aimed to bring positivist scientific rigor to philosophy.

Her mentor also urged her to attend graduate school at the highly ranked University of Michigan philosophy department, where her struggle with the discipline began. Allen, by her own account "completely apolitical" at the time, says she "knew about Angela Davis," the radical black woman philosopher (though she hadn't read her), and thought "other schools might want to have their own Angela Davis." So, with the help of one of the first Ford Foundation four-year grants that enabled African American students to pursue a PhD, she continued in philosophy.

Someday, perhaps, Allen will write a tell-all memoir that includes the bad things that followed, as well as the good. The colleagues who suggested she'd made it into philosophy only because of affirmative action. The dissertation director she had to dump after he "grabbed me and kissed me." The "constantly being hit on" by white male philosophy professors when she applied for a job. The uncertainty about whether people were "trying to talk to me to get into my panties, or trying to talk to me to offer me a job opportunity."

It's all a long time ago, but still fresh in mind. No wonder, then, that in her keynote address to the Collegium, "The White-Only Shade Tree," Allen reflected on integration over the last few decades, zapping Hannah Arendt's disapproval of southern parents who challenged segregated schools while incorporating her own encounters with racism. As Allen's political consciousness grew during her early career, she broke away from her first job teaching philosophy at Carnegie Mellon in Pittsburgh, took a position in Washington, turned to law, and rose steadily through legal academe to her current perch. Later, like Nussbaum, she tried to balance theoretical interests with engaged activities, such as chairing the West Philadelphia Alliance for Children.

"My hope," Allen said of the Nashville gathering, "is that this meeting will be for black women philosophers what the first meeting of black women lawyers was for us in the early nineties. . . . We have now arrived. And I think women in philosophy can also arrive."

NATIVE AMERICANS

Berkeley doctoral student Jennifer Vest rustled the printout before her like a trouper, realigning her pages with the nervy, ready-to-go edge dear to every academic panelist. She was on the scene in Albuquerque to do what most of the untenured do at the annual meeting of the American Philosophical Association's Pacific Division: deliver a paper.

The official topic was "Comparative African and Native American Philosophy." Suite 203 at the Hyatt Regency grew crowded with loyalists committed to the title's second half, from William Brave Bull, an under-graduate at North Dakota's Sitting Bull College, to eighty-two-year-old John Ladd, a Brown University emeritus professor whose anomalous book on Navajo ethics appeared forty-three years before. They'd been drawn by the unprecedented five sessions on American Indian philosophy, arranged by the three-year-old American Indian Philosophy Association.

The oddity—or are we talking alternate philosophical method?—was that Vest, part Seminole and part African American, and just on the verge of finishing her philosophy dissertation in Berkeley's ethnic studies department, kept breaking into her paper with stories. There was the one about her old undergraduate philosophy mentor at Hampshire College, when she'd been completing a master's in history at Howard and wanted to move on to a PhD in Native American philosophy. He'd told her he couldn't think of a place for her to go, but she might try "one of the more liberal departments, like Chapel Hill." There was the nasty tale of a few years later, when, still hoping to pursue a PhD, she showed up in the office of an esteemed Berkeley philosophy professor. He told her to read good old Lucien Lévy-Bruhl (*How Natives Think*), that pre-Foucault master of thought known for stressing the "primitive, prelogical mentality" of Vest's own ancestors.

"One of the major impediments to the inclusion of non-European philosophical concepts in discussions either of religion or philosophy," Vest declared in her talk, "has been the preoccupation in the West with categorizing the world's peoples into civilized and uncivilized, developed and undeveloped, primitive and sophisticated societies. Notions of civilization and savagery linked to race and culture have been central to the discipline of philosophy. The tendency of Europeans and Euro-Americans to view the indigenous peoples of Africa and America as prelogical, prerational savages has for many years guided studies of them by outsiders."

"Philosophy," she noted acidly, "has a lot of catching up to do." Who could disagree? As far back as 1943, in his classic, Pulitzer Prize–winning *The Growth of American Thought,* the great intellectual historian Merle Curti had written that as America's "Atlantic seaboard settlers" pushed westward and "indulged in brutal recriminations and even in massacres, they found it necessary to justify their actions on moral and rational grounds. . . . The Indian was condemned as a savage incapable of becoming civilized and Christianized. He was, in the words of Cotton Mather, a rabid animal, perfidious, bloody, cruel, a veritable devil in the flesh, an agent employed by Satan himself to overcome God's chosen people."

Most APA members knew that, compared to literary studies, where shaking up of the canon over the last three decades amounted to a motion picture, philosophy in American universities remained largely a frieze, a creaky ordering of Whitehead's "footnotes to Plato," a frozen lineup of Euro and Euro-American males in need of a *Critique of Pure Whiteness and Uptightness.* Until the alighting here of the APA's Pacific Division, which normally met in Los Angeles or San Francisco, it could fairly be said that "Red Men and Women"—who spurred the creation of so many admiring antebellum organizations as federal policy pushed Native Americans west—remained unread men and women.

Even in an age of diversity, boning up on the subject took some work. You might not expect to find an article on Native American philosophy in that aging reference *The Encyclopedia of Philosophy,* but neither could you find any coverage of Native American or American Indian philosophy (supporters used both terms) in more recent philosophy reference works, such as *The Cambridge Dictionary of Philosophy,* David Cooper's *World Philosophies* or Richard Wightman Fox and James T. Kloppenberg's *A Companion to American Thought.* Some Native American thinking pierced the wall around mainstream American thought, but in popular titles rather than scholarly ones, and more anthropo-logically and religiously than philosophically. The prime example was *Black Elk Speaks,* the visions of Oglala Lakota leader Nicholas Black Elk (1863–1950), as communicated by the poet and critic John Neihardt (1881–1973), who met Black Elk on the Pine Ridge Reservation in South Dakota in 1931. Still, most Americans probably knew more about Black Elk's fellow Lakotans: Crazy Horse (Black Elk's cousin) and Sitting Bull. Will Rogers, once America's hugely famous "cowboy philosopher," was one-quarter Cherokee, but did anyone remember that?

Part of the problem, Vest explained, was that "no cohesive, unified literature exists on the subject." While many established scholars refused to "accept Native American beliefs as philosophy," she said, many Native Americans also lacked the ambition to analyze the traditional beliefs that constituted their heritage. APA Pacific's weekend spasm of Native American philosophy, held just a mile from the Old Town tourist shops hawking headdresses, Indian blankets, walking sticks and Indian kitsch, masked the reality of its weak professional status—a marginalization so extreme that it made feminist philosophy look as central as Quinean epistemology, African American philosophy as accepted as new books on Kant.

According to Anne Waters, a lecturer at California State University at Bakersfield and the driving force behind the Albuquerque sessions, only six Native Americans, four of whom were present, held PhDs in philosophy. (She earned hers from Purdue University in 1992.) To make matters worse, she added, "there's not a single Native American PhD in philosophy who has a solid job in philosophy now." Only one journal, a Canadian publication at Lakehead University called *Ayaangwaamizin: International Journal of Indigenous Philosophy,* covered the territory. In Q-and-A sessions over the weekend, trench-level reasons become more concrete: department chairs who explained that no one on the campus was "really qualified" to direct a dissertation on Native American philos-ophy, or ruled that "Choctaw is not an appropriate scholarly language."

The scant scholarship on Native American philosophy exhibited similar shakiness. In one Albuquerque session, participants read aloud excerpts from the "Native American Philosophy" article in Routledge's newest *Encyclopedia of Philosophy,* the first prestigious reference work in the discipline to give the subject lengthy attention. Some listeners groaned when they heard the author's claims that Native American peoples lacked the "state-level societies" needed for "higher mathematics and, correlatively, symbolic logic," and that because Indian languages "were oral, philosophical thought often did not survive unless translated and transcribed by chroniclers literate in a European language."

Still, mainstream philosophers—the kind who rushed about the Hyatt Regency, ignoring the meeting's Indian offerings for run-of-the-mill sessions on justification and belief—might have sniffed that six PhDs was a weak showing for a people with 556 federally recognized tribes, 55 million acres of land, and about 1 percent of the nation's population. Of course, the notion of a "handful" of philosophers was right only if identifying Native American philosophers meant applying standard Western grids to American Indian thought—an idea some Native thinkers detested and others defended.

No matter. If, as James Wilson wrote in *The Earth Shall Weep* (1999), his exacting history of Native America, it's a "central belief" of American culture that the Indian "belongs essentially to the past rather than to the present," the paleface establishment's once vanishing nineteenth-century opponent had pulled the rug out from under the Zeitgeist with an eightfold increase in population in a hundred years, and then, of all things, a decision to grab a slice of the philosophy pie.

Throughout the Albuquerque sessions, Native American thinkers took pleasure in marking the differences between classical Western assumptions and Native styles of thought. "North American Indians," observed the Sioux scholar Vine Deloria Jr., regarded by many as the most distinguished Native American thinker, "would say, Socrates is mortal because I once met Socrates and he's mortal." Vest said that Native American axioms resemble African axioms in challenging Western clichés, mentioning the African thinker John Mbiti's alternative to Cartesian fundamentalism: "I am because we are, and because we are, therefore I am."

"Native Americans should play the role of questioning those who are never questioned," said Viola Cordova, an Apache who took her PhD in philosophy at the University of New Mexico in 1992, then taught environmental ethics at the University of Idaho. "They should be disturbers of the peace." In the discipline's impoverished state, she suggested, it could profit by switching to a comparative approach. For all the animus toward judging Native American philosophy's progress by conventional Western criteria, however, it was plainly gaining ground in that arena.

After one APA Pacific session, Anne Waters gathered the contributors to *American Indian Thought: Philosophical Essays*—a groundbreaking anthology edited by her—for a combined contract-signing and photo session. Thanks to aggressive efforts by Waters and others, the APA had established a Committee on Indians in Philosophy two years earlier (guaranteeing regular slots on conference programs for Native American philosophy), and the American Indian Philosophy Association would soon be starting its own APA newsletter.

More secondary work was also appearing from non–Native American scholars. In *The Primal Roots of American Philosophy: Pragmatism, Phenomenology, and Native American Thought,* Rutgers University philosopher Bruce Wilshire offered an audacious chapter entitled "Black Elk, Thoreau, Emerson, and Their Aura," drawing links between Black Elk's discussion of the "hoop of the world" and Emerson's notion of horizon. Even more impressive, and without question the finest book available on the place of Native American thought in American philosophy, was Scott Pratt's *Native Pragmatism: Rethinking the Roots of American Philosophy.* Pratt, chair of the University of Oregon philosophy department, boldly argued that "the central commitments of the later classical pragmatism of Charles S. Peirce, William James and John Dewey are apparent much earlier in Native American thought, particularly within Northeastern Native traditions."

Pratt brought a wealth of new material and perspective to pragmatism's origins. To set the context, he cited a 1952 essay by Felix S. Cohen, a City University of New York philosopher, which described "a meeting in which the commissioner-elect of the Bureau of Indian Affairs asked a group of native people how the bureau could best 'Americanize the Indian.'" According to Cohen, a Native American man in the audience responded as follows:

You will forgive me if I tell you that my people were American thousands of years before your people were. The question is not how you can Americanize us but how we can Americanize you. We have been working at that for a long time. Sometimes we are discouraged by the results. But we will keep trying. And the first thing we want to teach you is that, in the American way of life, each man has respect for his brother's vision. Because each of us respected his brother's dream, we enjoyed freedom here in America while your people were busy killing and enslaving each other across the water. The relatives you left behind are still trying to kill each other and enslave each other because they have not learned that freedom is built on my respect for my brother's vision and his respect for mine. We have a hard trail ahead of us in trying to Americanize you and your white brothers. But we are not afraid of hard trails.

Cohen agreed with the man, concluding that "the real job of the New World" was "Americanizing the white man." Pratt, building on that sentiment, unpacked a historical story in which, against the ethos of European colonial domination and takeover of an American wilderness, "an indigenous attitude characterized by commitments to interaction, pluralism, community, and growth emerged in Native responses. . . . This attitude came to be adopted by some non-Native people who also rejected the colonial attitude and became part of a long intellectual tradition that includes classical pragmatism, anti-racism, and feminism."

Pratt wrote about the Narragansett leader Miantonomi, his influence on his friend the Puritan minister and philosopher Roger Williams, and the broader impact of the Native American practices of *wunnegin*—welcome, or hospitality. He looked at the "logic of place" in the speeches of Sagoyewatha of the Seneca, Tenskwatawa of the Shawnee, and Neolin and Teedyuscung of the Delawares, noting that Teedyuscung's version of it brought him into contact with the government of Pennsylvania and Benjamin Franklin, whose own proto-pragmatism pointed forward to James and Dewey. In Pratt's book, Native American thought, far from being a marginalized bit of exotica in America the Philosophical, stood tall as a fundamental source, and gainsaid the old-fashioned view of Herbert Schneider, a key historian of American philosophy, that "it is useless to seek a 'native' tradition" in America, because "even our most genteel traditions are saturated with foreign inspirations."

But what American Indian philosophers in Albuquerque wanted even more than such a reverent bow from members of the tenured establishment, remarked Thomas M. Norton-Smith, an associate professor of philosophy at Kent State University and one of those handful of PhDs, was "to be in the academy" without becoming another token addition to "the rest of the isms." Cordova agreed, warning against the creation of another "ethno-philosophy," another "campus ghetto" in philosophy, insisting that Native American thinkers should grapple with the Euro-American tradition's unexamined assumptions.

In one session after another, when philosophy stepped offstage, the Native Americans bristled at the broader condescension toward them—expressed in hokey sports logos like that of the Cleveland Indians; the Europeanizing of Indian facial features in images such as

Sacajawea's on the dollar coin; the simplemindedness of dolls such as "Native American Barbie"—and the neglect with which mainstream thinkers treated their sessions here. Everywhere, a few suggested, Americans still identify them with buckskins, feathers, bows and arrows, and birch-bark canoes.

But when the talk returned to philosophy, internal differences replaced the differences with the establishment. Should Native American philosophers pursue what Vest called a "pan-tribal" approach, transcending differences because, as Waters noted, "[o]ur lingua franca is English"? Or should they insist that Native American philosophy be analyzed into Navajo thinking, Lakota thinking, Hopi thinking—keeping in mind that there are Mormon Hopis and Navajos, and other minorities, implying an infinite regress of classifications? Was any work produced by a Native American philosopher automatically Native American philosophy, even if it was on Kant's *Prolegomena*, or did the work have to discuss traditional Native beliefs?

A singular presence, as participants haggled over opposing viewpoints, was the octogenarian John Ladd—the only white male establishment philosopher who showed up regularly at the Native American presentations. Some of the younger American Indian scholars knew him and his 1957 book, *The Structure of a Moral Code: A Philosophical Analysis of Ethical Discourse Applied to the Ethics of the Navajo Indians.* It was so oddball for its time, Ladd confided between sessions, that his colleagues saw it as a kind of diversion, "as if I'd taken up sailing." Even more remarkable, Ladd recalled, the book helped him get tenure. "The fact that it was published by Harvard University Press," he said with a twinkle, "was what mattered."

Ladd drew respectful nods and smiles, but the time was gone when the Native American philosophers milling about might have worried about his backing. What was vanishing in the mind-set of this "doomed" people was the shame, the lingering assimilationist virus that fed it for so long. For the University of Oregon's Lorraine Brundige, who taught one of the few courses on American Indian thought, "to do Native American philosophy requires living a Native life," not publishing in refereed journals. Deloria believed that "eventually what we're going to do is regional philosophy—the Southwest is much different from the Plains." Urging young American Indian philosophers to be "very aggressive," he remarked that "white racism is not going to let you go very far with any of this."

But could it stop a people whose largest nation, the Navajo, ruled a territory the size of Belgium? So what if *The Cambridge Companion to Black Elk* and the standard Harvard course on "Political Philosophy from Locke to Lame Deer" were not around the corner? The indigenous people in Albuquerque didn't care. Let Harvard suffer, they implied, if it couldn't shake its fixation on individuals and turn more wisely to the mountains, land and community. As emphasized by Vest—who would go on to an associate professorship of philosophy at the University of Central Florida—in many Native American philosophies "the wisdom of a people is more important than the person who contributes to it." Let the casino money flow, and the endowed chairs rise along the plains, deserts and woodlands. Let conformists continue to joke about Tonto talk, or Rabbit Boy and Blood Clot and Standing Bear, as if their names were stranger than Learned Hand or Robert Frost. Waters and her Native American peers were safely distant from the sadness of Chief Joseph, unlikely to think, "From where the sun now stands, I will argue no more, forever."

Arguing, they had figured out, wasn't the point. And no pompous mandarin of establishment philosophy, that still-fearsome institution to Euro-American graduate students, was likely to convince them otherwise.

GAYS

For a discipline said to be founded in ancient Greece, where homosexuality enjoyed a degree of social respect that disappeared after Christianity's rise, mainstream professional philosophy in twentieth-century America devoted scant attention to gay life. "Queer studies" might be all the rage in American studies, cultural studies, comparative literature and other academic areas, but philosophy pretty much preferred that it stay in the closet. Indeed, the field evinced much of the same discomfort with the topic exhibited by American society for most of the twentieth century, before the percentage of people supporting gay marriage and gay rights began to zoom.

Good examples of that attitude could be seen in the brouhahas that arose when the gay aspects of two of the discipline's modern heroes—Ludwig Wittgenstein (1889–1951) and Michel Foucault (1926–1984)—leapt to public attention, threatening the nonpersonal, clinical image many professionals liked to maintain of their elite thinkers. The homosexuality of the two men, the status it gave them as sexual rebels and anomalies, melded with their assaults on conventional philosophy to make the topic even more uncomfortable.

With Wittgenstein, controversy over his homosexuality added to preexisting disagreement about him as a thinker and person, particularly in the Anglo-American world. After his death, his three literary executors, former students and disciples themselves—Rush Rhees, G. H. von Wright and G. E. M. Anscombe—began to issue works compiled from Wittgenstein's unpublished manuscript pages, notebook fragments, shoeboxes and shirt pockets. Those volumes included *The Blue and Brown Books, Philosophical Grammar, Philosophical Remarks, Zettel, On Certainty, Culture and Value* and *Remarks on Colour.* Like his two most important books, the early *Tractatus Logico-Philosophicus* (the only one published in his lifetime) and the later *Philosophical Investigations,* they consisted of paragraphs, aphorisms, and questions that expressed philosophical ideas in taut, conversational style. "We say a dog is afraid his master will beat him," wrote Wittgenstein in one typical query, "but not, he is afraid his master will beat him tomorrow. Why not?"

In the process of becoming the posthumous Wittgenstein, the man himself fell into the hands of the kind of academics who replace their proper names with three initials, scholars who leaned toward the conventional view at the time that philosophy was mainly about the theory of knowledge, and secondarily about philosophy of language and science insofar as those subjects illuminated epistemology. For them, the Wittgenstein engaged with those topics was all the Wittgenstein anyone needed to know. Conventional debate ensued on the merits of the "early Wittgenstein" (e.g., the *Tractatus*) versus the "later Wittgenstein" (e.g., the *Investigations*), but it remained a debate still largely centered on epistemology.

For many analytic philosophers who contributed to the huge industry of secondary texts and studies about him that began in the 1970s, Wittgenstein amounted to a master of piecemeal observation unable to state his larger business in proper, syllogistic journal form. They, graciously, would do it for him. An especially egregious example was the *Wittgenstein* volume by Robert Fogelin in a series entitled "Arguments of the Philosophers." Fogelin concluded that "the chief disappointment in Wittgenstein's later philosophy" came from "his failure to work out the constructive side of his view in detail," leaving his philosophy "radically incomplete."

But a fight had already begun for which of many Wittgensteins would endure. Because many outside the narrow world of professional Anglo-American philosophy knew that such a clipped, antiseptic view of Wittgenstein ignored whole dimensions of his life and thought hostile to both philosophy as a settled, professional occupation and to ordinary, middle-class academic life.

Wittgenstein, for instance, had spent six years teaching elementary school in provincial Austrian villages after jousting earlier in his life with Bertrand Russell in privileged Cambridge, England. As William Bartley III observed in a controversial biography, the argument doctors shepherding Wittgenstein's posthumous reputation usually passed over those years "in hurried bewilderment, as if they constituted an eccentric act best not dwelt upon." Academic philosophers eager to enlist Wittgenstein as a quirky officer in the march of British epistemological analysis, or in the Vienna Circle's mission to make philosophy "the logic of science," found much in the real Wittgenstein, on the intellectual side alone, to embarrass them: his passion for Tolstoy's account of the Gospels, his deep respect for Kierkegaard, and his insistence on reading from Rabindranath Tagore, the great Indian poet, at meetings of the science-minded Circle.

The foremost embarrassment on his philosophical side was his hostility to professional academic philosophy itself. Wittgenstein had vehemently declared to his American disciple, Norman Malcolm, that "he would gladly see all of his writings destroyed if along with them there would vanish the publications of his pupils and disciples." Wittgenstein repeatedly counseled students against becoming philosophy professors and described his calling, when he taught university philosophy, as a "living hell."

What unnerved professional philosophers most about the real Wittgenstein was the "later" one who wanted nothing but "to show the fly the way out of the fly bottle," who called the "real discovery" in philosophy "the one that makes me capable of stopping doing philosophy when I want to." Like Rorty, Wittgenstein wanted to end the campaign of misguided logic-chopping that supposedly demanded career officers—philosophy professors.

Wittgenstein's model, instead, was "therapeutic" philosophy meant to free us from "the bewitchment of our intelligence by means of language." Malcolm wrote of him after his death, "Unlike many other philosophers, who really want to retain the problems rather than solve them, Wittgenstein's desire was to clear them up, to get rid of them. He exclaimed to a friend, 'My father was a businessman and I am a businessman too!" In *Culture and Value,* the famously dissatisfied Austrian wrote, "A philosopher is a man who has to cure many intellectual diseases in himself before he can arrive at the notions of common sense."

That fear of Wittgenstein the rebel, the apostate who needed to be kept behind the curtain, helped explain why another rebel and apostate—Wittgenstein the homosexual—created such a stir when Bartley, more than anyone before, yanked his closet door open. In his biography, Bartley, a philosophy professor at California State University, turned journalist to explain Wittgenstein's period as a village schoolteacher. Claiming to have interviewed many who knew Wittgenstein both in Vienna and in the villages of Otterthal, Trattenbach and Puchsberg, Bartley emerged with a portrait of a deeply ashamed homosexual—more ashamed of *anything* sexual, it appeared, than of the homoerotic form his sexuality took—who, contrary to Cambridge assumptions, had not "given up" philosophy during the 1920s. Rather, he had sought to live out his deepest ethical beliefs, molded in part by Tolstoy, the Austrian school reform movements, and the notion of Otto Weininger that one must commit to and refine one's genius.

Bartley suggested that Wittgenstein was "either consciously or unconsciously, for better or worse, engaging in an imitation of Christ" during his village time. In doing so, Bartley argued, Wittgenstein attempted to live out his key theses in the *Tractatus* that some things can only be shown, not said, and that "ethics cannot be put into words." Weininger (1880–1903), himself a tortured thinker who killed himself in a Vienna house where Beethoven had lived, advocated "absolute sexual abstinence as a precondition of spiritual development and genius." According to Bartley, Wittgenstein's move to the villages came partly to protect himself against "the sort of rough blunt homosexual youth" he regularly sought out at the Prater in Vienna, and the "tough boys in London pubs." Sex, wrote Bartley, articulating Wittgenstein's attitude, "was immoral; by and large it was not for friends. . . . His life was lived in a kind of mourning, as it were, that he could not escape from sex entirely."

Bartley and his foes locked horns in the *Times Literary Supplement*. Anscombe attacked him for naming no sources and charged that, according to Bartley's interpreter, he'd drawn "a complete blank" from villagers on Wittgenstein's personal life. Bartley countercharged that Anscombe had threatened a defamation suit prior to publication in an effort to stop his book. He also claimed that Anscombe had made a career of squelching inquiries into Wittgenstein's personal life, even pressuring the distinguished economist F. A. Hayek, Wittgenstein's second cousin once removed, into dropping a planned biography of Wittgenstein (an accusation Anscombe confirmed).

Noting that Anscombe herself had indicated that even "to imply that a person is homosexual is libelous," he asked, "how can she expect me either to identify my informants or to facilitate their recognition in any way?" As *TLS* controversies often do, this one lingered. One friend of Wittgenstein, a psychiatrist, declared that "[s]ensuality in any form was entirely foreign to his ascetic personality. A Cornwall woman reported that Russell had remarked to her, 'Wittgenstein was witty, but was a homosexual.'"

All in all, it was an unworthy contretemps laced with homophobia from the Cambridge set. Years later, the writer Ray Monk, in his massive biography of Wittgenstein, attempted to put the controversy to rest by arguing that Wittgenstein's homosexual proclivities probably didn't lead to any corporeal sexuality. But that view appeared gainsaid by the Italian publication of a Wittgenstein diary, spirited out of the Wittgenstein estate without the approval of its executors, which indicated the opposite. In the meantime, outsiders and artists such as Derek Jarman, in his film *Wittgenstein,* happily included the thinker's homosexuality in its representation of his persona. Philosophers, on the whole, preferred to look elsewhere.

Michel Foucault's homosexuality hit the profession from a different direction, propelled by the French thinker's sometimes reckless cruising, and a book, *The Passion of Michel Foucault,* by New School professor James Miller, which sought to put that activity in a philosophical context. Foucault, who died of AIDS after a slow coming-out in his final years, dominated the center stage of philosophical Paris for two decades as a snarling putative maverick, a turtlenecked dandy whose authorial performances—colorful, historical studies of such subjects as insanity, sickness and punishment—amounted to stylized shows in which he thumbed his nose (and leveled his shaved head) at the establishment.

Foucault's most successful books—*Madness and Civilization* (1961), *The Birth of the Clinic* (1963) and *Discipline and Punish* (1975)—probed the supposedly rational foundations of psychiatry, medicine and criminal justice, finding those institutions undesirable systems of coercion against individual freedom. The idea most associated with Foucault at his death was that knowledge implies power—that divisions between concepts such as sane and insane, sick and healthy, or normal and abnormal (in regard to sex and other practices), depend on political structures imposed to control people's lives, not on natural or biological differences.

But Foucault also played footsie with the French establishment all his life. He attended France's most prestigious schools, served in several cultural posts for the foreign ministry (getting himself thrown out of Bucharest for an unwise homosexual affair), and campaigned for the best establishment jobs within the French university system. For years, when other gay intellectuals urged him to take a leadership role in their political activities, he demurred, explaining that too strong a "gay" identification would marginalize his work, and that terms such as "gay" were anyway simplistic.

Despite those internal biographical tensions, Foucault's image since his death has been mostly stable, his wish for his "gay" side to be minimized largely honored, except in the melee that broke out following the publication of Miller's book. In France, intellectuals debate his ideas, conscious of the many contradictions that color both his work and his personality, but his stature, unlike that of some deceased contemporaries, remains high. In America, anti-establishment academics and some gay theoreticians typically revere him, valuing his books as tools for opposing notions of objectivity or the "natural." His sexuality is rarely at the center of their concerns.

Miller's book, in contrast, built a bridge between Foucault's reckless life as a gay cruiser obsessed with death, suicide and sadomasochistic sex, and passages in the philosopher's work that suggest his obsessions were a Nietzschean attempt to test the limits of experience and thought. Acknowledging the influence on him of Alexander Nehamas's noted study, *Nietzsche: Life as Literature*, Miller, an ex-*Newsweek* critic with previous books on Rousseau, the New Left, and Marx, essentially produced *Foucault: Life as Limit-Experience*.

Miller credited Foucault with attempting, through gay S/M sex and what Foucault once called "the glory of torture," a "game of truth" by ordeal foreshadowed in his theoretical works. From a reportorial standpoint, Miller, to some extent, corroborated Didier Eribon's *Michel Foucault* (1991), the first full life of its subject. Eribon, a French journalist, revealed Foucault's hatred for his father, tortured attitude toward his homosexuality, viciousness toward others as a young adult, suicide attempts, self-mutilation, self-hatred, violent temper, fascination with the Marquis de Sade and other sensational matters. Offering solid fresh material about Foucault's experiments with LSD and San Francisco's leather scene, and useful perspectives from Foucault's intimates, Miller described his own book as an "account of one man's lifelong struggle to honor Nietzsche's gnomic injunction, to become what one is."

As Miller paraphrased Foucault's view, an "uninhibited exploration of sado-masochistic eroticism" might enable one to breach "the boundaries separating the conscious and unconscious, reason and unreason, pleasure and pain—and, at the ultimate limit, life and death—thus starkly revealing how distinctions central to the play of true and false are pliable, uncertain, contingent." It sounded academically admirable. It also sounded like the sort of worthy independent project a sly 1960s college senior might put over on a good-vibes professor. Miller didn't much consider whether Foucault's rhetoric about S/M sex was both a rationalization of his libido and a joke on his acolytes—one more instance of the way in which, Miller conceded, "truth" in Foucault's writing was often a kind of "game."

Miller, after all, had reported that Jean Daniel, a friend of Foucault, noted Foucault's "sharp temptation to sink into voluptuous delights." Miller also cited the observation of a Toronto friend of Foucault, who guided the philosopher to that city's leather scene, that Foucault *intellectualized* sexual practices. And Miller conceded that scholar Leo Bersani, who knew Foucault well, advised Miller after reading his manuscript that, in construing Foucault's sexuality, Miller was complicating something that "may not be that difficult."

In time, the controversy about Foucault's sexuality receded, as book-spawned controversies eventually do, and one more opportunity for demands of philosophy and issues of modern homosexuality to come together passed by. As in so many other areas, of course, America hardly needed to rely on professional philosophers to air those issues. The words and names that symbolized the rise of a gay rights movement in America—Stonewall, Harvey Milk, Larry Kramer, Act Up—affirmed that all issues needing discussion received their airtime. Writers and intellectuals outside the professional discipline of philosophy mainly filled the space.

Journalist Randy Shilts produced the enduring reportorial account of the AIDS crisis, *And the Band Played On*; investigative reporter Nathaniel Frank delivered *Unfriendly Fire: How the Gay Ban Undermines the Military and Weakens America*; and a more lighthearted journalist, Cathy Crimmins, contributed *How the Homosexuals Saved Civilization*, marking the cultural contributions of the gay aesthetic and camp attitudes. Historians, social scientists and other humanists, rather than official philosophers, tended to take on particular issues of homosexuality, such as Byrne Fone in *Homophobia: A History*, Harvard English professor Marjorie Garber in *Bisexuality and the Eroticism of Everyday Life*, and Rabbi Steven Greenberg in *Wrestling with God and Men: Homosexuality in the Jewish Tradition*. It fell to British classicists and historians, including Sir Kenneth Dover, in *Greek Homosexuality*, and James Davidson, in *The Greeks and Greek Love*, to shed light on the old days when philosophy and homosexuality were like fish and chips (or choose your own pairing).

In fact, as open discussion of homosexuality became the norm in the United States in the later years of the twentieth century, part of the academic field of cultural studies, and a whole new subfield of gay and lesbian studies, came on the scene and made it easier, arguably, for professional philosophers to avoid the topic. One *expected* a figure such as Joan Nestle, cofounder of the Lesbian Herstory Archives, rather than a philosopher, to be the coeditor of a volume such as *GenderQueer: Voices from Beyond the Sexual Binary*. Certainly it was hard to imagine the non-rebellious sorts who populated the APA, whatever their sexual orientation, producing a book such as *That's Revolting!: Queer Strategies for Resisting Assimilation*, edited by Mattilda Bernstein Sycamore, which sought to keep alive the tradition of gays not aspiring to join straights in conventional marriages, but forging their own rebel culture. Or *Mad for Foucault: Rethinking the Foundations of Queer Theory* by Lynne Huffer, an Emory University scholar in women's studies who wrestled with Foucault's alleged condescension toward women.

And yet outsiders pushing the envelope on borderline gay topics often displayed, in a way typical in America the Philosophical, enormous philosophical range and references. In *Unlimited Intimacy: Reflections on the Subculture of Barebacking*, Tim Dean, director of the Humanities Institute at the State University of New York, explored unsafe gay sex as a courageous endorsement of intimacy *despite* HIV and AIDS by invoking, along the way, enough philosophers to form a new Academy: Pierre Bourdieu, Judith Butler, Jacques Derrida, Umberto Eco, Frantz Fanon, Michel Foucault, Immanuel Kant, Jacques Lacan, Claude Levi-Strauss, Emmanuel Levinas, Friedrich Nietzsche, Susan Sontag, Charles Taylor and Slavoj Zizek.

All that philosophical vitality in American culture, regardless of its sources, helped the movement for civil unions and gay marriage take off in the first decade of this century. More and more readers found themselves in a classic philosophical situation created by social change: forced to reexamine their fundamental premises about a long-standing, putatively "natural" concept—marriage—and to ask what constitutes one, or any love relationship between two human beings with no family connection.

To be fair, the debates taking place outside professional philosophy mirrored some increased activity within the discipline as well. Butler, a philosopher by training who had built her career in the Department of Rhetoric and Comparative Literature at the University of California, Berkeley, ranked as the most successful lesbian philosopher. Nothing if not prolific, Butler, in books such as *Gender Trouble; Bodies That Matter: On the Discursive Limits of "Sex"; Excitable Speech: A Politics of the Performative; Precarious Life: The Powers of Mourning and Violence;*

and *Undoing Gender,* took on virtually every human concept under the sun through the prism of gender: sex, hate speech, personhood, post-9/11 America and more. To her votaries, she became the Joan of Arc of queer studies. To her critics, she brought turgid, unreadable, humorless academic prose—famously attacked in the *New Republic* by Martha Nussbaum—to unprecedented heights. To be sure, she demonstrated that a gay American philosopher could rival European stars in drawing the kind of secondary studies meant to explain the barely explicable.

A worthier warrior within the field was Richard Mohr, professor of philosophy at the University of Illinois at Urbana. A classicist whose first book was *The Platonic Cosmology* (1985), Mohr turned to issues closer to home in *Gays/Justice: A Study of Ethics, Society, and Law* (1988). Then came *Gay Ideas* (1992), which put him on the media map after twenty-three printers refused to handle it. The reason? *Gay Ideas* included Robert Mapplethorpe's notorious photos of gay lovers, as well as erotic art by Tom of Finland and Rex, artists Mohr described elsewhere as standing to "gay male life of the 1970s and 1980s" as Grandma Moses did to mainstream American communities of earlier times. (Months later, one recalcitrant printer, R. R. Donnelley and Sons, would draw stinging criticism in the *New York Times* and elsewhere for nonetheless taking on Madonna's 500,000-print-run *Sex,* with photos of the singer "in a compromising position with a dog" and having a knife held to her crotch by a bald, tattooed lesbian.)

A slew of university presses also rejected *Gay Ideas*—at least one, Mohr asserted in a *Chronicle of Higher Education* article, to protect state funding. To top things off, even Columbia University Press turned it down, despite Mohr being the general editor of its own series, "Between Men, Between Women: Lesbian and Gay Studies," one of the first series of books devoted to gay and lesbian studies in the U.S. "I was turned down by my own series," Mohr half joked, before resigning his editorship.

Gay Ideas, however, ultimately published by Beacon Press, pluckily became the first contemporary book in which a philosophy professor courageously stated his arguments, and not just his wish list, about crucial gay matters such as outing, gay pornography, AIDS and the radical tactics of Act Up. Popular writers about gay issues, accustomed to the philosophy profession mainly avoiding the subject, rose up in high praise. Michelangelo Signorile, the crusading *Advocate* columnist, praised its "brilliant, razor-sharp analysis of outing." Yale scholar Wayne

Koestenbaum applauded Mohr for being "fearlessly willing to articulate the unfashionable and the necessary, to proffer prescriptions or diagnoses we've never seen in print." John Preston, author of *Flesh and the Word,* noted the sudden new disciplinary support: "Richard Mohr brings the harsh but illuminating focus of philosophy to the arenas of modern gay life."

The book didn't achieve a runaway sales success, but it won a Lambda "Editor's Choice" Award for the best gay book of the year. And the publicity stirred by all the resistance brought a wider audience to Mohr's book and to philosophical approaches to gay issues, enabling it to be judged on its merits and flaws, and not just its illustrations.

Like many philosophers, Mohr was a foundationalist at heart, which meant he believed in building on principles that remained largely axiomatic. To Mohr, the best political foundation was liberal democracy, and the primary value for gays had to be "dignity" rather than "happiness or practicality." That meant refusing to act in ways that promoted society's denigration of gays. Mohr's angry opening-chapter defense of outing—the exposure of closeted gays against their wishes—extended that premise.

He contended that the one social practice binding the gay community was "The Secret": the tacit understanding that gays don't expose other gays to the outside world. To Mohr, however, that social convention amounted to "a belief in the community's worthlessness"—a belief rooted in self-hatred and shame. Commitment to outing, he maintained, was an "expected consequence of living morally" because it kept gays from participating in their own oppression.

Mohr's positions in later chapters proved equally forceful. He warned gays away from "[l]eftward-leaning ideological fixes," analyzed the awe-inspiring features of the NAMES Project's AIDS quilt and Wagner's opera *Parsifal,* and rejected the trendy notion that homosexuality was just a "social construction." He also boldly argued that promiscuous homosexuals nourished democracy, and traced the effect of court decisions about gay rights on traditional civil rights law. As a writer, Mohr occasionally unleashed a stinging image, as when he asserted that American gays possessed fewer rights than "barnyard animals in Sweden." Sometimes, like most academic philosophers, he displayed a deaf ear for good prose rhythms. A few of those houses that declined to publish the book perhaps nixed it for unnatural acts against the English sentence.

Yet it was Mohr's reasoning that made you want to paddle the Platonist in him without harming the gay activist. His defense of outing, for instance, depended on a foggy distinction between "privacy" and "secrecy." That division supposedly implied the further distinction that one has a right to privacy about one's sexual behavior, but not about one's sexual orientation. Both distinctions, unfortunately, possessed the solidity of warm soup, as Mohr might have realized if he'd questioned how one proved a person's homosexual orientation in the absence of sexual behavior. (Hello, Wittgenstein, are you there?)

Mohr seemed regularly unsure of his position when he tried to articulate the link between gay sex and the status of being gay. On one page he wrote that "to have relations of a certain sort" was "what it is to be gay." Five pages later, he attacked the 1952 McCarran-Walter Act for excluding foreign gays from the United States "based on a distinction of status rather than behavior." Yet if Mohr believed gays were gay because engaging in homosexual relations is "what it is to be gay," then being "gay" amounted to no more a status than being a jaywalker became a status once you illegally crossed a street. "Status" based on past behavior wasn't the sort of "status" that the law disfavored as discriminatory.

Mohr's position on outing also invited attack for its paternalistic interference with the rights of individuals—a violation of traditional liberalism. In *The Passion of Michel Foucault*, Miller had reported that Foucault for many years resisted requests to come out because he considered "gay" too simple a concept to describe his personality. Mohr, in contrast, accepted the "gay" label as part of the activist life. But his theory of gay dignity provided no space for those who, wisely or naively, considered sexual behavior so minor a part of their lives that they didn't want it distracting others from personal actions and achievements they considered more important. Mohr held that the "gay person who keeps another gay person's dirty little secret degrades himself, does an injustice to himself by going along with rather than resisting the values that oppress gays." But Mohr's abstract commitment to justice for the individual gay clashed with his concrete support for stripping individual gays of control over presentation of their personalities—a right already recognized in American privacy law.

Finally, Mohr's argument that outing all gays was key to gay dignity also ended up specious—as specious as the argument that outing all beneficiaries of cosmetic surgery (a voluntarily chosen condition) or all sufferers from Alzheimer's (an imposed condition) was essential to removing social stigma from either group. The social stigma on both groups has faded because of study, education and debate—not outing.

Still, many people with Alzheimer's or a history of cosmetic surgery prefer not to be revealed as "Alzheimer's sufferers" or "facelift veterans." If exposing such individuals isn't necessary to promoting the dignity of their conditions, and they view exposure as both "degrading" and "an injustice," how could Mohr justify outing them—or gays? Only, it seems, by always favoring activists over nonactivists in their right to justice. That itself, of course, violated justice—the right of equals to equal treatment. If gays enjoyed a right not to be gay activists, they also enjoyed a right not to be outed.

Regardless of whether one accepted his positions, Mohr, a resourceful thinker, merited sustained applause for living up to a general "Aristotelian" lesson implicit in his battle for publication, and stated in his own *Chronicle* article: "People become courageous by performing courageous acts and promote cowardice by performing cowardly acts." Two years later, he kept up his spirited engagement with gay issues in *A More Perfect Union: Why Straight America Must Stand Up for Gay Rights,* revised and republished a decade after that as *The Long Arc of Justice: Lesbian and Gay Marriage, Equality, and Rights.* There, happily, he could report much progress in the advance of gay rights in the U.S., and a "philosophical" acceptance of them by many straight Americans.

Mohr noted that the "taboo blanketing talk of lesbians and gay men" had "all but collapsed" in the U.S. (He gave wry credit to opponents, noting that "the more the Right has to talk about things gay," the more the taboo disintegrated.) The *New York Times* had gone from refusing, as late as 1987, to print the word "gay" to running gay wedding announcements in 2004. Television had begun to offer attractive gay characters in sitcoms such as *Will and Grace,* and mainstream advertisers from American Express to Wrigley's had started to use gay celebrities to pitch their products. Mohr detected an end, in most parts of American culture, to "demonization" of gays, and without demonization, he explained "it's hard, perhaps impossible, to think of homosexuality as a contagious disease." Still, philosophically attuned to nuances of language, he submitted that "gay marriage," which once had hit the American ear as not just "an oxymoron" but "a flat-out contradiction," had come to sound "about as unshocking as the phrase 'gay couples.' "

Mohr didn't mention Wittgenstein, but he couldn't resist noting a wonderful corroboration of Wittgenstein's notion of "meaning as use" in regard to "gay marriage": "Here linguistic reform has called into being a real-world possibility. Thanks to the Right's yammering, America, like the White Queen in *Alice in Wonderland,* is believing six impossible things before breakfast."

Professional philosophy as a discipline still paid only rare attention to gay issues, even as the legal movement for gay marriage gathered steam, but Mohr didn't seem to care. On a fine November day after the Ontario Supreme Court made that Canadian province "the first place on Earth where gay American couples could legally wed," Mohr tied the knot with his partner of twenty-five years. The following Sunday, the *Times* ran their announcement and photo in its Sunday Styles section. "We were," he wrote in *The Long Arc of Justice,* "the tenth same-sex couple to be announced as married in the *New York Times.*"

PART 4

GUTENBERG'S REVENGE: THE EXPLOSION OF CYBERPHILOSOPHY

THE BOOK LIVES!

Scrunched into a chair in his cramped West Village pied-à-terre years ago, a vision of rebel chic in trademark black shirt, boots and purple bandanna, bearded cyberphilosopher John Perry Barlow—called "the Coyote" by fellow digerati for his maverick, cowboy ways—looked atypically sheepish. Best known as the author of the "Declaration of Independence in Cyberspace," a much-read, widely downloaded manifesto of Net libertarianism, the former Grateful Dead lyricist and Wyoming cattle rancher deferred to no man, woman or genius-geek in his passion for the Web.

John Perry Barlow (1947–), former lyricist for the Grateful Dead, became one of the first outspoken cyberlibertarians with his "Declaration of Independence in Cyberspace."

He brandished a business card that blared "Cognitive Dissident." Way back in 1991, he played cover boy on the demo issue that *Wired* magazine's founders circulated to investors. As cofounder himself of the Electronic Frontier Foundation, Barlow roamed the country and the world attacking copyright lawyers, denouncing corporations for property grabs, exalting freedom in cyberspace.

Fellow digerati credited him with popularizing science fiction novelist William Gibson's metaphor of cyberspace as a new "frontier" to be "settled"—with energetically pushing the digital juggernaut's revolutionary edge. He liked to say that the Internet was "going to cause the renegotiation of every single power relationship on the planet." Given enough provocation, Barlow warned, he might even "kill to protect the Internet."

Yet late one Manhattan afternoon, deep in conversation about the digital revolution's glories, Barlow, by then middle-aged and reflective, ponied up an embarrassing, almost antediluvian admission. That book contract he'd signed many moons before with Viking? Well, he didn't think anyone should set up the publicity tour yet, but lately he'd been "thinking a lot about actually doing it." That's right—publishing a treeware product called a book. One of those old-fashioned objects made of paper.

"People don't read books much anymore," Barlow mused, a trace of apology in his voice, "but they do wave them at one another as totemic objects. And they come to symbolize the line of thought that is associated with an individual. Since there's a line of thought associated with me, I would just as soon have a symbol people can wave at one another."

A few months later, on that "left coast" of the country more identified with laptops than books on one's lap, Paul Saffo, then director of California's Institute for the Future, confessed to similar thoughts. Dubbed the "resident intellectual" of Silicon Valley at the time by cyberimpresario John Brockman, and the "industry's dancing bear" by *New York Times* cyberjournalist John Markoff because he could "conceptualize ideas and articulate them better than anybody," Saffo was, in the early days of cyberphilosophy, Barlow's top rival when it came to magisterial sound bites on things digital.

A self-described "technology forecaster," Saffo represented the cautionary edge of cyberthought, the voice of "plausible scenarios" based on careful homework. In his Menlo Park office, he surrounded himself with "doomed technologies" on which other people lost money. Smooth, savvy and wry, Saffo at first derided the idea that everyone who's anyone in digital culture needed to write a book and turn digital philosopher.

"Henry Ford wrote a book, *My Vision of Industry,* which I have at home," he observed drily. "The cry has always gone forward to the successful people in our society: Prophesize, prophesize! Tell us the answer! We're hungry for this."

Still, it turned out that Saffo, who earned law degrees from Harvard and Oxford, had been engaged in "sabbatical research" as a visiting scholar at Stanford, studying "a different way of thinking about how technology and culture interact." Main premise? That change in the digital revolution was "actually very slow, no faster than it was four centuries ago." The research, Saffo conceded, would "probably turn into a book."

"But I'm not going to turn it into a book until I'm convinced it's a very honest book," he insisted. "I don't want to look back twenty years from now and feel embarrassed. There are a lot of people spouting off things who are going to look ridiculous in five years."

How they would look in five years, as Saffo liked to point out, amounted to forecasting. What they'd begun to knock out in the pre-Kindle and pre-Nook 1990s, however—whether they styled themselves revolutionaries or number crunchers, true believers or cyberskeptics—was pure paper: reams and reams of cyberphilosophy. Digerati by the dozens began spouting off about the profound implications of the information revolution faster than you could say "America the Philosophical," giving the U.S. a whole new distinctive and cerebral cottage industry that no other country could rival.

Suddenly, it seemed, everyone wanted to update Marshall McLuhan (1911–1980), to upgrade the Canadian communications theorist who answered television's takeover of mass culture with books hypothesizing "the global village," the "medium" as "message" and other ideas that catalyzed mainstream thought. Cyberphilosophy's McLuhans took on the commitment of telling us how, as the digital revolution took hold, we would think, vote, read, pray, view art, listen to music, cover news, choose our lovers, tell the truth or lie.

"You have the people of the book, which is the East Coast," remarked Kevin Kelly, the former executive editor of *Wired,* "and the people of the screen, which is the West Coast." Both had turned philosophically ambitious in the wake of the cyber juggernaut. But it wasn't that traditional philosophy described by Whitehead as all "footnotes to Plato."

Kelly himself—a New Jerseyan transplanted to San Francisco—had produced *Out of Control: The New Biology of Machines, Social Systems, and the Economic World*, which the London *Spectator* thumbnailed as "an attempt to comprehend the possible future evolution of everything."

"You can read all these big-idea books, including mine," remarked Kelly, "and I would say 95 percent of the citations are things from the last ten or twenty years." The "big-idea" authors faced a phenomenon, Kelly suggested, that he and his longtime *Wired* colleagues had confronted every month: "There is an emerging philosophy. Part of what we're trying to do is identify it rather than create it. Label it, name it, make people self-aware of what it is." So while techies and Wall Streeters focused on digital convergence and gadget evolution—the combined laptop/television/phone/fax machine/printer/camera and maybe refrigerator we're all supposedly dying to buy and put in our pocket or wrap around our ear (as we wait for everything to malfunction at once)—a convergence was already taking place, at least among cybermoguls and "net-ellectuals," between what Kelly called the "Publish or Perish!" mentality of the East Coast and the "Demo or Die!" ethos of the Valley.

"As new media become ever more rapid paced," agreed John Pavlik, a leading academic expert on the subject and chair of the journalism and media studies department at Rutgers, "the people doing the thinking about these technologies are compelled to write in a medium that has much greater longevity. I think Kelly and some others are drawn to writing treatises because they see the new media as too fleeting."

"It's both paradoxical and sensible," continued Pavlik, who would add his own overview, *Media in the Digital Age,* to the pack in 2008. "New media have very short life spans—just try to find an eight-track player today. Yet a book will still be readable centuries from now. . . . The book's prestige is actually increasing in an age in which everything seems so ephemeral." In the very decade when Microsoft's omnipresent slogan asked, "Where do you want to go today?," net-ellectuals increasingly answered, "To my laptop, to write a book!"

It might have seemed that they were rejecting the admonition of one of their own gurus, Nicholas Negroponte, in the title of his hot book during early cyberphilosophy, *Being Digital.* Not quite. While Negroponte's groundbreaker now ironically reads more like *Being Digital 1.1,* its author, the founder and former head of MIT's Media Lab, assisted the boom in his preface to that book, entitled "The Paradox of a Book."

Asking himself why his publisher was shipping "atoms instead of bits," Negroponte offered three reasons: "not enough digital media" in the hands of potential readers; a huge print following among fans of his monthly *Wired* column; and a truly heretical third thought: "Interactive media leaves very little to the imagination. Like a Hollywood film, multimedia narrative includes such specific representations that less and less is left to the mind's eye. By contrast, the written word sparks images and evokes metaphors that get much of their meaning from the reader's imagination and experiences."

With that kind of okay from *Wired*'s first investor and chief cybercheerleader, even an alpha geek committed to nonfiction could feel guiltless about being literary and cyberphilosophical. And who knew that e-books and e-readers would, within a generation, narrow the page/bits gap even further? Sci-fi novelists and directors of dystopian movies like *Blade Runner* didn't get to have all the fun as the d-revolution thrust forward. The computer industry's first mega-billion-dollar man himself, Bill Gates, launched the CEO version of the genre in two editions of *The Road Ahead*. ("He changed highways," commented Saffo, referring to Gates's legendary late appreciation of the Internet.) Smaller entrepreneur/authors who brought up the rear included Webworking Services chairman David Whittle (*Cyberspace: The Human Dimension*) and Perspecta CEO Steven Holtzman (*Digital Mosaics: The Aesthetics of Cyberspace*).

But the publishing deluge spilled forth from every class of cybercitizen: computer academics like MIT's Michael Dertouzos (*What Will Be*) and Sherry Turkle (*Life on the Screen*); cyberjournalist insiders like Kelly and Esther Dyson (*Release 2.1*), long the publisher of a leading industry newsletter; even eternal '60s icon Timothy Leary, with *Design for Dying*, which flung open "a whole new range of beyond-death possibilities for the wired generation."

Typically, the first generation of cyberthinkers informed readers that colossal transformations awaited them. Turkle warned in *Life on the Screen* that the Net was "changing the way we think, the nature of our sexuality, the form of our communities, our very identities." Kelly declared that "the realm of the *born*—all that is nature—and the realm of the *made*—all that is humanly constructed—are becoming one."

For writers, thinkers and CEOs too pressured to uncork a whole book, or inclined to stay singles hitters, heavy-clicking editors quickly gathered their essays or industry talks into anthologies such as *The Internet and Society, High Noon on the Electronic Frontier,* and *Internet Culture*. As the digital revolution leapfrogged from practical, immediately affected areas of life (e.g., finance and retail marketing) to such practices as art, literature, music, religion, ethics, romance, politics and journalism, books promising a "macro" philosophical sense of the digital Zeitgeist began to be joined by "micro" works of greater focus and precision.

In *Politics on the Nets: Wiring the Political Process,* communications journalist Wayne Rash more or less inaugurated the "Net and politics" genre, predicting that online life would "drop the price of entry onto the national stage to a level that nearly anyone can afford." In *The Soul of Cyberspace: How New Technology Is Changing Our Spiritual Lives,* former *Parabola* editor Jeff Zaleski did the same for "Net and religion" books, reporting challenges to religious ritual in cyberspace's devaluation of the body, and warning that the "digital crusades are here, and this time the prize isn't Constantinople but the entire earth." In *Hamlet on the Holodeck: The Future of Narrative in Cyberspace,* Janet Murray suggested that linear storytelling itself might fade. In *Digital Mosaics,* Steven Holtzman explored virtual sculptures, self-perpetuating music and the possibly doomed distinction between artist and audience. Finally, as if three exploding genres of cyberphilosophy in its biblical age weren't enough to require extra memory in the hard drives between our ears, a fourth also arose: jeremiads from the cyberskeptics and cyberReveres (Bad stuff is coming! Bad stuff is coming!), whose titles stung as sharply as the latest flamer e-mail, that ancestor of blogger and Twitter vituperation.

In *Trapped in the Net,* Berkeley physicist Gene Rochlin hammered home, in the words of his subtitle, "the unintended consequences of computerization" for air traffic controllers and other challenged professionals. In *Moths to the Flame* and *Slaves of the Machine,* Indiana professor Gregory Rawlins emphasized equally troubling ramifications, such as how "future propaganda might compare to today's persuasions the way a child's crayon drawing compares to the Sistine Chapel." Just scanning the titles of cyberphilosophy's first wave—Sven Birkerts's *The Gutenberg Elegies,* Kirkpatrick Sale's *Rebels Against the Future,* Clifford Stoll's *Silicon Snake Oil,* Mark Slouka's *War of the Worlds*—you knew those cyberskeptics possessed the bandwidth to give Barlow and friends the philosophical and literary fight of their lives.

What explained America's cyberphilosophy boom? Faith that books remained the boffo vehicle for sustained reading and thinking—Pavlik's point—was clearly the key reason why treeware remained the preferred delivery system until the massification of e-books and e-readers, whose ultimate impact on the printed book remained uncertain. When it came to explaining the philosophical impulse itself, other reasons shot forth: widespread fear of the unknown on the part of ordinary Americans; the historic desire of intellectuals more broadly (from novelists Edward Bellamy, Jules Verne and H. G. Wells to social critics Norman Bel Geddes and Herman Kahn) to interpret new technologies through "futurism"; and the view of younger, hyperliterate, screen-friendly up-and-comers that cyberphilosophy constituted a cool epiphenomenon of the digital revolution, sharing its make-or-break, demo-or-die pragmatist spirit.

Dertouzos, who had overseen a number of breakthroughs during his nearly three decades of running MIT's computer lab, said he published his views in part because too many unqualified types were writing "hype" about the digital revolution, and "if someone reads *What Will Be*, it's impossible for that person to go around with some of these stupid ideas." More broadly, Dertouzos saw the cyberphilosophy boom responding to fear among laymen about technological change: "They're asking, 'How far will this go? Will machines get smarter than I am? Will complexity warp us? Will I lose my job?'"

"When I went on my book tour," Dertouzos recalled, "I found people out there overwhelmingly afraid, much more so than I thought. I knew it cerebrally, but after 106 appearances, I now know it in my gut."

Saffo pointed out that whenever people feared the future, futurism was seldom far behind. That is, futurism and technological change bred fear, which bred futurism, which bred technological change—and more fear. "Futurism is like a comet on some loopy, irregular orbit," remarked Saffo. "It comes back about every fifteen or twenty years." It flourished, for instance, around the time of the 1939 New York World's Fair, at which industrial designer Norman Bel Geddes produced a hugely successful "Futurama" exhibit for General Motors, consecrating his popular image as a "famed expert on future trends." Later, futurism commanded mass attention in the books of writers such as Herman Kahn and Alvin Toffler.

"In the end," Saffo asked, "why do people cry for prophecy? Because we don't like change, we don't like uncertainty. We all share Mark Twain's sentiment: 'I'm all for progress—it's change I object to.' Most people's idea of progress is change in everything else, so they can preserve their own places."

Esther Dyson, widely regarded as one of the best connected women in cyberspace, acknowledged, like Dertouzos, a desire, with her book *Release 2.1,* to calm nerves. Daughter of the distinguished physicist

Freeman Dyson, she agreed that some cyberphilosophy was "pretty lightweight." Nonetheless, in aiming to make the "stuff accessible," she characterized her book in a way that captured cyberfuturism's curious relation with philosophy, the genre that comes closest to describing it: "I tried to make sure what I said held up against reality, more than against the pantheon of philosophers."

It was, for sure, a remarkable aspect of the cyberphilosophy boom that it focused far more on real-world data than on other texts, and that so few philosophy professors participated in it. There, too, several reasons suggested themselves. Despite some increase of trained philosophers in so-called applied ethics (e.g., medical ethics, business ethics) and a handful of thinkers (including Daniel Dennett and Hubert Dreyfus) who specialized in the connections between computers, consciousness and artificial intelligence, many of America's professional philosophers remained beholden to ancient examples and issues rather than the up-to-date phenomena crucial for cyberphilosophers. In contrast to their cybercousins, professional philosophers reflexively sought comprehensive, static statements of the way things *were*, rather than how things were becoming. A disproportionately cited line among them ironically came from "Mr. Becoming" himself, Georg Wilhelm Friedrich Hegel, in his famous observation that "The Owl of Minerva arrives only after dusk"—that philosophy waits for the dust of history to clear before rendering judgment.

But Kelly, a kind of gatekeeper of short-form American cyberphilosophy in his days at *Wired*, highlighted aspects of it that suggested the genre—like the computer revolution as a whole—amounted to a living fulfillment of that distinctive American contribution to world philosophy: the "pragmatism" of James and Dewey that saw knowledge as the upshot of man's continual effort to test hypotheses in his organic environment—and to keep testing them until the results fulfilled his purposes.

"It's demo or die, demo or die!" Kelly repeated. "Demo or die is the motto by which this pragmatic lifestyle and philosophy comes out. A very important part of the evolutionary viewpoint that Stuart Kauffman [the theoretical biologist long associated with the Santa Fe Institute] and I and others are promoting is that you do *iterations*. You don't expect to get it right the first time. You keep pluggin' away."

In other words, consumers of cyberphilosophy, like consumers of software, sometimes got "the Beta version"—the new product with kinks—because part of demo or die was "the idea of releasing a prod-

Kevin Kelly (1952–), founding executive editor of *Wired*, the mass-media monthly for cyberthinkers, saw digital types as descendants of "the cowboys and scouts out in the Midwest."

uct to the public that you expect the public to finish at their expense." Because a large part of the market for cyberphilosophy came from netheads acculturated to that ethos, the symbiosis between cyberauthors and cyberreaders proved smooth. "People of the screen don't read a lot of books the way they're supposed to," Kelly said. "It's not that they don't buy them and go through them. It's that they read them as if they're Web sites." That is, updatable.

Kelly saw the denizens of cyberculture as descendants of "the cowboys and scouts out in the Midwest. They weren't hauling along Plato and Aristotle. There was too much to discover." Still, they wanted to know if they were going in the right direction. Cyberphilosophy, true to its pragmatist, interactive link to the demo-or-die culture, tested hypotheses the way companies tested product. That symbiosis between intelligent, well-prepared forecasting by intellectuals, and intrepid testing and innovation by the digital industry, said Saffo, indicated why "cheap-shot" critics who mocked wrong predictions by past and present futurists—Ma and Pa flying off to work in jetpacks, five-hundred-story buildings—missed the mark. The important point was that the symbiosis worked, driving American technological culture ahead.

Put differently, Arthur Clarke's famous observation—"The future isn't what it used to be"—was a good thing. It showed that futurists kept their adjustable pragmatist eyeglasses on, and abandoned "yesterday's tomorrows" when appropriate. Forecasts, Saffo pointed out, had "to be logical, internally consistent and plausible. Reality suffers under no such limitation." The lovely thing about uncertainty, he quipped, "is that it evaporates as present moves into past."

Not all Silicon Valley framers found the lure of cyberphilosophy powerful enough to turn their attention to that "killer application," the Nostradamean tome. Sun Microsystems' chief scientist John Gage—a member of cyberroyalty far more devoted to wiring schools as a modern Johnny Modemseed than to writing treatises—liked to observe that "[t]he future is always in the future." And writing in *Slate,* Nathan Myhrvold, Gates's longtime in-house visionary, mocked the new marketplace for "cybershamans."

"Being a visionary is a new profession," he declared, "but it is really just a variant on fortunetelling, which may be the world's oldest." After confessing that he fit the profile, and providing a recipe for how to succeed as a cybershaman (e.g., "Tell 'em that 'old media' are going to die"), Myhrvold advised that humans of the future won't need the cybervisionary, because they, by definition, will grow up comfortable with the technology that frightens us. We even know these people, he joked: "We call them children."

Nonetheless, by the end of the article—acknowledging the venerable philosophical insight that children grow up—even Myhrvold didn't really buy his own point: "They'll have their own fears about the future, and so—my last prediction—the future of the fortunetelling industry is secure."

So the explosion of cyberphilosophy formed another mighty dimension of America the Philosophical, with only minor competition in such sophisticated cultures as France, Germany and the United Kingdom, and none at all in most. Beginning in the 1990s, and continuing for two decades, American thinkers began turning out a more concrete genre of cyberphilosophy about the effect of the digital revolution on politics, religion, literature, romance, journalism, film, music, business and every other part of life. At the same time, a determined cadre of cyberskeptics—among them Rochlin, Slouka, and Stoll—while hardly matching the boosters tome for tome, unleashed a steady number of contrary books, asking whether we wouldn't be better off slowing down.

As with the great cavalcade of white male American philosophy, the rise of "other minds" muscling into their territory, the rising outsiders who've expanded the big tent of America the Philosophical, some selective reportorial exploration of the territory brings weight to the thesis that, in America, we do philosophy our way.

CYBERPOLITICS

The sign on the door of the meeting room at the Omni Shoreham Hotel in Washington, D.C., said "Cabinet Room," but the folks sweeping in looked unfamiliar. These were not the folks who sat at the long table in the White House. Here, in August, at the American Political Science Association's annual meeting, with sensible government types on summer recess, only hard-core *thinkers* about politics showed their faces. Yet that always included a good mix of practitioners. On a late Thursday afternoon, the Omni Cabinet Room ended up standing room only, packed with such noteworthies as former deputy secretary of state Joseph Nye Jr., and media scholar W. Russell Neuman. They were waiting for the session on "Political Communication Via the Internet."

Positioned amid what sometimes still goes for "high tech" at an academic convention—worn metal chairs and water pitchers on an aproned table—Richard Davis of Brigham Young University got started on a nonpartisan note.

"Speaking of technology," he remarked as people began to liquefy from the Potomac humidity, "I think they should issue fans."

It wasn't necessary. After only twenty sweat-filled minutes of a panel full of the expected oracular observations—that the Net was "potentially the most powerful political tool of the past fifty years," that "for those who are marginalized, the Internet provides a cyber village square"—two audience members, presumably on the edge of heat-induced dementia, rose up and did the unthinkable, or previously un-thought-of.

They examined the air conditioner switch.

They determined it was off.

They turned it on.

Smiles all around. The great convention master in the sky had sent a signal. *Beware, ye political junkies of great hubris, in the face of Future Tech. You're just barely on top of the stuff you've got.*

Everywhere at that APSA meeting—left, right, or undecided—panels of heavy thinking about the Net, the digital revolution, and the implications for politics were sure to follow. Among them: "The Future of Political Science and the Internet"; "Internet and Governance: Local, State, National, and Global Issues"; "Research on the Use of the Internet and Multimedia in Election Campaigns."

The questions—let alone the answers—couldn't be found in Locke, Rousseau or Weber:

- Did the Internet's speed and reach mean that representative democracy in America—a system the Founders explicitly favored over direct democracy—was doomed in favor of democracy by referenda and ballot initiatives? (Maybe.)
- Had the Net made traditional campaigning's telephone trees and rubber-chicken dinners so antiquated that political power within ten years would be controlled by the cybersavvy? (Yes. Obama would confirm it.)
- Was the youth-friendly nature of the Net sure to help Democrats more than Republicans? (Likely, but not certain.)
- Would future candidates have to respond interactively to voter queries, or suffer the consequences of providing mere "brochure-ware" on their Web pages? (To some extent.)
- Would the Net's ability to bind together far-flung people of similar interests lead to greater political power by fringe groups, and a Balkanization of American politics? (Maybe.)
- Could we expect the ability of politicians and their parties to communicate their messages *unfiltered* by major media to accelerate further marginalization of major media? (For sure.)

Those and other provocative questions all found themselves repeated. The attention paid at APSA, the many panel papers, confirmed that slews of books on "the Internet and politics" were stirring in embryo, slouching toward birth. You had to give the political scientists credit for Realpolitik. Cyberphilosophers in the field, much like the public at large, seemed to split into two mainstream parties identifiable by their rough approaches, both test-ballooning the big ideas that kibitzers and aspiring "poly-cyentists" would have to confront for years to come.

The "delegate counters"—let's call them that—concentrated on the nitty-gritty of day-to-day politics, bringing the best (empirical data) and worst (convoluted explanations of the obvious) from political science to the issue of who was using which technology to reach how many constituencies for what purpose. On that score, Rash Jr.'s *Politics on the Nets* provided the earliest blueprint of the trends that would later be analyzed in such books as *Web Campaigning* by Kirsten Foot and Steven Schneider (2006) and *Rebooting American Politics* by Jason Gainous and Kevin Wagner (2011). Drawing on the insights of scores of political and digital experts, evaluating the Web strategies of political parties and issue groups (even reproducing their Web pages on glossy stock), Rash, then senior technology editor for *Communications Week,* surveyed the field, explaining how small novelties such as a presidential candidate giving out his Web page address at the end of a debate had signaled the future.

By contrast, the "advance men and women"—so to speak—pondered democracy with a lower-case *d,* offering majestic thoughts about how the cyberrevolution would affect the state, the citizen, the polis and all those key classical abstractions of political theory debated from Aristotle to George Kennan. Here an early book that extended some of cyber-cynicism to politics was Lawrence Grossman's *The Electronic Republic: Reshaping Democracy in the Information Age.* In it, the former PBS and NBC News president warned that representative democracy, designed by the framers to inhibit the potential abuses of direct democracy (nicely described by the Twentieth Century Fund president as "a tyranny of whim"), now tottered on the brink of the technological revolution.

Rash made clear in *Politics on the Nets* that cyberpolitics in its infancy remained an "afterthought" for many political organizations, and netlag was to be expected from older politicians slow to learn about digital things. He also noted two factors that at first complicated e-mail efficiency for politicians: the need to authoritatively discern whether a person was "a constituent or not," and the early perception that sending e-mail was "so easy and cheap that it can be done without thought." Politicians, Rash reported, in pondering whether to reply to communications and its cost, tended to weigh heavily "the likelihood of voting."

Rash thought such foot-dragging was likely to fade, as it did, because "when the voters refuse to stand for such resistance, the government will be forced to find a way." Then the changes Rash envisioned—such as greater citizen-government business through the Net—would come, as they did, with the transaction costs of communication between government and citizens declining from direct mail to listserve postings to Twitter.

First, single-issue groups, less constrained geographically and financially, would increasingly be able to organize and lobby more successfully. Rash gave the now ancient example of Internet activist Jim Warren's 1993 effort to get the California legislature to make pending bills available over the Internet. Using e-mail messages to trigger more weightily valued letters and faxes, Warren's campaign, wrote Rash (of what is now standard practice), "became what the military refers to as a force multiplier. . . . [I]t makes your resources seem larger and more effective than they really are."

Second, while Rash stated the later commonplace that radical and fringe groups were also exploiting the Net for traditional political functions from public relations to recruitment to fund-raising, he noted that the need for fringe groups "to appear generally acceptable as a way to get the public to read an organization's Web site" was affecting them. According to Rash, "as groups that once seemed to be beyond normal politics come into closer contact with the mainstream, they also change to more closely reflect the mainstream."

Third, Rash felt confident that the huge increase in available political information, and access to it, would result in better-educated, better-informed voters, less easy to fool. Fourth, politicians with netlag would increasingly pay the price. (Hello, John McCain.) Net politics, he promised, was "far superior to anything else available for organizing and winning an election," and the future would confirm that.

Rash's approach kept to the largely and understandably ahistorical. Grossman, by contrast, placed our electronically pressured democracy in the broad context of the American experience. Even before the Web took over American life, Grossman contended, the country was turning into "an electronic republic," a democratic system that was "vastly increasing the people's day-to-day influence on the decisions of state." Grossman cited chapter and verse:

> Populist measures such as term limits, balanced budget amendments, direct state primaries and caucuses, and expanding use of ballot initiatives and referenda reduce the discretion of elected officials, enable voters to pick their own presidential nominees, bypass legislatures, and even empower the people to make their own laws. Incessant public-opinion polling and increasingly sophisticated interactive communications devices make government instantly aware of, and responsive to, popular will. . . . As

the elect seek to respond to every twist and turn of the electorate's mood, the people at large are taking on a more direct role in government than the Founders ever intended.

For Grossman, the people, not the press, were becoming the "fourth estate," supplementing the executive, legislative and judicial branches. He feared that the "electronic republic" would "undercut—if not fundamentally alter—some of our most cherished Constitutional protections against the excesses of majority impulses."

The Founders, he noted, feared both pure democracy and governmental authority: "The Constitution sought not only to protect the people against the overreaching power of government but also to protect the new nation against the overreaching demands of ordinary people, especially the poor." With the "electronic republic" a foregone conclusion, Grossman warned that the judiciary would bear "an increasingly difficult and heavy burden to protect individual rights against popular assault." In the meantime, "[a]s the power of public opinion rises, the roles of the traditional political intermediaries—the parties, the mass media experts, and the governing elite—decline. Institutions that obstruct the popular will or stand between it and the actions of government get bypassed."

In the end, Grossman argued, striking a Deweyan note, the only solution was better-educated citizens, more likely to be dedicated to "the common good." He took as his beacon a statement by Thomas Jefferson: "I know of no safe depository of the ultimate powers of the society but the people themselves, and if we think them not enlightened enough to exercise their control with a wholesome discretion, the remedy is not to take it from them, but to inform their discretion."

Did Grossman's and Rash's visions clash? On the contrary. Rash's details suggested that Grossman's better-educated citizenry would develop, allowing us all to breathe a sigh of relief. Another budding cyberphilosopher of the time, before he found writing about dogs more fulfilling—Jon Katz—argued in his book *Virtuous Reality* that such a citizenry would fulfill the democratic hopes of Jefferson and Paine: "Anyone online can recognize the idea of countless ordinary people participating in the creation of public opinion, their ideas 'expansible over all space.'"

The delay in politics *radically* changing on the ground meant that "advance men and women" could still safely battle over the big picture to come. One contrary voice at APSA, Jodi Dean of Hobart and William Smith Colleges, denounced the whole cliché of cyberspace as a "public sphere," charging that the media enable aggressive corporate and governmental designs on it by propagating the stereotype. "To territorialize cyberia as the public sphere," argued Dean, "is to determine in advance what sorts of engagements and identities are proper to the political and use this determination to homogenize political engagement, neutralize social space, and sanitize popular cultures."

Contrary to Grossman's fear that America's public conversation would become too *democratic,* or to the "romantic conception" of Jon Katz that the Net would level the power of the corporatized press, Dean contended that it was precisely the multifarious *private* nature of the Net that constituted its uniqueness. "The democratizing force of the Internet," she insisted, "is not about voting or expressing an opinion on particular political issues. It's about competing conceptions of the real as sites produced by ufologists, teenagers from New Jersey, CNN, and Nicholas Negroponte vie for hits even as they are linked together. It's about contests over whose words count and how this might be decided or fought out. It's about the unceasing disruption of official narratives of truth, authority, and reality."

Or so she said.

CYBERRELIGION

Looking around the hip, industrial-chic San Francisco newsroom of *Wired*—the monthly intellectual digest of the digital revolution—in its pre–Condé Nast infancy, you knew you were at the site of a contemporary Genesis, a world of sacred digital citizens created in fewer than seven years.

It was the part of cyberspace ordered into existence the old-fashioned way, the Old Testament way: a heavenly thought (courtesy of founding publisher Louis Rossetto), transformed into scripture (thanks to founding editor Kevin Kelly), put into action through slangy, clangy, know-it-all sentences and scoop reportage from the fringes of the emerging digital universe. Add *Wired*'s widely imitated, eyeball-mashing graphics on luxurious paper, and its endless "A New Dawn Is Rising!" cover teases—"PUSH! THE RADICAL FUTURE OF MEDIA BEYOND THE WEB," or "THE LONG BOOM: 25 YEARS OF PROSPERITY, FREEDOM AND A BETTER ENVIRONMENT FOR THE WHOLE WORLD"—and you had the miracle of the decade in magazine publishing: serial cyberphilosophy that sold.

"*Let there be Wired!*" the culture seemed to shout, so loudly that Si Newhouse eventually bought it, and yanked it to Manhattan, but generally left it alone.

Everywhere in the original, funky *Wired* newsroom, housed in a drab former factory building along Third Street in the neighborhood locals called "Multimedia Gulch," a cocky, superior attitude ruled. It surfaced amid the makeshift desks balanced on file cabinets, the tastefully exposed silver pipes and mechanicals.

On the cubicles of several staffers, photocopies hung of a classic reporter-to-editor sentiment ("Go Ahead, Make One More Change!"), with Dirty Harry's photo beside it to drive home the message. Around the gray-carpeted newsroom, posters with a bristly libertarian message

("Uncle Sam, Out of My Homepage!") competed with less aggressive forms of attitude ("Will Write for Food!").

Finally you came to the far corner cubicle, where Kelly, *Wired*'s top editor at the time, proposed and disposed. Crowding the geekosphere around his terminal, forming piles on the floor, were not monitor pets but books of cyberthink: *High Noon on the Electronic Frontier: Conceptual Issues in Cyberspace,* edited by Peter Ludlow and Mike Godwin; *The Ingenious Mind of Nature,* by George Hall; and even his own: *Out of Control.*

"I'm an idea junkie," confessed Kelly, ruddy-faced and quick to gesture, so familiar with cyberideas that he routinely started muttering, "Right, right, right" whenever the point of a visitor's question crested before the end of his sentence. "I swim in ideas. I wrote a book about *very big ideas.*" *Out of Control*'s revelations included the claim that "Machines are becoming biological and the biological is becoming engineered." (That would also become a signature theme of fellow cyberphilosopher Ray Kurzweil.)

A more immediate revelation screamed from Kelly's Mac, where a small card affixed to the screen bore one large message: "You are a visionary." Just a modest step down, a visitor noted, from a card declaring "You are a God"—the role, Kelly reported in his book, that software whizzes increasingly take on in the brave new world of computer-game simulacra.

"When I was researching *Out of Control,*" said Kelly, "the thing that struck me was how often computer scientists use the word 'God.' It actually accrues a kind of scientific meaning, with a small *g*. They're making all these worlds all the time, so they have to have some prime cause or source behind these things."

In a chapter of *Out of Control* titled "God Games," Kelly described computer god games such as *Populous II,* in which the player becomes a son of Zeus and has to "think like a god" to win. Another god game, *SimEarth,* began for its designers in an attempt to model the Gaia hypothesis of biologists James Lovelock and Lynn Margulis. According to their view, the "self-correcting cohesion" of the earth's global biochemistry makes it best understood as a living organism. Players of *SimEarth,* wrote Kelly, got a feel "of what it will be like to parry with autonomous vivisystems."

Digital empowerment, Kelly believed, helped secular-minded computer geeks accept the notion of "godly" intelligence. "There is a reintroduction of the idea of God to secular thought," he said, "but it's *engineers as gods.* Nothing propels your thoughts in that direction like having to think of a world that, given the initial conditions, will run and fold out."

"You start thinking about what kind of a God am I?" he continued. "Am I a God who's constantly intervening? Am I a God who just stands back as it rolls out? Am I a God who occasionally does miracles? There's not a lot of talk about it, but from an observer's point of view, yes, it's very rampant."

Yet despite Kelly's belief that the revolution bore huge implications for religion and theology, those subjects drew less attention from traditional media, cyberseers and bloggers than, for instance, the impact of the Net on politics.

Most books by cyberthinkers simply ignored the Net's religious ramifications. One exception—*What Will Be,* a wide-ranging 336-page study by Dertouzos—devoted three paragraphs to the subject. Religious organizations, noted the longtime director of MIT's Laboratory for Computer Science, would benefit, like everyone else, from electronic improvements in office work and proselytizing: the "ability of each church to reach hundreds of millions of people with information about their beliefs and functions will widen the possibilities for affiliation." Dertouzos predicted improved outreach by churches would be "felt mostly as an extension of the physical community, with totally virtual religious membership and fully virtual churches being rare and confined to cases where there is no other alternative." At the same time, he could not "foresee any ways in which the Information Marketplace" would "affect the spirituality of people one way or another, except perhaps indirectly by exposing many more people to the various options for spiritual fulfillment."

David Whittle, chairman of Webworking Services and author of *Cyberspace: The Human Dimension,* similarly spent just a few pages on religious issues in his 456-page tome. He, however, noticed something Dertouzos overlooked: "Many religions have doctrinal roots in ideas that might be construed to be related to cyberspace, such as collective consciousness, infinite knowledge, an oversoul, the all-seeing eye, and shared visions. These ideas may begin to influence religious perspectives in many ways as we interpret scripture and prophecies, share insights, and study sacred religious traditions with the help of cyberspace resources."

Some digitally savvy scholars of religion voiced their expectations of change more strongly. In an article entitled "The Unknown God of the Internet: Religious Communication from the Ancient Agora to the

Virtual Forum," Stephen O'Leary of the University of California and Brenda Brasher of Thiel College—who met and became friends on the Net—argued that we shouldn't be surprised if the "form of religion in the electronic communities of the future differs as greatly in its contemporary incarnations as the teachings of Jesus differ from the dialectical theology of Aquinas or as the eucharistic ceremonies of the earliest Christians differ from the Latin high mass."

One cyberphilosopher took that truth to heart and confronted the Net's religious implications head-on: Jeff Zaleski, a lapsed Catholic, fledgling Buddhist and former editor of *Parabola.*

"Jews, Christians, Muslims, Hindus, and Buddhists have established beachheads on the Internet," he declared in his introduction to *The Soul of Cyberspace,* the best, boldest and most comprehensive early guide to the subject. "So have Druids, Pagans, Taoists, Zoroastrians, Gnostics, Sikhs, Mormons, Jains, New Agers, Twelve-Steppers, and Satanists." A happy interfaith marriage between the journalistic and philosophical, *The Soul of Cyberspace* named names, gathered figures and filed dispatches from across online's religious terrain.

Zaleski reported back from Rabbi Yosef Kazen's Chabad Lubavitch Web site in Brooklyn as well as the Havienu L'Shalom "virtual congregation" that wanted to build the Third Temple in cyberspace. He discussed the formal blessing of cyberspace by Tibetan Buddhist monks and introduced us to Tariqas, a Sufi mailing list, and its spiritual presence, Sheikh Hisham Muhammad Kabbani, who declared that the "Internet is energy."

To the extent anyone possessed firm numbers on Net religiosity, Zaleski collected them. Christian Web sites, he reported, made up "more than 80 per cent of the Web sites of the world's five major (i.e., most influential) religions," even though Judaism, Islam, Buddhism and Hinduism combined claim "about 2 billion adherents, the same number Christianity claims." The explanation, according to Zaleski, was "domination of the Net by users from the United States and Western Europe, where Christianity reigns." (Those numbers have since grown more balanced.) In a final nod to shoe-leather reporting, Zaleski also provided a guide to Web sites for almost every religious interest. Want to discuss the righteousness of the veil, or whether dogs are "bad for Muslims"? He had a site for you. More interested in how Buddhist sutras should operate on the Web? He could offer a recommendation there too.

According to Zaleski, the seed for his project wasn't reportorial fervor, but philosophical perplexity. It had come a few years earlier when he began to research, with his wife, Tracy Cochran, a book entitled *Transformations: Awakening to the Sacred in Ourselves.* Using Net skills he'd mastered as a text writer for computer games, he went online to ask people about their moments of spiritual transformation.

"It dawned on me that no one mentioned having such a moment while online," said Zaleski during an interview at his office in Manhattan. "All the stories involved walking in nature, or making love, or something to do with our everyday physical world. So I flipped that into a question: Was something about cyberspace keeping people from having the sort of spiritual experiences they have in the real world?" That question became the seed for *The Soul of Cyberspace.* For all its information yield, the book took shape around a spine of probing questions—and tentative answers—in the face of profound issues raised by religion's encounter with digital innovation:

- Would the widely discussed cybernotion of the Net as an "emergent universal mind" alter people's traditional conception of God? (Possible, but unlikely.)
- Might the anarchic libertarianism of the Net lead to a proliferation of religious sects so extraordinary that the Reformation would seem a mild in-house splintering? (Also unlikely.)
- Could we expect all kinds of religious rituals and sacraments, such as the minyan in Judaism—the quorum of ten adult Jewish males required by Jewish law to be present to conduct public prayers—or confession and baptism in Catholicism, to lose their corporeal requirements and be replaced by ten-person chat rooms for the minyan and virtual water sprinkled over an avatar for baptism? (*Very* unlikely.)
- Were computer scientists, like some physicists in the generation before them, becoming more respectful of religion in the light of discoveries about networked intelligence? (No.)
- Would authoritarian religions, such as Catholicism, suffer as the Net became more influential, while less centralized ones, such as Buddhism, prospered? (Probably.)
- Would the singular importance of the body across *all* religions prove a kind of "Great Wall" keeping the Net from changing religion to the degree it changed other areas of life? (Probably.)
- Would emergent intelligences on the Net have souls and deserve reverence? (Unclear.)

Zaleski acknowledged that the notion of a "global brain" arising persisted as "a very dominant idea in cybercircles. It's a real catchy idea. It's certainly true that the Internet is connecting people. And insofar as it connects people, there's some sort of synergy that goes on through a multitude of brains. Perhaps something more intellectually powerful than one brain is emerging from it. People want a God—everyone has a spiritual thirst."

The idea bore a distinguished pedigree. The French Jesuit paleontologist Pierre Teilhard de Chardin (1881–1955), who argued that the mind of God develops along with the universe in an evolutionary way, exercised a powerful influence on cyberthinkers, as did the Gaia hypothesis. Yet another factor bolstering the idea of a "global brain" was the notion associated with physicists such as Sir Arthur Eddington that "[t]he stuff of the world is mind stuff." In the light of modern physics's discovery that matter, as it becomes infinitesimal, is not so much a *thing* as a "state of organization" describable solely by mathematical equations, Eddington wrote in *The Nature of the Physical World* (1935) that "modern scientific theories have broken away from the common standpoint which identifies the real with the concrete."

His contemporary and Einstein's colleague Sir James Jeans—often remembered for remarking that "God is a mathematician"—asserted in *The Mysterious Universe* (1930) that in the light of modern mathematical physics, "the universe can best be pictured . . . as consisting of pure thought, the thought of what, for want of a wider word, we must describe as a mathematical thinker."

All the same, Zaleski derided as "total hooey" the idea that an intelligence built up of the mathematically based intelligences of various computers approximated the traditional notion of God. "The reason it's hooey," he said, "is that there's a difference between intelligence and consciousness." While machines would get smarter and smarter, and more and more like us, he conceded, they would not *be* us—or God: "The traditional definition of God requires that he is self-aware."

Zaleski agreed that some of God's other traditional attributes— omniscience, omnipotence, immanence through all space and time, freedom from the laws of science and logic—made it hard for even the most amazing of machines, or machine-like intelligences, to catch up. He pooh-poohed Kelly's notion that the global mind might lead us to redefine God as a very smart superextended being—as complex, so to speak, as our technology will allow. "That would be like a god with a little *g*," Zaleski remarked, "like the Greek gods. Gods like that will arise. But my sense of God or what God might be comes mostly from the testimony of the mystics. If the mystics come back and say that God is *that* and yet he is *not that,* God breaks the barriers set up by science. God is alogical. Spiritual truth is alogical."

In Zaleski's view, that scientists saw "God" as an emergent networked intelligence showed that the Net wasn't, in fact, drawing them closer to traditional religion. It just showed that a lot of scientists "believe consciousness is simply an epiphenomenon of the neurological circuitry of the brain." They differed, then, from those twentieth-century physicists who had grown more appreciative of religion as they came to understand the irreducible need for metaphor in explaining the universe.

Bill Gates, Zaleski suggested, aptly represented such folks: "As far as I can tell, he doesn't have a religious bone in his body." Nonetheless, Zaleski saw an irony in the cyberpriesthood's enthusiasm for a global mind. "They seem to scoff at traditional gods," he noted, "but they clearly hunger for something to worship. That's something embedded in human beings. Worship is a natural stance for humanity." Rather than scientists being lured into traditional religion, Zaleski believed "more religious-oriented people" were "being lured by the Net into becoming more involved with science. That may be what transforms science's attitude toward its limits more than anything else." A key reason was that science could never "satisfactorily explore spiritual experience." Science remained "based on rationality, the scientific method and measurement. And you can't measure spiritual experiences."

Perhaps the key dividing line between religion and cyberculture, Zaleski emphasized, came in the non-negotiable importance every world religion places on rituals that require the body. "It's a bedrock of every religion," said Zaleski of corporeal presence. Whether, he noted in *The Soul of Cyberspace,* one expressed the concept as *prana*—a Sanskrit word alternately translated as "breath" or "life force"—or through the Chinese concept of *chi,* or "the Judeo-Christian-Islamic concept of *spirit,*" all the major traditions possessed "this insistence on the sacredness of the flesh—the flesh animated with holy breath." Catholicism, he explained, reflected that in the significance of Christ coming to earth in a human body, and of the Catholic mass asserting, "This is my body, this is my blood, partake of it."

Why was corporeal presence so important? "Because," answered Zaleski, "to know God you have to know yourself. To know yourself, you have to be aware of yourself in this moment. And the only way to do that is to ground your attention in your body. You have to have the body, because there's no other ground. The mind can't ground itself. Beyond that, the great religions teach that in the body itself are manifested certain sacred energies, which don't manifest themselves just in the mind.

"A Catholic priest would *not* say that if you took this host and examined the chemicals, you're going to find human flesh," Zaleski continued. "But whatever the Christ substance is that's in the flesh is now in the host. It's not a metaphor. It is the thing itself."

"Take confession," he said, offering another example. "Confession is the sacrament that most easily could be performed on the Net because, as someone in the book mentions, you could have communication between one person and another at least as secure as you do in the booth. I personally don't see why you have to be in the body. But the Catholic Church says you do."

And it's the same with baptism, he concluded. You *could* sprinkle virtual water over an avatar, but the Church says no. You could conduct a minyan in a chat room, but the rabbis say no. "You're talking about Mystery here with a capital *M*," remarked Zaleski.

Even beyond mystery, Zaleski thought one could come up with *scientific* rationales for emphasizing the importance of the body for religion. One, he pointed out, was taking the approach of Candace Pert, an expert on the role of endorphins in the body who had "become a leading spokesperson for the idea that consciousness exists not just in the brain, but throughout the body, in the limbic system."

"Of course," Zaleski continued, "someone like Kelly might say, 'We can digitize the brain, we can digitize the limbic system.' So my question in the book became, 'Is there something that can't be digitized?' Because if there's not, we might as well leave our bodies and be on software. My guess is that there *is* something that cannot be digitized, because it's not digital. It does not translate into ones and zeros, into yeses and nos. That is what we want to call primal sacred energy. It's what can't be represented through software."

"What Heaven's Gate said to me," Zaleski explained, referring to the thirty-nine San Diego cultists who committed mass suicide, "was, 'Here is the danger—when the Internet takes people away from their bodies and the natural world.' When you're cut off from the natural world and your sense of the body, you're cut off from sacred energies. That's where madness begins."

"What we're really going back to here," Zaleski said, "is that old medieval demonization of the body. It's coming back through cyberculture. *The body's bad, we have to leave it behind.* And of course it's bad because we're not immortal. As Jaron Lanier [the coiner of the term "virtual reality"] points out, part of what's going on here is death denial. These scientists don't want to die. They want to become immortal, and to do it through software." That is, as Lanier said, they want to survive death by backing themselves up on disc.

Beyond the threshold question of the body's centrality to religion, Zaleski found it notable that "other than the very vague, worshipful attitude toward the überbrain, there's been no even mildly powerful religion that's arisen from the Internet." He suspected that even with the proliferation of Web sites, a gigantic fragmentation of established religions into sects would not occur: "People like to be told what to do. People like to be told what the truth is. Insofar as that's the case, the centralized hierarchical religions will continue to flourish."

At the same time, Zaleski did think that "the Net will affect some religions more than others. It's a very fluid, nonhierarchical, noncentralized, anarchistic medium. As people spend more and more time in it, they're going to gravitate toward religions that reflect that particular structure. The religion that reflects such a structure most easily is Buddhism, which has no center. And the religion most antithetical to that is Roman Catholicism."

"Curiously enough," he added, that was reflected in the Web sites. When the Vatican's Web site began, for instance, it was not interactive and could not receive e-mail. "It was like visiting St. Peter's," Zaleski joked, "and the Web site of the Latter-day Saints was the same way." Further, Zaleski thought that given America's initial dominance of the Web, "American brands of religion" would likely win adherents around the world, spreading values of democracy and emphasis on "the role of individual conscience." He believed the Net would also help correct distortions of religion encouraged by selective mass-media coverage (such as regular identification of Islam with terrorism), and place every official religion under scrutiny: "Blasphemy and heretical attitudes are going to proliferate like crazy on the Net, and personally I'm all for it. I think every religion needs a challenge. . . . If you have fifteen thousand Web sites devoted to Roman Catholicism, probably ten thousand of them are going to be heretical in some way, because human nature tends to veer from dictated truth."

So what could the powers of established religion do? Will the pope have to maintain more bandwidth than any other Catholic? Will religions have to compete to get the latest Intel chip to stay a step ahead?

"I don't think there really is a way to stay ahead," Zaleski replied.

"Whoever really attracts the best techies is going to put on the best show."

As Zaleski elaborated in his book, the multiple implications of the Net for religion—at first, so uncertain—poured forth. Might a cyberliterate, forty-two-year-old cardinal elected to the papacy alter traditions irrevocably? ("It's imaginable," said Zaleski.) How about an e-mail election for a new pope, without the traditional wisps of white smoke? (Also conceivable, he said, while warning that "whatever is digitized will be hacked"—including a papal election.)

In the end, Zaleski confessed to much uncertainty about the cyber-religious future. "It's really unfathomable to figure out from here what's going to happen over the long run," he said. "We're dealing with forever." But he ventured a thought. "The most profound effect the Net is going to have on religion," he predicted, will be "something we haven't even touched upon: the Net's generation of intelligences that are not human."

Zaleski recalled that he'd already conducted Net conversations through as many as ten back-and-forths before realizing he was talking to a "bot."

"Once humanity is dealing with and interacting with artificial intelligences that for all perceptible purposes are as conscious and intelligent as us, and this will happen," he concluded, "it's going to throw into question everything by which we define ourselves as human. It will throw our very natures into question. And that will shake up religions tremendously."

Stephen O'Leary and Brenda Brasher agreed that the "cyborg" phenomenon would prove daunting for religion. As computer intelligences became more sophisticated, the so-called Turing test would lose its usefulness. Alan Turing, the famous British mathematician, suggested the test in 1950 to determine whether a machine could "think." If a computer can answer questions so that the questioner can't tell if a computer or human being is answering, then "intelligence" is at hand.

The problem of applying the test to a higher consciousness, however, boggled the mind. O'Leary and Brasher believed traditional "philosophical conceptions of the embodiment of the Logos in human form are profoundly challenged by the human-machine coupling." If, they suggested, such a creature decided to echo Jesus in Matthew 8:29 and ask, "Who do you say that I am?," what would we be likely to answer?

Which brought one back to Kelly's thought that as the digital revolution continued to push forward on the fronts of interconnected and "artificial" intelligence, there was a subject—he called it "the theology of computation"—that bore watching.

"The thing about computers is that they're actually changing science," Kelly said. "There were two parts of science: theory and experiment. An hypothesis and a test of it. And there was back-and-forth between the two. But computers are the third way. Computers are neither theory nor experiment—they're both. When you do a model in computer systems, you *embody that theory*, you give it behavior, a world in which to live."

"It's no longer just abstract theory," he continued. "The model itself becomes *something more than a model*, it becomes something in itself, that you have to deal with. So, artificial life, in some sense, you could say, is just a theory of life. But it's also become something in its own. A computer world like *SimEarth* has its own dynamics. Is a computer virus, replicating around, a theory? Is it an experiment? No. It's something in itself, a new creation, a third way."

"The new way of doing science is that you actually create a model that I call 'hyperreal,'" Kelly said, "after Umberto Eco's term: it's a fake so real that it has its own realness. That hyperreality is how science is being done more and more. You model the oceans, you model the atmosphere, and the model itself takes on something distinctive: you're not quite studying the real world, you're not quite studying the experiment: it has its own being."

Simply put, suggested Kelly, we were in "a period of second-order Godhood," following in the footsteps of our maker. In *Out of Control*, Kelly ended his account of god games by reflecting on the original: Yahweh's creation of man on the sixth day of Genesis. Yahweh, Kelly wrote, had built his universe "merely by thinking aloud." But the creation of man proceeded differently, requiring an "almost playful gesture."

"This one was to be a model in imitation of the great Yahweh himself," maintained Kelly. "In some cybernetic way the man was to be a simulacra of Yahweh. As Yahweh was a creator, this model would also create a simulation of Yahweh's creativity. As Yahweh had free will and loved, this model was to have free will and love in reflection of Yahweh. So Yahweh endowed the model with the same type of true creativity he himself possessed."

It's all there in Genesis, Kelly implied. So it came to pass, he continued, that "[a] few bold man-things have had a recurring dream: to do as Yahweh did and make a model of themselves—a simulacra that

CYBERLITERATURE

William Gibson, sci-fi demigod and coiner of the term "cyberspace" in his story "Burning Chrome," conceded that he often didn't live up to his forbidding image as digital desire seized the world of literature. For one thing, he remained a nice enough guy to meet a visitor to his adopted hometown, Vancouver, British Columbia, at the Web Cafe, even though he admitted being sick of showing up at such an obvious setting, with its "Cyber Nachos" (predictable tortilla chips smothered in cheese) and "Web Salad" (fresh greens tossed with carrots, no pixels in sight).

Wimpy behavior, especially for the creator of Case, that outlaw computer hacker who plugged into the sensory apparatus of strangers in Gibson's *Neuromancer* (1984), the Old Testament of cyberpunk novels. "There was an assistant district attorney in Arizona," laughed Gibson, tall (six foot six), gentle, lanky and as bent over as a study lamp, "who was convinced for a while that [fellow cyberpunk writer] Bruce Sterling and I were completely responsible for every act of computer terrorism ever committed in her jurisdiction."

"Sterling ran into her at a computer conference," Gibson recalled, "and she said, 'Yeah, we know we've got a bad one when we break the door down and there's a copy of *Neuromancer* on top of the terminal! Then we *really* take them apart.'"

Eventually, Gibson said, Sterling won her over with charm and the argument that "we were no more responsible for that stuff than Elmore Leonard is for people becoming hit men."

But failing the criminal mastermind test was not the only way Gibson failed to measure up. There are also those "distressing experiences" with fans.

"I don't know what they expect from Stephen King," he said, "maybe an ax in his head, or something. But some people still really believe that I'll turn out to be the king of the hackers. That I do my hacking on some-

will spring from their own hands and in its turn create novelty freely as Yahweh and man-things can."

That's where we were heading, according to Kelly, facing some ultimate questions: "Would creating our own simulacra *complete* Yahweh's genesis in an act of true flattery? Or did it commence mankind's demise in the most foolish audacity? Was the work of the model-making-its-own-model a sacrament or a blasphemy?"

It was only a matter of time, Kelly and other cyberthinkers believed, before the religious implications of the digital revolution became more widely apparent and perplexing. As O'Leary and Brasher wrote, "If humans have spent the last two millennia pondering the implications of the Gospel's statement that 'the Word became flesh, and dwelt among us' (John 1:14), is it even possible for us to imagine—let alone assimilate—the incarnation of the Logos in an age of technologized humans and humanized machines? . . . What creature is it that the cool, abstract discourse of cybernetics summons toward Bethlehem to be born?"

By 2010, Kelly, in a new treatise titled *What Technology Wants,* had decided that the name of the new deity was—technology. Or what Kelly dubbed "the technium"—the whole system of technology in which we're now embedded. It had developed its own desires and instincts, and now constituted, in the words of Paul Hawken, "a self-organizing universe better understood through the metaphors of biology than engineering." As Kelly put it, "We can't demand that technology obey us any more than we can demand that life obey us. Sometimes we should surrender to its lead and bask in its abundance."

It sounded as if the impulse to worship was alive and well.

thing that looks like a stealth bomber, with the serial numbers filed off, that's been built by disaffiliated Sun/Microsoft rogues in Puerto Rico. When they discover I'm not that, they're really disappointed. I never know what to do. I give them an extra book or T-shirt or something."

No, the literary father of cyberspace and cyberpunk was not inclined to bestow his blessing on the two most obvious philosophical (as opposed to commercial) consequences of the digital revolution on literature: 1) the explosion of novels dealing with digitally savvy themes, characters and settings, and 2) the separate, much-hyped genre of hyperfiction, touted by some academics as the hip literature of the future that might change the nature of narrative.

On the whole, Gibson didn't much care for computers.

"I can't fetishize them," he said. "They're about the only things I can't fetishize. They don't *look very good.* They're always obsolete. It's like buying ice cream—you buy some and take it home from the store, it's kind of melting in the trunk while you try to get it home." The same wild enthusiasm issued forth when you asked him about hyperfiction, in which digital prose chunks can be read in almost any order. Back in the mid-1980s, various people kept singing its praises. Whatever happened to it?

"Beats me," said Gibson, chuckling. "I'm just a words-in-a-row kind of guy myself. My idea of hypertext fiction is James Joyce's *Ulysses* or, you know, reading after a couple of stiff Scotches. That's close enough for me. I just never got the idea."

But in absorbing the material of the digital revolution into fiction (when not leading the charge), Gibson managed to stay well in line with many others. Just as Victorian novels like Dickens's *Hard Times* reflected the impact of the Industrial Revolution, and post–World War II novels such as Norman Mailer's *The Naked and the Dead* distilled a generation's experience, so the wares of America's novelists increasingly showed the impact of the digital revolution from the last two decades of the twentieth century on. From John Updike's *Roger's Version* (1984), with its manipulation of computer metaphors, to *Exegesis* (1997), by Astro Teller, a first novel composed entirely of e-mail, to multiple novels by the brainy Richard Powers and Charles Yu's *How to Live Safely in a Science Fictional Universe,* a critics' favorite in 2010, the themes and technical furniture of digital culture gradually and comfortably entered the mainstream.

Yet true to the many paradoxes spawned by digital culture—such as whether machines can be people, and people machines—the literary realm offered its own version: Did digital culture create the literature, or did the literature create digital culture? While literary writers drew on computer culture for decades—think as far back as Kurt Vonnegut's *Player Piano* (1952) or Thomas Pynchon's *The Crying of Lot 49* (1964)—its first real impact on fiction came in the 1980s, with the rise of "cyberpunk" fiction.

First used by writer Bruce Bethke in his 1983 story, the term "cyberpunk" was then applied by science fiction anthologist Gardner Dozois to describe a new genre of science fiction mainly set, according to science fiction scholar Peter Nicholls, "in computer-driven, high-tech near-future venues inhabited by a slum-bound citizenry for whom the new world is an environment, not a project." Pioneer writers included Gibson, Sterling, Rudy Rucker, and Lewis Shiner, with Gibson's *Neuromancer* the urtext. Cyberpunk fiction tended to imagine future scenarios in which political or economic power lay in huge national or international networks. In *Neuromancer,* for instance, Gibson's protagonist, Case, entered into the world's mysterious database by jacking himself into it and propelling "his disembodied consciousness into the consensual hallucination that was the matrix."

The prefix "cyber," etymologically derived from the Greek word "to steer," had returned to modern usage in the new science of "cybernetics" proclaimed by mathematician Norbert Weiner in his 1947 book of that title. For Weiner, the term captured the study of intelligent systems—organic, mechanical or potentially a mixture of both—and how they process information and govern themselves through feedback loops.

"Cyber," however, increasingly came to connote "having to do with electronic computer systems," and the "punk" part of "cyberpunk" then brought in a flavor from rock lingo of the time. According to Nicholls, it stood for "young, streetwise, aggressive, alienated and offensive to the Establishment." The phrase also evoked, Nicholls wrote, the ethos of "the film *Blade Runner* (1982), whose near-future milieu—mean, drizzling, populous streets lit up by enormous advertisements for Japanese products, alternating street junk with high tech—is, in the intensity of its visual info-dumps, like a template for a cyberpunk scenario."

Reflecting back on that period, Gibson acknowledged his role: "Yeah, I kind of took the means of science fiction I'd inherited from my culture and I wed them with rock and roll and street stuff. That just hadn't been done before. I remember thinking when I did it, 'This is too obvious. This is a *little too obvious.*' But it worked. I could see right away that it had immediate impact. I made it possible for the post-hippy Microsoft guys to wear black leather jackets and feel they were cool."

One younger writer affected was Mark Frauenfelder, an editor and writer for *Wired* in its early days. Frauenfelder later founded what some regard as the most popular blog in the world, BoingBoing.net, and also became the editor-in-chief of *Make*, the top magazine in the "do-it-yourself" movement, a phenomenon he recounted in *Made by Hand: Searching for Meaning in a Throwaway World* (2010). Among his youthful achievements at *Wired* was shepherding cyberpunk classics back into print as part of a defunct Wired Books series called *Cortext: Science Fiction That Changed the World.*

"I'd given up on science fiction in the '80s," said Frauenfelder, chatting in San Francisco. "It had lost its juice for me.... I became much more interested in things like punk rock and zines, and second- or third-generation underground comics. Then I started to realize there was science fiction that was picking up on stuff in the cultural Zeitgeist: the do-it-yourself revolution, the end of government ... disillusionment about ever going into space, designer drugs, global corporations. I became really interested in science fiction again. It became relevant again."

More than that, asserted Frauenfelder, it became influential—a prod to science. "Silicon Valley is probably the only industry that uses fiction as a guiding principle or philosophy for what it does," said Frauenfelder, noting that there was a long history of fictional scenarios anticipating Silicon Valley realities. One reissued Cortext book was *The Artificial Kid*, by Bruce Sterling, along with Gibson the figure most identified with cyberpunk thanks to his fanzine *Cheap Truth* and influential anthology *Mirrorshades*. Replete with televised gang warfare, superpowerful technology, and "ultra-rich satellite dwellers who orbit the planet Reverie," the novel suggested what might be down the road.

A second reissue, Charles Platt's *The Silicon Man*, proved particularly "ahead of its time," noted Frauenfelder. It explored what it would be like "to download your consciousness onto a computer network"—a possibility always fondly discussed by experts in artificial intelligence. In the novel, an FBI agent happened on a secret research project that left him "an unwilling inhabitant of a world that exists entirely within cyberspace." Cortext also reissued *White Light*, by Rudy Rucker, a two-time winner of the Philip K. Dick Award who came with a unique credential for predicting where the Zeitgeist might head: he was the great-great-grandson of the German philosopher Hegel, who popularized the notion. In *White Light,* a university teacher of math got "lost in a multidimensional astral universe of warped time-scales and fractal landscapes" that bore some resemblance to reality as currently understood by physicists and mathematicians.

Cyberpunk authors also intuited the Internet boom, a phenomenon even Bill Gates initially missed. One novel Frauenfelder cited was *Métrophage,* by Richard Kadrey: "He's got something in there called the 'grid,' which is a network everybody uses. He talks about it being a system that spreads misinformation, rumors and gossip, and how that just whips through the grid. *Pretty insightful.*"

"The novels were like blueprints," mused Frauenfelder. "Cyberpunk didn't really do much to change science fiction. It's still really bad—endless *Star Trek* novelizations and 'sharecropper' shared universes where one author comes up with the idea for a world and a bunch of hack writers knock out stories for it. But what it did do was get a lot of people in Silicon Valley very excited by its concepts and ideas." As Cortext's catalog once put it, "The high-tech industry lifted concepts and vocabulary straight from the pages of these books to write their business plans, effectively creating a self-fulfilling prophecy."

Gibson agreed, in general, that there had been a lot of lifting from science fiction to applied science: "Most frequently," he joked, "people name their start-up companies after characters in my book. I wish I had a file." Gibson particularly remembered one outfit's attempt to register "cyberspace" as a trademark: "I was extremely grumpy about it. I could see it moving into common parlance. I thought, 'Wow, this is so cool, my neologism is going to become a word!' And I thought, one day, it might even appear in newspapers." The trademark attempt went nowhere, leaving Gibson at peace: "Now I think it pretty well appears in every English-language newspaper in the world at least once daily. Which is pretty good for a guy with a yellow legal pad and a felt pen who also thought, 'Hmm, "infospace," "dataspace" . . .'"

At the same time, Gibson mocked the idea that any high-tech executives might actually employ him or his peers as a fount of ideas. "We're the licensed court jesters of technological society," he said of himself and his fellow sci-fi writers. "Besides, the corporate people are too smart. They can tell that no matter how successful I may be at what I do, or how many useful little pieces of ideas I turn up, I'm still some sort of *antibody.*"

More like a middleman *antibody,* he suggested. "I'm quite a lazy person," Gibson asserted, "and I've learned to turn that to my advantage. I use more scientifically literate science fiction writers as a filtering mechanism for all of that hard-core futurism. I wait until I hear a squeal of glee or horror from a scientifically literate SF writer, and I run over and say, 'What hurts, what hurts?,' and he says, 'Nicholas Negroponte predicts . . . ,' and I go, 'Okay.' So I use these other guys like pulp testers."

"I'm in a perverse relationship with futurism," Gibson remarked, seeking to situate his fiction properly, "because it's ostensibly what I do, but I've been declaring from the beginning that it's *not* what I do. For me, the world we live in right this minute is just as weird as it can possibly be. Weirder than anyone has been able to describe. So I'm using this tool kit that I inherited from science fiction to attempt a kind of naturalism. Sometimes it seems to me the only real naturalism that we can do today is 99 percent science fiction. Because that's our scenario."

"What I'm trying to do," he concluded, "is get a handle on an *unthinkable present.*" That even a cyberpunk guru like Gibson found the fast-moving present challenging as a novelist may explain why more and more mainstream fiction writers—lacking the utopian or dystopian urges of sci-fi peers—took the cyberpresent as their territory. They thus edged into that "non-genre" traditionally defined—once you've eliminated all the Westerns, romances, mysteries, thrillers, potboilers and sappy bestsellers—as "literature."

Relaxing in a sparely furnished San Francisco townhouse he was sharing with friends, novelist and journalist Po Bronson, author of *The First $20 Million Is Always the Hardest: A Silicon Valley Novel,* figured as a literary pioneer in mainstreaming cyberculture. A longtime player in the Bay Area's publishing world beyond his career as a writer—he was associate publisher of Mercury House and founder and chairman of Consortium Book Sales, a national distributor of small literary presses—Bronson recalled a time when the literary community, while "writing left and right about all sorts of things, completely ignored this topic."

"They didn't see it as a real topic, a worthy topic," said the tousle-haired writer, whose hunky good looks—he resembled Richard Gere—were exploited on the back flap of *The First $20 Million.* "Silicon Valley and high tech was not about what's real. They wanted to get at the small wonders of life, and that was all distracting. It was not a legitimate topic for serious writers to take on."

A Seattle-born graduate of Bill Gates's high school who went to Stanford, studied economics and began to absorb the area's high-tech business ethos, Bronson considered that a big mistake. It also seemed an ugly irony given that, Bronson said, many aspiring fiction writers in the Bay Area found that if they needed writing or editing work to pay the bills, the jobs were in "computer media," which, he said, "swallow up writers here like you wouldn't believe." So after writing *Bombardiers,* a successful satire of greedy Wall Street bond traders, Bronson decided that if he didn't "find out what was going on in Silicon Valley," he'd "really regret it later."

The First $20 Million tracked idealistic twenty-six-year-old Andy Caspar, who abandoned a foot-dragging midsize computer company for the more exciting task of leading a research institute project to develop the "VWPC"—a Volkswagen network personal computer that would sell for under $300 and thus threaten the stranglehold of established companies in the computer biz. Trying to cut Caspar and pals off at the pass was the evil François Benoit, a genius chip designer who would break any rule to position himself as absolute ruler of the Net.

Some locals zeroed in on the book's roman à clef aspects, wondering whether Benoit was Sun's Bill Joy, and the book's magical "hypnotizer" language a takeoff on Java. But Bronson, who had called fiercely competitive Silicon Valley "the most ruthless business environment" he'd ever witnessed, trained his novelistic eye on the dweebs, the little people, the "ironmen" programmers behind the fabled honchos, the still idealistic second or third generation that tried to stay pure amid corporate culture.

While regretting that the book didn't offer much cybersex or hacking, Random House made it sound like a jazzy airport read in its promotional material: "As Caspar's team gets closer and closer to a major breakthrough, it becomes clear that this simple computer will threaten the 'bigger is better' machismo of the industry. As Andy and his team of programming wizards toil around the clock, conflicts mount, venture capital scurries away, careers are suddenly jeopardized, and the very industry that once championed the product is now the villain that may undermine it."

Yet Bronson's potentially harshest critics—area reviewers—applauded *The First $20 Million* as a step toward the longtime project of local writers to produce the Great Silicon Valley Novel. The *San Jose Mercury News,* the Valley's chief newspaper, found it "drenched in Silicon Valley verisimilitude." Salon deemed it the first Silicon Valley novel to live up to that title. *Time* suggested it might turn out to be "the *Primary Colors* of Silicon Valley."

One thing was clear: other cyberwriters and journalists started clicking, like Bronson, on "fiction" as the next step in their career evolutions. Publishing houses kicked in by committing to new media books and starting imprints, such as HarperEdge. That imprint published *Ecstasy Club,* a first novel by well-known digital journalist Douglas Rushkoff (*Cyberia*). The come-on: "When the young, hypertalented idealists who call themselves ECSTASY CLUB find an abandoned piano factory in Oakland, they make it the focus of a round-the-clock rave the likes of which the Bay Area has never seen before. They also make the factory a base camp in their search for a method of time travel that combines computer wizardry, esoteric spirituality, and mind-altering substances. The Club's mesmeric leader, Duncan, and our resourceful narrator, Zach, actually manage to 'break time' online, only to discover that an unsettling array of characters has beaten them to it."

HarperEdge also published *Signal to Noise,* a first novel by Carla Sinclair, author of *Net Chick: A Smart-Girl Guide to the Wired World.* Billed as "a fabulously biting and hair-raising satire of wired culture," *Signal to Noise* offered, according to the publisher, an insider plot worthy of Bronson's own: "Living at opposite ends of new media's hierarchy, Jim Knight—features editor of the ultra cool *Signal*—and Kat Astura—unpaid 'zine drudge—are tossed together when Kat, mouse-clicking her way into trouble, blows almost $200,000 of Jim's money in a virtual blackjack game backed by all-too-real thugs. Kidnapped to the hinterlands by Way New mobsters, Jim and Kat race through the electronic byways of the San Francisco multimedia ghetto and the streets of Las Vegas in a run for their money and their lives."

Signal to Noise, like Bronson's novel, trailed roman à clef mists behind it. Said one San Francisco cyberjournalist, "That's the first one I've seen where you can figure out who everyone is." Presumably the verisimilitude wasn't hurt by the fact that Sinclair was married to Frauenfelder. In addition, the novel's marketing reflected a phenomenon barely noted by East Coast publishers at the time: digital literati, particularly on the West Coast, already formed a network not unlike the extended MFA-program families of the East, whose members regularly blurbed one another's books and even reviewed them (if they could get away with it).

Sinclair's novel, for instance, came with advance blurbs from Rushkoff ("The hilarious *Upstairs Downstairs* of the South of Market hi-tech publishing world"), Rudy Rucker ("A transreal Gen-X career quest amidst the enchantment that is San Francisco"), and Bruce Sterling ("This jewel-like artifact . . . should be preserved in amber for the sake of our remote descendants").

Rushkoff's novel, in turn, offered blurbs from Rucker ("A juicy tale of the early . . . San Francisco psychedelic scene") and Gibson ("A darkly comic contemporary fable: a brave, very funny, very knowing trip through the neo-psychedelic substrate of the wired world").

In short, the literary combustion of West Coast fictional digerati may have been a tad incestuous, but it helped launch the philosophical issues and challenges of the cyberrevolution into the minds of larger and larger sets of American readers, helpfully wrapped in the plot turns of just-plain-human characters. The rise of the Silicon Valley novel even occasioned an East Coast/West Coast critical fissure. In the *New York Times*, critic Edward Rothstein treated Bronson like a bandwagon jumper, grouping *The First $20 Million* with Pat Dillon's *The Last Best Thing* and Douglas Coupland's earlier novel, *Microserfs*, writing that they were "almost enough to constitute a genre."

"As if three makes a genre," Bronson harrumphed, "when you can count three legal thrillers being published per week."

Rothstein, one of the few critics to ponder the Silicon Valley novel as genre, noted that it hewed "to novelistic convention. Business in much nineteenth-century fiction is disruptive, even evil—who can forget the Dickens counterpart to Silicon Valley in *Hard Times*, in which the owners scorn their serfs and factories belch smoke? Business did not fare much better in American novels by Frank Norris, Sinclair Lewis and William Dean Howells.

"The Valley novel," Rothstein continued, "preserves the hostility but injects a new sort of faith: that a new kind of business can evolve, one that in its devotion to the glory of code, in its communion of like-minded nerds and in its devotion to the liberating character of technology, might make some other way of life possible."

For Rothstein, the three books he considered failed on technical grounds and ended up "very smart, but very limited." A key reason he offered was that the Valley culture they took as territory, despite the "fluidity, hierarchy and energy that gave birth to the great social novels of the past," lacked "structures like religion, politics, family and history." Those structures were necessary to create strong identities, capable of resisting what Rothstein saw as Silicon Valley's "only salient forces," reduced to "money and code, television shows and pop culture."

Californians could be forgiven for detecting an old genre in East Coast critical writing: a Woody-Allenish reduction of West Coast intellectual culture, perhaps spawned by fear that, as Bay Area or Seattle intellectual engines liked to brag, the center of the next century was in their backyard. Perhaps it was truer to say of Bronson's book, as *San Francisco Chronicle* reviewer Michael Stern did, that "Silicon Valley novels aren't a genre yet, but the outlines of the form are beginning to crystallize."

Distinguishing them from "technothrillers" and "technomelodramas"—and thus from cyberpunk—Stern took a stab at definition:

> They are true to the myth of Valley life, which is about the dream—and price—of getting rich quick and sometimes deserving it. . . . The recipe includes various elements. There's "Jack and the Beanstalk" (little magic beans of start-ups can grow seemingly overnight into big, big beanstalks of public companies with huge markets and lots of newly rich employee shareholders). There's "The Underground Man" (geeks desperately coding away in anonymous cubes until their stock options get liquid). And of course there's "Dilbert" (the graveyard humor of the right-sized and reengineered), with a dash of *roman à clef* on the side.

If, in any event, the mainstream Silicon Valley novel was coming into focus—ironically, the most successful rendition of that world would come much later in the film *The Social Network*, created from Aaron Sorkin's screenplay—the other prime shape over the past twenty-five years of the digitally impacted literary novel was also detectable: the philosophical story that focused on a particular technological aspect of digital life, and consequences that might stem from it.

One popular subject became artificial intelligence embodied in a computer program. Richard Powers's widely acclaimed *Galatea 2.2* probed a character, not unlike its hyperintellectual author, who became involved with a cognitive neurologist interested in modeling the human brain through computerized neural networks. The task: to train a computer intelligence "on a canonical list of Great Books until the machine becomes capable of passing a comprehensive exam in English literature." For Powers and the reader, the fun came in watching the device grow in self-consciousness and enter a rivalry with a real twenty-two-year-old master's candidate.

A novel with a similar concern—*Exegesis,* by Carnegie Mellon doctoral candidate Astro Teller—consisted entirely of e-mail, making it the first *e*-pistolary novel. *Exegesis* recorded the relationship between Alice Lu, a grad student in artificial intelligence, and her thesis project—Edgar. Unsurprisingly, Edgar evolved into an autonomous being, with the species' predictable bent for more freedom and information. Before long, he was in trouble with the Feds, in love with Alice, in jail and planning an escape.

Teller, grandson of "Father of the H-bomb" Edward Teller, acknowledged that he wrote *Exegesis* conscious of such literary antecedents as *Frankenstein, Pygmalion* and the myth of Galatea. So the digital novel of "created intelligence" found itself part of a much older genre way before we'd reached the stage, forecast long ago by Isaac Asimov, when we would consider ourselves lucky vis-à-vis computer intelligences if they even kept us on "as pets."

The second most appealing digital hook for mainstream novelists became the allure of anonymous intimate communication. An early instance, Richard de Combray's novel *Lost in the City of Light,* examined an American sculptor manqué in Paris who turns to the "Minitel"—France's ancient government-operated computer system—to begin an anonymous infatuation with a mysterious woman named Lea. Considerably more graphic in its focus on the traps of computer anonymity was *As Francesca,* by Martha Baer, a longtime San Francisco editor. It scrutinized Elaine Botsch, a hard-driving professional by day who logged on at night as "Francesca." In doing so, she submitted utterly to Inez, "her brilliant on-line dominatrix," who forced Elaine "to the thrilling edge of her sexual limits." When Elaine mistakenly logged on as herself, Inez disappeared.

Over lunch at South Park Cafe, one epicenter of San Francisco's South Park digital culture (despite courtesy newspapers still on the racks), Baer suggested that fiction intent on merely *spotlighting* digital culture was already passé. "When I was shopping my book," she said, "before editors read it, their first reaction was often, 'We already have an Internet book.'"

As Francesca, Baer countered, shouldn't have been seen that way. Still, while the novel drew both positive and mixed reviews, Baer thought it suffered with East Coast reviewers "already sick of the Net," engaging in the very real phenomenon of "Internet backlash." To escape such literary retribution, Baer believed, serious writers steeped in cyberculture would need to produce literature that did what literature had always done—transcend its immediate setting by zeroing in on specific elements that reveal larger truths beneath surfaces. In the case of *As Francesca,* Baer tried to do that by showing how Net-enabled anonymity and role playing accurately reflected our real psychologies—that none of us really has "a unified stable self."

"For me," she said of her novel, "it's not an Internet book. It's not *about* the Net. It *assumes* the Net. There's a difference."

Content, in short, lay in the eye of the beholder. And form? The digital revolution's chief formal impact on literature came in its encouragement of new styles of narrative, particularly interactive narrative. But did such changes revolutionize the act of storytelling or undermine it?

The Hungarian literary critic Georg Lukacs argued that every epoch produces its own literary genre. If that's so, the most academically promoted new form of the digital age remained "hypertext." The term itself came from Theodor H. Nelson in the 1960s. "By hypertext," Nelson explained in a later publication, *Literary Machines,* "I mean non-sequential writing—text that branches and allows choices to the reader, best read at an interactive screen. As popularly conceived, this is a series of text chunks connected by links which offer the reader different pathways."

In literary hypertext, prose came in blocks of words that academics called "lexias," borrowing the term of the late French literary theorist Roland Barthes. The blocks came electronically linked to other blocks. Instead of the prose being readable in only one direction, as dictated by the author, the reader could zigzag in a variety of multilinear directions.

Hypertext fiction's best-known specimen remained Michael Joyce's novel, confusingly titled *afternoon: a story,* which invited the reader to probe the thoughts of a writer named Peter who was bothered by expectations of loss and tragedy. Using a hypertext program called Storyspace, Joyce composed it in 539 lexias, hoping it would change "every time you read it." It was as if someone took all the chapters of a novel one was reading, scissored them into separate lexias, and put the novel back together again.

Hypertext's main advocates largely resided in the academy. A leading figure there, George Landow, proved that digitally literate humanities scholars could learn a few tricks from the computer pros. He updated and republished his *Hypertext: The Convergence of Contemporary Critical Theory and Technology* as *Hypertext 2.0.* True to his subtitle,

Landow believed, like many academic fans of hypertext, that it mirrored the view of postmodern philosophers such as Jacques Derrida that "we must abandon conceptual systems founded upon ideas of center, margin, hierarchy and linearity and replace them with ones of multilinearity, nodes, links, and networks."

According to Landow, almost "all parties to this paradigm shift, which marks a revolution in human thought, see electronic writing as a direct response to the strengths and weaknesses of the written book." Hypertext, it followed, "decenters" the book and "blurs the distinction" between what is inside and outside a text. It undermines such Aristotelian requirements for plot as fixed sequence and a definite beginning and end. Finally, by merging the role of reader and writer, it questions the very notion of an "author."

As such ideas flourished in literary academe, Landow enjoyed company on the bookshelves. In *Cybertext: Perspectives on Ergodic Literature*, Norwegian critic Espen Aarseth examined hypertext fiction and other digital genres of narrative, such as computer games, computer-generated poetry and interactive game/texts such as MUDs (multi-user domains). Taking the term "ergodic" from physics, Aarseth saw them as continuing a traditional genre of open texts such as the *I Ching*, which require a reader to make choices. In another study, *From Text to Hypertext*, postmodernist scholar Silvio Gaggi similarly saw resemblances between hypertext fiction and earlier avant-garde art, including such literary experiments as the nonsequential prose of Italo Calvino.

Perhaps the most insightful work of cyberphilosophy that welcomed nouveau narratives was Murray's *Hamlet on the Holodeck*. Murray, an MIT research scientist who also taught interactive fiction writing, argued that computers were on the verge of becoming "spellbinding" storytellers that would stretch "the spectrum of narrative expression, not by replacing the novel or the movie but by continuing their timeless bardic work within another framework." Murray accepted that the holodeck—a fantasy machine from *Star Trek* that creates illusory worlds with controllable characters—was not on the release schedule of any major firm. But she believed that the technological options we already possessed—from hypertext to the Net itself—placed us in the fledgling days of a spectacular future.

"It's the ideal medium for Tolstoys of the future," remarked Murray over the phone, "because it's so capacious, it's ideally suited to multiple points of view."

Unfortunately, like Landow, Murray assumed rather than argued in her book that multiform narratives, alternate versions of reality, were "now part of the way we think, part of the way we experience the world." She touched the requisite bases of "multlinear" traditional works of art—*Don Quixote, Tristram Shandy,* the stories of Borges, the Talmud, the film *Rashomon,* multi-plot TV shows—and then described her cherished computer analogs: MUDs, in which netizens created collective, interactive fantasy in a common virtual space; video games; hypertext soap operas; running dialogues with intelligent computer agents. Then Murray more or less sat down to await our narrative future, alternating between apologies for the shallowness of much computer narrative and paeans to a future "James Joyce of the electronic age."

The difficulty with her optimism about such interactive narratives was that almost no one in the nonacademic world of publishing and literature shared it. As critic Michiko Kakutani observed of Murray in a *New York Times* review of *Hamlet on the Holodeck,* "Although she tries hard to inflate the significance of her examples, they always end up sounding more like the mindless computer games we already know than emotionally engaging works of art." Even such steeped-in-cyberculture types as Gibson, Frauenfelder and Baer showed little enthusiasm.

Gibson remarked that while a friend occasionally sent him a chunk of a complex MUD text the latter participated in, and that it offered some "quotable bits," it was "not like reading fiction. It's just some other activity." And while Murray believed "the postmodern hypertext tradition celebrates the indeterminate text as a liberation from the tyranny of the author," Baer and Frauenfelder, like Gibson, owned up to a fondness for "words-in-a-row."

"None of those experiments has really gone anywhere," said Baer. "If you look around, there's no evidence that they've gained interest. There's never been a breakthrough." Nor did she feel that's regrettable: "I don't think there's a lot of merit to the idea. People like to read to be directed—not to make choices."

Frauenfelder didn't even like going on the Net for a long *linear* narrative. "For me," he said, before e-readers and e-books began to catch fire, "the Net isn't a very good place for literature. I first became interested in the Net because there were other people out there to hook up with, who share similar interests. That's the killer application of the Net. For me, it's a waste of the Net to have long texts that are just meant to be read. The more people try to make the Net a place for publishing long stuff, the more we look at books and realize what a cool thing they are."

Would hypertext fiction and other forms of digital narrative ever succeed in their step-up to literature? To be sure, as digital technology evolved, new ways of harnessing fiction to it quickly followed. With the rise of social networking and Facebook, efforts to extend the joy of hypertext and the boundaries of literature increased, as did competition for who would be first off the mark with a "Facebook novel."

In 2007, Penguin Canada announced its publication of established writer Michael Winter's new novel as the first "Facebook novel"—it came in forty-seven parts over ten weeks. In 2008, a collaborative online writing project called "LiveBook" aimed at the writing of two distinct novels through applications on Facebook and Bebo, respectively. The narratives were to be built by having users vote each new sentence up or down, with sentences that reached a certain threshold added to the stories. In the winter of 2009, an American writer, Leif Peterson, found himself the author of *Missing: The Facebook Novel.* He posted a short story on his Facebook page, received requests from friends for new installments (what old-fogey writers might call chapters) and ended up, by June 2009, with eighty-four installments. In 2010, Deutsche Welle reported that an Austria-based writer from Hungary, Gergely Teglasy, was claiming to have posted the first Facebook novel to which fans could contribute—thousands quickly "liked" the idea.

Well-known cultural critic Katie Roiphe took stock that year in a column for the *New York Times.* She called attention to a novel being written at the online magazine *Slate* titled *My Darklyng.* Its plot played out on Facebook and Twitter. The two young-adult novelists composing it, Lauren Mechling and Laura Moser, created a fake Facebook page for a sixteen-year-old girl named Natalie Pollack. The posting expressed familiar teenage-girl breathless speech ("OMG!") and mannerisms ("HAHAHAHA"). Roiphe opined that it was "a brilliant stroke to use Facebook for novel writing, because in general Facebook feeds on fiction; it consumes it, and spits it out in every direction." She added: "It is not, alas, *The Sun Also Rises,* but Facebook is the novel we are all writing."

Maybe, maybe not, as Robert Fulghum might have chirped. Search for "collaborative writing projects" or "Internet novels" on the Web and you'll find a slew of projects, including a wiki novel. One problem with "Facebook novel" taking off as a term and genre is that the phrase already means something in online slang: a Facebook message so long (e.g., more than two thousand words) that it looks as if it will take forever to read.

Lasting judgments on whether the latest digital literature succeeds more than hypertext will depend not just on readers but also on those supposedly dwindling literary gatekeepers who go by such meatspace IDs as book editor, book-review editor, book critic and book reviewer. Most still largely ignore hypertext and any purely digital fiction. So long as traditional book publishing hangs on, with authors eager to see their work in bound form, gatekeepers, like general readers, will likely remain focused on well-shaped traditional texts. Nothing in the recent packaging triumph of e-books and e-readers suggests any greater desire for zig-zag or open narratives than before.

CYBERCYNICS

After decades of teaching at the University of California, Berkeley, Gene Rochlin knew all the putdowns of his home base as a nest of wacky ideas scorned by mainstream America: *Berserkeley*, the *People's Republic of Berkeley*, the *Looneversity of California* and so on. He didn't mind. Berkeley, after all, was where the Free Speech Movement of the 1960s took off, where the *Berkeley Barb* seemed an apt name for the town's vitriolic anti-establishment weekly.

Besides, the Chicago native suggested, it was not such a bad thing to live in a place that banned Styrofoam cups and other threats from cookie-cutter America. That's why he took his Saturday-morning breakfast at Rick and Ann's, one of those good-vibe eateries where you endured the wait and nonstop chatter because no chain-management recipe would *dare* infringe on Rick and Ann's judgment about eggs and pancakes.

"Is Berkeley a part of the United States?" Rochlin asked good-naturedly. "It may not even be a part of Earth! It's a very strange community that in no way represents the broader society. The general feeling here is that everybody outside is a dope and nobody is to be trusted."

Or, to put it in the words of a polite local guidebook, Berkeley, "more than any other American town," remained synonymous with dissent and intense skepticism about what other people considered progress. No shock, then, that cybercynics thrived here like starlets in L.A. Rochlin's *Trapped in the Net* was one of the first studies to empty its ammunition on bright-eyed and bushy-tailed cyberphilosophers.

"The core thesis of the book," this professor of "energy and resources" explained over coffee, was "that people don't understand what they've bought into when they go for these interconnected computer systems. They don't understand the implications, and they're constantly surprised by them."

"Most people still believe that the computer is a liberating, freeing, empowering, stand-alone technology. In fact, it creates the greatest web of social dependencies the world has ever seen. You're constrained at every turn by the way computer designers want you to behave." Rochlin acknowledged that every Tom, Dick and Esther in the computer business was publishing a book eligible for the archetypal title snagged by Dertouzos: *What Will Be.*

Rochlin's reply was that we could use more books titled *What Should Be.*

"I hear too much about the inevitable march of technology," he said. "Technology *does* have a logic, but it's not self-shaping. It's formed." And his Berkeley-bred political antennae helped him identify where and by *what* it was formed. "The inevitable," Rochlin asserted, "comes not from the technology, but from social formations, political stuff."

"Why don't we have lightweight cars with great miles per gallon instead of urban assault vehicles?" Rochlin asked. "Because it's in the corporate interest to promote them. Why do I need to upgrade my computer system? Because you have a market system in which people are actually marketing change and innovation." Rochlin sniffed at the notion that we can't resist technological change: "Hey, we've resisted bicycles and lightweight cars! We've resisted all kinds of things."

So why did so much cyberphilosophy exalt only positive possibilities in the future? Because, he said, it absorbed the buoyant attitude of the "techie" community. People "in the business," said Rochlin—referring to the high-tech industry that stretches from Silicon Valley through the Bay Area—found that "all their friends, their professional colleagues, the people they went to school with" were working right alongside them. Together, Rochlin argued, "they build a representation of optimism, enthusiasm and positive consequences that seems to slap into everybody. Even people who are not financially involved tend to express themselves as if they were."

Such types, Rochlin concluded, were unlikely to generate cynicism about the cyberrevolution once they'd been trained to focus on their technical scientific tasks and ignore both users and the consequences of their inventions. Unfortunately, Rochlin observed, "thoughtlessness gets reinforced socially and institutionally within the profession."

"If you have a dog defending your yard," he mused, "you don't want it to ask people whether they're friendly. You just want it to bite."

The apotheosis of cyberspace by self-anointed philosophers took the literati and other humanists by surprise. Excited by expanding computer access, by the breathless message that we needed to run full speed to keep up with the digital juggernaut, by the sudden appetite of old media for Quotations from Chairman Somebody in the digital world, cyberphilosophers booted up every sci-fi fantasy they could think of and served them up.

Barlow, the former Grateful Dead lyricist, became a one-man quip show and cybervangelist, declaring that our minds would be "uploaded into the Internet." Nicholas Negroponte urged everyone to *be digital* or be dim. John Brockman, a New York agent and impresario for some of the leading scientists of our time, declared the "digerati" a new intellectual elite, a "Third Culture."

Yet despite the ever more bullish tomes that trumpeted superimproved cyberversions of our world, such as Kelly's *Out of Control*—and perhaps because of them—the digital votaries couldn't remove the contrarian spirit at the core of America the Philosophical. Two principles in what might be called "the physics of culture" kicked in to correct the balance.

Intellectual life, like nature, abhors a vacuum.

Every intellectual trend calls forth an equal and opposite intellectual trend.

So while Rochlin was right—scientists bankrolled by the digital revolution were hardly leading the league in producing critiques of cyberhype—the opposed genre of "cybercynicism" predictably took off. The impulse dated back to classical times. If the celebration of calculation, algorithms and machine-like rules of procedure first surfaced in Socrates's quest for exact definitions, the seeds of cybercynicism arose in his opponents: the rhetoricians, sophists and cynics, who rejected and sometimes mocked Socrates's search for exact answers as false to the messiness of concepts in real life. Diogenes, the paradigm cynic, earned his tag (derived from the Greek word for "dog") because of his frank willingness to "bark" against the entrenched beliefs of his time, to "deface the currency" of conventional wisdom in search of simplicity and freedom.

More commonly cited ancestors of the cybercynics included the politically committed, machine-wrecking Luddites, who battled the Industrial Revolution in early-nineteenth-century Britain—they were alternately seen as enemies of progress or heroic opponents of rapacious capitalism. Yet another role model was that quintessential American early-warning system, Henry David Thoreau, who—some may recall—made lead pencils for a living. "Our inventions are wont to be pretty toys," Thoreau wrote in *Walden,* "which distract our attention from serious things. They are but improved means to an unimproved end. We are in great haste to construct a magnetic telegraph from Maine to Texas; but Maine and Texas, it may be, have nothing important to communicate."

Two prescient works of cybercynicism loomed large in the infancy of America's digital revolution: Hubert Dreyfus's classic and influential *What Computers Can't Do,* updated and republished as *What Computers Still Can't Do,* and Theodore Roszak's *The Cult of Information,* updated later for a second edition. The bête noire of Dreyfus, a Berkeley philosophy professor who started out at MIT, was artificial intelligence and the hubris of its proponents, several of them his former MIT colleagues.

"Almost half a century ago," Dreyfus recalled in his second edition, "computer pioneer Alan Turing suggested that a high-speed digital computer, programmed with rules and facts, might exhibit intelligent behavior." By the late 1960s, Marvin Minsky, director of MIT's artificial intelligence program, declared that "[w]ithin a generation the problem of creating 'artificial intelligence' will be substantially solved."

Not so, Dreyfus argued.

"After fifty years of effort," according to him, it was clear "to all but a few diehards that this attempt to produce general intelligence has failed." It had become, he added, what philosophers of science called "a degenerating research program." The core reason for the failure could be put in sophisticated terms, but, Dreyfus explained, it boiled down to the inability of scientists to program "common sense" into a computer or neural network. The vast contextualization required for common sense and its generalizations was "a kind of *know-how*" acquired through life, rather than the propositional knowledge translatable into symbols for the computer.

As a result, all sorts of human intelligence—such as good judgment in extending a past practice in innovative ways—couldn't be translated into representational bits of knowledge without, so to speak, getting the computer a life. "No one in AI believes anymore," Dreyfus concluded, that "we will have an artificial intelligence like HAL," the rebellious computer in the movie *2001.*

Roszak, a historian, agreed with Dreyfus on the roadblocks to artificial intelligence. Happily quoting Dreyfus, he took it as axiomatic that "the mind thinks, not with data, but with ideas whose creation and elaboration cannot be reduced to a set of predictable rules." But he also attacked the computer revolution from another angle—the sociological.

Roszak started out suspicious of corporate motivations for the computer revolution's pie-in-the-sky ideology. He found that the computer, "like the too-susceptible emperor," came "overdressed in fabulous claims." And he regarded such media clichés as "the information society" as "the mumbo jumbo of a widespread public cult" aimed at substituting "low-grade mechanical counterfeits" in schools for the traditional process of strengthening "powers of reason and imagination."

"If we wish to reclaim the true art of thinking from this crippling confusion," Roszak wrote, "we must begin by cutting our way through an undergrowth of advertising hype, media fictions, and commercial propaganda." Roszak did that by castigating what he called the "data merchants"—all those in consumer society who "find their careers or their investments tied to the extravagant promises that attach to computers," from manufacturers to media outfits eager to increase upbeat coverage of computer products in order to draw advertising from the industry.

"The result has been the creation of a mystique of information," Roszak charged. He felt as if he had "strayed into some strange sect" involved in "worshipping light bulbs." Mused Roszak, "I would not want to live without them. But I never would have thought of them as objects of veneration." So Roszak deemed his book "a small protest on behalf of the naked human mind, its creative powers, its animal resiliency, its undiscovered evolutionary potential, its deep enigmas of aspiration and self-transcendence." It was also a protest against the failure of corporately owned mass media to pay attention to the mercenary aims behind paeans to the cyberrevolution.

"The merchandising of hardware and software," Roszak wrote, "remains as much of a carnival act as ever, with endless new attractions along the midway, all of them being brazenly oversold. While the price of such basic items as memory chips and hard disks continues to fall, new fascinations like desktop publishing and interactivity serve to keep the consumers consuming . . . [W]hat P. T. Barnum earned by convincing everybody in the nation that they just *had* to buy a ticket to see Jumbo the elephant amounts to peanuts compared to the billions that Bill Gates of Microsoft has taken in."

Roszak sounded one of the first bells in the clang of warnings that Rochlin took up and scored like a neo-Luddite symphony: "the overweening confidence of computer scientists in their systems," and "the power of the computer to concentrate ever-greater decision-making power in the wrong few hands." Long before turmoil in Asian markets or the worldwide recession of 2008, Roszak insightfully observed that use of computers in high finance had "radically altered international economic affairs." He presciently charged that "programmed trading," developed by some of the nation's best mathematicians, had "become a disruptive and all but dictatorial force in world finance—to such a degree that patterns of investment and speculation generated by computers have become an independent factor determining the shape of the market."

Indeed, noting "the temptation to make overnight billions by shuffling electronic values," Roszak quoted financier Felix Rohatyn on the danger: "Twenty-six-year-olds with computers are creating financial hydrogen bombs."

"The cult of information is theirs, not ours," intoned Roszak, summing up the threats of the computer age. "They use it, and they use it against us . . . while the rest of us cling to the margins, the power and profit of the technology gravitate elsewhere."

Masses of pacified Americans did not rise up in arms after reading Dreyfus and Roszak. But both caught the ear of later cybercynics, who built upon their work. Some, like Mark Slouka, a humanities lecturer at the University of California, San Diego, who later gravitated to writing fiction, zapped cyberboosterism across a comprehensive front—its unconvincing sell job on cyberspace as *new, improved* reality. Volunteering to be "a speed bump on the fiber-optic highway" in his *War of the Worlds: Cyberspace and the High-Tech Assault on Reality*, Slouka attacked the media for covering the computer business with a passive lack of criticism except on matters of technical performance. Instead, he urged them to focus on one of the biggest power grabs in history: the effort by computer and communications empires to lure Americans into a sedentary, abstract relation to life while convincing us that it was progress.

Under their influence, Slouka warned, we were experiencing a "growing separation from reality. More and more of us, whether we realize it or not, accept the copy as the original. . . . Reality, in other words, may someday come with an asterisk." Slouka particularly targeted Net religionists like Kelly and Barlow who talked up the idea of ditching the messily material for the pure immaterial, the inconvenient body for the efficient electronic mind, perhaps in the hope of achieving the "hard-wiring of collective consciousness," the old idealist aim of a Universal Mind. It was an impulse, Slouka wrote, reminiscent of nothing so much as early Christianity.

In such a world, "feedback technology would provide the illusion of touch directly to your nervous system. . . . Physical presence would become optional; in time, an affectation." A key strain in the thinking of all such cyberphilosophy, Slouka pointed out, was a myth of inevitability, exemplified in Barlow's well-known crack, "When you're about to be swept over the falls, you might as well enjoy the ride."

Slouka hammered at the immaturity of such pseudo-truths, comparing them to the child's pre-ethical sense that only resistance marks the line between the moral and immoral. "The implicit motto seemed to be," Slouka wrote, "we tinker because we can." In a similar way, he remarked, children "tear the wings off flies because they can—until someone suggests that they stop." No more convincing, he thought, were cybersalesmen who exploited frontier rhetoric ("the open road") to make nerdish Net surfing seem like classic American adventurism.

"What it comes down to," Slouka declared, "is this: the digital revolution represents a $3.5 trillion market. Vitally important to the success of that revolution is our willingness to move indoors, to renounce the external world (where so many things are free, after all) in favor of the internal one (which can be commodified to the heart's delight by selling us substitutes of the things we've given up)." Digital revolutionaries pushed that goal, in his view, by turning the meanings of public and private upside down: "You're not alone, the argument goes; you're connected. You're not isolated in your room, tapping on a keyboard; you're in touch, linked up, wired to the world."

But cyberspace, countered Slouka, was "quite literally nowhere; an electronic space that mimics the forms of social life even as it confirms us in our isolation." Not all cybercynics heeded Slouka's call to the barricades. At least one, computer scientist Gregory J. E. Rawlins of Indiana University, combined gentle cyberbashing with a collaborationist ethic. In two books for his school's university press, *Moths to the Flame: The Seductions of Computer Technology* and *Slaves of the Machine: The Quickening of Computer Technology,* Rawlins counseled accommodation. Contrary to Roszak, Rochlin and most of his skeptical peers, Rawlins stressed the inevitability of the digital revolution, likening it—and our adaptation to it—to organic evolution. We needed, he believed, to steer it for the good of humanity, and therefore we needed to "dance to the flame."

Far more typical of cyberskeptical outbursts, however—and more influential due to its mass-market publication—was Clifford Stoll's whimsical and folksy *Silicon Snake Oil: Second Thoughts on the Information Highway.* Stoll, a former Berkeley astronomer and computer security expert, enjoyed instant media credibility as an Internet apostate, and rapid media appreciation for his cutesy approach. He lived up to the role. Beginning with the signature lament of cybercynics—the feeling of being alone and isolated amid a plethora of cyberphilosophical hucksters—Stoll complained that there was "damned little critical discussion of the online world." Then he unleashed a few emerging tenets of the genre.

He bewailed the poverty of true sensation on the Net, its irrelevance to much of life: "You don't need a keyboard to bake bread, play touch football, piece a quilt, build a stone wall, recite a poem, or say a prayer." He warned that planned obsolescence of hardware and software endangered our future record keeping, just as the advent of the CD ruined musical record keeping. He explained that the computer offered only false promises in the classroom. He charged that Net relationships lacked "depth, commitment, and ordinary etiquette." Stoll compared the insidiousness of the information highway to the horrors of the superhighway system promoted by Robert Moses, which gave us "hour-long commutes" and turned "our society from one of neighborhoods to that of suburbs." In the spirit of Slouka, Stoll declared, "Life in the real world is far more interesting, far more important, far richer, than anything you'll ever find on a computer screen."

Yet another group of cybercynics declined to take on the whole megilla of cyberspace, picking their shots. Literary critic Sven Birkerts, for instance, concentrated on its fallout for reading and verbal intelligence in his widely praised *The Gutenberg Elegies,* offering a thesis summarized by one critic as "Book Good, Screen Bad."

Birkerts argued that an encroaching "communications net" was leading to the decline of print culture. As a result, "[t]he complexity and distinctiveness of spoken and written expression . . . will gradually be replaced by a more telegraphic form of 'plainspeak.' . . . [A]mbiguity, paradox, irony, subtlety and wit are fast disappearing. . . . The greater part of any articulate person's energy will be deployed in dumbing-down her discourse."

Elsewhere, in the world of business, University of Colorado psychology professor Thomas K. Landauer examined the similarly depressing upshot of computers on a core value of the business world—productivity. In *The Trouble with Computers: Usefulness, Usability, and Productivity,* Landauer targeted the supposed "productivity paradox" of computers—mere marginal improvement in productivity despite an American corporate investment of more than a trillion dollars in information technology since roughly 1980. According to Landauer, the increase in productivity of major economies since the mid-1970s was only half that of the immediate post–World War II years. Landauer conceded that computers had "helped put men on the moon, totally revised warfare, finally made it possible to solve centuries-old mathematics problems, led to bursts of new scientific knowledge, taken over our bookkeeping and our telephone switches."

But, he wrote, "the promise that they would contribute to economics, to a vast improvement in the standard of living, has not been kept. The nations, industries, and people who have invested in them heavily have not prospered proportionately (except those who sell computers)." In his view, the problem was partly "that they are still too hard to operate and get misused and applied badly to the wrong jobs. But mostly the problem is that they don't yet do enough sufficiently useful things."

Other reasons, according to Landauer, also accounted for the limited productivity. Too many companies failed to "reengineer" their businesses to make them cohere with computer capabilities. Badly designed hardware and software proved difficult to master and thus ate up staff time. One California study found that typical users spent 43 percent of online time "futzing" with their computer—fooling with software, experimenting with applications, navigating the interface. Landauer's solution was "user-centered design, user-centered development, user-centered deployment." Until the computer industry took users seriously, and permitted their feedback to govern design, Landauer believed, the "productivity paradox" would not disappear.

In the meantime, Landauer assuaged his anxiety—and that of his readers—by stringing *New Yorker* cartoons through chapters teeming with research data about corporate screwups. In the frontispiece, a waiter delivered entrees to a couple. The dishes looked exactly the same as what everyone else in the dining room was getting.

"Sorry, folks," the waiter explained. "It's not what you ordered, but everyone is getting fettucine until we fix the computer."

Did Landauer change his mind about the usefulness of computers to business in the smartphone Age of Jobs that postdated his book? Well, he did go into business himself, at Pearson Education.

Rochlin's brand of cybercynicism, though, retained a political edge during his long years in Berkeley, and he advanced the tradition. Still partly the working-class "tech weenie" who grew up on *Popular Mechanics* magazine, he found himself "on the ground early in the days of computing." (He worked at Berkeley on the Von Neumann–designed MANIAC III computer, which needed a basketball court to hold it.)

As a result, Rochlin pooh-poohed neither the reality of the technological transformation he lived through ("This *is* a revolutionary time"), as Dreyfus sometimes did, nor the possibility of politically resisting it where appropriate, à la Rawlins. Instead, in his meticulously documented book, Rochlin showed that the chief danger of computer systems didn't lie in any wild scenario from futuristic fiction. It rested in an already demonstrable fact—computer systems took our hands off the controls of too many things.

Rochlin explained how program trading contributed to a stock market crash. He detailed how a "smart" system caused the USS *Vincennes* to accidentally shoot down an Iranian airliner. He reported how air traffic controllers had resisted attempts to automate aspects of their work, fearing it would lead to disaster, but were losing that battle. Such defeats, said Rochlin, might mean that "increasingly the people who operate the system will not be able to recover if something goes wrong."

In all these technical areas, Rochlin argued, even the best designed systems failed. When they failed in unanticipated circumstances, their automation, which distanced experts from understanding how a system worked, made it harder for the humans to fix them.

"What you really want people for," Rochlin remarked, "is for the things you never thought would happen." Humans, Rochlin asserted, possessed an ability to respond correctly to ambiguity that no computer had yet matched. "Things happen out there that you can never anticipate, and no one has ever satisfied me that anyone but a human being can solve a completely human problem."

Unfortunately, as experts lost direct control over the equipment they operated, they also lost trial-and-error expertise necessary to triumph over the unexpected. In Rochlin's view, "taking away the easy part of an operator's tasks" made "the hard ones more difficult."

Yet he was not, he insisted, opposed to automation in all cases. "The more confined and narrow a job is," he explained, "and the smaller the range of options, the more likely it is you can automate that job." Rochlin gave the example of a plane's automatic landing system: "I love automatic landing systems. They let me land in a fog in Frankfurt instead of circling the airport for nine hours. An airliner is a very predictable device landing in a very predictable place. The computer's got one job to do, something a pilot really can't do. But do I trust the computer to fly me out of the Frankfurt landing pattern? Would I trust an automatic landing system on an aircraft carrier?"

There was also another problem: automation bores people. Rochlin noted in regard to it that those "who run repetitive jobs often make mistakes. It surprises some that the harder and more complex a job is, the better the performance you get out of people. Well, that's not really surprising."

The reason, Rochlin said, is that challenges "engage the one capacity of human beings you can't replicate—understanding the constantly changing nature of their environment and interpreting it from moment to moment." Such a capacity, in fact, derived from the "common sense" that, Dreyfus pointed out, computer scientists still hadn't *instilled* into systems.

Nonetheless, automation by computer was on the rise, and Rochlin feared it was propelling a mind-set of resignation into all areas of our lives. "People have given up understanding things," Rochlin remarked. "When was the last time you opened the lid of your car? What would you do if you did? You'd look at it in horror and close it! There's nothing you can do under that hood anymore!"

"Gradually," Rochlin continued, "people have lost control over their artifacts and become dumb users of smart systems. They don't think they're passive, but they are more unconsciously accepting." In return, computer engineers allow them "enormous discretion" to do lots of remarkable new things (as in a software program) so long as they do it in a "highly structured" domain.

If Rochlin sounded rebellious, he was. In that respect, his most activist literary and philosophical allies among cybercynics resided on the East Coast. One was journalist and historian Kirkpatrick Sale, whose critical history *Rebels Against the Future: The Luddites and Their War on the Industrial Revolution* refused to stereotype his subjects as maniacal opponents of progress. Rather, Sale investigated and reestablished them as English textile workers desperate, in the years 1811 and 1812, to protect their livelihoods with guns and hammers from the assault of industrial capitalism.

A lighter-hearted bunch, also in sync with the protest style of critique one associated with Berkeley radicalism, was the Lead Pencil Club, a vaguely tongue-in-cheek group that gave new meaning to the obsolete term "pencilpusher." In *Minutes of the Lead Pencil Club: Pulling the Plug on the Electronic Revolution,* publisher Bill Henderson recalled its founding on a December night, when he was reading "some Luddite sentiments" in Doris Grumbach's memoir, *Extra Innings.* She was sick of her computer and other gadgets and wished they could "catch a virus for which there was no cure.

" 'Why not use a lead pencil?' I asked myself. 'Why not a lead pencil club, for those of us who agree with her?' "

Henderson quickly won Grumbach's cooperation and penciled a manifesto ("We will avoid fax and hang up on voice mail. We will receive no e-mail and send none . . ."). After some enterprising shilling for the event, Henderson drew notices in *Time, Newsweek,* the *International Herald Tribune* and other publications. "From all areas of the earth," he said, "letters arrived in pencil." They responded, in part, to Henderson's wry voice in taking up the neo-Luddite cause. As the savvy founder of Pushcart Press and a student of media spin, Henderson recognized that older-generation cyberphilosophers like Barlow and Stewart Brand won allegiance partly because they'd mastered the art of the glib cyberaphorism, such as "Information wants to be free."

Brand, the maverick former editor of the *Whole Earth Catalog,* excelled so much at the task that you could find his one-liners on either side of most issues in the literature. In his popular book, *The Media Lab,* Brand played booster: "If you're not part of the steamroller, you're part of the road." Yet he could also crack, in a 1985 interview, "This generation swallowed computers whole, like dope."

Henderson answered in sarcastic kind. He warned that "[t]he Info Highway is paving us over," mocked $39.95 software programs "that duplicate handwriting fast and neatly," and predicted that the lead pencil would become "a symbol of defiance at the digital colonialization of this planet, just as Gandhi's spinning wheel symbolized the resistance of the people of India." Material submitted by group members, Henderson wrote, confirmed that "behind the current blather about a free, unfettered international Internet community lurks a universal trust of business interests with billions of dollars to invest in fiber optic connections to every living room on earth."

"The priests of this particular cyberspace sect . . . ," he went on, "see consumers pinned to the map like cockroaches, sorted according to buying preferences, age, sex, and every other detail and sold to accordingly." Nonetheless, all digital hype would eventually fall before the truth telling of Thoreau's progeny.

"The Lead Pencil Club declares," he summed up, "that the World Wide Web is a duck primed for slaughter. Soon, with every individual, organization, and company owning a site, the World Wide Web will resemble the World Wide Yellow Pages, and you know how much fun it is to flip through the phone book."

That didn't happen. In some ways, a balancing took place between two types of cyberphilosophy that were more distinct in the activity's first wave: the upbeat "what will be" exploration of the future, and the skeptical assessment that saw both good and bad. Thinkers at the heart of Internet studies stopped gushing so much and did more worrying.

Two law professors, Daniel J. Solove and Jonathan Zittrain, both saw storm clouds ahead in the digital revolution. In *The Future of Reputation: Gossip, Rumor, and Privacy on the Internet,* Solove concentrated on the clash between free expression and privacy. He believed digital communication added new worries to traditional concerns, and worried that "the free flow of information on the Internet" might "make us less free."

"As social reputation-shaping practices such as gossip and shaming migrate to the Internet," he asserted, "they are being transformed in significant ways. Information that was once scattered, forgettable, and localized is becoming permanent and searchable" as "chatrooms, online discussion groups, and blogs," as well as social networking Web sites such as MySpace and Facebook, continue "proliferating at a breakneck pace." Thanks to innovations such as YouTube, it now seemed that "foolish deeds are preserved for eternity on the Internet." Growth in the permanence and availability of private information, aided by mass linking, was one Solove concern. Blogs, he noted, expanded from "about 50" in 1999 to "approximately 50 million" by July 2006.

Also growing was the problem that such information could be of "dubious reliability," "false and defamatory" or "true but deeply humiliating or discrediting." The Internet made "gossip a permanent reputational stain, one that never fades." He added to that another difference: "Traditional gossip occurs in a context, among people who know the person gossiped about. But the Internet strips away that context, and this can make gossip even more pernicious."

Those sounded like gloomy trends. But since Solove, like most Anglo-American law professors, reasoned his way through case studies, *The Future of Reputation* also offered an eye-opening tour along with its somber philosophical atmosphere. One famous case on the Internet, that of the "dog poop girl," illustrated several of the "Generation Google" phenomena that disturbed Solove.

A young woman's small dog fouled a South Korean subway train. When other passengers asked her to clean it up, she "told them to mind their own business." Someone took photos of her and posted them on a popular blog. Criticism of the girl, and attacks on her, quickly followed.

Widely known as "dog poop girl" before long, she discovered that her personal information was being sought and distributed. Soon she became national news. Publicly shamed and embarrassed, the girl "dropped out of her university."

"Whereas before," Solove observed, "the girl would have been remembered by a few . . . now her image and identity are eternally preserved in electrons. Forever, she will be 'the dog poop girl'; forever, she will be captured in Google's unforgiving memory; and, forever, she will be in the digital doghouse."

Solove gave many other examples: a thirty-four-year-old American professional who could not escape his juvenile criminal record; "Little Fatty," a "pudgy sixteen-year-old in China," whose plump countenance began to get posted everywhere in ways that left the boy "humiliated"; Jessica Cutler, the twenty-five-year-old staffer to a U.S. senator who lost her job after her lascivious blog became public; Laura, a student who sought to plagiarize a paper on Hinduism, then ended up the subject of a mass Net conversation on appropriate punishment for her misdeed.

While Solove conceded that some enforcing of social norms by Internet shaming could have "benefits," he pointed out that Net shaming, unlike legal sanctioning, "occurs without any formal procedures, investigation, or direct feedback to the accused offender. As a result, Internet shaming can readily get out of hand." This was especially so given the burgeoning of sites that invited shaming of others for activities such as miserly tipping ("BitterWaitress"), making crude remarks to women ("Hollaback NYC") and cheating on one's lover ("Revenge World").

As Solove put it, "The Internet is bringing back the Scarlet Letter in digital form." Was there a solution? Solove thought the answer lay mainly in improved law, in "recognizing a new and broader notion of privacy and by reaching a better balance between privacy and free speech." We must "protect privacy to ensure that the freedom of the Internet doesn't make us less free." That meant splitting the difference between regulatory and absolutist approaches to free speech. While Solove recognized that "there is a limit to what law can do," he believed it was an "instrument capable of subtle notes."

Zittrain, by contrast, was a romantic about the "Live Free or Die" ethos of original Internet culture, while doubling as a technical master of its legal and manufacturing history. In *The Future of the Internet,* he expressed concern that regulators, manufacturers and frightened citizens might converge to snatch technological freedom from Internet culture. In Zittrain's view, the hallmark of both the Internet and the personal computer had been their "generative" quality, an openness to change in some respects by anyone with access to them. That quality had produced unexpected good things like Google and YouTube, instant messaging and search engines, and unexpected bad things like "viruses, spam, identity theft, crashes," not to mention worms and "botnets," those networks of maliciously compromised computers that make people's Internet lives miserable.

On the whole, Zittrain thought, we'd done well. Yet too many people had forgotten that the freedom of the Internet was largely a happy accident. In some of his best passages, about how the PC eclipsed the mainframe, and how the Internet left controlled environments like AOL in the dust (if not buried), Zittrain vaunted the benefits of freedom. The accelerating problem he saw, however, was that negative upshots of Internet freedom, such as viruses and spyware, were driving ordinary Internet users—those with no special desire for inventive interactivity with their devices, who saw themselves "only as consumers whose participation is limited to purchasing decisions"—to demand devices that offer the reliability and security of appliances.

Welcome to the brave new "present" of iPods, iPhones, Xboxes and TiVos, devices that don't permit end users to program them but remain under the control of their corporate manufacturers. The Internet's "sea change" would come, Zittrain cautioned, with "control over the endpoint," because if you "lock down the device . . . network censorship and control can be extraordinarily reinforced."

Zittrain thus confronted the same freedom-versus-loss-of-control issue as Solove, but in a wider sphere—Net technology itself. True to his Net romanticism, however, Zittrain saw solutions not primarily in law. Rather, he looked to the original "communitarian" ethos of the Net. Whereas Solove hoped for legal doctrines that carefully balanced between privacy and free expression, Zittrain called on community cooperation of the sort one saw in Wikipedia. Just as "neighborhood watch" programs staffed by citizens protected neighborhoods, Zittrain believed more netizens needed to enlist in the fight against Internet gangsterism.

He also urged technical solutions. We needed better PCs whose "wiki" technology would provide histories of documents that enabled them to be examined and corrected. He suggested "virtual machines" on PCs that would allow users to divide safe and risky activities. He imagined a Manhattan Project–type commitment of Internet players to defeat bad guys who drove the growing public wish for locked-down, "tethered" devices that barred third-party or user tinkering, but provided security.

Both Zittrain and Solove exhibited a common trait of technologically oriented futurists imbued with cyberskepticism: they assumed current values and a wish to preserve them in the face of fresh logistical forces. That was often a reasonable assumption. Several new privacy crises in cyberspace—as when Facebook users objected to the site's compiling and exploiting their individual purchases for marketing purposes—indicated that young Internet users treasured the same traditional privacy values that Solove did.

Zittrain, too, could doubtless find many young whizzes who wanted cyberspace to remain as wild and woolly as promised in the early days of Barlow's "Declaration," before the subject became so complex (and buttoned down). At the same time, Solove's examples, such as Jennifer Ringley, the twenty-year-old student who opened her whole life to regular webcam monitoring in 1996 and didn't shut down until 2004, evoked truths more explored by Frankfurt School philosophers than American futurists—that technology also changed our values, or at least adjusted them. The iPod, for instance, pressured us to tolerate forms of behavior formerly considered rude, such as the teenager who made her purchase at the cash register without removing her earplugs.

How, then, could one mark the state of cyberphilosophy and cybercynicism by 2011? As Saffo had warned, some of yesterday's fortune-tellers increasingly looked like yesterday's dimbos, particularly in the real-world economy. Who had predicted Google? YouTube? Twitter? The direction social networking would take with the decline of MySpace and the explosion of Facebook? The creation of the blogosphere?

In some ways, cybercynics, trained on human beings rather than devices, had been better prognosticators than the true believers. Facebook, as Rochlin had warned about such phenomena, controlled vital information about its registrees, which would provoke regular controversies with them. Facebook also extended the arguable deception that Slouka and Henderson had mocked: the idea that "[y]ou're not alone—you're connected."

But perhaps the best answer to where cyberphilosophy and cybercynicism stood in the first decades of this century was on all sides of the issues, resolutely pumping up Gutenberg's revenge. There were still the cyberenthusiasts and gurus, like Barlow years before, exulting over the newest flavor in the cyber-ice-cream dispenser and then thinking, "Book!"

The hottest technology was Twitter. David Pogue, weekly tech columnist and digital explainer for the *Times*, described it for the terminally ignorant as "a Web site where you can broadcast very short messages—140 characters max—to anyone who's signed up to receive them," a group that came to be dubbed one's "followers." Pogue tagged Twitter as "a cross between a blog and a chat room."

Pogue swore that he began, like many people, as a Twitter skeptic: "The first time I covered Twitter for *The New York Times*, I wrote, 'Like the world needs another ego-massaging, social-networking time drain?'" But then he began to "get it." The quickness with which everyone could shoot out wry observations. The useful links sent and received. The way breaking news increasingly got twittered first, and hard-to-get news sometimes could only be twittered, a phenomenon powerfully confirmed by the postelection crackdown of Iran's government in 2009, and the Cairo revolution of 2011.

Pogue tried an experiment. While giving a talk in Las Vegas in which he was on tap to explain Twitter, he "fired up Twitter on the big-screen and typed to my 5,000 followers: 'I need a cure for hiccups . . . right now!'" Responses poured in immediately: "Check your 401K. That should scare the hiccups right out of ya"; "Take 9 sips of water and say 'January.' Laugh now, but you'll thank me when the hiccups are gone!"

The "weird, wonderful, funny" material that poured in—instantaneously—stunned Pogue. He thought its quality confirmed Twitterers as intellectually a cut above the "people who populate MySpace, Facebook or YouTube." According to Pew and Quantcast, he subsequently learned, they were "an older, better-educated, higher-earning group." The only problem was how to share all the brilliant repartee. A problem, Pogue explained, with a solution: "With certain exceptions, when you get a reply on Twitter, you're the only person who sees it.

When I got home from that speaking trip, I mentioned that problem to my wife, Jennifer. 'You know what you should do,' she said. 'You should ask a question every night, and then publish the best answers in a book.'"

And so he did: *The World According to Twitter*, by "David Pogue and his 500,000 Followers." A few hundred pages of hilarious replies to questions such as "Add 1 letter to a famous person's name; explain." (One reply: "Chez Guevara: Revolutionary Franco/Latino restaurant.") Or, "You've lived your life this far. What have you learned?" (One gem: "You are your own worst enemy. Fortunately, you can be defeated.")

In turning to "the book" to express and display the digital revolution's latest, greatest and temporarily hottest form of expression, Pogue was, of course, simply gathering fresh samples of one of literature and philosophy's oldest forms, the aphorism. Remember Emerson, the rocket manufacturer? Remember Sontag, and her determination to mirror Nietzsche? If, in fact, the Internet and other new technologies were lessening attention spans, or pressuring people to express their thoughts more compactly, that didn't mean philosophy wasn't getting done.

True, "serious thinkers" worried about the issue. In a book quite different from Pogue's—George Myerson's *Heidegger, Habermas, and the Mobile Phone,* which didn't get a multi-hundred-thousand-copy run—the King's College, London, literature professor raised the issue in regard to a formerly hot device in modern life: Europe's "mobile," America's "cell phone."

Hadn't Jürgen Habermas, Germany's greatest living philosopher, the intellectual conscience of German democracy, long promoted a theory of communication that emphasized rational discussion among people, marked by the deliberate exchange of reasons, in an atmosphere where everyone aimed at understanding? Mobile phones, like Twitter, idealized and encouraged "the swiftest possible route to the most direct response," in part because idle chatter at first cost so much. (Twitter's terseness, by contrast, was self-imposed by the company—an example of Zittrain's worrisome constraint from on high.)

As mobiles and cells continued their evolution into multi-app smartphones that included e-mail, video and more, the priority of quick message exchange over deliberate, critical conversation would only grow. Habermas, Myerson argued, would consider "a society that arranged its affairs by exchanging 20 or 30 messages an hour" to be likely to "forget what is involved in a meaningful expression" and turn "pathological." In mobile communication, Myerson warned, "[t]here are no reasons." He feared an oncoming world that could not "distinguish between a credit card transaction and a conversation." Philosophically, we needed communication in which people pressured one another's premises, not just triggered their ringtones.

Were Myerson's fears overwrought? Wasn't it possible to pressure premises one by one? He, too, managed to make his points in a book, without his call to the culture being dropped. As Barlow's inclination and Pogue's choice indicated—as Gutenberg's revenge highlighted—both cyberphilosophy and cybercynicism arose out of a philosophical tradition dating back millennia. A wise take on the issues involved, and the responsibility of cyberphilosophy toward them, could be found among Roszak's final thoughts in *The Cult of Information*:

> The history of technology has always been a faltering search for Promethean power and utopian perfection. Every mature technology brings a minimal immediate gain followed by enormous long-term liabilities. The computer is the latest entry in that history, still bright with promise for its enthusiasts but surely destined to join the lengthening file of modern technological treachery that Aldous Huxley began compiling in his prophetic *Brave New World.* By now we should know what the Luddites of old learned before us: every tool ever invented is a mixed blessing. How things will balance out is a matter of vigilance, moral courage, and the distribution of power.

By 2011, the wisdom of Roszak's warning began to play out in a second—or was it the third?—wave of cybercynicism, books so invested in warning us that they amounted to a new subgenre called cyberRevere-ism. Mark Helprin's *Digital Barbarism* argued that its title phenomenon, rooted in the so-called Creative Commons movement, amounted to "a well organized effort to cut away at intellectual property rights until they disappear." In *The Net Delusion: The Dark Side of Internet Freedom,* Stanford visiting scholar Evgeny Morozov, catching the media's attention just as young Arab cyberactivists in the Middle East battled their supposedly less adept state-security opponents, showed how repressive regimes as well as freedom fighters could turn digital savvy to their purposes by increasing surveillance and suppressing dissent. In *The Shallows: What the Internet Is Doing to Our Brains,* Nicholas Carr echoed Kevin Kelly's point that technology was altering our personalities. In *Alone Together,* Sherry Turkle continued her lifetime work of investigating the digital revolution's impact on our emotions.

But perhaps Jaron Lanier's *You Are Not a Gadget* presented the most telling coda to the intellectual tale told here. The well-known programmer and musician, like Morozov, situated himself simultaneously in both the fresh philosophical tradition mapped in Part 4 and the one more familiarly cataloged under philosophy as previously conceived. In their pages, one could find nods to Barlow, Brand, Dreyfus, Dyson, Kelly and Negroponte, as well as Plato, Marx, Freud, Heidegger, Maslow, Arendt, Marcuse, Fukuyama and Zizek.

One might have expected Lanier, who identified himself as a former member of the "merry band of idealists" that included Barlow and Kelly, to sing the praises of a third wave of cyberinnovation. Instead, positioning himself squarely within cybercynicism, and describing his book as "pro-human" rather than "anti-technology," he warned that "something started to go wrong with the digital revolution around the turn of the twenty-first century."

Lanier cautioned that certain "anti-human software designs" of the moment pulled us into life patterns "that gradually degrade the ways in which each of us exists as an individual." He predicted the rise of widespread "digital serfdom," and asserted that we already "get certain free cloud services in exchange for being spied on." Would computing clouds "become effectively infinite"? If so, he feared, "all meaningful expression would become impossible."

Not yet, however. Sure enough, when his book appeared in paper-

Jaron Lanier (1960–), a computer scientist and composer, helped popularize the term "virtual reality" and expressed his concerns about the digital revolution in his book, *You Are Not a Gadget*.

back in 2011, with a question-and-answer afterword, the first question asked was "Isn't it absurd to release *You Are Not a Gadget* as a book?"

Lanier's answer: "The important things don't really change that fast."

The long view of the digital revolution and cyberphilosophy reminded us that when we speak of cybercynics and cyberskeptics, the very words we use declare that much of our conception of philosophy remains controlled by the ancient Greeks, whose schools and dominating figures shape our categories. We speak (misleadingly) of "platonic" love between friends. We talk of Socratic questioning in the courtroom, of defendants who take their verdicts "stoically," of Wall Streeters who refuse to give up their epicurean delights.

Occasionally, modern scholars help us amend our off-kilter understanding of what these words actually mean. A good example in recent times was misunderstanding of the Stoics, who supposedly showed or experienced no emotion. Martha Nussbaum helped clarify that Stoics were perfectly comfortable with emotion, thank you very much, so long as it was properly modulated.

It is, however, an ancient Greek thinker even more lost in the mists of history, and his style of thought, whose proper rediscovery provides the best explanation of why America the Philosophical is not only an empirical reality but a historically sound judgment. It sweeps from the eighteenth century to modern cyberthinking once one corrects the story of how Western philosophy began.

Isocrates, despite his remarkably up-to-date mind-set, was largely and unfairly dropped from the pantheon of crucial Western thinkers. That is why we have no adjective "Isocratic."

Until now.

PART 5

ISOCRATES:
A MAN, NOT A TYPO

BUSTING ISOCRATES

What a difference a letter makes. Even truck drivers know Socrates (469–399 B.C.), thanks to his fame in both high and pop culture. By contrast, intellectuals outside classics often blank on Isocrates (436–338 B.C.), despite his being judged "the father of humanistic culture" by stellar German classicist Werner Jaeger, and one of "Plato's foremost intellectual rivals" by Josiah Ober, one of today's leading scholars of ancient Athens.

If you walk about the tourist-packed neighborhood of Plaka in Athens, you'll find shops selling hundreds, even thousands, of busts of ancient Athenians. Socrates and Plato lead the pack, but other favorites abound: Homer, Pythagoras, Euripides, Aristotle, Pindar.

Isocrates? Not a one to be found. Of six or seven gift shop owners asked if any busts existed of Isocrates, only one had heard of him. The leading Athenian dealer in old prints and lithographs can't remember ever seeing one of Isocrates. Indeed, Isocrates can't even get a portrait of himself on his own books. See that well-toned, unidentified fellow clutching the scroll on the cover of the University of Texas's volume of Isocrates's writings? Alas, it's Demosthenes, courtesy of the Ny Carlsberg Glyptotek in Copenhagen. The only public place in modern Athens with an image of Isocrates is the interactive "Agora" established a few years ago on the highway, clogged by auto repair shops, that leads from the city to Piraeus. It comes from the sole extant bust of Isocrates, itself a copy, that ended up (oddly enough) in Moscow's Pushkin Museum.

But Isocrates should be as famous as Socrates. The so-called battle between rhetoric and philosophy in the heyday of ancient Athens, with rhetoric supposedly represented by Isocrates and philosophy represented by Socrates, actually took place between two visions of philosophy, not philosophy and something else. As Alasdair MacIntyre observed in his book *Whose Justice? Which Rationality?*, Isocrates offered "an alternative to philosophy as Socrates, Plato and Aristotle had defined it."

Socrates, as depicted by Plato (427–347 B.C.), viewed philosophy as a rational, scientific, dialectical process that led one to eternal verities and right answers. Popular mentioners and worshippers of Socrates often identify him with his famous statement that he knew nothing except his own ignorance. It's more true, however, as classicist Emily Wilson wrote in *The Death of Socrates*, that his "own beliefs are never called into serious question." Considerable dogmatism lies behind the Platonic Socrates's guise as an open-minded investigator of ideas, and the hero worship of Socrates—not shared, as we saw, by I. F. Stone—often comes from

Isocrates (436–338 B.C.) argued that his form of practical reasoning amounted to the wisest form of philosophy, but despite his immense fame in his own time, Plato successfully derided him as a mere rhetorician.

intellectuals who don't know ancient Greek philosophy well, and simply adopt a conventional position toward him.

Isocrates, in contrast, saw philosophy as an imprecise form of "civilized discourse" or "public deliberation," what he called *logos politikos*, aimed at persuasion about great matters. His vision of philosophy jibes with American pragmatism and philosophical practice far more than Socrates's view. Indeed, he is the single intellectual of ancient Greece who incarnates the contradictions, pragmatism, ambition, bent for problem solving and getting things done that mark Americans. In reality, the triumph of Isocrates over Socrates in American life took place a long time ago. What remains for American intellectual historians, as well as foreign thinkers saddled with false clichés about the U.S., is to recognize that and describe intellectual life here correctly. America the Philosophical operates under the sign of Isocrates. We simply haven't heard of him.

Almost all of our biographical information about Isocrates comes from his surviving work—one of the most extensive extant bodies of writing of any classical Greek thinker aside from Plato—and a few other sources such as Pseudo-Plutarch and Dionysius of Halicarnassus. Many facts about his life remain uncertain. George Norlin, translator of the three Isocrates volumes in the Loeb Classical Library, warns that "much of the tradition regarding his life must be received with caution."

By all accounts, he came from a wealthy Athenian family. His father, Theodorus, was the prosperous owner of a flute workshop, an employer of slave girls in the business who spent a good deal of money benefiting Athens and educating Isocrates to reach great heights. His mother was named Heduto—that's all we know about her—and he had three brothers and a sister. Tradition holds that Isocrates studied with Tisias, the Sicilian student of Corax believed to have launched rhetorical practice along with his master, and possibly Prodicus, Gorgias and Socrates. In his comprehensive scholarly study *The Greeks and Greek Love,* British classicist James Davidson notes only a single fact about Isocrates, whom he describes as "an orator": that Isocrates is referred to as a "*paidika* of Socrates," a "favorite" of his whose writings Socrates admired.

Isocrates informs us that he lost most of the wealth he inherited from his family in the Peloponnesian War. Tradition tells us that around 403 B.C., Isocrates, short of money, became a logographer—a ghostwriter of speeches for the law courts. In *Antidosis,* his late apologia modeled on Plato's *Apology* about Socrates, Isocrates denies that he ever worked as a speechwriter. That denial contradicts a claim of Aristotle (384–322 B.C.), who some sources say was a student at Isocrates's school before transferring to Plato's Academy and turning snippy toward his former headmaster. Aristotle noted that volumes and volumes of Isocrates's legal speeches could be found in Athenian bookshops. Jaeger mentions the tradition that Aristotle liked to say, when he came to Isocrates in his lectures, "It would be a shame to remain silent while Isocrates is permitted to speak."

Scholars today divide on the issue despite six surviving speeches attributed to Isocrates. The majority surmise that Isocrates's late-life denials amount to the embarrassment of a successful philosopher-teacher over his youthful job as a spokesman and publicist. Most nonetheless take Isocrates at his word that he never actually delivered a speech himself. In *To Philip,* Isocrates famously wrote, "I did not have a voice sufficiently strong nor the self-assurance to enable me to cope with the mob, to be reviled and to abuse those who parade on the speaker's platform."

We also know that, later in life, Isocrates is said to have married Plathane, daughter of the sophist Hippias, and to have adopted Aphareus, her son by a previous marriage. By 390 B.C., Isocrates was plainly concentrating his time on educational and philosophical writing, and it's generally agreed that he didn't write speeches in his middle and later years. The school he founded in Athens, which began some four years before Plato founded the Academy, and served as its chief rival, produced many leaders of Athenian society, including the general Timotheus. Isocrates reportedly taught more than one hundred students at a time, and the Forbes 400 of his day listed him as one of the twelve hundred wealthiest Athenians. Isocrates tells us in *Antidosis* that he took fees only from foreigners, rejecting the charge that he made a profit on fellow citizens. He insisted that he always gave more in public service than he took—that he benefited Athens by his teaching, and never corrupted anyone. He retired from teaching, sources say, in 351 B.C., at the age of eighty-five.

Apart from his general views on philosophy, rhetoric and argument, Isocrates won the most attention in his time, and remains best known among classical scholars, for his "Panhellenism," his oft-argued belief that Greek cities should unite under Athenian leadership, and later under Philip of Macedonia, to defeat the "barbarians," i.e., the Persians. Isocrates promoted a cultural and political rather than racial and ethnic theory of "being Greek," similar to our contemporary notion of "being American." Someone could become Greek, in Isocrates's view, by possessing Greek values, a Greek education, and intellectual and linguistic ability. While a consistent supporter of democracy (unlike Plato) in his works, he did so from a decidedly aristocratic and critical stance, and addressed many of his letters and appeals to leaders and kings of the ancient world. According to tradition, Isocrates starved himself to death at age ninety-eight after learning that Philip had defeated the Athenians at the Battle of Chaeronea in 338 B.C.

Despite the triumph of Plato and Aristotle in excluding Isocrates from the philosophical tradition, almost all scholars agree that Isocrates's school exerted a far greater influence on subsequent Greek and Roman education than did the Academy or Aristotle's Lyceum. Athens, the classical scholar Yun Lee Too reminds us, placed "a premium on the ability to speak in public." The prejudice of the time held that oral presentation surpassed written expression because the latter eliminated many of the rhetorical resources a speaker possesses, especially the ability to adjust tactics in the wake of audience response. In that milieu, Too observes, "Isocrates is the ancient author who more than any other establishes writing as a medium of political expression and activity." Add, then, to his proper status as philosophical founding father a possible niche as the father of blogging, albeit of a fairly formal sort. He was read in the Renaissance, and, according to Too, his *To Nicocles* and *Nicocles* (two separate essays) were quite popular in Latin.

Finally, Pseudo-Plutarch gives evidence of Isocrates's wit. Once, when he was being entertained by the Cypriot tyrant Nicocreon, a name believed to be a variant of the more commonly used Nicocles, Isocrates was asked to give a speech. As a great believer that understanding the right thing to do at any given moment—what the Greeks called an appreciation for *kairos*—constituted the highest intellectual faculty a person could possess, Isocrates declined. He remarked, "[F]or the matters in which I am capable this is not the moment, and in the matters for which this is the moment, I am not capable."

IMAGES AND CLICHÉS OF ISOCRATES

Various classical scholars praise Isocrates for one virtue or another. According to Norlin, Isocrates "is always clear." He "fixed the form of rhetorical prose for the Greek world, and, through the influence of Cicero, for modern times as well." Norlin gives us an admirable Isocrates whose qualities mirror those of Socrates in some respects:

> his aloofness from public life; his critical attitude toward the excesses of the Athenian democracy, and his hatred of demagogues; his contempt for the sham pretensions of some of the sophists; his logical clearness and his insistence on the proper definition of objectives and terms; his prejudice against the speculations of philosophy on the origin of things as being fruitless; his feeling that ideas are of value only as they can be translated into action, and that education should be practical and aim at right conduct in private and in public life; his rationalism in religion combined with acquiescence in the forms of worship, his emphasis upon ethics and his earnest morality.

Jaeger, who deems Isocrates a "happy mean" between Socrates and Plato in various respects, urges us not to forget that he has, "like Plato, his admirers and exponents, and there is no doubt that since the Renaissance he has exercised a far greater influence on the educational methods of humanism than any other Greek or Roman teacher." Allan Bloom, the firebrand author of *The Closing of the American Mind,* who wrote his doctoral dissertation on Isocrates under no less than Leo Strauss, declared, "When we do not understand Isocrates and Xenophon, we do not understand Thucydides and Plato."

These positive images of Isocrates, however, coexist and sometimes clash with many negative ones, what scholar Kathryn Morgan calls "a long tradition of Isocrates-bashing." In *The Classical Greek Reader,* editor Kenneth Atchity describes Isocrates as "a self-promoter." Ober in one place interprets Isocratean philosophy as simply "the mastery of elegant verbal expression." Norlin himself calls Isocrates a "political pamphleteer." Norman Baynes says he's "a bundle of contradictions."

To Robert Wardy in *The Birth of Rhetoric,* Isocrates "evades rather than engages in the conflict between philosophy and rhetoric." Too, a student of Wardy, labels Isocrates "a figure of inadequacy" and "peripheral." In his early work, *The Art of Persuasion in Greece,* George Kennedy, one of the foremost American experts on ancient Greek rhetoric, describes Isocrates as "tiresome," "longwinded," "superficial" and an "opportunist" fond of obfuscation. Kathleen Welch, a recent scholar who appreciates Isocrates and gathers some of these disparagements, notes that Kennedy declined to repeat his negative judgments in later work, suggesting Isocrates's rise in reputation. Yet she acknowledges that "Isocrates as windbag is in fact a recurrent idea."

Unlike Socrates, revered as a hero by most philosophers (though a countertradition of opprobrium from Nietzsche and others also exists), Isocrates suffers a surfeit of condescension, minimization, marginalization and dismissal, with a minority strain of scholars standing up for him as a thinker rather than just a teacher and influence on the history of European education. The latter, tellingly, are almost always the scholars who have read him rather than heard about him from others.

Isocrates, then, is not only obscure to the general educated public, but a prisoner of clichés within the field of classics. With some exceptions, scholars who don't study Isocrates directly, but know him mainly as a background figure, adopt those clichés. Those who study him directly realize that he's more a thinker than a teacher of style, and a thinker who challenges assumptions that have been ruling the pedagogy of ancient Greek philosophy for centuries.

To appreciate why Isocrates matters, then, to both American and ancient Greek intellectual history, and ought to be rediscovered and revived, it's crucial to unpack the difference between a sophist, a rhetorician and a philosopher in ancient Greece, emphasizing, as will be seen, that those words, or their Greek equivalents, remained unstable and in flux in the fourth century B.C.

SOPHISTS AND SOPHISTRY

Who were the sophists? Scholars disagree on many nuances here. Even Socrates, who plainly opposed the sophists, was identified as one by Aristophanes in *The Clouds.* Canonically, the figures most typically on the list include Gorgias of Leontini, Hippias, Prodicus, Protagoras and, sometimes, Isocrates, though he, like Socrates, rejected the label.

In general, sophists were educated, traveling intellectuals who, for a fee, taught argument and persuasion in a democratic culture where public speaking was very important and essential to political participation. Writes Taxis Poulakos, "with some training in verbal quibbles, a good grip on paradoxical argumentation, and an overall dexterity in language use, one was sufficiently equipped to call himself a 'sophist.'" Some charged big money for their lectures. Protagoras supposedly charged as much as 100 minai, or 10,000 drachmas, more than the sum earned by Phidias and ten sculptors put together. In the famous formulation promoted by Plato in such dialogues as *Protagoras, Gorgias* and later *Sophist,* sophists professed to teach virtue and promised to show acolytes how "to make the weaker of two arguments the stronger"—an ability first attributed to Protagoras and cited by Aristophanes. As itinerants who, scholar W. K. C. Guthrie says, tended to share Isocrates's Panhellenism (though all taught at Athens at some time in the second half of the fifth century B.C.), they exhibited tricky skills at speaking, and claimed to know a great deal about everything.

In Plato's view, they were cheats and sharpies oblivious to truth. In *Sophist,* Plato offers a definition, calling such a teacher a hunter for rich young men, a merchant of learning, and an imitator of the wise, more concerned with the interest of the speaker than the listener. Xenophon reports Socrates calling sophists "prostitutes of wisdom" because they provided their version of it for money. Disparagement of sophists was widespread in Athens, and reflected the view of Socrates, Plato and their circle, whose derogatory stance became the standard story of Western intellectual history, leaving the modern word "sophistry" synonymous with crafty and deceptive thinking.

But the great French scholar of sophistry, Jacqueline de Romilly, pointed out that the "entire collection of fragments from the Sophists would amount to no more than 20 pages." To be sure, she concedes, Plato "is the best guide we have. But here we're confronted with another paradox: our guide is quite clearly a biased one, for although Plato sets the Sophists on stage, he assigns Socrates to refute their theses. We are accordingly bound to be wary of following his testimony, sensing that the Sophists are in danger of being ill served by this distorting spotlight." Indeed, Romilly adds, "the Sophists were under attack from all sides." Jaeger maintains that Plato produced "caricatures" of Isocrates, sophists and rhetoricians that are, unfortunately, "quite as immortal as his idealized portrait of Socrates."

Edward Schiappa, another leading scholar of the sophists, agrees that Plato is a biased source: "If Plato could identify the 'product' of his rival Isocrates' training as something unnecessary or undesirable, so much the better for the reputation of Plato's school. Gorgias, it should be remembered, was the teacher of Isocrates, hence a dialogue on public discourse titled *Gorgias* that included thinly veiled references to Isocrates would easily have been recognized in the fourth century as an attack on the training afforded by Isocrates."

Moreover Plato, in the *Euthydemus*, mocks sophistry as eristics—controversy for the sake of controversy. In Plato's view, it's the sophists who are intolerant, proud, averse to dialogue, concerned more with success than the truth—characteristics, as we'll see, not shared by Isocrates. For those uncomfortable with the relativism and pragmatism of Protagoras, it amounted to lack of interest in truth. One could also, however, see Protagoras as Diogenes Laertius saw him, as "the first to maintain that there are two sides to every question," the first pluralist, the first democrat of argument.

Indeed, Plato's subtle identification of Isocrates with the worst features of sophists—preference for success over truth, willingness to vaunt weaker arguments over stronger arguments—is a complete distortion. Isocrates, like Socrates, privileged truth and virtue above mere persuasion. Isocrates, like Plato, disparaged eristics. A key problem with deeming Isocrates a sophist is his pamphlet *Against the Sophists* (ca. 390 B.C.). Too writes that Isocrates, in *Against the Sophists,* asserts his opposition to sophists because "the discourse of these individuals poses the greatest obstacle to achieving Greek unity and Athenian hegemony, for they engage in modes of writing, e.g., eristic, paradox, logography, which bring no profit to their societies." And Isocrates brings to bear against them his trademark cleverness: he notes that sophists require students to make deposits of their tuition money to a third party for safekeeping, suggesting a lack of confidence, contrary to advertised claims, that they will successfully teach their students justice and virtue.

In making plain his opposition to the sophists, Isocrates granted that the word "sophist" had once been neutral or even positive (those nice traveling word people), but had taken on a negative connotation even in his own day, partly because Plato almost always used the word and its cognates pejoratively, denoting the opposite of a philosopher or philosophy. Indeed, Noboru Notomi, the Japanese classicist, argues that "attacking the sophist as the antithesis of the philosopher is for Plato the only way to make philosophy possible."

In their volume of essays, *Isocrates and Civic Education,* Takis Poulakos and David Depew sum up the powerful view of a top expert on the movement, John Poulakos, author of *Sophistical Rhetoric in Classical Greece*: "Isocrates is anything but a Sophist. He demands reflection and deliberative choice, not unthinking response. He is far from a nomadic intellectual. He is a sedentary, somewhat conservative citizen of democratic Athens. His conceptual scheme does not revolve around what is powerful (*dunastes*), as did that of the Sophists whose experience was formed by the rise of tyrants."

There is no question that Isocrates distinguished himself from the sophists. Was he then a rhetorician?

Rhetoric in ancient Greece was not what one of its present meanings denotes—empty verbiage—but oratory, neutrally described (at least at first), and made famous by Gorgias. Soon Athenians came to see it as fine words, and perhaps dangerous ones. It meant language used for persuasion, and Gorgias, even in Plato's dialogue named after him, recognizes that rhetoric can be used for good or evil. In neither that dialogue nor the *Meno* is Gorgias presented as an immoral or amoral person. In the *Meno*, he claims no more than to produce good orators, not virtue. Rhetoric is associated with injustice only in regard to Polus and Callicles. Plato presents rhetoric in regard to them as mere blandishment, though, later, in the *Phaedrus,* he recognizes a better, higher form of dialectical rhetoric.

Schiappa points out that Gorgias himself never used the word *rhetorike*. He used *logos*. Neither did Isocrates use the word to describe what he did, or *rhetor* to describe himself. Isocrates specifically denies, in *To Philip* and elsewhere, that he is a *rhetor,* and while he employs the term *rhetorikos* on rare occasions, he never uses it to describe his own method. Rather, as noted in passing and soon to be seen in detail, Isocrates used the word "philosophy" to describe his practice. It is Plato and Aristotle who used the Greek equivalents of the words "rhetoric" and "rhetorician." Plato uses it nearly ninety times in *Gorgias,* where it's defined and originates in the late fourth century B.C. According to Schiappa, "the term *rhetor* in the fourth century designated a specific class of individuals who spoke often in court or the assembly. Plato opposed education aimed at such orators because he did not trust the training to produce proper statesmen." Schiappa adds, "There is a tendency to treat rhetoric as a given in Plato's *Gorgias.* That is, it is usually assumed that there was a discrete set of activities or a body of teachings that were consensually regarded as *rhetorike* and toward which Plato directed his critical abilities."

Not so, Schiappa asserts. In fact, Plato coined the word, then attached a derogatory meaning to it of "duplicitous" or "deceptive" argumentation. For Plato in the *Euthydemus, Republic* and elsewhere, rhetoric is then a practice that puts successful persuasion ahead of everything. Thomas Cole agrees that "the word rhetoric itself bears every indication of being a Platonic invention." Too, picking up on Schiappa and Cole, says that Plato invented *rhetorike* "as a means of differentiating his own discourse, i.e., dialectic, from non-dialectical language, and of asserting the privileged status of the former."

And yet many classical scholars and others dependent on them still often write as though there were two vastly different intellectual practices—dubious rhetoric and noble philosophy—with Isocrates representing the first and Socrates and Plato the second. The difficulties in this area, and the degree to which differences of scholarly opinion are partly matters of semantic choice, is indicated by Too's statement that, for Isocrates, philosophy is "the term he employs to designate the whole art and discipline of his rhetoric." One can easily think, "six of one, a half dozen of the other," as classicists bandy about these terms.

The important point is that just as Isocrates distanced himself from the worst, nonphilosophical aspects of sophistry, so he distanced himself from the worst, nonphilosophical aspects of rhetoric. According to Pseudo-Plutarch, Isocrates, when asked to define rhetoric, replied disparagingly that its goal was "to make small things great and great things small." In *Against the Sophists,* Isocrates censures rhetoricians, observes Stephen Halliwell in his contribution to *The Rhetoric Canon,* "for professing a 'knowledge' that they cannot validate . . . with a technical self-confidence that transcends both experience and individual ability."

Isocrates does not accept that rhetoric can be a formulaic *techne,* or art. In *Against the Sophists,* Too observes, "Isocrates stresses the need for rhetoric to be taught by other than rigid or theoretical, abstract means. . . . For the rhetorician, true 'technicality' paradoxically entails the avoidance of theory. . . . [I]t ideally resists rigidity and fixed forms of teaching. . . . [G]ood speeches will satisfy the particular circumstance that defines the opportune moment of performance (*kairos*), the requirement of appropriateness." Ekaterina Haskins, author of *Logos and Power in Isocrates and Aristotle,* agrees that Isocrates in *Against the*

Sophists opposes the idea of rhetoric having "cookie-cutter methods." Isocrates himself writes in that oration, "I am amazed when I see these men claiming students for themselves. They fail to notice that they are using an ordered art as a model for a creative activity."

One scholar who remains comfortable with regarding Isocrates as a rhetorician is Takis Poulakos, author of *Speaking for the Polis: Isocrates' Rhetorical Education.* But his position actually corroborates the element of semantic choice in this area: some scholars, in effect, prefer to say that Isocrates *took* rhetoric away from its bad elements, and made it philosophy. So Poulakos writes, "In Isocrates' hands, rhetoric became the art of politics." Poulakos speaks, in regard to Isocrates, of "the uniqueness of his version of rhetoric in relation to contemporary practices of rhetoric." And he states that Isocrates's task as a political thinker, eager to promote citizenship, was "to disassociate rhetoric from its reputation as a tool for individual self-advancement and to associate rhetoric instead with social interactions and civil exchanges between human beings."

Nonetheless, Poulakos, too, concedes that Isocrates "avoids using the term rhetoric in reference to his profession," and Poulakos understands why: "The term *rhetoric* would have connected him too closely to teachers of oratory for whom, like Plato, rhetoric meant the art of eloquence applied to the specific oratorical demands in the courts and the assembly. Thus he opted for the term *philosophy.*" Ober also understands Isocrates's rationale: Plato's *Gorgias* and *Phaedrus* had made it clear that "neither practitioners nor teachers of rhetoric could ever be regarded as philosophers. For the Academy, rhetoric was a branch of Sophism and as such was inevitably foreign to philosophy proper."

ISOCRATES, PHILOSOPHER

Who counted as a philosopher in the heyday of Plato and Isocrates? Some, like German scholar Walter Burkert, held that the word originated with Pythagoras, supposedly the first to call himself a "philosopher" in the sense of "wise man." Plato then tweaked it to mean the more activist "lover and pursuer of wisdom." That strongly implied that the philosopher does not possess wisdom or knowledge (mainly the property of the gods) but must seek it. According to Romilly, Plato reacted against the "practical haste" of the sophists by calling on Pythagoras's "wise man" to be someone satisfied only with truth, which he identified as an ideal, eternal truth. Philosophy, for Plato, aimed at understanding the "transcendent essences" of the concepts it addressed.

Isocrates, however, disagreed. He wasn't eccentric or idiosyncratic for doing so because, as Notomi notes, the word *philosophia* "was still contestable at the time of Isocrates." Those who pursued more theoretical studies during Isocrates's time had no more an established claim to the word than did Isocrates. Jaeger agrees that the word was in play: "Today, when Plato's definition of 'philosophy' has been universally accepted for centuries, Isocrates's procedure appears to have been a mere whim. But really it was not. In his time, those concepts were still developing, and had not yet fully hardened into their ultimate shapes." As Haskins writes, they were "up for grabs." Ober, in turn, highlights the competitiveness of the intellectual situation: "The title *philosophos* was a valued prize well worth contending for."

Isocrates, in designating his own method as *philosophia,* stands as one philosopher challenging others over what philosophy should do and what it could be. In his various works, he sets out his views, promising in *Antidosis* that he'll "prove that philosophy has been unjustly slandered by many people and that it deserves much more to be liked than hated." Much like Rorty, Isocrates begins by frowning on epistemological queries that amount to empty logic-chopping and hair-splitting, mere eristics. Such exercises sharpen the wits, but that's all. They're of little importance except as stepping stones for young people on the way to worthwhile, genuine philosophy. Isocrates writes in *Antidosis* that he does not "think it proper to apply the term 'philosophy' to a training which is no help to us in the present either in our speech or in our actions, but rather I would call such training mental gymnastics and a preparation for philosophy."

In a similar way, Isocrates voices a grudging acceptance of metaphysical queries, again on the pedagogical rationale that it could help students start thinking. Otherwise, he can be scathing about the metaphysics of early Greek thinkers in regard to the nature of things, as evidenced by his droll recitation of the scorecard in *Antidosis*: "Anaxagoras maintained that the elements of being were infinite in number; Empedocles, that there were four; Ion, that there were three; Alcmaeon, that there were two; Parmenides, that there was one; and Gorgias, that there were none at all."

Similarly, writes Romilly, for Isocrates "the great truths pursued by Plato seemed far too distant." He preferred productive arguments to useless ones, and urged "studies that will enable us to govern wisely both our own households and the commonwealth." In his *Helen*, he observed that "it is far superior to have decent judgments about useful matters, than to have precise knowledge about useless things."

The principle lies at the heart of his thought: for a philosopher, development of judgment trumps acquisition of knowledge. In that respect, his image over many centuries as the father of what we now call "liberal arts education," the instilling in students of a flexible, critical spirit and a mastery of language, is perfectly accurate. The paramount importance of language to Isocrates—to civilization and its institutions, which include civilized good judgment—is articulated by him in *Nicocles*, where he writes: "Since we have the ability to persuade one another and to make clear to ourselves what we want, not only do we avoid living like animals, but we have come together, built cities, made laws, and invented arts. Speech is responsible for nearly all our inventions. It legislated in matters of justice and injustice, and beauty and baseness, and without these laws, we could not live with one another."

That jibes with his view in *Antidosis*, where Isocrates writes that those gifted in eloquence, "those who have gained this power by the study of philosophy and the exercise of reason, never speak without weighing their words, and so are less often in error as to a course of action." There, too, he condemns the verbal games of older sophists because they keep people from paying attention to what matters to true lovers of philosophy: politics and the issues of citizens. At the core a modern pragmatist, he thought the great upshot of philosophy to be applying notions of virtue and excellence to public life and practical problems, and preparing young people to be effective political actors. True to that spirit, he said he'd be happy if posterity judged him by the quality of his students (far more of whom became leaders in ancient Greece than did students of Plato).

Genuine philosophy, then, must always engage the real problems of real people in everyday life. (Think of Isocrates here as Dewey-onicus.) The philosopher seeks sound judgment (*doxa*) and doesn't fetishize unlikely exact knowledge (*episteme*). Real philosophy makes students "stronger in their thinking" and produces "the ability to think and speak well."

Because Isocrates helped move philosophy from speech to writing, he also assists us in understanding that philosophy of all sorts begins internally, with our private thinking about alternate ideas. He writes in *Antidosis*: "The same arguments that we use in persuading others when we speak in public, we employ also when we deliberate in our own thoughts, and while we call articulate those who are able to speak before a crowd, we regard as wise those who most effectively deliberate their problems in their own minds. . . . [N]one of the things which are done with intelligence take place without the help of *logos*. . . . In all our actions as well as in all our thoughts language is our guide, and is more employed by those who have the most wisdom."

Isocrates doesn't identify philosophy with a formulaic style of argumentative reasoning, in the manner of many contemporary analytic philosophers, just as America the Philosophical does not. It is reasonably careful thinking, sensitive to reality. Philosophy is also a form of education, and so Isocrates states, once again laying claim to the word and practice, "I direct students of philosophy."

Amusingly, he also expresses himself on what other people consider philosophy to be: "Since I hold that what some people call philosophy is not entitled to that name . . . my view of this question is, as it happens, very simple. For since it is not in the nature of man to attain a science [*episteme*] by the possession of which we can know positively what we should do or what we should say, in the next resort I hold that man to be wise who is able by his powers of conjecture [*doxa*] to arrive generally at the best course, and I hold that man to be a philosopher who occupies himself with the students from which he will most quickly gain that kind of insight [*phroneo*]."

Finally, unlike the sophists or rhetoricians targeted by Plato, Isocrates throughout his work voices a moral sensibility. One can't guarantee honesty, but one can try, and philosophy is the best training for it. A first step toward honesty is recognizing that all we have is opinion, the highest, soundest form of opinion, based on educated good judgment. Sounding like a contemporary pragmatist, dismissive of the artificial ethical views argued by analytic philosophers based on far-fetched hypothetical examples, Isocrates in *Antidosis* says that dogmatic philosophers of the Platonic type "exhort their followers to a kind of virtue and wisdom that is ignored by the rest of the world and is disputed among themselves—I, to a kind which is recognized by all." He rejects the possibility of ethical principles that can have prior validity for all possible situations, stressing the contingency of such judgments.

It all sounds very reasonable. Nonetheless, as David Timmerman writes in his article "Isocrates' Competing Conceptualization of Philosophy" (*Philosophy and Rhetoric*, 1998), "Plato was the winner of this definitional battle" over *philosophia*, Isocrates the loser. (We would amend that to, maybe he was the winner for most of Western intellectual history, but not in the future.) David Depew and Takis Poulakis observe of Isocrates that, "against his own explicit wishes, he has been extruded entirely from the philosophical canon." Welch remarks, "Isocrates' use of the word *philosophia* is very different from our conception of the word philosophy. Our construction of philosophy is largely the Platonic and Cartesian construction and indicates the foundational principles that underlie Western knowledge and being (or reality) in the fourth century B.C.E."

The catch here is in that phrase "our conception of the word philosophy," and the too-easy use of the word "our." In truth, intellectuals have always contested the concept of philosophy, even over the long reign of Platonic thinking. The foundationalist approach of Plato gained steam from the professionalization of philosophy and apotheosis of epistemology that Rorty punctured. But now, in his wake, as well as that of the earlier pragmatists and Wittgenstein, "philosophy" is returning to the heavily contested state that existed in ancient Athens. Given, for instance, that such Platonic ideas as that the soul "recollects" knowledge now strike us as malarkey, why should Plato's conception of philosophy still automatically hold the upper hand?

Many classicists, to be sure, do not take kindly to the notion of

Isocrates as philosopher. Some acknowledge Isocrates's decision to call his practice and style of thinking philosophy, then mock it. Wardy, for instance, described Isocrates's definition of philosophy in *Antidosis* as of "almost heroic vapidity." M. I. Finley says Isocrates simply uses *philosophia* to mean a "virtuous, therefore wise, way of life." Again, it is almost always classics scholars, operating with an uncritical view of the idea of philosophy anchored in Platonic definition, who pooh-pooh Isocrates's claim to it.

Some of the issues relating to Isocrates's battle against Plato over philosophy undoubtedly turn on the vagaries of translation. *Philosophia* and *philosophos*, like words such as *phronesis, paideia, doxa* and *logos*, were, as noted, in formation during Isocrates's life. Compare the debate, despite its differences, with the contemporary one over who is a journalist in the age of blogging. Words and occupations come under pressure from changing practices. Add the inevitable inexactness between cultures and languages, and there is wiggle room on translation. Different classicists, with equally prestigious credentials, make different decisions on key words in ancient Greek culture. *Logos*, for instance, has been translated as speech, discourse, reasoning, rational thinking with language, rhetoric and eloquence. *Doxa* is sometimes opinion, sometimes sound judgment. So Guthrie writes that by philosophy Isocrates "meant above all rhetoric." Others go for "cultivated life" or "higher education."

But one central fact remains: Isocrates used the word *philosophia*. It is only by privileging Plato's particular philosophical program that one defaults into the view that one must use a word other than philosophy for what Isocrates does. Timmerman, who has closely examined the Socrates/Isocrates rivalry over the word, argues that our usage today "is predicated on a Platonically colored view of what constitutes philosophy." Timmerman counts Plato using the *philosoph* stem 357 times in his writings, Isocrates 87 times in his own. Timmerman also points out that all the strands involved in Isocrates's conception—reasoning, public testing of ideas, expertise in discourse, knowledge of culture— come together in what we see as philosophy today. Timmerman aptly shows that philosophy is not a vague process for Isocrates, but, in different places, an "area of study," a subject matter" that can be taught, an "education," a "virtue," an "occupation," a "training" and "an honorable pursuit"—all notions that fit with a modern Rortyan conception of philosophy stripped of epistemological hubris.

Like America the Philosophical, Isocrates neither identifies philosophy with a single kind of thinking nor believes that "any" sort of thinking amounts to philosophy. Isocrates demarcates sloppy thinking from dedicated thinking. It is reasonably careful thinking, sensitive to an array of information and considerations. As Timmerman documents, that gives Isocrates confidence in repeatedly referring to his practice as philosophy, advising students to study it, and using *philosophia* to indicate "serious study" or "close examination."

Isocrates thus merits the status of philosopher as much as Plato or Socrates, and remains more compatible as a thinker with what counts as philosophy in America. That is true in one more way as well—when we connect their dispute over "philosophy" not just to "politics," but to the specific sort of politics each endorsed.

ISOCRATES, GREECE AND AMERICA

As noted at the outset, the best known aspect of Isocrates's politics was his Panhellenism. As foreign policy, it was the belief that Greek city-states such as Athens, Sparta and Thebes should unite under Athens's leadership to defeat the "barbarians," the Persians. As cultural philosophy, it held that being Greek was a state of mind, sensibility and education, not ethnicity—a notion, as suggested earlier, similar to the way we think of being American. Cosmopolitan in outlook, Isocrates, much as he revered Athens, viewed the Greek-speaking (and, one might say, Greek-thinking) world as far larger than one's own city-state. Norlin describes Isocrates's cultural Panhellenism as a "brotherhood of culture, transcending the bounds of race," so that the description of "Greek," in Isocrates's words, "is applied rather to those who share our culture than to those who share a common blood." His Panhellenism deems it a virtue always to think about his adored Athens in the larger context of Hellas.

Isocrates's proselytization for the foreign policy aspect of his cause did not arise out of a warmongering temperament or, despite some suggestions to the contrary, an imperialistic bent against a foreign culture happy to mind its own business. Under the Peace of Antalcidas in 387 B.C., the Greek city-states had, in fact, lost a considerable part of their freedom to the "King's Peace" imposed by the Persian monarch Artaxerxes II. Isocrates first unpacked his Panhellenism in *Panegyricus,* an oration composed for the Panhellenic Olympic Games of 380 B.C. At that point, writes Norlin, who describes Isocrates's politics at length, Athens was renewing its naval strength and "was acknowledged to be the intellectual capital of the Greek world."

In *Panegyricus,* which took Isocrates ten years to write and is considered by some classicists his masterpiece, he emphasized the love of freedom that united Greeks. Later in his nearly century-long life, in works such as *Panathenaicus* and *To Philip*, he lost faith that the differences among Athens, Sparta and Thebes could ever be overcome, and began to promote the powerful monarch Philip of Macedonia as ideal leader of a unified Greek military campaign against the Persians.

Norlin argues that "'[f]reedom and autonomy'—the catch-words of Greek politics," were "as precious to Isocrates as to any other. He differs from his contemporaries only in cherishing these ideals for all the cities of Hellas." But Isocrates's position is not Attic neoconservatism. Norlin notes that Isocrates regards "[a]ggression—the passion to dominate" as "the disease of Greek foreign policy, resulting soon or late in weakness and disaster." So too, adds Norlin, Isocrates laments "imperialism," which has been "the curse of Athens, its only fruits being hatred, wars, and an empty treasure."

Other leading scholars concur. Jaeger says Isocrates "believed that Athens could play a leading part in Greek affairs only in peaceful agreement with Sparta and the other Greek states, with entire equality between victor and vanquished; for then the intellectual superiority of Athens to her coarser rivals would assure that she acquired the balance of power."

In contrast to aggression or imperialism, Isocrates advocated the virtue of *sophrosyne*, or self-control, which Norlin unpacks as "the disposition to live and let live, to cherish freedom for oneself and respect freedom in others." In *Panegyricus*, Isocrates recalls it at length as a virtue present in both Athenians and Spartans in happier times: "They treated the Hellenes with consideration and not with insolence, deeming it their right to take command in the field but not to tyrannize over them, desiring rather to be addressed as leaders than as masters, and rather to be greeted as saviors than to be reviled as destroyers."

Isocrates is thus "a pronounced believer in democracy," in Norlin's judgment, so long as democracy does not deteriorate into mob rule. Jaeger also sees Isocrates as against "radical mob rule" while asserting that "in every one of his writings" Isocrates "condemned oligarchy and praised *genuine* equality and democracy." However, because Isocrates criticizes excesses of popular democracy and praises aristocratic virtues, controversy continues over his democratic credentials. Too says he advances "an ideology of oligarchic elitism" and Takis Poulakis finds "oligarchic sympathies" because Isocrates called for a restricted form of democracy in his *Areopagiticus*, opposed the democratic practice of appointing officials through a lottery and admired strongman leaders such as Philip. Too also chides Isocrates for hypocrisy, for always praising Panhellenism but ending up himself "paradoxically at odds, at 'war,' with the rest of Greece, with Sparta and with the sophists."

A broader perspective is provided by Ober, who contends that Isocrates's democratic credentials must be understood in the context of his time and peers: "The content of several of Isocrates' speeches makes it quite clear that by the mid-fourth century, if one claimed to be an intellectual—a practitioner of *philosophia*—one must also be a critic of the rule of the people. Plato and his associates tried to claim as their own not only the terminology of *philosophia*, but the project of criticizing democracy from a critical perspective." Isocrates, in doing so, expressed much more support for it than Plato. He sought, for instance, to build citizens, not just ruling guardians. To Ober, Isocrates is "very eager to avoid the 'oligarchic tarbrush,'" a thinker who described "his ideal regime as an ancestral democracy." Jaeger says plainly, "The ideal he settles on finally is a democracy with strongly aristocratic elements."

Isocrates's stature as a political thinker suffers somewhat because another old derider, Aristotle, condescended to him in that realm, just as he minimized Isocrates's standing as a philosopher. Ekaterina Haskins, author of a comparative study of the two, finds that reaction unfair. Aristotle, she charges, "minimizes the political importance and timeliness of Isocrates's writings by tearing them into stylistically interesting but ultimately decontextualized fragments. Apparently, this practice did not escape Isocrates's notice. In his last extant pamphlet, *Panathenaicus,* he protests against those who gather in the Lyceum to abuse his discourses, 'reading them in the worst possible manner side by side with their own, dividing them at the wrong places, mutilating them, and in every way spoiling their effect.'"

To Aristotle, according to Haskins, Isocrates, whom Aristotle cites fifty-nine times in his works, is largely a teacher of "parts of speech." That distorts him, she asserts. In *Areopagiticus,* he "extols wise governance under representative democracy" and he is, she contends, no more xenophobic than "Aeschylus, Herodotus," and, she zings, Aristotle himself. Indeed, Isocrates is more democratic than Aristotle, in her view, because "Isocrates' educational program strives to reform Athenian democracy by the cultivation of its future leaders."

For the great advocate of public deliberation, she continues, "power is explicitly a product of a discursive negotiation of civic identity and authority." Aristotle, by contrast, wants to "discipline the demos into substantively and procedurally restricted roles within a constitutional regime." As a result, Haskins sees Isocrates as engaged in "an elitist correction of popular democracy." Kathryn Morgan, like Haskins a younger scholar who breaks away from traditional dismissal of Isocrates, also endorses Isocrates's democratic bent, writing that as philosopher he "rejects the platonic model wherein a democracy is incapable of rationality and orderly deliberation."

Is Isocrates nonetheless jingoistic in his championing of Athens and Greece? Jaeger defends him against the charge: "Isocrates' nationalistic ideology (in which Athens is the founder of all civilization), along with all the other ideas implicit in his *paedeia,* was later taken over by humanism as part of its general view of history." We can see that as imperialistic, just as we can see as imperialistic the world's adoption of various American values, habits and cultural practices while often resisting American rule.

Jaeger's point is that we can't easily place all blame on the sources of these universalized cultures. He also thinks we should be honest in toting up the pros and cons of thinking in such expansive ways: "Without the idea which [Isocrates] here expresses for the first time, the idea that Greek *paedaia* was something universally valuable, there would have been no Macedonian Greek world-empire, and the universal culture which we call Hellenistic would never have existed." In short, when we talk of the "glory that was Greece," we're speaking Isocratean, but he didn't exactly force us to do so.

All scholars concede that, as Cole writes, "Socrates at the end of the *Phaedrus . . .* acknowledges the existence of a certain element of philosophy (*tis philosophia*) in Isocrates' make-up." While scholars argue about the degree of sarcasm in those remarks, the admission ought to be replaced by far greater recognition of Isocrates, whatever Socrates thought. Socrates, in the predominant picture of him drawn by Plato, favors discourse that presumes there's a right answer, an eternally valid truth, at the end of the discursive road. Isocrates favors discourse, but thinks, like Rorty and Habermas, that right answers emerge from appropriate public deliberation, from what persuades people at the end of the road.

That helps Isocrates resonate with contemporary America, and with America the Philosophical. Isocrates's use of the term *philosophia,* notes Halliwell, "is a calculated eschewal of any notion of philosophy as an esoteric discipline that requires admission into a special way of life or an exclusive domain of theory." Writes Jaeger, "The terrain [Isocrates] chooses is that of ordinary common sense. He appeals to the instincts of the man in the street—who, without comprehending the philosophers' technical secrets, sees that those who would lead their followers to wisdom and happiness have nothing themselves and get nothing from their students."

The resemblances between Athens, Isocrates's model for a greater Greece and America are hard not to notice. Jaeger, a refugee from Nazi Germany who became Harvard's preeminent classicist for decades, spots one aspect of Athens that contributes to them. Isocrates, he writes, "sees the city, which had at all times been the refuge for every unfortunate, as at the same time the favored home of those who sought the sweets of life. The essence of Athenian culture, in contradistinction to the exclusive Spartan attitude, is not to repel strangers but to attract them."

In understanding the great resonances between Isocrates's vision and American culture, and why it makes sense to see America the Philosophical as a place that honors his shrewd grasp of what philosophy must be, it's helpful to keep in mind the inspired work of contemporary historian Carl J. Richard. In a trio of fine books—*The Founders and the Classics: Greece, Rome, and the American Enlightenment* (1994); *Greeks and Romans Bearing Gifts: How the Ancients Inspired the Founding Fathers* (2008); and *The Golden Age of the Classics in America: Greece, Rome, and the Antebellum United States* (2009)—Richard, professor of history at the University of Louisiana/Lafayette, has bolstered earlier magisterial historians of American thought in regard to crucial truths: Merle Curti, for instance, in his claim that the classics provided the founders with "lessons of patriotism and statesmanship," and Gordon Wood in his assertion that Revolutionary classicism "was not only a scholarly ornament of educated Americans; it helped to shape their values and their ideals of behavior."

With far more detailed attention to the connections between classical writers and the founders (as well as their antebellum successors) than any previous scholar, Richard has shown that the classics, as he wrote in his first book, "contributed a great deal to the founders' conception of human nature, their understanding of the nature and purpose of virtue, and their appreciation of society's essential role in its production. . . . In short, the classics supplied a large portion of the founders' intellectual tools."

It is no fey, flashy conceit, then, to vaunt the importance of Isocrates for comprehending today's United States as a philosophical society extraordinaire. We, no less than the founders, would not be bold, quintessentially independent Americans if we did not have the confidence to look our classical heritage in the eye and see history's big picture as accurately as we can. In the United States, we don't have to teach people how to philosophize because the country's immense diversity forces them to it. And if, in America, we've come to recognize that truth emerges from consensus—from decision as much as discovery—Isocrates, not Socrates, is our man. That point can be driven home even in a culture that has been lobbied for centuries to prefer his similar-sounding peer. As Isocrates wrote in a famous line, if you can teach bears to dance, you can teach humans anything.

John Rawls learned a different kind of lesson—that no matter how much reverence one commands as a teacher, one cannot convince Americans of principles they choose not to accept. For fifty years, America's foremost political philosopher acknowledged that no country exhibits a pluralism of philosophical and political beliefs as strongly as the United States. At the same time, he tried to construct a systematic theory of justice all could accept and be convinced by *despite* their disagreements on multiple matters of policy and ultimate good. That Rawls failed at justifying his theory of justice, while generating tremendous activity within political philosophy and policy debate, left no one judging his philosophical abilities weaker than previously thought. Rather, it testified to the extraordinary intellectual diversity that made America the Philosophical unique. In the end, even John Rawls could not overcome that.

PART 6

JUST SAYING NO TO JUSTIFICATION: THE MAGNIFICENT FAILURE OF JOHN RAWLS

NOT SINCE JOHN STUART MILL

No work of modern American philosophy ever received the unstinting praise that greeted *A Theory of Justice* when it first appeared in 1971. No twentieth-century American philosopher basked in the critical warmth—the near-unanimous judgment that he stood head and shoulders above all others in his field—that John Rawls experienced from fellow philosophy professors.

Shortly after the publication of *A Theory of Justice*, the *New York Times Book Review* devoted its front page and two inside pages to a review of it by Marshall Cohen, then professor of philosophy at City University of New York and editor of *Philosophy and Public Affairs*, the era's leading academic journal of political philosophy.

Cohen noted that while the U.S. Constitution relied on the social contract theory of Locke and Kant, the tradition of such thinking had long since faltered as a guide to our considered moral and political judgments thanks to the success of Jeremy Bentham's and John Stuart Mill's nineteenth-century utilitarian approach. Cohen credited Rawls with creating, in a "magisterial," "peerless," "bold and rigorous" work that Cohen deemed a future classic, the "most formidable defense" that social contract thinking had ever received. The *Times Literary Supplement* in London chimed in: "It is a convincing refutation, if indeed one is needed, of any lingering suspicions that the tradition of English-speaking political philosophy might be dead."

Three years after the book appeared, Rawls's Harvard colleague Robert Nozick, despite disagreeing with many of Rawls's conclusions in his own *Anarchy, State, and Utopia*, tipped his hat as well: "*A Theory of Justice* is a powerful, deep, subtle, wide-ranging, systematic work in political and moral philosophy which has not seen its like since the writings of John Stuart Mill, if then. It is a fountain of illuminating ideas." Philosopher of law Ronald Dworkin judged it "one of those

John Rawls (1921–2002)
won singular acclaim
for his ambitious trea-
tise *A Theory of Justice*
(1971), but decades later
even admirers conceded
that it had exerted little
influence on the eco-
nomics of contemporary
American society.

books, rare but essential to philosophy, that define the state of the art."
Percy Lehning, a leading political theorist in Holland, ranked it "one of
the all-time great works in moral and political philosophy." Years later,
Thomas Pogge, a former Rawls PhD student and teaching fellow at
Harvard—subsequently professor of philosophy at Yale and author of
two books on Rawls—recalled how students referred to the book as
"TJ," or "green monster," because of its size (607 pages) and bright green
cover, while saluting it as "uniquely ambitious and illuminating . . . a
brilliant achievement in political philosophy, the best there is."

The lavish praise directed at the book over the years triggered homage toward its author from inside and outside academe. Thomas Nagel,
a leading NYU philosopher and, like Pogge, a former Rawls PhD student, declared his onetime dissertation director "the most important
political philosopher of the twentieth century." Jeremy Waldron, another
internationally regarded legal and political thinker, pronounced Rawls a
"monumental theorist." Martha Nussbaum lauded Rawls as "the most
distinguished moral and political philosopher of our age." Cohen, in his

Times review, remarked that "it is not unheard of for admirers to invoke the name of Immanuel Kant in the search for an adequate comparison."

That supreme regard for Rawls existed on the national and international landscape as well, if not in national and international mass media. No less than President Bill Clinton marked Rawls's greatness by awarding him the National Humanities Medal in 1999. In his citation, Clinton—echoing Nagel while adding a politician's impulse toward hedging—announced, "John Rawls is perhaps the greatest political philosopher of the twentieth century. In 1971, when Hillary and I were in law school, we were among the millions moved by a remarkable book he wrote, *A Theory of Justice,* that placed our right to liberty and justice upon a strong and brilliant new foundation of reason. Almost single-handedly, John Rawls revived the disciplines of political and ethical philosophy. . . . [H]e has helped a whole generation of learned Americans revive their faith in democracy itself." That same year, the Swedish Academy of Sciences bestowed on Rawls the Rolf Shock Prize in Logic and Philosophy, an award seen by many, and intended by its endower, as the "Nobel Prize in Philosophy."

After Rawls's death in 2002 at the age of eighty-one, the superlatives settled into a boilerplate consensus, at least among elite, and usually white-male, political theorists. A biographical squib typical of those found on prestigious academic books appeared on the jacket of Samuel Freeman's *Rawls* (2007). It simply declared, "John Rawls (1921–2002) was the most influential political philosopher of the twentieth century." On a collection of essays, *Rawls's Law of Peoples: A Realistic Utopia?* (2006), edited by Rex Martin and David Reidy, the copy began, "John Rawls is considered the most important theorist of justice in much of Western Europe and the English-speaking world." As if all that prestige weren't enough, Rawls stood as the furthest thing imaginable in philosophy from an institutional outsider like Richard Mohr, or a hepped-up cyberphilosopher like Jaron Lanier. For most of his life, Rawls flourished as the ultimate philosophical insider: the James Bryant Conant University Professor at Harvard University's philosophy department, traditionally the country's most powerful.

With credentials like those, and the nonpareil reception his work received, you would think it almost impossible that Rawls failed to convince most Americans of his ideas. After all, for students who encountered his work in the 1970s and '80s, he stood as the ultimate argument machine and grand systematizer. And the distance he kept from popular culture enhanced the sense of his philosophical grandeur. Except among his intimates, little was known about his life and personal background. Like many analytic philosophers, who typically disdain connections between their personal histories and their philosophical ideas, Rawls offered virtually no insight into his life within his published writings, and attracted practically no attention from the press. Rawls compounded the scarcity of biographical information about him by an almost complete refusal to grant interviews, a bent attributed by those who knew him to his modesty, his stammer and his determination to express his ideas only in a published form he could rigorously oversee. (He once politely declined an interview request from this writer, then a Princeton University undergraduate, with a friendly smile and the comment, "I wouldn't want to be seen as promoting my book.")

But Rawls did fail at the task of justifying his vision of justice to a wide American audience. That failure underlined a firm truth about America the Philosophical: academic philosophers generally can't prove what they claim they can prove, and most Americans don't buy philosophical justifications unless, well, they buy them—by their own criteria. As more information began to come out about Rawls after his death—particularly thanks to *John Rawls: His Life and Theory of Justice* (2007) by Pogge, who interviewed his diffident former adviser multiple times—Rawls began to look more like other American thinkers: a complicated product of his life and emotions, notwithstanding the peculiar systematic force of his ideas.

Certainly no one could justify to Rawls what he later called life's "arbitrary" contingencies. He learned about them quite early.

A LUCKY LIFE

John Bordley Rawls—friends called him "Jack"—experienced life's fierce unfairness before he was ten, and in an especially cruel form. Born on February 21, 1921, in Baltimore, he began, in the vocabulary he'd later employ in his theory of justice, with "social advantages." His father, William Lee Rawls (1883–1946), a North Carolinian who never finished high school, worked as a "runner" for a law firm, educated himself in its library and passed the bar. He eventually became a top Maryland corporate attorney at the Marbury firm (the name stretched back to the *Marbury v. Madison* case that launched Supreme Court review in the U.S.), an activist in Maryland gubernatorial politics and president of the Baltimore Bar Association. His mother, Anna Abel Stump (1892–1954), traced her family to Germany, but the Stumps also boasted a long history in Maryland. She served for a time as president of the Baltimore chapter of the League of Women Voters and as a volunteer for presidential candidate Wendell Willkie.

The family's elite status could not protect it from the vagaries of chance. Those struck in the form of disease, claiming two of Rawls's four brothers. Pogge recounted the awful series of events:

> [J]ack fell gravely ill. Although Bobby, twenty-one months younger, had been sternly told not to enter Jack's room, he did so anyway a few times to keep Jack company. Soon both children were lying in bed with high fever. Because the family physician initially misdiagnosed the disease, much time passed until it was finally discovered that both were suffering from diphtheria. The correct diagnosis and antitoxin came too late to save Bobby. His death was a severe shock to Jack and may have (as their mother thought) triggered his stammer, which was a serious (though gradually receding) handicap for him for the rest of his life.

Jack recovered from the diphtheria, but the very next winter, while recovering from a tonsillectomy, caught a severe pneumonia, which soon infected his brother Tommy [two years old]. The tragedy of the previous year repeated itself. While Jack was recovering slowly, his little brother died in February of 1929.

Late in life, as Rawls continued designing a theory of justice that sought in every way to counter arbitrary twists of fate with carefully thought-out principles of justice, Rawls indicated that the death of his brothers—like the unfair economic position of poor children that he remembered from his childhood—remained fresh in his mind, having stirred, Pogge writes, "his sense of injustice."

In high school, Rawls's economically privileged status continued to play out. He attended the elite Kent School, an Episcopalian private institution in Connecticut for boys. The religious obligations Kent imposed on its students—services six days a week—may well have pushed Rawls toward a stronger faith even as he engaged in multiple secular activities, such as playing trumpet in the school's jazz orchestra and winning a place on the football and wrestling teams.

Immediately after graduating in 1939, Rawls, following in the footsteps of his older brother, Richard, entered Princeton University, a member of its 630-strong Class of '43. They arrived just as Hitler invaded Poland, triggering World War II. Like many of his classmates, Rawls felt certain he'd be called up to fight, and spent time reading up on World War I in the school library. For four years, he experienced the challenges and privileges of a Princeton education. He joined the freshman football team, signed up with Ivy Club, traditionally one of the school's most prestigious, and contributed to the *Daily Princetonian* for two years as a music critic. Having sampled such fields as chemistry, math and music, he decided to major in philosophy.

At Princeton, his first influences in the discipline included Walter T. Stace, a dyed-in-the-wool utilitarian who taught moral philosophy (and had once served as mayor of Colombo, Ceylon), and David Bowers, a Kantian. Yet, Rawls told Pogge, the greatest influence on him was Norman Malcolm, an American philosopher most remembered as one of Wittgenstein's closest students and friends at Cambridge—Malcolm's *Ludwig Wittgenstein: A Memoir* (1958) became an essential text for any student of the Austrian philosopher.

Malcolm, according to Rawls, communicated the same sense of philosophy's enormous importance and intensity to Rawls that Wittgenstein conveyed to Malcolm—it had to be done with almost saint-like care and seriousness. Malcolm's severe criticism of his new student's undergraduate efforts, Rawls confided to Pogge, proved a large influence on his "own way of doing philosophy." Before Malcolm left Princeton in 1942 to join the U.S. Navy, Rawls took a course with him on human evil, in which they read thinkers such as Plato, Augustine and Reinhold Niebuhr. The class inspired Rawls so much that, his religious side aroused, he considered applying to Virginia Theological Seminary so he could become a priest.

We now know, thanks to the recent publication of Rawls's undergraduate thesis at Princeton—*A Brief Inquiry into the Meaning of Sin and Faith* (2009)—that Rawls remained a committed believer during his senior year, though by the heyday of *A Theory of Justice* he wrote in the voice of a typically secular analytic philosopher. Included in the volume was a private paper Rawls wrote for family and friends in the 1990s, "On My Religion," that explained some of his thinking, and its origins.

In January 1943, Rawls graduated from Princeton summa cum laude. One month later he entered the Army as an enlisted man in the 128th Infantry regiment of the 32nd Infantry Division. He completed a course in the Signal Corps, then served in New Guinea, the Philippines and Japan, where, from his troop train, he saw Hiroshima after the atomic bombing. Pogge explained, "He served both in the regimental headquarters company and in an intelligence and reconnaissance (I&R) unit that, in squads of seven or eight men, reconnoitered enemy positions. He claims not to have seen much combat, but his division was in heavy fighting in Leyte, and he was awarded the Bronze Star for his radio work behind enemy lines along the treacherous Villa Verde Trail in Luzon toward the end of the war. His only wound came about when he removed his helmet to drink from a stream and was grazed by a sniper's bullet."

Again, Jack Rawls had been lucky.

He gradually worked his way up to sergeant during his time in the Pacific, but was busted back to private while in Japan for, as Pogge relates it, "refusing to punish a soldier as ordered by a first lieutenant whom this soldier had insulted."

Rawls left the Army in 1946, still a private. In "On My Religion," he recorded how three galvanizing moral experiences in the war shook his faith. The first, he wrote, was "Deacon's death," in May 1945. It took place "high up on the Villa Verde trail on Luzon."

"Deacon was a splendid man," Rawls began.

[W]e became friends and shared a tent at Regiment. One day the First Sergeant came to us looking for two volunteers, one to go with the Colonel to where he could look at the Japanese positions, the other to give blood badly needed for a wounded soldier in the small field hospital nearby. We both agreed and the outcome depended on who had the right blood type. Since I did and Deacon didn't, he went with the Colonel. They must have been spotted by the Japanese, because soon 150 mortar shells were falling in their direction. They jumped into a foxhole and were immediately killed when a mortar shell also landed in it. I was quite disconsolate and couldn't get the incident out of my mind. I don't know why this incident so affected me, other than my fondness for Deacon, as death was a common occurrence. But I think it did.

Rawls then wrote of a day in the middle of December 1944, after the struggle of his F Company "to take a ridge overlooking the town of Limon." He and his fellow troops were stationary for the moment, holding their ground.

[A] Lutheran pastor came up and during his service gave a brief sermon in which he said that God aimed our bullets at the Japanese while God protected us from theirs. I don't know why this made me so angry, but it certainly did. I upbraided the Pastor (who was a First Lieutenant) for saying what I assumed he knew perfectly well—Lutheran that he was—were simple falsehoods about divine providence. What reason could he have possibly had but his trying to comfort the troops. Christian doctrine ought not to be used for that, though I knew perfectly well that it was.

Rawls closed "On My Religion" with a third war experience that upset him, while adding—ironically for one who would later commit so strongly to the possibility of justifying beliefs—"I don't profess to understand at all why my beliefs changed, or believe it is possible fully to comprehend such changes." It took place in April 1945, while his regiment rested up at Asingan. "We went to the Army movies shown in the evening," he writes. For the first time, he saw newsreels of and "heard about the Holocaust."

"These incidents," he explained,

and especially the third as it became widely known, affected me in the same way. This took the form of questioning whether prayer was possible. How could I pray and ask God to help me, or my family, or my country, or any other cherished thing I cared about, when God would not save millions of Jews from Hitler? When Lincoln interprets the Civil War as God's punishment for the sin of slavery, deserved equally by North and South, God is seen as acting justly. But the Holocaust can't be interpreted in that way, and all attempts to do so that I have read of are hideous and evil. To interpret history as expressing God's will, God's will must accord with the most basic ideas of justice as we know them. For what else can the most basic justice be? Thus, I soon came to reject the idea of the supremacy of the divine will as also hideous and evil. . . . The following months and years led to an increasing rejection of many of the main doctrines of Christianity, and it became more and more alien to me.

Over the centuries, most participants in the debate between atheists and believers have called that the "problem of evil." Sophisticated theologians often treat loss of faith because of it as a simplistic intellectual reflex. There can be multiple subtle explanations, they argue, for why God would permit evil. But the "problem of evil" seemed good enough for Rawls, as for legions of others throughout history without his philosophical sophistication.

Rawls's postwar life took a conventional academic path, leaving aside the swiftness and brilliance of his professional ascent, and the magnitude of his ultimate achievement. He began graduate school in philosophy at Princeton on the GI Bill in 1946. Apart from a year at Cornell, where he reunited with Malcolm, he remained at Princeton and completed a dissertation on ethics under Stace. In June 1949, he married Margaret (Mardy) Fox, a senior at Pembroke College, Brown University, with whom he had four children in a marriage that lasted fifty-three years. They spent that first summer together in Princeton, composing, for $500, the index to Princeton professor Walter Kaufmann's classic biography, *Nietzsche: Philosopher, Psychologist, and Antichrist*—a crossing of the cordon sanitaire between analytic and continental philosophy that tends to amuse anyone in professional philosophy who learns of Rawls's unexpected "deviation."

For the next two years, Rawls taught at Princeton as an instructor in philosophy. A Fulbright year followed at Oxford, where he met and studied with several future British philosophers of distinction, such as Isaiah Berlin and Stuart Hampshire. From there he took a position in Cornell's highly regarded philosophy department, achieving tenure in 1956 at age thirty-five following the publication of several important papers in which he'd begun to work out his core notion of "Justice as Fairness." A year as a visiting professor at Harvard (1959–60) produced the offer of a full professorship, with tenure, from nearby MIT. Two years later, Rawls returned, this time as a full professor, to Harvard, where he taught—even after his official retirement in 1991—until the first of a series of strokes stopped him in 1995. He died at his Lexington, Massachusetts, home in 2002.

Throughout his career, Rawls impressed colleagues with his modesty, integrity, kindness and lack of airs. Typical was his remark, in the preface to the first edition of *A Theory of Justice,* that "I must disclaim any originality for the views I put forward"—a disclaimer roundly rejected by everyone else. When Harvard bestowed on him in 1972 the rarely given rank of a "University Professorship," which permits a faculty member wide-ranging freedom to teach beyond the constraints of departments and schools, Rawls told the *New York Times,* "I'm somewhat ambivalent about being made different from other people, but that's the way universities are."

After his death, Samuel Freeman, his most devoted student, and the editor or author of several volumes of Rawls scholarship, contributed a reminiscence to the *Chronicle of Higher Education.* Freeman, Avalon Professor in the Humanities at the University of Pennsylvania, fondly remembered his teacher and friend, "a tall, lanky man, with piercing blue eyes," an "excellent sailor" who "exercised well into his 70s, biking, jogging" and took "daily walks until a few days before his death." He explained that Rawls "did not enjoy the spotlight" and "chose not to take an active role in public life. In part, that was because he felt uncomfortable speaking before strangers and large groups, and often stuttered in those settings." But it also had to do with his decency and character, his awareness of how dumb luck had made his life of acclaimed philosophical achievement possible. Freeman recalled that Mardy Rawls understood his character so well that when Japan sent a message offering him the $500,000 Kyoto Prize, "she declined on his behalf without even consulting him." It turned out she'd decided correctly. When Rawls learned that the prize required him to "have lunch and dinner with the emperor of Japan," he endorsed the rejection. Wrote Freeman, "His daughter Liz said he was willing to do a lot of things, but not have lunch with the emperor." Freeman added that Rawls in private "regularly denounced the practice of royalty and the corrupting effects of privilege."

As a teacher, Freeman remembered, Rawls "made his lecture notes available to his students, acknowledging that he sometimes stuttered and was not sure that he could be understood." Long resistant to publishing those notes or many of his papers, he relented late in life only when his students appealed to his sense of fairness, explaining that while those who attended Harvard had the notes and could read them, others without that privilege could not.

Freeman ended his reminiscence by observing that Rawls had always taught him and his other students "to look behind the intricate or clever arguments that philosophers make, to see whether those thinkers are doing anything important. . . . [H]e encouraged us to try to discover the best in positions we disagree with, and to respond to that."

The last time Freeman saw Rawls came a month before his death, when he'd driven to Lexington to show him a collection of essays he'd just edited, *The Cambridge Companion to Rawls,* only the second volume in that distinguished series to be devoted to a living philosopher. Although the portrait of Rawls on its cover had been painted by his wife, Mardy, Rawls "vigorously objected to any picture, saying that he did not see why people cared what he looked like." Rawls stopped protesting only when Freeman pointed out to him that every other volume in the series bore a cover portrait. Yet Rawls also possessed, Freeman wrote in the preface to his own thoughtful book on Rawls, a "self-effacing sense of humor" about his humility.

Toward the end of his life, Freeman explained, Rawls wrote a short autobiography for friends titled "Just Jack." The title grew out of an anecdote Rawls had been told by the Chicago legal scholar Paul Freund. For a time in Chicago, Freund had related, there were two federal judges named Julius Hoffman. "To distinguish them," Freeman wrote, "Chicago lawyers called one, who was highly respected, 'Julius the Just.'" The other, less respected Julius Hoffman was the judge who presided over the 1970s Chicago Seven trial. "They called him 'just Julius,'" Freeman continued. "So Jack took to signing letters and inscribing books for his friends 'just Jack.'" Freeman and others thought he had it backward, and "was indeed Jack the Just."

For all his shining personal modesty, however, Rawls's philosophical ambition proved outsize. He wanted to convince others—all others—that we could reason fairly and unselfishly about justice. A tireless reviser and rethinker throughout his life, he believed that if he could just find the right words, the right phrase, the right conceptual architecture, he could justify his vision to those critics who ritually acknowledged his greatness, then zapped his theory for failing to justify one claim or another. Indeed, "justification" proved the concept that most concerned him after "justice" itself, because if he couldn't provide a convincing account of justification, he couldn't win over people to his notion of justice either.

Yet Rawls's failure, in the end, to persuade even as devoted a student as Pogge that his theory worked in its most popularly known provisions—that we should choose as our basic principles of justice those we'd select in a hypothetical "original position" where none of us knows our exact position in society, or the principle that goods in a situation of inequality should ultimately be distributed in a way that benefits the least well off—ultimately harkened back to his failure to provide a cogent account of justification. Rawls's peculiarly abstract, ahistorical approach to the concept, the colorless prose in which he explained it, his unwillingness—unlike Rorty—to consider the relation of any act of justification to its flesh-and-blood context in American life, or the words and metaphors in which it was expressed, amounted to a fatal flaw. This was not the dramatic, gun-toting, ethics-testing sense of *Justified* that American viewers and TV critics applauded in the FX drama series of that name. Ordinary Americans, as the audience for that show indicated, seemed to understand how justification worked just fine, but not because *A Theory of Justice* had explained it to them.

JUST ANOTHER WORD FOR
NOTHING LEFT TO ARGUE ABOUT

Every American endlessly encounters the words "justify" and "justification" in popular journalism, newspaper editorials and serious books. Their use extends over every area of social life. But saying that something is justified or justifiable doesn't necessarily make it so—at least to others. Consider some examples from the *New York Times*.

On July 12, 2010, the *Times* ran a story headlined "Israeli Military Find Flotilla Killings Justified." Six weeks before, on May 31, Israeli navy commandos had boarded a Turkish ship bound for Gaza to break through Israel's blockade of that territory. The commandos met immediate violent resistance and ended up killing nine Turks. According to the *Times* story, Israeli military investigators had determined that more than sixty-five Turkish Islamic militants "armed with metal sticks and knives" had been aboard the ship, that the commandos had been attacked as soon as they landed on the ship, and that they'd been fired on in four to six separate events. "All the shooting," according to a senior Israeli official quoted, "was either when the soldiers were in immediate danger of their lives or when they had to rescue fellow soldiers."

But Prime Minister Recep Tayyip Erdogan of Turkey rejected both the Israelis' version of the incident and the "justification" of Israeli force. Having downgraded Turkish-Israeli relations, Erdogan continued to demand an "apology" from Israel—an admission whose logical upshot would be that Israeli force was *not* justified—before returning those relations to normal. Israel, according to reports, would at best offer its "regrets," which, unlike an apology, would not logically concede that the killings were unjustified. A case, then, of "justification" asserted, and "justification" denied.

In November 2010, the *Times* ran another story, this one headlined

"In Rare Cases, Pope Justifies Use of Condoms." Speaking to a German journalist, Pope Benedict XVI had said that the wearing of a condom by a male prostitute to prevent AIDS would constitute "a first assumption of responsibility" and be welcomed by the Church. Since, under Catholic doctrine, the pope's direct endorsement of a policy constitutes a kind of justification *eo ipso*, or by itself, the comment naturally triggered not only the *Times* story, but commentary around the world.

Yet much "justification" talk occurs in realms where authority is not so clear-cut. Later the same month, the *Times* ran a "Deal Book" article in its business section headlined "Can Wall Street Justify Its Existence?" The author, Chris Nicholson, began by quoting Lord Adair Turner, chair of Britain's securities regulator, who had stated that much of what takes place in banks and on Wall Street is "socially useless activity." Nicholson asked of the world of finance, "Can it justify its existence, or will it simply purchase the political favors to continue as before? What does it do for the rest of humanity?" Here, Nicholson noted, justification might be in the eye of the beholder: "Banks often design complicated trading strategies that help a customer, such as a pension fund or a wealthy individual, circumvent regulatory requirements or reduce tax liabilities. From the client's viewpoint, these types of financial products can create value, but from society's perspective they merely shift money around." The criterion of justification of "finance" as a respectable part of the business world, like the justification of the Israeli action, seemed open to debate.

And what of justification in art? In January 2011, the *Times* took a lengthy look at the long-delayed opening of the Broadway musical *Spider-Man: Turn Off the Dark*, under the headline " 'Spider-Man' Producers Say Delay Is Justified." The producers argued that any reasons they possessed to keep fine-tuning the production were justified, since no one else had a right to determine a production's opening date. Critics and others quoted, however, argued that the producers' departure from time-honored theater traditions—a faster opening, lower ticket prices for previews—rendered the delay unjustified.

What is plain to most people on the receiving end of "justification talk" is that it's not always obvious which concepts or actions the words "justify" and "justification" communicate or require. It's not an easy matter to think about. The words and notions operate too close to the foundation of everyday thought. They're too crucial to the way we reason for us to enjoy examining them. And yet they haven't been entirely ignored by cultural critics.

One of the most influential essays of the 1960s in aesthetics and criticism, Sontag's "Against Interpretation," expressed her insistence that art should not be forced to "justify itself." Sontag added, "None of us can ever retrieve that innocence before all theory when art knew no need to justify itself." Use of the word unites logic-chopping analytic philosophers and their continental, historically oriented colleagues, not to mention the pastor in the church, the lawyer in the courtroom, the doctor in the hospital, the politician on the stump, and just about everyone who uses language. Wittgenstein once wrote that "justification must end somewhere," but use of the word plainly doesn't. You figure it must be pretty important.

A thorough explanation of justification talk from a deep philosophical and scholarly perspective is best left aside for now—it would require an in-depth analysis of legal metaphors, their rhetorical effect on how we think about truth, and how they interconnect (as in, "I consider that a *legitimate justification*"). I hope to undertake that analysis elsewhere. The important point here is that Americans, irreverent by a kind of birthright, intuitively grasp the surface logic of justification and why it doesn't compel anyone by logical force alone to accept a particular justification. That, in turn, explains why Americans could never be pushovers for Rawls's redistributionist theory of justice. Simply put, every American understands the formal emptiness of the logic of justification (more on that in a moment), which provides excellent armor for resisting any specific claim of justification—a justified war, a justified divorce, a justified punch in the nose, a justified use of a condom—that one doesn't like.

The first thing every American understands about justification is that the attempt to establish it takes place only when we're not agreeing with others because of differing values and practices. Many claims in life aren't challenged or opposed. For example, one doesn't attempt to "justify" the logical inference of *modus ponens* (if P then Q; P, therefore Q), or that the name of Detroit is Detroit, or that the Yankees won the pennant if they did it according to the rules. Saying that Harry was unjustified in hitting you because he had no reason to does not just call attention to the idea that unprovoked violence is wrong, but that criticism of it ought to continue, and perhaps be accompanied by punishment. Saying that you're justified in hitting Harry back because Harry hit you first does not just draw a questioner's attention to one's reason, but demands a stop to any questioning of your action.

The second thing every American understands about the logic of justification, and particularly an *accepted* justification, is that it's meant to put an end to debate and all *further* justification. Columnist Ray Kerrison, in the *New York Post*, once reflected on a letter he'd received from a mother angry at his support of the first U.S. war against Iraq. It said, Kerrison reported, that "nothing I had written justified any of her three children and a son-in-law, who are in the military, 'being placed in harm's way on the other side of the globe.'" Kerrison observed that "the hottest debate in the country" was whether the war "is justifiable." The headline that accompanied his column read "For some, no war can be justified" (even if, as scholars know, there is a tradition of "just war" theory). Toward the column's end, Kerrison quoted the sister of a dead soldier: "No one can justify his death."

Those readers who wrote to Kerrison exemplified how ordinary Americans employ "justification talk" with striking confidence, even though our individual criteria for justifying specific moral and political actions differ sharply. Imagine a media critic unpacking the logic of that headline over Kerrison's column—"For some, no war can be justified"—to a length no copy editor would permit. That is, to something like, "For some, it is absolutely true that it is impossible to justify a war." One suspects many people—like many philosophers—would ditch the claim, understanding that justification, when it happens, depends on compatibility between a persuader's criteria and those of whoever is meant to be persuaded.

The third thing that Americans understand about the logic of justification is that using the "J word" introduces an extra dimension of spin that simply speaking of "reasons" lacks. In a dispatch from the Mideast about press opposition to the Pentagon's use of "pools," a *New York Times* correspondent wrote, "In addition to the correspondents' safety, military officers have put forward a number of justifications for the highly restricted pool system: Difficulties of transportation and logistics, the need to insure that they can screen stories to assure that security is not violated and the confusion that could ensue in battle if hordes of journalists were present."

Here, "justifications" operated as a virtual synonym for "reasons," yet one notes a difference. If the reporter or officers had used the word "reasons," it would seem perfectly natural to follow the laid-out reasons with a counterclaim that the reasons were not merely bad, but perhaps badly motivated. Reasons, for instance, can be selfish. Yet when the reporter or officers use "justifications," there's added meaning. Characterizing one's reasons as "justifications" implies that a preestablished set of criteria for *good* reasons—established by the person making the argument—has been met. It makes sense to reply to someone's reasons by saying, "But those aren't good reasons to me because I reject your basic values and views." Similarly, it would make sense for the officers to say, "We've put forth a number of reasons," while acknowledging that no one else does or should agree with them. But it wouldn't make sense for them to say, "We've put forth a number of justifications," and then hold that no one else does or should agree with them. To say that some claim is "justified" implies that *others should accept the claim, and one's criteria for the claim.*

These three characteristics of how we talk about justification—what I've called its surface logic—explain why Americans use "J words" with high confidence about what can or can't be accomplished. When we describe a claim as justified, we're implying that we can offer a good reason or reasons that ought to be accepted, or some fact that will put us over the top. Sometimes, we believe that something is justified—say, the execution of a murderer who raped and dismembered his child victims—by just one reason or fact or principle. ("Someone who does that just doesn't deserve to live.") At the same time, there's always an "all things considered" aspect to the logic of justification. If we believe some unconsidered factor might undermine the claim we think justified ("You say someone else confessed to the crime?"), we don't invoke the word.

Americans, in short, think about justification the way the classical pragmatists argued we *should* think about any idea or action. Crediting his chief pragmatist predecessor as usual, William James wrote in "What Pragmatism Means" that "Peirce, after pointing out that our beliefs are really rules for action, said that, to develop a thought's meaning, we need only determine what conduct it is fitted to produce: that conduct is for us its whole significance." To attain "perfect clearness in our thoughts" about the meaning of an idea or action, James continued, we need to know "what sensations we are to expect from it" and "what reactions we must prepare. Our conception of these effects, whether immediate or remote, is then for us the whole of our conception."

Americans don't ask what justification is, but what it *does*. The effect of a justification, when it's recognized as such, is that the person on the receiving end drops further challenges, forsakes further appeals. If we imagine President Obama justifying his budget to the Republicans, or the Afghan war to Congress, or why he should be elected president again to the American people, and all parties to the situation share assumptions about what's needed for a justification, it violates our understanding of the word to suggest that further argument is necessary.

Justification means *nothing else* needs to be done—the issue is closed. At best, "justify" conveys the sense in American English of "to persuade through the presentation of reasons, or facts, or evidence, or states of affairs *or something* short of a gun to the head." When people involved in an effort to justify a claim share values and assumptions, it's not hard to achieve a justification—that is, an agreement that permits subsequent action without challenge. It's when they don't that trouble happens.

One can see these philosophical phenomena at work in commentary on the action that provoked perhaps the most intense use of the word "justified" in recent American history: the killing by American Navy Seal commandos of Osama bin Laden.

When President Obama announced bin Laden's death on the evening of May 1, 2011, he declared that "justice had been done." Not everyone agreed that the killing of bin Laden was justified. In a *Times* article headlined "In Europe, Disquiet over Bin Laden and U.S.," British human rights attorney Geoffrey Robertson, whose clients included WikiLeaks founder Julian Assange, asserted to the BBC that Obama's claim that "justice was done" amounted to "a total misuse of language," adding, "This is the justice of the Red Queen; sentence first, trial later." Yet in a *Times* op-ed titled "Thinking Through Assassination," Jim Rasenberger, author of *The Brilliant Disaster: JFK, Castro, and America's Doomed Invasion of Cuba's Bay of Pigs,* illustrated that the logic of justification is not parallel to the logic of legal justification. Bin Laden presented a special case, Rasenberger contended, and not just because he'd taken credit for the 9/11 massacres, making his guilt in an empirical sense, if not a legal sense, clear. Rather, Rasenberger submitted, broad agreement among Americans that it was justified for the U.S. to kill bin Laden was so clear-cut—however much it might be based in a desire for vengeance—that "[t]here is no conceivable argument against assassination that could stand up to the overwhelming desire in this country to see the man die." Sure enough, an Associated Press–GfK poll conducted that month showed, the AP wrote, "the nation supporting the raid with rare unanimity." In the poll, 87 percent of those questioned judged bin Laden's killing "justified," while 9 percent did not. A USA Today–Gallup poll reported similar results: 93 percent of those interviewed approved of the killing, and 5 percent disapproved. By a month or so after bin Laden's killing, discussion in the U.S. over the justification of his killing largely disappeared from all but fringe venues, even while a Pew survey found that 63 percent of Pakistanis judged the killing unjustified.

Two other controversial killings in 2011—the taking out by drone attack of radical Islamic cleric and American citizen Anwar al-Awlaki in Yemen, and the summary elimination of Muammar el-Qaddafi by Libyan rebels who captured him—further delineated the logical space between narrow public conceptions of justification such as legal justification (spurring disagreement even on that limited terrain) and a broader public form of justification.

After al-Awlaki's killing in September 2011, the *New York Times* reported that a secret, roughly fifty-page Justice Department memo had laid out a legal justification for it despite his American citizenship. The article analyzed several of the document's alleged arguments—*Times* reporter Charlie Savage indicated he hadn't seen the memo but had received descriptions of it from some who'd read it—for why al-Awlaki was not protected by such legal safeguards as an executive order against assassination, elements of the Bill of Rights, and a federal law against murder. The memo presumably persuaded the administration and the article took no stand.

But in an editorial three days later headlined "Justifying the Killing of an American," the *Times* declared that the memo, at least as reported, provided an "insufficient foundation" for the killing, and that the administration had "set aside Mr. Awlaki's rights to due process." The editorial then hinted, in classic American fashion, at the *Times*'s own criterion for a justification. If the White House had released what evidence it had to back the claim that Awlaki was involved in "operational planning of attacks," then it "would have a better chance of justifying the cleric's death."

At least to the *Times*.

Colonel Qaddafi's killing, in contrast, forced onlookers around the world to weigh whether that action could be justified apart from a legal process and its criteria, even (or especially?) given the particularly brutal manner in which it took place. Hadn't Qaddafi treated thousands during his dictatorship to equal brutality? One Web commentator asked whether Qaddafi had offered due process to the hundreds of passengers killed on the Pan Am 103 flight presumed to have been attacked on his orders. Suddenly, one of the oldest philosophical justifications in Western history—an eye for an eye—was being debated on the world's front pages and around the Internet. An op-ed piece in the *Times* by historian

Simon Sebag Montefiore bore a simple headline: "Dictators Get the Deaths They Deserve."

The problem that these ordinary understandings of justification presented for Rawls and his theory was that he knew the same thing ordinary Americans did—that successful justifications require people to agree at the beginning, when they're making their assumptions, and not just at the end of a 607-page book of conclusions deduced from those assumptions. When Rawls drily turned to the concept of "justification" in *A Theory of Justice,* he pretty much gave the game away, though the sterility of his language made it hard to notice his concessions. Bear with me, then, as we enter just a few pages of Rawls's highly abstract prose. It's important to understand why even *A Theory of Justice,* for all its magisterial reputation, rested only on what most Americans hope for when they start arguing with their office mates—voluntary, shared agreement.

RAWLS ON JUSTIFICATION

Rawls's own foundational thoughts on justification came in two key sections of *A Theory of Justice*: at the beginning, in "The Original Position and Justification," and, at the end, in "Concluding Remarks on Justification." In the first of those, he asserted that

> one conception of justice is more reasonable than another, or justifiable with respect to it, if rational persons in the initial situation would choose its principles over those of the other for the role of justice. Conceptions of justice are to be ranked by their acceptability to persons so circumstanced. Understood in this way the question of justification is settled by working out a problem of deliberation: we have to ascertain which principles it would be rational to adopt given the contractual situation. This connects the theory of justice with the theory of rational choice.

He added, "If this view of the problem of justification is to succeed, we must, of course, describe in some detail the nature of this choice problem."

Justification of an idea of justice for Rawls thus required acceptance of the idea in a hypothetical situation. That is, he *stipulated*, or assumed, the specific audience that needed to accept his notion of justice: those in his imagined original position. And he invoked a kind of synonymy between the justifiable and the reasonable, with both being forms of objective truth capable of being discovered. In these moves—the link between the justifiable and the reasonable, and the need for acceptance by a specific audience—Rawls reflected ideas already in the philosophical air, in the work of the Belgian thinker Chaim Perelman and German philosopher Jürgen Habermas, about how deliberation leads to justification. Yet Rawls projected a certainty about justification missing from Perelman or Habermas.

A key part of Rawls's approach came across as classically rhetorical, even though he seemed oblivious to that dimension of his work. He sought, that is, to draw the reader into his project with subtly inveigling phrases such as, "If this view of the problem of justification is to succeed . . ." A particular reader, of course, might not have wanted Rawls's theory to succeed, or cared whether it did. But the effect of Rawls's gentle language was to make the reader more tolerant of the criteria Rawls assumed. If the reader wanted the "theory" to fail, he could reject Rawls's assumptions at the outset and close the book. If he wanted it to succeed—which he perhaps did if he kept reading—he was almost obliged as a matter of civility to nod yes, and not object as Rawls genially assumed this, that and the next thing. In *A Theory of Justice*, Rawls did not give the reader any criterion of success except meeting his own: the satisfaction of a hypothetical community of fair-minded deciders.

So Rawls kept stipulating: "I assume, for one thing, that there is a broad measure of agreement that principles of justice should be chosen under certain conditions. To justify a particular description of the initial situation one shows that it incorporates these commonly shared presumptions." Again, ponder the logical relations at play. The reader had already been asked to accept an assumption about the relation of presented evidence (i.e., the folks in the original position agree) to conclusive justification (i.e., of the principles of justice). Now Rawls was asking the reader to accept a further stipulation: that the first "justifying" device Rawls had introduced, the original position (or "initial situation"), was itself already justified by its agreeing with our conventional beliefs about justice. As he wrote, there is "another side to justifying a particular description of the original position. This is to see if the principles which would be chosen match our considered convictions of justice or extend them in an acceptable way." Thomas Nagel once paraphrased this aspect of Rawls's theory as the proviso that "[a]bstract principles, whatever their *a priori* plausibility, must not be permitted to sweep away concrete moral judgments too easily. . . . [W]e should not disregard the pre-theoretical voice of conscience."

Rawls gave some examples of what conditions should obtain in his original position: "Thus it seems reasonable and generally acceptable that no one should be advantaged or disadvantaged by natural fortune or social circumstances in the choice of principles. It also seems widely agreed that it should be impossible to tailor principles to the circumstances of one's own case." Yet as Rawls would come to realize after years of scholarly criticism, plenty of thinkers and ordinary people thought we *should* be able to take into account the advantages of natural fortune (e.g., intelligence, drive) in choosing principles, just as we should be able to know the circumstances of our own case. Nonetheless, in *A Theory of Justice,* after discussing how one goes back and forth between principles and judgments to reach "reflective equilibrium," Rawls wrote, "[F]or the time being we have done what we can to render coherent and to justify our convictions of social justice."

A skeptic might have said—and naysayers did—that he had merely adopted his convictions, or articulated them. More of Rawls's general thoughts about justification followed. The justification of principles of justice was that "they would be agreed to in an initial situation of equality." But the justification of "a conception of justice" could not be "deduced from self-evident premises or conditions on principles." It depended, rather, on "the mutual support of many considerations, of everything fitting together into one coherent view."

Here Rawls essentially acknowledged that justification amounted to the considered preference of one omnibus theory over any other theory—regardless of particular flaws, achievements, principles. Thus, no single test or criterion invalidated the justification of a theory, because the theory might boast compensating virtues elsewhere. It sounded as if the justification of a theory rested on a preference for how things hung together in that theory, not on any Talmudically or Jesuitically drawn-out deductions. Was that rationale for accepting a theory terribly different from a less sophisticated thinker declaring, "I don't know—I just like the way things hang together in Catholicism, even though it's flawed"?

At the end of the book, Rawls corroborated the impression that it wasn't, returning to these meta-problems one more time in his "Concluding Remarks on Justification." There he offered a broad statement that should be quoted at length, because it reveals the down-to-earth basis on which Rawlsian justification takes place despite all the high-falutin abstractions with which the author surrounds it:

> Philosophers commonly try to justify ethical theories in one of two ways. Sometimes they attempt to find self-evident principles from which a sufficient body of standards and precepts can be derived to account for our considered judgments. A justification of this sort we may think of as Cartesian. It presumes that

first principles can be seen to be true, even necessarily so; deductive reasoning then transfers this conviction from premises to conclusion. A second approach . . . is to introduce definitions of moral concepts in terms of presumptively non-moral ones, and then to show by accepted procedures of common sense and the sciences that the statements thus paired with the asserted moral judgments are true. Although on this view the first principles of ethics are not self-evident, the justification of moral convictions poses no special difficulties. They can be established, granting the definitions, in the same fashion as other statements about the world.

Rawls then insisted that he had "not adopted either of these conceptions of justification." He rejected the first because "there is no set of conditions or first principles that can be plausibly claimed to be necessary or definitive of morality and thereby especially suited to carry the burden of justification." He rejected the second because "for the justification to succeed, a clear theory of meaning is presupposed and this seems to be lacking. . . . [I]n any case, definitions become the main part of the ethical doctrine, and thus in turn they need to be justified."

So Rawls announced his own, "third way" of justification, that tracked with his earlier idea of it as based on a comprehensive set of factors or elements: "I have not proceeded then as if first principles, or conditions thereon, or definitions either, have special features that permit them a peculiar place in justifying a moral doctrine. They are central elements and devices of theory, but justification *rests upon the entire conception and how it fits in with and organizes our considered judgments in reflective equilibrium.* [Emphasis added.] And, as we have noted before, justification is a matter of the mutual support of many considerations, of everything fitting together into one coherent view."

Rawls appeared to realize that he'd gotten himself into a logical fix. A "general complaint" against him, he admitted, was that his model of justification "appeals to the mere fact of agreement." (One might faintly hear Isocrates calling out across the ages, "I told you so . . .") A second was that his position—Rawls preferred to think of it as an "argument"—depended upon "a particular list of conceptions of justice between which the parties in the original position are to choose," and "an agreement among persons" in both their considered judgments and notion of "reasonable conditions to impose on the choice of first principles." Rawls addressed the problems directly, leading slowly to the closest thing in *A Theory of Justice* to a *definition* of justification: because, Rawls argued, justification is "argument addressed to those who disagree with us, or to ourselves when we are of two minds," it always "presumes a clash of views." But being "designed to reconcile by reason," justification starts "from what all parties to the discussion hold in common."

"Ideally," Rawls contended, justifying a notion of justice to someone required giving that person "a proof of its principles from premises that both parties accept," those principles producing consequences that match our considered judgments. Thus, according to Rawls, "mere proof is not justification. A proof simply displays logical relations between propositions." Rather, "proofs become justifications once the starting points are mutually recognized, or the conclusions so comprehensive and compelling" that they "persuade us of the soundness of the conception expressed by their premises. It is perfectly proper, then, that the argument for the principles of justice should proceed from some consensus. This is the nature of justification."

The problem? Rawls's view of justification didn't match that of most Americans once you packed in all the assumptions. For one thing, his notion that justification is "designed to reconcile by reason" addressed only one type of traditional justification—reasoning—that particularly appeals to philosophers. Usage showed that most people thought you could justify a position in a variety of ways, such as bringing to bear a fresh fact or fresh information in general. ("The DNA test shows he wasn't there. He's innocent.") For another, Rawls's judgment that ideal justification was a "proof" from premises shared by people that also squared with our "considered judgments," privileged both mainstream moral beliefs and the kind of systematic rational enterprise he'd spent years constructing—admired by professional academic philosophers, but looked upon with skepticism by many thinkers outside the guild. If the only clear-cut message that a successful justification sent was that all challenge to one's claims should end ("I am one hundred feet tall, with a long white beard, and am omniscient, omnipresent and eternal as well—now stop doubting I'm God!"), it was not self-evident that a string-of-reasonings "proof" plus status-quo morality (which once included, for instance, acceptance of slavery) delivered that best. Common usage didn't require that "justification" entail a long chain of reasoning, such as Rawls's theory. Yet Rawls took that for granted, writing that "the question of justification is settled by working out a problem of deliberation." In doing so, he employed a common strategy of analytic philosophers that drove outsiders batty. He acknowledged in muted form that justifications are a relative matter, announced the criteria of his own, then fell into a language that implied that once *his* criteria of justification were met, the general problem of justification disappeared.

A Theory of Justice, for all the praise it drew, was thus anchored by enough assumptions to fill a cargo container. It made perfect sense, then, that many of the same philosophers and thinkers who lauded *A Theory of Justice* for its systematic ambition, its philosophical heft, its sophisticated conceptual architecture, its humane values, *didn't agree with it.* As Robert Talisse noted in his *On Rawls: A Liberal Theory of Justice and Justification,* what seemed like a thousand criticisms bloomed. R. M. Hare, a leading moral philosopher, accused Rawls of subjectivism, a rejection of objective moral truths. Michael Walzer detected, in contrast, "universalism," a belief in universal truths about social justice "that can be applied to any society." Nozick found Rawls "too radical on economic justice and governmental interference." Feminist philosopher Virginia Held, like Nussbaum, worried that Rawls's theory of justice remained too narrow to address issues of justice for women. Michael Sandel thought justice as fairness still left holders of some religious beliefs unfairly treated. Robert Paul Wolff and Benjamin Barber both feared that justice as fairness remained too abstract to propel concrete political policies. Over time, some political theorists, such as Charles W. Mills of Northwestern University, also attacked Rawls on far tougher grounds, dispensing with the ritual praise for his greatness.

Mills, a black philosopher whose work in "oppositional political theory" and issues of class, race and gender placed him outside the arena of so-called ideal justice theory occupied by almost all of Rawls's disciplinary admirers, criticized the "person seen as the most important twentieth-century American philosopher and theorist of social justice" for having "nothing to say about the remediation of racial injustice, central to American society and history."

In hardnosed, crystal-clear journal articles such as "Racial Liberalism" (*PMLA,* 2008), and "Rawls on Race / Race in Rawls" (*The Southern Journal of Philosophy,* 2009), Mills, whose incisive books included *The Racial Contract* (1997) and *Blackness Visible: Essays on Philosophy and Race* (1998), pointed out that in Rawls's articulation of his theory through more than two thousand pages in five books over five decades, all the sentences that mentioned race might "add up to half a dozen pages."

Even worse, Mills argued, Rawls did not once mention affirmative action—which Mills deemed "the most important American postwar measure of corrective racial justice"—or Native Americans, who "are completely absent from every page of these five books."

Was it any wonder, Mills asked, that "race" was one of those features that a person in Rawls's hypothetical "original position" was not permitted to know about himself? The fatal flaw undermining Rawls's theory of justice from top to bottom, for Mills, was its artificial "ideal" character, its unwillingness to recognize that all real societies contain injustice at both their inception and later on, and thus any adequate justice theory needs to address the rectification of *injustice*. Mills acknowledged that Rawls personally condemned racism and had his heart in all the right liberal places. As Samuel Freeman noted, "Jack frequently quoted Lincoln's assertion—'If anything is wrong, slavery is wrong'—as the best example of a fixed moral conviction that anyone with a sense of justice must believe." But that didn't keep Mills from reaching a damning judgment: "The postwar struggle for racial justice in practice and theory, and the Rawlsian corpus on justice, are almost completely separate and non-intersecting universes."

As criticisms mounted over the years, Rawls conceded the complaint that his account of justice appealed to the "mere fact of agreement." He seemed to know that nothing he said really refuted it. Some critics thought that deep recognition prompted Rawls's retreat from universal claims in his later published work, such as *Political Liberalism* (1993), his slightly revised edition of *A Theory of Justice* (1999), and *The Law of Peoples* (1999), in which Rawls extended his thinking about justice to international society and justice among nations.

The truth was that in multi-voiced, pluralistic, kaleidoscopically complicated America, people powerfully disagreed on what assumptions must be adopted, what arguments must be made, what facts must be in place, what consequences must follow, for a position in any number of fields—politics, art, morality, criticism—to be justified. Americans knew that if nothing marked debate in philosophy so much as its eternal failure to take yes for an answer, the key reason wasn't that philosophers (like politician, lawyers and movie critics) failed to "justify" their views with reasons or evidence that fit their *own* criteria for a justification. Rather, it was that others didn't agree that meeting those criteria sufficed for a justification. Radicals and iconoclasts, for instance, didn't have to respect Rawls's concern for our considered moral beliefs as opposed to spontaneous, outré, push-the-envelope beliefs. Nor did they have to accept the moral cachet of consent among equals as opposed to a Nietzschean attitude that aristocratic might makes right.

But perhaps the most painful nail in the coffin of Rawls's theory—in the notion that sophisticated academic philosophy could "justify" Americans into philosophical unanimity, rather than catalyze us into brash nitpickers who make the U.S. the world's top agora of arguers—was that even one of Rawls's most devoted students and scholars ultimately couldn't defend it.

"THE THEORY IS NOT SUCCESSFUL"

In a large auditorium at the College of New Jersey—known as Trenton State College until it won its present name by arguing that Princeton *unjustly* clung to legal ownership of the name "College of New Jersey"—Morton Winston of the school's philosophy department appeared to have pulled off a nervy symposium in the spirit of the college's name-game battle.

Just months before the fortieth anniversary of the publication of *A Theory of Justice,* on a nippy October afternoon in 2010, he'd managed to attract three of the most distinguished Rawls scholars in the world—Samuel Freeman, Erin Kelly and Thomas Pogge—to a symposium entitled "John Rawls's *A Theory of Justice: Forty Years On.*" Even nervier, he'd convinced several prominent public-minded citizens—among them Douglas Forrester, a former Republican candidate for both governor of New Jersey and senator from New Jersey, and Helen E. Hoens, a member of New Jersey's Supreme Court, to join them onstage to figure out the impact and legacy of *A Theory of Justice.*

Having announced, in standard academic fashion, the endless CV credentials of his three main speakers, and noted that all of them had received their PhD in philosophy at Harvard under Rawls, Winston quipped, "You may have noticed that there's a pattern here." If he wanted to imply that proximity in philosophy leads to loyalty on doctrine, he was in for a surprise.

In the first part of the three-section, all-day session, Freeman, who as a lawyer had clerked for both the Fourth Circuit Court of Appeals and the North Carolina Supreme Court before *A Theory of Justice* convinced him to become a philosopher instead, explained some broad aspects of Rawls's exercise in "ideal theory." Freeman conceded that it didn't track very well with the real society we live in. Rawls's theory, for instance, assumed that all citizens want to do justice, and nothing in the newspapers indicated that was the case. Similarly, Freeman observed, "We don't live in a well-ordered society" of the sort Rawls aspired to.

Making frequent reference to Milton Friedman, the late conservative economist whose ideas Freeman employed as a counterpoint to Rawlsian thinking, he noted the strong influence they'd had during the Reagan years and admitted, "I'm not optimistic about the evolution of American capitalism toward anything resembling Rawls's difference principle or his account of economic justice."

When the nonacademic guests and audience got their chance to participate, the questioners steered the discussion to considerably more concrete topics. What did Rawls think about affirmative action? Freeman couldn't recall him writing directly about the subject, but remembered his teacher saying things "in both directions." When an audience member suggested that "Rawls really didn't have anything to say about employment . . . that was a point where Rawls missed the boat," Freeman responded that Rawls favored full employment, and would have seen employment as a crucial part of being an equal citizen and having self-respect, but probably wouldn't have said, "You have a right to a job."

Then someone asked Freeman where, if anywhere, he disagreed with Rawls. "Well, I think there were certain arguments that didn't work," Freeman shot back. "But I think he came around to realize that himself." Freeman spoke of the so-called stability argument in *A Theory of Justice,* devised to "hold this whole scheme together." Rawls believed that everyone would endorse a kind of "Kantian autonomy," a form of moral and rational independence, as "an essential good for all persons," but that assumption plainly didn't hold in a world where some religions and ideologies seek compliance, not independence. Rawls, Freeman further explained, came to understand that many people "were not going to be Kantians," and were "not going to agree" with Rawls's liberal democratic assumptions. "That was just too unrealistic," Freeman noted, calling it "the most serious problem in *A Theory of Justice.*"

The next questioner consequently wondered, "Where are we with John Rawls," if his theory couldn't accommodate the wider world, if one couldn't "universalize" it? Freeman, frustration showing on his face, replied in broad, casual, conversational style. Rawls wasn't "trying to present a universally true theory of justice, true of all societies," he said. He didn't think that "any society is unjust" that didn't "aspire to" his model. Rawls, he suggested, would have replied, "I'm addressing modern democratic societies where people regard themselves as free and equal, and that's mostly true of at least half the world, and most of the rest of the world aspires to something like that. So insofar as these ideals are part of the people's political and mental culture, this model would apply to them."

Freeman clearly felt the edge of the questioner's challenge. Rawls scholars did recognize that, at least in *A Theory of Justice*, Rawls had included a "kind of Kantian argument" that he later "distanced himself from," and had sounded as if "he was making claims about objectivity that apply across all societies."

The gathering sense that the intricate academic sophistication of Rawls's system perhaps did not count for much in the complicated real world of American life continued during Erin Kelly's presentation. After the Tufts University political theorist set out a generally admiring account of the theory's rational architecture, and Rawls's desire to see differences in distribution managed for the least well off, Forrester, with the polite yet firm tone of a politician used to public challenges, asked her bluntly about the fastidiously "rational" aspect of Rawls's system: "Do you think that for any significant number of people, 'reason' is enough to give up power?"

Kelly immediately snapped into real-world mode. "No," she replied. Winston added his own thought, directing it to Forrester as if in defense of his troops and his discipline: "Most political philosophers are not that naive."

But it was Pogge—German by birth, lean and quick-witted in manner—who most incisively expressed the growing sense that if Rawls's theory of justice ranked as one of modern America's great philosophical achievements, it wasn't because it had persuaded lots of people.

"So what's so great about Rawls?" Pogge pugnaciously began, speaking with hardly a look at his notes before him. Pogge himself, of course, had helped the wider reading public understand Rawls the man better than anyone yet, thanks to his biographically driven interviews with his ex-adviser. And in his earlier book Pogge had expressed an appreciation of Rawls and his accomplishment that matched standard raves—Rawls's theory was, he had written, "the best there is." But now, after many years, something seemed to have changed.

In rapid-fire style, Pogge identified one after another weakness in the theory that was "supposed" to establish this, or "supposed" to establish that. Rawls's two principles of justice—that everyone is entitled to the maximum of equal liberty, and that in situations of inequality the distribution of goods should be shaped to the advantage of those worse off—couldn't be "applied transparently" to resolve differences. When viewed together, the two principles and the thought experiment of the "original position" was "incoherent." The two principles, in any case, "did not match our considered judgments" about morality, as Rawls thought they must. Moreover, the "original position" *itself* didn't match those judgments.

"The theory is not successful," Pogge asserted. "We're at the point where we're no longer talking about the theory. . . . We're talking about the man, what did he think."

"That, in a way," Pogge stingingly continued, "is already indicative of the bankruptcy of the theory." Calling attention to the huge growth in income inequality in America over the past several decades, Pogge contended that, by his lights, Rawls's theory of justice "didn't do anything in the United States. . . . Things went backward by any conceivable Rawlsian standard ever since he wrote." Indeed, in 1970, the year before *A Theory of Justice* was published, the top 1 percent of U.S. households made 9 percent of all income. By 2010, it made more than 20 percent of all income. Other statistics corroborated the anti-Rawlsian trend. By 2011, the top 1 percent of Americans possessed a greater collective net worth than the bottom 90 percent. And according to an analysis by economists Thomas Piketty and Emmanuel Saez, income for Americans in the top-1-percent tax bracket rose by 30 percent from 2002 to 2008, while income for those in the bottom 90 percent dropped by 4 percent.

In the discussion afterward, Freeman resisted some of Pogge's more aggressive dismissals. ("We've had these arguments before," Freeman commented with a smile to the audience, seemingly acknowledging that these birds of an academic feather had flocked together from one conference to another.) "You know," Freeman ventured, "the argument that Rawls went one way and the United States the other, well—all philosophical theories take forever to leak down. It took hundreds of years for Locke to filter down."

Yet Freeman—or the lawyer in him, if not the political philosopher—conceded in response to another question directed at the real-world upshot of Rawls's theory, "If it doesn't have some practical applications, there's not much interest in it. It is a theory of *justice*, so it's got to somehow be applicable to our world."

The College of New Jersey symposium appeared to underline a core truth. The virtues of *A Theory of Justice* as an elaborate exercise in reasoning did not mean that the book was "right" or convincing about its subject. A product of its time and profession that unquestionably spurred further work, it took the notion of justification for granted. And if the greatest moral and political philosopher of modern times couldn't find a magic key to justification, Rorty must have been right—there wasn't any.

Rawls's true accomplishment, which Pogge gracefully acknowledged before leaving the stage, segued with an aim Rorty would have applauded. Rawls had, "more than anyone else," in Pogge's view, been responsible for "reinvigorating the discussion of social justice" in America. And catalytic contributions like that were what philosophy came down to in a huge, diverse, pluralistic democracy full of people with the courage to argue. Almost as a confirmation of that, when Occupy Wall Street and its allied protests around the country focused Americans on income inequality in the fall of 2011, political theorist Steven V. Mazie of Bard College urged protestors to "find inspiration by reading *A Theory of Justice* and Rawls's other books in study circles from Zuccotti Park to Washington, D.C., to Des Moines." In his October 2011 article for—what else?—the *Times*'s online philosophy forum, The Stone, Mazie argued that Rawls's work made "a perfect intellectual touchstone" for the Occupy movement.

Perhaps. And perhaps some future American historian of ideas would also show, with an inspired feat of scholarship, that Rawls laid the conceptual groundwork for a society capable of electing, as its president, a man born far from the upper rungs of American life: a child, born to a white mother and a largely absent black father, whose original position, to be sure, lacked advantages.

EPILOGUE:

OBAMA, PHILOSOPHER IN CHIEF

In the spring of 2009, in the great hall of Cairo University, President Barack Obama delivered the most ballyhooed speech of his first year in office. A week later, another intellectual of complicated global lineage, the Anglo-Dutch scholar Ian Buruma, gave a less heralded but important related address in Vienna. In the elegant Wiener Börsensäle, the historic former stock exchange of a city whose vulnerability to Islam had symbolized strife between Europe and Muslim culture for centuries, Buruma, the Henry Luce Professor of Human Rights and Journalism at Bard College, spoke on "The Virtues and Limits of Cosmopolitanism," providing sophisticated context for an idea at the core of Obama's approach in Cairo.

Cosmopolitanism is a "tricky" notion, Buruma observed. In one regard, we think of it as "a positive term denoting a high degree of cultivation and even glamor." We recognize, with the *Oxford English Dictionary*, that it connotes "ease in many different countries and cultures." In another regard, Buruma noted, the "same word, spoken with a sneer and contempt," and often preceded by "bourgeois" or "rootless," played an ugly role in Nazi and Soviet propaganda. In that slanderous argot, the person "of too many places" simply "cannot be one of us"—whoever we may be.

Buruma's etymology lesson, appropriately offered in a "Jan Patocka Memorial Lecture" honoring the Prague Spring philosopher who inspired Václav Havel's heroic open-mindedness, suggested the delicate intellectual maneuver Obama tried to pull off in Cairo. There Obama had expressed what lay behind many of his surface "nonpartisan" positions, those flexible postures so many pundits on right and left attacked as mere wussiness: a cosmopolitan ideal of the American thinker. The thinker committed to cooperative conversation. The thinker described nearly two and a half millennia ago by Isocrates, powerfully outlined by Richard Rorty toward the end of the twentieth century, then echoed in *Cosmopolitanism: Ethics in a World of Strangers* by Kwame Anthony Appiah, the Ghanaian-American philosopher whose leadership of many U.S. high-cultural organizations paralleled Obama's own classically American ascent.

As Appiah noted in his book, cosmopolitanism dates back to the fourth-century Cynics, who "rejected the conventional view that every civilized person belonged to a community among communities." Stoics from Cicero to Marcus Aurelius picked up the idea, as did St. Paul ("There is neither Jew nor Greek . . . for ye are all one in Christ Jesus") and thinkers from Kant to Arendt and Derrida. For Appiah, two strands intertwined in the notion of cosmopolitanism: "One is the idea that we have obligations to others, obligations that stretch beyond those to whom we are related by the ties of kith and kind, or even the more formal ties of a shared citizenship. The other is that we take seriously the value not just of human life but of particular human lives."

The special "trickiness" of cosmopolitanism for an American president was to shape it in the face of a double challenge: maintaining pride in the allure of America's own values while resisting the bluster of academic Americanists who too often exalted our pluses over our minuses. Even a relatively skeptical sort, such as British-born historian Simon Schama in *The American Future: A History,* gushed over America's "perennial capacity for reinvention" and declared that the "American future is all vision, numinous, unformed, lightheaded with anticipation."

William H. Goetzmann, a University of Texas intellectual historian, stood as one example of the overly appreciative Americanist. In *Beyond the Revolution: A History of American Thought from Paine to Pragmatism,* published in the year of Obama's inauguration, Goetzmann announced his theme as "the American quest for the climactic model of world civilization that not only would incorporate the best ideas, the best lifestyles, and the most important spiritual values, but also would forever remain free and open to the new. It would be the world's first truly cosmopolitan civilization."

Goetzmann thus understandably began his book with Thomas Paine, who insisted that "the cause of America is in great measure the cause of all mankind." Paine believed, Goetzmann reminded us, that "America was God's country of the future," with its "spirit of revival, constant regeneration, and future-oriented habits of pragmatic thinking." The author wrote that Paine, like other revolutionary leaders, helped shape certain Enlightenment habits of mind into "traditional American values," among which are "a reverence for principles, particularly individual liberty, a dedication to reason and the rational solution, a belief in order and at the same time constant change, [and] a talent for practicality."

Obama plainly agreed with some of those views, but he proved subtler on that five-day international trip in his first year, marked by several significant speeches, including the Cairo centerpiece. He signaled what made Americans wonderful without declaring that Americans *were* wonderful. Leaving business moguls and Americanists at home, he relied on an entourage of ideas. The *New York Times* and others had joked that Obama increasingly sounded like a professor in chief, and there was truth to that. But professors needed students to sign up for their courses and agree to be graded. Obama, by sticking his neck out in front of free agents—foreign audiences—continued the process of fashioning himself as both philosopher and cosmopolitan in chief.

The first part of Obama's Cairo teach-in combined the best of rhetoric and philosophy. In the shrewd tradition of Isocrates and Aristotle, the president softened up his audience in Cairo University's ornate auditorium by quoting the Koran and dispensing rich praise. He related how Islamic culture had given us "the order of algebra, our magnetic compass and tools of navigation, our mastery of pens and printing, our understanding of how disease spreads and how it can be healed." Despite next launching into a sustained "on the one hand, on the other hand" structure, he sidestepped what might have been called the Bernard Lewis counterpoint to Islam: But what have you done for us lately?

Obama balanced almost every point in favor of Israel as a Jewish state with one that favored Palestinian Arabs. That his audience didn't immediately absorb the lesson in evenhandedness disappointed. The audience applauded only points directly in Islam's or the Arab world's self-interest. Though Obama observed that "the aspiration for a Jewish homeland is rooted in a tragic history that cannot be denied," he chose not to voice a further thought: that "the day this audience applauds a point made on behalf of others will be the day peace comes."

That might have driven home his approach far more strongly. But it would not have been Obama—cool, polite, generous, cosmo.

All the same, he imparted rules for philosophical discourse: "We must say openly the things we hold in our hearts and that too often are said only behind closed doors. There must be sustained effort to listen to each other, to learn from each other, to respect one another, and to

Barack Obama (1961–) angered some during his presidency for his inclination to compromise and avoid hardball rhetoric against supposed enemies, but others credited him with an admirable philosophical temperament.

seek common ground." At its core, his teaching was ethical and political, using logic to illuminate hypocrisy and contradiction: "None of us should tolerate these extremists," he said.

"They have killed in many countries. They have killed people of different faiths—but more than any other, they have killed Muslims. Their actions are irreconcilable with the right of human beings, the progress of nations, and with Islam. The holy Koran teaches that whoever kills an innocent, it is as if he has killed all mankind."

Without weighing the pros and cons of American egalitarianism, Obama simply affirmed that "a woman who is denied an education is denied equality." Countering Machiavelli without mentioning Madison, he spoke straight to the Mideast prince: "You must maintain your power through consent, not coercion; you must respect the rights of minorities, and participate with a spirit of tolerance and compromise; you must place the interests of your people and the legitimate workings of the political process above your party." Weaving the ethical, political and pragmatic together, Obama told Palestinians that if they forswore violence and took the high road, a la Gandhi and King, they would get their state.

During the final two days of his international lecture tour, in Germany and France, policy again vanished behind Obama's philosophical non-negotiables, boldly submitted as starting points for negotiation. At Buchenwald, addressing Holocaust denial, Obama denounced "a denial of fact and truth that is baseless and ignorant and hateful." At Omaha Beach, the president followed stories of heroic soldiers with a hybrid principle of existential pragmatism, pitch perfect for the occasion and redolent of Camus, whom Elie Wiesel, at the president's side in Buchenwald, had quoted the day before. "Our history has always been the sum total of the choices made and the actions taken by each individual man and woman," said Obama. "It has always been up to us." Schama, reviewing the oratory in the *Financial Times,* dubbed Obama "our new American Pericles."

Overall, Obama's most singular philosophical breakthrough was to project the cosmopolitan idea that the U.S. president must care about non-Americans. True, Obama had observed months before that he was the president of the United States, not the president of China, and had to put the needs and safety of Americans first. But to an extraordinary extent, Obama announced that the U.S. president, because of the United States' effect on and involvement with the rest of the world, must think of other global citizens as constituents. He'd made the point as far back as a campaign speech to the Chicago Council on Global Affairs, when, as reported by Australian ethicist Peter Singer, "he called for a president who can speak directly to everyone in the world who longs for dignity and security, and say, 'You matter to us. Your future is our future.'" Two years after Cairo, when faced with the choice of intervening in Libya or turning away as its leader threatened to massacre his own people, Obama put his military where his mouth had been, embodying his cosmopolitan ethos in action.

A truly cosmopolitan culture permitted its members to choose different styles of life and thought, including antiquated ones, so long as they didn't harm the neighbors. Obama, like no president before him, put the rest of the world on notice that the United States would continue to express, rather than export, its philosophy, values and political theory—but through conversation, not declamation, seeking free adoption, not grudging acquiescence.

"Obama would like to believe you can lead the world by the power of ideas," Henry Kissinger had observed to Fareed Zakaria on the latter's CNN show. Yes, he did seem to believe that. But in the extraordinary policy bustle that constituted a president's life, and that of the media that cover him, Obama's expert articulation in key speeches of his philosophical beliefs—a rich moral idealism tempered by astute pragmatism—went terribly underreported. In its typical unstable fashion, the elite media that anointed him a master of oratory during his presidential campaign began to voice the countercliché that the magic was gone. In a November 2009 *New York Times* article with the headline "The President Whose Words Once Soared," White House correspondent Peter Baker asked, "Has Mr. Obama lost his oratorical touch?" The story ultimately acknowledged that the answer most likely was no—that the volume and necessary policy detail of presidential pronouncements had probably created an unkind oratorical illusion. More disreputably, Michael Gerson, President George W. Bush's former chief speechwriter, argued in a January 2010 *Washington Post* op-ed that "with President Obama's declining public standing has come a declining rhetorical reputation." Mocking Obama's designation in *New York* magazine way back as "our national oratorical superhero—a honey-tongued Frankenfusion of Lincoln, Gandhi, Cicero, Jesus and all our most cherished national acronyms (MLK, JFK, RFK, FDR)," Gerson—apparently oblivious to his role in leaving his former boss with the reputation of a tongue-tied incompetent—accused Obama of "workmanlike utterances" and "oddly disconnected" performances at times of crisis.

One had only to read Obama's visionary speeches—to Ghanaians in Accra, to his Oslo audience in accepting the Nobel Prize for Peace, to the people of Tucson after the shooting of Representative Gabrielle Giffords and others, to State Department employees on the Arab Spring—to recognize how off the mark and fired by *ressentiment* such judgments were. In Ghana, Obama expanded the cosmopolitanism of his Cairo speech to his father's continent, declaring that we live in "a time when the boundaries between people are overwhelmed by our connections." Foreshadowing the principle of humanitarian intervention that would propel his decision to use force in Libya, he asserted that "in the twenty-first century, we are called to act by our conscience but also by our common interest, because when a child dies of a preventable disease in Accra, that diminishes us everywhere." With courageous concreteness for a guest, he reeled off a litany of African political ills:

> This is about more than just holding elections. It's also about what happens between elections. . . . No country is going to create wealth if its leaders exploit the economy to enrich themselves, or if police can be bought off by drug traffickers. No business wants to invest in a place where the government skims 20 percent off the top, or the head of the port authority is corrupt. No person wants to live in a society where the rule of law gives way to the rule of brutality and bribery. That is not democracy, that is tyranny, even if occasionally you sprinkle an election in there. . . . Africa doesn't need strongmen, it needs strong institutions.

With similar panache, Obama in Oslo, conscious of wide criticism that his Peace Prize arrived prematurely, launched into a taut philosophical probing of war and peace, acknowledging that he came to the podium as "Commander-in-Chief of the military of a nation in the midst of two wars." Obama's inadequately reported Nobel address proved a model of crisp analysis, thumbnailing the cultural history of war, the development of "just war" criteria, and of America's role "in constructing an architecture to keep the peace" after World War II. Remarkably, in speaking to the peace-loving elite of neutral Norway, with appropriate and sincere nods to Gandhi, King and the moral beauty of non-violence, he then bravely articulated the unfortunate, occasional need for force in the service of peace: "A non-violent movement could not have halted Hitler's armies. Negotiations cannot convince al Qaeda's leaders to lay down their arms. To say that force may sometimes be necessary is not a call to cynicism—it is a recognition of history; the imperfections of man and the limits of reason."

And so, the Nobel Laureate for Peace announced that "the instruments of war do have a role to play in preserving the peace." In no other speech had Obama so clearly and conceptually laid out the pragmatically shaped moral idealism that guides his foreign policy decisions. "I believe that force can be justified on humanitarian grounds," he told his Oslo audience, "as it was in the Balkans. . . . Inaction tears at our conscience and can lead to more costly intervention later. . . . The belief that peace is desirable is rarely enough to achieve it. Peace requires responsibility. Peace entails sacrifice."

Then, with the thread of detail that marked him as writer-president as well as philosopher-president, Obama explained his inclination to both excoriate dictatorial regimes in words—he invoked the "quiet dignity" of Aung Sang Suu Kyi, the "bravery of Zimbabweans who cast their ballots in the face of beatings," the "hundreds of thousands who have marched silently through the streets of Iran"—and remain open to them diplomatically.

"I know that engagement with repressive regimes lacks the satisfying purity of indignation," Obama firmly observed, in a line that vaporized Gerson's literary condescension in a flash. "But I also know that sanctions without outreach—condemnation without discussion—can carry forward only a crippling status quo. No repressive regime can move down a new path unless it has the choice of an open door." True to his pragmatist inclinations, Obama backed up his argument with historical evidence:

> In light of the Cultural Revolution's horrors, Nixon's meeting with Mao appeared inexcusable—and yet it surely helped set China on a path where millions of its citizens have been lifted from poverty and connected to open societies.
>
> Pope John Paul's engagement with Poland created space not just for the Catholic Church, but for labor leaders like Lech Walesa. Ronald Reagan's efforts on arms control and embrace of perestroika not only improved relations with the Soviet Union, but empowered dissidents throughout Eastern Europe.

Eloquent formulations continued to grace his speeches. One example came in the profound common sense of his Tucson speech, when he advised that "none of us can know exactly what triggered this vicious attack. None of us can know with any certainty what might have stopped those shots from being fired, or what thoughts lurked in the inner recesses of a violent man's mind. . . . But what we can't do is use this tragedy as one more occasion to turn on one another." A second stood out in his State Department lecture on the Arab Spring, where he declared that Americans, as a people, "have a stake not just in the stability of nations, but in the self-determination of individuals"—that to defend that stake we must "broaden our engagement beyond elites." Obama could not have been any clearer about where he stood on the

Arab Spring than in stating, "The United States supports a set of universal rights. And these rights include free speech, the freedom of peaceful assembly, the freedom of religion, equality for men and women under the rule of law, and the right to choose your own leaders—whether you live in Baghdad or Damascus, Sanaa or Tehran."

While journalists tended to pass over the philosophical content of Obama's speeches as mere boilerplate—preferring, as always, play by play on whichever political battle was in progress, from midterm elections to health care struggles to debt ceiling follies—others with a longer view, and more sensitive ear, paid attention to the rare statesman before them, because to take Obama seriously as a philosopher hardly amounted to a showy conceit.

One was the chair of the Harvard University history department, the distinguished intellectual historian James Kloppenberg, who voiced the judgment at book length. In *Reading Obama: Dreams, Hope, and the American Political Tradition,* Kloppenberg, coeditor of *A Companion to American Thought,* praised the president's "intellectual acuity and suppleness," crediting him with an "exceptionally sophisticated and sustained engagement with the history of American thought." For Kloppenberg, Obama counted as a "man of ideas" whose writings merited discussion as much as those of "John Adams, Jefferson, Madison, and John Quincy Adams."

In placing Obama as writer and intellectual in the "broader contexts of the American political tradition," Kloppenberg maintained that Obama had "a deeper interest in, and a firmer grasp on, America's past than has any President of the United States since Theodore Roosevelt and Woodrow Wilson." He judged Obama's two main books—*Dreams from My Father* and the usually less praised *The Audacity of Hope*—to be "the most substantial books written by anyone elected President of the United States since Woodrow Wilson." To Kloppenberg's mind, the books had made "original and important contributions" to American political thought.

Were these just the subjective kudos of a political fan of the president? It didn't seem so. In extending collegial respect to Obama as a thinker, Kloppenberg hadn't delivered an armchair effort, though the book included the scholar's rich thinking about America's intellectual tradition. Rather, he accumulated material and perspectives from many of Obama's friends and former teachers, among them Roger Boesche (an Obama professor and mentor at Occidental College), Harvard constitutional law scholar Laurence Tribe (Obama served as Tribe's research assistant from 1988 to 1989), and Brazilian philosopher and Harvard Law professor Roberto Mangabeira Unger, whose classes Obama took twice and with whom the young law student experienced "some sharp exchanges." As a result, Kloppenberg could offer penetrating observations on how writers and thinkers as varied as Emerson, Ralph Ellison, Langston Hughes, Max Weber, Friedrich Nietzsche, Reinhold Niebuhr, Gordon Wood and Howard Zinn had influenced Obama. Kloppenberg even gave intense attention to easily overlooked early writings by Obama, such as his article "Why Organize?" in the journal *Illinois Issues,* and his case note for the *Harvard Law Review* (January 1990) on fetal rights against mothers.

Whether the rest of the world, still in recovery from disenchantment with America during the George W. Bush administration—still coming down from a peak of virulent anti-Americanism that shot off the charts—would be willing to listen to an American president who spoke to them like Aurelius rather than Augustus, remained to be seen. But in doing so, his country, the United States, had his back.

Mocked overseas as a nation concerned only with the almighty buck and projection of power, America contained the broadest spectrum of ethnicities, philosophies and means of communication, the widest boundaries of freedom of expression, of any country in history.

Stereotyped by many of its own thinkers as a land of casual anti-intellectuals who lowered discourse to a crass demotic level, America used its insouciant independence to question all elite thought unable to make its case. Sneered at by some for predictable self-interested behavior and an inability to shift historic gears, it stunned the world, and delighted itself, by trusting a half-white, half-black man not yet fifty, a writer of books, partly raised in far-off Indonesia by a single mother, from a family without power or connections, to lead it into the new century and articulate its foremost ideals.

Would it be another "American century"? Probably not. But it looked to be the century of America the Philosophical.

So what, as Judith Moyers liked to ask?

And what did it mean for Americans?

For the man at the top, it meant "philosopher in chief" was the right tag. For Americans, it meant we were entitled to one.

Acknowledgments

In a world too full of mayhem, tragedy, injustice and sadness, it's a great privilege to live for decades as a writer and teacher. Writers and teachers should never forget how fortunate they are. I'm grateful to the multiple professional institutions—academic, journalistic and literary—that have permitted me to be so lucky for more than thirty years.

Institutions, of course, help and inspire you through people, and I'd like to offer my professional thanks here. I will always be grateful to Shelby Coffey, former Style editor at *The Washington Post,* for plucking a Yale philosophy grad student out of a pile of applications before him and introducing that young man to the excitement that was Style-section journalism in its glory days. To Gene Roberts, ambitious and principled former editor of *The Philadelphia Inquirer* and managing editor of *The New York Times,* I owe enduring thanks for his trust in making me book editor of the *Inquirer,* and later its book critic, at the untested age of thirty. Thank you, Gene, for my journalism career.

I also thank Maxwell King, Robert J. Rosenthal, Amanda Bennett, Walker Lundy and Anne Gordon—all top editors at the *Inquirer* in later years—for allowing me to flourish as a critic even when my academic ambitions beyond the newspaper, and mounting economic pressures on daily journalism, caused friction that made such support a tough call. For twelve years, I've also had the singular honor of being critic-at-large of *The Chronicle of Higher Education,* the finest, most sophisticated publication in the world on the many complex subjects it covers. To write for the *Chronicle* is to enjoy the best-educated readers and editors around. To Scott Jaschik, Doug Lederman and Ted Weidlein, who originally brought me aboard; to Malcolm Scully, who encouraged me with warm gentlemanly support; to Corbin Gwaltney, who keeps a top-notch publication humming; and to the whole superb crew I work with at the *Chronicle* today—Liz McMillen, Evan Goldstein, Jean Tamarin, Karen Winkler and my blood brother (and editor) Alexander Kafka, I owe you much, and cannot thank you enough.

In my academic life, I wish to fondly remember John Strassburger, the dynamic former president of Ursinus College, who died the month I began teaching there (September, 2010). I thank him for enthusiastically welcoming me to a wonderful new academic home. I can see why J. D. Salinger remained sweet on the place despite running away to Manhattan, and find it easy to visualize John Updike's parents falling in love there (as they did) amid its gentle charms. Other professional debts come to my mind as well. My years as professor of philosophy at Bennington College ended up fireworks from start to finish—thank you to my Bennington students and colleagues for making life up on the old dairy farm a nonstop philosophical, emotional and moral whirlwind. I also warmly thank one of academe's most rightly appreciated deans, Michael Delli Carpini of the Annenberg School for Communication, for many happy years of teaching at the University of Pennsylvania.

I've been fortunate in my career to receive generous support and invitations from a variety of other institutions that immeasurably broadened my outlook on philosophy, America and life. I thank Columbia University for my two exciting fellowships there, and the Shorenstein Center and Adams House for a bracing time at Harvard. The Fulbright Program—America's finest ambassadorial enterprise—has my gratitude forever for life-changing appointments in Germany and Russia. In the latter country, I especially thank my colleagues and students at Smolny College of St. Petersburg State University, and at Herzen University, for their bravery and ability to force me to think in new ways about my country—and theirs. To be invited to research and write at Vienna's Institut für die Wissenschaften vom Menschen as a Milena Jesenska Fellow—indeed, merely to be associated with the name of that tremendously courageous Czech journalist and translator of Kafka—was a privilege. I similarly thank the University of Cambridge in England and Tel Aviv University for enriching times there.

My agent, Georges Borchardt, the most distinguished practitioner of his trade, somehow manages to return e-mails quickly even from this minor member of his list. Georges—thank you for prodding me as this book inched its way to the finish line. Jonathan Segal, my distinguished editor at Knopf, combined toughness, critical acuity and steadfastness, and *America the Philosophical* is much better for it. My thanks, as well, to his always meticulous and helpful assistant, Joey McGarvey, for leading me through the thickets of production, and to Sonny Mehta and everyone else at Knopf. Their high standards, evident in every catalogue and book, keep it the great publishing house it has always been.

•

Bibliography

For a career book critic, there can never be enough books. My hope is that this bibliography, a mark, in part, of the singular productivity of writers and scholars in America, will assist readers in pursuing topics and issues discussed in *America the Philosophical*. The bibliography, like the text, is an argument for America the Philosophical.

Aarseth, Espen. *Cybertext: Perspectives on Ergodic Literature.* Johns Hopkins University Press. 1997.

Abt, Vicki, and Leonard Mustazza. *Coming After Oprah: Cultural Fallout in the Age of the TV Talk Show.* Bowling Green State University Popular Press. 1997.

Adler, Mortimer J. *Philosopher at Large: An Intellectual Autobiography, 1902–1976.* Macmillan. 1977.

———. *A Second Look in the Rearview Mirror.* Macmillan. 1992.

Aiken, William, and John Haldane, eds. *Philosophy and Its Public Role.* Imprint Academic. 2004.

Allen, Anita. *Why Privacy Isn't Everything: Feminist Reflections on Personal Accountability.* Rowman and Littlefield. 2003.

———. *The New Ethics: A Guided Tour of the Twenty-first-Century Moral Landscape.* Miramax Books. 2004.

———. *Unpopular Privacy: What Must We Hide?* Oxford University Press, 2011.

Allen, Gay Wilson. *William James: A Biography.* Viking. 1967.

Alston, William P. *Beyond Justification.* Cornell University Press. 2005.

Anderson, Walter. *The Upstart Spring: Esalen and the American Awakening.* Addison-Wesley. 1983.

Anton, John P. *American Naturalism and Greek Philosophy.* Prometheus Books. 2005.

Apel, Karl-Otto. *Charles S. Peirce: From Pragmatism to Pragmaticism.* Translated by John Michael Krois. Humanities Press. 1995.

Apolito, Paolo. *The Internet and the Madonna: Religious Visionary Experience on the Web.* University of Chicago Press. 2005.

Appiah, Kwame Anthony. *In My Father's House: Africa in the Philosophy of Culture.* Oxford University Press. 1992.

———. *The Ethics of Identity.* Princeton University Press. 2005.

———. *Cosmopolitanism: Ethics in a World of Strangers.* W. W. Norton. 2006.

———. *Experiments in Ethics.* Harvard University Press. 2008.

———. *The Honor Code: How Moral Revolutions Happen.* W. W. Norton. 2010.

Arcilla, Rene Vincente. *For the Love of Perfection: Richard Rorty and Liberal Education.* Routledge. 1995.

Arendt, Hannah. *The Origins of Totalitarianism.* Harcourt Brace. 1951.

———. *The Human Condition: A Study of the Central Dilemmas Facing Modern Man.* University of Chicago Press. 1958.

———. *Eichmann in Jerusalem: A Report on the Banality of Evil.* Viking Press. 1963.

———. *The Life of the Mind.* Harcourt Brace Jovanovich. 1978.

———. *Responsibility and Judgment.* Edited by Jerome Kohn. Schocken Books. 2003.

Arendt, Hannah, and Martin Heidegger. *Letters: 1925–1975.* Edited by Ursula Ludz. Translated from the German by Andrew Shields. Harcourt. 2004.

Aristophanes. *Clouds, Wasps, Birds.* Translated by Peter Meineck. Hackett Publishing Company. 1998.

Atchity, Kenneth, ed. *The Classical Greek Reader.* Oxford University Press. 1998.

Audard, Catherine. *John Rawls.* McGill-Queen's University Press. 2007.

Auxier, Randall E., and Lewis Edwin Hahn. *The Philosophy of Richard Rorty.* Library of Living Philosophers, vol. XXXII. Open Court Publishing Company. 2010.

Babbitt, Susan E., and Sue Campbell, eds. *Racism and Philosophy.* Cornell University Press. 1999.

Baer, Martha. *As Francesca.* Broadway Books. 1997.

Barber, Benjamin R. *The Truth of Power: Intellectual Affairs in the Clinton White House.* W. W. Norton. 2001.

Barrett, William. *Irrational Man: A Study in Existential Philosophy.* Doubleday. 1962.

———. *The Illusion of Technique.* Anchor Press/Doubleday. 1978.

———. *The Truants: Adventures Among the Intellectuals.* Anchor Press/Doubleday. 1982.

Barsky, Robert F. *Noam Chomsky: A Life of Dissent.* MIT Press. 1997.

Bartley, W. W. III. *Wittgenstein.* Quartet Books. 1977.

Bartscherer, Thomas, and Roderick Coover. *Switching Codes: Thinking Through Digital Technology in the Humanities and the Arts.* University of Chicago Press. 2011.

Barzun, Jacques. *A Stroll with William James.* University of Chicago Press. 1983.

Bauerlein, Mark. *The Dumbest Generation: How the Digital Age Stupefies Young Americans and Jeopardizes Our Future.* Jeremy Tarcher. 2008.

Bayoumi, Moustafa, and Andrew Rubin, eds. *The Edward Said Reader.* Vintage Books. 2000.

Beard, Charles. *An Economic Interpretation of the Constitution of the United States.* Free Press. 1941.

Beard, Henry, and Christopher Cerf. *The Official Politically Correct Dictionary and Handbook.* Villard Books. 1993.

Beauvoir, Simone de. *The Second Sex.* Translated by Constance Borde and Sheila Malovany-Chevallier. Alfred A. Knopf. 2010.

Becker, Gary, and Richard Posner. *Uncommon Sense: Economic Insights, from Marriage to Terrorism.* University of Chicago Press. 2009.

Bell, Daniel. *The End of Ideology.* Free Press. 1960.

Bellah, Robert N., Richard Madsen, William M. Sullivan, Ann Swidler, and Steven Tipton. *Habits of the Heart: Individualism and Commitment in American Life.* University of California Press. 1985.

Bell-Villada, Gene. *The Pianist Who Liked Ayn Rand: A Novella and 13 Stories.* Amador Press. 1998.

Benda, Julien. *The Betrayal of the Intellectuals.* Beacon Press. 1955.

Bender, Thomas. *A Nation Among Nations: America's Place in World History.* Hill & Wang. 2006.

Ben-Jochannan, Yosef A. A. *Africa: Mother of Western Civilization.* Black Classic Press. 1971.

Berman, Paul. *A Tale of Two Utopias: The Political Journey of the Generation of 1968.* W. W. Norton. 1996.

Berman, Paul, ed. *Debating P.C.: The Controversy over Political Correctness on College Campuses.* Delta. 1995.

Bernal, Martin. *Black Athena.* 2 vols. Rutgers University Press. 1989, 2001.

———. *Black Athena Writes Back: Martin Bernal Responds to His Critics.* Edited by David Chioni Moore. Duke University Press. 2001.

Birkerts, Sven. *The Gutenberg Elegies: The Fate of Reading in an Electronic Age.* Faber & Faber. 1994.

Bjork, Daniel. *B. F. Skinner: A Life.* Basic Books. 1993.

Bloom, Allan. *The Closing of the American Mind: How Higher Education Has Failed Democracy and Impoverished the Souls of Today's Students.* Simon & Schuster. 1987.

———. *Giants and Dwarfs: Essays, 1960–1990.* Simon & Schuster. 1990.

Bloom, Harold. *The Visionary Company: A Reading of English Romantic Poetry.* Cornell University Press. 1971.

———. *The Anxiety of Influence.* Oxford University Press. 1973

———. *Kabbalah and Criticism.* Seabury Press. 1975.

———. *A Map of Misreading.* Oxford University Press. 1975.

———. *The American Religion: The Emergence of the Post-Christian Nation.* Simon & Schuster. 1992.

———. *Omens of Millennium: The Gnosis of Angels, Dreams, and Resurrection.* Riverhead Books. 1996.

———. *The Anatomy of Influence.* Yale University Press. 2011.

Boler, Megan, ed. *Digital Media and Democracy.* MIT Press. 2008.

Bollinger, Lee. *Uninhibited, Robust, and Wide-Open: A Free Press for a New Century.* Oxford University Press. 2010.

Boyd, Melba Joyce. *Discarded Legacy: Politics and Poetics in the Life of Frances E. W. Harper, 1825–1911.* Wayne State University Press. 1994.

Brand, Stewart. *The Media Lab: Inventing the Future at M.I.T.* Viking Penguin. 1987.

Branden, Barbara. *The Passion of Ayn Rand.* Anchor Books. 1987.

Branden, Nathaniel. *My Years with Ayn Rand.* Jossey-Bass. 1999.

Brandom, Robert B., ed. *Rorty and His Critics.* Blackwell. 2000.

Branham, R. Bracht, and Marie-Odile Goulet-Caze, eds. *The Cynics: The Cynic Movement in Antiquity and Its Legacy.* University of California Press. 1996.

Brent, Joseph. *Charles Sanders Peirce: A Life.* Indiana University Press. 1993.

Britting, Jeffrey. *Ayn Rand.* Overlook. 2004.

Brockman, John. *The Third Culture: Beyond the Scientific Revolution.* Simon & Schuster. 1995.

Bronson, Po. *The First $20 Million Is Always the Hardest: A Silicon Valley Novel.* Random House. 1997.

Brook, James, and Iain A. Boal. *Resisting the Virtual Life: The Culture and Politics of Information.* City Lights. 1995.

Brooks, Thom, and Fabian Freyenhagen, eds. *The Legacy of John Rawls.* Continuum. 2005.

Brown, David S. *Richard Hofstadter: An Intellectual Biography.* University of Chicago Press. 2006.

Buell, Lawrence. *Emerson.* Harvard University Press. 2003.

Burke, Kenneth. *Language as Symbolic Action: Essays on Life, Literature, and Method.* University of California Press. 1966.

———. *Counter-Statement.* University of California Press. 1968.

———. *A Grammar of Motives.* University of California Press. 1969.

———. *A Rhetoric of Motives.* University of California Press. 1969.

———. *The Philosophy of Literary Form.* University of California Press. 1974.

Burns, Jennifer. *Goddess of the Market: Ayn Rand and the American Right.* Oxford University Press. 2009.

Burns, Timothy, ed. *After History? Francis Fukuyama and His Critics.* Littlefield, Adams. 1994.

Buruma, Ian, and Avishai Margalit. *Occidentalism: The West in the Eyes of Its Enemies.* Penguin Press. 2004.

Butler, Judith. *Bodies That Matter: On the Discursive Limits of "Sex."* Routledge. 1993.

———. *Excitable Speech: A Politics of the Performative.* Routledge. 1997.

———. *Precarious Life: The Powers of Mourning and Violence.* Verso. 2003.

———. *Undoing Gender.* Routledge. 2004.

———. *Gender Trouble: Feminism and the Subversion of Identity.* Routledge. 2006.

Campbell, James. *Recovering Benjamin Franklin: An Exploration of a Life of Science and Service.* Open Court. 1999.

Campbell, Joseph. *The Hero with a Thousand Faces.* Pantheon Books. 1949.

———. *The Masks of God.* 4 vols. Viking Press. 1959–1968.

———. *The Way of the Animal Powers.* Alfred Van Der Marck Editions. 1983.

———. *The Inner Reaches of Outer Space; Metaphor as Myth and as Religion.* Alfred Van Der Marck Editions. 1986.

———. *An Open Life: Joseph Campbell in Conversation with Michael Toms.* Selected and edited by John M. Maher and Dennie Briggs. Larson Publications. 1988.

———. *Sake & Satori: Asian Journals—Japan.* Edited and with a foreword by David Kudler. New World Library. 2002.

Capper, Charles. *Margaret Fuller: An American Romantic Life.* 2 vols. Oxford University Press. 2006.

Carr, Nicholas. *The Big Switch: Rewiring the World, from Edison to Google.* W. W. Norton. 2008.

———. *The Shallows: What the Internet Is Doing to Our Brains.* W. W. Norton. 2010.

Cathcart, Thomas, and Daniel Klein. *Plato and a Platypus Walk into a Bar . . . : Understanding Philosophy Through Jokes.* Abrams Image. 2007.

———. *Aristotle and an Aardvark Go to Washington.* Abrams Image. 2007.

———. *Heidegger and a Hippo Walk Through Those Pearly Gates.* Viking. 2009.

Cavell, Stanley. *The World Viewed: Reflections on the Ontology of Film.* Viking Press. 1971.

———. *Pursuits of Happiness: The Hollywood Comedy of Remarriage.* Harvard University Press. 1984.

———. *Themes Out of School: Effects and Causes.* North Point Press. 1984.

———. *In Quest of the Ordinary: Lines of Scepticism and Romanticism.* University of Chicago Press. 1989.

———. *The Senses of Walden.* Expanded ed. University of Chicago Press. 1992.

———. *A Pitch of Philosophy: Autobiographical Exercises.* Harvard University Press. 1994.

———. *Contesting Tears: The Hollywood Melodrama of the Unknown Woman.* University of Chicago Press. 1996.

———. *The Claim of Reason: Wittgenstein, Skepticism, Morality, and Tragedy.* Oxford University Press. 1999.

———. *Cities of Words: Pedagogical Letters on a Register of the Moral Life.* Harvard University Press. 2004.

———. *Philosophy the Day After Tomorrow.* Harvard University Press. 2005.

Ceaser, James W. *Reconstructing America: The Symbol of America in Modern Thought.* Yale University Press. 1997.

Chaplin, Tamara. *Turning on the Mind: French Philosophers on Television.* University of Chicago Press. 2007.

Chester, Jeff. *Digital Destiny: New Media and the Future of Democracy.* New Press. 2007.

Ching, Barbara, and Jennifer A. Wagner-Lawlor, eds. *The Scandal of Susan Sontag.* Columbia University Press. 2009.

Chomsky, Noam. *Chomsky on Miseducation.* Edited and introduced by Donaldo Macedo. Rowman and Littlefield. 2000.

———. *A New Generation Draws the Line: Kosovo, East Timor, and the Standards of the West.* Verso. 2001.

———. *9–11.* Seven Stories Press. 2001.

———. *Chomsky on Democracy and Education.* Edited by Carlos Otero. Routledge. 2002.

———. *Hegemony or Survival: America's Quest for Global Dominance.* Metropolitan Books. 2003.

Clack, Beverley. *Misogyny in the Western Philosophical Tradition: A Reader.* Routledge. 1999.

Cobb, Jennifer. *Cybergrace: The Search for God in the Digital World.* Crown Books. 1998.

Colaiaco, James A. *Frederick Douglass and the Fourth of July.* Palgrave. 2006.

Cole, Thomas. *The Origins of Rhetoric in Ancient Greece.* Johns Hopkins University Press. 1991.

Coles, Robert. *The Moral Life of Children.* Houghton Mifflin. 1986.

———. *The Political Life of Children.* Houghton Mifflin. 1986.

———. *The Call of Stories.* Houghton Mifflin. 1989.

———. *The Spiritual Life of Children.* Houghton Mifflin. 1990.

———. *The Call of Service: A Witness to Idealism.* Houghton Mifflin. 1993.

———. *Simone Weil: A Modern Pilgrimage.* Skylight Paths Publishing. 2001.

Commager, Henry Steele. *The American Mind: An Interpretation of American Thought and Character Since the 1880s.* Yale University Press. 1950.

Conley, John J. *The Suspicion of Virtue: Women Philosophers in Neoclassical France.* Cornell University Press. 2002.

Cotkin, George. *Existential America*. Johns Hopkins University Press. 2002.

Cottee, Simon, and Thomas Cushman, eds. *Christopher Hitchens and His Critics: Terror, Iraq, and the Left*. New York University Press. 2008.

Countryman, Edward. *Americans: A Collision of Histories*. Hill & Wang. 1996.

Coupland, Douglas. *Microserfs*. Harper Perennial. 2008.

Crimmins, Cathy. *How the Homosexuals Saved Civilization: The True and Heroic Story of How Gay Men Shaped the Modern World*. Jeremy Tarcher. 2004.

Crompton, Louis. *Homosexuality and Civilization*. Harvard University Press. 2003.

Cruse, Harold. *The Crisis of the Negro Intellectual*. William Morrow. 1967.

Curti, Merle. *The Growth of American Thought*. 2nd ed. Harper and Brothers. 1951.

D'Agostino, Fred. *Chomsky's System of Ideas*. Oxford University Press. 1986.

Damrosch, Leo. *Tocqueville's Discovery of America*. Farrar, Straus and Giroux. 2010.

Danto, Arthur C. *The Transfiguration of the Commonplace*. Harvard University Press. 1981.

———. *The Philosophical Disenfranchisement of Art*. Columbia University Press. 1986.

———. *Connections to the World: The Basic Concepts of Philosophy*. Harper & Row. 1989.

———. *Encounters and Reflections: Art in the Historical Present*. Farrar, Straus and Giroux. 1990.

———. *Beyond the Brillo Box: The Visual Arts in Post-historical Perspective*. Farrar, Straus and Giroux. 1992.

———. *Embodied Meanings: Critical Essays and Aesthetic Reflections*. Farrar, Straus and Giroux. 1994.

———. *The Madonna of the Future: Essays in a Pluralistic Art World*. Farrar, Straus and Giroux. 2000.

———. *The Abuse of Beauty: Aesthetics and the Concept of Art*. Open Court. 2003.

———. *Unnatural Wonders: Essays from the Gap Between Art and Life*. Farrar, Straus and Giroux. 2005.

Davidson, Donald. *Problems of Rationality*. Oxford University Press. 2004.

———. *Truth and Predication*. Harvard University Press. 2005.

———. *The Essential Davidson*. Oxford University Press. 2006.

Davidson, James. *The Greeks and Greek Love: A Bold New Exploration of the Ancient World*. Random House. 2009.

Davis, Angela Y. *Blues Legacies and Black Feminism: Gertrude "Ma" Rainey, Bessie Smith, and Billie Holiday*. Pantheon Books. 1998.

Deakin, Michael A. B. *Hypatia of Alexandria: Mathematician and Martyr*. Prometheus Books. 2007.

Dean, Tim. *Unlimited Intimacy: Reflections on the Subculture of Barebacking*. University of Chicago Press. 2009.

Dearborn, Mary. *Love in the Promised Land: The Story of Anzia Yezierska and John Dewey*. Free Press. 1988.

De Botton, Alain. *The Consolations of Philosophy*. Random House. 2000.

De Combray, Richard. *Lost in the City of Light*. Alfred A. Knopf. 1989.

Delany, Martin. *The Condition, Elevation, Emigration, and Destiny of the Colored People of the United States Politically Considered*. 1852. Arno. 1969.

De Romilly, Jacqueline. *The Great Sophists in Periclean Athens.* Oxford University Press. 1992.

Dertouzos, Michael. *What Will Be: How the New World of Information Will Change Our Lives.* HarperEdge. 1997.

———. *The Unfinished Revolution: How to Make Technology Work for Us—Instead of the Other Way Around.* Harper Perennial. 2002.

Dewey, John. *Democracy and Education.* Macmillan. 1916.

———. *Reconstruction in Philosophy.* Enlarged ed. Beacon Press. 1948.

———. *The Quest for Certainty: A Study of the Relation of Knowledge and Action.* Capricorn Books. 1960.

Dickstein, Morris, ed. *The Revival of Pragmatism: New Essays on Social Thought, Law, and Culture.* Duke University Press. 1998.

Diliberto, Gioia. *A Useful Woman: The Early Life of Jane Addams.* Scribner. 1999.

Douglass, Frederick. *Selected Speeches and Writings.* Edited by Philip S. Foner. Abridged and adapted by Yuval Taylor. Lawrence Hill Books. 1999.

Dover, Kenneth. *Greek Homosexuality.* Duckworth. 1978.

Dreyfus, Hubert L. *What Computers Still Can't Do: A Critique of Artificial Reason.* MIT Press. 1993.

D'Souza, Dinesh. *What's So Great About America.* Regnery Publishing. 2002.

Du Bois, W. E. B. *Writings.* Edited by Nathan Higgins. Library of America. 1986.

Durant, Will. *The Story of Philosophy.* Simon & Schuster. 1926.

———. *On the Meaning of Life.* Ray Long and Richard R. Smith, Inc. 1932.

———. *The Greatest Minds of All Time.* Compiled and edited by John Little. Simon & Schuster. 2002.

Durant, Will, and Ariel Durant. *The Story of Civilization.* 11 vols. Simon & Schuster. 1966.

Dworkin, Ronald. *Taking Rights Seriously.* Harvard University Press. 1977.

———. *A Matter of Principle.* Harvard University Press. 1985.

———. *Law's Empire.* Harvard University Press. 1986.

———. *Life's Dominion: An Argument About Abortion, Euthanasia, and Individual Freedom.* Alfred A. Knopf. 1993.

———. *Freedom's Law: The Moral Reading of the American Constitution.* Harvard University Press. 1996.

———. *Sovereign Virtue: The Theory and Practice of Equality.* Harvard University Press. 2000.

———. *Justice in Robes.* Harvard University Press. 2006.

———. *Justice for Hedgehogs.* Harvard University Press. 2011.

Dykhuizen, George. *The Life and Mind of John Dewey.* Southern Illinois University Press. 1973.

Dyson, Esther. *Release 2.0: A Design for Living in the Digital Age.* Broadway Books. 1997.

Dyson, Michael Eric. *Reflecting Black: African-American Cultural Criticism.* University of Minnesota Press. 1993.

———. *Between God and Gangsta Rap: Bearing Witness to Black Culture.* Oxford University Press. 1995.

——. *Making Malcolm: The Myth and Meaning of Malcolm X.* Oxford University Press. 1996.

——. *Race Rules: Navigating the Color Line.* Addison-Wesley. 1996.

——. *Holler If You Hear Me: Searching for Tupac Shakur.* Basic Civitas Books. 2001.

——. *Open Mike: Reflections on Philosophy, Race, Sex, Culture, and Religion.* Basic Civitas Books. 2003.

——. *Why I Love Black Women.* Basic Civitas Books. 2003.

——. *The Michael Eric Dyson Reader.* Basic Civitas Books. 2004.

——. *Pride: The Seven Deadly Sins.* Oxford University Press. 2006.

——. *Know What I Mean? Reflections on Hip Hop.* Basic Books. 2007.

Dzielska, Maria. *Hypatia of Alexandria.* Harvard University Press. 1995.

Eddington, Arthur. *The Nature of the Physical World.* Ann Arbor Paperbacks. 1968.

Edel, Leon. *Henry James.* 5 vols. J. P. Lippincott. 1953–1972.

Edgar, Andrew. *The Philosophy of Habermas.* McGill-Queen's University Press. 2005.

Edmundson, Mark. *Literature Against Philosophy: Plato to Derrida.* Cambridge University Press. 1995.

Elshtain, Jean Bethke. *Public Man, Private Woman: Women in Social and Political Thought.* Princeton University Press. 1981.

——. *Women and War.* Basic Books. 1987.

——. *Democracy on Trial.* Basic Books. 1995.

——. *Jane Addams and the Dream of American Democracy: A Life.* Basic Books. 2002.

——. *Just War Against Terrorism.* Basic Books. 2003.

Elshtain, Jean Bethke, ed. *The Jane Addams Reader.* Basic Books. 2002.

Emerson, Ralph Waldo. *Essays and Lectures.* Edited by Joel Porte. Library of America. 1983.

Eribon, Didier. *Michel Foucault.* Harvard University Press. 1992.

Etcoff, Nancy. *Survival of the Prettiest: The Science of Beauty.* Doubleday. 1999.

Ettinger, Elzbieta. *Hannah Arendt/Martin Heidegger.* Yale University Press. 1995.

Fallows, James. *Breaking the News: How the Media Undermine American Democracy.* Pantheon Books. 1996.

Faye, Emmanuel. *Heidegger: The Introduction of Nazism into Philosophy.* Yale University Press. 2009.

Feinstein, Howard M. *Becoming William James.* Cornell University Press. 1984.

Finley, M. I. *The Use and Abuse of History.* Viking Press. 1975.

Fisher, Paul. *House of Wits: An Intimate Portrait of the James Family.* Henry Holt. 2008.

Fite, David. *Harold Bloom: The Rhetoric of Romantic Vision.* University of Massachusetts Press. 1985.

Fletcher, George. *A Crime of Self-Defense: Bernhard Goetz and the Law on Trial.* University of Chicago Press. 1990.

——. *Loyalty: An Essay on the Morality of Relationships.* Oxford University Press. 1993.

Fletcher, George, and Jens David Ohlin. *Defending Humanity: When Force Is Justified and Why.* Oxford University Press. 2008.

Flower, Elisabeth, and Murray G. Murphey. *A History of Philosophy in America.* 2 vols. G. P. Putnam's Sons. 1977.

Fogelin, Robert. *Wittgenstein.* 2nd ed. Routledge. 1987.

Fone, Byrne. *Homophobia: A History.* Henry Holt. 2000.

Fontaine, William. *Reflections on Segregation, Desegregation, Power, and Morals.* Charles C. Thomas. 1967.

Foot, Kirsten A., and Steven M. Schneider. *Web Campaigning.* MIT Press. 2006.

Foucault, Michel. *Madness and Civilization.* Pantheon Books. 1965.

———. *The Order of Things.* Pantheon Books. 1971.

———. *The Birth of the Clinic: An Archeology of Medical Perception.* Pantheon Books. 1973.

———. *Discipline and Punish: The Birth of the Prison.* Pantheon Books. 1978.

Fox, Jeremy. *Chomsky and Globalization.* Icon Books. 2001.

Fox, Richard Wightman, and James T. Kloppenberg. *A Companion to American Thought.* Wiley-Blackwell. 1998.

Frank, Nathaniel. *Unfriendly Fire: How the Gay Ban Undermines the Military and Weakens America.* St. Martin's Press. 2009.

Frankfurt, Harry. *On Bullshit.* Princeton University Press. 2005.

Franklin, Benjamin. *Writings.* Edited by J. A. Leo Lamay. Library of America. 1987.

Fraterrigo, Elizabeth. Playboy *and the Making of the Good Life in Modern America.* Oxford University Press. 2009.

Frauenfelder, Mark. *Made by Hand: Searching for Meaning in a Throwaway World.* Portfolio/Penguin Group. 2010.

Freeland, Cynthia, and Thomas E. Wartenberg, eds. *Philosophy and Film.* Routledge. 1995.

Freeman, Samuel. *Justice and the Social Contract: Essays on Rawlsian Political Philosophy.* Oxford University Press. 2007.

———. *Rawls.* Routledge. 2007.

Freeman, Samuel, ed. *The Cambridge Companion to Rawls.* Cambridge University Press. 2003.

Freud, Sigmund. *The Future of an Illusion.* Hogarth Press. 1961.

Fricker, Miranda, and Jennifer Hornsby, eds. *The Cambridge Companion to Feminism in Philosophy.* Cambridge University Press. 2000.

Friedan, Betty. *The Second Stage.* Summit Books. 1981.

———. *The Feminist Mystique.* With a new introduction. W. W. Norton. 1997.

———. *Life So Far: A Memoir.* Simon & Schuster. 2000.

Fukuyama, Francis. *The End of History and the Last Man.* Free Press. 1992.

———. *The Great Disruption: Human Nature and the Reconstitution of Social Order.* Free Press. 1999.

———. *Our Posthuman Future: Consequences of the Biotechnology Revolution.* Farrar, Straus and Giroux. 2002.

———. *State-Building: Governance and World Order in the 21st Century.* Cornell University Press. 2004.

———. *America at the Crossroads: Democracy, Power, and the Neoconservative Legacy.* Yale University Press. 2006.

———. *The Origins of Political Order: From Prehuman Times to the French Revolution.* W. W. Norton. 2011.

Fulghum, Robert. *All I Really Need to Know I Learned in Kindergarten.* Ballantine Books. 1986.

———. *It Was on Fire When I Lay Down on It.* Ivy Books. 1991.

———. *Uh-oh: Some Observations from Both Sides of the Refrigerator Door.* Ballantine Books. 1991.

———. *Maybe (Maybe Not): Second Thoughts from a Secret Life.* Villard Books. 1993.

———. *From Beginning to End: The Rituals of Our Lives.* Villard Books. 1995.

———. *What On Earth Have I Done? Stories, Observations, and Affirmations.* St. Martin's Press. 2007.

Fuller, Margaret. *Woman in the Nineteenth Century.* 1845. Edited by Larry J. Reynolds. W. W. Norton. 1998.

Fussell, Paul. *The Great War and Modern Memory.* Oxford University Press. 1977.

———. *Class: A Guide Through the American Status System.* Simon & Schuster. 1983.

———. *Bad or, The Dumbing of America.* Summit Books. 1991.

Gaarder, Jostein. *Sophie's World: A Novel About the History of Philosophy.* Translated by Paulette Moller. Farrar, Straus and Giroux. 1994.

Gaggi, Silvio. *From Text to Hypertext: Decentering the Subject in Fiction, Film, the Visual Arts, and Electronic Media.* University of Pennsylvania Press. 1997.

Gainous, Jason, and Kevin M. Wagner. *Rebooting American Politics: The Internet Revolution.* Rowman and Littlefield. 2011.

Garber, Marjorie. *Bisexuality and the Eroticism of Everyday Life.* Routledge. 2000.

Gardner, Howard. *Creating Minds: An Anatomy of Creativity as Seen Through the Lives of Freud, Einstein, Picasso, Stravinsky, Eliot, Graham, and Gandhi.* Basic Books. 1994.

———. *Frames of Mind.* Basic Books. 2004.

Gascoigne, Neil. *Richard Rorty: Liberalism, Irony, and the Ends of Philosophy.* Polity. 2008.

Gaskins, Richard H. *Burdens of Proof in Modern Discourse.* Yale University Press. 1992.

Gates, Bill. *The Road Ahead.* Rev. ed. Penguin Books. 1996.

Gates, Henry Louis Jr., and Cornel West. *The Future of the Race.* Alfred A. Knopf. 1996.

Geary, James. *I Is an Other: The Secret Life of Metaphor and How It Shapes the Way We See the World.* Harper. 2011.

Gerlernter, David. *Americanism: The Fourth Great Western Religion.* Doubleday. 2007.

Gibson, Roger F. Jr. *The Philosophy of W. V. Quine: An Expository Essay.* University of South Florida. 1982.

Gibson, William. *Neuromancer.* Ace Books. 1984.

Gladstein, Mimi, and Chris Sciabarra, eds. *Feminist Interpretations of Ayn Rand.* Penn State University Press. 1999.

Glaude, Eddie S. Jr. *In a Shade of Blue: Pragmatism and the Politics of Black America.* University of Chicago Press. 2007.

Goetzmann, William H. *Beyond the Revolution: A History of American Thought from Paine to Pragmatism.* Basic Books. 2009.

Gordon, Lewis R. *Existence in Black. An Anthology of Black Existential Philosophy.* Routledge. 1997.

———. *Existentia Africana: Understanding African Existentialist Thought.* Routledge. 2000.

Gottlieb, Anthony. *The Dream of Reason: A History of Philosophy from the Greeks to the Renaissance*. W. W. Norton. 2000.

Gould, Timothy. *Hearing Things: Voice and Method in the Writing of Stanley Cavell*. University of Chicago Press. 1998.

Graham, Gordon. *The Internet: A Philosophical Inquiry*. Routledge. 1999.

Greenberg, Rabbi Steven. *Wrestling with God and Men: Homosexuality in the Jewish Tradition*. University of Wisconsin Press. 2004.

Greene, Rachel. *Internet Art*. Thames & Hudson. 2004.

Gross, Neil. *Richard Rorty: The Making of an American Philosopher*. University of Chicago Press. 2008.

Grossman, Lawrence. *The Electronic Republic: Reshaping Democracy in the Information Age*. Viking. 1995.

Grudin, Robert. *American Vulgar: The Politics of Manipulation Versus the Culture of Awareness*. Shoemaker and Hoard. 2006.

Gura, Philip F. *American Transcendentalism: A History*. Hill & Wang. 2007.

Guthrie, W. K. C. *The Greek Philosophers from Thales to Aristotle*. Harper & Row. 1950.

Gutmann, Amy, and Dennis Thompson. *Democracy and Disagreement: Why Moral Conflict Cannot Be Avoided in Politics, and What Should Be Done About It*. Harvard University Press. 1996.

Guttenplan, D. D. *American Radical: The Life and Times of I. F. Stone*. Farrar, Straus and Giroux. 2009.

Haapala, Arto, Jerrold Levinson, and Veikko Rantala. *The End of Art and Beyond: Essays After Danto*. Humanities Press. 1997.

Hall, David L. *Richard Rorty: Prophet and Poet of the New Pragmatism*. State University of New York Press. 1994.

Hall, George. *The Ingenious Mind of Nature: Deciphering the Patterns of Man, Society, and the Universe*. Basic Books. 2001.

Hall, John, and Charles Lindholm. *Is America Breaking Apart?* Princeton University Press. 1999.

Hamilton, Alexander, John Jay, and James Madison. *The Federalist*. Edited and with an introduction by Robert Scigliano. Modern Library. 2000.

Harris, Leonard, ed. *The Critical Pragmatism of Alain Locke*. Rowman and Littlefield. 1999.

Harris, Leonard, and Charles Molesworth. *Alain L. Locke: The Biography of a Philosopher*. University of Chicago Press. 2008.

Harris, Leonard, Scott Pratt, and Anne Waters, eds. *American Philosophies: An Anthology*. Blackwell. 2002.

Harris, Randy Allen. *The Linguistics Wars*. Oxford University Press. 1993.

Hartz, Louis. *The Liberal Tradition in America*. Harcourt Brace. 1983.

Haskins, Ekaterina. *Logos and Power in Isocrates and Aristotle*. University of South Carolina Press. 2004.

Hefner, Hugh. *The Playboy Philosophy*. HMH Publishing Company. 1963.

Heilbrun, Carolyn. *Writing a Woman's Life*. W. W. Norton. 1988.

Heim, Michael. *The Metaphysics of Virtual Reality*. Oxford University Press. 1993.

Heller, Anne Conover. *Ayn Rand and the World She Made*. Anchor Books. 2010.

Helprin, Mark. *Digital Barbarians: A Writer's Manifesto.* Harper. 2009.

Henderson, Bill, ed. *Minutes of the Lead Pencil Club: Pulling the Plug on the Electronic Revolution.* Pushcart Press. 1996.

Hennessee, Judith. *Betty Friedan: A Life.* Random House. 1999.

Henriksen, Louise Levitas. *Anzia Yezierska: A Writer's Life.* Rutgers University Press. 1988.

Herman, Andrew, and Thomas Swiss, eds. *The World Wide Web and Contemporary Cultural Theory.* Routledge, 2000.

Hietala, Thomas R. *Manifest Design: American Exceptionalism and Empire.* Rev. ed. Cornell University Press. 2003.

Hinks, Peter P. *To Awaken My Afflicted Brethren: David Walker and the Problem of Antebellum Slave Resistance.* Penn State University Press. 1997.

Hirsch, E. D. Jr. *Cultural Literacy: What Every American Needs to Know.* Houghton Mifflin. 1987.

———. *The Making of Americans: Democracy and Our Schools.* Yale University Press. 2009.

Hitchens, Christopher. *The Missionary Position: Mother Teresa in Theory and Practice.* Verso. 1997.

———. *No One Left to Lie To: The Values of the Worst Family.* Verso. 2000.

———. *Letters to a Young Contrarian: The Art of Mentoring.* Basic Books. 2001.

———. *God Is Not Great: How Religion Poisons Everything.* Twelve. 2009.

Hoffer, Eric. *The True Believer: Thoughts on the Nature of Mass Movements.* Harper & Row. 1951.

Hoffman, Edward. *The Right to Be Human: A Biography of Abraham Maslow.* Jeremy Tarcher. 1989.

Hofstadter, Richard. *Anti-Intellectualism in American Life.* Alfred A. Knopf. 1963.

Holland, A. J. *Philosophy, Its History and Historiography.* D. Reidel. 1985.

Hollinger, David A. *Postethnic America: Beyond Multiculturalism.* Revised and updated. Basic Books. 2000.

Hollinger, David A., and Charles Capper. *The American Intellectual Tradition.* Vol. I, 1630–1865. Vol. II, 1865 to the Present. Oxford University Press. 1997.

Holtzman, Steven. *Digital Mosaics: The Aesthetics of Cyberspace.* Simon & Schuster. 1997.

Hook, Sidney. *Out of Step: An Unquiet Life in the 20th Century.* Harper & Row. 1987.

———. *Convictions.* Prometheus Books. 1990.

Hookway, Christopher. *Quine: Language, Experience, and Reality.* Stanford University Press. 1988.

Horowitz, Daniel. *Betty Friedan and the Making of* The Feminist Mystique: *The American Left, the Cold War, and Modern Feminism.* University of Massachusetts Press. 1998.

Howe, Irving. *World of Our Fathers: The Journey of the East European Jews to America and the Life They Found and Made.* Simon & Schuster. 1976.

———. *A Margin of Hope: An Intellectual Autobiography.* Harcourt Brace Jovanovich. 1982.

Hughes, Robert. *Culture of Complaint: The Fraying of America.* Oxford University Press. 1993.

Hussein, Abdirahman A. *Edward Said: Criticism and Society.* Verso. 2002.

Hutchinson, George. *The Harlem Renaissance in Black and White.* Harvard University Press. 1995.

Isocrates. *Works.* Vols. I and II, with an English translation by George Norlin. Vol. III, with an English translation by Larue Van Hook. Edited by George Norlin. Loeb Classical Library. Harvard University Press. 1928–1945.

———. *Isocrates I.* Translated by David Mirhady and Yun Lee Too. University of Texas Press. 2000.

Jacobs, Margaret C. *Strangers Nowhere in the World: The Rise of Cosmopolitanism in Early Modern Europe.* University of Pennsylvania Press. 2006.

Jacoby, Russell. *The Last Intellectuals: American Culture in the Age of Academe.* Basic Books. 1987.

Jacoby, Susan. *The Age of American Unreason.* Pantheon. 2008.

Jaeger, Werner. *Paedeia: The Ideals of Greek Culture.* 3 vols. Oxford University Press. 1943–1945.

James, William. *The Principles of Psychology.* 2 vols. Henry Holt. 1890.

———. *The Varieties of Religious Experience: A Study in Human Nature.* Longmans, Green. 1902.

———. *Pragmatism.* Harvard University Press. 1975.

———. *A Pluralistic Universe.* Harvard University Press. 1977.

———. *Writings, 1902–1910.* Edited by Bruce Kuklick. Library of America. 1987.

Jeans, James. *The Mysterious Universe.* E. P. Dutton. 1958.

Johnson, Mark. *The Body in the Mind: The Bodily Basis of Meaning, Imagination, and Reason.* University of Chicago Press. 1987.

———. *The Meaning of the Body: Aesthetics of Human Understanding.* University of Chicago Press. 2007.

Johnson, Steven. *Interface Culture: How New Technology Transforms the Way We Create and Communicate.* HarperEdge. 1997.

Jones, Dylan. *IPod, Therefore I Am: Thinking Inside the White Box.* Bloomsbury. 2005.

Joseph, Lawrence E. *Common Sense: Why It's No Longer Common.* Addison-Wesley. 1994.

Joyce, Michael. *afternoon: a story.* Eastgate Systems CD-ROM. 1999.

Kadrey, Richard. *Métrophage.* Gollancz. 1989.

Kagan, Robert. *Dangerous Nation: America's Place in the World from Its Earliest Days to the Dawn of the Twentieth Century.* Alfred A. Knopf. 2006.

Kallen, Horace. *Culture and Democracy in the United States.* Transaction Publishers. 1997.

Kammen, Michael. *A Machine That Would Go of Itself: The Constitution in American Culture.* Alfred A. Knopf. 1986.

———. *Mystic Chords of Memory: The Transformation of Tradition in American Culture.* Alfred A. Knopf. 1991.

———. *The Lively Arts: Gilbert Seldes and the Transformation of Cultural Criticism in the United States.* Oxford University Press. 1996.

———. *American Culture, American Tastes: Social Change and the 20th Century.* Alfred A. Knopf. 1999.

Kaplan, Robert. *The Nothing That Is: A Natural History of Zero.* Oxford University Press. 2000.

Kaplan, Robert, and Ellen Kaplan. *Hidden Harmonies: The Lives and Times of the Pythagorean Theorem.* Bloomsbury. 2011.

Karasu, Bilge. *Night.* Louisiana State University Press. 1994.

Kasulis, Thomas P., and Robert Cummings Neville. *The Recovery of Philosophy in America: Essays in Honor of John E. Smith.* State University of New York Press. 1997.

Katz, Jon. *Virtuous Reality: How America Surrendered Discussion of Moral Values to Opportunists, Nitwits, and Blockheads like William Bennett.* Random House. 1997.

Katz, Michael B., and Mark J. Stern. *One Nation Divisible: What America Was and What It Is Becoming.* Russell Sage Foundation. 2006.

Kaufman, Michael T. *Soros: The Life and Times of a Messianic Billionaire.* Alfred A. Knopf. 2002.

Kazin, Alfred. *On Native Grounds: An Interpretation of Modern American Prose Literature.* Harcourt, Brace. 1942.

Kazin, Michael, and Joseph A. McCartin, eds. *Americanism: New Perspectives on the History of an Ideal.* University of North Carolina. 2006.

Kelly, Kevin. *Out of Control: The New Biology of Machines, Social Systems, and the Economic World.* Addison-Wesley. 1994.

———. *New Rules for the New Economy: 10 Radical Strategies for a Connected World.* Viking. 1998.

———. *What Technology Wants.* Viking. 2010.

Kelly, Mary, ed. *The Portable Margaret Fuller.* Penguin Books. 1994.

Kennan, George. *Around the Cragged Hill: A Personal and Political Philosophy.* W. W. Norton. 1994.

Kennedy, George A. *Classical Rhetoric and Its Christian and Secular Tradition from Ancient to Modern Times.* University of North Carolina Press. 1980.

———. *A New History of Classical Rhetoric.* Princeton University Press. 1994.

Kennedy, Liam. *Susan Sontag: Mind as Passion.* Manchester University Press. 1995.

Kennedy, Paul. *The Rise and Fall of the Great Powers: Economic Change and Military Conflict from 1500 to 2000.* Random House. 1998.

Kloppenberg, James. *Reading Obama: Dreams, Hope, and the American Political Tradition.* Princeton University Press. 2011.

Knobe, Joshua, and Shaun Nichols. *Experimental Philosophy.* Oxford University Press. 2008.

Kolenda, Konstantin. *Rorty's Humanistic Pragmatism: Philosophy Democratized.* University of South Florida Press. 1990.

Kraut, Richard. *Socrates and the State.* Princeton University Press. 1984.

Kukathas, Chandran, and Philip Pettit. *Rawls: A Theory of Justice and Its Critics.* Stanford University Press. 1990.

Kuklick, Bruce. *The Rise of American Philosophy: Cambridge, Massachusetts, 1860–1930.* Yale University Press. 1977.

———. *Churchmen and Philosophers: From Jonathan Edwards to John Dewey.* Yale University Press. 1985.

———. *A History of Philosophy in America, 1720–2000.* Oxford University Press. 2002.

———. *Black Philosopher, White Academy: The Career of William Fontaine.* University of Pennsylvania Press. 2008.

Kurtz, Howard. *Media Circus: The Trouble with America's Newspapers.* Times Books. 1993.
———. *Hot Air: All Talk, All the Time.* Times Books. 1996.
———. *Spin Cycle: Inside the Clinton Propaganda Machine.* Free Press. 1998.
Kurtz, Paul, ed. *American Philosophy in the Twentieth Century.* Macmillan. 1966.
Lacey, A. R. *Robert Nozick.* Princeton University Press. 2001.
Ladd, John. *The Structure of a Moral Code: A Philosophical Analysis of Ethical Discourse Applied to the Ethics of the Navajo Indians.* Harvard University Press. 1957.
Lakoff, George. *Women, Fire, and Dangerous Things: What Categories Reveal About the Mind.* University of Chicago Press. 1987.
———. *Moral Politics: What Conservatives Know That Liberals Don't.* University of Chicago Press. 1996.
———. *The Political Mind: Why You Can't Understand 21st-Century American Politics with an 18th-Century Brain.* Viking. 2008.
Lakoff, George, and Mark Johnson. *Philosophy in the Flesh: The Embodied Mind and Its Challenge to Western Thought.* Basic Books. 1999.
———. *Metaphors We Live By.* University of Chicago Press. 1980. Reprinted with afterword, 2003.
Lakoff, George, and Rafael E. Nunez. *Where Mathematics Comes From: How the Embodied Mind Brings Mathematics into Being.* Basic Books. 2000.
Lakoff, George, and Mark Turner. *More than Cool Reason: A Field Guide to Poetic Metaphor.* University of Chicago Press. 1989.
Lakoff, Sanford. *Max Lerner: Pilgrim in the Promised Land.* University of Chicago Press. 1998.
Lambert, Ellen Zetzel. *The Face of Love: Feminism and the Beauty Question.* Beacon Press. 1995.
Landauer, Thomas K. *The Trouble with Computers: Usefulness, Usability, and Productivity.* MIT Press. 1995.
Landow, George. *Hypertext 2.0: The Convergence of Contemporary Critical Theory and Technology.* 2nd ed. Johns Hopkins University Press. 1997.
Lang, Beryl. *Heidegger's Silence.* Cornell University Press. 1996.
Lanier, Jaron. *You Are Not a Gadget: A Manifesto.* Alfred A. Knopf. 2010.
Lear, Linda. *Rachel Carson: Witness for Nature.* Henry Holt. 1997.
Lears, Jackson. *Rebirth of a Nation: The Making of Modern America, 1877–1920.* Harper. 2009.
Lefkowitz, Mary. *Not Out of Africa: How Afrocentrism Became an Excuse to Teach Myth as History.* Basic Books. 1996.
———. *History Lesson: A Race Odyssey.* Yale University Press. 2008.
Lefkowitz, Mary R., and Guy MacLean Rogers, eds. *Black Athena Revisited.* University of North Carolina Press. 1996.
Lehning, Percy B. *John Rawls: An Introduction.* Cambridge University Press. 2009.
Lerner, Gerda. *The Creation of Patriarchy.* Oxford University Press. 1987.
———. *The Creation of Feminist Consciousness: From the Middle Ages to Eighteen-seventy.* Oxford University Press. 1993.
Lerner, Max. *It Is Later Than You Think: The Need for a Militant Democracy.* Viking Press. 1938.

———. *America as a Civilization: Life and Thought in the United States Today.* Simon & Schuster. 1957.

———. *Thomas Jefferson, America's Philosopher-King.* Edited and with an introduction by Robert Schmuhl. Transaction Publishers. 1996.

Levine, Lawrence W. *Highbrow/Lowbrow: The Emergence of Cultural Hierarchy in America.* Harvard University Press. 1988.

———. *The Opening of the American Mind: Canons, Culture, and History.* Beacon Press. 1996.

Levine, Robert S. *Martin Delany, Frederick Douglass, and the Politics of Representative Identity.* University of North Carolina Press. 1997.

Levy, Bernard-Henri. *American Vertigo: Traveling America in the Footsteps of Tocqueville.* Random House. 2006.

Levy-Bruehl, Lucien. *How Natives Think.* Princeton University Press. 1985.

Lewis, David Levering. *When Harlem Was in Vogue.* Penguin. 1997.

———. *W. E. B. Du Bois: Biography of Race, 1868–1919.* Owl Books. 1993.

———. *W. E. B. Du Bois: The Fight for Equality and the American Century, 1919–1963.* Henry Holt. 2000.

Lind, Michael. *The Next American Nation: The New Nationalism and the Fourth American Revolution.* Free Press. 1995.

Linn, James Weber. *Jane Addams: A Biography.* University of Illinois Press. 2000.

Lippmann, Walter. *Public Opinion.* Mentor Books. 1955.

———. *A Preface to Morals.* Transaction Publishers. 1982.

Lipset, Seymour Martin. *American Exceptionalism: A Double-Edged Sword.* W. W. Norton. 1996.

Lipset, Seymour Martin, and Gary Marks. *It Didn't Happen Here: Why Socialism Failed in the United States.* W. W. Norton. 2000.

Livingston, James. *Pragmatism, Feminism, and Democracy: Rethinking the Politics of American History.* Routledge. 2001.

Lloyd, Genevieve. *The Man of Reason: "Male" and "Female" in Western Philosophy.* Methuen. 1984.

Locke, Alain, ed. *The New Negro.* Albert and Charles Boni Inc. 1925.

Locke, Alain LeRoy. *Race Contacts and Interracial Relations.* Edited and with an introduction by Jeffrey C. Stewart. Howard University Press. 1992.

Lombard, Jean. *Isocrate: Rhetorique et Education.* Editions Klincksieck. 1990.

Lopate, Philip. *Notes on Sontag.* Princeton University Press. 2009.

Ludlow, Peter, and Mike Godwin, eds. *High Noon on the Electronic Frontier: Conceptual Issues in Cyberspace.* A Bradford Book. 1996.

MacIntyre, Alasdair. *Whose Justice? Which Rationality?* University of Notre Dame Press. 1988.

Mailloux, Steven, ed. *Rhetoric, Sophistry, Pragmatism.* Cambridge University Press. 1995.

Malachowski, Alan. *Richard Rorty.* Princeton University Press. 2002.

Malachowski, Alan, ed. *Reading Rorty.* Blackwell. 1999.

Malcolm, Norman. *Ludwig Wittgenstein: A Memoir.* Oxford University Press. 1967.

Marcus, Greil. *The Shape of Things to Come: Prophecy and the American Voice.* Farrar, Straus and Giroux. 2006.

Marcuse, Herbert. *Eros and Civilization: A Philosophical Inquiry into Freud.* Beacon Press. 1955.

———. *One-Dimensional Man: Studies in the Ideology of Advanced Industrial Society.* Beacon Press. 1970.

Marinoff, Lou. *Plato, Not Prozac! Applying Philosophy to Everyday Problems.* Harper-Collins. 1999.

———. *The Big Questions: How Philosophy Can Change Your Life.* Bloomsbury. 2003.

———. *The Middle Way: Finding Happiness in a World of Extremes.* Sterling. 2007.

Martin, Jay. *The Education of John Dewey: A Biography.* Columbia University Press. 2002.

Martin, Rex, and David A. Reidy, eds. *Rawls's Law of Peoples: A Realistic Utopia?* Blackwell. 2006.

Maslow, Abraham. *Toward a Psychology of Being.* 2nd ed. Van Nostrand Reinhold. 1968.

———. *Motivation and Personality.* HarperCollins. 1987.

Matthiessen, F. O. *American Renaissance: Art and Expression in the Age of Emerson and Whitman.* Oxford University Press. 1941.

———. *The James Family.* Alfred A. Knopf. 1947.

Mayers, David. *Dissenting Voices in America's Rise to Power.* Cambridge University Press. 2007.

McCarthy, Thomas. *The Critical Theory of Jürgen Habermas.* MIT Press. 1978.

McCaughey, Martha, and Michael D. Ayers, eds. *Cyberactivism: Online Activism in Theory and Practice.* Routledge. 2003.

McCloskey, Deirdre. *The Rhetoric of Economics.* 2nd ed. University of Wisconsin Press. 1998.

McCormick, John. *George Santayana: A Biography.* Alfred A. Knopf. 1987.

McCumber, John. *Time in the Ditch: American Philosophy and the McCarthy Era.* Northwestern University Press. 2001.

McDonald, Forrest. *Novis Ordo Seclorum: The Intellectual Origins of the Constitution.* University Press of Kansas. 1986.

McGary, Howard. *Between Slavery and Freedom: Philosophy and American Slavery.* Indiana University Press. 1992.

McGinn, Colin. *Mindfucking: A Critique of Mental Manipulation.* Acumen. 2008.

McIlwain, Charles. *Constitutionalism Ancient and Modern.* Cornell University Press. 1947.

Melkonian, Markar. *Richard Rorty's Politics: Liberalism at the End of the American Century.* Humanity Books. 1999.

Menand, Louis. *Pragmatism: A Reader.* Vintage Books. 1997.

———. *The Metaphysical Club: A Story of Ideas in America.* Farrar, Straus and Giroux. 2001.

———. *American Studies.* Farrar, Straus and Giroux. 2002.

Mencken, H. L. *The American Language.* 4th ed. Alfred A. Knopf. 1962.

Miller, Dennis. *I Rant, Therefore I Am.* Doubleday. 2000.

Miller, James. *The Passion of Michel Foucault.* Simon & Schuster. 1993.

———. *Examined Lives: From Socrates to Nietzsche.* Farrar, Straus and Giroux. 2010.

Miller, Perry. *The Life of the Mind in America from the Revolution to the Civil War.* Harcourt, Brace & World. 1965.

Mills, Charles W. *The Racial Contract.* Cornell University Press. 1997.

———. *Blackness Visible: Essays on Philosophy and Race.* Cornell University Press. 1998.

Misak, Cheryl, ed. *The Oxford Handbook of American Philosophy.* Oxford University Press. 2008.

Mohr, Richard. *Gays/Justice: A Study of Ethics, Society, and Law.* Columbia University Press. 1988.

———. *Gay Ideas: Outing and Other Controversies.* Beacon Press. 1992.

———. *A More Perfect Union: Why Straight America Must Stand Up for Gay Rights,* revised and republished as *The Long Arc of Justice: Lesbian and Gay Marriage, Equality, and Rights.* Columbia University Press. 2005.

Mooney, Chris, and Sheril Kirshenbaum. *Unscientific America: How Scientific Illiteracy Threatens Our Future.* Basic Books. 2009.

Moor, James H., and Terrell Ward Bynum. *Cyberphilosophy: The Intersection of Computing and Philosophy.* Blackwell. 2002.

Morgenbesser, Sidney, ed. *Dewey and His Critics.* Journal of Philosophy Inc. 1977.

Morozov, Evgeny. *The Net Delusion: The Dark Side of Internet Freedom.* PublicAffairs. 2011.

Morris, Thomas. *Philosophy for Dummies.* IDG Books. 1999.

Moses, Wilson Jeremiah. *Black Messiahs and Uncle Toms: Social and Literary Manipulations of a Religious Myth.* Penn State University Press. 1993.

———. *Creative Conflict in African American Thought: Frederick Douglass, Alexander Crummell, Booker T. Washington, W. E. B. Du Bois, and Marcus Garvey.* Cambridge University Press. 2004.

Moses, Wilson Jeremiah, ed. *Classical Black Nationalism: From the American Revolution to Marcus Garvey.* New York University Press. 1996.

Mossberger, Karen, Caroline J. Tolbert, and Ramona S. McNeal. *Digital Citizenship: The Internet, Society, and Participation.* MIT Press. 2008.

Moyers, Bill. *A World of Ideas.* Doubleday. 1989.

———. *Healing and the Mind.* Doubleday. 1993.

———. *Moyers on Democracy.* Doubleday. 2008.

Muelder, Walter G., and Laurence Sears, eds. *The Development of American Philosophy.* Houghton Mifflin. 1940.

Murdoch, Iris. *Under the Net.* Viking Press. 1954.

Murray, Janet. *Hamlet on the Holodeck: The Future of Narrative in Cyberspace.* Free Press. 1997.

Myers, Gerald. *William James: His Life and Thought.* Yale University Press. 1986.

Myerson, George. *Heidegger, Habermas, and the Mobile Phone.* Icon Books. 2001.

Nadell, Martha Jane. *Enter the New Negroes: Images of Race in American Culture.* Harvard University Press. 2004.

Navia, Luis E. *Socrates: A Life Examined.* Prometheus Books. 2007.

Negroponte, Nicholas. *Being Digital*. Alfred A. Knopf. 1995.

Nehamas, Alexander. *Nietzsche: Life as Literature*. Harvard University Press. 1985.

Neihardt, John G. *Black Elk Speaks: Being the Life Story of a Holy Man of the Oglala Sioux*. State University of New York Press. 2008.

Neiwert, David. *The Eliminationists: How Hate Talk Radicalized the American Right*. PoliPointPress. 2009.

Nestle, Joan, Riki Wilchins, and Clare Howell, eds. *GenderQueer: Voices from Beyond the Sexual Binary*. Alyson Books. 2002.

Nizan, Paul. *The Watchdogs: Philosophers and the Established Order*. Monthly Review Press. 1971.

Notomi, Noburu. *The Unity of Plato's 'Sophist': Between the Sophist and the Philosopher*. Cambridge University Press. 1999.

Nozick, Robert. *Anarchy, State, and Utopia*. Basic Books. 1974.

———. *Philosophical Explanations*. Harvard University Press. 1981.

———. *The Examined Life*. Simon & Schuster. 1989.

———. *The Nature of Rationality*. Princeton University Press. 1993.

———. *Socratic Puzzles*. Harvard University Press. 1997.

———. *Invariances: The Structure of the Objective World*. Harvard University Press. 2001.

Nunez, Sigrid. *Sempre Susan: A Memoir of Susan Sontag*. Atlas Books. 2011.

Nussbaum, Martha. *The Fragility of Goodness: Luck and Ethics in Greek Tragedy and Philosophy*. Cambridge University Press. 1986.

———. *Love's Knowledge: Essays on Philosophy and Literature*. Oxford University Press. 1990.

———. *The Therapy of Desire: Theory and Practice in Hellenistic Ethics*. Princeton University Press. 1994.

———. *Poetic Justice: The Literary Imagination and Public Life*. Beacon Press. 1996.

———. *Cultivating Humanity: A Classical Defense of Reform in Liberal Education*. Harvard University Press. 1997.

———. *Sex and Social Justice*. Oxford University Press. 1999.

———. *Women and Human Development: The Capabilities Approach*. Cambridge University Press. 2000.

———. *Upheavals of Thought: The Intelligence of Emotions*. Cambridge University Press. 2001.

———. *Hiding from Humanity: Disgust, Shame, and the Law*. Princeton University Press. 2004.

———. *Frontiers of Justice: Disability, Nationality, Species Membership*. Harvard University Press. 2006.

———. *The Clash Within: Democracy, Religious Violence, and India's Future*. Harvard University Press. 2007.

———. *Liberty of Conscience: In Defense of America's Tradition of Religious Equality*. Basic Books. 2008.

———. *Not for Profit: Why Democracy Needs the Humanities*. Princeton University Press. 2010.

Obama, Barack. *Dreams from My Father: A Story of Race and Inheritance.* Three Rivers Press. 2004.

———. *The Audacity of Hope: Thoughts on Reclaiming the American Dream.* Three Rivers Press. 2006.

Ober, Josiah. *Political Dissent in Democratic Athens: Intellectual Critics of Popular Rule.* Princeton University Press. 1998.

Orend, Brian. *Michael Walzer on War and Justice.* University of Wales Press. 2000.

Ortony, Andrew, ed. *Metaphor and Thought.* 2nd ed. Cambridge University Press. 1993.

Ott, Hugo. *Martin Heidegger: A Political Life.* Translated by Allan Blunden. Basic Books. 1993.

Outlaw, Lucius. *On Race and Philosophy.* Routledge. 1996.

Paglia, Camille. *Sexual Personae: Art and Decadence from Nefertiti to Emily Dickinson.* Yale University Press. 1990.

———. *Sex, Art, and American Culture.* Viking. 1993.

———. *Vamps and Tramps: New Essays.* Viking. 1995.

———. *Break, Blow, Burn: Camille Paglia Reads Forty-three of the World's Best Poems.* Pantheon Books. 2005.

Palmen, Connie. *The Laws.* Translated by Richard Huijing. George Braziller. 1993.

Parrington, V. L. *Main Currents in American Thought.* 2 vols. 1927. University of Oklahoma Press. 1987.

Paulos, John Allen. *I Think, Therefore I Laugh.* Columbia University Press. 1985.

Pavlik, John V. *Media in the Digital Age.* Columbia University Press. 2008.

Perelman, Chaim. *The Idea of Justice and the Problem of Argument.* Humanities Press. 1963.

———. *Justice.* Random House. 1967.

Perlmutter, David A. *Blog Wars.* Oxford University Press. 2008.

Perry, Lewis. *Intellectual Life in America: A History.* University of Chicago Press. 1984.

Perry, Ralph Barton. *The Thought and Character of William James.* 2 vols. Harvard University Press. 1935.

Persons, Stow. *American Minds: A History of Ideas.* Holt, Rinehart and Winston. 1958.

Phillips, Christopher. *Socrates Café: A Fresh Taste of Philosophy.* W. W. Norton. 2001.

———. *Six Questions of Socrates: A Modern-Day Journey of Discovery Through World Philosophy.* W. W. Norton. 2005.

———. *Socrates in Love: Philosophy for a Passionate Heart.* W. W. Norton. 2007.

Pierce, Charles P. *Idiot America: How Stupidity Became a Virtue in the Land of the Free.* Doubleday. 2009.

Pierson, George Wilson. *Tocqueville in America.* Johns Hopkins University Press. 1996.

Pirsig, Robert M. *Zen and the Art of Motorcycle Maintenance: An Inquiry into Values.* William Morrow. 1974.

Pitzulo, Carrie. *Bachelors and Bunnies: The Sexual Politics of Playboy.* University of Chicago Press. 2011.

Plato. *The Collected Dialogues of Plato Including the Letters.* Edited by Edith Hamilton and Huntington Cairns. Princeton University Press. 2005.

Platt, Charles. *The Silicon Man.* Wired Books. 1997.

Pogge, Thomas. *John Rawls: His Life and Theory of Justice.* Oxford University Press. 2007.

———. *World Poverty and Human Rights.* 2nd ed. Polity. 2008.

———. *Politics as Usual: What Lies Behind the Pro-Poor Rhetoric.* Polity. 2010.

Pogue, David. *The World According to Twitter.* Black Dog and Leventhal Publishers. 2009.

Polish, Ed, and Darren Wotz. *I Bitch, Therefore I Am.* Ten Speed Press. 2007.

Popper, Sir Karl. *The Open Society and Its Enemies.* 2 vols. Routledge. 1947.

Posner, Richard. *The Economics of Justice.* Harvard University Press. 1981.

———. *Sex and Reason.* Harvard University Press. 1992.

———. *The Problems of Jurisprudence.* Harvard University Press. 1993.

———. *Aging and Old Age.* University of Chicago Press. 1995.

———. *Law, Pragmatism, and Democracy.* Harvard University Press. 2003.

———. *How Judges Think.* Harvard University Press. 2008.

———. *A Failure of Capitalism: The Crisis of '08 and the Descent into Depression.* Harvard University Press. 2009.

Postman, Neil. *Amusing Ourselves to Death: Public Discourse in the Age of Show Business.* Penguin. 2005.

Poulakos, John. *Sophistical Rhetoric in Classical Greece.* University of South Carolina Press. 2008.

Poulakos, Takis. *Speaking for the Polis: Isocrates' Rhetorical Education.* University of South Carolina Press. 1997.

Poulakos, Takis, and David Depew. *Isocrates and Civic Education.* University of Texas Press. 2004.

Powers, Richard. *Galatea 2.2.* Farrar, Straus and Giroux. 1995.

Pratkanis, Anthony, and Elliot Aronson. *Age of Propaganda: The Everyday Use and Abuse of Persuasion.* Holt Paperbacks. 2001.

Pratt, Scott L. *Native Pragmatism: Rethinking the Roots of American Philosophy.* Indiana University Press. 2002.

Putnam, Hilary. *Renewing Philosophy.* Harvard University Press. 1992.

Putnam, Robert. *Bowling Alone: The Collapse and Revival of American Community.* Simon & Schuster. 2000.

Pynchon, Thomas. *The Crying of Lot 49.* J. P. Lippincott. 1964.

Quine, W. V. *Word and Object.* MIT Press. 1960.

———. *From a Logical Point of View.* 2nd ed., revised. Harvard University Press. 1961.

———. *The Ways of Paradox and Other Essays.* Random House. 1966.

———. *Ontological Relativity and Other Essays.* Columbia University Press. 1969.

———. *Theories and Things.* Harvard University Press. 1981.

———. *The Time of My Life: An Autobiography.* MIT Press. 1985.

———. *Pursuit of Truth.* Rev. ed. Harvard University Press. 1992.

———. *Quintessence: Basic Readings from the Philosophy of W. V. Quine.* Harvard University Press. 2004.

Rand, Ayn. *We the Living.* Macmillan. 1936.

———. *Anthem.* Cassell. 1938.

———. *The Fountainhead*. Bobbs-Merrill. 1943.

———. *Atlas Shrugged*. Random House. 1957.

———. *The Virtue of Selfishness: A New Concept of Egoism*. Signet. 1963.

———. *Philosophy: Who Needs It?* Edited by Leonard Peikoff. Signet. 1982.

Rash, Wayne. *Politics on the Nets: Wiring the Political Process*. W. H. Freeman. 1997.

Rawlins, Gregory. *Moths to the Flame: The Seductions of Computer Technology*. MIT Press. 1996.

———. *Slaves of the Machine. The Quickening of Computer Technology*. MIT Press. 1997.

Rawls, John. *A Theory of Justice*. Harvard University Press. 1971.

———. *Political Liberalism*. Columbia University Press. 1993.

———. *Collected Papers*. Edited by Samuel Freeman. Harvard University Press. 1999.

———. *The Law of Peoples*. Harvard University Press. 1999.

———. *A Theory of Justice*. Rev. ed. Harvard University Press. 1999.

———. *Lectures on the History of Moral Philosophy*. Edited by Barbara Herman. Harvard University Press. 2000.

———. *Lectures on the History of Political Philosophy*. Edited by Samuel Freeman. Harvard University Press. 2007.

———. *A Brief Inquiry into the Meaning of Sin and Faith*. With "On My Religion." Edited by Thomas Nagel. Harvard University Press. 2009.

Remnick, David. *The Bridge: The Life and Rise of Barack Obama*. Alfred A. Knopf. 2010.

Rhu, Lawrence F. *Stanley Cavell's American Dream: Shakespeare, Philosophy, and Hollywood Movies*. Harvard University Press. 2004.

Richard, Carl J. *The Founders and the Classics: Greece, Rome, and the American Enlightenment*. Harvard University Press. 1994.

———. *The Battle for the American Mind: A Brief History of a Nation's Thought*. Rowman and Littlefield. 2004.

———. *Greeks and Romans Bearing Gifts: How the Ancients Inspired the Founding Fathers*. Rowman and Littlefield. 2008.

———. *The Golden Age of the Classics in America: Greece, Rome, and the Antebellum United States*. Harvard University Press. 2009.

Richards, David A. J. *The Case for Gay Rights: From Bowers to Lawrence and Beyond*. University Press of Kansas. 2005.

Richardson, Robert D. *William James: In the Maelstrom of American Modernism*. Houghton Mifflin, 2006.

———. *Emerson: A Mind on Fire*. University of California Press. 1995.

Rieff, David. *Swimming in a Sea of Death: A Son's Memoir*. Simon & Schuster. 2008.

Roberts, Sam. *Who We Are: The Changing Face of America in the Twenty-first Century*. Times Books. 2004.

Rochlin, Gene. *Trapped in the Net: The Unintended Consequences of Computerization*. Princeton University Press. 1997.

Rockefeller, Steven. *John Dewey: Religious Faith and Democratic Humanism*. Columbia University Press. 1991.

Rockwell, Geoffrey. *Defining Dialogue: From Socrates to the Internet*. Humanity Books. 2003.

Rollins, Mark, ed. *Danto and His Critics*. Blackwell. 1993.

Rollyson, Carl. *Reading Susan Sontag: A Critical Introduction to Her Work.* Ivan R. Dee. 2001.

Rollyson, Carl, and Lisa Paddock. *Susan Sontag: The Making of an Icon.* W. W. Norton. 2000.

Rorty, Richard. *Consequences of Pragmatism: Essays, 1972–1980.* University of Minnesota Press. 1982.

———. *Contingency, Irony, and Solidarity.* Cambridge University Press. 1989.

———. *Essays on Heidegger and Others. Philosophical Papers, Vol. 2.* Cambridge University Press. 1991.

———. *Objectivity, Relativism, and Truth. Philosophical Papers, Vol. 1.* Cambridge University Press. 1991.

———. *Achieving Our Country: Leftist Thought in Twentieth-Century America.* Harvard University Press. 1998.

———. *Truth and Progress. Philosophical Papers, Vol. 3.* Cambridge University Press. 1998.

———. *Philosophy as Cultural Politics. Philosophical Papers, Vol. 4.* Cambridge University Press. 2007.

———. *Philosophy and Social Hope.* Penguin Books. 1999.

———. *Take Care of Freedom and Truth Will Take Care of Itself.* Interviews edited by Eduardo Mendieta. Stanford University Press. 2005.

———. *Philosophy and the Mirror of Nature.* Thirtieth anniversary edition, with an introduction by Michael Williams. Princeton University Press. 2009.

Rorty, Richard, ed. *The Linguistic Turn.* University of Chicago Press. 1967.

Rorty, Richard, and Pascal Engel. *What's the Use of Truth?* Columbia University Press. 2007.

Rose, Steven, ed. *From Brains to Consciousness?: Essays on the New Sciences of the Mind.* Allen Lane. 1998.

Rosen, Jonathan. *The Talmud and the Internet: A Journey Between Worlds.* Farrar, Straus and Giroux. 2000.

Rosen, Norma. *John and Anzia: An American Romance.* E. P. Dutton. 1989.

Rosenfeld, Sophia. *Common Sense: A Political History.* Harvard University Press. 2011.

Roszak, Theodore. *The Cult of Information: The Folklore of Computers and the True Art of Thinking.* Pantheon. 1986.

Rubin, Joan Shelley. *The Making of Middlebrow Culture.* University of North Carolina Press. 1992.

Rucker, Rudy. *White Light.* Wired Books. 1997.

Rushkoff, Douglas. *Ecstasy Club.* HarperEdge. 1997.

———. *Cyberia: Life in the Trenches of Cyberspace.* Clinamen Press. 2002.

Ryan, Alan. *John Dewey and the High Tide of American Liberalism.* W. W. Norton. 1995.

Saatkamp, Herman J. Jr. *Rorty and Pragmatism: The Philosopher Responds to His Critics.* Vanderbilt University Press. 1999.

Sacks, Oliver. *An Anthropologist on Mars: Seven Paradoxical Tales.* Vintage. 1996.

———. *The Man Who Mistook His Wife for a Hat and Other Clinical Tales.* Simon & Schuster. 2006.

———. *Musicophilia: Tales of Music and the Brain.* Alfred A. Knopf. 2007.

————. *The Mind's Eye.* Alfred A. Knopf. 2010.

Said, Edward. *Beginnings: Intention and Method.* Basic Books. 1975.

————. *Orientalism.* Vintage Books. 1978.

————. *The World, the Text, and the Critic.* Harvard University Press. 1983.

————. *The Question of Palestine.* Vintage Books. 1992.

————. *Culture and Imperialism.* Alfred A. Knopf. 1993.

————. *Representations of the Intellectual.* Vintage Books. 1994.

————. *Covering Islam: How the Media and the Experts Determine How We See the Rest of the World.* Vintage Books. 1997.

————. *Out of Place: A Memoir.* Alfred A. Knopf. 1999.

————. *Humanism and Democratic Criticism.* Columbia University Press. 2004.

————. *On Late Style: Music and Literature Against the Grain.* Pantheon. 2006.

Sale, Kirkpatrick. *Rebels Against the Future: The Luddites and Their War on the Industrial Revolution.* Addison-Wesley. 1996.

Santayana, George. *The Sense of Beauty.* Charles Scribner's Sons. 1896.

————. *Interpretations of Poetry and Religion.* Charles Scribner's Sons. 1900.

————. *The Life of Reason.* 5 vols. Charles Scribner's Sons. 1905–06.

————. *Three Philosophical Poets: Lucretius, Dante, and Goethe.* Harvard University Press. 1910.

————. *Winds of Doctrine: Studies in Contemporary Opinion.* Charles Scribner's Sons. 1913.

————. *Egotism in German Philosophy.* Charles Scribner's Sons. 1916.

————. *Scepticism and Animal Faith.* Charles Scribner's Sons. 1923.

————. *Realms of Being.* 4 vols. Charles Scribner's Sons. 1927–40.

————. *The Last Puritan: A Memoir in the Form of a Novel.* Charles Scribner's Sons. 1936.

————. *Persons and Places.* Charles Scribner's Sons. 1963.

————. *The Genteel Tradition in American Philosophy and Character and Opinion in the United States.* Edited by James Seaton. Yale University Press. 2009.

Schama, Simon. *The American Future: A History.* Ecco. 2009.

Schiappa, Edward. *Protagoras and Logos: A Study in Greek Philosophy and Rhetoric.* University of South Carolina Press. 1991.

————. *The Beginnings of Rhetorical Theory in Classical Greece.* Yale University Press. 1999.

Schildgren, Brenda Dean, ed. *The Rhetoric Canon.* Wayne State University Press. 1997.

Schilpp, Paul Arthur, ed. *The Philosophy of George Santayana.* Tudor Publishing Company. 1951.

Schlesinger, Arthur Jr. *The Disuniting of America: Reflections on a Multicultural Society.* Rev. and enlarged ed. W. W. Norton. 1998.

Schmidtz, David, ed. *Robert Nozick.* Cambridge University Press. 2002.

Schuyler, Robert. *The Constitution of the United States: An Historical Survey of Its Formation.* Macmillan. 1923.

Sciabarra, Chris Matthew. *Ayn Rand: The Russian Radical.* Penn State University Press. 1995.

Sclove, Richard E. *Democracy and Technology.* Guilford Press. 1995.

Scott, Gary Alan, ed. *Does Socrates Have a Method? Rethinking the Elenchus in Plato's Dialogues and Beyond.* Penn State University Press. 2002.

Segal, Robert A. *Joseph Campbell: An Introduction.* Garland Publishing. 1987.

Seigfried, Charlotte Haddock. *Pragmatism and Feminism: Reweaving the Social Fabric.* University of Chicago Press. 1996.

Seldes, Gilbert. *The Seven Lively Arts.* Harper and Brothers. 1924.

Seligman, Craig. *Sontag and Kael: Opposites Attract Me.* Counterpoint. 2004.

Shelby, Tommie. *We Who Are Dark: The Philosophical Foundations of Black Solidarity.* Harvard University Press. 2005.

Shilts, Randy. *And the Band Played On: Politics, People, and the AIDS Epidemic.* St. Martin's Press. 1987.

Signorile, Michelangelo. *Queer in America: Sex, the Media, and the Closets of Power.* Random House. 1993.

Simmons, A. John. *Justification and Legitimacy: Essays on Rights and Obligations.* Cambridge University Press. 2001.

Sinclair, Carla. *Signal to Noise.* HarperSanFrancisco. 1997.

Skinner, B. F. *Beyond Freedom and Dignity.* Alfred A. Knopf. 1971.

Skotheim, Robert Allen. *American Intellectual Histories and Historians.* Princeton University Press. 1966.

Slouka, Mark. *War of the Worlds: Cyberspace and the High-Tech Assault on Reality.* Basic Books. 1995.

Smith, John E. *The Spirit of American Philosophy.* Oxford University Press. 1963. Rev. ed. State University of New York Press. 1983.

———. *Themes in American Philosophy: Purpose, Experience, and Community.* Harper Torchbooks. 1970.

———. *Purpose and Thought: The Meaning of Pragmatism.* Yale University Press. 1978.

———. *America's Philosophical Vision.* University of Chicago Press. 1992.

Smolla, Rodney. *Free Speech in an Open Society.* Alfred A. Knopf. 1992.

———. *The Constitution Goes to College.* New York University Press. 2011.

Snyder, Ilana. *Hypertext: The Electronic Labyrinth.* New York University Press. 1997.

Solomon, Robert C. *A Passion for Justice: Emotions and the Origins of the Social Contract.* Addison-Wesley. 1990.

Solomon, Robert C., and Kathleen M. Higgins, eds. *From Africa to Zen: An Invitation to World Philosophy.* Rowman and Littlefield. 1993.

Solove, Daniel J. *The Future of Reputation: Gossip, Rumor, and Privacy on the Internet.* Yale University Press. 2007.

Sommers, Christine. *Who Stole Feminism?: How Women Have Betrayed Women.* Simon & Schuster. 1994.

Sontag, Susan. *The Benefactor.* Farrar, Straus and Giroux. 1963.

———. *Against Interpretation.* Farrar, Straus and Giroux. 1966.

———. *Death Kit.* Farrar, Straus and Giroux. 1967.

———. *Styles of Radical Will.* Farrar, Straus and Giroux. 1969.

———. *On Photography.* Farrar, Straus and Giroux. 1977.

———. *I, etcetera.* Farrar, Straus and Giroux. 1978.

———. *Illness as Metaphor.* Farrar, Straus and Giroux. 1978.

————. *Under the Sign of Saturn.* Farrar, Straus and Giroux. 1980.

————. *AIDS and Its Metaphors.* Farrar, Straus and Giroux. 1989.

————. *The Volcano Lover: A Romance.* Farrar, Straus and Giroux. 1992.

————. *In America.* Farrar, Straus and Giroux. 1999.

————. *Where the Stress Falls.* Farrar, Straus and Giroux. 2002.

————. *Regarding the Pain of Others.* Farrar, Straus and Giroux. 2003.

————. *Reborn: Journals and Notebooks, 1947–1963.* Edited by David Rieff. Farrar, Straus and Giroux. 2008.

Soros, George. *Open Society: Reforming Global Capitalism.* PublicAffairs. 2000.

Sperlich, Wolfgang B. *Noam Chomsky.* Reaktion Books. 2006.

Sprinker, Michael, ed. *Edward Said: A Critical Reader.* Blackwell. 1992.

Starobin, Paul. *After America: Narratives for the Next Global Age.* Viking. 2009.

Stauffer, Devin. *The Unity of Plato's Gorgias: Rhetoric, Justice, and the Philosophic Life.* Cambridge University Press. 2006.

Stavans, Ilan, ed. *Becoming Americans: Four Centuries of Immigrant Writing.* Library of America. 2009.

Sterling, Bruce. *Holy Fire.* Bantam Books. 1996.

————. *The Artificial Kid.* Hardwired Books. 1997.

————. *Tomorrow Now: Envisioning the Next Fifty Years.* Random House. 2003.

Stevenson, Jay. *The Complete Idiot's Guide to Philosophy.* 3rd ed. Alpha Books. 2005.

Stoll, Clifford. *Silicon Snake Oil: Second Thoughts on the Information Highway.* Doubleday. 1995.

Stone, I. F. *The Trial of Socrates.* Little, Brown. 1998.

Storr, Anthony. *Feet of Clay: Saints, Sinners, and Madmen: A Study of Gurus.* Free Press. 1996.

Strouse, Jean. *Alice James: A Biography.* Houghton Mifflin. 1980.

Sunstein, Cass. *Republic.com 2.0.* Princeton University Press. 2007.

Sycamore, Matilda Bernstein. *That's Revolting!: Queer Strategies for Resisting Assimilation.* Soft Skull Press. 2008.

Talisse, Robert B., and Scott F. Aiken, eds. *The Pragmatism Reader: From Peirce Through the Present.* Princeton University Press. 2011.

Tannen, Deborah. *The Argument Culture: Moving from Debate to Dialogue.* Random House. 1998.

Taylor, Astra, ed. *Examined Life: Excursions with Contemporary Thinkers.* New Press. 2009.

Teller, Astro. *Exegesis.* Vintage Books. 1997.

Thayer, H. S. *Meaning and Action: A Critical History of Pragmatism.* 2nd ed. Hackett Publishing Company. 1981.

Thompson, Dennis F. *Political Ethics and Public Office.* Harvard University Press. 1987.

————. *Just Elections: Creating a Fair Electoral Process in the United States.* University of Chicago Press. 2002.

Thoreau, Henry David. *Walden and Civil Disobedience.* Penguin Books. 1983.

Tobar, Hector. *Translation Nation: Defining a New American Identity in the Spanish-Speaking United States.* Riverhead Books. 2005.

Tocqueville, Alexis de. *Democracy in America.* Translated, edited, and with an introduction by Harvey C. Mansfield and Delba Winthrop. University of Chicago Press. 2000.

Too, Yun Lee. *The Rhetoric of Identity in Isocrates: Text, Power, Pedagogy.* Cambridge University Press. 1995.

Torres, Louis, and Michelle Marder Kamhi. *What Art Is: The Esthetic Theory of Ayn Rand.* Open Court. 2000.

Troy, Tevi. *Intellectuals and the American Presidency: Philosophers, Jesters, or Technicians? 1960 to Present.* Rowman and Littlefield. 2002.

Turkle, Sherry. *Life on the Screen: Identity in the Age of the Internet.* Simon & Schuster. 1995.

———. *Alone Together: Why We Expect More from Technology and Less from Each Other.* Basic Books. 2011.

Turner, Frederick Jackson. *Rereading Frederick Jackson Turner.* With commentary by John Mack Faragher. Henry Holt. 1994.

Twitchell, James. *Carnival Culture: The Trashing of Taste in America.* Columbia University Press. 1992.

———. *AdCultUSA: The Triumph of Advertising in American Culture.* Columbia University Press. 1996.

———. *For Shame: The Loss of Common Decency in American Culture.* St. Martin's Press. 1997.

———. *Shopping for God: How Christianity Went from in Your Heart to in Your Face.* Simon & Schuster. 2007.

Tworkov, Helen. *Zen in America: Five Teachers and the Search for an American Buddhism.* Kodansha. 1994.

Unamuno, Miguel de. *The Tragic Sense of Life in Men and in Peoples.* Macmillan. 1931.

Updike, John. *Roger's Version.* Alfred A. Knopf. 1984.

Vander Waerdt, Paul A., ed. *The Socratic Movement.* Cornell University Press. 1994.

Van Hooft, Stan. *Cosmopolitanism: A Philosophy for Global Ethics.* McGill-Queen's University Press. 2009.

Vlastos, Gregory. *Socrates: Ironist and Moral Philosopher.* Cornell University Press. 1991.

Vonnegut, Kurt. *Player Piano.* Dial Press. 1999.

Waithe, Mary Ellen. *A History of Women Philosophers.* 4 vols. Martinus Nijhoff Publishers. 1987.

Walia, Shelley. *Edward Said and the Writing of History.* Icon Books. 2001.

Walker, Jeff. *The Ayn Rand Cult.* Open Court. 1998.

Walzer, Michael. *Spheres of Justice: A Defense of Plurality and Equality.* Basic Books. 1983.

———. *Just and Unjust Wars: A Moral Argument with Historical Illustrations.* 2nd ed. Basic Books. 1992.

———. *What It Means to Be an American: Essays on the American Experience.* Marsilio. 1992.

———. *On Toleration.* Yale University Press. 1997.

———. *The Company of Critics: Social Criticism and Political Commitment in the Twentieth Century.* Basic Books. 2002.

————. *Arguing About War.* Yale University Press. 2005.

————. *Thinking Politically: Essays in Political Theory.* Edited by David Miller. Yale University Press. 2007.

Wardy, Robert. *The Birth of Rhetoric: Gorgias, Plato, and Their Successors.* Routledge. 1996.

Warner, Michael, ed. *American Sermons: The Pilgrims to Martin Luther King Jr.* Library of America. 1999.

Warraq, Ibn. *Defending the West: A Critique of Edward Said's Orientalism.* Prometheus Books. 2007.

Washington, Johnny. *Alain Locke and Philosophy: A Quest for Cultural Pluralism.* Greenwood Press. 1986.

————. *A Journey into the Philosophy of Alain Locke.* Greenwood Press. 1994.

Waters, Anne. *American Indian Thought: Philosophical Essays.* Wiley-Blackwell. 2008.

Watts, Steven. *Mr. Playboy: Hugh Hefner and the American Dream.* 2007. John Wiley and Sons. 2008.

Welch, Kathleen E. *Electric Rhetoric: Classical Rhetoric, Oralism, and a New Literacy.* MIT Press. 1999.

Welchman, Jennifer. *Dewey's Ethical Thought.* Cornell University Press. 1995.

Werkmeister, W. H. *A History of Philosophical Ideas in America.* Greenwood Press. 1949.

Wertheim, Margaret. *The Pearly Gates of Cyberspace: A History of Space from Dante to the Internet.* W. W. Norton. 1999.

West, Cornel. *The American Evasion of Philosophy: A Genealogy of Pragmatism.* University of Wisconsin Press. 1989.

————. *Keeping Faith: Philosophy and Race in America.* Routledge. 1993.

————. *Prophetic Reflections: Notes on Race and Power in America.* Common Courage Press. 1993.

————. *Prophetic Thought in Postmodern Times.* Common Courage Press. 1993.

————. *Race Matters.* Beacon Press. 1993.

Westbrook, Robert B. *John Dewey and American Democracy.* Cornell University Press. 1991.

White, Curtis. *The Middle Mind: Why Americans Don't Think for Themselves.* HarperSanFrancisco. 2003.

White, Morton. *Social Thought in America: The Revolt Against Formalism.* Rev. ed. Beacon Press. 1957.

————. *Documents in the History of American Philosophy: From Jonathan Edwards to John Dewey.* Oxford University Press. 1972.

————. *Philosophy,* The Federalist, *and the Constitution.* Oxford University Press. 1987.

————. *A Philosopher's Story.* Penn State University Press. 1999.

————. *From a Philosophical Point of View: Selected Studies.* Princeton University Press. 2005.

Whittle, David. *Cyberspace: The Human Dimension.* W. H. Freeman. 1997.

Wiebe, Robert H. *Self-Rule: A Cultural History of American Democracy.* University of Chicago Press. 1995.

Williams, Raymond. *Keywords: A Vocabulary of Culture and Society.* Oxford University Press. 1981.

Wilshire, Bruce. *The Primal Roots of American Philosophy: Pragmatism, Phenomenology, and Native American Thought.* Penn State University Press. 2000.

Wilson, Emily. *The Death of Socrates.* Harvard University Press. 2007.

Wilson, James. *The Earth Shall Weep: A History of Native America.* Picador. 1998.

Winograd, Morley, and Michael D. Hais. *Millennial Makeover: MySpace, YouTube, and the Future of American Politics.* Rutgers University Press. 2008.

Wiredu, Kwasi. *Philosophy and an African Culture.* Cambridge University Press. 1980.

Witham, Larry. *A City upon a Hill: How Sermons Changed the Course of American History.* HarperOne. 2007.

Wittgenstein, Ludwig. *Tractatus Logicus-Philosophicus.* Routledge & Kegan Paul. 1922.

———. *Philosophical Investigations.* Basil Blackwell. 1953.

———. *On Certainty.* Basil Blackwell. 1969.

———. *Culture and Value.* University of Chicago Press. 1980.

Wolin, Richard. *Heidegger's Children: Hannah Arendt, Karl Lowith, Hans Jonas, and Herbert Marcuse.* Princeton University Press. 2001.

Wood, Ellen, and Neal Wood. *Class Ideology and Ancient Political Theory.* Blackwell. 1978.

Woodward, Anthony. *Living in the Eternal: A Study of George Santayana.* Vanderbilt University Press. 1988.

Wright, Ronald. *What Is America? A Short History of the New World Order.* Da Capo Press. 2008.

Yancy, George, ed. *Cornel West: A Critical Reader.* Blackwell. 2001.

———. *Philosophy in Multiple Voices.* Rowman and Littlefield. 2007.

Yezierska, Anzia. *All I Could Never Be.* Brewer, Warren and Putnam. 1932.

———. *Bread Givers.* Persea Books. 2003.

———. *Salome of the Tenements.* Transaction. 2009.

Young-Bruehl, Elisabeth. *Hannah Arendt: For Love of the World.* 2nd ed. Yale University Press. 2004.

———. *Why Arendt Matters.* Yale University Press. 2006.

Yu, Charles. *How to Live Safely in a Science Fictional Universe.* Pantheon Books. 2010.

Zaleski, Jeff. *The Soul of Cyberspace: How New Technology Is Changing Our Spiritual Lives.* HarperSanFrancisco. 1997.

Zhang, Wei. *Heidegger, Rorty, and the Eastern Thinkers.* State University of New York Press. 2006.

Zittrain, Jonathan. *The Future of the Internet—And How to Stop It.* Yale University Press. 2008.

Interviews

I am grateful to the following people, who, over many years, granted me interviews that illuminated my understanding of philosophy, the Internet, America, and other matters discussed in this book.

Mortimer J. Adler
Anita Allen
Ayaan Hirsi Ali
Shirley Anderson
Sybol Cook Anderson
Violaine Ares
Shlomo Avineri
A. J. Ayer
Martha Baer
John Perry Barlow
Brian Barry
Jacques Barzun
Elizabeth Beardsley
Monroe Beardsley
Sara Beardsworth
Saul Bellow
Jeff Bezos
Andrei Bitov
Harold Bloom
Wayne Booth
Norman Bowie
Jo Ann Boydston
John Brockman
William F. Buckley Jr.
Kenneth Burke
Sam Butler
Joseph Campbell
Jim Cappio
Jimmy Carter
Dick Cavett
Noam Chomsky

Joanne B. Ciulla
Robert Coles
Edward Craig
Arthur C. Danto
Donald Davidson
Alain de Botton
Richard T. DeGeorge
Michael Dertouzos
Vincent Descombes
Phil Donahue
Alan Donagan
Mike Douglas
Roger-Pol Droit
Esther Dyson
Michael Eric Dyson
Umberto Eco
Abraham Edel
Jose Ferrater Mora
Luc Ferry
Alain Finkelkraut
Max Fisch
Elisabeth Flower
Michel Foucault
Reuven Frank
Mark Frauenfelder
Betty Friedan
Ivan Frolov
Robert Fulghum
Paul Fussell
Jostein Gaarder
John Gage

Howard Gardner
William Gass
Peter Gay
Kathryn Gines
William Gibson
Alan Goldman
Nelson Goodman
Samuel Gorvitz
Anna Gotlib
Stephen Jay Gould
Anthony Grayling
Phil Grier
Marjorie Grene
Merv Griffin
Jürgen Habermas
Sir Stuart Hampshire
Leonard Harris
Charles Hartshorne
Hugh Hefner
Virginia Held
David Hills
Jaaako Hintikka
Christopher Hitchens
David Hoekema
Eric Hoffman
Howard V. Hong
Sidney Hook
Vittorio Hosle
Paulin Houtoundji
Irving Howe
Richard Howey
Michael Ialacci
Ramin Jahanbegloo
Steven Johnson
Francois Jullien
Gary Kamiya
Kevin Kelly
Tracy Kidder
Yersu Kim
Michael Kinsley
George Kline
Ken Knisely
Ioanna Kucuradi
Thomas Kuhn
Bruce Kuklick

Hans Kung
John Ladd
Andrew Lamey
Archibald Laud-Hammond
Doris Lessing
Rick Lewis
Bernard-Henri Levy
Victor Lowe
Alasdair MacIntyre
Joseph Margolis
Ruth Barcan Marcus
Gordon Marino
Lou Marinoff
Qrescent Mali Mason
Thomas McCarthy
John McDermott
Louis Menand
Truman Metzel
Czeslaw Milosz
Francisco Miro Quesada
Terence Moore
Jeremy Morris
Ferdinand Mount
Bill Moyers
Martha C. Nussbaum
John O'Connor
Hans Oberdiek
Kenzaburo Oe
Alan M. Olson
Lucius Outlaw
Camille Paglia
John Pavlik
Octavio Paz
Alvin Plantinga
Richard Powers
Hilary Putnam
W. V. Quine
Lord Anthony Quinton
Jeff Rice
Paul Ricoeur
Gene Rochlin
Mary Rorty
Richard Rorty
Stanley Rosen
Louis Rossetto

Salman Rushdie
Oliver Sacks
Paul Saffo
Edward Said
Mike Sandbothe
Giovanni Sartori
Andre Schiffrin
David Schrader
George Seldes
Richard Shusterman
David Sidorsky
Margaret A. Simons
John E. Smith
Robert C. Solomon
Christine Sommers
Susan Sontag
George Soros
Tom Stoppard
Wole Soyinka

Frank Sulloway
David Talbot
Georg Theiner
Neil Thomason
Julius Tomin
Imamichi Tomonobu
Roberto Mangabeira Unger
Jennifer Vest
Johnny Washington
Anne Waters
G. Edward White
Michael Williams
Bernard Williams
Bruce Wilshire
Arnold Wilson
Edward O. Wilson
Kwasi Wiredu
Yirmiahu Yovel
Jeff Zaleski

Index

Page numbers in *italics* refer to illustrations.